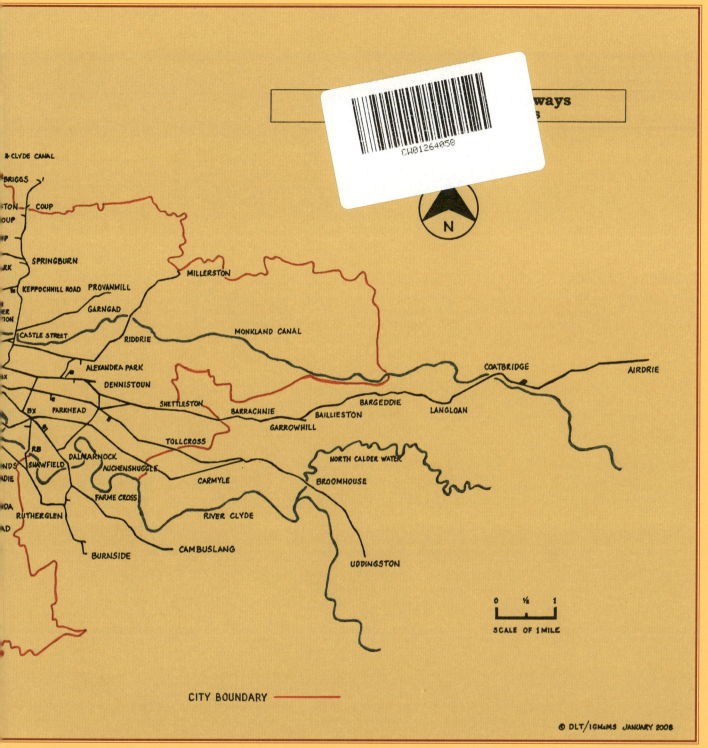

from Dunbartonshire (Knightswood) were all taken over. In 1931 there was a small addition of Hogganfield and Carntyne East. Finally in 1938, what were then largely undeveloped areas of Lanarkshire (Balmuildy, Auchinairn, Cardowan, Gartloch, Easterhouse and Queenslie); of Renfrewshire (Linn Park, Jenny Lind, Darnley and Penilee); and of Dunbartonshire (Drumry, Drumchapel and Summerston) were all absorbed. For all that expansion, the trams still operated far outwith the city limits and served during their lifetime, as well as landward areas of Lanarkshire, Renfrewshire and Dunbartonshire, no fewer than nine independent Burghs, namely the Royal Burgh of Rutherglen along with the Burghs of Airdrie, Barrhead, Clydebank, Coatbridge, Johnstone, Milngavie, Paisley (Scotland's largest Burgh) and Renfrew. Some thirteen other towns were also reached by Glasgow trams. These were Baillieston, Bargeddie, Bearsden, Bishopbriggs, Cambuslang, Carmyle, Clarkston, Duntocher, Elderslie, Giffnock, Kilbarchan, Thornliebank and Uddingston.

(Information sourced from The Third Statistical Account of Scotland – Glasgow published 1958)

GLASGOW TRAM SERVICES

by

David L Thomson

DEDICATION
This volume is dedicated to the memory of the tramway men and women who operated Glasgow's tramcars throughout the years and at all times provided the citizens with a transport service second to none.

Published Jointly By

The Scottish Tramway & Transport Society

and

Venture Publications Ltd

© 2009 SCOTTISH TRAMWAY & TRANSPORT SOCIETY

Published jointly by the STTS and Venture Publications Ltd

ISBN 978 190530 430 1

All rights reserved. Except for normal review purposes no part of this book may be reproduced or utilised in any form by any means, electrical or mechanical, including photocopying, recording or by an information storage and retrieval system, without the prior written consent of the STTS or Venture Publications Ltd, Glossop, Derbyshire, SK13 8EH.

Design and computer origination by John and Mark Senior

Glasgow Bridge in 1936 with cars on Green and Yellow Services prominent. *(T&R Annan)*

CONTENTS

ACKNOWLEDGEMENTS & PROLOGUE	4, 5
SERVICE & ROUTE IDENTIFICATION	6
EXPLANATORY NOTES	8
DEVELOPMENT OF SERVICES: DIARY OF EVENTS	10
APPENDIX A - GLASGOW CORPORATION TRAMWAYS DEPOTS	188
FARE STAGE MAP	208
APPENDIX B - GLASGOW CORPORATION SERVICES	210
APPENDIX C - SLIPBOARDS	281
APPENDIX D - HEADCODES	282
APPENDIX E - GLASGOW CORPORATION NIGHT SERVICES	285
APPENDIX F - DESTINATION DISPLAYS	290
SYSTEM MAP	*Front End Papers*
CITY CENTRE MAP	*Rear End Papers*

The need for the George V Bridge is amply demonstrated in this view by Annan Galleries of Glasgow Bridge taken in 1924. Trams of all colours jostle for space with other traffic, mainly horse-drawn. The numbers displayed below the destination indicators are "route" or "running" numbers immediately prior to the introduction of Headcodes.
(T&R Annan)

AUTHOR'S ACKNOWLEDGEMENTS

I thank those who have assisted unstintingly in the preparation and production of this publication.

The basis of the information was ingathered over the years from personal observation and through the co-operation of the late Eric Fitzpayne, the General Manager of Glasgow Corporation Transport Department, and his staff in allowing access for a teenage schoolboy to study the Traffic Logs on Saturday mornings. These Logs were amongst the many documents later rescued by Brian Longworth when the Head Office subsequently closed and further reference to them has been readily made available by Brian whose own knowledge of all records has proved invaluable. My thanks go to him for all his help so willingly given.

Without Ian G McM Stewart, the Editor, this volume would never have seen the light of day. He has been instrumental in transforming what had been compiled as a record effectively for personal use into something presentable to the world at large. His knowledge and experience in preparing and publishing transport works, which is expansive; his considerable effort in sourcing illustrations, and his practical expertise in the preparation of the maps have all been of tremendous value. Not least has the volume been enhanced by the inclusion of many of his superb drawings. Alan Brotchie kindly allowed Ian to revise his city centre map which had originally been published in *A Handbook of Glasgow Tramways* in 1961. James Sinclair assisted with extra photography.

Thanks also go to Alan Carlaw for images from actual Destination Screens, to BJ ("Curly") Cross for considerable support and to Glynn Wilton of the National Tramway Museum for making images available from their archives.

Maureen Campbell tirelessly transposed the text into a form acceptable for Mark and John Senior whose expertise and publishing efforts are the icing on the cake.

The photographs are credited to the sources that have been identified. If anyone has been wrongly named or missed out, my apologies are placed on record. Any errors in the facts stated in the text are wholly mine for which I accept full responsibility.

Editor's Footnote

This publication is intended to be a long-promised companion volume to *The Glasgow Tramcar* published by the then Scottish Tramway Museum Society (STMS) in 1983 revised and reprinted by the STTS in 1993, *Glasgow Buses* published jointly by the STTS and Transport Publishing Company (TPC) in 1990 and *The Glasgow Horse Tramways* published by the STTS in 2000.   IGMcMS

PROLOGUE

Acclaimed worldwide as the finest and greatest of its kind, in its heyday the Glasgow Tramway System received representatives, emissaries and delegates from all corners of the globe charged with the task of finding out just how such an operation should really be run and determined to carry back that knowledge and apply it to their own countries and cities. It unquestionably had world-class status. These pages, which set down the development, peak and decline of the electric tram routes and services provided by Glasgow Corporation, do more than merely record the life of a system which the citizens loved and of which they were justifiably proud. Also can be gleaned a slice of social history as the structure and expansion of the city is determined; as its changing shape and the developing travelling habits of its citizens are illustrated; and as what made a large and industrial and commercial conurbation of the first half of the 20th century tick is demonstrated.

Against all that the reader must keep in mind the background: namely for nearly the whole period that the trams served the city, private transport, whether by horse-carriage or by motor car, was the luxury enjoyed by few; the working year lasted for 50 weeks; the working week for five-and-a-half, sometimes six, days; Sunday was universally a day of rest; New Year's Day was always, and Christmas Day was never, an industrial holiday; relaxation and entertainment were sought in the homes of relatives and of friends, or in city parks, museums, theatres, music halls, dance halls, picture-houses and football grounds; and travel for distances which could not readily be walked was undertaken on the tramcars. The web of routes covered every major street and sought to embrace all areas within the city boundaries as well as reaching out into many surrounding burghs. The whole operation was structured and integrated to provide cars every few minutes throughout the system. There was, literally, always a car in sight. Above all there existed a tremendous sense of civic pride of which the presence of the tramcars was constantly a visual and tangible reminder.

It gives me enormous pleasure to place this information garnered over the years into a form which will provide a lasting record of the heartbeat of my native city in the hope I have provided but a slight means to glimpse a past way of life now gone for ever.

David L Thomson
Gourock
December 2008

"There was, literally, always a car in sight". A look up Hope Street in 1958 confirms this to be the case with four trams visible, including two cars on Service 22 heading north for Lambhill. *(BJ Cross Collection)*

GLASGOW CORPORATION TRAMWAYS SERVICES
SERVICE AND ROUTE IDENTIFICATION

Background Information

Identification of Glasgow Tram Services was based originally on a system of Route Colours, carried on the upper deck panels, so that prospective passengers could identify the car of their choice easily and quickly from afar and also, as illiteracy was still a reality with a portion of the population at that time, without needing to be able to read.

However, the Corporation also devised an internal system of identification of the different groups of services using the letters of the alphabet. This system was also used on the tickets but apart from that was seldom made public although it continued to be used within the Department until the outbreak of the Second World War and indeed to appear on certain records until the final closure of the tramway system in 1962.

Headcodes

In 1924 a numbering system was introduced based on Headcode principles but following the Route-colour groupings. It was based on numbers, applied unidirectionally, paired for each group of Services utilising the Numbers from 1 to 40, omitting 13, and allocating a different suffix letter for intermediate terminal points. This system was advertised to the travelling public and displayed on the cars using digital three-track roller-blind indicators. An earlier version of these indicators had been originally fitted about 1913. The suffix Letters provided on the Screens were: A B C D E H J K L M P R S T, although the highest letter in use was, in fact, J. Because, by its nature, it was a fairly complicated system, it failed to catch on with the public who were, after all, fully thirled to the Route Colours. Additionally, the Headcode nature of the system involved the crews' changing the number screens at every terminus with an awareness of the different suffix Letter identifying each intermediate terminal point. This did not make the correct display of the information an easy nor a popular job. It fell into disuse fairly quickly although, in theory, the system lasted until 1937 when the number screens on the new Coronation trams rejuvenated, for a time, the Headcode numbers and letters. Also there were some Services withdrawn in the late 1920s and early 1930s which never had Headcode identification allocated to them. The digital indicators had originally been used to display the Departmental Route or Running Numbers of the individual cars much to the confusion to the public and thus no doubt reducing markedly the chances of the Headcode System's ever being accepted!

Final Numbering System and Phasing-out of Route Colours

However, it had been decided to introduce a more straightforward system of Service Numbers in time for the 1938 Empire Exhibition in Bellahouston Park, mainly to allay, possibly unfounded, fears that strangers to the city would find the Route Colour system difficult to master, although this would not be helped by the need to draft in cars of whatever colour was available to handle crowds travelling to and from the Exhibition.

The Route Colour system was not displayed by the new Coronation trams which had adopted the then Bus- or Standard-Green livery on their upper deck panels, so perhaps after all there would have been an element of confusion! It should be explained that the Standard-Green colour did differ from the Route-Colour Green which latter was a darker shade. The new Service Numbers, in May 1938, were structured on the then-existing system of Motorbus Service Numbers but still retained, by use of suffix letters, the tram services in their Route Colour groups. The Numbers from 1 to 20 were initially allocated with suffix identification being associated with Services 1/1A, 4/4A/4B, 5/5A, 8/8A/8B, 9/9A/9B and 15/15A. The numbers 3A, 30/30A and 31 were allocated for temporary Empire Exhibition Services. A new Service introduced at the close of the Exhibition was numbered 21. By the outbreak of the Second World War, with the repainting of White cars and Green cars, mainly into the Standard-Green Livery carried by the Coronation trams and the Motorbuses, there was a greater and greater dependence by the travelling public on the Service Numbers. A major reorganisation of tram services in August 1943 caused the splitting into two of some of the longer services and the renumbering of all the services then carrying suffix letters. This brought into use the numbers from 22 to 32 but along with new 3A and 5A Services. Service 40 was introduced at the end of 1943, followed by 10A and 33 in 1944, 34 in 1946, 14A in 1947, 14B in 1948, 35 and 36 in 1949 and 24A in 1951. 31 was out of use from 1946 until early 1949. The numbers 37, 38 and 39 were never used in this series. Subsequent changes to Services saw the introduction of 18A and 26A in 1955. Repainting of Route-coloured Cars in Standard-Green brought about the final demise of the Red, Yellow and Blue cars in the early 1950s.

The density of city centre services can be seen in this 1950s commercial postcard, looking north in Renfield Street. Standard trams dominate, as usual, with one Cunarder about to cross St Vincent Street. The lower view is in complete contrast and shows that, as late as 1960 the Glasgow trams went through undeveloped territory – in this case between Garrowhill and Barrachnie.
(Upper: IG Stewart Collection, Lower: BJ Cross Collection)

EXPLANATORY NOTES

ROUTE COLOURS — Route colour bands were carried on the upper deck side panels and dashes. At night, the colour was also displayed through an appropriately illuminated lens on the bulkhead that could be changed over so that red was always displayed at the rear.

SLIPBOARDS — Refers to Route Boards carried on the upper deck side panels.

ROUTE — The Route Description details all the streets traversed by each Service. Reference should be made to the List of Changes to determine the position at any given time.

PART DAY SERVICES — Part Day Services usually ran at Weekdays and Saturdays Peak Periods but in some cases at other times and also provided some service on Sundays.

SPECIALS — In addition to extra peak-hour cars covering regular routes, many additional runs were provided by "Specials" comprising timetabled duties with their own series of Route Numbers (qv) often connecting two or three areas otherwise without a direct service. These cars usually displayed a blank service number. The best examples were the Shipyard Specials connecting many areas of the system with Partick, Whiteinch, Scotstoun, Clydebank, Dalmuir, Govan, Linthouse and Shieldhall. Some depots would thus provide cars into areas not normally served by that particular Shed (e.g. Maryhill Depot cars along Dumbarton Road and Langside Depot cars into Renfrew and Paisley). Other Specials would cover journeys over a basic service route and thus, to the public, would be scarcely distinguishable from regular service cars.

DEPOT — Depot Allocations changed from time to time for certain Services. Information provided refers to the established Service and may not necessarily record all allocations.

DEPOT WORKINGS — Very few tram services actually passed by the Depot doors resulting in specific routes being followed by cars going into or coming off service. With the exception of Elderslie Depot between July 1932 and February 1940, such cars were always deemed to be in service and would carry any passengers offering. Details of routes followed appear under the Depot listings. These are described outwards from the Depots. Inwards journeys followed the same routes except where otherwise indicated.

ROUTE NUMBERS — The term "Route Numbers" refers to each individual tram's Running Number. These were displayed on the side of the car initially with oval enamel plates, then on metal stencil plates and, latterly, sometimes on white plastic tabs. These were not advertised to the public. However, they were also displayed prominently from about 1913 on digital number screens on vestibuled and unvestibuled Round Dash Standard cars below the canopy bends, much to the mystery and confusion of the travelling public. These indicators were replaced by three-track displays on all cars and utilised for the Headcode system introduced in 1925.

SERVICE NUMBERS — The term "Service Numbers" applies to the numbering system introduced in 1938 for the identification of the different tram services.

CAR TYPES — There were certain restrictions in the types of tramcar permitted to operate on certain services due, for example, to tight radii and limited clearances or to height restriction. There were also some operating practices governing usage of cars on certain services. Reference is made to these under the individual services.

IDENTIFICATION OF INDIVIDUAL SERVICES — Originally, services were identified, internally and in the public domain, solely by their Route Colours and terminal points. A system of identification by Letter, used also on the Bell-punch tickets, was introduced for internal use by the Corporation. In order to assist in the understanding of the history of the services in the following records, this Letter identification has been used, along with the Route Colours, from the outset in 1898, changing over to the Service Number system upon its introduction in 1938.

STREET NAMES — As the City of Glasgow expanded and individual burghs were absorbed, there were, mainly in the 1920s, high numbers of renamings of streets including principal thoroughfares. Often, this was to eliminate duplication. For the sake of clarity, the later names are used throughout in the route descriptions with the exception of Garngad Road which had its name changed as late as 1942, only seven years before the trams were withdrawn from that thoroughfare. Those changes that affected tram routes are as follows:

Later Name	Former Name
Abercromby Street	
Canning Street to Stevenson Street	Clyde Street
Admiral Street	Wellington Street
Albert Drive	
Pollokshaws Road to Shields Road	Albert Road
Argyle Street	
Anderston Cross to Finnieston	Main Street Anderston
Ballater Street	Govan Street
Bogmoor Road	Maxwell Road
Celtic Street	Lennox Street
Clyde Street	Great Clyde Street
Fulbar Road Paisley	Chain Road
Gallowgate	
Camlachie Foundry to Parkhead Cross	Great Eastern Road
Garscube Road	Garscube Street
Gibson Street	King Street
Golspie Street	White Street
Gorbals Street	Main Street Gorbals
Govan Road	
Paisley Road Toll to Lorne Street	Old Govan Road
Graving Docks to Fairfields	Main Road Govan
Greenview Street	Pollok Street
Hawthorn Street	Eastfield Street
Kilmarnock Road Giffnock	Fenwick Road
Lawmoor Street	South Wellington Street
London Road	
Glasgow Cross to Ross Street	London Street
Ross Street to Green Street	Great Hamilton Street
Green Street to Bridgeton Cross	Canning Street
Maryhill Road	
St George's Cross to Queen's Cross	New City Road
Queen's Cross to Gairbraid Avenue	Gairbraid Street
Gairbraid Avenue to Canal Aqueduct	Wyndford Street
Canal Aqueduct to Celtic Street	Main Street Maryhill
Millerston Street	East Miller Street
Milnpark Street	Park Street
Paisley Road West	Paisley Road
Pollokshaws Road	
Leckie Street to Pollok Street	Maxwell Street
Rutherglen Road	
Crown Street to South Wellington St	Rutherglen Loan
Rouken Glen Road	Eastwood Mains Road West
Royston Road	Garngad Road
Sauchiehall Street	
Argyle Street to Kelvingrove Street	Sandyford Street
Seaward Street	St James Street
Shawbridge Street	Main Street Pollokshaws
Shawfield Drive	Richmond Drive
Springfield Road	
Parkhead Cross to London Road	Dalmarnock Street
Strachur Street	Drummond Street
Tollcross Road	Great Eastern Road
Tullis Street	John Street Bridgeton
Turriff Street	Elgin Street
Woodlands Road	
Willowbank Street to Park Road	South Woodside Road
Wyndford Street	Garscube Road

9

DEVELOPMENT OF TRAMWAY SERVICES
DIARY OF EVENTS

Time Frame 1898 – 1902: Electrification

Having seen off the Glasgow Tramway & Omnibus Company at the expiry of their operating lease in 1894, within two years the Glasgow Corporation Tramways are already setting their sights on replacing horse traction with something better and, after several alternatives in a Report on "Mechanical Motors" were considered, electric traction using the overhead wire wins the day. Having researched state-of-the-art systems in America, many ideas sourced there are put into practice, including the most emphatic advice not to rely on any other municipal departments to supply traction power – hence the bold move in constructing the Tramways' own Power Station at Pinkston. So the years 1898 – 1902 mainly feature the electrification of existing lines with some extensions added for operational convenience.

The new electric trams obviously attracted a great deal of attention but evidently had to share the operation of the inaugural route with horse cars.
(BJ Cross collection)

A 'Room & Kitchen' car, newly into service, heads south along Springburn Road.

13th October 1898
  Commencement of Electric Traction Operation.
  Electrified Line Opened in Springburn Road, Castle Street, Parliamentary Road, Sauchiehall Street, West Nile Street and Mitchell Street.
  The following Service introduced:
  White Service S SPRINGBURN & MITCHELL STREET from Springburn Road at Balgrayhill via Springburn Road, Castle Street, Parliamentary Road, Sauchiehall Street, West Nile Street, Mitchell Street to Mitchell Street north end.
  ➢   *Springburn Depot, Keppochhill Road opened for Electric Traction.*
  Power generation provided from small Power Station adjoining Springburn Depot.

23rd January 1899
  Electrified Line Opened in Castle Street from Parliamentary Road and in High Street to Glasgow Cross.
  The following Service Alteration takes place:
  White Service S SPRINGBURN & MITCHELL STREET split to become SPRINGBURN & GLASGOW CROSS via former route to Castle Street, then via Castle Street, High Street to High Street at Glasgow Cross; and SPRINGBURN & MITCHELL STREET via former route.

8th November 1899

Electrified Line Opened in Saltmarket, Albert Bridge, Crown Street, Cathcart Road as far as Dixon Avenue.

Electrified Line Opened in Coplaw Street to link Coplawhill Car Works with electrified system.
Not used by cars in service.

The following Service Alteration takes place:

White Service S SPRINGBURN & GLASGOW CROSS section extended to become
SPRINGBURN & GOVANHILL via former route to Glasgow Cross then via Saltmarket, Albert Bridge, Crown Street, Cathcart Road to Cathcart Road at Dixon Avenue;
SPRINGBURN & MITCHELL STREET section unaltered.

19th February 1900

Electrified Line Opened in Monkland Street linking Parliamentary Road and Castle Street.
Not used for Service Cars.

27th April 1901

Pinkston Power Station inaugurated.
Power generation from Power Station at Springburn Depot phased out.

The extension of White Service S to Dixon Avenue featured trams lettered "GOVANHILL AND SPRINGBURN". It was a further five years before detachable Slipboards were introduced. The oval enamel disc displaying the car's Route Number is mounted over the centre window of the saloon.
(IG Stewart Collection)

Before the electrified link from Cathcart Road to Coplawhill Car Works was completed, cars requiring attention had to be dragged there by horses. Destination displays relied on rotating boards.
(BJ Cross collection)

28th April 1901

Electric Operation commences on Main Street Bridgeton, London Road and to Partick and Whiteinch. The following Services commence:

Red Service F PARTICK & DALMARNOCK from Dumbarton Road at Hayburn Street via Dumbarton Road, Argyle Street, Trongate, Glasgow Cross, London Road, Bridgeton Cross, Dalmarnock Road to Dalmarnock Road at Dalmarnock Bridge;

Red Service L WHITEINCH & LONDON ROAD from Dumbarton Road at Westland Drive via Dumbarton Road, Argyle Street, Trongate, Glasgow Cross, London Road, Bridgeton Cross, London Road to London Road at Kinnear Road.

White Service Y FINNIESTON & RUTHERGLEN BRIDGE from Argyle Street at Finnieston Street via Argyle Street, Trongate, Glasgow Cross, London Road, Bridgeton Cross, Main Street Bridgeton to Main Street Bridgeton at French Street.

> Partick Depot, Hayburn Street opened to Electric Traction.
> Dalmarnock Depot, Ruby Street opened to Electric Traction.

Cars operating Red Service F were lettered "PARTICK AND DALMARNOCK". Car 909 was fairly new and had still to be fitted with gate-and-tray lifeguards. It was photographed at a featureless location somewhere in the east end.
(BJ Cross collection)

1st May 1901

Electric Operation commences on Victoria Road, Eglinton Street, Bridge Street, Glasgow Bridge, Jamaica Street, Union Street, Renfield Street, Sauchiehall Street. The following Service commences:

Yellow Service C KELVINGROVE & QUEEN'S PARK from Sauchiehall Street west of Radnor Street via Sauchiehall Street, Charing Cross, Sauchiehall Street, Renfield Street, Union Street, Jamaica Street, Glasgow Bridge, Bridge Street, Eglinton Street, Eglinton Toll, Victoria Road to Queen's Park Gates.

Hand-coloured postcards of the period can be misleading. These are both yellow cars on Yellow Service C in a deserted Victoria Road with Queen's Park in the background.
(IG Stewart collection)

3rd May 1901

Opening of International Exhibition in Kelvingrove Park.
Line Opened in Radnor Street.
RADNOR STREET terminus renamed EXHIBITION.
The following Special Service commences:
White Service [Horse Shoe] QUEEN STREET & ST VINCENT STREET via RADNOR STREET from Argyle Street at Queen Street Lye via Argyle Street, Radnor Street, Sauchiehall Street, Charing Cross, Sauchiehall Street, Renfield Street, St Vincent Street to St Vincent Place. Cars show EXHIBITION on leaving Queen Street and St Vincent Place.

White cars operated special services to the 1901 International Exhibition at Kelvingrove Park but cars on Yellow Service C also displayed "EXHIBITION" for the duration.
(Courtesy: Struan JT Robertson)

5th May 1901

Electric Operation commences on Langside Road and Grange Road.
Electric Line Opened on Battlefield Road.
The following Service Alteration takes place:
Yellow Service C KELVINGROVE & QUEEN'S PARK extended to operate between
KELVINGROVE & LANGSIDE [Battlefield] via former route to Queen's Park Gates then via Langside Road, Grange Road, Battlefield Road to Battlefield Road at Langside Depot.
➢ *Langside Depot, Battlefield Road opened to Electric Traction.*

May 1901

Power distribution problems with the newly commissioned Pinkston Power Station require slower Horse Cars running on several routes along with electric cars.

Mixed horse and electric traction was still in operation when this 1901 view of Eglinton Toll was taken. The tram on White Service E turning into Maxwell Road is lettered "Gilmorehill" which preceded the "**UNIVERSITY**" destination.
(BJ Cross collection)

9th May 1901

Electric Operation commences on University route and through Pollokshields.

The following Service commences:

White Service E Weekdays and Saturdays: UNIVERSITY & POLLOKSHIELDS from University Avenue at Kelvin Way via University Avenue, Gibson Street, Eldon Street, Woodlands Road, St George's Road, Charing Cross, Sauchiehall Street, Renfield Street, Union Street, Jamaica Street, Glasgow Bridge, Bridge Street, Eglinton Street, Eglinton Toll, Maxwell Road, Kenmure Street, Albert Drive, St Andrew's Drive to St Andrew's Drive north of Nithsdale Road.

No Sundays Service.

Further Services for International Exhibition at Kelvingrove Park.

The following Service Alteration takes place:

White Service Y FINNIESTON & RUTHERGLEN BRIDGE extended to become EXHIBITION & RUTHERGLEN BRIDGE from Radnor Street via Argyle Street and former route.

11th May 1901

Electric Operation commences on St George's Road and on Maryhill Road between St George's Cross and Seamore Street.

The following Service commences:

Yellow Service H NEW CITY ROAD & LANGSIDE [Battlefield] from Maryhill Road at Seamore Street via Maryhill Road, St George's Cross, St George's Road, Charing Cross, Sauchiehall Street, Renfield Street, Union Street, Jamaica Street, Glasgow Bridge, Bridge Street, Eglinton Street, Victoria Road, Langside Road, Grange Road, Battlefield Road to Battlefield Road at Langside Depot.

12th May 1901

The following Service Alteration takes place:

Red Service F Sundays: PARTICK & DALMARNOCK extended to become
WHITEINCH & DALMARNOCK from Dumbarton Road at Westland Drive via Dumbarton Road and former route;
Weekdays and Saturdays: PARTICK & DALMARNOCK unaltered.

The Botanic Gardens terminus outside the station of that name featured a loop on the north side of Great Western Road.
(BJ Cross collection)

5th June 1901

Problems with power distribution from Pinkston Power Station resolved.

Electric Operation commences on Great Western Road, Park Road, Elmbank Street, Bothwell Street, Hope Street between Argyle Street and Gordon Street, and on Rutherglen Road; on Pollokshaws Road between Eglinton Toll and Shawlands, and on Kilmarnock Road, Coustonholm Road and Pleasance Street.

The following Services commence:

Blue Service O BOTANIC GARDENS & OATLANDS via PARK ROAD, CROWN STREET from Great Western Road west of Byres Road via Great Western Road, Park Road, Woodlands Road, St George's Road, Charing Cross, Sauchiehall Street, Elmbank Street, Bothwell Street, Hope Street, Argyle Street, Trongate, Glasgow Cross, Saltmarket, Albert Bridge, Crown Street, Rutherglen Road to Rutherglen Road at Braehead Street;

Red Service R SPRINGBURN & SHAWLANDS or POLLOKSHAWS from Springburn Road at Balgrayhill via Springburn

Road, Castle Street, Parliamentary Road, Sauchiehall Street, Renfield Street, Union Street, Jamaica Street, Glasgow Bridge, Bridge Street, Eglinton Street, Eglinton Toll, Pollokshaws Road, Shawlands Cross, Kilmarnock Road, Coustonholm Road.
➢ *Pollokshaws Depot, Pleasance Street opened to Electric Traction.*

A Red Service R car in Union Street photographed with Argyle Street eastbound track in the foreground. This view dates from 1901.
(BJ Cross collection)

8th June 1901

Line Opened on Church Street and Byres Road.
The following Service Alteration takes place:
Yellow Service C KELVINGROVE & LANGSIDE [Battlefield] extended to become
BOTANIC GARDENS or KELVINGROVE & LANGSIDE [Battlefield] from Great Western Road at Botanic Gardens via Byres Road, Church Street, Dumbarton Road, Argyle Street, Sauchiehall Street and former route.

13th June 1901

Electric Operation commences on Great Western Road and Dennistoun Services.
The following Service commences:
Green Service A KELVINSIDE & DENNISTOUN from Great Western Road at Hyndland Road via Great Western Road, St George's Cross, New City Road, Cambridge Street, Sauchiehall Street, Renfield Street, St Vincent Street, St Vincent Place, George Square west and north, George Street, Duke Street to Duke Street at Millerston Street.
➢ *Dennistoun Depot, Paton Street opened to Electric Traction.*

30th June 1901

Electric Operation commences on Maryhill to Gorbals routes.
The following Services commence:
Red Service M MARYHILL & MOUNT FLORIDA via NEW CITY ROAD from Maryhill Road at Maryhill Station via Maryhill Road, Queen's Cross, Maryhill Road, St George's Cross, New City Road, Cowcaddens, West Nile Street, St Vincent Street, St Vincent Place, George Square south, South Frederick Street, Ingram Street, Glassford Street, Stockwell Street, Victoria Bridge, Gorbals Street, Cathcart Road to Cathcart Road at McLennan Street;
Red Service N GAIRBRAID STREET & QUEEN'S PARK via NEW CITY ROAD from Maryhill Road at Northpark Street via Maryhill Road, Queen's Cross, Maryhill Road, St George's Cross, New City Road, Cowcaddens, West Nile Street, St Vincent Street, St Vincent Place, George Square south, South Frederick Street, Ingram Street, Glassford Street, Stockwell Street, Victoria Bridge, Gorbals Street, Pollokshaws Road, Eglinton Toll, Victoria Road to Queen's Park Gates;
Red Service T Weekdays & Saturdays: GAIRBRAID STREET & TRONGATE via NEW CITY ROAD from Maryhill Road at Northpark Street via Maryhill Road, Queen's Cross, Maryhill Road, St George's Cross, New City Road, Cowcaddens, West Nile Street, St Vincent Street, St Vincent Place, George Square south, South Frederick Street, Ingram Street, Glassford Street to Glassford Street at Trongate;
Sundays: MARYHILL & TRONGATE via NEW CITY ROAD from Maryhill Road at Maryhill Station via Maryhill Road and above route.

St Vincent Place was a terminal point for cars servicing the 1901 Exhibition at Kelvingrove Park. Car 971 on Red Service T was photographed there at that time. (BJ Cross collection)

The following Service Alteration takes place:
White Service S SPRINGBURN & MITCHELL STREET section withdrawn;
SPRINGBURN & GOVANHILL via GLASGOW CROSS section unaltered.
➢ *Maryhill Depot, Celtic Street, opened to Electric Traction.*
Prospecthill Road **opened to Electric Traction** for Langside Depot workings.
Mitchell Street and West Nile Street between St Vincent Street and Gordon Street **closed** to trams.

5th July 1901

Electric Operation commences on Garscube Road.
The following Service Alteration takes place:
Red Service N GAIRBRAID STREET & QUEEN'S PARK via NEW CITY ROAD diverted to become
GAIRBRAID STREET & QUEEN'S PARK via GARSCUBE ROAD from Maryhill Road at Northpark Street via Maryhill Road, Queen's Cross, Garscube Road, Round Toll, Garscube Road, Cowcaddens and former route.

14th July 1901

Introduction of Sunday Services on Pollokshields route.
White Service E Sundays: UNIVERSITY & POLLOKSHIELDS introduced;
Weekdays and Saturdays: UNIVERSITY & POLLOKSHIELDS unaltered.

28th July 1901

Electric Operation commences on Paisley Road and Parkhead routes.
The following Service commences:
Green Service B PAISLEY ROAD & PARKHEAD from Paisley Road Toll via Paisley Road, Morrison Street, Nelson Street, Bridge Street, Glasgow Bridge, Jamaica Street, Argyle Street, Trongate, Glasgow Cross, Gallowgate to Parkhead Cross.
➢ *Whitevale Depot, Rowchester Street opened to Electric Traction.*
➢ *Kinning Park Depot, Admiral Street, opened to Electric Traction.*

10th August 1901

Electric Operation commences on Possilpark and Govan routes.
The following Service commences:
Blue Service G POSSILPARK & GOVAN [Linthouse] via LORNE STREET from Saracen Cross via Saracen Street, Mosshouse, Possil Road, Round Toll, Garscube Road, Cowcaddens, Renfield Street, Union Street, Jamaica Street, Glasgow Bridge, Bridge Street, Nelson Street, Morrison Street, Paisley Road, Paisley Road Toll, Paisley Road West, Lorne Street, Govan Road, to Govan Road at Linthouse Burn.
➢ *Possilpark Depot, Hawthorn Street, opened for service.*

17th August 1901

Electric Operation commences between Paisley Road Toll and Halfwayhouse.
The following Service Alteration takes place:
Green Service B Weekdays and Saturdays: PAISLEY ROAD & PARKHEAD extended to become
HALFWAY, IBROX or PAISLEY ROAD TOLL & PARKHEAD from Paisley Road West at Halfwayhouse via Paisley Road West; from IBROX, Paisley Road West east of Copland Road via Paisley Road West, Paisley Road Toll and former route;
Sundays: PAISLEY ROAD & PARKHEAD extended to become HALFWAY or PAISLEY ROAD TOLL & PARKHEAD.

16

9th September 1901

Electric Operation commences on Bellgrove route.
The following Service commences:
Yellow Service J Weekdays and Saturdays: ALEXANDRA PARK & BRIDGETON CROSS from Cumbernauld Road at Kennyhill Square via Cumbernauld Road, Duke Street, Bellgrove Street, Abercromby Street, London Road to Bridgeton Cross;
No Sundays Service.

2nd October 1901

Line Opened on Alexandra Parade.
Line in Monkland Street **opened** to Service trams.
The following Service Alteration takes place:
Red Service R SPRINGBURN & SHAWLANDS or POLLOKSHAWS some cars diverted and extended, service split to become SPRINGBURN or ALEXANDRA PARK & POLLOKSHAWS; SPRINGBURN & SHAWLANDS;
ALEXANDRA PARK cars from Cumbernauld Road at Kennyhill Square via Cumbernauld Road, Alexandra Parade, Castle Street, Monkland Street, Parliamentary Road and former route;
Sundays: SPRINGBURN & SHAWLANDS or POLLOKSHAWS diverted and extended to become SPRINGBURN or ALEXANDRA PARK & POLLOKSHAWS.

October 1901

Closure of International Exhibition in Kelvingrove Park.
EXHIBITION terminus in Radnor Street renamed KELVINGROVE.
White Service [Horse Shoe] QUEEN STREET & ST VINCENT STREET via RADNOR STREET withdrawn.

25th November 1901

Line Opened on Great Western Road from Hyndland Road to Anniesland.
The following Service Alteration takes place:
Green Service A KELVINSIDE & DENNISTOUN part extended to become
ANNIESLAND or KELVINSIDE & DENNISTOUN from Anniesland Cross via Great Western Road and former route.

2nd December 1901

Line Opened on Keppochhill Road.
The following Service Alteration takes place:
Blue Service G POSSILPARK & GOVAN [Linthouse] via LORNE STREET part diverted and extended to become KEPPOCHHILL ROAD or POSSILPARK & GOVAN [Linthouse] via LORNE STREET from Keppochhill Road east end via Keppochhill Road, Mosshouse and former route.

12th December 1901

The following Service Alteration takes place:
White Service Y KELVINGROVE & RUTHERGLEN BRIDGE extended to become
WHITEINCH & RUTHERGLEN BRIDGE from Dumbarton Road at Westland Drive via Dumbarton Road, Argyle Street and former route.

6th January 1902

Green Service B was extended to Shettleston on 26th February 1902 and a Standard car on this service is seen here passing thatched houses still extant at that time.
(IG Stewart collection)

Springburn Power Station **closed** and plant sold to Rothesay Tramways. All power now supplied from Pinkston.
Line Opened in Hawthorn Street between Springburn Road and Possilpark Depot.
The following Operational Alterations take place:
Springburn Depot operation of
Red Service R SPRINGBURN or ALEXANDRA PARK & POLLOKSHAWS
Red Service R SPRINGBURN & SHAWLANDS
White Service S SPRINGBURN & GOVANHILL via GLASGOW CROSS
all transferred to Possilpark Depot.
Adjustment to Depot Allocation for Yellow Services C and H.
Yellow Service C BOTANIC GARDENS or KELVINGROVE & QUEEN'S PARK
Yellow Service H NEW CITY ROAD [Seamore Street] & LANGSIDE [Battlefield]
both transferred from Coplawhill Depot to Langside Depot.
Springburn Depot **closed** to trams. Remaining cars transferred to Possilpark Depot
Coplawhill Depot **closed** to trams. Remaining cars transferred to Langside Depot.

3rd February 1902

The following Operational Alterations take place:
Red Service R frequency to SPRINGBURN reduced and to ALEXANDRA PARK increased.
Red Service R SPRINGBURN or ALEXANDRA PARK & POLLOKSHAWS;
SPRINGBURN & SHAWLANDS adjusted accordingly.

26th February 1902

Electric Operation commences between Parkhead and Shettleston.
The following Service Alteration takes place:
Green Service B Weekdays and Saturdays: HALFWAY, IBROX or PAISLEY ROAD TOLL & PARKHEAD extended to become
HALFWAY or IBROX & PARKHEAD or SHETTLESTON via former route to Parkhead Cross then via Westmuir Street, Shettleston Sheddings, Shettleston Road to Shettleston Road at Gartocher Road;
Sundays: HALFWAY or PAISLEY ROAD TOLL & PARKHEAD altered and split to become
HALFWAY & SHETTLESTON; IBROX & PARKHEAD.
Increase in Services to Mount Florida.
The following Service Alteration takes place:
White Service S SPRINGBURN & GOVANHILL via GLASGOW CROSS extended to become
SPRINGBURN & GOVANHILL or MOUNT FLORIDA via GLASGOW CROSS via former route to Cathcart Road at Dixon Avenue then via Cathcart Road to Cathcart Road at McLennan Street.

24th March 1902

Electric Operation commences from Linthouse to Shieldhall and on Govan Road (Old Govan Road) between Paisley Road Toll and Lorne School.
GOVAN terminus renamed LINTHOUSE
The following Service Alterations take place:
Blue Service G KEPPOCHHILL ROAD or POSSILPARK & GOVAN [Linthouse] via LORNE STREET split and extended to become:
Blue Service G POSSILPARK & LINTHOUSE via LORNE STREET via former route; and
Blue Service K KEPPOCHHILL ROAD & SHIELDHALL via former route from Keppochhill Road to Paisley Road Toll then via Govan Road (Old Govan Road) and then former route to Govan Road at Linthouse Burn then via Renfrew Road to Shieldhall.

2nd April 1902

Line Opened from Dalmarnock to Rutherglen.
The following Service Alterations take place:
Red Service F Weekdays and Saturdays: PARTICK & DALMARNOCK extended to become
PARTICK & DALMARNOCK or RUTHERGLEN via former route to Dalmarnock Bridge then via Dalmarnock Road, Farme Cross, Farmeloan Road, Main Street Rutherglen to Main Street Rutherglen west of Castle Street;
Sundays: WHITEINCH & DALMARNOCK extended to become WHITEINCH & RUTHERGLEN via DALMARNOCK.

14th April 1902

Line Opened from Shettleston to Barrachnie.
Electric Operation commences between Parkhead and Tollcross.
Electrification of Services B & U completed.
The following Service Alterations take place:
Green Service B HALFWAY or IBROX & PARKHEAD or SHETTLESTON split and extended to become:
Green Service B Weekdays: IBROX & SHETTLESTON or BARRACHNIE via former route to Shettleston Road then via

Shettleston Road, Baillieston Road to Baillieston Road at Barrachnie Road/Mount Vernon Avenue;
Saturdays: IBROX & BARRACHNIE;
Sundays: IBROX & PARKHEAD extended to become IBROX & BARRACHNIE; and
Green Service U Weekdays and Saturdays: HALFWAY or IBROX & PARKHEAD;
IBROX & TOLLCROSS via former route to Parkhead Cross then via Tollcross Road to Tollcross Road at Causewayside Street;
Sundays: HALFWAY & SHETTLESTON diverted to become HALFWAY & TOLLCROSS.
Last Horse Car operation, between Parkhead and Tollcross, withdrawn. Never originally a horse car service, this had been a temporary expedient pending electrification.

5th June 1902

> **Résumé**
>
> **1st June 1902**
>
> The following Tram Services operating:
>
> | | | |
> |---|---|---|
> | A | Green | ANNIESLAND or KELVINSIDE & DENNISTOUN |
> | B | Green | IBROX & SHETTLESTON or BARRACHNIE |
> | C | Yellow | BOTANIC GARDENS or KELVINGROVE & LANGSIDE [Battlefield] |
> | E | White | UNIVERSITY & POLLOKSHIELDS |
> | F | Red | WHITEINCH or PARTICK & DALMARNOCK or RUTHERGLEN |
> | G | Blue | POSSILPARK & LINTHOUSE via LORNE STREET |
> | H | Yellow | NEW CITY ROAD [Seamore Street] & LANGSIDE [Battlefield] |
> | J | Yellow | ALEXANDRA PARK & BRIDGETON CROSS |
> | K | Blue | KEPPOCHHILL ROAD & SHIELDHALL |
> | L | Red | WHITEINCH & LONDON ROAD |
> | M | Red | MARYHILL & MOUNT FLORIDA via NEW CITY ROAD |
> | N | Red | GAIRBRAID STREET & QUEEN'S PARK via GARSCUBE ROAD |
> | O | Blue | BOTANIC GARDENS & OATLANDS via PARK ROAD, CROWN STREET |
> | R | Red | SPRINGBURN or ALEXANDRA PARK & SHAWLANDS or POLLOKSHAWS |
> | S | White | SPRINGBURN & GOVANHILL or MOUNT FLORIDA via GLASGOW GROSS |
> | T | Red | MARYHILL or GAIRBRAID STREET & TRONGATE via NEW CITY ROAD |
> | U | Green | HALFWAY or IBROX & PARKHEAD or TOLLCROSS |
> | Y | White | WHITEINCH & RUTHERGLEN BRIDGE |

St George's Road looking north from Charing Cross finds a White car about to bear left into Woodlands Road heading for the University. St George's Road swings to the right and at the time carries only the Yellow Service H bound for New City Road [Seamore Street].
(Commercial Postcard courtesy NTM Archive)

Time Frame 1902 – 1914: Expansion

With the last of the horse trams out of the way, new lines and extensions are laid down with amazing vigour and rapidity right up to the 1914 -1918 War. The pace of doing so compares very favourably with 21st Century practice anywhere other than the United Kingdom. Coupled with this are constant refinement and adjustment of services at a frequency that would not be out of place today where ever-changing bus services and frequencies are wearily accepted as the norm by the hapless travelling public.

Looking west along Dumbarton Road from Partick (North British Railway) Station bridge, alterations to the track to improve access to Hayburn Street and Partick Depot are under way.
(IG Stewart collection)

Line Opened from Whiteinch to Scotstoun.
The following Service Alterations take place:
Red Service L Weekdays and Saturdays: WHITEINCH & LONDON ROAD extended to become
SCOTSTOUN or WHITEINCH & LONDON ROAD from Dumbarton Road at Queen Victoria Drive via Dumbarton Road and former route;
Sundays: WHITEINCH & LONDON ROAD extended to become SCOTSTOUN & LONDON ROAD;
White Service Y Weekdays and Saturdays: WHITEINCH & RUTHERGLEN BRIDGE cut back to become
PARTICK & RUTHERGLEN BRIDGE from Dumbarton Road at Hayburn Street and former route;
Sundays: WHITEINCH & RUTHERGLEN BRIDGE unaltered.

14th June 1902

Line Opened on Pollokshaws Road from Shawlands Cross to Greenview Street.
Greenview Street **opened** between Pollokshaws Depot and Pollokshaws Road.
POLLOKSHAWS renamed POLLOKSHAWS EAST.
The following Service Alterations take place:
Red Service R Weekdays and Saturdays: SPRINGBURN or ALEXANDRA PARK & POLLOKSHAWS altered to become
ALEXANDRA PARK & POLLOKSHAWS EAST from Alexandra Park via former route to Coustonholm Road east end;
Weekdays and Saturdays: SPRINGBURN & SHAWLANDS extended to become
SPRINGBURN & SHAWLANDS or POLLOKSHAWS WEST via former route to Shawlands Cross then via Pollokshaws Road to Pollokshaws Road at Greenview Street;
Sundays: SPRINGBURN or ALEXANDRA PARK & POLLOKSHAWS altered and extended to become
 ALEXANDRA PARK & POLLOKSHAWS EAST; and SPRINGBURN & SHAWLANDS or POLLOKSHAWS WEST.

19th June 1902

The following Service Alteration takes place:
White Service Y Weekdays and Saturdays: PARTICK & RUTHERGLEN BRIDGE re-extended to become
WHITEINCH or PARTICK & RUTHERGLEN BRIDGE from Dumbarton Rd at Westland Drive via Dumbarton Rd and former route;
Sundays: WHITEINCH & RUTHERGLEN BRIDGE unaltered.

5th July 1902

The following Service Alterations take place:
Red Service F Saturdays: PARTICK & DALMARNOCK or RUTHERGLEN extended to become
WHITEINCH or PARTICK & DALMARNOCK or RUTHERGLEN from Dumbarton Road at Westland Drive via former route;
Weekdays: PARTICK & DALMARNOCK or RUTHERGLEN unaltered;
Sundays: WHITEINCH & RUTHERGLEN via DALMARNOCK unaltered;
White Service Y Saturdays: WHITEINCH or PARTICK & RUTHERGLEN BRIDGE cut back to become
PARTICK & RUTHERGLEN BRIDGE;
Weekdays: WHITEINCH or PARTICK & RUTHERGLEN BRIDGE unaltered.
Sundays: WHITEINCH & RUTHERGLEN BRIDGE unaltered.

17th July 1902

Line Opened on Pollokshaws Road from Greenview Street to Barrhead Road.
POLLOKSHAWS WEST terminus extended to Pollokshaws Road at Barrhead Road.
Red Service R SPRINGBURN & SHAWLANDS or POLLOKSHAWS WEST section extended accordingly via Pollokshaws Road to Pollokshaws Road at Barrhead Road.

6th August 1902

Line Opened from Oatlands to Rutherglen.
The following Service Alteration takes place:
Blue Service O Weekdays and Saturdays: BOTANIC GARDENS & OATLANDS via PARK ROAD, CROWN STREET extended to become BOTANIC GARDENS & OATLANDS or RUTHERGLEN via PARK ROAD, CROWN STREET via former route to Rutherglen Road at Braehead Street then via Rutherglen Road, Glasgow Road, Main Street Rutherglen to Main Street Rutherglen west of Castle Street; Sundays: BOTANIC GARDENS & OATLANDS via PARK ROAD, CROWN STREET extended to become BOTANIC GARDENS & RUTHERGLEN via PARK ROAD, CROWN STREET.

25th August 1902

Line Opened on Duke Street from Paton Street to Carntyne Road.
The following Service Alteration takes place:
Green Service A Weekdays and Saturdays: ANNIESLAND or KELVINSIDE & DENNISTOUN altered to become
ANNIESLAND & DENNISTOUN via former route;
Sundays: ANNIESLAND or KELVINSIDE & DENNISTOUN altered to become ANNIESLAND or BOTANIC GARDENS & CARNTYNE via former route to Dennistoun then via Duke Street to Duke Street at Carntyne Road.
The following Service commences:
Green Service D Weekdays and Saturdays. BOTANIC GARDENS & CARNTYNE from Great Western Road west of Byres Road via Great Western Road, St George's Cross, New City Road, Cambridge Street, Sauchiehall Street, Renfield Street, St Vincent Street, St Vincent Place, George Square west and north, George Street, Duke Street to Duke Street at Carntyne Road; No Sundays Service.
Line Opened on Aikenhead Road from Cathcart Road to Govanhill Street.
The following Service Alteration takes place:
White Service S SPRINGBURN & GOVANHILL or MOUNT FLORIDA via GLASGOW CROSS diverted, altered, split and part extended to become SPRINGBURN & MOUNT FLORIDA via GLASGOW CROSS via former route; and
SPRINGBURN & POLMADIE via GLASGOW CROSS via former route to Cathcart Road then via Aikenhead Road to Aikenhead Road at Govanhill Street.

8th September 1902

Line Opened from Battlefield Road to Cathcart.
The following Service Alteration takes place:
Yellow Service C BOTANIC GARDENS or KELVINGROVE & LANGSIDE [Battlefield] altered and extended to become
BOTANIC GARDENS & CATHCART and
KELVINGROVE & LANGSIDE [Battlefield] via former route to Battlefield Road at Langside Depot then via Battlefield Road, Holmlea Road, Clarkston Road to Clarkston Road at Dairsie Street.

25th September 1902

The following Service Alterations take place:
Green Service A Weekdays and Saturdays: ANNIESLAND & DENNISTOUN extended to become
ANNIESLAND & CARNTYNE via former route to Duke Street at Millerston Street then via Duke Street to Duke Street at Carntyne Road;

Sundays: ANNIESLAND or BOTANIC GARDENS & CARNTYNE unaltered;

Green Service D Weekdays and Saturdays: BOTANIC GARDENS & CARNTYNE altered to become KELVINSIDE & DENNISTOUN from Great Western Road at Hyndland Road via Great Western Road and former route to Duke Street at Millerston Street; No Sundays Service.

10th October 1902

Line Opened in Grange Road to Battle Place.
The following Service Alteration takes place:

Yellow Service H NEW CITY ROAD [Seamore Street] & LANGSIDE [Battlefield] diverted to become NEW CITY ROAD [Seamore Street] & BATTLE PLACE via former route to Langside Road then via Langside Road to Battle Place.

12th October 1902

The following Service Alteration takes place:

Green Service A Sundays: ANNIESLAND or BOTANIC GARDENS & CARNTYNE altered to extend all shortworking cars to become ANNIESLAND & CARNTYNE;
Weekdays and Saturdays: ANNIESLAND & CARNTYNE unaltered.

29th October 1902

Line Opened from Scotstoun to Yoker.
The following Service Alteration takes place:

Red Service L SCOTSTOUN or WHITEINCH & LONDON ROAD extended to become YOKER or WHITEINCH & LONDON ROAD from Dumbarton Road at Yoker Burn via Dumbarton Road and former route;
Sundays: SCOTSTOUN & LONDON ROAD extended to become YOKER & LONDON ROAD.

3rd November 1902

Line Opened from Halfwayhouse to Crookston.
The following Service Alteration takes place:

Green Service U Weekdays and Saturdays: HALFWAY or IBROX & PARKHEAD extended to become CROOKSTON or IBROX & PARKHEAD from Paisley Road West at Crookston Road via Paisley Road West and former route;
Weekdays and Saturdays: IBROX & TOLLCROSS section unaltered;
Sundays: HALFWAY & TOLLCROSS extended to become CROOKSTON & TOLLCROSS.

22nd November 1902

Line Opened from Shieldhall to Renfrew.
The following Service Alteration takes place:

Blue Service K Weekdays and Saturdays: KEPPOCHHILL ROAD & SHIELDHALL extended to become KEPPOCHHILL ROAD & SHIELDHALL or RENFREW via former route to Shieldhall then via Renfrew Road, Govan Road Renfrew, High Street Renfrew to Renfrew Cross;
Sundays: KEPPOCHHILL ROAD & SHIELDHALL extended to become KEPPOCHHILL ROAD & RENFREW.

24th November 1902

The following Service Alterations take place:

Red Service N Weekdays and Saturdays: GAIRBRAID STREET & QUEEN'S PARK via GARSCUBE ROAD extended to become BARRACKS GATE & LANGSIDE [Battlefield] via GARSCUBE ROAD from Maryhill Road at Maryhill Barracks Gate via Maryhill Road and former route to Queen's Park Gates then via Langside Road, Grange Road to

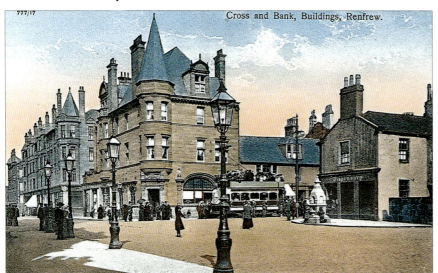

Glasgow Corporation trams reached Renfrew Cross before the Paisley District Tramways arrived. Here is a Glasgow tram waiting to depart for the city prior to laying track and erecting overhead for the Paisley trams.
(IG Stewart collection)

Battlefield Road;

Sundays: GAIRBRAID STREET & QUEEN'S PARK via GARSCUBE ROAD extended to become
MARYHILL & LANGSIDE [Battlefield] via GARSCUBE ROAD;

Red Service T Weekdays and Saturdays: GAIRBRAID STREET & TRONGATE via NEW CITY ROAD extended to become
BARRACKS GATE & TRONGATE via NEW CITY ROAD from Maryhill Road at Maryhill Barracks Gate via Maryhill Road and former route;

Sundays: MARYHILL & TRONGATE via NEW CITY ROAD unaltered.

1st December 1902

Alteration to terminal names in Langside and Battlefield area.

LANGSIDE terminus renamed BATTLEFIELD.

BATTLE PLACE terminus renamed LANGSIDE.

The following Service Alterations take place:

Yellow Service C KELVINGROVE & LANGSIDE [Battlefield] section becomes
KELVINGROVE & BATTLEFIELD all via former route;

Yellow Service H NEW CITY ROAD [Seamore Street] & BATTLE PLACE [Langside] becomes
NEW CITY ROAD [Seamore Street] & LANGSIDE all via former route;

Red Service N Weekdays and Saturdays: BARRACKS GATE & LANGSIDE [Battlefield] via GARSCUBE ROAD becomes
BARRACKS GATE & BATTLEFIELD via GARSCUBE ROAD all via former route;

Sundays: MARYHILL & LANGSIDE [Battlefield] via GARSCUBE ROAD becomes
MARYHILL & BATTLEFIELD via GARSCUBE ROAD.

2nd February 1903

On 23rd February 1903 White Service E was part diverted to New City Road. Here, electrified Horse Car No.51 is seen entering the Seamore Street loop.
(IG Stewart collection)

Line Opened from Springburn to Bishopbriggs.

The following Service Alteration takes place:

Red Service R SPRINGBURN & SHAWLANDS or POLLOKSHAWS WEST section extended to become
BISHOPBRIGGS or SPRINGBURN & SHAWLANDS or POLLOKSHAWS WEST from Kirkintilloch Road north of Springfield Road Bishopbriggs via Kirkintilloch Road, Springburn Road and former route;
ALEXANDRA PARK & POLLOKSHAWS EAST section unaltered.

16th February 1903

Line Opened from Rutherglen Bridge to Glasgow Road at Rutherglen Road.

White Service Y Weekdays and Saturdays: WHITEINCH or PARTICK & RUTHERGLEN BRIDGE extended to become
WHITEINCH or PARTICK & RUTHERGLEN BRIDGE or RUTHERGLEN via former route to Main Street Bridgeton at French Street then via Main Street Bridgeton, Rutherglen Bridge, Shawfield Road, Glasgow Road, Main Street Rutherglen to Main Street Rutherglen west of Castle Street;

Sundays: WHITEINCH & RUTHERGLEN BRIDGE extended to become
WHITEINCH & RUTHERGLEN via RUTHERGLEN BRIDGE.

23rd February 1903

Services Yellow CH and White E to and from New City Road [Seamore Street] switched.

The following Service Alterations take place:
White Service E UNIVERSITY & POLLOKSHIELDS part diverted to become
UNIVERSITY or NEW CITY ROAD [Seamore Street] & POLLOKSHIELDS from Maryhill Road at Seamore Street via Maryhill Road, St George's Cross, St George's Road; from University unaltered via former route and then all via former route;
Yellow Service C KELVINGROVE & BATTLEFIELD section withdrawn, replaced by Yellow Service H;
Yellow Service C BOTANIC GARDENS & CATHCART section unaltered;
Yellow Service H NEW CITY ROAD [Seamore Street] & LANGSIDE diverted to become KELVINGROVE & LANGSIDE from Radnor Street via Sauchiehall Street, Charing Cross, Sauchiehall Street and former route.

23rd March 1903

Line Opened from Alexandra Park to Riddrie (Cumbernauld Road at Lomax Street).
The following Service Alteration takes place:
Red Service R ALEXANDRA PARK & POLLOKSHAWS EAST section extended to become
RIDDRIE or ALEXANDRA PARK & POLLOKSHAWS EAST from Cumbernauld Road at Lomax Street via Cumbernauld Road and former route;
The following Service Alterations also take place:
Weekdays: BISHOPBRIGGS or SPRINGBURN & SHAWLANDS or POLLOKSHAWS WEST section part-extended to become BISHOPBRIGGS or SPRINGBURN & POLLOKSHAWS WEST;
Saturdays: BISHOPBRIGGS or SPRINGBURN & SHAWLANDS or POLLOKSHAWS WEST unaltered;
Sundays: BISHOPBRIGGS or SPRINGBURN & POLLOKSHAWS WEST altered to become
BISHOPBRIGGS & POLLOKSHAWS WEST.

29th March 1903

Introduction of Sundays Service on Bellgrove route.
The following Service commences:
Yellow Service J Sundays: ALEXANDRA PARK & BRIDGETON CROSS.

27th April 1903

Service to Rutherglen and Sundays Service to Renfrew improved.
The following Service Alterations take place:
White Service Y Weekdays and Saturdays: WHITEINCH or PARTICK & RUTHERGLEN BRIDGE or RUTHERGLEN altered to become WHITEINCH or PARTICK & RUTHERGLEN via RUTHERGLEN BRIDGE;
Sundays: WHITEINCH & RUTHERGLEN via RUTHERGLEN BRIDGE unaltered;
Blue Service G Sundays: POSSILPARK & LINTHOUSE via LORNE STREET part extended to become
POSSILPARK & LINTHOUSE or RENFREW via LORNE STREET;
Weekdays and Saturdays: POSSILPARK & LINTHOUSE via LORNE STREET unaltered.

By the time the Paisley District trams served Renfrew, their tracks remained unconnected to the Glasgow network. Compare this view with that on page 22. (IG Stewart collection)

During 1903
Line Opened in Clyde Street between Saltmarket and Mart Street to provide siding for the High Court of Justiciary for movement of prisoners.

14th May 1903
Line Opened at Mount Florida from Cathcart Road at McLennan Street via Clincart Road to Clincart Road at Florida Street.
MOUNT FLORIDA terminus moved southwards to Clincart Road at Florida Street.
Red Service M MARYHILL & MOUNT FLORIDA via NEW CITY ROAD
White Service S SPRINGBURN & MOUNT FLORIDA via GLASGOW CROSS both extended accordingly.

30th May 1903
Line Opened from Yoker to Clydebank (Glasgow Road at Bon Accord Street).
The following Service Alterations take place:
Red Service F Weekdays: PARTICK & DALMARNOCK or RUTHERGLEN extended to become
WHITEINCH & DALMARNOCK or RUTHERGLEN from Dumbarton Rd at Westland Dr via Dumbarton Rd and former route;
Saturdays: WHITEINCH or PARTICK & DALMARNOCK or RUTHERGLEN altered to become
WHITEINCH & DALMARNOCK or RUTHERGLEN;
Sundays: WHITEINCH & RUTHERGLEN via DALMARNOCK unaltered;
Red Service L Weekdays and Saturdays: YOKER or WHITEINCH & LONDON ROAD extended to become
CLYDEBANK or WHITEINCH & LONDON ROAD from Glasgow Road Clydebank at Bon Accord Street via Glasgow Road Clydebank, Dumbarton Road and former route:
Sundays: YOKER & LONDON ROAD extended to become CLYDEBANK & LONDON ROAD;
White Service Y WHITEINCH or PARTICK & RUTHERGLEN via RUTHERGLEN BRIDGE cut back to become
PARTICK & RUTHERGLEN via RUTHERGLEN BRIDGE all week.

8th June 1903
Increase in Weekdays frequency to Crookston.
Green Service U Weekdays: CROOKSTON or IBROX & PARKHEAD extended to become CROOKSTON & PARKHEAD;
IBROX & TOLLCROSS section unaltered;

20th June 1903
The following Service Alteration takes place:
Red Service L Saturdays: CLYDEBANK or WHITEINCH & LONDON ROAD altered to become
CLYDEBANK & LONDON ROAD;
Weekdays: CLYDEBANK or WHITEINCH & LONDON ROAD unaltered;
Sundays: CLYDEBANK & LONDON ROAD unaltered.

20th August 1903
Line Opened from Bridgeton Cross to Nelson Street.
The following Service Alteration takes place:
Yellow Service J ALEXANDRA PARK & BRIDGETON CROSS extended to become
ALEXANDRA PARK & PAISLEY ROAD TOLL via BRIDGETON CROSS via former route to Bridgeton Cross then via James Street, King's Drive, King's Bridge, Ballater Street, Norfolk Street, Nelson Street, Morrison Street, Paisley Road to Paisley Road east of Paisley Road Toll.

7th September 1903
Provision of additional cars on Saturdays to Linthouse.
The following Service Alteration takes place:
Yellow Service J Saturdays: ALEXANDRA PARK & PAISLEY ROAD TOLL via BRIDGETON CROSS
part extended to become ALEXANDRA PARK & PAISLEY ROAD TOLL or LINTHOUSE via BRIDGETON CROSS via former route to Paisley Road Toll then via Old Govan Road, Govan Road to Govan Road at Linthouse Burn;
Weekdays and Sundays: ALEXANDRA PARK & PAISLEY ROAD TOLL via BRIDGETON CROSS unaltered.

26th November 1903
Line Opened from Crookston to meet Paisley District Tramways at Hawkhead Road.
The following Service Alteration takes place:
Green Service U Weekdays and Saturdays: CROOKSTON or IBROX & PARKHEAD section extended to become
PAISLEY & PARKHEAD from Glasgow Road Paisley at Hawkhead Road via Glasgow Road Paisley, Paisley Road West and former route;
IBROX & TOLLCROSS section unaltered;
Sundays: CROOKSTON & TOLLCROSS extended to become PAISLEY & TOLLCROSS.

2nd December 1903
Line Opened from Farme Cross to Cambuslang.

NEW CITY ROAD terminus at Seamore Street renamed SEAMORE STREET.
Further rearrangement of Services terminating at Seamore Street.
The following Service commences:

Red Service X PARTICK & CAMBUSLANG via BOTHWELL STREET from Dumbarton Road at Hayburn Street via Dumbarton Road, Argyle Street, St Vincent Street, Bothwell Street, Argyle Street, Trongate, Glasgow Cross, London Road, Bridgeton Cross, Dalmarnock Road, Farme Cross, Cambuslang Road, Glasgow Road Cambuslang, Main Street Cambuslang to Main Street Cambuslang east end.

The following Service Alterations take place:

White Service E UNIVERSITY or NEW CITY ROAD [Seamore Street] & POLLOKSHIELDS reverts to UNIVERSITY & POLLOKSHIELDS via former route;

Weekdays and Saturdays Specials: GORDON STREET & POLLOKSHIELDS introduced from Gordon Street via Gordon Street, Union Street and former route;

White Service Y PARTICK & RUTHERGLEN via RUTHERGLEN BRIDGE diverted to become SEAMORE STREET & RUTHERGLEN via RUTHERGLEN BRIDGE from Maryhill Road at Seamore Street via Maryhill Road, St George's Cross, St George's Road, Charing Cross, Sauchiehall Street, Elmbank Street, Bothwell Street, Hope Street, Argyle Street and former route.

27th December 1903

Frequency of Sundays Services to Renfrew reduced.
The following Service Alteration takes place:

Blue Service K Sundays: KEPPOCHHILL ROAD & RENFREW part cut back to become KEPPOCHHILL ROAD & LINTHOUSE or RENFREW;

Weekdays and Saturdays: KEPPOCHHILL ROAD & SHIELDHALL or RENFREW unaltered.

23rd January 1904

Adjustments to provide improved service to Cambuslang on Saturday afternoons.
The following Service Alterations take place:

Red Service F Saturdays: WHITEINCH & DALMARNOCK or RUTHERGLEN altered to become WHITEINCH & DALMARNOCK, RUTHERGLEN or CAMBUSLANG with alternate Cars after 1300 proceeding from Farme Cross via Cambuslang Road, Glasgow Road Cambuslang, Main Street Cambuslang to Main Street Cambuslang east end;

Weekdays: WHITEINCH & DALMARNOCK or RUTHERGLEN unaltered;
Sundays: WHITEINCH & RUTHERGLEN via DALMARNOCK unaltered;

Red Service X Saturdays: PARTICK & CAMBUSLANG via BOTHWELL STREET adjusted after 1300 hrs.

21st February 1904

POLLOKSHAWS EAST terminus extended from Coustonholm Road east end to Coustonholm Road at Coustonhill Street.

Red Service R RIDDRIE or ALEXANDRA PARK & POLLOKSHAWS EAST section extended via Coustonholm Road to Coustonholm Road at Coustonhill Street.

Regular cars commence operation on Coustonholm Road.

29th February 1904

Reduction in frequency of Weekdays Service to Paisley.
The following Service Alteration takes place:

Green Service U Weekdays: PAISLEY & PARKHEAD altered to become PAISLEY or IBROX & PARKHEAD;
IBROX & TOLLCROSS section unaltered;
Saturdays: IBROX & TOLLCROSS; PAISLEY & PARKHEAD unaltered;
Sundays: PAISLEY & TOLLCROSS unaltered.

During 1904

Starting with new Top-covered (Phase II) Standard cars, Slipboards introduced on upper-deck side-panels. Eventually also applied to all remaining open-top cars.

17th April 1904

Line Opened on Duke Street from Carntyne Road to Parkhead Cross.
DENNISTOUN terminus moved from Duke Street at Millerston Street to Duke Street at Fleming Street. Crossover at Millerston Street retained for Depot Workings.
The following Service Alteration takes place:

Green Service A ANNIESLAND & CARNTYNE extended to become ANNIESLAND & PARKHEAD via former route to Duke Street at Carntyne Road then via Duke Street to Parkhead Cross;

Green Service D KELVINSIDE & DENNISTOUN (No Sunday Service) extended accordingly.
The following Specials introduced:

Green Service B Saturdays: QUEEN STREET & BARRACHNIE;
Green Service U Saturdays and Sundays: PAISLEY & QUEEN STREET.

During 1904

The following Service Alteration takes place:

White Service E Weekdays and Saturdays Specials: GORDON STREET & POLLOKSHIELDS extended to become ST VINCENT STREET & POLLOKSHIELDS from St Vincent Street west of Renfield Street via St Vincent Street, Renfield Street, Union Street and former route.

4th June 1904

Lines Opened on Finnieston Street and on North Street.

The following Service commences:

Green Service W ST GEORGE'S CROSS & STOBCROSS FERRY via NORTH STREET from St George's Cross via St George's Road, Charing Cross, Sauchiehall Street, North Street, St Vincent Street, Argyle Street, Finnieston Street, Stobcross Quay to Stobcross Quay at Harbour Tunnel.

13th August 1904

Increase in frequency of Paisley Services on Saturday afternoons.

The following Service Alterations take place:

Green Service B Saturdays: IBROX & SHETTLESTON or BARRACHNIE extended to become PAISLEY & SHETTLESTON or BARRACHNIE from Glasgow Road Paisley at Hawkhead Road via Glasgow Road Paisley, Paisley Road West and former route;

Weekdays: IBROX & SHETTLESTON or BARRACHNIE unaltered;

Sundays: IBROX & BARRACHNIE unaltered;

Green Service U Saturdays: IBROX & TOLLCROSS section extended to become PAISLEY & TOLLCROSS from Glasgow Road Paisley at Hawkhead Road via Glasgow Road Paisley, Paisley Road West and former route;

Saturday Specials: PAISLEY & QUEEN STREET withdrawn;

PAISLEY & PARKHEAD section unaltered;

Weekdays: PAISLEY or IBROX & PARKHEAD; IBROX & TOLLCROSS unaltered;

Sundays: PAISLEY & TOLLCROSS unaltered.

14th September 1904

Line Opened on St George's Road from St George's Cross to Round Toll.

The following Service Alteration takes place:

Green Service W ST GEORGE'S CROSS & STOBCROSS FERRY via NORTH STREET extended to become KEPPOCHHILL ROAD & STOBCROSS FERRY via NORTH STREET from Keppochhill Road east end at Millarbank Street via Keppochhill Road, Mosshouse, Possil Road, Round Toll, St George's Road, St George's Cross, St George's Road and former route.

10th October 1904

Line Opened from Clydebank at Bon Accord Street to Dalmuir.

The following Service Alteration takes place:

Red Service L Weekdays: CLYDEBANK or WHITEINCH & LONDON ROAD extended to become DALMUIR or WHITEINCH & LONDON ROAD from Dumbarton Road Clydebank east of Dalmuir Canal Bridge at Beardmore Street via Dumbarton Road Clydebank, Glasgow Road Clydebank and former route;

Saturdays and Sundays: CLYDEBANK & LONDON ROAD extended to become DALMUIR & LONDON ROAD.

6th November 1904

The following Operational Alteration takes place:

Green Service W KEPPOCHHILL ROAD & STOBCROSS FERRY via NORTH STREET Route Numbers altered.

26th November 1904

Frequency of Paisley Services on Saturdays revised.

Green Service B Saturdays Specials: QUEEN STREET & BARRACHNIE withdrawn;

Green Service B Saturdays: PAISLEY & SHETTLESTON or BARRACHNIE and

Green Service U Saturdays: PAISLEY or IBROX & PARKHEAD and PAISLEY & TOLLCROSS both altered accordingly.

20th March 1905

Agreement finally reached with Paisley District Tramways Co. for **Running Powers** between Hawkhead Road and Paisley Cross.

PAISLEY terminus moved westwards to PAISLEY CROSS.

The following Service Alterations take place:

Green Service B Saturdays: PAISLEY & SHETTLESTON or BARRACHNIE extended to become PAISLEY CROSS & SHETTLESTON or BARRACHNIE from east of Paisley Cross via St James Bridge, Smithhills, Gauze Street Paisley, Glasgow Road Paisley and former route;

Weekdays: IBROX & SHETTLESTON or BARRACHNIE unaltered;

Sundays: IBROX & BARRACHNIE unaltered;
Green Service U Weekdays and Saturdays: PAISLEY or IBROX & PARKHEAD or TOLLCROSS extended to become PAISLEY CROSS & TOLLCROSS from east of Paisley Cross via St James Bridge, Smithhills, Gauze Street Paisley, Glasgow Road Paisley and former route;
Sundays: PAISLEY & TOLLCROSS extended to become PAISLEY CROSS & TOLLCROSS.

3rd April 1905

The following Service Alteration takes place:
Red Service T Weekdays and Saturdays: BARRACKS GATE & TRONGATE via NEW CITY ROAD extended to become MARYHILL & TRONGATE via NEW CITY ROAD from Maryhill Road at Maryhill Station via Maryhill Road and former route;
Sundays: MARYHILL & TRONGATE via NEW CITY ROAD unaltered.

30th April 1905

Rearrangement of Whiteinch, Scotstoun and Stobcross Ferry Services.
The following Service Alterations take place:
Red Service F Weekdays and Saturdays: WHITEINCH & DALMARNOCK, RUTHERGLEN or CAMBUSLANG extended to become SCOTSTOUN & DALMARNOCK, RUTHERGLEN or CAMBUSLANG from Dumbarton Road at Queen Victoria Drive via Dumbarton Road and former route;
Sundays: WHITEINCH & RUTHERGLEN via DALMARNOCK extended to become DALMUIR (Summer only) or SCOTSTOUN & RUTHERGLEN via DALMARNOCK from Dumbarton Road Clydebank east of Dalmuir Canal Bridge at Beardmore Street via Dumbarton Road Clydebank, Glasgow Road Clydebank, Dumbarton Road and former route;
Red Service L DALMUIR or WHITEINCH & LONDON ROAD altered to become
DALMUIR or SCOTSTOUN & LONDON ROAD;
Green Service W KEPPOCHHILL ROAD & STOBCROSS FERRY via NORTH STREET diverted to become
KEPPOCHHILL ROAD & WHITEINCH via NORTH STREET via former route to Argyle Street then via Argyle Street, Dumbarton Road to Dumbarton Road at Westland Drive;
Red Service X PARTICK & CAMBUSLANG via BOTHWELL STREET diverted to become
STOBCROSS FERRY & CAMBUSLANG via ANDERSTON CROSS from Stobcross Quay at Harbour Tunnel via Stobcross Quay, Finnieston Street, Argyle Street, Anderston Cross, Argyle Street and former route.
Regular cars cease to operate on St Vincent Street between North Street and Elmbank Street.

28th May 1905

Increase in Summer Sundays Service to Cathcart.
The following Service Alteration takes place:
Red Service N Sundays: MARYHILL & BATTLEFIELD via GARSCUBE ROAD extended on Summer Sundays to become (Summer only): MARYHILL & CATHCART via GARSCUBE ROAD via former route to Battlefield Road then via Holmlea Road, Clarkston Road to Clarkston Road at Dairsie Street;
Weekdays and Saturdays: BARRACKS GATE & BATTLEFIELD via GARSCUBE ROAD unaltered.

17th June 1905

Line Opened from Coustonholm Road to Giffnock.

The Glasgow Corporation Red Service R reached "Nellie's Toll" (later Eastwood Toll) at Giffnock in 1905. Although the road has long since been realigned with a large roundabout, the mansion to the right of the tram still stands. *(IG Stewart collection)*

The following Service Alteration takes place:
Red Service R Weekdays and Saturdays: RIDDRIE or ALEXANDRA PARK & POLLOKSHAWS EAST extended to become RIDDRIE or ALEXANDRA PARK & POLLOKSHAWS EAST or GIFFNOCK via former route to Kilmarnock Road at Coustonholm Road then via Kilmarnock Road, Fenwick Road to Eastwood Toll;
Sundays: RIDDRIE or ALEXANDRA PARK & POLLOKSHAWS EAST extended to become RIDDRIE or ALEXANDRA PARK & GIFFNOCK

1st July 1905

Frequency of Paisley Service on Saturdays increased.
Green Service B Saturdays: PAISLEY CROSS & SHETTLESTON or BARRACHNIE
Green Service U Saturdays: PAISLEY CROSS & TOLLCROSS increased in frequency.

26th August 1905

Frequency of Paisley Service on Saturdays reverts to former timetable.
Green Service B Saturdays: PAISLEY CROSS & SHETTLESTON or BARRACHNIE adjusted to become PAISLEY CROSS or IBROX & SHETTLESTON or BARRACHNIE;
Green Service U Saturdays: PAISLEY CROSS & TOLLCROSS adjusted to become PAISLEY CROSS or IBROX & TOLLCROSS.

3rd September 1905

The following Service Alteration takes place:
Red Service X STOBCROSS FERRY & CAMBUSLANG via ANDERSTON CROSS rerouted to become STOBCROSS FERRY & CAMBUSLANG via BOTHWELL STREET via former route to Argyle Street then via St Vincent Street, Bothwell Street, Hope Street, Argyle Street and former route.
Regular cars resume operation on St Vincent Street between North Street and Elmbank Street.

15th October 1905

Frequency and Running Times to Paisley reduced.
The following Service Alteration takes place:
Green Service U Weekdays and Saturdays: PAISLEY CROSS & TOLLCROSS part cut back to become PAISLEY CROSS or IBROX & TOLLCROSS;
Sundays: PAISLEY CROSS & TOLLCROSS unaltered.

11th November 1905

Reduction in Service to Giffnock on Saturdays.
The following Service Alteration takes place:
Red Service R Saturdays: RIDDRIE or ALEXANDRA PARK & POLLOKSHAWS EAST or GIFFNOCK section ratio of cars turned back at Pollokshaws East increased to 50%.

19th November 1905

Winter Sunday Services resume on Dalmuir route.
The following Service Alteration takes place:
Red Service F Sundays: DALMUIR or SCOTSTOUN & RUTHERGLEN via DALMARNOCK altered to become WHITEINCH & RUTHERGLEN via DALMARNOCK;
Weekdays: SCOTSTOUN & DALMARNOCK or RUTHERGLEN unaltered;
Saturdays: SCOTSTOUN & DALMARNOCK, RUTHERGLEN or CAMBUSLANG unaltered.

27th November 1905

Shortworkings to Scotstoun cut back to Whiteinch.
The following Service Alterations take place:
Red Service F Weekdays: SCOTSTOUN & DALMARNOCK or RUTHERGLEN altered to become WHITEINCH & DALMARNOCK or RUTHERGLEN;
Saturdays: SCOTSTOUN & DALMARNOCK, RUTHERGLEN or CAMBUSLANG altered to become WHITEINCH & DALMARNOCK, RUTHERGLEN or CAMBUSLANG;
Sundays: WHITEINCH & RUTHERGLEN via DALMARNOCK unaltered;
Red Service L Weekdays and Saturdays: DALMUIR or SCOTSTOUN & LONDON ROAD altered to become DALMUIR or WHITEINCH & LONDON ROAD;
Sundays: DALMUIR & LONDON ROAD unaltered.

10th December 1905

Sunday Service to Giffnock reduced.
The following Service Alteration takes place:
Red Service R Sundays: RIDDRIE or ALEXANDRA PARK & GIFFNOCK section altered to become RIDDRIE or ALEXANDRA PARK & POLLOKSHAWS EAST or GIFFNOCK;
Weekdays and Saturdays: RIDDRIE or ALEXANDRA PARK & POLLOKSHAWS EAST or GIFFNOCK unaltered.

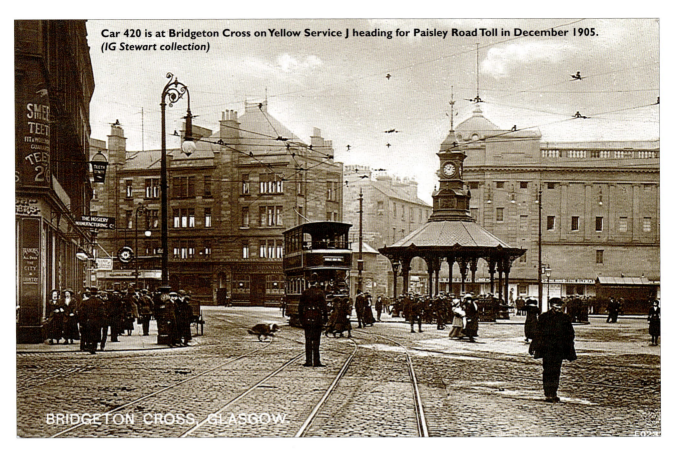

Car 420 is at Bridgeton Cross on Yellow Service J heading for Paisley Road Toll in December 1905. (IG Stewart collection)

23rd December 1905

Saturday runs by Yellow Service J to Linthouse withdrawn.
The following Service Alteration takes place:
Yellow Service J Saturdays: ALEXANDRA PARK & PAISLEY ROAD TOLL or LINTHOUSE cut back to become ALEXANDRA PARK & PAISLEY ROAD TOLL via BRIDGETON CROSS;
Weekdays and Sundays: ALEXANDRA PARK & PAISLEY ROAD TOLL via BRIDGETON CROSS unaltered.

During 1906

Line Opened on Clyde Street westwards from Stockwell Street and on Customhouse Quay for Permanent Way Department access alongside shipping, for unloading and delivering granite setts.
Line laid Dumbarton Road Clydebank west of Dalmuir Canal Bridge as far as Dumbarton Road at Duntocher Burn, but not wired or opened.

16th February 1906

Line Opened from St Andrew's Drive to Sherbrooke Church Pollokshields.
POLLOKSHIELDS terminus moved from St Andrew's Drive at Nithsdale Road to Nithsdale Road at Sherbrooke Avenue.
White Service E UNIVERSITY & POLLOKSHIELDS extended accordingly.

3rd March 1906

Line Opened from Barrachnie to Baillieston.
The following Service Alteration takes place:
Green Service B Weekdays: IBROX & SHETTLESTON or BARRACHNIE extended to become
IBROX & SHETTLESTON or BAILLIESTON via former route to Baillieston Road at Barrachnie Road then via Glasgow Road Baillieston, Main Street Baillieston to Main Street Baillieston east of Dyke Street;
Saturdays: PAISLEY CROSS or IBROX & SHETTLESTON or BARRACHNIE extended to become
PAISLEY CROSS or IBROX & SHETTLESTON or BAILLIESTON;
Sundays: IBROX & BARRACHNIE extended to become IBROX & BAILLIESTON.

28th March 1906

OATLANDS crossover moved from Rutherglen Road at Braehead Street eastwards to Rutherglen Road at Shawfield Drive.
Blue Service O BOTANIC GARDENS & OATLANDS or RUTHERGLEN via PARK ROAD, CROWN STREET altered accordingly.

8th April 1906

30

Line Opened on Springfield Road.
The following Service Alteration takes place:
Green Service A Weekdays and Saturdays: ANNIESLAND & PARKHEAD extended to become
ANNIESLAND & SPRINGFIELD ROAD via former route to Parkhead Cross then via Springfield Road to Springfield Road south end;
Sundays: ANNIESLAND & PARKHEAD altered to become ANNIESLAND & DENNISTOUN or SPRINGFIELD ROAD.
Summer Sunday Service to Paisley increased.
The following Service Alteration takes place:
Green Service B Sundays: IBROX & BAILLIESTON extended to become PAISLEY CROSS & BAILLIESTON;
Weekdays: IBROX & SHETTLESTON or BAILLIESTON unaltered;
Saturdays: PAISLEY CROSS or IBROX & SHETTLESTON or BAILLIESTON unaltered.

13th April 1906

Line Opened from Maryhill to Killermont.
The following Service Alterations take place:
Red Service M MARYHILL & MOUNT FLORIDA via NEW CITY ROAD extended to become
KILLERMONT & MOUNT FLORIDA via NEW CITY ROAD from Maryhill Road at Killermont Bridge (or Garscube Bridge) via Maryhill Road and former route;
Red Service T Weekdays and Saturdays: MARYHILL & TRONGATE via NEW CITY ROAD extended at peak periods to become MARYHILL & TRONGATE or GORBALS via NEW CITY ROAD via former route to Glassford Street then via Stockwell Street, Victoria Bridge, Gorbals Street to Gorbals Street at Cleland Street;
Sundays: MARYHILL & TRONGATE via NEW CITY ROAD unaltered.
Line Opened from Giffnock to Rouken Glen.
The following Service Alteration takes place:
Red Service R Weekdays and Saturdays: RIDDRIE or ALEXANDRA PARK & POLLOKSHAWS EAST or GIFFNOCK extended to become RIDDRIE or ALEXANDRA PARK & POLLOKSHAWS EAST or ROUKEN GLEN via GIFFNOCK via former route to Fenwick Road at Eastwood Toll then via Rouken Glen Road to Rouken Glen Road at Rouken Glen Park Gates;
Sundays: RIDDRIE or ALEXANDRA PARK & POLLOKSHAWS EAST or GIFFNOCK extended to become RIDDRIE or ALEXANDRA PARK & ROUKEN GLEN via GIFFNOCK.
Section BISHOPBRIGGS or SPRINGBURN & POLLOKSHAWS WEST unaltered.

20th May 1906

Line Opened in Riddrie from Cumbernauld Road at Lomax Street to Smithycroft Road at Naver Street.
RIDDRIE terminus extended to Smithycroft Road at Naver Street.
The following Service Alteration takes place:
Red Service R RIDDRIE or ALEXANDRA PARK & POLLOKSHAWS EAST or ROUKEN GLEN via GIFFNOCK extended to operate from Smithycroft Road at Naver Street via Smithycroft Road, Cumbernauld Road and former route.

27th May 1906

The following Service Alteration takes place:
Red Service T Sundays: MARYHILL & TRONGATE via NEW CITY ROAD extended in Summer to become
Sundays (Summer only) KILLERMONT & TRONGATE via NEW CITY ROAD from Killermont Bridge via Maryhill Road and former route;
Weekdays and Saturdays: MARYHILL & TRONGATE or GORBALS via NEW CITY ROAD unaltered.

13th July 1906

White Service E was extended from St Andrew's Drive to Sherbrooke Church. Car 748 is seen citybound turning from Nithsdale Road into St Andrew's Drive around that time.
(BJ Cross collection)

Line Opened from Possilpark to Lambhill.
The following Service Alteration takes place:
Blue Service G Weekdays and Saturdays: POSSILPARK & LINTHOUSE via LORNE STREET extended to become LAMBHILL or POSSILPARK & LINTHOUSE via LORNE STREET from Strachur Street via Strachur Street, Balmore Road, Saracen Cross, Saracen Street and former route;
Sundays: POSSILPARK & LINTHOUSE or RENFREW via LORNE STREET extended to become LAMBHILL or POSSILPARK & LINTHOUSE or RENFREW via LORNE STREET.

13th August 1906

Line Opened from Pollokshields to Dumbreck.
The following Service Alteration takes place:
White Service E UNIVERSITY & POLLOKSHIELDS extended to become UNIVERSITY & DUMBRECK via POLLOKSHIELDS via former route to Nithsdale Road at Sherbrooke Avenue then via Nithsdale Road to Nithsdale Road at Dumbreck Road.
POLLOKSHIELDS terminus reverts to St Andrew's Drive north of Nithsdale Road.

During 1906

The following Special Service becomes established:
Service "Hampden Wheel" TRONGATE & FOOTBALL SPECIALS [Mount Florida] operates one way only from Trongate westbound via Trongate, Stockwell Street, Victoria Bridge, Gorbals Street, Pollokshaws Road, Eglinton Toll, Victoria Road, Langside Road, Grange Road, Prospecthill Road, (Cars line up in Prospecthill Road during the Match), returning via Prospecthill Road, Cathcart Road, Crown Street, Albert Bridge, Saltmarket, Glasgow Cross, Trongate; [Operated for Football Internationals and Cup Finals at Hampden Park].

13th October 1906

Line Opened between Cathcart Road and Paisley Road Toll.
The following Service commences:
Yellow Service Q MOUNT FLORIDA & PAISLEY ROAD TOLL via SHIELDS ROAD from Clincart Road at Florida Street via Clincart Road, Cathcart Road, Allison Street, Nithsdale Street, Nithsdale Road, Shields Road, Scotland Street, Seaward Street, Milnpark Street, Admiral Street to Admiral Street north end.

15th October 1906

Subsidence at Lambhill.
The following Temporary Service Alteration takes place:
Blue Service G LAMBHILL or POSSILPARK & LINTHOUSE via LORNE STREET split to operate between LAMBHILL & POSSILPARK and POSSILPARK & LINTHOUSE via LORNE STREET.

22nd October 1906

Subsidence at Lambhill repaired.
Blue Service G temporary service LAMBHILL & POSSILPARK and POSSILPARK & LINTHOUSE via LORNE STREET withdrawn and normal service LAMBHILL or POSSILPARK & LINTHOUSE via LORNE STREET restored.

12th November 1906

Line Opened in Garngad Road.
The following Service Alteration takes place:
White Service S SPRINGBURN & POLMADIE via GLASGOW CROSS section withdrawn and replaced by new **White Service V**;
SPRINGBURN & MOUNT FLORIDA via GLASGOW CROSS section unaltered.
The following Service commences:
White Service V GARNGAD & POLMADIE via GLASGOW CROSS from Garngad Road at Blochairn Road via Garngad Road, Castle Street, High Street, Glasgow Cross, Saltmarket, Albert Bridge, Crown Street, Cathcart Road, Aikenhead Road to Aikenhead Road at Govanhill Street.

19th November 1906

Reduction in service to Killermont.
The following Service Alterations take place:
Red Service M Weekdays and Saturdays: KILLERMONT & MOUNT FLORIDA via NEW CITY ROAD altered to become KILLERMONT or MARYHILL & MOUNT FLORIDA via NEW CITY ROAD;
Sundays: KILLERMONT & MOUNT FLORIDA via NEW CITY ROAD unaltered.
Red Service T Weekdays and Saturdays: MARYHILL & TRONGATE or GORBALS via NEW CITY ROAD some peak journeys to GORBALS cut back to TRONGATE;
Sundays: MARYHILL & TRONGATE via NEW CITY ROAD unaltered.

15th December 1906

Line Opened from Tollcross to Broomhouse Village Post Office.
The following Service Alteration takes place:
Green Service U Weekdays and Saturdays: PAISLEY CROSS or IBROX & TOLLCROSS extended to become
PAISLEY CROSS or IBROX & TOLLCROSS or BROOMHOUSE via former route to Tollcross Road at Causewayside Street then via Tollcross Road, Hamilton Road to Hamilton Road at Broomhouse Post Office;
Sundays: PAISLEY CROSS & TOLLCROSS extended to become
PAISLEY CROSS or IBROX & TOLLCROSS or BROOMHOUSE.

16th January 1907

Reduction in Weekdays and Saturdays service on Springfield Road.
The following Service Alteration takes place:
Green Service A Weekdays and Saturdays: ANNIESLAND & SPRINGFIELD ROAD part cut back to become
ANNIESLAND & PARKHEAD or SPRINGFIELD ROAD;
Sundays: ANNIESLAND & DENNISTOUN or SPRINGFIELD ROAD unaltered.

20th January 1907

Lanarkshire Tramways Company line opened from east to Cambuslang abutting on to GCT tracks in Main Street Cambuslang at corner of Hamilton Road.
LTC Service CAMBUSLANG & NEWMAINS operated.

21st April 1907

Increase in Sunday Service to Broomhouse.
Green Service U Sundays: PAISLEY CROSS or IBROX & TOLLCROSS or BROOMHOUSE all cars extended to BROOMHOUSE after 1200.

4th May 1907

Line Opened from Broomhouse Village Post Office to Uddingston CR Station
The following Service Alteration takes place:
Green Service U Weekdays and Saturdays: PAISLEY CROSS or IBROX & TOLLCROSS or BROOMHOUSE extended to become PAISLEY CROSS or IBROX & TOLLCROSS or UDDINGSTON via former route to Broomhouse Post Office then via Hamilton Road, Glasgow Road Uddingston to Glasgow Rd Uddingston at Caledonian Railway Station;
Sundays: PAISLEY CROSS or IBROX & TOLLCROSS or BROOMHOUSE extended to become
PAISLEY CROSS & TOLLCROSS or UDDINGSTON.

8th June 1907

Line Opened in Uddingston from CR Station to Uddingston Cross.
UDDINGSTON terminus moved south from Caledonian Railway Station to Main Street Uddingston north of Bellshill Road.
The following Service Alteration takes place:
Green Service U PAISLEY CROSS or IBROX & TOLLCROSS or UDDINGSTON extended accordingly via Main Street Uddingston to Main Street Uddingston north of Bellshill Road.

9th June 1907

The following Service Alteration takes place:
White Service Y SEAMORE STREET & RUTHERGLEN via RUTHERGLEN BRIDGE extended to become
BARRACKS GATE & RUTHERGLEN via RUTHERGLEN BRIDGE from Maryhill Road at Maryhill Barracks Gate via Maryhill Road, Queen's Cross, Maryhill Road and former route.

4th August 1907

The following Service Alteration takes place:
Yellow Service J ALEXANDRA PARK & PAISLEY ROAD TOLL via BRIDGETON CROSS extended to become
RIDDRIE or ALEXANDRA PARK & PAISLEY ROAD TOLL via BRIDGETON CROSS from Smithycroft Road at Naver Street via Smithycroft Road, Cumbernauld Road and former route.

10th November 1907

Reduction in Sunday Service to Uddingston.
The following Operational Alteration takes place:
Green Service U Sundays: PAISLEY CROSS & TOLLCROSS or UDDINGSTON reduced in frequency beyond TOLLCROSS accordingly.

4th December 1907

Line Opened in Highburgh Road and Hyndland.
The following Service Alteration takes place:
Yellow Service H KELVINGROVE & LANGSIDE extended to become
HYNDLAND & LANGSIDE from Hyndland Road south of Clarence Drive via Hyndland Road, Highburgh Road,

The first top covered Standard trams featured the "Unobtrusive Top Cover" design that was largely unsuccessful. Here is one such car, 878 in Sauchiehall Street on Yellow Service H. In their latter years, all were gathered together on the Red Service N. *(BJ Cross collection)*

Byres Road, Church Street, Dumbarton Road, Argyle Street, Sauchiehall Street and former route.

30th January 1908

Line Opened in Aikenhead Road between Govanhill Street and Polmadie Street.
POLMADIE terminus moved southwards to Aikenhead Road at Polmadie Street.
The following Service Alteration takes place:
White Service V GARNGAD & POLMADIE extended to operate to Aikenhead Road at Polmadie Street.

25th June 1908

Dumbarton Burgh and County Tramways Co. Ltd. line opened from the west to Dalmuir West abutting on to unused GCT tracks in Dumbarton Road Clydebank at Duntocher Burn.
DB&CT Service BALLOCH & DALMUIR introduced.

15th October 1908

Line Opened to Burnside.
The following Service Alteration takes place:
White Service Y BARRACKS GATE & RUTHERGLEN via RUTHERGLEN BRIDGE extended to become
BARRACKS GATE & BURNSIDE via RUTHERGLEN BRIDGE via former route to Main Street Rutherglen west of Castle Street then via Main Street Rutherglen, Stonelaw Road to Stonelaw Road at Duke's Road.

26th October 1908

The following Service Alteration takes place:
Yellow Service C Weekdays: BOTANIC GARDENS & CATHCART part diverted to become
BOTANIC GARDENS or HYNDLAND & CATHCART from HYNDLAND on Hyndland Road south of Clarence Drive via Hyndland Road, Highburgh Road and Byres Road then both via former route;
Saturdays and Sundays: BOTANIC GARDENS & CATHCART unaltered.

2nd December 1908

Line Opened from Dalmuir West to Dalmuir Canal Bridge, isolated from main system.
Dumbarton Burgh and County Tramways Co. Ltd commence operation over Glasgow Corporation tracks isolated west of Dalmuir Canal Bridge.
Dumbarton Burgh and County Tramways DALMUIR terminus moved eastwards from Dumbarton Road Clydebank at Duntocher Burn to Dumbarton Road Clydebank at Duntocher Road west of Dalmuir Canal Bdge.
DB&CT Service BALLOCH & DALMUIR extended accordingly.

9th January 1909
Line Opened on Bilsland Drive.
The following Service Alteration takes place:
White Service Y BARRACKS GATE & BURNSIDE via RUTHERGLEN BRIDGE diverted and extended to become SPRINGBURN & BURNSIDE via BILSLAND DRIVE, RUTHERGLEN BRIDGE from Springburn Road at Balgrayhill via Springburn Road, Hawthorn Street, Bilsland Drive, Maryhill Road and former route.

1st April 1909
The following Service Alteration takes place:
Red Service T Weekdays and Saturdays: MARYHILL & TRONGATE or GORBALS via NEW CITY ROAD extended at peak hours to become MARYHILL & TRONGATE or JAMIESON STREET via NEW CITY ROAD via former route to Gorbals then via Gorbals Street, Cathcart Road to Cathcart Road at Jamieson Street;
Sundays: KILLERMONT (Summer only) or MARYHILL & TRONGATE via NEW CITY ROAD unaltered.

30th April 1909
Line Opened from Pollokshaws Road at Barrhead Road to Rouken Glen.
The following Service Alterations take place:
Red Service R Weekdays and Saturdays: BISHOPBRIGGS or SPRINGBURN & POLLOKSHAWS WEST section extended to become BISHOPBRIGGS or SPRINGBURN & POLLOKSHAWS WEST or ROUKEN GLEN Circle via THORNLIEBANK via former route to Pollokshaws Road then via Cross Street, Harriet Street, Thornliebank Road, Main Street Thornliebank, Spiersbridge Road, Rouken Glen Road to Rouken Glen Road at Rouken Glen Gates.
Through running instituted at Rouken Glen with Circle Cars returning via Giffnock to ALEXANDRA PARK or RIDDRIE;
Sundays: BISHOPBRIGGS & POLLOKSHAWS WEST extended to become
BISHOPBRIGGS & ROUKEN GLEN Circle via THORNLIEBANK;
RIDDRIE or ALEXANDRA PARK & POLLOKSHAWS EAST or ROUKEN GLEN via GIFFNOCK section altered to become RIDDRIE or ALEXANDRA PARK & POLLOKSHAWS EAST or ROUKEN GLEN Circle via GIFFNOCK.
Through running instituted at Rouken Glen with Circle Cars returning via Thornliebank to SPRINGBURN or BISHOPBRIGGS.

30th May 1909
Line Opened in south end of Crow Road.
PARTICK terminus moved into Crow Road south end.
Stobcross Ferry route temporarily closed.
The following Service Alteration takes place:
Red Service X STOBCROSS FERRY & CAMBUSLANG via BOTHWELL STREET diverted and extended to become PARTICK & CAMBUSLANG via BOTHWELL STREET from Crow Road south end via Crow Road, Dumbarton Road, Argyle Street, St Vincent Street and former route.
Regular cars cease to operate on Stobcross Quay and Finnieston Street.

During 1909
Siding Opened in East King Street Rutherglen alongside Substation

21st June 1909
Stobcross Ferry route reopened
The following Service commences:
Green Service SF STOBCROSS FERRY & FINNIESTON from Stobcross Quay at Harbour Tunnel via Stobcross Quay, Finnieston Street to Finnieston Street north end.
Regular cars resume operation on Stobcross Quay and Finnieston Street

28th September 1909
The following Service Alteration takes place:
Red Service T Weekdays and Saturdays: MARYHILL & TRONGATE or JAMIESON STREET via NEW CITY ROAD altered to become
Weekdays: BARRACKS GATE & TRONGATE or GOVANHILL via NEW CITY ROAD and
Saturdays: MARYHILL or BARRACKS GATE & TRONGATE or GOVANHILL via NEW CITY ROAD via former route to Cathcart Road at Jamieson Street then via Cathcart Road to Cathcart Road at Dixon Avenue;
Sundays: KILLERMONT (Summer only) or MARYHILL & TRONGATE via NEW CITY ROAD unaltered.

7th December 1909
The following Service Alteration takes place:
Red Service T Weekdays and Saturdays: MARYHILL or BARRACKS GATE & TRONGATE or GOVANHILL via NEW CITY ROAD frequency to GOVANHILL adjusted.

13th December 1909

The following Service Alteration takes place:

White Service E Weekdays and Saturdays: UNIVERSITY & DUMBRECK part cut back to become UNIVERSITY & POLLOKSHIELDS or DUMBRECK;
Sundays: UNIVERSITY & DUMBRECK unaltered.

19th December 1909

Burnside provided with additional route to and from Glasgow via Dalmarnock.
The following Service Alterations take place:

Red Service F Weekdays: WHITEINCH & DALMARNOCK or RUTHERGLEN part extended to become WHITEINCH & DALMARNOCK, RUTHERGLEN or BURNSIDE via former route to Rutherglen Cross then Burnside cars proceeding via Stonelaw Road to Stonelaw Road at Duke's Road;
Saturdays: WHITEINCH & DALMARNOCK, RUTHERGLEN or CAMBUSLANG extended to become DALMUIR or WHITEINCH & DALMARNOCK, RUTHERGLEN, BURNSIDE or CAMBUSLANG;
Sundays: WHITEINCH & RUTHERGLEN via DALMARNOCK extended to become WHITEINCH & RUTHERGLEN or BURNSIDE via DALMARNOCK;

White Service Y Weekdays and Saturdays: SPRINGBURN & BURNSIDE via BILSLAND DRIVE, RUTHERGLEN BRIDGE altered to become
SPRINGBURN or VERNON STREET & RUTHERGLEN or BURNSIDE via BILSLAND DRIVE, RUTHERGLEN BRIDGE;
Sundays: SPRINGBURN & BURNSIDE via BILSLAND DRIVE, RUTHERGLEN BRIDGE altered to become
SPRINGBURN & RUTHERGLEN or BURNSIDE via BILSLAND DRIVE, RUTHERGLEN BRIDGE.

20th December 1909

GAIRBRAID STREET terminus renamed QUEEN'S CROSS.
The following Service Alteration takes place:

Red Service N Weekdays and Saturdays: BARRACKS GATE & BATTLEFIELD via GARSCUBE ROAD cut back to become QUEEN'S CROSS & BATTLEFIELD via GARSCUBE ROAD from Maryhill Road at Northpark Street via Maryhill Road and former route;
Sundays: MARYHILL & BATTLEFIELD or CATHCART via GARSCUBE ROAD unaltered.

6th March 1910

Line Opened on Shettleston Road between Duke Street and Shettleston Sheddings.
The following Service Alteration takes place:

Green Service A Weekdays and Saturdays: ANNIESLAND & PARKHEAD or SPRINGFIELD ROAD part-diverted and altered to become ANNIESLAND & SPRINGFIELD ROAD or SHETTLESTON via former route, Cars for SHETTLESTON proceeding from Duke Street via Shettleston Road, Shettleston Sheddings, Shettleston Road to Shettleston Road at Gartocher Road;
Sundays: ANNIESLAND & DENNISTOUN or SPRINGFIELD ROAD altered to become
ANNIESLAND & SPRINGFIELD ROAD or SHETTLESTON;

Green Service D Sundays: ANNIESLAND & DENNISTOUN introduced;
Weekdays and Saturdays: KELVINSIDE & DENNISTOUN unaltered.

Line Opened on Crow Road from Partick to Broomhill Cross.
The following Service Alteration takes place:

Red Service X PARTICK & CAMBUSLANG via BOTHWELL STREET extended to become
BROOMHILL CROSS & CAMBUSLANG via BOTHWELL STREET from Broomhill Cross via Crow Road and former route.

10th April 1910

Line Opened on Clarence Drive from Hyndland to Broomhill Cross.
The following Service Alteration takes place:

Yellow Service C Weekdays: BOTANIC GARDENS or HYNDLAND & CATHCART part extended to become
BOTANIC GARDENS or BROOMHILL CROSS & CATHCART from Broomhill Cross via Clarence Drive, Hyndland Road and former route;
Saturdays and Sundays: BOTANIC GARDENS & CATHCART unaltered;

Yellow Service H HYNDLAND & LANGSIDE extended to become BROOMHILL CROSS & LANGSIDE via HYNDLAND from Broomhill Cross via Clarence Drive, Hyndland Road and former route.

1st May 1910

Line Opened on Cathcart Road from Mount Florida to Holmlea Road.
The following Service Alterations take place:

Red Service N Summer Sundays: MARYHILL & CATHCART via GARSCUBE ROAD cut back to basic route to become
Sundays: MARYHILL & BATTLEFIELD via GARSCUBE ROAD;
Weekdays and Saturdays: QUEEN'S CROSS & BATTLEFIELD via GARSCUBE ROAD unaltered.

White Service S SPRINGBURN & MOUNT FLORIDA via GLASGOW CROSS extended to become
SPRINGBURN & MOUNT FLORIDA or CATHCART via GLASGOW CROSS via former route to Mount Florida then Cathcart

The northern extension of Yellow Services C and H and Red Service X on 15th May 1910 saw trams running beyond Broomhill Cross for the first time. The Cross is in the distance to the right of Red Car 846.
(BJ Cross collection)

cars continue via Cathcart Road, Holmlea Road, Clarkston Road to Clarkston Road at Dairsie Street.

8th May 1910

Summer Sunday frequency to Dalmuir increased.
The following Service Alteration takes place:

Red Service F Summer Sundays: WHITEINCH & RUTHERGLEN or BURNSIDE via DALMARNOCK extended to become DALMUIR or WHITEINCH & RUTHERGLEN or BURNSIDE via DALMARNOCK.
Weekdays: WHITEINCH & DALMARNOCK, RUTHERGLEN or BURNSIDE unaltered;
Saturdays: WHITEINCH & DALMARNOCK, RUTHERGLEN, BURNSIDE or CAMBUSLANG unaltered.

15th May 1910

Line Opened on Crow Road from Broomhill Cross to Jordanhill Station.
The following Service Alterations take place:

Yellow Service C Weekdays: BOTANIC GARDENS or BROOMHILL CROSS & CATHCART part extended to become BOTANIC GARDENS or JORDANHILL & CATHCART from Jordanhill Station via Crow Road, Broomhill Cross and former route;
Saturdays and Sundays: BOTANIC GARDENS & CATHCART unaltered;

Yellow Service H BROOMHILL CROSS & LANGSIDE via HYNDLAND extended to become
JORDANHILL & LANGSIDE via HYNDLAND from Jordanhill Station via Crow Road, Broomhill Cross and former route;

Red Service X BROOMHILL CROSS & CAMBUSLANG via BOTHWELL STREET extended to become
JORDANHILL & CAMBUSLANG via BOTHWELL STREET from Jordanhill Station via Crow Road, Broomhill Cross and former route.

21st May 1910

Increase in frequency to Rouken Glen on Saturday afternoons.
The following Service Alteration takes place:

Red Service R Saturday Afternoons: POLLOKSHAWS EAST cars extended to ROUKEN GLEN Circle via GIFFNOCK.

During 1910

Line in Clyde Street between Saltmarket and Mart Street, for High Court of Justiciary **closed** to trams.

30th May 1910

Increase in frequency of Parkhead via Dennistoun service.
The following Service Alteration takes place:

Green Service D Weekdays and Saturdays: KELVINSIDE & DENNISTOUN part extended to become
KELVINSIDE & DENNISTOUN or PARKHEAD;
Sundays: ANNIESLAND & DENNISTOUN unaltered.

May 1910

Pollokshaws Depot, Pleasance Street, **closed** to trams. Cars transferred to Newlands Depot.
➢ *Newlands Depot, Newlandsfield Road opened for service.*
The following Operational Alterations take place:
Pollokshaws Depot operation of
White Service E UNIVERSITY & POLLOKSHIELDS or DUMBRECK
Red Service R BISHOPBRIGGS or SPRINGBURN & POLLOKSHAWS WEST or ROUKEN GLEN Circle via THORNLIEBANK; RIDDRIE or ALEXANDRA PARK & POLLOKSHAWS EAST or ROUKEN GLEN Circle via GIFFNOCK
all transferred to Newlands Depot.

During 1910

Loop Opened from citybound track in Cathcart Road north of GOVANHILL also known as DIXON AVENUE crossover.

5th June 1910

The following Service Alterations take place:
Red Service T Weekdays: BARRACKS GATE & TRONGATE or GOVANHILL via NEW CITY ROAD and
Saturdays: MARYHILL or BARRACKS GATE & TRONGATE or GOVANHILL via NEW CITY ROAD divided to become
Weekdays and Saturdays: MARYHILL or BARRACKS GATE & GOVANHILL via NEW CITY ROAD and
KILLERMONT & TRONGATE via NEW CITY ROAD;
Sundays: KILLERMONT & TRONGATE via NEW CITY ROAD unaltered.

27th June 1910

The following Service Alterations take place:
Green Service A Weekdays and Saturdays: ANNIESLAND & SPRINGFIELD ROAD or SHETTLESTON part diverted to become ANNIESLAND & PARKHEAD or SPRINGFIELD ROAD via former route;
Sundays: ANNIESLAND & SPRINGFIELD ROAD or SHETTLESTON unaltered;
Green Service D Weekdays and Saturdays: KELVINSIDE & DENNISTOUN or PARKHEAD diverted to become KELVINSIDE & DENNISTOUN or SHETTLESTON via former route to Dennistoun then via Duke Street, Shettleston Road, Shettleston Sheddings, Shettleston Road to Shettleston Road at Gartocher Road;
Sundays: ANNIESLAND & DENNISTOUN unaltered;
Yellow Service C Weekdays: BOTANIC GARDENS or JORDANHILL & CATHCART part cut back to become BOTANIC GARDENS or HYNDLAND & CATHCART via former route;
Saturdays and Sundays: BOTANIC GARDENS & CATHCART unaltered;
Yellow Service H Weekdays: JORDANHILL & LANGSIDE via HYNDLAND part cut back to become JORDANHILL or HYNDLAND & LANGSIDE;
Saturdays and Sundays: JORDANHILL & LANGSIDE via HYNDLAND unaltered.

10th July 1910

Line Opened from Jordanhill to Anniesland.
The following Service Alteration takes place:

Coustonholm Road bears right where the shop awnings can be seen, and led to Pollokshaws East terminus and the Pollokshaws Depot. Car 410 on Red Service R is heading south to Giffnock. *(BJ Cross collection)*

Red Service X JORDANHILL & CAMBUSLANG via BOTHWELL STREET extended to become ANNIESLAND & CAMBUSLANG via BOTHWELL STREET from Crow Road north end via Crow Road and former route.

1st August 1910

Conversion of Stobcross Ferry route to one-man operation.
The following Operational Alteration takes place:
Green Service SF STOBCROSS FERRY & FINNIESTON becomes one-man operated, with Pay-as-You-Enter Fare collection, operated by Single-deck Car.

15th August 1910

POLLOKSHAWS EAST terminus moved from Coustonholm Road at Coustonhill Street to Pollokshaws Town House at corner of Pleasance Street and Shawbridge Street.
The following Service Alteration takes place:
Red Service R RIDDRIE or ALEXANDRA PARK & POLLOKSHAWS EAST or ROUKEN GLEN Circle via GIFFNOCK section POLLOKSHAWS EAST cars extended to new terminus via Coustonholm Road, Pleasance Street to Pleasance Street west end at Town House.
Regular cars commence operation on Pleasance Street.

12th September 1910

The following Service commences, for an experimental period of three months:
Blue Service Z HYNDLAND & ALEXANDRA PARK from Hyndland Road south of Clarence Drive via Hyndland Road, Highburgh Road, Byres Road, Church Street, Dumbarton Road, Argyle Street, Sauchiehall Street, Charing Cross, Sauchiehall Street, Parliamentary Road, Monkland Street, Castle Street, Alexandra Parade to Alexandra Parade at Kennyhill Square.

21st November 1910

Line Opened in Kelvinside Avenue.
New terminus KELVINSIDE AVENUE provided in Kelvinside Avenue north end for short workings on **Red Services M, N and T** and **White Service Y**.
The following Service Alteration takes place:
Red Service N Weekdays and Saturdays: QUEEN'S CROSS & BATTLEFIELD via GARSCUBE ROAD extended to become KELVINSIDE AVENUE & BATTLEFIELD via GARSCUBE ROAD from Kelvinside Avenue north end via Kelvinside Avenue, Maryhill Road, Queen's Cross, Garscube Road and former route;
Sundays: MARYHILL & BATTLEFIELD via GARSCUBE ROAD unaltered;
White Service Y Weekdays and Saturdays: SPRINGBURN or VERNON STREET & RUTHERGLEN or BURNSIDE via BILSLAND DRIVE, RUTHERGLEN BRIDGE short workings to and from VERNON STREET cut back to become SPRINGBURN or KELVINSIDE AVENUE & RUTHERGLEN or BURNSIDE via BILSLAND DRIVE, RUTHERGLEN BRIDGE;
Sundays: SPRINGBURN & RUTHERGLEN or BURNSIDE via BILSLAND DRIVE, RUTHERGLEN BRIDGE unaltered.

12th December 1910

Upon end of experimental period, the following Service to remain in operation:
Blue Service Z HYNDLAND & ALEXANDRA PARK.

6th March 1911

Line Opened in Clincart Road, Mount Florida between Florida Street and Bolton Drive.
MOUNT FLORIDA terminus extended from Clincart Road at Florida Street to Clincart Road at Bolton Drive.
Red Service M KILLERMONT or MARYHILL & MOUNT FLORIDA via NEW CITY ROAD
Yellow Service Q MOUNT FLORIDA & PAISLEY ROAD TOLL
White Service S SPRINGBURN & MOUNT FLORIDA or CATHCART via GLASGOW CROSS
all extended accordingly.

8th April 1911

Pollokshaws East section withdrawn.
The following Service Alteration takes place:
Red Service R RIDDRIE or ALEXANDRA PARK & POLLOKSHAWS EAST or ROUKEN GLEN Circle via GIFFNOCK altered to become RIDDRIE or ALEXANDRA PARK & NEWLANDS or ROUKEN GLEN Circle via GIFFNOCK:
NEWLANDS terminus in Kilmarnock Road at Newlandsfield Road.
Coustonholm Road and Pleasance Street closed to regular service trams but along with Greenview Street retained for Newlands Depot workings.
Line Opened on London Road from Kinnear Road to Williamson Street.
LONDON ROAD terminus moved east from London Rd at Kinnear Road to London Rd at Williamson Street.
The following Service Alteration takes place:
Red Service L DALMUIR or WHITEINCH & LONDON ROAD extended accordingly.

3rd May 1911

Opening of Scottish National Exhibition in Kelvingrove Park.
Line Opened in Kelvingrove Street between Argyle Street and Sauchiehall Street.
The following Temporary Services commence:
Service [Horse Shoe] QUEEN STREET & ST VINCENT PLACE via RADNOR STREET (Part Day) and QUEEN STREET & ST VINCENT PLACE via KELVINGROVE STREET (Part Day) from Argyle Street at Queen Street Loop via Argyle Street, either via Radnor Street or via Kelvingrove Street, then via Sauchiehall Street, Charing Cross, Sauchiehall Street, Renfield Street, St Vincent Street, St Vincent Place to St Vincent Place Loop;
Cars show EXHIBITION on leaving Queen Street and St Vincent Place;
White Service E UNIVERSITY & ST VINCENT PLACE Specials introduced from University via normal route to Renfield Street then via Renfield Street, St Vincent Street, St Vincent Place to St Vincent Place Loop.
Blue Service Z Specials HYNDLAND & ALEXANDRA PARK for Exhibition.

13th May 1911

The following Service Alteration takes place:
Temporary Service [Horse Shoe] QUEEN STREET & ST VINCENT PLACE via KELVINGROVE STREET (Part Day) withdrawn, all cars operate as QUEEN STREET & ST VINCENT PLACE via RADNOR STREET (Part Day).

11th June 1911

The following Service Alteration takes place:
White Service Y Sundays: SPRINGBURN & RUTHERGLEN or BURNSIDE via BILSLAND DRIVE, RUTHERGLEN BRIDGE; Shortworkings to RUTHERGLEN withdrawn and altered to become
SPRINGBURN & BURNSIDE via BILSLAND DRIVE, RUTHERGLEN BRIDGE;
Weekdays and Saturdays: SPRINGBURN or KELVINSIDE AVENUE & RUTHERGLEN or BURNSIDE via BILSLAND DRIVE, RUTHERGLEN BRIDGE unaltered.

25th June 1911

Line Opened in Kirklee Road.
The following Service Alteration takes place:
Yellow Service C Weekdays: BOTANIC GARDENS or HYNDLAND & CATHCART withdrawn from Hyndland and extended from Botanic Gardens to become
KIRKLEE & CATHCART via BOTANIC GARDENS from Kirklee Road south end via Kirklee Road, Great Western Road, Botanic Gardens, Byres Road and former route;
Saturdays and Sundays: BOTANIC GARDENS & CATHCART extended to become
KIRKLEE & CATHCART via BOTANIC GARDENS;
Yellow Service H Weekdays: JORDANHILL or HYNDLAND & LANGSIDE altered to become
JORDANHILL & LANGSIDE via HYNDLAND;
Saturdays and Sundays: JORDANHILL & LANGSIDE via HYNDLAND unaltered.

3rd July 1911

The following Service Alteration takes place:
Red Service R RIDDRIE or ALEXANDRA PARK & NEWLANDS or ROUKEN GLEN Circle via GIFFNOCK altered to become
RIDDRIE or ALEXANDRA PARK & MERRYLEE or ROUKEN GLEN Circle via GIFFNOCK:
MERRYLEE crossover on Kilmarnock Road at Merrylee Road.

5th July 1911

The following Service Alteration takes place:
Temporary Service [Horse Shoe] QUEEN STREET & ST VINCENT PLACE via RADNOR STREET (Part Day) reduced and altered to become RADNOR STREET [EXHIBITION] & ST VINCENT PLACE (Part Day) from Radnor Street via Radnor Street, Sauchiehall Street and former route.

During 1911

Siding Opened in Cooperswell Street to serve Partick Substation.

11th September 1911

Increase in frequency to Crookston.
The following Service Alterations take place:
Green Service B Weekdays: IBROX & SHETTLESTON or BAILLIESTON extended to become
CROOKSTON & SHETTLESTON or BAILLIESTON from Paisley Road West at Crookston Road via Paisley Road West and former route;
Saturdays: PAISLEY CROSS or IBROX & SHETTLESTON or BAILLIESTON extended to become
PAISLEY CROSS or CROOKSTON & SHETTLESTON or BAILLIESTON;
Sundays: PAISLEY CROSS & BAILLIESTON unaltered;
Green Service U Weekdays and Saturdays: PAISLEY CROSS or IBROX & TOLLCROSS or UDDINGSTON altered to become
PAISLEY CROSS, CROOKSTON or IBROX & TOLLCROSS or UDDINGSTON;

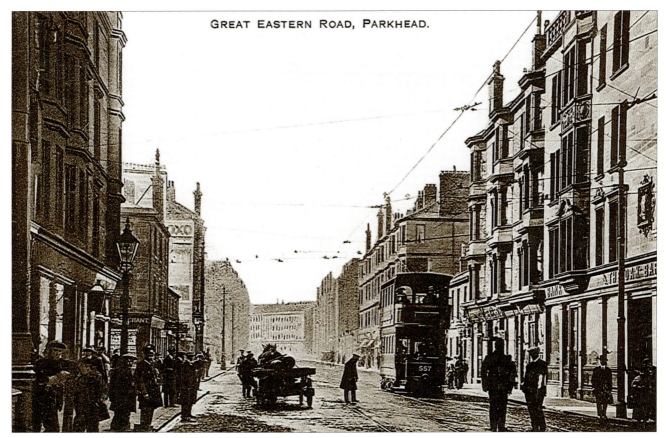

The Green Services were popularly associated with the east end although they served many other parts of the City. Here is Car 557 on Green Service B or U at Great Eastern Road (later Gallowgate) approaching Parkhead Cross.
(BJ Cross collection)

Sundays: PAISLEY CROSS & TOLLCROSS or UDDINGSTON unaltered.

6th November 1911

Closure of Scottish National Exhibition, Kelvingrove Park.
The following Temporary Services withdrawn:
Service [Horse Shoe] RADNOR ST. [EXHIBITION] & ST VINCENT PLACE (Part Day) withdrawn;
White Service E Specials UNIVERSITY & ST VINCENT PLACE withdrawn;
Blue Service Z Specials HYNDLAND & ALEXANDRA PARK withdrawn.
Further Rearrangement of Hyndland Services.
The following Service Alterations take place:
Yellow Service C Weekdays: KIRKLEE & CATHCART via BOTANIC GARDENS part diverted to become
KIRKLEE or HYNDLAND & CATHCART Hyndland cars from Hyndland Road south of Clarence Drive via Hyndland Road, Highburgh Road, Byres Road and former route;
Saturdays and Sundays: KIRKLEE & CATHCART via BOTANIC GARDENS unaltered;
Yellow Service H Weekdays: JORDANHILL & LANGSIDE via HYNDLAND altered to become
JORDANHILL or HYNDLAND & LANGSIDE;
Saturdays and Sundays: JORDANHILL & LANGSIDE via HYNDLAND unaltered.

12th November 1911

Frequency to Crookston reduced.
The following Service Alterations take place:
Green Service B Weekdays: CROOKSTON & SHETTLESTON or BAILLIESTON cut back to become
IBROX & SHETTLESTON or BAILLIESTON;
Saturdays: PAISLEY CROSS or CROOKSTON & SHETTLESTON or BAILLIESTON altered to become
PAISLEY CROSS or IBROX & SHETTLESTON or BAILLIESTON;
Sundays: PAISLEY CROSS & BAILLIESTON unaltered;
Green Service U Weekdays and Saturdays: PAISLEY CROSS, CROOKSTON or IBROX & TOLLCROSS or UDDINGSTON altered to become PAISLEY CROSS & TOLLCROSS or UDDINGSTON;
Sundays: PAISLEY CROSS & TOLLCROSS or UDDINGSTON unaltered.

5th February 1912

Line Opened in Turriff Street linking Eglinton Street and Pollokshaws Road.
The following Service commences:
Blue Service P Weekdays and Saturdays only: ST VINCENT PLACE & SHAWLANDS via GORBALS from St Vincent Place Loop via St Vincent Place, George Square south, South Frederick Street, Ingram Street, Glassford Street, Stockwell Street, Victoria Bridge, Gorbals Street, Pollokshaws Road, Turriff Street, Eglinton Street, Eglinton Toll, Pollokshaws Road, to Pollokshaws Road at Shawlands Cross. No Sundays Service.

During 1912

Siding Opened in Fleming Street, Dennistoun, southwards from Duke Street for Permanent Way Yard access. Also available for DENNISTOUN shortworking cars.

11th March 1912

Further rearrangement of Hyndland Services.
The following Service Alteration takes place:
Blue Service Z Weekdays: HYNDLAND & ALEXANDRA PARK part extended to become
JORDANHILL or HYNDLAND & ALEXANDRA PARK from Jordanhill Station via Crow Road, Broomhill Cross, Clarence Drive, Hyndland Road and former route;
Saturdays and Sundays: HYNDLAND & ALEXANDRA PARK unaltered.

May 1912

Line Opened in Aitken Street from Cumbernauld Road to Marwick Street.
ALEXANDRA PARK terminus moved from Cumbernauld Road at Kennyhill Square to Aitken Street north end.
Yellow Service J RIDDRIE or ALEXANDRA PARK & PAISLEY ROAD TOLL via BRIDGETON CROSS
Red Service R RIDDRIE or ALEXANDRA PARK & MERRYLEE or ROUKEN GLEN Circle via GIFFNOCK
Blue Service Z JORDANHILL or HYNDLAND & ALEXANDRA PARK all altered accordingly.

September 1912

Siding and Loop Opened in Kent Road between North Street and Granville Street for loading Special Cars serving events in the St Andrew's Halls.

5th October 1912

Line Opened in Elmvale Street, Springburn.
SPRINGBURN terminus for cars from the south moved from Springburn Road at Balgrayhill to Elmvale Street east end.
Springburn (Balgrayhill) crossover moved northwards in Springburn Road to a position between Elmvale Street and Hawthorn Street.
Red Service R BISHOPBRIGGS or SPRINGBURN & POLLOKSHAWS WEST or ROUKEN GLEN Circle via THORNLIEBANK;
White Service S SPRINGBURN & MOUNT FLORIDA or CATHCART via GLASGOW CROSS
both altered to use Elmvale Street accordingly;
White Service Y SPRINGBURN or KELVINSIDE AVENUE & RUTHERGLEN or BURNSIDE via BILSLAND DRIVE, RUTHERGLEN BRIDGE continues to turn in Springburn Road using re-sited crossover.

10th February 1913

Further rearrangement of Hyndland Services.
The following Service Alterations take place:
Yellow Service H Weekdays: JORDANHILL or HYNDLAND & LANGSIDE Hyndland shortworking cars re-extended to become
JORDANHILL & LANGSIDE via HYNDLAND;
Saturdays and Sundays JORDANHILL & LANGSIDE via HYNDLAND unaltered;
Blue Service Z Weekdays: JORDANHILL or HYNDLAND & ALEXANDRA PARK cut to become
HYNDLAND & ALEXANDRA PARK;
Saturdays and Sundays: HYNDLAND & ALEXANDRA PARK unaltered.

During 1913

Digital Number Screen Boxes fitted to cars above Motorman's vestibule window and used to display each car's individual Route Number (see Notes).

24th February 1913

Cars shortworking to Whiteinch extended to Scotstoun.
The following Service Alterations take place:
Red Service F Weekdays: WHITEINCH & DALMARNOCK, RUTHERGLEN or BURNSIDE altered to become
SCOTSTOUN & DALMARNOCK, RUTHERGLEN or BURNSIDE from Dumbarton Road west of Queen Victoria Drive via Dumbarton Road and former route;
Saturdays: DALMUIR or WHITEINCH & DALMARNOCK, RUTHERGLEN, BURNSIDE or CAMBUSLANG altered to become

From 10th August 1913, Sunday cars on Blue Services G and K operating to Renfrew were rearranged. Note the Paisley District Tramways tracks in the foreground, still unconnected to the GCT metals.
(IG Stewart collection)

DALMUIR or SCOTSTOUN & DALMARNOCK, RUTHERGLEN, BURNSIDE or CAMBUSLANG;
Sundays: DALMUIR (Summer only) or WHITEINCH & RUTHERGLEN or BURNSIDE via DALMARNOCK unaltered;
Red Service L Weekdays and Saturdays DALMUIR or WHITEINCH & LONDON ROAD altered to become DALMUIR or SCOTSTOUN & LONDON ROAD;
Sundays: DALMUIR & LONDON ROAD unaltered.

10th August 1913

Adjustments to Possil-Govan-Renfrew Sundays Services.
The following Service Alterations take place:
Blue Service G Sundays: LAMBHILL or POSSILPARK & LINTHOUSE or RENFREW via LORNE STREET altered to become LAMBHILL & LINTHOUSE via LORNE STREET;
Weekdays and Saturdays: LAMBHILL or POSSILPARK & LINTHOUSE via LORNE STREET unaltered;
Blue Service K Sundays: KEPPOCHHILL ROAD & LINTHOUSE or RENFREW altered to become KEPPOCHHILL ROAD & RENFREW;
Weekdays and Saturdays: KEPPOCHHILL ROAD & SHIELDHALL or RENFREW unaltered.

11th January 1914

Extension of Gorbals Blue Car Service to Maryhill.
The following Service Alterations take place:
Blue Service P Weekdays and Saturdays: ST VINCENT PLACE & SHAWLANDS via GORBALS extended to become MARYHILL & SHAWLANDS via ST GEORGE'S CROSS, GORBALS from Maryhill Road at Maryhill Station via Maryhill Road, Queen's Cross, Maryhill Road, St George's Cross, New City Road, Cowcaddens, West Nile Street, St Vincent Street, St Vincent Place and former route;
Sundays: MARYHILL & SHAWLANDS via ST GEORGE'S CROSS, GORBALS introduced;
Red Service T Weekdays and Saturdays: KILLERMONT & TRONGATE via NEW CITY ROAD section withdrawn;
MARYHILL or BARRACKS GATE & GOVANHILL via NEW CITY ROAD section unaltered;
Sundays: KILLERMONT or MARYHILL & TRONGATE via NEW CITY ROAD withdrawn.

26th April 1914

Extension of Blue Service to Killermont on Sundays.
The following Service Alteration takes place:
Blue Service P Sundays: MARYHILL & SHAWLANDS via ST GEORGE'S CROSS, GORBALS extended to become KILLERMONT & SHAWLANDS via ST GEORGE'S CROSS, GORBALS from Killermont Bridge via Maryhill Road and former route;
Weekdays and Saturdays: MARYHILL & SHAWLANDS via ST GEORGE'S CROSS, GORBALS unaltered.

6th September 1914
   Line Opened in Sinclair Drive.
   The following Service Alteration takes place:
   Red Service N Weekdays and Saturdays: KELVINSIDE AVENUE & BATTLEFIELD via GARSCUBE ROAD
   diverted and extended to become KELVINSIDE AVENUE & SINCLAIR DRIVE via GARSCUBE ROAD via former route to
   Grange Road then via Sinclair Drive to Sinclair Drive at Cartside Street;
   Sundays: MARYHILL & BATTLEFIELD via GARSCUBE ROAD diverted and extended to become
   MARYHILL & SINCLAIR DRIVE via GARSCUBE ROAD.

Résumé

6th September 1914

The following Tram Services operating:

A	Green	ANNIESLAND & PARKHEAD or SPRINGFIELD ROAD
		ANNIESLAND & SPRINGFIELD RD or SHETTLESTON (Sundays only)
B	Green	PAISLEY CROSS or IBROX & SHETTLESTON or BAILLIESTON
C	Yellow	KIRKLEE & CATHCART via BOTANIC GARDENS
		HYNDLAND & CATHCART
D	Green	KELVINSIDE & DENNISTOUN or SHETTLESTON
		ANNIESLAND & DENNISTOUN (Sundays only)
E	White	UNIVERSITY & POLLOKSHIELDS or DUMBRECK
F	Red	DALMUIR or SCOTSTOUN & DALMARNOCK, RUTHERGLEN, BURNSIDE or CAMBUSLANG
G	Blue	LAMBHILL or POSSILPARK & LINTHOUSE via LORNE STREET
H	Yellow	JORDANHILL & LANGSIDE via HYNDLAND
J	Yellow	RIDDRIE or ALEXANDRA PARK & PAISLEY ROAD TOLL via BRIDGETON CROSS
K	Blue	KEPPOCHHILL ROAD & SHIELDHALL or RENFREW
L	Red	DALMUIR or SCOTSTOUN & LONDON ROAD
M	Red	KILLERMONT or MARYHILL & MOUNT FLORIDA via NEW CITY ROAD
N	Red	MARYHILL or KELVINSIDE AVENUE & SINCLAIR DRIVE via GARSCUBE ROAD
O	Blue	BOTANIC GARDENS & OATLANDS or RUTHERGLEN via PARK ROAD, CROWN STREET
P	Blue	KILLERMONT or MARYHILL & SHAWLANDS via ST GEORGE'S CROSS, GORBALS
Q	Yellow	MOUNT FLORIDA & PAISLEY ROAD TOLL via SHIELDS ROAD
R	Red	BISHOPBRIGGS or SPRINGBURN & POLLOKSHAWS WEST or ROUKEN GLEN Circle via THORNLIEBANK
		Circle Cars return to ALEXANDRA PARK or RIDDRIE
		RIDDRIE or ALEXANDRA PARK & MERRYLEE or ROUKEN GLEN Circle via GIFFNOCK
		Circle Cars return to SPRINGBURN or BISHOPBRIGGS
S	White	SPRINGBURN & MOUNT FLORIDA or CATHCART via GLASGOW CROSS
T	Red	MARYHILL or BARRACKS GATE & GOVANHILL via NEW CITY ROAD
U	Green	PAISLEY CROSS & TOLLCROSS or UDDINGSTON
V	White	GARNGAD & POLMADIE via GLASGOW CROSS
W	Green	KEPPOCHHILL ROAD & WHITEINCH via NORTH STREET
X	Red	ANNIESLAND & CAMBUSLANG via BOTHWELL STREET
Y	White	SPRINGBURN or KELVINSIDE AVENUE & RUTHERGLEN or BURNSIDE via BILSLAND DRIVE, RUTHERGLEN BRIDGE
Z	Blue	HYNDLAND & ALEXANDRA PARK
SF	Green	STOBCROSS FERRY & FINNIESTON

Proposals for Night Tram Services shelved due to outbreak of First World War.

Facing page: Life was leisurely in the months leading to The Great War. It was possible to wheel a bicycle along the tramlines behind this Green Service B tramcar in Trongate. *(T&R Annan)*

Time Frame 1914 - 1918: Frustration

The pace with which tram services had been extended and refined since completion of their electrification is severely curtailed during World War I. Indeed, General Manager James Dalrymple's zeal in recruiting for the Highland Light Infantry (HLI) from his own staff, although doubtless of great benefit to the Regiment where the "Tramways Battalion" is formed, leaves him short of motormen, conductors and maintenance staff. Timetable cut-backs are inevitable at the start of the war and also at the end, (although this time due to a shortage of coal for the Power Station). The following shows that the Corporation Tramways do not stand still, despite difficulties, although certain major works had probably been under construction prior to war being declared.

15th September 1914
Cut-backs brought about by staff shortages with onset of First World War
The following Operational Alterations take place:
Green Service B PAISLEY CROSS or IBROX & SHETTLESTON or BAILLIESTON reduced in frequency;
Green Service U PAISLEY CROSS & TOLLCROSS or UDDINGSTON reduced in frequency;
Green Service W KEPPOCHHILL ROAD & WHITEINCH via NORTH STREET reduced in frequency;
Red Service X ANNIESLAND & CAMBUSLANG via BOTHWELL STREET reduced in frequency;
Blue Service Z HYNDLAND & ALEXANDRA PARK reduced in frequency.

16th September 1914
Further cut-backs brought about by staff shortages with onset of First World War
Blue Service Z HYNDLAND & ALEXANDRA PARK temporarily withdrawn.

17th September 1914
Further cut-backs brought about by staff shortages with onset of First World War.
The following Operational Alterations take place:
Yellow Service H JORDANHILL & LANGSIDE via HYNDLAND reduced in frequency;
Red Service M KILLERMONT or MARYHILL & MOUNT FLORIDA via NEW CITY ROAD reduced in frequency;
Blue Service P Weekdays and Saturdays: MARYHILL & SHAWLANDS via ST GEORGE'S CROSS, GORBALS withdrawn.

23rd September 1914
Red Service M KILLERMONT or MARYHILL & MOUNT FLORIDA via NEW CITY ROAD normal frequency restored
Blue Service P Weekdays and Saturdays: MARYHILL & SHAWLANDS via ST GEORGE'S CROSS, GORBALS reintroduced.

2nd October 1914
Green Service B PAISLEY CROSS or IBROX & SHETTLESTON or BAILLIESTON normal frequency restored;
Green Service U PAISLEY CROSS & TOLLCROSS or UDDINGSTON normal frequency restored.

5th October 1914
Red Service X ANNIESLAND & CAMBUSLANG via BOTHWELL STREET normal frequency restored.

7th October 1914
Blue Service Z HYNDLAND & ALEXANDRA PARK normal service reintroduced.

8th October 1914
Yellow Service H JORDANHILL & LANGSIDE via HYNDLAND normal frequency restored.
Green Service W KEPPOCHHILL ROAD & WHITEINCH via NORTH STREET normal frequency restored.

10th February 1915
New Dalmuir Canal Swing Bridge formally opened.

11th February 1915
Line opened over Dalmuir Canal Swing Bridge.
Line from Dalmuir to Dalmuir West Opened to GCT Service Cars.
Dumbarton Burgh and County Tramways Co Ltd DALMUIR terminus reverts to former site in Dumbarton Road Clydebank at Duntocher Burn.
DB&CT Service BALLOCH & DALMUIR cut back accordingly.
The following Service Alterations take place:
Red Service F Weekdays: SCOTSTOUN & DALMARNOCK, RUTHERGLEN or BURNSIDE extended to become

From 11th February 1915 the Balloch service of the Dumbarton Burgh & County Tramways retreated to Dalmuir West and the Glasgow Red Services F and L extended from the Dalmuir Canal Bridge. Prior to that date Dumbarton Car 6 is ready to set off for Balloch from its terminus on Glasgow metals.
(STTS collection)

DALMUIR WEST & DALMARNOCK, RUTHERGLEN or BURNSIDE from Dumbarton Road Clydebank at Duntocher Burn via Dumbarton Road Clydebank, Glasgow Road Clydebank, Dumbarton Road and former route;

Saturdays: DALMUIR or SCOTSTOUN & DALMARNOCK, RUTHERGLEN, BURNSIDE or CAMBUSLANG extended to become DALMUIR WEST & DALMARNOCK, RUTHERGEN, BURNSIDE or CAMBUSLANG;

Sundays: DALMUIR or WHITEINCH & RUTHERGLEN or BURNSIDE via DALMARNOCK extended to become DALMUIR WEST or WHITEINCH & RUTHERGLEN or BURNSIDE via DALMARNOCK;

Red Service L Weekdays and Saturdays: DALMUIR or SCOTSTOUN & LONDON ROAD extended to become DALMUIR WEST or SCOTSTOUN & LONDON ROAD from Dumbarton Road Clydebank at Duntocher Burn via Dumbarton Road Clydebank and former route;

Sundays: DALMUIR & LONDON ROAD extended to become DALMUIR WEST & LONDON ROAD.

8th March 1915

Frequency to Dalmuir West reduced.

Red Service F Weekdays: DALMUIR WEST & DALMARNOCK, RUTHERGLEN or BURNSIDE cut back to become DALMUIR & DALMARNOCK, RUTHERGLEN or BURNSIDE from Dumbarton Road Clydebank east of Dalmuir Canal Swing Bridge via former route;

Saturdays: DALMUIR WEST & DALMARNOCK, RUTHERGLEN or BURNSIDE or CAMBUSLANG cut back to become DALMUIR or SCOTSTOUN & DALMARNOCK, RUTHERGLEN, BURNSIDE or CAMBUSLANG;

Sundays: DALMUIR WEST or WHITEINCH & RUTHERGLEN or BURNSIDE via DALMARNOCK unaltered.

3rd April 1915

Line opened in Calderciult Road from Maryhill Road to Crosbie Street.

MARYHILL terminus moved from Maryhill Road at Maryhill Station to Calderciult Road west end.

Red Service M KILLERMONT or MARYHILL & MOUNT FLORIDA via NEW CITY ROAD

Red Service N MARYHILL or KELVINSIDE AVENUE & SINCLAIR DRIVE via GARSCUBE ROAD;

Blue Service P KILLERMONT or MARYHILL & SHAWLANDS via ST GEORGE'S CROSS, GORBALS;

Red Service T MARYHILL or BARRACKS GATE & GOVANHILL via NEW CITY ROAD all extended accordingly.

Blackout precautions introduced during the 1914-18 war comprised blinding of headlamps and application of black paper to the upper half of all windows. This can be seen on 'Unobtrusive' top covered car 472 on Red Service N.
(G Hunter)

Yellow car 631 and Red 368 on the siding laid for the Greystone Special School for physically handicapped pupils. Both cars have blackout paper applied to their windows.
(Strathclyde Regional Archives)

18th April 1915

Line opened from Cathcart to Netherlee.
The following Service Alterations take place:
Yellow Service C Weekdays: KIRKLEE or HYNDLAND & CATHCART extended to become
KIRKLEE or HYNDLAND & NETHERLEE via former route to Clarkston Road then via Clarkston Road to Clarkston Road at Ormonde Drive;
Saturdays and Sundays: KIRKLEE & CATHCART extended to become KIRKLEE & NETHERLEE.

June 1915

Sidings opened in Tullis Street Bridgeton between Main Street Bridgeton and Landressy Street and in Greystone Avenue Burnside between Stonelaw Road and Springfield Park Road for Special Cars conveying physically handicapped pupils between Bridgeton School and Burnside (later Greystone) Special School.

10th August 1915

Kinning Park Depot, Admiral Street, **closed** to traffic. Cars transferred to Govan Depot. Building retained as Sand Drier and Hopper facilities. Part also used for Uniform Clothing Store.
➢ *Govan Depot, Brand Street, opened for service.*
Curves opened between Lorne Street to and from Paisley Road West westwards for Depot Journeys.
The following Operational Alterations take place:
Kinning Park Depot operation of
Green Service B PAISLEY CROSS or IBROX & SHETTLESTON or BAILLIESTON
Blue Service G LAMBHILL or POSSILPARK & LINTHOUSE via LORNE STREET
Blue Service K KEPPOCHHILL ROAD & SHIELDHALL or RENFREW
Yellow Service J RIDDRIE or ALEXANDRA PARK & PAISLEY ROAD TOLL via BRIDGETON CROSS
Green Service U PAISLEY CROSS & TOLLCROSS or UDDINGSTON
all transferred to Govan Depot.

6th November 1915

Major works in Balmore Road.
The following Temporary Service Alteration takes place:
Blue Service G LAMBHILL or POSSILPARK & LINTHOUSE via LORNE STREET split to operate between
LAMBHILL & POSSILPARK and POSSILPARK & LINTHOUSE via LORNE STREET.

24th January 1916

Increase in frequency to Scotstoun.
The following Service Alteration takes place:
Green Service W Weekdays: KEPPOCHHILL ROAD & WHITEINCH via NORTH STREET part extended to become
KEPPOCHHILL ROAD & WHITEINCH or SCOTSTOUN via NORTH STREET via former route to Dumbarton Road then via Dumbarton Road to Dumbarton Road west of Queen Victoria Drive;
Saturdays and Sundays: KEPPOCHHILL ROAD & WHITEINCH via NORTH STREET unaltered.

With so many of the "Green Staff" volunteering for military duties, the Tramways Department recruited and trained female staff for driving and conducting. This is a photograph of maybe the first group "passing-out".
(BJ Cross collection)

11th February 1917

Balmore Road reopened to through traffic.

Blue Service G temporary service LAMBHILL & POSSILPARK and POSSILPARK & LINTHOUSE or RENFREW via LORNE STREET withdrawn and normal service LAMBHILL or POSSILPARK & LINTHOUSE via LORNE STREET restored.

During 1917

Line opened in Duncryne Place from Kirkintilloch Road to Permanent Way Coup.

3rd September 1917

Increase in frequency to Clydebank.
The following Service Alteration takes place:

Green Service W Weekdays: KEPPOCHHILL ROAD & WHITEINCH or SCOTSTOUN via NORTH STREET, cars turning at SCOTSTOUN extended to become KEPPOCHHILL ROAD & WHITEINCH or CLYDEBANK via NORTH STREET via former route at Dumbarton Road then via Dumbarton Road, Glasgow Road Clydebank to Glasgow Road Clydebank at Bon Accord Street;

Saturdays: KEPPOCHHILL ROAD & WHITEINCH via NORTH STREET part extended to become KEPPOCHHILL ROAD & WHITEINCH or CLYDEBANK via NORTH STREET;

Sundays: KEPPOCHHILL ROAD & WHITEINCH via NORTH STREET unaltered.

21st January 1918

Further cut-backs brought about by shortages of coal for electricity generation.

Blue Service Z HYNDLAND & ALEXANDRA PARK temporarily withdrawn

As can be seen, the lady drivers and "conductor-esses" wore Black Watch skirts as part of their uniform. The lengths seemed to vary as can be seen from these two views. Car 806 is on Red Service M.
(IG Stewart collection)

1st November 1918

Temporary reduction in services due to shortages of coal for electricity generation.
The following Operational Alteration takes place:
Green Service W KEPPOCHHILL ROAD & WHITEINCH or CLYDEBANK via NORTH STREET reduced in frequency.

11th November 1918

Armistice brings hostilities of First World War to a close.
Temporary reduction in services due to shortages of coal for electricity generation.
The following Operational Alterations take place:
Yellow Service C KIRKLEE or HYNDLAND & NETHERLEE
Yellow Service H JORDANHILL & LANGSIDE via HYNDLAND reduced in frequency.

23rd November 1918

Reduction in services to Clydebank.
Green Service W Saturdays: KEPPOCHHILL ROAD & WHITEINCH or CLYDEBANK via NORTH STREET cut back to become KEPPOCHHILL ROAD & WHITEINCH via NORTH STREET;
Weekdays: KEPPOCHHILL ROAD & WHITEINCH or CLYDEBANK via NORTH STREET unaltered;
Sundays: KEPPOCHHILL ROAD & WHITEINCH via NORTH STREET unaltered.

23rd December 1918

Yellow Service C KIRKLEE or HYNDLAND & NETHERLEE and
Yellow Service H JORDANHILL & LANGSIDE via HYNDLAND normal frequency restored.

After the end of the 1914-18 War it became possible to renew expansion and consolidation of tram services. The superb reserved track from Baillieston to Coatbridge was an example of this. (DL Thomson collection)

Time Frame 1919 – 1938: Reinvigoration, Competition and Inspiration

After the end of hostilities it takes a little while for normality to resume but soon construction of new trams and line extensions are under way again, not forgetting the acquisition and integration of the services operated by the Airdrie & Coatbridge Tramways Company and the Paisley District Tramways Company which, respectively, increase the fleet by 15 and 73 trams of which 87 are used. It is during this time that the trams suffer their first serious threat, from unregulated buses which lead to modernisation of the fleet. This period also includes the first abandonments but there is a continuing need for additional trams, culminating in the first Coronations, and the period ends with the opening of the Empire Exhibition which results in major changes to the tramway system.

30th January 1919
Green Service W KEPPOCHHILL ROAD & WHITEINCH or CLYDEBANK via NORTH STREET normal frequency restored.

30th June 1919
Blue Service Z HYNDLAND & ALEXANDRA PARK normal service reintroduced.

25th March 1920
Renewal of cables in Govan Road (Old Govan Road) between Paisley Road Toll and Lorne School. All cars temporarily diverted to run via Paisley Road West and Lorne Street.
Blue Service K KEPPOCHHILL ROAD & SHIELDHALL or RENFREW diverted between Paisley Road Toll and Lorne School to run via Paisley Road West and Lorne Street.

During 1920
Work on renewing cabling in Govan Road completed.
Blue Service K KEPPOCHHILL ROAD & SHIELDHALL or RENFREW reverts to normal route.

7th February 1921
Night Services introduced. See details in separate listings.

March 1921
Line Opened in Broomloan Road providing Siding and Football Lye.
BROOMLOAN ROAD siding opened for Football Specials.
IBROX service terminus remains in Paisley Road West east of Copland Road.

16th August 1921
Line Opened from Netherlee to Clarkston (Stamperland).
The following Service Alteration takes place:
Yellow Service C Weekdays: KIRKLEE or HYNDLAND & NETHERLEE extended to become KIRKLEE or HYNDLAND & NETHERLEE or CLARKSTON via former route to Clarkston Road at Ormonde Drive then via Clarkston Road to temporary terminus at Stamperland;
Saturdays: KIRKLEE & NETHERLEE extended to become KIRKLEE & NETHERLEE or CLARKSTON;
Sundays: KIRKLEE & NETHERLEE extended to become KIRKLEE & CLARKSTON.

1st October 1921
Line Opened from Stamperland to Clarkston Mearns Road.
CLARKSTON terminus extended from temporary site at Stamperland to Mearns Road.
The following Service Alteration takes place:
Yellow Service C KIRKLEE or HYNDLAND & NETHERLEE or CLARKSTON extended via Clarkston Road, Busby Road, Mearns Road to Mearns Road east end.

19th December 1921
Morning and Midday frequency to Clydebank reduced.
The following Service Alteration takes place:
Green Service W Weekdays: KEPPOCHHILL ROAD & WHITEINCH or CLYDEBANK via NORTH STREET altered to become

KEPPOCHHILL ROAD & WHITEINCH, SCOTSTOUN or CLYDEBANK via NORTH STREET;

Saturdays and Sundays: KEPPOCHHILL ROAD & WHITEINCH via NORTH STREET unaltered.

1st January 1922

Glasgow Corporation acquires Airdrie & Coatbridge Tramways Company.

The following Service operated by Airdrie & Coatbridge Tramways Company was acquired:

Service [Airdrie Local] LANGLOAN & AIRDRIE from Bank Street Coatbridge west of Woodside Street via Bank Street, Main Street Coatbridge, Deedes Street Coatbridge, Alexander Street Airdrie, Stirling Street, Airdrie New Cross, Graham Street, Clerk Street, Forrest Street to Forrest Street west end, east of Carlisle Road.

➢ *Coatbridge Depot, Main Street Coatbridge acquired.*

Fleet of 15 trams acquired.

29th January 1922

The following Operational Alteration takes place:

Part of Yellow Service Q transferred from Langside Depot to Govan Depot.

Yellow Service Q MOUNT FLORIDA & PAISLEY ROAD TOLL via SHIELDS ROAD adjusted accordingly.

6th March 1922

Saturday frequency to Dalmuir reduced.

The following Service Alteration takes place:

Red Service F Saturdays: DALMUIR or SCOTSTOUN & DALMARNOCK, RUTHERGLEN, BURNSIDE or CAMBUSLANG cut back to become

CLYDEBANK or SCOTSTOUN & DALMARNOCK, RUTHERGLEN, BURNSIDE or CAMBUSLANG;

Weekdays: DALMUIR & DALMARNOCK, RUTHERGLEN or BURNSIDE unaltered;

Sundays: DALMUIR WEST or WHITEINCH & RUTHERGLEN or BURNSIDE via DALMARNOCK unaltered.

May 1922

Speeding up of Airdrie and Coatbridge Services.

The following Operational Alteration takes place:

Service [Airdrie Local] LANGLOAN & AIRDRIE end to end Running Time reduced from 30 to 23 minutes.

May 1922

Line Opened in Holmfauld Road.

LINTHOUSE terminus moved from Govan Road at Linthouse Burn to Holmfauld Road south end.

Blue Service G LAMBHILL or POSSILPARK & LINTHOUSE via LORNE STREET altered accordingly.

Until the Linthouse terminal siding was opened on Holmfauld Road, trams had to use the crossover on the main Govan Road.
(Commercial Postcard, Courtesy NTM Archive)

10th June 1922

The following Service Alteration takes place:

White Service S Saturdays: SPRINGBURN & MOUNT FLORIDA or CATHCART via GLASGOW CROSS extended to become SPRINGBURN & MOUNT FLORIDA, CATHCART or NETHERLEE via GLASGOW CROSS via former route to Clarkston Road at Dairsie Street then via Clarkston Road to Clarkston Road at Ormonde Drive;

Sundays: SPRINGBURN & CATHCART via GLASGOW CROSS extended to become SPRINGBURN & NETHERLEE via GLASGOW CROSS;

Weekdays: SPRINGBURN & MOUNT FLORIDA or CATHCART via GLASGOW CROSS unaltered

16th July 1922

Line Opened on Garngad Road from Blochairn Road to east of Provanmill Road.

The following Service Alteration takes place:

White Service V GARNGAD & POLMADIE via GLASGOW CROSS extended to become PROVANMILL & POLMADIE via GLASGOW CROSS from Garngad Road east of Provanmill Road via Garngad Road and former route.

18th September 1922

Line Opened in Primrose Street.

WHITEINCH terminus moved from Dumbarton Road at Westland Drive to Primrose Street north end.

Red Service F DALMUIR WEST, DALMUIR, SCOTSTOUN or WHITEINCH & DALMARNOCK, RUTHERGLEN, BURNSIDE or CAMBUSLANG;

Green Service W KEPPOCHHILL ROAD & WHITEINCH, SCOTSTOUN or CLYDEBANK via NORTH STREET;

both adjusted accordingly.

1st October 1922

Line Opened from Killermont to Canniesburn.

The following Service Alteration takes place:

Red Service M Weekdays and Saturdays: KILLERMONT or MARYHILL & MOUNT FLORIDA via NEW CITY ROAD extended to become CANNIESBURN or MARYHILL & MOUNT FLORIDA via NEW CITY ROAD from Maryhill Road south of Bearsden Road via Maryhill Road and former route;

Sundays: KILLERMONT & MOUNT FLORIDA via NEW CITY ROAD extended to become CANNIESBURN & MOUNT FLORIDA via NEW CITY ROAD.

14th October 1922

Parkhead Depot, Tollcross Road opened at 1700 hrs.

15th October 1922

Whitevale Depot, Rowchester Street, **closed to traffic**. Cars transferred to Parkhead Depot.

➢ *Parkhead Depot, Tollcross Road opened for service*

The following Operational Alterations take place:

Whitevale Depot Operation of

Green Service A ANNIESLAND & SHETTLESTON or SPRINGFIELD ROAD

Green Service B PAISLEY CROSS or IBROX & SHETTLESTON or BAILLIESTON

Green Service U PAISLEY CROSS & TOLLCROSS or UDDINGSTON all transferred to Parkhead Depot.

Rowchester Street retained as WHITEVALE terminus.

The following Service Alterations take place:

Green Service B Weekdays: PAISLEY CROSS or IBROX & SHETTLESTON or BAILLIESTON and

Green Service U Weekdays: PAISLEY CROSS & TOLLCROSS or UDDINGSTON portion of shortworking cars extended from IBROX to HALFWAY.

4th November 1922

Removal of Centre Poles on Great Western Road between Botanic Gardens and Park Road commences. Alignment of tracks not altered.

5th November 1922

Line Opened on London Road from Williamson Street to Tollcross Station Road.

The following Service Alteration takes place:

Red Service L Weekdays: DALMUIR WEST & LONDON ROAD extended to become DALMUIR WEST or SCOTSTOUN & LONDON ROAD or AUCHENSHUGGLE via former route to London Road at Williamson Street then via London Road to London Road at Tollcross Station Road;

Saturdays: DALMUIR WEST or SCOTSTOUN & LONDON ROAD extended to become DALMUIR WEST & LONDON ROAD or AUCHENSHUGGLE;

Sundays: DALMUIR WEST & LONDON ROAD extended to become DALMUIR WEST & AUCHENSHUGGLE;

Red Service F Weekdays: DALMUIR & DALMARNOCK, RUTHERGLEN or BURNSIDE cut back to become

SCOTSTOUN & DALMARNOCK, RUTHERGLEN or BURNSIDE;
Saturdays: DALMUIR or SCOTSTOUN & DALMARNOCK, RUTHERGLEN, BURNSIDE or CAMBUSLANG cut back to become CLYDEBANK or SCOTSTOUN & DALMARNOCK, RUTHERGLEN, BURNSIDE or CAMBUSLANG;
Sundays: DALMUIR WEST or WHITEINCH & RUTHERGLEN or BURNSIDE via DALMARNOCK unaltered.

24th December 1922

The following Service Alteration takes place:
Blue Service O Weekdays and Saturdays: BOTANIC GARDENS & OATLANDS or RUTHERGLEN via PARK ROAD, CROWN STREET extended to become KIRKLEE & OATLANDS or RUTHERGLEN via PARK ROAD, CROWN STREET from Kirklee Road south end via Kirklee Road, Great Western Road and former route;
Sundays: BOTANIC GARDENS & RUTHERGLEN via PARK ROAD, CROWN STREET extended to become KIRKLEE & RUTHERGLEN via PARK ROAD, CROWN STREET.
BOTANIC GARDENS Loop on north side of Great Western Road west of Byres Road closed to traffic and removed. Crossover retained.

28th December 1922

Removal of Centre Poles on Great Western Road between Botanic Gardens and Park Road completed.

11th March 1923

Demolition of Tolbooth Buildings (apart from Tolbooth Steeple) on north side of Trongate at corner of High Street, Glasgow Cross.
High Street closed to traffic at Glasgow Cross.
The following Temporary Service Alterations take place:
White Service S SPRINGBURN & MOUNT FLORIDA, CATHCART or NETHERLEE via GLASGOW CROSS;
White Service V PROVANMILL & POLMADIE via GLASGOW CROSS
both split to turn on temporary crossovers on either side to operate
White Service S SPRINGBURN & GLASGOW CROSS and
GLASGOW CROSS & MOUNT FLORIDA, CATHCART or NETHERLEE;
White Service V PROVANMILL & GLASGOW CROSS and GLASGOW CROSS & POLMADIE.

25th March 1923

The following Service Alteration takes place:
Blue Service P Sundays: KILLERMONT & SHAWLANDS via ST GEORGE'S CROSS, GORBALS extended to become CANNIESBURN & SHAWLANDS via ST GEORGE'S CROSS, GORBALS from Maryhill Road at Canniesburn via Maryhill Road and former route:
Weekdays and Saturdays: MARYHILL & SHAWLANDS via ST GEORGE'S CROSS, GORBALS unaltered.

21st April 1923

The following Service Alteration takes place:
Red Service M Saturdays: CANNIESBURN or MARYHILL & MOUNT FLORIDA via NEW CITY ROAD, shortworking MARYHILL cars extended to become CANNIESBURN & MOUNT FLORIDA via NEW CITY ROAD;
Weekdays: CANNIESBURN or MARYHILL & MOUNT FLORIDA via NEW CITY ROAD unaltered;
Sundays: CANNIESBURN & MOUNT FLORIDA via NEW CITY ROAD unaltered.

3rd June 1923

IBROX terminus moved from Paisley Road West east of Copland Road to existing siding in Broomloan Road south end.
Green Service B PAISLEY CROSS, HALFWAY or IBROX & SHETTLESTON or BAILLIESTON ;
Green Service U PAISLEY CROSS & TOLLCROSS or UDDINGSTON shortworkings
both altered accordingly.

July 1923

Junction installed at Turriff Street and MacKinlay Street for proposed Carlton Place route.

15th July 1923

Gas Main repairs at junction of Maryhill Road and Bilsland Drive.
White Service Y SPRINGBURN or KELVINSIDE AVENUE & RUTHERGLEN or BURNSIDE via BILSLAND DRIVE, RUTHERGLEN BRIDGE split to operate SPRINGBURN & VERNON STREET via BILSLAND DRIVE and KELVINSIDE AVENUE & RUTHERGLEN or BURNSIDE via RUTHERGLEN BRIDGE.

27th July 1923

Gas Main repairs at junction of Maryhill Road and Bilsland Drive completed.
White Service Y SPRINGBURN or KELVINSIDE AVENUE & RUTHERGLEN or BURNSIDE via BILSLAND DRIVE, RUTHERGLEN BRIDGE reverts to normal service.

The former Paisley District fleet was quickly repainted in GCT colours. Car 1004, seen above, at Renfrew Ferry on Service KIL with the distinctive pylon in the background for the high tension cabling for the Yoker Power Station across the river carries Green route colours while 1062 at Elderslie Depot, below, is a blue car. *(STTS Collection)*

1st August 1923

Glasgow Corporation acquires Paisley District Tramways Company.

The following Services operated by Paisley District Tramways Co. were acquired:

Green Service ABB PAISLEY CROSS & SPRINGBANK ROAD or ABBOTSINCH from Gilmour Street beneath railway overbridge via Gilmour Street, Old Sneddon Street, Love Street, Inchinnan Road; either to Inchinnan Road at Loop at south end; or via Inchinnan Road, Abbotsinch Road to Abbotsinch Road at Douglas Terrace; No Sundays Service;

Green Service KIL KILBARCHAN or JOHNSTONE CENTRE & RENFREW FERRY from High Barholm at Churchill Place via High Barholm, Low Barholm, Easwaldbank, Overjohnstone Bridge, Cartside, Kilbarchan Road, Graham Street, Macdowall Street, High Street Johnstone, Houston Square north; JOHNSTONE CENTRE cars from Houston Square north; then via High Street Johnstone, Thorn Brae, Thornhill, Main Street Elderslie, Main Road Elderslie, Ferguslie, Broomlands Street, West End Cross, Wellmeadow Street, High Street Paisley, Paisley Cross, Gilmour Street, County Square, Gilmour Street, Old Sneddon Street, Weir Street, Renfrew Road Paisley, Paisley Road Renfrew, Hairst Street, Renfrew Cross, Canal Street Renfrew, Ferry Road to Renfrew Ferry, Ferry Road south of Clyde Street Renfrew;

Blue Service ROUKEN GLEN [Spiersbridge], BARRHEAD (PRINCES SQUARE), BARRHEAD CENTRE or POTTERHILL & RENFREW FERRY from Spiersbridge Road south of Rouken Glen Road via Spiersbridge Road, Private Track on north side of Nitshill Road, Darnley, Private Track on north side of Parkhouse Road, Parkhouse, Darnley Road, Main Street Barrhead, Allan's Corner, Cross Arthurlie Street, Paisley Road Barrhead, Caplethill Road, Neilston Road, Causeyside Street, St Mirren Street, Paisley Cross, Gilmour Street, County Square, Gilmour Street, Old Sneddon Street, Weir Street, Renfrew Road Paisley, Paisley Road Renfrew, Hairst Street, Renfrew Cross, Canal Street Renfrew, Ferry Road to Renfrew Ferry, Ferry Road south of Clyde Street Renfrew;

Green Service [Paisley Local] PAISLEY CROSS & HAWKHEAD ROAD from High Street Paisley west of Paisley Cross via Paisley Cross, St James Bridge, Smithhills Street, Gauze Street, Glasgow Road Paisley to Glasgow Road Paisley at Hawkhead Road;

Blue Service [Paisley Local] POTTERHILL & PAISLEY CROSS or SPRINGBANK ROAD from Neilston Road at Potterhill Station via Neilston Road, Causeyside Street, St Mirren Street, Paisley Cross, County Square, Gilmour Street, Old Sneddon Street, Love Street, Inchinnan Road to Loop at south end.

> *Elderslie Depot and Workshops,* Main Road Elderslie, **acquired.**
> *Renfrew Depot,* Paisley Road Renfrew, **acquired.**
> *Barrhead Depot,* Aurs Road Barrhead, **acquired.**
> *Permanent Way Yard and Coup*, Beith Road Johnstone, **acquired,**

Access Line in Aurs Road Barrhead from Main Street Barrhead to Barrhead Depot, **acquired**.
Access Line from Paisley Road Barrhead to Boylestone Quarry **acquired**.
Access Line in Beith Road Johnstone from Thornhill to Permanent Way Yard and Coup **acquired**.
Fleet of 73 trams acquired.

56

With the rolling stock of the Paisley District Tramways came three depots: Elderslie (complete with workshops), a small outstation in Barrhead and that at Renfrew, shown opposite.
(IG Stewart Collection)

Car 1050 carrying a Blue route band was allocated to Renfrew Depot when new. It here operates a special duty covering the Local Service to Hawkhead Road over the original alignment at Paisley Cross. Work on widening the adjacent St James Bridge and realigning these tracks was eventually completed in June 1929.
(DL Thomson collection)

The extension from Dumbreck to Corkerhill Road, below, featured this fine roadside reservation. The Municipal housing estate in Mosspark was still under construction at the time.
(GCT)

August 1923
Line Opened in Spiersbridge Road linking system with former Paisley system.

August 1923
Right-angled Crossing installed at intersection of South Portland Street and Norfolk Street on proposed Carlton Place route.

12th August 1923
Line Opened on Mosspark Boulevard from Dumbreck to Corkerhill Road.
The following Service Alteration takes place:
White Service E Weekdays and Saturdays: UNIVERSITY & POLLOKSHIELDS or DUMBRECK extended to become UNIVERSITY & MOSSPARK via POLLOKSHIELDS via former route to Dumbreck Road then via Dumbreck Road, Private Track on north side of Mosspark Boulevard to Mosspark Boulevard east of Corkerhill Road;
Sundays: UNIVERSITY & DUMBRECK via POLLOKSHIELDS extended to become
UNIVERSITY & MOSSPARK via POLLOKSHIELDS.

10th September 1923
Line Opened from Turriff Street to Carlton Place.
The following Service commences:
Red Service CP CARLTON PLACE & BATTLEFIELD (Part Day) from South Portland Street north end at Carlton Place via South Portland Street, Abbotsford Place, Mackinlay Street, Turriff Street, Eglinton Street, Eglinton Toll, Victoria Road, Langside Road, Grange Road, Battlefield Road to Battlefield Road at Grange Road.

16th September 1923
Line Opened from Govan to Craigton Road.
The following Service Alteration takes place:
Yellow Service J RIDDRIE or ALEXANDRA PARK & PAISLEY ROAD TOLL via BRIDGETON CROSS extended to become RIDDRIE or ALEXANDRA PARK & CRAIGTON ROAD via BRIDGETON CROSS via former route to Paisley Road Toll then via Old Govan Road, Govan Road, Golspie Street, Langlands Road, Elder Street, Crossloan Road, Craigton Road to Craigton Road south end north of railway bridge over Joint Line.

30th September 1923
Line Opened linking High Street Renfrew tracks with former Paisley system at Renfrew Cross southwards into Hairst Street.

6th October 1923
Line Opened in Balmoral Street, Scotstoun.
SCOTSTOUN terminus moved from Dumbarton Road west of Queen Victoria Drive to Balmoral Street north end.
Red Service F DALMUIR WEST, CLYDEBANK, SCOTSTOUN or WHITEINCH & DALMARNOCK, RUTHERGLEN, BURNSIDE or CAMBUSLANG
Red Service L DALMUIR WEST or SCOTSTOUN & LONDON ROAD or AUCHENSHUGGLE
Green Service W KEPPOCHHILL ROAD & WHITEINCH, SCOTSTOUN or CLYDEBANK via NORTH STREET
all adjusted accordingly.

18th November 1923
Line Opened from Baillieston to Bargeddie.
The following Service Alterations take place:
Green Service B Weekdays and Saturdays: PAISLEY CROSS, HALFWAY or IBROX & SHETTLESTON or BAILLIESTON extended to become PAISLEY CROSS, HALFWAY or IBROX & SHETTLESTON, BAILLIESTON or BARGEDDIE via former route to Main Street Baillieston then via Main Street Baillieston, Private Track on south side of Coatbridge Road to Bargeddie Village east of intersection of Langmuir Road;
Sundays: IBROX & BAILLIESTON extended to become IBROX & BAILLIESTON or BARGEDDIE.

25th November 1923
Line Opened from Canniesburn to Hillfoot.
Siding Opened in Kessington Road to Bearsden Substation.
The following Service Alteration takes place:
Red Service M Weekdays: CANNIESBURN or MARYHILL & MOUNT FLORIDA via NEW CITY ROAD extended to become HILLFOOT or MARYHILL & MOUNT FLORIDA via NEW CITY ROAD from Milngavie Road south of Hillfoot railway bridge via Milngavie Road, Maryhill Road and former route;
Saturdays and Sundays: CANNIESBURN & MOUNT FLORIDA via NEW CITY ROAD extended to become
HILLFOOT & MOUNT FLORIDA via NEW CITY ROAD

8th December 1923
Connection at Spiersbridge opened to service cars.

The following Service Alterations take place:

Blue Service P Weekdays and Saturdays: MARYHILL & SHAWLANDS via ST GEORGE'S CROSS, GORBALS extended to become MARYHILL & SHAWLANDS or BARRHEAD CENTRE via ST GEORGE'S CROSS, GORBALS via former route to Shawlands then via Pollokshaws Road, Cross Street, Harriet Street, Thornliebank Road, Main Street Thornliebank, Spiersbridge Road, Private Track on north side of Nitshill Road, Darnley, Private Track on north side of Parkhouse Road, Parkhouse, Darnley Road, Main Street Barrhead, Allan's Corner, Cross Arthurlie Street to Cross Arthurlie Street at Robertson Street;

Sundays: CANNIESBURN & SHAWLANDS via ST GEORGE'S CROSS, GORBALS extended to become

CANNIESBURN & SHAWLANDS or BARRHEAD CENTRE via ST GEORGE'S CROSS, GORBALS;

Blue Service ROUKEN GLEN [Spiersbridge], BARRHEAD (PRINCES SQUARE), BARRHEAD CENTRE or POTTERHILL & RENFREW FERRY cut back and split to become

BARRHEAD (PRINCES SQUARE), BARRHEAD CENTRE or POTTERHILL & RENFREW FERRY from Main Street Barrhead at Aurs Road via Main Street Barrhead, Allan's Corner, Cross Arthurlie Street, Paisley Road Barrhead and former route; and

PAISLEY CROSS & RENFREW FERRY from County Square via Gilmour Street and former route.

ROUKEN GLEN [Spiersbridge] terminus in Spiersbridge Road renamed SPIERSBRIDGE.

Blue Service [Paisley Local] POTTERHILL & PAISLEY CROSS or SPRINGBANK ROAD unaltered.

28th December 1923

Physical link completed between Glasgow system and former Airdrie system at Langloan.

30th December 1923

Line Opened from Bargeddie to Langloan.

The following Service Alterations take place:

Green Service B Weekdays and Saturdays: PAISLEY CROSS, HALFWAY or IBROX & SHETTLESTON, BAILLIESTON or BARGEDDIE extended to become

PAISLEY CROSS, HALFWAY or IBROX & SHETTLESTON, BAILLIESTON or COATBRIDGE [Langloan] via former route to Bargeddie village then via Private Track on south side of Glasgow Road Coatbridge to east end of Private Track at Langloan;

Sundays: IBROX & BAILLIESTON or BARGEDDIE extended to become

IBROX & BAILLIESTON or COATBRIDGE [Langloan];

Through Booking available to and from

Green Service [Airdrie Local] LANGLOAN & AIRDRIE.

January 1924

Track doubled in Cross Arthurlie Street and Paisley Road Barrhead.

BARRHEAD CENTRE crossover provided in Cross Arthurlie Street at Robertson Street.

Line linking Paisley Road Barrhead with Boylestone Quarry **closed** to trams.

31st March 1924

Demolition of Tolbooth Buildings at Glasgow Cross completed.

High Street reopened to through tram traffic.

White Service S Weekdays: SPRINGBURN & MOUNT FLORIDA or CATHCART via GLASGOW CROSS;

Saturdays: SPRINGBURN & MOUNT FLORIDA, CATHCART or NETHERLEE via GLASGOW CROSS;

Sundays: SPRINGBURN & NETHERLEE via GLASGOW CROSS and

White Service V PROVANMILL & POLMADIE via GLASGOW CROSS

both resume normal through services.

During 1924

Siding opened from Main Street Baillieston west of Church Street, to serve Baillieston Substation.

19th April 1924

Frequency of service to Coatbridge increased.

Green Service B PAISLEY CROSS, HALFWAY or IBROX & SHETTLESTON, BAILLIESTON or COATBRIDGE [Langloan] adjusted accordingly.

20th April 1924

The following Service Alteration takes place:

Blue Service P Sundays: CANNIESBURN & SHAWLANDS or BARRHEAD CENTRE via ST GEORGE'S CROSS, GORBALS extended to become HILLFOOT & SHAWLANDS or BARRHEAD CENTRE via ST GEORGE'S CROSS, GORBALS from Milngavie Road south of Hillfoot railway bridge via Milngavie Road, Maryhill Road and former route;

Weekdays and Saturdays: MARYHILL & SHAWLANDS or BARRHEAD CENTRE via ST GEORGE'S CROSS, GORBALS unaltered.

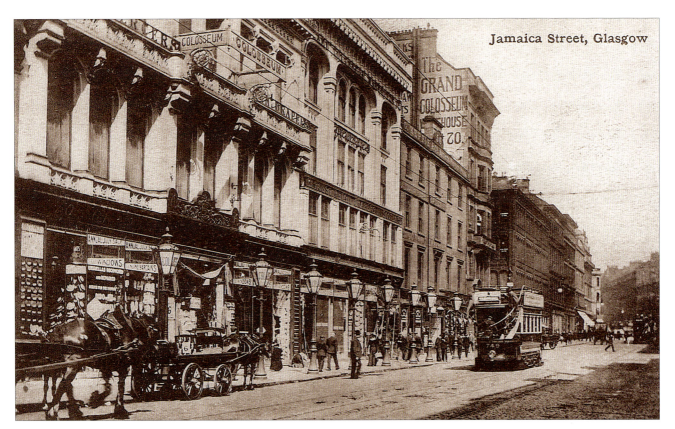

The Summer of 1924 saw the last of the Standard Cars placed in service reaching an eventual total of 1,004. At this time, also, the final open top Standard cars were top-covered. Number 749, here, was one of the last to be upgraded.
(Commercial Postcard, BJ Cross Collection)

10th May 1924

The following Service Alteration takes place:

Blue Service P Saturdays: MARYHILL & SHAWLANDS or BARRHEAD CENTRE via ST GEORGE'S CROSS, GORBALS extended to become HILLFOOT & BARRHEAD CENTRE via ST GEORGE'S CROSS, GORBALS from Milngavie Road south of Hillfoot railway bridge via Milngavie Road, Maryhill Road and former route;
Weekdays: MARYHILL & SHAWLANDS or BARRHEAD CENTRE via ST GEORGE'S CROSS, GORBALS
Sundays: HILLFOOT & SHAWLANDS or BARRHEAD CENTRE via ST GEORGE'S CROSS, GORBALS, both unaltered.

3rd June 1924

Former Airdrie and Coatbridge system closed down for reconstruction and refurbishment.
Green Service [Airdrie Local] LANGLOAN & AIRDRIE temporarily withdrawn and replaced by Motorbus Service.
Coatbridge Depot closed. Cars transferred to Elderslie Depot and Renfrew Depot.

16th June 1924

Line Opened in Gairbraid Avenue.
GAIRBRAID AVENUE terminal point available for shortworking journeys on
Red Service M HILLFOOT or MARYHILL & MOUNT FLORIDA via NEW CITY ROAD
Red Service N MARYHILL or KELVINSIDE AVENUE & SINCLAIR DRIVE via GARSCUBE ROAD
Blue Service P HILLFOOT or MARYHILL & SHAWLANDS or BARRHEAD CENTRE via ST GEORGE'S CROSS, GORBALS.
Red Service T MARYHILL or BARRACKS GATE & GOVANHILL via NEW CITY ROAD.

4th July 1924

Line Opened from Riddrie to Millerston.
The following Service Alteration takes place:
Red Service R Weekdays & Saturdays: RIDDRIE or ALEXANDRA PARK & MERRYLEE or ROUKEN GLEN Circle via GIFFNOCK section extended to become
MILLERSTON, RIDDRIE or ALEXANDRA PARK & MERRYLEE or ROUKEN GLEN Circle via GIFFNOCK from Station Road south end via Station Road, Cumbernauld Road, Smithycroft Road and former route;
Sundays: RIDDRIE or ALEXANDRA PARK & ROUKEN GLEN Circle via GIFFNOCK extended to become
MILLERSTON, RIDDRIE or ALEXANDRA PARK & ROUKEN GLEN Circle via GIFFNOCK.

13th July 1924

Line Opened in Kilbowie Road from Clydebank to Radnor Park.

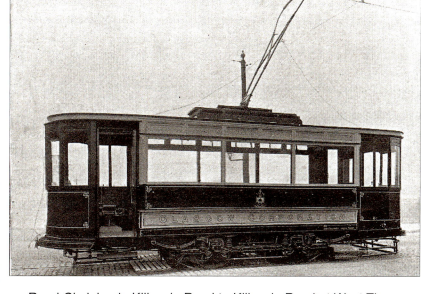

The opening of the Kilbowie Road Service with its single-deck trams introduced air braking to the fleet – an event whose potential for future orders was not lost on the suppliers, Westinghouse, who featured the first tram thus equipped in its trade advertising.
(BJ Cross Collection)

Additional YOKER crossover provided in Dumbarton Road east of Ferry Road.
The following Service commences:
Red Service RP [Single Deck Cars] YOKER & RADNOR PARK from Dumbarton Road east of Ferry Road via Dumbarton Road, Glasgow Road Clydebank, Kilbowie Road to Kilbowie Road at West Thomson Street.

19th July 1924

The following Operational Alteration takes place:
To provide space in Partick Depot for Single Deck Cars for Service RP, allocation of Blue Cars for Blue Service O transferred to Dalmarnock Depot.
Blue Service O KIRKLEE & OATLANDS or RUTHERGLEN via PARK ROAD, CROWN STREET adjusted accordingly.

21st July 1924

Emergency Specials provided on all services during strike of railwaymen.

29th July 1924

Following resumption of normal railway services, Emergency Specials withdrawn.

10th August 1924

Line Opened on Hyndland Road from Clarence Drive to Great Western Road.
KELVINSIDE CROSS crossover sited in Hyndland Road north end.
KELVINSIDE terminus moved from Great Western Road at Hyndland Road to Hyndland Road north end.
The following Service Alterations take place:
Blue Service Z HYNDLAND & ALEXANDRA PARK extended to become
KELVINSIDE CROSS & ALEXANDRA PARK from Hyndland Road north end via Hyndland Road, Highburgh Road and former route;
Green Service D Weekdays and Saturdays: KELVINSIDE & DENNISTOUN or SHETTLESTON adjusted accordingly.

17th August 1924

Lowering of track beneath railway bridges in Barrhead and in Capelthill Road at the Brownside Loop permits operation of top-covered Standard cars through from Barrhead to Paisley.
The following Service Alterations take place:
Blue Service P Weekdays: MARYHILL & SHAWLANDS or BARRHEAD CENTRE via ST GEORGE'S CROSS, GORBALS extended to become
MARYHILL & SHAWLANDS, PAISLEY CROSS or RENFREW FERRY via ST GEORGE'S CROSS, GORBALS, BARRHEAD via former route to Cross Arthurlie Street then via Paisley Road Barrhead, Capelthill Road, Neilston Road, Causeyside Street, St Mirren Street, Paisley Cross, Gilmour Street, County Square, Gilmour Street, Old Sneddon Street, Weir Street, Renfrew Road Paisley, Paisley Road Renfrew, Hairst Street, Renfrew Cross, Canal Street, Ferry Road to Renfrew Ferry, Ferry Road south of Clyde Street;
Saturdays: HILLFOOT & BARRHEAD CENTRE via ST GEORGE'S CROSS, GORBALS extended to become
HILLFOOT & PAISLEY CROSS or RENFREW FERRY via ST GEORGE'S CROSS, GORBALS, BARRHEAD;
Sundays: HILLFOOT & SHAWLANDS or BARRHEAD CENTRE via ST GEORGE'S CROSS, GORBALS, extended to become
HILLFOOT & SHAWLANDS, PAISLEY CROSS or RENFREW FERRY via ST GEORGE'S CROSS, GORBALS, BARRHEAD;
Blue Service BARRHEAD (PRINCES SQUARE), BARRHEAD CENTRE or POTTERHILL & RENFREW FERRY and
Blue Service [Paisley Local] POTTERHILL & PAISLEY CROSS or SPRINGBANK ROAD
both altered to become

Blue Service [Paisley Local] BARRHEAD (PRINCES SQUARE), BARRHEAD CENTRE or POTTERHILL & PAISLEY CROSS from Main Street Barrhead at Aurs Road via Main Street Barrhead, Allan's Corner, Cross Arthurlie Street, Paisley Road Barrhead, Caplethill Road, Neilston Road, Causeyside Street, St Mirren Street, Paisley Cross, Gilmour Street to County Square.

Blue Service [Paisley Local] PAISLEY CROSS & RENFREW FERRY unaltered.

12th October 1924

Line Opened from Anniesland to Scotstounhill.
The following Service Alteration takes place:

Green Service A Weekdays and Saturdays: ANNIESLAND & PARKHEAD or SPRINGFIELD ROAD extended to become SCOTSTOUNHILL & PARKHEAD or SPRINGFIELD ROAD from Anniesland Road at Southbrae Drive via Anniesland Road, Anniesland Cross, Great Western Road and former route;

Sundays: ANNIESLAND & SPRINGFIELD ROAD or SHETTLESTON altered to become SCOTSTOUNHILL & SPRINGFIELD ROAD;

Green Service D Sundays: ANNIESLAND & DENNISTOUN extended to become ANNIESLAND & SHETTLESTON via former route to Duke Street then via Duke Street, Shettleston Road, Shettleston Sheddings, Shettleston Road to Shettleston Road at Gartocher Road;

Weekdays and Saturdays: KELVINSIDE & DENNISTOUN or SHETTLESTON unaltered.

1st January 1925

System of Headcodes introduced to supplement Route Colours. Displayed on three-track digital number screens, formerly used for Route Numbers, the system, using suffix letters, allocated a separate identity to each turning point. Details appear under Appendix D.

The Service Headcode system made use of the digital indicators hitherto employed to display running numbers on Round Dash cars, as seen here. The Hexagonal Dash cars, however, needed to have an aperture fitted into their vestibule framing to display the new Headcodes. The system was over-complicated and latterly tended to be ignored by crews.
(IG Stewart Collection)

The following are the Numbers:

1	ROUKEN GLEN to BISHOPBRIGGS or MILLERSTON
2	BISHOPBRIGGS or MILLERSTON to ROUKEN GLEN
3	CLARKSTON or LANGSIDE to KIRKLEE or JORDANHILL
4	JORDANHILL or KIRKLEE to LANGSIDE or CLARKSTON
5	RENFREW to KEPPOCHHILL ROAD or LAMBHILL
6	LAMBHILL or KEPPOCHHILL ROAD to RENFREW
7	MOSSPARK to UNIVERSITY
8	UNIVERSITY to MOSSPARK
9	MOUNT FLORIDA to HILLFOOT
10	HILLFOOT to MOUNT FLORIDA
11	SINCLAIR DRIVE to KELVINSIDE AVENUE
12	KELVINSIDE AVENUE to SINCLAIR DRIVE
9	RENFREW FERRY to HILLFOOT
14	HILLFOOT to RENFREW FERRY
15	NETHERLEE to SPRINGBURN
16	SPRINGBURN to NETHERLEE
17	POLMADIE to PROVANMILL
18	PROVANMILL to POLMADIE
19	SCOTSTOUNHILL to SHETTLESTON or SPRINGFIELD ROAD
20	SPRINGFIELD ROAD or SHETTLESTON to SCOTSTOUNHILL
21	PAISLEY CROSS to UDDINGSTON or COATBRIDGE
22	COATBRIDGE or UDDINGSTON to PAISLEY CROSS
23	DALMUIR to AUCHENSHUGGLE, BURNSIDE or CAMBUSLANG
24	CAMBUSLANG, BURNSIDE or AUCHENSHUGGLE to DALMUIR
25	ANNIESLAND to CAMBUSLANG
26	CAMBUSLANG to ANNIESLAND
27	KIRKLEE to RUTHERGLEN
28	RUTHERGLEN to KIRKLEE
29	SPRINGBURN to BURNSIDE
30	BURNSIDE to SPRINGBURN
31	CRAIGTON ROAD to RIDDRIE
32	RIDDRIE to CRAIGTON ROAD
33	MOUNT FLORIDA to PAISLEY ROAD TOLL
34	PAISLEY ROAD TOLL to MOUNT FLORIDA
35	WHITEINCH to KEPPOCHHILL ROAD
36	KEPPOCHHILL ROAD to WHITEINCH
37	KELVINSIDE CROSS to ALEXANDRA PARK
38	ALEXANDRA PARK to KELVINSIDE CROSS
39	RADNOR PARK to YOKER
40	YOKER to RADNOR PARK

17th January 1925

The following Service Alterations take place:

Green Service B Weekdays and Saturdays: PAISLEY CROSS, HALFWAY or IBROX & SHETTLESTON, BAILLIESTON or COATBRIDGE [Langloan] extended to become
FERGUSLIE MILLS, CROOKSTON, HALFWAY or IBROX & SHETTLESTON, BAILLIESTON or COATBRIDGE [Langloan] from Ferguslie at Thomas Street via Ferguslie, Broomlands Street, West End Cross, Wellmeadow Street, High Street Paisley, Paisley Cross, St James Bridge and former route;
Sundays: IBROX & BAILLIESTON or COATBRIDGE [Langloan] unaltered;

Green Service U Weekdays and Saturdays: PAISLEY CROSS & TOLLCROSS or UDDINGSTON extended to become FERGUSLIE MILLS, CROOKSTON or IBROX & TOLLCROSS or UDDINGSTON from Ferguslie at Thomas Street via Ferguslie, Broomlands Street, West End Cross, Wellmeadow Street, High Street Paisley, Paisley Cross, St James Bridge and former route;
Sundays: PAISLEY CROSS & TOLLCROSS or UDDINGSTON extended to become
FERGUSLIE MILLS & TOLLCROSS or UDDINGSTON.

1st February 1925

Line Opened from Radnor Park to Duntocher.
The following Service Alteration takes place:
Red Service RP [Single Deck Cars] YOKER & RADNOR PARK extended to become
YOKER & DUNTOCHER via former route to Kilbowie Road at West Thomson Street then via Kilbowie Road, Glasgow Road Duntocher, Dumbarton Road Duntocher to Dumbarton Road Duntocher at Roman Road.

1st March 1925

The following Service Alteration takes place:
Red Service T MARYHILL or BARRACKS GATE & GOVANHILL via NEW CITY ROAD altered to become
HILLFOOT or MARYHILL & MOUNT FLORIDA via NEW CITY ROAD from Milngavie Road south of Hillfoot railway bridge via Milngavie Road, Canniesburn Toll, Maryhill Road and former route to Cathcart Road then via Cathcart Road, Clincart Road to Clincart Road at Bolton Drive.

March 1925

Siding Opened in Abercorn Street Paisley to serve Substation.

During 1925

Crossover installed at RUCHILL in Bilsland Drive at Ruchill Hospital Gates.

29th March 1925

The following Operational Alteration takes place:
Red Service R Weekdays and Saturdays: BISHOPBRIGGS or SPRINGBURN & POLLOKSHAWS WEST or ROUKEN GLEN Circle via THORNLIEBANK;
Sundays: BISHOPBRIGGS & ROUKEN GLEN Circle via THORNLIEBANK; MILLERSTON & ROUKEN GLEN Circle via GIFFNOCK amended timetables introduced.

20th April 1925

Line Opened in Moir Street. Queen Street lye in Argyle Street closed for cars from and to the west.
City Centre Shortworkings from west to Queen Street extended to run to Moir Street.
Peak-hour Cars and Specials on the following services run via Argyle Street, Trongate, Glasgow Cross, Gallowgate, Moir Street:
Green Service B IBROX & QUEEN STREET extended to become IBROX & GLASGOW CROSS;
Green Service U FERGUSLIE MILLS or PAISLEY CROSS & QUEEN STREET extended to become
FERGUSLIE MILLS or PAISLEY CROSS & GLASGOW CROSS;
Peak-hour Cars and Specials on the following services run via Argyle Street, Trongate, Glasgow Cross, London Road, and Moir Street:

The short Finnieston – Stobcross Ferry Service was the first to be withdrawn along with its one man operated converted Horse Car No. 92 which was subsequently transferred to the quiet Abbotsinch route.
(DL Thomson Collection)

Before Burnside terminus was moved round the corner from Stonelaw Road to Dukes Road to ease congestion, Car 137 is seen here in Stonelaw Road still with its experimental front exit.
(Commercial Postcard, BJ Cross Collection)

Red Service F SCOTSTOUN & QUEEN STREET extended to become SCOTSTOUN & GLASGOW CROSS;
Red Service L DALMUIR WEST & QUEEN STREET extended to become DALMUIR WEST & GLASGOW CROSS;
Blue Service O KIRKLEE & QUEEN STREET via PARK ROAD extended to become
KIRKLEE & GLASGOW CROSS via PARK ROAD;
Red Service X ANNIESLAND & QUEEN STREET via BOTHWELL STREET extended to become
ANNIESLAND & GLASGOW CROSS via BOTHWELL STREET;
White Service Y SPRINGBURN or KELVINSIDE AVENUE & QUEEN STREET extended to become
SPRINGBURN or KELVINSIDE AVENUE & GLASGOW CROSS.

4th May 1925

Closure of Stobcross Ferry route.
Green Service STOBCROSS FERRY & FINNIESTON withdrawn and replaced by Motorbus Service.
Stobcross Quay and Finnieston Street **closed** to trams.

23rd May 1925

Line Reopened to Airdrie.
The following Service Alteration takes place:
Green Service B FERGUSLIE MILLS, CROOKSTON, HALFWAY or IBROX & SHETTLESTON, BAILLIESTON or COATBRIDGE [Langloan] extended to become FERGUSLIE MILLS, CROOKSTON or IBROX & SHETTLESTON, BAILLIESTON or AIRDRIE via former route to east end of Private Track at Langloan then via Bank Street Coatbridge, Main Street Coatbridge, Deedes Street, Alexander Street Airdrie, Stirling Street, Airdrie New Cross, Graham Street, Clark Street, Forrest Street to Forrest Street west end beyond Carlisle Road.
The following Service recommences:
Green Service [Airdrie Local] LANGLOAN & AIRDRIE from Langloan Bank Street Coatbridge at Woodside Street via Bank Street Coatbridge, Main Street Coatbridge, Deedes Street, Alexander Street Airdrie, Stirling Street, Airdrie New Cross, Graham Street, Clark Street, Forrest Street to Forrest Street west end beyond Carlisle Road.
COATBRIDGE terminus moved eastwards to Main Street Coatbridge west end.

7th June 1925

Line Opened in Duke's Road Burnside.
BURNSIDE terminus moved from Stonelaw Road at Duke's Road into Duke's Road west end.
Additional crossover provided at Springburn in Hawthorn Street east end.
Adjustment to turning point of Springburn services.
SPRINGBURN terminus for White Service Y cut back from Springburn Road between Hawthorn Street and Elmvale Street to Hawthorn Street east end.
The following Service Alterations take place:
Red Service F DALMUIR WEST, CLYDEBANK, SCOTSTOUN or WHITEINCH & DALMARNOCK, RUTHERGLEN, BURNSIDE or CAMBUSLANG extended at Burnside accordingly;
White Service Y SPRINGBURN or KELVINSIDE AVENUE & RUTHERGLEN or BURNSIDE via BILSLAND DRIVE, RUTHERGLEN BRIDGE cut back at Springburn and extended at Burnside accordingly.

21st June 1925

Extension of further cars to Airdrie.
The following Service Alteration takes place:
Green Service D Weekdays and Saturdays: KELVINSIDE & DENNISTOUN or SHETTLESTON extended to become KELVINSIDE & DENNISTOUN, SHETTLESTON or AIRDRIE via former route to Shettleston Road then via Shettleston Road, Baillieston Road, Glasgow Road Baillieston, Main Street Baillieston, Private Track on south side of Coatbridge Road, Private Track on south side of Glasgow Road, Langloan, Bank Street Coatbridge, Main Street Coatbridge, Deedes Street, Alexander Street Airdrie, Stirling Street, Airdrie New Cross, Graham Street, Clark Street, Forrest Street to Forrest Street west end beyond Carlisle Road;
Sundays: ANNIESLAND & SHETTLESTON extended to become ANNIESLAND & AIRDRIE.

5th July 1925

Increase in service to Millerston.
The following Service Alteration takes place:
Yellow Service J RIDDRIE or ALEXANDRA PARK & CRAIGTON ROAD via BRIDGETON CROSS extended to become MILLERSTON, RIDDRIE or ALEXANDRA PARK & CRAIGTON ROAD via BRIDGETON CROSS from Station Road south end via Station Road, Cumbernauld Road, Smithycroft Road and former route.

9th August 1925

North end of Saracen Street Opened to regular Service cars.
Extension of Possilpark cars to Springburn via Hawthorn Street.
The following Service Alteration takes place:
Blue Service G Weekdays and Saturdays: LAMBHILL or POSSILPARK & LINTHOUSE via LORNE STREET extended to become LAMBHILL or SPRINGBURN & LINTHOUSE, SHIELDHALL or RENFREW via POSSILPARK, LORNE STREET from Springburn at Hawthorn Street east end via Hawthorn Street, Saracen Street, Saracen Cross and former route;
Sundays: LAMBHILL & LINTHOUSE via LORNE STREET altered to become
LAMBHILL or SPRINGBURN & LINTHOUSE via POSSILPARK, LORNE STREET.

17th August 1925

The following Service Alterations take place:
Green Service W Weekdays: KEPPOCHHILL ROAD & WHITEINCH, SCOTSTOUN or CLYDEBANK via NORTH STREET cut back to become KEPPOCHHILL ROAD & WHITEINCH or SCOTSTOUN via NORTH STREET;
Saturdays and Sundays: KEPPOCHHILL ROAD & WHITEINCH via NORTH STREET unaltered;
Blue Service Z Weekdays: KELVINSIDE CROSS & ALEXANDRA PARK part extended and part diverted to become JORDANHILL or KELVINSIDE CROSS & ALEXANDRA PARK or RIDDRIE from JORDANHILL Crow Road at Jordanhill Station via Crow Road, Broomhill Cross, Clarence Drive, Hyndland Road and former route to Alexandra Park then via Cumbernauld Road, Smithycroft Road to Smithycroft Road at Naver Street;
Saturdays and Sundays: KELVINSIDE CROSS & ALEXANDRA PARK unaltered.

January 1926

Trials commence using Bow Collectors in place of Trolley Poles on the Mount Florida-Paisley Road Toll
Yellow Service Q.

1st February 1926

The following Service Alteration takes place:
Red Service RP [Single Deck Cars] YOKER & DUNTOCHER cut back to become
Weekdays and Saturdays: CLYDEBANK & RADNOR PARK or DUNTOCHER from Kilbowie Road south end via Kilbowie Road and former route;
Sundays: YOKER & DUNTOCHER cut back to become CLYDEBANK & DUNTOCHER.

Résumé

1st February 1926

The following Tram Services operating:

A	Green	SCOTSTOUNHILL & PARKHEAD or SPRINGFIELD ROAD
ABB	Green	PAISLEY CROSS & SPRINGBANK ROAD or ABBOTSINCH (No Sundays Service)
B	Green	FERGUSLIE MILLS, CROOKSTON or IBROX & SHETTLESTON or AIRDRIE
C	Yellow	KIRKLEE or HYNDLAND & NETHERLEE or CLARKSTON
D	Green	ANNIESLAND or KELVINSIDE & DENNISTOUN, SHETTLESTON or AIRDRIE
E	White	UNIVERSITY & MOSSPARK via POLLOKSHIELDS
F	Red	DALMUIR WEST, CLYDEBANK, SCOTSTOUN or WHITEINCH & DALMARNOCK, RUTHERGLEN, BURNSIDE or CAMBUSLANG
G	Blue	LAMBHILL or SPRINGBURN & LINTHOUSE, SHIELDHALL or RENFREW via POSSILPARK, LORNE STREET
H	Yellow	JORDANHILL & LANGSIDE via HYNDLAND
J	Yellow	MILLERSTON, RIDDRIE or ALEXANDRA PARK & CRAIGTON ROAD via BRIDGETON CROSS
K	Blue	KEPPOCHHILL ROAD & SHIELDHALL or RENFREW
KIL	Green	KILBARCHAN or JOHNSTONE CENTRE & RENFREW FERRY
L	Red	DALMUIR WEST or SCOTSTOUN & LONDON ROAD or AUCHENSHUGGLE
M	Red	HILLFOOT or MARYHILL & MOUNT FLORIDA via NEW CITY ROAD
N	Red	MARYHILL or KELVINSIDE AVENUE & SINCLAIR DRIVE via GARSCUBE ROAD
O	Blue	KIRKLEE & OATLANDS or RUTHERGLEN via PARK ROAD, CROWN STREET
P	Blue	HILLFOOT or MARYHILL & SHAWLANDS, PAISLEY CROSS or RENFREW FERRY via ST GEORGE'S CROSS, GORBALS, BARRHEAD
Q	Yellow	MOUNT FLORIDA & PAISLEY ROAD TOLL via SHIELDS ROAD
R	Red	BISHOPBRIGGS or SPRINGBURN & POLLOKSHAWS WEST or ROUKEN GLEN Circle via THORNLIEBANK
		Circle Cars return to ALEXANDRA PARK, RIDDRIE or MILLERSTON
		MILLERSTON, RIDDRIE or ALEXANDRA PARK & MERRYLEE or ROUKEN GLEN Circle via GIFFNOCK
		Circle Cars return to SPRINGBURN or BISHOPBRIGGS
RP	Red	[Single Deck Cars] CLYDEBANK & RADNOR PARK or DUNTOCHER
S	White	SPRINGBURN & MOUNT FLORIDA, CATHCART or NETHERLEE via GLASGOW CROSS
T	Red	HILLFOOT or MARYHILL & MOUNT FLORIDA via NEW CITY ROAD
U	Green	FERGUSLIE MILLS, CROOKSTON or IBROX & TOLLCROSS or UDDINGSTON
V	White	PROVANMILL & POLMADIE via GLASGOW CROSS
W	Green	KEPPOCHHILL ROAD & WHITEINCH or SCOTSTOUN via NORTH STREET
X	Red	ANNIESLAND & CAMBUSLANG via BOTHWELL STREET
Y	White	SPRINGBURN or KELVINSIDE AVENUE & RUTHERGLEN or BURNSIDE via BILSLAND DRIVE, RUTHERGLEN BRIDGE
Z	Blue	JORDANHILL or KELVINSIDE CROSS & ALEXANDRA PARK or RIDDRIE
CP	Red	CARLTON PLACE & BATTLEFIELD (Part Day)
-	Blue	[Paisley Local] BARRHEAD (PRINCES SQUARE), BARRHEAD CENTRE or POTTERHILL & PAISLEY CROSS
-	Blue	[Paisley Local] PAISLEY CROSS & RENFREW FERRY
-	Green	[Paisley Local] PAISLEY CROSS & HAWKHEAD ROAD
-	Green	[Airdrie Local] LANGLOAN & AIRDRIE

A car on Green Service D at Anniesland terminus loading up before crossing over to the city-bound track for its departure to Parkhead.
(Commercial Postcard, BJ Cross Collection)

15th February 1926

Reduction in Service to Mosspark.
The following Service Alteration takes place:
White Service E Weekdays and Saturdays: UNIVERSITY & MOSSPARK via POLLOKSHIELDS altered to become UNIVERSITY & DUMBRECK or MOSSPARK via POLLOKSHIELDS;
Sundays: UNIVERSITY & MOSSPARK via POLLOKSHIELDS unaltered.

21st February 1926

The following Service Alterations take place:
Green Service KIL KILBARCHAN or JOHNSTONE CENTRE & RENFREW FERRY split to become
KILBARCHAN & RENFREW FERRY via former route; and
JOHNSTONE CENTRE & HAWKHEAD ROAD or RENFREW FERRY via former route with alternate cars proceeding from Paisley Cross via St James Bridge, Smithhills Street, Gauze Street, Glasgow Road Paisley to Glasgow Road at Hawkhead Road;
Green Service [Paisley local] PAISLEY CROSS & HAWKHEAD ROAD withdrawn.

28th February 1926

The following Operational Alterations take place:
➤ *Coatbridge Depot reopened for traffic*
Coatbridge Depot resumes operation of the following Services:
Green Service B FERGUSLIE MILLS, CROOKSTON or IBROX & SHETTLESTON or AIRDRIE;
Green Service D ANNIESLAND or KELVINSIDE & DENNISTOUN, SHETTLESTON or AIRDRIE;
Green Service [Airdrie Local] LANGLOAN & AIRDRIE

22nd March 1926

Service to Mosspark restored to former frequency.
The following Service Alteration takes place;
White Service E Weekdays and Saturdays: UNIVERSITY & DUMBRECK or MOSSPARK via POLLOKSHIELDS altered to become UNIVERSITY & MOSSPARK via POLLOKSHIELDS;
Sundays: UNIVERSITY & MOSSPARK via POLLOKSHIELDS unaltered.

26th March 1926

Construction of new deep-water King George V Dock at Shieldhall.

Renfrew Road realigned from Shieldhall crossover to High Street Renfrew near intersection of Glebe Street. Renfrew tram services diverted to run over new alignment.
Blue Service G LAMBHILL or SPRINGBURN & LINTHOUSE, SHIELDHALL or RENFREW via POSSILPARK, LORNE STREET;
Blue Service K KEPPOCHHILL ROAD & SHIELDHALL or RENFREW
both rerouted for journeys to and from RENFREW accordingly.

1st May 1926

Alteration to Clydebank terminus.
CLYDEBANK terminus moved from Glasgow Road at Bon Accord Street to Kilbowie Road south end; Catchpoints provided in Kilbowie Road to prevent Double-deck cars proceeding under low Railway Bridge at Clydebank LNER Station;
Crossover in Glasgow Road Clydebank renamed BON ACCORD STREET.
Red Service F DALMUIR WEST, CLYDEBANK, SCOTSTOUN or WHITEINCH & DALMARNOCK, RUTHERGLEN, BURNSIDE or CAMBUSLANG. Clydebank cars altered to run from Kilbowie Road south end via Kilbowie Road, Glasgow Road and former route.

4th May 1926

General Strike commences. All Services Suspended.

6th May 1926

Volunteer Students and others operate restricted Services on certain routes.

The track along Old Renfrew Road was abandoned when the new King George V deep water dock was constructed and services were diverted. Car 951 saunters along this country road in pre-World War I days while the lower view, taken in 1964, confirms that the old track was still in existence 50 years later – long outliving the trams themselves.
(Both: STTS Collection)

12th May 1926

General Strike over. Normal Services resume.

5th July 1926

Withdrawal of Carlton Place trams.

Red Service CP CARLTON PLACE & BATTLEFIELD (Part Day) withdrawn without replacement.

Regular cars cease to operate on MacKinlay Street, Abbotsford Place and South Portland Street.

Adjustments to Paisley Main Line services.

The following Service Alterations take place:

Green Service B Weekdays or Saturdays: FERGUSLIE MILLS, CROOKSTON or IBROX & SHETTLESTON or AIRDRIE cut back to become PAISLEY WEST, PAISLEY CROSS, CROOKSTON or IBROX & SHETTLESTON or AIRDRIE;

Sundays: FERGUSLIE MILLS & SHETTLESTON or AIRDRIE cut back to become IBROX & SHETTLESTON or AIRDRIE;

Green Service U Weekdays: FERGUSLIE MILLS, CROOKSTON or IBROX & TOLLCROSS or UDDINGSTON cut back to become PAISLEY CROSS, CROOKSTON or IBROX & TOLLCROSS or UDDINGSTON from St James Bridge and former route;

Saturdays: PAISLEY CROSS or IBROX & TOLLCROSS or UDDINGSTON extended to become PAISLEY WEST or IBROX & TOLLCROSS or UDDINGSTON;

Sundays: FERGUSLIE MILLS & TOLLCROSS & UDDINGSTON cut back to become PAISLEY CROSS & TOLLCROSS or UDDINGSTON.;

The following Operational Alteration takes place:

Green Service D KELVINSIDE & DENNISTOUN, SHETTLESTON or AIRDRIE timetable adjusted to interwork with revised Green Service B timings.

18th July 1926

Adjustments to Paisley Main Line Sundays Services.

The following Service Alterations take place:

Green Service B Sundays: IBROX & SHETTLESTON or AIRDRIE extended to become PAISLEY WEST & AIRDRIE from Broomlands Street east end via West End Cross, Wellmeadow Street, High Street Paisley, Paisley Cross, St James Bridge, Smithhills Street, Gauze Street. Glasgow Road, Paisley Road West and former route;

Weekdays and Saturdays: PAISLEY WEST, PAISLEY CROSS, CROOKSTON or IBROX & SHETTLESTON or AIRDRIE unaltered;

Green Service U Sundays: PAISLEY CROSS & TOLLCROSS or UDDINGSTON extended to become PAISLEY WEST & UDDINGSTON from Broomlands Street east end via West End Cross, Wellmeadow Street, High Street Paisley, Paisley Cross, St James Bridge and former route;

Weekdays and Saturdays: PAISLEY CROSS, CROOKSTON or IBROX & TOLLCROSS or UDDINGSTON unaltered.

The Tramways Department always seemed to be re-arranging the yellow services to the West End. Here are two yellow cars 871 and 363 at Charing Cross in the mid-1920s.
(Commercial Postcard, BJ Cross Collection)

8th August 1926

Rearrangement of Services in Hyndland and to Dalmuir West.
Introduction of circle Services for Hyndland.
KIRKLEE terminus for Yellow cars moved from Kirkee Road to Hyndland Road north end (also called KELVINSIDE for Green Cars). Blue Cars KIRKLEE terminus unaltered.
The following Service Alterations take place:

Yellow Service C Weekdays and Saturdays: KIRKLEE or HYNDLAND & NETHERLEE or CLARKSTON linked at Hyndland Road as circular to become KIRKLEE Circle via BOTANIC GARDENS or Circle via HYNDLAND & NETHERLEE or CLARKSTON from Hyndland Road north end either via Hyndland Road, Highburgh Road and former route or via Hyndland Road, Great Western Road, Byres Road and former route, with through Circle Cars at Hyndland Road;
Sundays: KIRKLEE & CLARKSTON extended as circular to become
KIRKLEE Circle via BOTANIC GARDENS or Circle via HYNDLAND & CLARKSTON;

Blue Service Z JORDANHILL or KELVINSIDE CROSS & ALEXANDRA PARK or RIDDRIE diverted and extended to become
Weekdays: DALMUIR WEST & ALEXANDRA PARK or RIDDRIE from Dumbarton Road Clydebank at Duntocher Burn via Dumbarton Road Clydebank, Glasgow Road Clydebank, Dumbarton Road and former route;
Saturdays and Sundays: KELVINSIDE CROSS & ALEXANDRA PARK diverted and extended to become
DALMUIR WEST & ALEXANDRA PARK;

Red Service L Saturdays: DALMUIR WEST & LONDON ROAD or AUCHENSHUGGLE altered to become
DALMUIR WEST, CLYDEBANK or SCOTSTOUN & LONDON ROAD or AUCHENSHUGGLE;
Sundays: DALMUIR WEST & AUCHENSHUGGLE cut back to become
WHITEINCH & LONDON ROAD or AUCHENSHUGGLE;
Weekdays: DALMUIR WEST or SCOTSTOUN & LONDON ROAD or AUCHENSHUGGLE unaltered.

August 1926

Councillors are invited to inspect five modernised tramcars produced to combat competition from buses and enable services to be speeded up. One of these was new and in that month the new Experimental Single-Deck Car enters service from Newlands Depot.

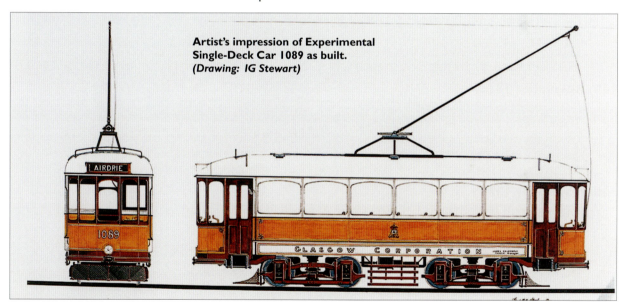

Artist's impression of Experimental Single-Deck Car 1089 as built.
(Drawing: IG Stewart)

22nd August 1926

Sunday Repairs to railway bridge at Airdrie terminus.
Service to and from Airdrie cut back to turn at AIRDRIE CROSS.
Green Service B Sundays: PAISLEY WEST & AIRDRIE
Green Service D Sundays: ANNIESLAND & AIRDRIE
Green Service [Airdrie Local] Sundays: LANGLOAN & AIRDRIE all altered accordingly.

27th August 1926

Sunday Repairs to railway bridge at Airdrie terminus additionally on one weekday only.
Service to and from Airdrie cut back to turn at AIRDRIE CROSS.
Green Service B Weekdays: PAISLEY WEST, PAISLEY CROSS, CROOKSTON or IBROX & SHETTLESTON or AIRDRIE;
Green Service D Weekdays: KELVINSIDE & DENNISTOUN, SHETTLESTON or AIRDRIE;
Green Service [Airdrie Local] Weekdays: LANGLOAN & AIRDRIE;
AIRDRIE runs altered on all services accordingly.

12th September 1926

Sunday Repairs to railway bridge at Airdrie terminus.
Arrangements for 22nd August 1926 repeated.

11th October 1926

The following Service Alteration takes place:

Green Service U Weekdays: PAISLEY CROSS, CROOKSTON or IBROX & TOLLCROSS or UDDINGSTON extended to become PAISLEY WEST & TOLLCROSS or UDDINGSTON from Broomlands Street east end via West End Cross, Wellmeadow Street, High Street Paisley, Paisley Cross, St James Bridge and former route;

Saturdays: PAISLEY WEST or IBROX & TOLLCROSS or UDDINGSTON altered to become PAISLEY WEST & TOLLCROSS or UDDINGSTON.

Sundays: PAISLEY WEST & UDDINGSTON unaltered.

31st October 1926

Restoration of former weekend Red Services to and from Dalmuir West.
The following Service Alteration takes place:

Red Service L Saturdays: DALMUIR WEST, CLYDEBANK or SCOTSTOUN & LONDON ROAD or AUCHENSHUGGLE altered to become DALMUIR WEST & LONDON ROAD or AUCHENSHUGGLE;

Sundays: WHITEINCH & LONDON ROAD or AUCHENSHUGGLE re-extended to become DALMUIR WEST & AUCHENSHUGGLE;

Weekdays: DALMUIR WEST or SCOTSTOUN & LONDON ROAD or AUCHENSHUGGLE unaltered.

During 1926

Automatic Light Signals fitted to control trams at Crossing Loops and Single Line sections in Caplethill Road between Glenfield and Cross Stobs Inn.

8th November 1926

Further adjustments to Dalmuir West services.
The following Service Alteration takes place:

Blue Service Z Weekdays: DALMUIR WEST & ALEXANDRA PARK or RIDDRIE part cut back to become DALMUIR WEST or SCOTSTOUN & ALEXANDRA PARK or RIDDRIE. Scotstoun cars from Balmoral Street north end, Dumbarton Road and former route;

Saturdays: DALMUIR WEST & ALEXANDRA PARK part cut back to become DALMUIR WEST or SCOTSTOUN or ALEXANDRA PARK; Sundays: DALMUIR WEST & ALEXANDRA PARK unaltered.

14th November 1926

Adjustments to Sundays Airdrie Service.
The following Service Alteration takes place:

Green Service D Sundays: ANNIESLAND & AIRDRIE altered to become ANNIESLAND & DENNISTOUN or AIRDRIE;

Weekdays and Saturdays: KELVINSIDE & DENNISTOUN, SHETTLESTON or AIRDRIE unaltered;

Green Service B Sundays: IBROX & SHETTLESTON or AIRDRIE timings adjusted accordingly.

30th November 1926

Line Opened on Great Western Road from Anniesland to Railway Crossing at Munro Place (Knightswood Brick Works).
The following Service Alterations take place:

Green Service D Weekdays and Saturdays: KELVINSIDE & DENNISTOUN, SHETTLESTON or AIRDRIE extended to become KNIGHTSWOOD or KELVINSIDE & DENNISTOUN, SHETTLESTON or AIRDRIE from Great Western Road at Munro Place via Great Western Road Private Track, Anniesland Cross, Great Western Road and former route;

Sundays: ANNIESLAND & DENNISTOUN or AIRDRIE extended to become KNIGHTSWOOD & DENNISTOUN or AIRDRIE.

2nd December 1926

New Extension to Knightswood (Munro Place) closed upon instruction of the Master of Works.
Green Service D reverts to former route.

3rd December 1926

New Extension to Knightswood (Munro Place) reopened.
Green Service D resumes Service previously introduced on 30th November 1926.

5th December 1926

Sunday work widening of road beneath railway bridge at Coatdyke.
Service to and from AIRDRIE cut back to turn at COATDYKE.
Green Service B Sundays: PAISLEY WEST & AIRDRIE
Green Service D Sundays: KNIGHTSWOOD & DENNISTOUN or AIRDRIE
Green Service [Airdrie Local] Sundays: LANGLOAN & AIRDRIE all altered accordingly.

15th and 16th January 1927

Weekend work widening of road beneath railway bridge at Coatdyke.
Service to and from AIRDRIE cut back to turn at COATDYKE.
Arrangements operating on 5th December 1926 apply for Saturday and Sunday.

20th March 1927

The following Service Alteration takes place:
Green Service KIL Sundays: JOHNSTONE CENTRE & HAWKHEAD ROAD or RENFREW FERRY section cut back become
JOHNSTONE CENTRE & PAISLEY CROSS or RENFREW FERRY via former route;
KILBARCHAN & RENFREW FERRY section unaltered; and
Weekdays and Saturdays: KILBARCHAN & RENFREW FERRY and
JOHNSTONE CENTRE & HAWKHEAD ROAD or RENFREW FERRY unaltered.

During 1927

Line in Duncryne Place and Permanent Way Coup **closed** to trams.

3rd April 1927

Removal of Centre Poles and realignment of citybound track between Hyndland Road and west of Botanic Gardens resulting in Track Alteration Works proceeding on Great Western Road in Kirklee area.
The following Temporary Service Alterations take place:
Yellow Service C KIRKLEE Circle via BOTANIC GARDENS or Circle via HYNDLAND & NETHERLEE or CLARKSTON split to operate separately as BOTANIC GARDENS & NETHERLEE or CLARKSTON from Botanic Gardens in Great Western Road west of Byres Road via Byres Road and normal route; and KELVINSIDE CROSS & NETHERLEE or CLARKSTON via HYNDLAND from Hyndland Road north end via Hyndland Road, Highburgh Road, Byres Road and normal route;
Blue Service O KIRKLEE & OATLANDS or RUTHERGLEN via PARK ROAD, CROWN STREET cut back to become
BOTANIC GARDENS & OATLANDS or RUTHERGLEN via PARK ROAD, CROWN STREET from Botanic Gardens in Great Western Road west of Byres Road via Great Western Road and normal route.
Green Service A SCOTSTOUNHILL & SPRINGFIELD ROAD and
Green Service D KNIGHTSWOOD or KELVINSIDE & DENNISTOUN, SHETTLESTON or AIRDRIE both continue to maintain services through trackworks and over temporary tracks on citybound line as work proceeds.

10th April 1927

The following Service Alteration takes place:
Green Service KIL Weekdays and Saturdays: JOHNSTONE CENTRE & HAWKHEAD ROAD or RENFREW FERRY section cut at off-peak to become
JOHNSTONE CENTRE & PAISLEY CROSS, HAWKHEAD ROAD or RENFREW FERRY;
KILBARCHAN & RENFREW FERRY section unaltered;
Sundays: KILBARCHAN or JOHNSTONE CENTRE & PAISLEY CROSS or RENFREW FERRY unaltered.

Although the centre poles had been removed from Great Western Road from Park Road to Botanic Gardens by 4th November 1922, they continued in use from this latter location westwards until April 1927 as can be seen here.
(DL Thomson Collection)

April 1927
Single Line section doubled on Neilston Road Paisley between Falside Road and Potterhill.
Crossovers provided at FALSIDE and at POTTERHILL for shortworking and Local cars.

25th April 1927
The following Service Alteration takes place:
Red Service N Weekdays and Saturdays: KELVINSIDE AVENUE & SINCLAIR DRIVE via GARSCUBE ROAD extended to become GAIRBRAID AVENUE & SINCLAIR DRIVE via GARSCUBE ROAD from Gairbraid Avenue east end via Gairbraid Avenue, Maryhill Road and former route;
Sundays: MARYHILL & SINCLAIR DRIVE via GARSCUBE ROAD unaltered.

5th June 1927
Increase in level of service on Paisley Road West.
Additional cars from east to HALFWAY and CROOKSTON provided on the following Services:
Green Service B Weekdays: PAISLEY WEST, PAISLEY CROSS, CROOKSTON or IBROX & SHETTLESTON or AIRDRIE altered to become
PAISLEY WEST, PAISLEY CROSS, CROOKSTON, HALFWAY or IBROX & SHETTLESTON or AIRDRIE;
Saturdays: PAISLEY WEST, CROOKSTON or IBROX & BAILLIESTON or AIRDRIE altered to become
PAISLEY WEST, CROOKSTON, HALFWAY or IBROX & BAILLIESTON or AIRDRIE;
Sundays: PAISLEY WEST & AIRDRIE unaltered;
Green Service U Weekdays and Saturdays: PAISLEY WEST & TOLLCROSS or UDDINGSTON altered to become
PAISLEY WEST, CROOKSTON, HALFWAY or IBROX & TOLLCROSS or UDDINGSTON;
Sundays: PAISLEY WEST & UDDINGSTON unaltered.

During 1927
Construction of Line on London Road to Mount Vernon.
To alleviate unemployment, construction proceeds of new line from Auchenshuggle to Mount Vernon along London Road to link with Uddingston line on Hamilton Road.

24th July 1927
Track Alteration Works on Great Western Road in Kirklee area near completion.
The following Temporary Service Alteration ceases:
Blue Service O BOTANIC GARDENS & OATLANDS or RUTHERGLEN via PARK ROAD, CROWN STREET reverts to normal service KIRKLEE & OATLANDS or RUTHERGLEN via PARK ROAD, CROWN STREET.

7th August 1927
Track Alteration Works on Great Western Road in Kirklee area finally completed.
The following Temporary Service Alteration ceases:
Yellow Service C BOTANIC GARDENS & NETHERLEE or CLARKSTON and
KELVINSIDE CROSS & NETHERLEE or CLARKSTON via HYNDLAND revert to normal service
KIRKLEE Circle via BOTANIC GARDENS or Circle via HYNDLAND & NETHERLEE or CLARKSTON.

10th October 1927
Increase in Service to Netherlee.
The following Service Alteration takes place:
White Service S Weekdays: SPRINGBURN & MOUNT FLORIDA or CATHCART via GLASGOW CROSS part extended to become SPRINGBURN & MOUNT FLORIDA, CATHCART or NETHERLEE via GLASGOW CROSS via former route to Clarkston Road at Dairsie Street then via Clarkston Road to Clarkston Road at Ormonde Drive;
Saturdays: SPRINGBURN & MOUNT FLORIDA, CATHCART or NETHERLEE via GLASGOW CROSS unaltered;
Sundays: SPRINGBURN & NETHERLEE via GLASGOW CROSS unaltered.

14th November 1927
Service to Netherlee reduced.
The following Service Alteration takes place:
White Service S Weekdays: SPRINGBURN & MOUNT FLORIDA, CATHCART or NETHERLEE via GLASGOW CROSS cut back to become SPRINGBURN & MOUNT FLORIDA or CATHCART via GLASGOW CROSS;
Saturdays: SPRINGBURN & MOUNT FLORIDA, CATHCART or NETHERLEE via GLASGOW CROSS unaltered;
Sundays: SPRINGBURN & NETHERLEE via GLASGOW CROSS unaltered.

January 1928
Following withdrawal of Burnside Special School Specials, Tullis Street Bridgeton and Greystone Avenue Sidings **closed** to trams.

February 1928
Programme of modernising Standard trams commences.

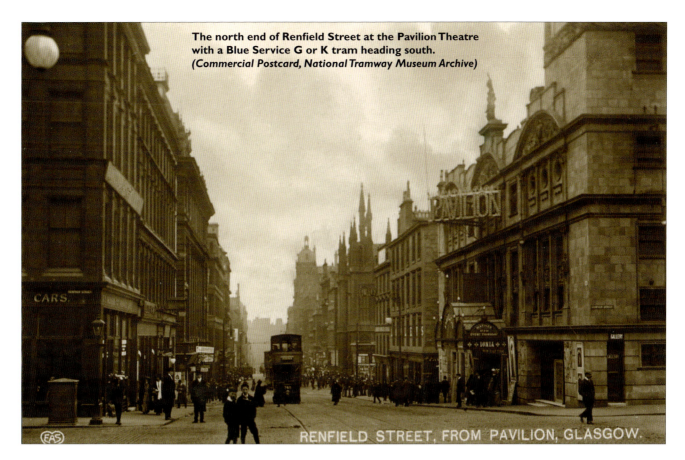

The north end of Renfield Street at the Pavilion Theatre with a Blue Service G or K tram heading south. (Commercial Postcard, National Tramway Museum Archive)

27th February 1928

George V Bridge linking Oswald Street and Commerce Street officially opened by H.M. King George V.

3rd March 1928

Dumbarton Burgh and County Tramways Co. Ltd. ceases operation.
DB&CT Service BALLOCH & DALMUIR withdrawn.

5th March 1928

Line Opened on Great Western Road Boulevard from Munro Place to Knightswood Cross.
KNIGHTSWOOD terminus moved from Great Western Road at Munro Place to Great Western Road west of Knightswood Cross.
The following Service Alteration takes place:
Green Service D KNIGHTSWOOD or KELVINSIDE & DENNISTOUN, SHETTLESTON or AIRDRIE extended to run from Great Western Road west of Knightswood Cross via Great Western Road Private Track and former route.

18th March 1928

TOLLCROSS crossover moved from Tollcross Road at Causewayside Street to Tollcross Road at Carmyle Avenue.
Green Service U PAISLEY WEST, CROOKSTON, HALFWAY or IBROX & TOLLCROSS or UDDINGSTON altered accordingly.

29th March 1928

Following experiments on Mount Florida-Paisley Road Toll **Yellow Service Q** line, decision taken to convert from Trolley Pole to Bow Collector current collection on Paisley-Airdrie/Uddingston **Green Services BU** and Abbotsinch **Green Service ABB**.

2nd April 1928

The following Service Alteration takes place:
Yellow Service J Sundays: MILLERSTON or RIDDRIE & CRAIGTON ROAD via BRIDGETON CROSS altered to become MILLERSTON, RIDDRIE or ALEXANDRA PARK & CRAIGTON ROAD via BRIDGETON CROSS;
Weekdays and Saturdays: MILLERSTON, RIDDRIE or ALEXANDRA PARK & CRAIGTON ROAD via BRIDGETON CROSS unaltered.

12th April 1928

Line Opened on St Vincent Street between Hope Street and Wellington Street.
Additional ST VINCENT STREET terminus provided west of Hope Street.

This official view of ex-works Standard Car 33 has been published before but it illustrates like no other the thorough job the Coplawhill Car Works made of modernising the Standard Cars. Note that this is a Green car. They were turned out first to combat competition from independent buses where the most serious inroads into tramway revenue had occurred, on the inter-urban services that connected Paisley with Airdie and Uddingston. The earliest examples started appearing in February 1928 and around four per week were being placed in service during a period of frenetic activity. Note the single magnetic brake and protective bar beneath the truck side frame; features found on the earliest modernised cars. The long point iron was retained at first and can be seen attached to the staircase stringer. The running or "route" number was by this time carried within the bracket attached to the corner pillar and took the form of a metallic stencil, back-lit by the interior lighting. *(GCT)*

14th April 1928

The following Operational and Service Alteration takes place:
Green Service ABB PAISLEY CROSS & SPRINGBANK ROAD or ABBOTSINCH converted to one-man operation with Pay-As-You-Enter fare collection and altered to become PAISLEY CROSS & ABBOTSINCH; No Sundays Service.

27th May 1928

The following Service Alteration takes place:
Red Service N Sundays: MARYHILL & SINCLAIR DRIVE via GARSCUBE ROAD part extended to become HILLFOOT or MARYHILL & SINCLAIR DRIVE via GARSCUBE ROAD from Milngavie Road south of Hillfoot railway bridge via Milngavie Road, Maryhill Road and former route;
Weekdays and Saturdays: GAIRBRAID AVENUE & SINCLAIR DRIVE via GARSCUBE ROAD unaltered.

22nd July 1928

The following Operational Alterations take place:
To provide additional space in Parkhead Depot for Motorbuses, reallocation of Green Car Duties effected.
Green Service B PAISLEY WEST, PAISLEY CROSS, CROOKSTON, HALFWAY or IBROX & SHETTLESTON, BAILLIESTON or AIRDRIE 6 Duties (4 on Sundays) transferred from Parkhead Depot to Elderslie Depot;
Green Service D KNIGHTSWOOD or KELVINSIDE & DENNISTOUN, SHETTLESTON or AIRDRIE;
5 Duties (3 on Sundays) transferred from Parkhead Depot to Dennistoun Depot.

September 1928

Track improvements carried out realigning single track in Old Sneddon Street Paisley on Green Service ABB PAISLEY CROSS & ABBOTSINCH.

October 1928

Production models of Standard Double Bogie Cars start entering service from Govan Depot on Green Services BU.

28th October 1928

Lines Opened in Kingston Street between Bridge Street and Commerce Street, in Commerce Street from Nelson Street northwards, George V. Bridge, Oswald Street and Hope Street from St Vincent Street to Cowcaddens.

The following Service Diversions take place:
Blue Service G LAMBHILL or SPRINGBURN & LINTHOUSE, SHIELDHALL or RENFREW via POSSILPARK, LORNE STREET and
Blue Service K KEPPOCHHILL ROAD & SHIELDHALL or RENFREW
diverted between Cowcaddens and Nelson Street to run via Hope Street, Oswald Street, George V. Bridge, Commerce Street (instead of via Renfield Street, Union Street, Jamaica Street, Glasgow Bridge, Bridge Street and Nelson Street).
The following Service commences:
Green Service UM UDDINGSTON & HOPE STREET via GLASSFORD STREET from Main Street, Uddingston north of Bellshill Road via Main Street Uddingston, Glasgow Road, Hamilton Road, Tollcross Road, Parkhead Cross, Gallowgate, Trongate, Glassford Street, Ingram Street, South Frederick Street, George Square south, St Vincent Place, St Vincent Street, Renfield Street, Cowcaddens returning via Cowcaddens, Hope Street, St Vincent Street and inward route.
The following Service Alterations take place:
Green Service B Weekdays: PAISLEY WEST, PAISLEY CROSS, CROOKSTON or IBROX & SHETTLESTON or AIRDRIE altered to become
PAISLEY WEST, CROOKSTON, HALFWAY or IBROX & SHETTLESTON or AIRDRIE;
Saturdays: PAISLEY WEST, CROOKSTON, HALFWAY or IBROX & BAILLIESTON or AIRDRIE unaltered;
Sundays: PAISLEY WEST & AIRDRIE unaltered;
Green Service U Weekdays: PAISLEY WEST, CROOKSTON, HALFWAY or IBROX & TOLLCROSS or UDDINGSTON cut back to become PAISLEY WEST or IBROX & TOLLCROSS;
Uddingston service replaced by Green Service UM;
Saturdays: PAISLEY WEST, CROOKSTON, HALFWAY or IBROX & TOLLCROSS or UDDINGSTON unaltered;
Sundays: PAISLEY WEST & UDDINGSTON unaltered.
Regular cars cease to operate southbound on Renfield Street between Cowcaddens and Sauchiehall Street.

During 1928

The following Service Alteration takes place:
Green Service KIL Weekdays and Saturdays: JOHNSTONE CENTRE & PAISLEY CROSS, HAWKHEAD ROAD or RENFREW FERRY section HAWKHEAD ROAD journeys withdrawn to combine with KILBARCHAN & RENFREW FERRY section to become
KILBARCHAN or JOHNSTONE CENTRE & PAISLEY CROSS or RENFREW FERRY;
Sundays: KILBARCHAN or JOHNSTONE CENTRE & PAISLEY CROSS or RENFREW FERRY unaltered.
The following Service reintroduced:
Green Service [Paisley Local] PAISLEY WEST or PAISLEY CROSS & HAWKHEAD ROAD (Part Day) from West End Cross at Broomlands Street via Wellmeadow Street, High Street Paisley, Paisley Cross, St James Bridge, Gauze Street Paisley, Glasgow Road Paisley to Glasgow Road Paisley at Hawkhead Road.

The Green Services from Paisley and the West End to Airdrie and Uddingston were speeded up due to their being given the first allocation of High-Speed Standard cars. Here is No. 252 on Green Service B at the Mercat Cross in 1929. *(Commercial Postcard, BJ Cross Collection)*

Mercat Cross, Glasgow

2nd December 1928
>The following Service Alterations take place:
>Green Service A Weekdays and Saturdays: SCOTSTOUNHILL & PARKHEAD or SPRINGFIELD ROAD altered to become SCOTSTOUNHILL or ANNIESLAND & PARKHEAD or SPRINGFIELD ROAD;
>Sundays: SCOTSTOUNHILL & SPRINGFIELD ROAD unaltered;
>Green Service D Weekdays and Saturdays: KNIGHTSWOOD or KELVINSIDE & SHETTLESTON or AIRDRIE altered to become KNIGHTSWOOD or KELVINSIDE & DENNISTOUN, SHETTLESTON or AIRDRIE;
>Sundays: KNIGHTSWOOD & DENNISTOUN or AIRDRIE unaltered.

February 1929
>**Line Opened** in Carntyne Road from Duke Street to Todd Street.
>Siding in Fleming Street **closed** to trams.

13th March 1929
>Resiting of Dennistoun turning point eastwards.
>DENNISTOUN terminus moved from Duke Street at Fleming Street to Carntyne Road west end.
>CARNTYNE terminus moved from Duke Street at Carntyne Road to Shettleston Road at Muiryfauld Drive.
>Green Service D KNIGHTSWOOD or KELVINSIDE & DENNISTOUN, SHETTLESTON or AIRDRIE adjusted accordingly.

19th May 1929
>Speeded-up Service inaugurated on Airdrie and Uddingston routes.
>Green Service A SCOTSTOUNHILL or ANNIESLAND & PARKHEAD or SPRINGFIELD ROAD
>Green Service B PAISLEY WEST, PAISLEY CROSS, CROOKSTON or IBROX & SHETTLESTON or AIRDRIE;
>Green Service D KNIGHTSWOOD or KELVINSIDE & DENNISTOUN, SHETTLESTON or AIRDRIE;
>Green Service U PAISLEY WEST or IBROX & TOLLCROSS or UDDINGSTON all adjusted accordingly.

26th May 1929
>Speeded-up Service on Airdrie and Uddingston routes Suspended.
>Former Timetables restored on Green Services A, B, D and U.

During 1929
>Track doubled in Spiersbridge Road between Rouken Glen Road and Nitshill Road and crossover provided for SPIERSBRIDGE terminus.

2nd June 1929
>Speeded-up Service on Airdrie and Uddingston routes reintroduced.
>Timetables inaugurated on 19th May 1929 restored on Green Services A, B, D and U.

June 1929
>New curve laid from Gilmour Street into Old Sneddon Street Paisley connecting to double track on route of Green Service ABB PAISLEY CROSS & ABBOTSINCH.
>St James' Bridge, Paisley and associated street widening at Paisley Cross and to the east completed with realigned tram tracks brought into use.

24th June 1929
>Increase in provision of Cars to and from Shettleston.
>Green Service D Sundays: KNIGHTSWOOD & DENNISTOUN or AIRDRIE altered to become KNIGHTSWOOD & SHETTLESTON or AIRDRIE.

21st July 1929
>Increase in Service to Burnside.
>The following Service Alteration takes place:
>Blue Service O Weekdays and Saturdays: KIRKLEE & OATLANDS or RUTHERGLEN via PARK ROAD, CROWN STREET part extended to become KIRKLEE & OATLANDS, RUTHERGLEN or BURNSIDE via PARK ROAD, CROWN STREET via former route to Main Street Rutherglen then via Main Street Rutherglen, Stonelaw Road, Duke's Road to Duke's Road west end;
>Sundays: KIRKLEE & RUTHERGLEN via PARK ROAD, CROWN STREET part extended to become KIRKLEE & RUTHERGLEN or BURNSIDE via PARK ROAD, CROWN STREET.

15th September 1929
>**Line Opened** from Scotstounhill to link with Dumbarton Road at Scotstoun West.
>The following Service Alteration takes place:
>Green Service A Weekdays and Saturdays: SCOTSTOUNHILL or ANNIESLAND & PARKHEAD or SPRINGFIELD ROAD extended to become
>DALMUIR WEST, SCOTSTOUNHILL or ANNIESLAND & PARKHEAD or SPRINGFIELD ROAD from Dumbarton Road Clydebank at Duntocher Burn via Dumbarton Road Clydebank, Glasgow Road Clydebank, Dumbarton

Road, Kingsway, Anniesland Road and former route;
Sundays: SCOTSTOUNHILL & SPRINGFIELD ROAD extended to become
DALMUIR WEST & SPRINGFIELD ROAD.

19th September 1929

The following Service Alteration takes place:
Green Service ABB PAISLEY CROSS & ABBOTSINCH (to facilitate reversal of Bow Collector) extended at Gilmour Street from under railway bridge to turn in County Square running from County Square Loop via Gilmour Street and former route.

21st October 1929

The following Service Alteration takes place:
Red Service N Weekdays and Saturdays: GAIRBRAID AVENUE & SINCLAIR DRIVE via GARSCUBE ROAD cut back to become KELVINSIDE AVENUE & SINCLAIR DRIVE via GARSCUBE ROAD from Kelvinside Avenue north end via Kelvinside Avenue, Maryhill Road and former route;
Sundays: HILLFOOT or MARYHILL & SINCLAIR DRIVE via GARSCUBE ROAD cut back to become
GAIRBRAID AVENUE & SINCLAIR DRIVE via GARSCUBE ROAD from Gairbraid Avenue east end via Gairbraid Avenue, Maryhill Road and former route.

4th November 1929

Increase in frequency to Riddrie.
The following Service Alteration takes place:
Yellow Service J Weekdays and Saturdays: MILLERSTON, RIDDRIE or ALEXANDRA PARK & CRAIGTON ROAD via BRIDGETON CROSS altered to become
MILLERSTON or RIDDRIE & CRAIGTON ROAD via BRIDGETON CROSS;
Sundays: MILLERSTON, RIDDRIE or ALEXANDRA PARK & CRAIGTON ROAD via BRIDGETON CROSS unaltered.

18th November 1929

Increase in frequency on Knightswood and on Springfield Road Services.
Green Service A Saturdays: DALMUIR WEST or ANNIESLAND & PARKHEAD or SPRINGFIELD ROAD adjusted accordingly;
Green Service D Weekdays: KNIGHTSWOOD or KELVINSIDE & DENNISTOUN, SHETTLESTON or AIRDRIE adjusted accordingly.

In 1895 the newly built City Chambers had become the home of Glasgow Town Council. They form a backdrop to two Standard trams on Red Service N passing each other on the south side of George Square.
(T&R Annan)

March 1930
Line on Kelvingrove Street between Argyle Street and Sauchiehall Street removed.

16th March 1930
The following Service Alteration takes place:
Red Service N Sundays: GAIRBRAID AVENUE & SINCLAIR DRIVE via GARSCUBE ROAD re-extended to become MARYHILL & SINCLAIR DRIVE via GARSCUBE ROAD from Caldercuilt Road west end via Caldercuilt Road, Maryhill Road and former route;
Weekdays and Saturdays: KELVINSIDE AVENUE & SINCLAIR DRIVE via GARSCUBE ROAD unaltered.

6th April 1930
The following Service Alteration takes place:
Green Service UM UDDINGSTON & HOPE STREET via GLASSFORD STREET diverted and extended to become UDDINGSTON & GAIRBRAID AVENUE via GLASSFORD STREET via former route to St Vincent Street then via West Nile Street, Cowcaddens, New City Road, St George's Cross, Maryhill Road, Queen's Cross, Maryhill Road, Gairbraid Avenue to Gairbraid Avenue east end.
Regular cars cease to operate on Renfield Street between Sauchiehall Street and Cowcaddens. Section retained for emergency diversions.

24th May 1930
The following Service Alteration takes place:
White Service V Saturdays: PROVANMILL & POLMADIE via GLASGOW CROSS altered to become
PROVANMILL or GARNGAD & POLMADIE via GLASGOW CROSS;
GARNGAD cars turn in Garngad Road at Blochairn Road;
Weekdays and Sundays: PROVANMILL & POLMADIE via GLASGOW CROSS unaltered.

14th June 1930
Re-opening of Line on South Portland Street to Carlton Place.
The following Service commences:
Red Service CP Saturdays and Sundays: CARLTON PLACE & ROUKEN GLEN Circle via GIFFNOCK or Circle via THORNLIEBANK from South Portland Street north end at Carlton Place via South Portland Street, Abbotsford Place, MacKinlay Street, Turriff Street, Eglinton Street, Eglinton Toll, Pollokshaws Road, Shawlands Cross then either via Kilmarnock Road, Fenwick Road, Eastwood Toll, Rouken Glen Road to Rouken Glen Road at Park Gates returning via Rouken Glen Road, Spiersbridge Road, Main Street Thornliebank, Thornliebank Road, Harriet Street, Cross Street, Pollokshaws Road, Shawlands Cross and outwards route or via Pollokshaws Road, Cross Street, Harriet Street, Thornliebank Road, Main Street Thornliebank, Spiersbridge Road, Rouken Glen Road to Rouken Glen Road at Park Gates returning via Rouken Glen Road, Eastwood Toll, Fenwick Road, Kilmarnock Road, Shawlands Cross and outwards route; No Weekdays Service.
Regular cars resume operation on MacKinlay Street, Abbotsford Place and South Portland Street.

23rd June 1930
The following Service Alteration takes place:
Red Service N Weekdays and Saturdays: KELVINSIDE AVENUE & SINCLAIR DRIVE via GARSCUBE ROAD
re-extended to become GAIRBRAID AVENUE & SINCLAIR DRIVE via GARSCUBE ROAD from Gairbraid Avenue east end via Gairbraid Avenue, Maryhill Road and former route;
Sundays: MARYHILL & SINCLAIR DRIVE via GARSCUBE ROAD unaltered.

During 1930
New crossover provided in Hawthorn Street west end at Lomond Street.
BALMORE ROAD turning point sited at Hawthorn Street west end.

6th September 1930
Withdrawal of Carlton Place trams.
Red Service CP Saturdays and Sundays: CARLTON PLACE & ROUKEN GLEN Circle via GIFFNOCK or Circle via THORNLIEBANK

withdrawn without replacement.
MacKinlay Street, Abbotsford Place and South Portland Street **closed** to trams.

22nd September 1930

King's Bridge (James Street Bridge) closed for major reconstruction.
Tram Service split to turn on special crossovers on either side each showing the destination JAMES ST. BRIDGE.

Yellow Service J Weekdays and Saturdays: MILLERSTON or RIDDRIE & CRAIGTON ROAD via BRIDGETON CROSS split to operate MILLERSTON or RIDDRIE & JAMES ST. BRIDGE and JAMES ST. BRIDGE & CRAIGTON ROAD;

Sundays: MILLERSTON, RIDDRIE or ALEXANDRA PARK & CRAIGTON ROAD via BRIDGETON CROSS split to operate MILLERSTON, RIDDRIE or ALEXANDRA PARK & JAMES ST. BRIDGE and JAMES ST. BRIDGE & CRAIGTON ROAD.

6th October 1930

Lanarkshire Tramways Co. ceases operation on their Cambuslang route.
LTC Service CAMBUSLANG & NEWMAINS withdrawn.

2nd November 1930

Line Opened on Aikenhead Road between Polmadie Street and north of Calder Street.
POLMADIE terminus moved from Aikenhead Road at Polmadie Street to Aikenhead Road north of Calder Street.
White Service V PROVANMILL or GARNGAD & POLMADIE via GLASGOW CROSS extended accordingly.

November 1930

Decision taken to re-equip all remaining Services with Fischer Bow Collectors in place of Trolley Poles. Fischer Bow patents purchased to allow Corporation to manufacture and fit Bow Collectors themselves. Conversion proceeds.

16th November 1930

Service to Burnside reduced.
The following Service Alteration takes place:

Blue Service O Weekdays and Saturdays: KIRKLEE & OATLANDS, RUTHERGLEN or BURNSIDE via PARK ROAD, CROWN STREET cut back to become
KIRKLEE & OATLANDS or RUTHERGLEN via PARK ROAD, CROWN STREET;
Sundays: KIRKLEE & RUTHERGLEN or BURNSIDE via PARK ROAD, CROWN STREET cut back and split operationally to become KIRKLEE & RUTHERGLEN via PARK ROAD, CROWN STREET and
QUEEN STREET & OATLANDS via CROWN STREET (Part Day).

Modernised Standard car No.642 in Kirklee Road on Blue Service O which had been cut back again from Burnside to Rutherglen on 16th November 1930.
(IG Stewart Collection)

23rd November 1930

Service to Mosspark reduced.
The following Service Alteration takes place:
White Service E UNIVERSITY & MOSSPARK via POLLOKSHIELDS part cut back to become
UNIVERSITY & POLLOKSHIELDS or MOSSPARK;
Cars turning at POLLOKSHIELDS in St Andrew's Drive just north of Nithsdale Road.

24th November 1930

The following Service Alteration takes place:
Yellow Service Q Weekdays and Saturdays: MOUNT FLORIDA & PAISLEY ROAD TOLL via SHIELDS ROAD extended Part Day to become
MOUNT FLORIDA & PAISLEY ROAD TOLL or IBROX via SHIELDS ROAD via former route to Paisley Road Toll then via Paisley Road West, Broomloan Road to Broomloan Road north end;
Sundays: MOUNT FLORIDA & PAISLEY ROAD TOLL via SHIELDS ROAD unaltered.

15th December 1930

The following Service Alteration takes place:
White Service E Weekdays and Saturdays: UNIVERSITY & POLLOKSHIELDS or MOSSPARK altered to become
UNIVERSITY & DUMBRECK or MOSSPARK via POLLOKSHIELDS;
Sundays: UNIVERSITY & POLLOKSHIELDS or MOSSPARK unaltered.

25th January 1931

The following Service Alteration takes place:
Blue Service [Paisley Local] BARRHEAD (PRINCES SQUARE), BARRHEAD CENTRE or POTTERHILL & PAISLEY CROSS cut back and altered to become
[Paisley Local] GLENFIELD & PAISLEY CROSS from Caplethill Road east of Glenfield Road via Caplethill Road and former route; and
[Paisley Local] POTTERHILL & RENFREW FERRY from Neilston Road at Potterhill Station via Neilston Road and former route.
Blue Service [Paisley Local] PAISLEY CROSS & RENFREW FERRY withdrawn.

27th April 1931

The following Service Alteration takes place:
White Service Y Weekdays and Saturdays: SPRINGBURN or KELVINSIDE AVENUE & RUTHERGLEN or BURNSIDE via BILSLAND DRIVE, RUTHERGLEN BRIDGE altered to become
SPRINGBURN or BALMORE ROAD & RUTHERGLEN or BURNSIDE via BILSLAND DRIVE, RUTHERGLEN BRIDGE;
Sundays: SPRINGBURN & BURNSIDE via BILSLAND DRIVE, RUTHERGLEN BRIDGE unaltered.

22nd and 23rd June 1931

Dumbarton Road Dalmuir partially closed between Dalmuir and Dalmuir West.

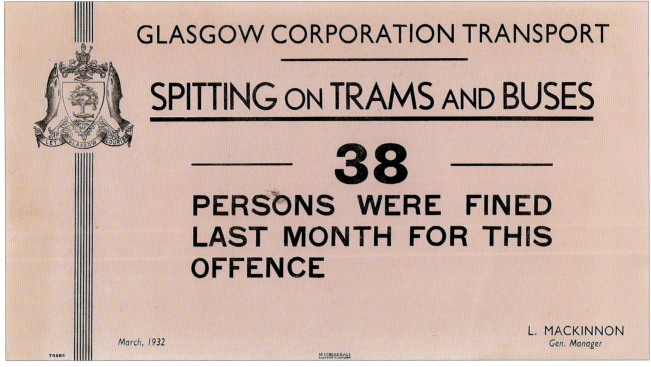

Single-line working instituted between Dalmuir and Dalmuir West.
Red Service L Weekdays: DALMUIR WEST or SCOTSTOUN & LONDON ROAD or AUCHENSHUGGLE half service curtailed at DALMUIR, every second car proceeds to DALMUIR WEST.

11th October 1931

The following Service Alteration takes place:
Blue Service [Paisley Local] GLENFIELD & PAISLEY CROSS cut back to become POTTERHILL & PAISLEY CROSS from Neilston Road at Potterhill Station via Neilston Road and former route.
Blue Service [Paisley Local] POTTERHILL & RENFREW FERRY unaltered.

1st November 1931

Adjustment to Uddingston Service.
Green Service UM UDDINGSTON & GAIRBRAID AVENUE via GLASSFORD STREET withdrawn.
The following Service Alteration takes place:
Green Service U Weekdays: PAISLEY WEST or IBROX & TOLLCROSS re-extended to become PAISLEY WEST or IBROX & TOLLCROSS or UDDINGSTON;
Saturdays: PAISLEY WEST, CROOKSTON, HALFWAY or IBROX & TOLLCROSS or UDDINGSTON and
Sundays: PAISLEY WEST & UDDINGSTON;
frequency to UDDINGSTON increased accordingly to replace **Green Service UM**.

9th November 1931

Yellow Car Peak-hour service to Ibrox withdrawn.
The following Service Alteration takes place:
Yellow Service Q Weekdays and Saturdays: MOUNT FLORIDA & PAISLEY ROAD TOLL or IBROX via SHIELDS ROAD cut back to become MOUNT FLORIDA & PAISLEY ROAD TOLL via SHIELDS ROAD;
Sundays: MOUNT FLORIDA & PAISLEY ROAD TOLL via SHIELDS ROAD unaltered.

30th November 1931

The following Service Alteration takes place:
Red Service R Weekdays: BISHOPBRIGGS or SPRINGBURN & POLLOKSHAWS WEST or ROUKEN GLEN Circle via THORNLIEBANK section POLLOKSHAWS WEST cars part extended to become BISHOPBRIGGS or SPRINGBURN & POLLOKSHAWS WEST, SPIERSBRIDGE or ROUKEN GLEN Circle via THORNLIEBANK;
Cars for SPIERSBRIDGE run via Spiersbridge Road to Spiersbridge Road south of Rouken Glen Road.

12th December 1931

Subsidence in Main Street Rutherglen. Citybound track closed.
The following Temporary Service Alterations take place:
Blue Service O KIRKLEE & OATLANDS or RUTHERGLEN via PARK ROAD, CROWN STREET cut back to become KIRKLEE & OATLANDS via PARK ROAD, CROWN STREET;

Glasgow Corporation Transport.

TRAMWAY & MOTOR BUS SERVICES

CHARITIES' DAY,
SATURDAY, 16th JANUARY, 1932.

Between the hours of 9.45 a.m. and 12 noon, Tram Cars and Buses on various routes may require to be diverted from the streets along which the Students' procession will pass, and journeys to fare stages on these Streets cannot therefore be guaranteed.

46 Bath Street,
6th January, 1932.

L. MACKINNON,
General Manager.

White Service Y SPRINGBURN or BALMORE ROAD & RUTHERGLEN or BURNSIDE via BILSLAND DRIVE, RUTHERGLEN BRIDGE; Cars to and from RUTHERGLEN withdrawn and citybound cars from BURNSIDE diverted between Rutherglen Cross and Bridgeton Cross to operate via Farmeloan Road, Farme Cross, Dalmarnock Road, Bridgeton Cross and then normal route;
Cars to BURNSIDE unaltered.

28th February 1932

Works on subsidence in Main Street Rutherglen completed.
Temporary Service Alterations cease:
Blue Service O KIRKLEE & OATLANDS via PARK ROAD, CROWN STREET reverts to normal service
KIRKLEE & OATLANDS or RUTHERGLEN via PARK ROAD, CROWN STREET;
White Service Y SPRINGBURN or BALMORE ROAD & RUTHERGLEN or BURNSIDE via BILSLAND DRIVE, RUTHERGLEN BRIDGE reverts to normal route and service.

1st May 1932

Abandonment of Kilbarchan trams.
Green Service KIL KILBARCHAN or JOHNSTONE CENTRE & PAISLEY CROSS or RENFREW FERRY withdrawn and replaced between Kilbarchan and Paisley Cross by Motorbus Service 12, and between Paisley Cross and Renfrew Ferry by revised Paisley Local Services.
Permanent Way Yard and Coup at Beith Road Johnstone **closed**.
High Barholm, Low Barholm, Easwaldbank, Overjohnstone Bridge, Cartside, Kilbarchan Road, Graham Street Johnstone, Macdowall Street, Houston Square, High Street Johnstone, Thorn Brae, Thornhill, Beith Road, Main Street Elderslie, Main Road Elderslie as far as Elderslie Depot **closed** to trams;
Elderslie Depot Workings only operate on Main Road Elderslie from Elderslie Depot, Beith Road, Ferguslie, Broomlands Street to Paisley West terminus.
Green Service B PAISLEY WEST, CROOKSTON, HALFWAY or IBROX & SHETTLESTON or AIRDRIE;
Green Service U PAISLEY WEST or IBROX & TOLLCROSS or UDDINGSTON both adjusted accordingly.
The following Service Alterations take place:
Blue Service [Paisley Local] POTTERHILL & PAISLEY CROSS and
Blue Service [Paisley Local] POTTERHILL & RENFREW FERRY
both integrated into and replaced by the following revised services:
Blue Service [Paisley Local] POTTERHILL & PAISLEY CROSS from Neilston Road at Potterhill Station via Neilston Road, Causeyside Street, St Mirren Street, Paisley Cross, Gilmour Street, to County Square;
Blue Service [Paisley Local] BRAIDS ROAD & RENFREW FERRY from Neilston Road at Braids Road via Neilston Road, Causeyside Street, St Mirren Street, Paisley Cross, Gilmour Street, County Square, Gilmour Street, Old Sneddon Street, Weir Street, Renfrew Road Paisley, Paisley Road Renfrew, Hairst Street Renfrew, Renfrew Cross, Canal Street, Ferry Road to Renfrew Ferry;
Blue Service [Paisley Local] PAISLEY CROSS & RENFREW FERRY from County Square via Gilmour Street, Old Sneddon Street, Weir Street, Renfrew Road Paisley, Paisley Road Renfrew, Hairst Street Renfrew, Renfrew Cross, Canal Street, Ferry Road to Renfrew Ferry (to replace Green Service KIL cars).
Extension of Renfrew services.
RENFREW terminus renamed RENFREW CROSS.
The following Service Alterations take place:
Blue Service G LAMBHILL or SPRINGBURN & LINTHOUSE, SHIELDHALL or RENFREW via POSSILPARK, LORNE STREET becomes LAMBHILL or SPRINGBURN & LINTHOUSE, SHIELDHALL or RENFREW CROSS via POSSILPARK, LORNE STREET via former route;
Blue Service K Weekdays and Saturdays: KEPPOCHHILL ROAD & SHIELDHALL or RENFREW extended to become KEPPOCHHILL ROAD & SHIELDHALL or PORTERFIELD ROAD via former route to Renfrew Cross then via Hairst Street Renfrew, Paisley Road Renfrew to Paisley Road Renfrew at Porterfield Road;
Sundays: KEPPOCHHILL ROAD & RENFREW extended to become
KEPPOCHHILL ROAD & PORTERFIELD ROAD.
Line at Renfrew Cross linking High Street Renfrew and Hairst Street Renfrew brought into use by regular cars.

17th July 1932

All cars proceeding from and to Elderslie Depot run empty as far as Paisley West.
Regular cars cease to operate on Main Road Elderslie from Elderslie Depot, Beith Road, Ferguslie and Broomlands Street to Paisley West terminus.

17th and 18th September 1932

Air Pageant at Renfrew Aerodrome.
Blue Service K KEPPOCHHILL ROAD & SHIELDHALL or PORTERFIELD ROAD extended to become
KEPPOCHHILL ROAD & RENFREW DEPOT via Paisley Road Renfrew to Paisley Road Renfrew at Newmains Road (Renfrew Depot).

After an aborted attempt to run top covered cars converted to low-height configuration, the evident inevitability was accepted and the last open top cars were withdrawn from the Kilbarchan route on 1st May 1932 when the service closed. This view of Green 1002 at Kilbarchan is a last-day scene.
(Courtesy, DL Thomson)

27th September 1932

The following Service Alteration takes place:
Red Service R Weekdays: BISHOPBRIGGS or SPRINGBURN & POLLOKSHAWS WEST, SPIERSBRIDGE or ROUKEN GLEN Circle via THORNLIEBANK section part cut back to revert to become
BISHOPBRIGGS or SPRINGBURN & POLLOKSHAWS WEST or ROUKEN GLEN Circle via THORNLIEBANK.

1st October 1932

Further adjustments to Paisley Local Services.
The following Service Alterations take place:
Blue Service [Paisley Local] POTTERHILL & PAISLEY CROSS cut back to become
BRAIDS ROAD & PAISLEY CROSS from Neilston Road at Braids Road and former route;
Blue Service [Paisley Local] BRAIDS ROAD & RENFREW FERRY and
Blue Service [Paisley Local] PAISLEY CROSS & RENFREW FERRY combined to become
GLENFIELD or POTTERHILL & RENFREW FERRY from Caplethill Road at Glenfield Road via Caplethill Road, Neilston Road and former route.

20th November 1932

The following Operational Alteration takes place:
Red Service N MARYHILL or GAIRBRAID AVENUE & SINCLAIR DRIVE via GARSCUBE ROAD portion of service operated by Langside Depot transferred to Newlands Depot.

11th December 1932

The following Operational Alteration takes place:
Red Service N MARYHILL or GAIRBRAID AVENUE & SINCLAIR DRIVE via GARSCUBE ROAD portion of service operated by Newlands Depot reverts to Langside Depot.

16th January 1933

GARNGAD crossover moved eastwards from Garngad Road at Blochairn Road to Garngad Road at LNER railway tunnel.
White Service V PROVANMILL or GARNGAD & POLMADIE via GLASGOW CROSS adjusted accordingly.

13th February 1933

Gordon Street between Hope Street and Union Street **closed** to trams.

16th February 1933

Trials with sample Pantograph current collectors from various manufacturers commence fitted to several Green cars operating from Parkhead Depot.

The short Abbotsinch route outlasted the Kilbarchan route by nearly eleven months and this view shows the One-Man-Operated car No. 92 at Abbotsinch in its final condition before withdrawal. It was put into storage initially at Renfrew Depot but not scrapped until 1938.
(Courtesy, DL Thomson)

26th March 1933

Abandonment of Abbotsinch trams.
Green Service ABB PAISLEY CROSS & ABBOTSINCH withdrawn and replaced by Motorbus Service 17.
Old Sneddon Street, St James Place, Love Street, Inchinnan Road **closed** to trams.
The following Service Alteration takes place:
Red Service T HILLFOOT or MARYHILL & MOUNT FLORIDA via NEW CITY ROAD integrated into Red Service M.
Red Service M HILLFOOT or MARYHILL & MOUNT FLORIDA via NEW CITY ROAD adjusted accordingly.

20th until 22nd May 1933

Air Pageant at Renfrew Aerodrome.
Special Extension of Blue Service K to RENFREW DEPOT (as on 17th September 1932) operates.

During 1933

Line Opened in Colston Road westwards from Springburn Road to new Permanent Way Coup on north side of Colston Road.

30th May 1933

Junction at Old Sneddon Street Paisley with former Abbotsinch route disconnected.

8th and 9th July 1933

Air Pageant at Renfrew Aerodrome.
Special Extension of Blue Service K to RENFREW DEPOT (as on 17th September 1932) operates.

10th September 1933

Air Pageant at Renfrew Aerodrome.
Special Extension of Blue Service K to RENFREW DEPOT (as on 17th September 1932) operates.

21st October 1933

Completion of reconstruction of King's Bridge (James Street Bridge).
The following Temporary Service Alteration ceases:
Yellow Service J MILLERSTON, RIDDRIE or ALEXANDRA PARK & JAMES ST. BRIDGE and JAMES ST. BRIDGE & CRAIGTON ROAD revert to normal service:
Weekdays and Saturdays: MILLERSTON or RIDDRIE & CRAIGTON ROAD via BRIDGETON CROSS;
Sundays: MILLERSTON, RIDDRIE or ALEXANDRA PARK & CRAIGTON ROAD via BRIDGETON CROSS.

November 1933

Single line curve from Hawthorn Street westbound into Balmore Road southbound removed.

13th November 1933

Increase in Late Afternoon and Evening Service to Barrachnie.
The following Service Alteration takes place:
Green Service D Weekdays and Saturdays: KNIGHTSWOOD or KELVINSIDE & DENNISTOUN, SHETTLESTON or AIRDRIE Shettleston cars extended (1630-1930 and 2130-2300) to become
KNIGHTSWOOD or KELVINSIDE & DENNISTOUN, SHETTLESTON, BARRACHNIE or AIRDRIE;
Sundays: KNIGHTSWOOD & SHETTLESTON or AIRDRIE unaltered.

10th December 1933

The following Service Alteration takes place:

Blue Service O Sundays: QUEEN STREET & OATLANDS via CROWN STREET (Part Day) section extended to become
ST VINCENT STREET & OATLANDS via CROWN STREET (Part Day) from St Vincent Street at Wellington Street via St Vincent Street, Hope Street, Argyle Street and former route;
Sundays: KIRKLEE & RUTHERGLEN via PARK ROAD, CROWN STREET main section unaltered;
Weekdays and Saturdays: KIRKLEE & OATLANDS or RUTHERGLEN via PARK ROAD, CROWN STREET unaltered.

29th January 1934

The following Service Alteration takes place:

White Service Y Weekdays and Saturdays: SPRINGBURN or BALMORE ROAD & RUTHERGLEN or BURNSIDE via BILSLAND DRIVE, RUTHERGLEN BRIDGE altered to become
SPRINGBURN, RUCHILL (BALMORE ROAD) or KELVINSIDE AVENUE & RUTHERGLEN or BURNSIDE via BILSLAND DRIVE, RUTHERGLEN BRIDGE;
Sundays: SPRINGBURN & BURNSIDE via BILSLAND DRIVE, RUTHERGLEN BRIDGE unaltered.

14th April 1934

The following Service Alteration takes place:

Blue Service O Saturdays: KIRKLEE & OATLANDS or RUTHERGLEN via PARK ROAD, CROWN STREET part cut back and diverted to become
KIRKLEE or ST VINCENT STREET & OATLANDS or RUTHERGLEN via PARK ROAD, CROWN STREET;
St Vincent Street cars from St Vincent Street at Wellington Street via St Vincent Street, Hope Street and former route;
Weekdays: KIRKLEE & OATLANDS or RUTHERGLEN via PARK ROAD, CROWN STREET unaltered;
Sundays: KIRKLEE & RUTHERGLEN via PARK ROAD, CROWN STREET and
ST VINCENT STREET & OATLANDS via CROWN STREET (Part Day) unaltered.

23rd April 1934

Resiting of Jordanhill crossover to facilitate bow collector reversal clear of railway overbridges.
JORDANHILL terminus moved from Jordanhill Station to Crow Road north of Southbrae Drive.
Yellow Service H JORDANHILL & LANGSIDE via HYNDLAND
Red Service X ANNIESLAND & CAMBUSLANG via BOTHWELL STREET Shortworkings
both adjusted accordingly.

April 1934

Disused tracks in Gordon Street removed.

19th and 20th May 1934

Air Pageant at Renfrew Aerodrome.
Special Extension of **Blue Service K** to RENFREW DEPOT (as on 17th September 1932) operates.

20th May 1934

Subsidence in Maryhill Road between Queen's Cross and St George's Cross. Citybound track blocked.
The following Temporary Service Alterations take place:

Red Service M HILLFOOT or MARYHILL & MOUNT FLORIDA via NEW CITY ROAD cars from HILLFOOT and MARYHILL diverted between Queen's Cross and Cowcaddens to run via Garscube Road, Cowcaddens and then normal route;
Blue Service P MARYHILL & SHAWLANDS, PAISLEY CROSS or RENFREW FERRY via ST GEORGE'S CROSS, GORBALS, BARRHEAD cars from MARYHILL diverted between Queen's Cross and Cowcaddens to run via Garscube Road, Cowcaddens and then normal route;
White Service Y SPRINGBURN or KELVINSIDE AVENUE & RUTHERGLEN or BURNSIDE via BILSLAND DRIVE, RUTHERGLEN BRIDGE cars from SPRINGBURN and KELVINSIDE AVENUE diverted between Queen's Cross and Hope Street at Bothwell Street to run via Garscube Road, Cowcaddens, Hope Street and then normal route.

The following Operational Alteration takes place:
City Centre Timing Point for Green Services BU moved from Union Street to Queen Street.
Green Service B PAISLEY WEST, CROOKSTON or IBROX & SHETTLESTON or AIRDRIE
Green Service U PAISLEY WEST, PAISLEY CROSS or IBROX & TOLLCROSS or UDDINGSTON
Timeboards for both adjusted accordingly.

22nd May 1934

Subsidence in Maryhill Road between Queen's Cross and St George's Cross.
Citybound track blocked.
Motorbus Shuttle Service QUEEN'S CROSS & HOPE STREET introduced.

Blue Services G and K traversed George V. Bridge and would become the test bed for a major experiment with Regenerative Braking cars.
(Commercial Postcard, BJ Cross Collection)

28th May 1934

Subsidence in Maryhill Road repaired.
Temporary Service Alterations cease:
Red Service M HILLFOOT or MARYHILL & MOUNT FLORIDA via NEW CITY ROAD
Blue Service P MARYHILL & SHAWLANDS, PAISLEY CROSS or RENFREW FERRY via ST GEORGE'S CROSS, GORBALS, BARRHEAD;
White Service Y SPRINGBURN or KELVINSIDE AVENUE & RUTHERGLEN or BURNSIDE via BILSLAND DRIVE, RUTHERGLEN BRIDGE; all revert to normal service;
Motorbus Shuttle Service QUEEN'S CROSS & HOPE STREET withdrawn.

10th July 1934

Burst Water Main in Garscube Road between Raglan Street and North Woodside Road.
The following Temporary Service Alteration takes place for one day only:
Blue Service G Weekdays: LAMBHILL or SPRINGBURN & LINTHOUSE, SHIELDHALL or RENFREW CROSS via POSSILPARK LORNE STREET and
Blue Service K Weekdays: KEPPOCHHILL ROAD & SHIELDHALL or PORTERFIELD ROAD
both diverted between Round Toll and Hope Street at Sauchiehall Street via St George's Road, St George's Cross, St George's Road, Charing Cross, Sauchiehall Street, Hope Street then normal route;
Red Service N Weekdays: GAIRBRAID AVENUE & SINCLAIR DRIVE via GARSCUBE ROAD diverted between Queen's Cross and Normal School via Maryhill Road, St George's Cross, New City Road, Cowcaddens then normal route.

16th September 1934

Line from Paisley West to Ferguslie Mills reopened to passenger traffic.
The following Service Alterations take place:
Green Service B Weekdays: PAISLEY WEST, CROOKSTON, HALFWAY or IBROX & SHETTLESTON or AIRDRIE extended to become FERGUSLIE MILLS, CROOKSTON, HALFWAY or IBROX & SHETTLESTON or AIRDRIE from Ferguslie at Thomas Street via Ferguslie, Broomlands Street, West End Cross and former route;
Saturdays: PAISLEY WEST, CROOKSTON, HALFWAY or IBROX & BAILLIESTON or AIRDRIE extended to become FERGUSLIE MILLS, CROOKSTON, HALFWAY or IBROX & BAILLIESTON or AIRDRIE;
Sundays: PAISLEY WEST & AIRDRIE extended to become FERGUSLIE MILLS & AIRDRIE;
Green Service U Weekdays: PAISLEY WEST or IBROX & TOLLCROSS or UDDINGSTON extended to become FERGUSLIE MILLS or IBROX & TOLLCROSS or UDDINGSTON from Ferguslie at Thomas Street via Ferguslie, Boomlands Street, West End Cross and former route;

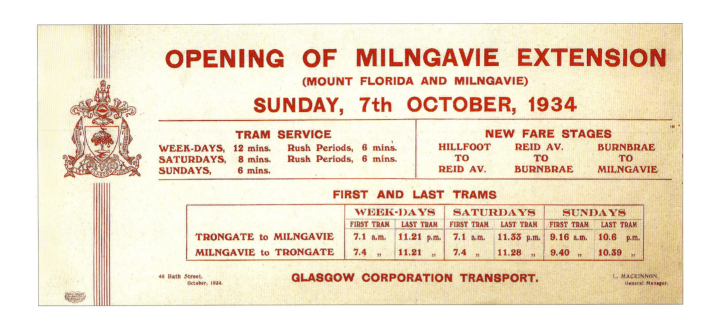

Saturdays: PAISLEY WEST, CROOKSTON, HALFWAY or IBROX & TOLLCROSS or UDDINGSTON extended to become FERGUSLIE MILLS, CROOKSTON, HALFWAY or IBROX & TOLLCROSS or UDDINGSTON;

Sundays: PAISLEY WEST & UDDINGSTON extended to become FERGUSLIE MILLS & UDDINGSTON.

Cars proceeding from and to ELDERSLIE DEPOT run empty between Elderslie Depot and Ferguslie Mills.

Regular cars resume operation on Ferguslie eastwards from Thomas Street and on Broomlands Street as far as Castle Street Paisley.

7th October 1934

Line Opened from Hillfoot to Milngavie.

Following the opening of the line to Hillfoot on 25th November 1923, work had proceeded with the construction of the line beyond to Milngavie. The LNER was, however, extremely reluctant to allow the Corporation to operate tramcars over the railway bridge at Hillfoot Station and what became a long and extremely acrimonious dispute between the railway company and the Tramways Department followed, delaying the opening of the already-finished extension of the route for another 11 years. In the run-up to the resolution of the argument, the Corporation was anxious to "test the route", that is, to satisfy itself as to the integrity of the infrastructure (track, overhead, polarity, etc.) and also to allow route-learning for motormen to take place. This was carried out in the weeks immediately preceding opening but, in order to keep the LNER placated before sanction had been formally granted to traverse the offending bridge, only trams with a light axle load were used. **Thus the frequent passage of Single-Decker** [cut down ex-Paisley District] **cars from Partick Depot occurred**, during this period, carrying out these very duties between Hillfoot and Milngavie.

The following Service Alterations take place:

Red Service M Weekdays: HILLFOOT or MARYHILL & MOUNT FLORIDA via NEW CITY ROAD extended to become MILNGAVIE, HILLFOOT or MARYHILL & MOUNT FLORIDA via NEW CITY ROAD from Main Street Milngavie at Park Road via Main Street Milngavie, Milngavie Road and former route;

Saturdays and Sundays: HILLFOOT & MOUNT FLORIDA via NEW CITY ROAD extended to become MILNGAVIE & MOUNT FLORIDA via NEW CITY ROAD;

Blue Service P Sundays: HILLFOOT & SHAWLANDS, PAISLEY CROSS or RENFREW FERRY via ST GEORGE'S CROSS, GORBALS, BARRHEAD extended to become MILNGAVIE & SHAWLANDS, PAISLEY CROSS or RENFREW FERRY via ST GEORGE'S;CROSS, GORBALS, BARRHEAD from Main Street Milngavie at Park Road via Main Street Milngavie, Milngavie Road and former route;

Saturdays: HILLFOOT & PAISLEY CROSS or RENFREW FERRY via ST GEORGE'S CROSS, GORBALS, BARRHEAD extended to become MILNGAVIE & PAISLEY CROSS or RENFREW FERRY via ST GEORGE'S CROSS, GORBALS, BARRHEAD;

Weekdays: MARYHILL & SHAWLANDS, PAISLEY CROSS or RENFREW FERRY via ST GEORGE'S CROSS, GORBALS, BARRHEAD unaltered.

10th November 1934

The following Service Alteration takes place:

Blue Service O Saturdays: KIRKLEE or ST VINCENT STREET & OATLANDS or RUTHERGLEN via PARK ROAD, CROWN STREET part diverted and extended to become KIRKLEE or PARTICK & OATLANDS or RUTHERGLEN via CROWN STREET from Crow Road Partick via Crow Road, Dumbarton Road, Argyle Street, Anderston Cross, Argyle Street and former route;

The Official Opening of the long-delayed extension from Hillfoot to Milngavie was performed by a very ordinary Yellow (!) Standard car No. 465 after extensive proving of the route with Duntocher Single-Deckers.
(IG Stewart Collection)

The Milngavie route soon settled down to be operated with red cars. Typical was Standard Car 487 photographed around 1936 when it was still fitted with louvred ventilators in the lower deck. These would soon be replaced by the usual perforated strip variety. They were less susceptible to damage each time they were removed in the course of repainting the cars.
(Courtesy, R Morant)

Weekdays: KIRKLEE & OATLANDS or RUTHERGLEN via PARK ROAD, CROWN STREET unaltered;
Sundays: KIRKLEE & RUTHERGLEN via PARK ROAD, CROWN STREET and
ST VINCENT STREET & OATLANDS via CROWN STREET (Part Day) unaltered.

19th November 1934

Revision of Netherlee and Clarkston services.
The following Service Alterations take place:
Yellow Service C Weekdays and Saturdays: KIRKLEE Circle via BOTANIC GARDENS or Circle via HYNDLAND & NETHERLEE or CLARKSTON altered to become
KIRKLEE Circle via BOTANIC GARDENS or Circle via HYNDLAND & CLARKSTON;
Sundays: KIRKLEE Circle via BOTANIC GARDENS or Circle via HYNDLAND & CLARKSTON unaltered;
White Service S Weekdays: SPRINGBURN & MOUNT FLORIDA or CATHCART via GLASGOW CROSS extended to become SPRINGBURN & MOUNT FLORIDA or NETHERLEE via GLASGOW CROSS via former route to Clarkston Road at Dairsie Street then via Clarkston Road to Clarkston Road at Ormonde Drive;
Saturdays: SPRINGBURN & MOUNT FLORIDA, CATHCART or NETHERLEE via GLASGOW CROSS altered to become SPRINGBURN & MOUNT FLORIDA or NETHERLEE via GLASGOW CROSS;
Sundays: SPRINGBURN & NETHERLEE via GLASGOW CROSS unaltered.

During 1935

Right-angled crossing at South Portland Street and Norfolk Street built up for smooth running through via Norfolk Street.

During 1935

Crossover in Bilsland Drive at Ruchill Hospital Gates removed.

Standard car No. 51 leaves Glasgow Cross on White Service S, heading down Saltmarket. The Tolbooth Steeple dating from 1626 is in the background.
(Commercial Postcard, BJ Cross Collection)

RUCHILL terminus moved for all services to BALMORE ROAD crossover in Hawthorn St west end at Lomond St.
White Service Y RUCHILL shortworkings already using BALMORE ROAD crossover unaltered.

8th February 1935

Line Opened in Annan Street linking Grange Road and Prospecthill Road to facilitate Football Specials for Hampden Park operating the "Hampden Wheel".
The following Service Alteration takes place:
Service "Hampden Wheel" TRONGATE & FOOTBALL SPECIALS [Mount Florida] (one-way outwards via Victoria Road returning via Cathcart Road) diverted between Grange Road and Prospecthill Road to run via Annan Street instead of via Grange Road and Prospecthill Road.

15th and 16th June 1935

Air Pageant at Renfrew Aerodrome.
Special Extension of Blue Service K to RENFREW DEPOT (as on 17th September 1932) operates.

25th August 1935

The following Service Alteration takes place:
Green Service A Weekdays and Saturdays: DALMUIR WEST, SCOTSTOUNHILL or ANNIESLAND & PARKHEAD or SPRINGFIELD ROAD altered to become
DALMUIR WEST, SCOTSTOUN WEST or ANNIESLAND & PARKHEAD or SPRINGFIELD ROAD;
SCOTSTOUN WEST cars turn in Dumbarton Road west of Burnham Road;
Sundays: DALMUIR WEST & SPRINGFIELD ROAD unaltered.

29th September 1935

SCOTSTOUNHILL turning point withdrawn and crossover removed.
Additional SCOTSTOUN WEST crossover provided in Kingsway west end for use of Green Cars.
SCOTSTOUN WEST turning point for Green Cars moved from Dumbarton Road west of Burnham Road to Kingsway west end. Dumbarton Road services unaltered.
Green Service A DALMUIR WEST, SCOTSTOUN WEST or ANNIESLAND & PARKHEAD or SPRINGFIELD ROAD adjusted accordingly.

8th November 1935

Doubling of track in Garngad Road completed.

13th December 1935

Adjustments at Cambuslang terminus to address traffic congestion.
Lying time position moved westwards on citybound track to opposite 64 Main Street Cambuslang.
Red Service F Saturdays: CLYDEBANK or SCOTSTOUN & DALMARNOCK, RUTHERGLEN, BURNSIDE or CAMBUSLANG ;
Red Service X ANNIESLAND & CAMBUSLANG via BOTHWELL STREET both adjusted accordingly.

25th December 1935

CLYDEBANK terminus for cars from and to City moved from Kilbowie Road south end to Dumbarton Road Clydebank just east of LMS railway overbridge.
Green Service A DALMUIR WEST, SCOTSTOUN WEST or ANNIESLAND & PARKHEAD or SPRINGFIELD ROAD Shortworkings

Red Service F DALMUIR WEST, CLYDEBANK, SCOTSTOUN or WHITEINCH & DALMARNOCK, RUTHERGLEN, BURNSIDE or CAMBUSLANG;
Red Service L DALMUIR WEST or SCOTSTOUN & LONDON ROAD or AUCHENSHUGGLE Shortworkings
Blue Service Z DALMUIR WEST or SCOTSTOUN & ALEXANDRA PARK or RIDDRIE Shortworkings
all adjusted accordingly;
Red Service RP CLYDEBANK & RADNOR PARK or DUNTOCHER unaltered.

15th January 1936

SHAWLANDS terminus moved from Pollokshaws Road north of Shawlands Cross to Pollokshaws Road south of Shawlands Cross at Shawlands Academy.
Blue Service P MILNGAVIE or MARYHILL & SHAWLANDS, PAISLEY CROSS or RENFREW FERRY via ST GEORGE'S CROSS, GORBALS, BARRHEAD;
Red Service R BISHOPBRIGGS or SPRINGBURN & POLLOKSHAWS WEST or ROUKEN GLEN Circle via THORNLIEBANK; MILLERSTON or RIDDRIE & MERRYLEE or ROUKEN GLEN Circle via GIFFNOCK Shortworkings
all adjusted accordingly.

8th February 1936

Eglinton Toll shelter removed.

18th February 1936

Junction at Turriff Street and MacKinlay Street with former Carlton Place route removed.

24th February 1936

The following Service Alteration takes place:
Red Service R Weekdays and Saturdays: MILLERSTON or RIDDRIE & MERRYLEE or ROUKEN GLEN Circle via GIFFNOCK altered to become MILLERSTON or RIDDRIE & GIFFNOCK or ROUKEN GLEN Circle via GIFFNOCK.
GIFFNOCK terminus in Fenwick Road north of Eastwood Toll;
Sundays: MILLERSTON & ROUKEN GLEN Circle via GIFFNOCK unaltered;
BISHOPBRIGGS or SPRINGBURN & POLLOKSHAWS WEST or ROUKEN GLEN Circle via THORNLIEBANK section unaltered.

24th March 1936

Sailing of Cunard Liner "Queen Mary" from Clydebank to Tail of the Bank.
The following Temporary Service Alterations take place between 0630 and 1500:
Green Service A DALMUIR WEST, SCOTSTOUN WEST or ANNIESLAND & PARKHEAD or SPRINGFIELD ROAD;
All ANNIESLAND and SCOTSTOUN WEST shortworking Cars extended to DALMUIR WEST;
Blue Service G LAMBHILL or SPRINGBURN & LINTHOUSE, SHIELDHALL or RENFREW CROSS via POSSILPARK, LORNE STREET and
Blue Service K KEPPOCHHILL ROAD & SHIELDHALL or PORTERFIELD ROAD
All LINTHOUSE and SHIELDHALL Cars extended to RENFREW CROSS;
Blue Service P MARYHILL & SHAWLANDS, PAISLEY CROSS or RENFREW FERRY via ST GEORGE'S CROSS, GORBALS, BARRHEAD
Additional Cars operated between SHAWLANDS & RENFREW FERRY;
Red Service L DALMUIR WEST, CLYDEBANK or SCOTSTOUN & LONDON ROAD or AUCHENSHUGGLE;
All SCOTSTOUN and CLYDEBANK shortworking Cars extended to DALMUIR WEST;

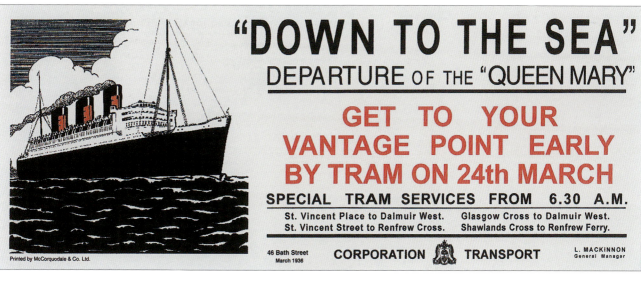

Blue Service Z DALMUIR WEST or SCOTSTOUN & ALEXANDRA PARK or RIDDRIE
All SCOTSTOUN shortworking Cars extended to DALMUIR WEST.

May 1936

Easing of traffic congestion with queuing motor traffic for the Renfrew Ferry.
RENFREW FERRY terminus moved back from Ferry Road south of Clyde Street to Ferry Road south of London Street.
Blue Service P MILNGAVIE or MARYHILL & SHAWLANDS, PAISLEY CROSS or RENFREW FERRY via ST GEORGE'S CROSS, GORBALS, BARRHEAD;
Blue Service [Paisley Local] GLENFIELD or POTTERHILL & RENFREW FERRY
both adjusted accordingly.

17th June 1936

Installation of Traffic Lights at Eglinton Toll to address congestion problems.
The following Service Alteration takes place:
Red Service N MARYHILL or GAIRBRAID AVENUE & SINCLAIR DRIVE via GARSCUBE ROAD;
Northbound cars rerouted at Eglinton Toll to proceed from Victoria Road via Eglinton Street, Turriff Street, Pollokshaws Road and former route;
Southbound cars unaltered continue to run directly from Pollokshaws Road to Victoria Road.

6th September 1936

BAILLIESTON terminus moved eastwards from Main Street Baillieston east of Dyke Street to west end of Private Track on south side of Coatbridge Road.
Green Service B FERGUSLIE MILLS, CROOKSTON, HALFWAY or IBROX & SHETTLESTON, BAILLIESTON or AIRDRIE
extended accordingly and
Green Service D Weekdays and Saturdays: KNIGHTSWOOD or KELVINSIDE & DENNISTOUN, SHETTLESTON, BARRACHNIE or AIRDRIE Shortworkings extended to become
KNIGHTSWOOD or KELVINSIDE & DENNISTOUN, SHETTLESTON, BAILLIESTON or AIRDRIE;
Sundays: KNIGHTSWOOD & SHETTLESTON or AIRDRIE unaltered.

4th October 1936

Renfrew Depot **closed** to trams. Cars transferred to Elderslie Depot, Govan Depot and Newlands Depot.
Barrhead Depot **closed** to trams. Cars transferred to Elderslie Depot.
The following Operational Alteration takes place:
Renfrew Depot operation and Barrhead Depot operation of
Blue Service P MILNGAVIE or MARYHILL & SHAWLANDS, PAISLEY CROSS or RENFREW FERRY via ST GEORGE'S CROSS, GORBALS;
Blue Service [Paisley Local] BRAIDS ROAD & PAISLEY CROSS
Blue Service [Paisley Local] GLENFIELD or POTTERHILL & RENFREW FERRY
all transferred to Elderslie Depot.
Line in Aurs Road Barrhead leading to Substation and former Barrhead Depot **closed** to trams.

When the Depot at Renfrew and the small outstation at Barrhead were closed in 1936, their allocation and responsibility for the lengthy Blue Service P were transferred to Elderslie Depot. This view taken from another car awaiting access to the single track between Cross Stobs and Glenfield confirms its rural terrain.
(W Fisher, Courtesy DW Fisher)

1st November 1936

LONDON ROAD terminus moved eastwards from crossover at Williamson St to London Rd at Maukinfauld Rd.
Red Service L DALMUIR WEST or SCOTSTOUN & LONDON ROAD or AUCHENSHUGGLE adjusted accordingly.

30th November 1936

Railway Bridge in Duke Street Dennistoun closed for repairs.
Cars turned on either side and access to Dennistoun Depot restricted to be available from and to the east only.
The following Temporary Service Alterations take place:
Green Service A DALMUIR WEST, SCOTSTOUN WEST or ANNIESLAND & PARKHEAD or SPRINGFIELD ROAD;
Green Service D KNIGHTSWOOD or KELVINSIDE & DENNISTOUN, SHETTLESTON or AIRDRIE
both split to turn in Duke Street at Bluevale Street crossover in the west and in Paton Street Depot access in the east.
Yellow Service J MILLERSTON, RIDDRIE or ALEXANDRA PARK & CRAIGTON ROAD via BRIDGETON CROSS;
Red Service R MILLERSTON or RIDDRIE & GIFFNOCK or ROUKEN GLEN Circle via GIFFNOCK and BISHOPBRIGGS or SPRINGBURN & POLLOKSHAWS WEST or ROUKEN GLEN Circle via THORNLIEBANK;
Blue Service Z DALMUIR WEST or SCOTSTOUN & ALEXANDRA PARK or RIDDRIE.
Depot Workings from and to Dennistoun Depot diverted via Duke Street, Parkhead Cross, Gallowgate, Trongate, either to Argyle Street at Queen Street crossover or via Glassford Street, Ingram Street, South Frederick Street, George Square south, St Vincent Place.

6th December 1936

The following Service Alteration takes place:
Blue Service K KEPPOCHHILL ROAD & SHIELDHALL or PORTERFIELD ROAD extended to become
KEPPOCHHILL ROAD & SHIELDHALL or RENFREW AERODROME (RENFREW DEPOT) via former route to Paisley Road Renfrew at Porterfield Road then via Paisley Road Renfrew to Paisley Road Renfrew at Renfrew Depot (crossover at Newmains Road).

25th December 1936

Railway Bridge repairs in Duke Street Dennistoun completed.
Temporary Service Alterations cease:
Green Service A DALMUIR WEST, SCOTSTOUN WEST or ANNIESLAND & PARKHEAD or SPRINGFIELD ROAD;
Green Service D KNIGHTSWOOD or KELVINSIDE & DENNISTOUN, SHETTLESTON or AIRDRIE
both revert to normal service.
Yellow Service J MILLERSTON, RIDDRIE or ALEXANDRA PARK & CRAIGTON ROAD via BRIDGETON CROSS;
Red Service R MILLERSTON or RIDDRIE & GIFFNOCK or ROUKEN GLEN Circle via GIFFNOCK and
BISHOPBRIGGS or SPRINGBURN & POLLOKSHAWS WEST or ROUKEN GLEN Circle via THORNLIEBANK;
Blue Service Z DALMUIR WEST or SCOTSTOUN & ALEXANDRA PARK or RIDDRIE.
Dennistoun Depot workings revert to normal routes.

Although intended for the interurban service between Airdrie and Paisley, the experimental Single-Deck car 1089 was put out to graze on the Clydebank – Duntocher service.
(W Fisher, Courtesy DW Fisher)

18th January 1937

Sandyhills Railway Bridge at City Boundary in Shettleston Road / Baillieston Road closed for repairs.
Cars turned on either side on temporary crossovers.
The following Temporary Service Alterations take place:
Green Service B FERGUSLIE MILLS, CROOKSTON, HALFWAY or IBROX & SHETTLESTON, BAILLIESTON or AIRDRIE;
Green Service D KNIGHTSWOOD or KELVINSIDE & DENNISTOUN, SHETTLESTON, BAILLIESTON or AIRDRIE both split to turn on temporary crossovers either side in west on Shettleston Road and in east on Baillieston Road

28th February 1937

Repairs to Sandyhills Railway Bridge completed.
Temporary Service Alterations cease:
Green Service B FERGUSLIE MILLS, CROOKSTON, HALFWAY or IBROX & SHETTLESTON, BAILLIESTON or AIRDRIE;
Green Service D KNIGHTSWOOD or KELVINSIDE & DENNISTOUN, SHETTLESTON, BAILLIESTON or AIRDRIE;
revert to normal service.

30th March 1937

The following Service Alteration takes place
White Service V Saturdays: PROVANMILL or GARNGAD & POLMADIE via GLASGOW CROSS altered to become PROVANMILL & POLMADIE via GLASGOW CROSS;
Weekdays: PROVANMILL or GARNGAD & POLMADIE via GLASGOW CROSS unaltered.
Sundays: PROVANMILL & POLMADIE via GLASGOW CROSS unaltered.

10th April 1937

Water Main repairs in Springfield Road.
The following Temporary Service Alteration takes place:
Green Service A DALMUIR WEST, SCOTSTOUN WEST or ANNIESLAND & PARKHEAD or SPRINGFIELD ROAD cut back to turn on crossover in Springfield Road at Bogside Street.

11th April 1937

Water Main repairs in Springfield Road completed.
Green Service A DALMUIR WEST, SCOTSTOUN WEST or ANNIESLAND & PARKHEAD or SPRINGFIELD ROAD reverts to normal service.

18th April 1937

Replacement of Railway Overbridge and widening of roadway on Great Western Road at Anniesland Station.
Sunday closure of roadway with tram services turning on temporary crossovers on either side.
Green Service A Sundays: DALMUIR WEST & SPRINGFIELD ROAD
Green Service D Sundays: KNIGHTSWOOD & SHETTLESTON or AIRDRIE split to turn on either side of the bridge.

30th May 1937

Replacement of Railway Overbridge and widening of roadway on Great Western Road at Anniesland Station. Arrangements for 18th April 1937 repeated.

6th June 1937

Replacement of Railway Overbridge and widening of roadway on Great Western Road at Anniesland Station. Arrangements for 18th April 1937 repeated.

29th August 1937

Increase in frequency of Paisley Road West Services.
Cars shortworking to IBROX extended to CROOKSTON.
The following Service Alterations take place:
Green Service B Weekdays and Saturdays: FERGUSLIE MILLS, CROOKSTON, HALFWAY or IBROX & SHETTLESTON, BAILLIESTON or AIRDRIE altered to become
FERGUSLIE MILLS or CROOKSTON & SHETTLESTON, BAILLIESTON or AIRDRIE; Cars from CROOKSTON from Paisley Road West at Crookston Road and former route;
Sundays: FERGUSLIE MILLS & AIRDRIE unaltered;
Green Service U Weekdays: FEGUSLIE MILLS or IBROX & TOLLCROSS or UDDINGSTON altered to become
FEGUSLIE MILLS or CROOKSTON & TOLLCROSS or UDDINGSTON;
Saturdays: FERGUSLIE MILLS, CROOKSTON, HALFWAY or IBROX & TOLLCROSS or UDDINGSTON altered to become
FERGUSLIE MILLS or CROOKSTON & TOLLCROSS or UDDINGSTON;
Sundays: FERGUSLIE MILLS & UDDINGSTON unaltered.

October 1937

Production models of Coronation Cars start entering service from Newlands Depot on White Service E.

When the first production Coronation cars were placed in service they adhered to the use of the Headcode system of Service differentiation, which began to assume an importance hitherto absent as route colours were dispensed with in favour of the Corporation's Bus Green. The Headcodes can be seen on the two pre-production prototypes, 1141 and 1142. The drawbacks of the Headcode system are illustrated in the view of 1142. Although the destination and via Screens have been changed, the Headcode still shows the Renfrew South code; it should be 5C for Keppochhill Road.
(W Fisher, Courtesy DW Fisher)

14th November 1937

The following Service Alteration takes place:
Green Service D Sundays: KNIGHTSWOOD & SHETTLESTON or AIRDRIE altered to become KNIGHTSWOOD & BARGEDDIE or AIRDRIE;
Weekdays and Saturdays: KNIGHTSWOOD or KELVINSIDE & DENNISTOUN, SHETTLESTON, BAILLIESTON or AIRDRIE unaltered.

5th December 1937

Repair work on Railway Underbridge on Cumbernauld Road between Provan Road and Dee Street. Sunday closure of road to all traffic.
The following Temporary Service Alterations take place:
Yellow Service J Sundays: MILLERSTON, RIDDRIE or ALEXANDRA PARK & CRAIGTON ROAD via BRIDGETON CROSS curtailed to ALEXANDRA PARK & CRAIGTON ROAD via BRIDGETON CROSS;
Red Service R Sundays: MILLERSTON & ROUKEN GLEN Circle via GIFFNOCK section curtailed to ALEXANDRA PARK & ROUKEN GLEN Circle via GIFFNOCK;
Motorbus Shuttle Service MILLERSTON & ALEXANDRA PARK.

Time Frame 1938 – 1945: Hostilities Again

This time frame starts with the preparations for the Empire Exhibition at Bellahouston Park when war is seen by many to be inevitable. Glasgow Corporation Transport continues to build new Coronation trams in batches of 100, 25 and 25 until this is halted by shortages of supplies and diversion of effort when the Second World War eventually comes. Plans to replace the oldest Standard trams are put on hold after only five experimental examples are built and soon the effects of hostilities become ever more tangible. The new service numbering system introduced for the Exhibition is modified in 1943 to allow more manageable operation, the service colour differentiation is on its way out and modern trams are dispersed to depots less vulnerable to attack. This is a short but eventful period as will be seen and it will have long-lasting consequences.

The simplified Service numbering system introduced in 1938 was based on the existing Motorbus Service numbers. Hence Mosspark, served by the "3" bus was then also served by the "3" tram. This view of Glasgow Bridge in the previous year shows two Red Standard cars 227 and 73 passing a bus on Service "5A" that would later be paralleled by Service 5 trams.
(Courtesy: Online Transport Archive)

22nd January 1938

Increase in Saturdays service to Auchenshuggle.
The following Service Alteration takes place:
Red Service L Saturdays: DALMUIR WEST & LONDON ROAD or AUCHENSHUGGLE altered to become DALMUIR WEST & AUCHENSHUGGLE;
Weekdays: DALMUIR WEST or SCOTSTOUN & LONDON ROAD or AUCHENSHUGGLE unaltered;
Sundays: DALMUIR WEST & AUCHENSHUGGLE unaltered.

6th February 1938

Line opened in Jura Street.
The following Service Alteration takes place:
Yellow Service J Weekdays and Saturdays: MILLERSTON or RIDDRIE & CRAIGTON ROAD via BRIDGETON CROSS extended to become MILLERSTON or RIDDRIE & BELLAHOUSTON via BRIDGETON CROSS via former route to Craigton Road then via Jura Street to Jura Street south end;
Sundays: MILLERSTON, RIDDRIE or ALEXANDRA PARK & CRAIGTON ROAD via BRIDGETON CROSS extended to become MILLERSTON, RIDDRIE or ALEXANDRA PARK & BELLAHOUSTON via BRIDGETON CROSS.

During 1938

Colston Road Permanent Way Coup closed.
Line in Colston Road **closed** to trams.
Eastfield Permanent Way Coup east of Eastfield Locomotive Shed Opened.
Access Line Opened to Eastfield Coup running off west side of Springburn Road south of junction with Huntershill Street.

10th April 1938

Increase in Sunday Service to Dumbreck.
The following Service Alteration takes place:
White Service E Sundays: UNIVERSITY & POLLOKSHIELDS or MOSSPARK altered to become UNIVERSITY & DUMBRECK or MOSSPARK via POLLOKSHIELDS;
Weekdays and Saturdays: UNIVERSITY & DUMBRECK or MOSSPARK via POLLOKSHIELDS unaltered.

3rd May 1938

New Service Number scheme handselled, based on existing Motorbus Service Numbers. Headcode System abandoned.
Use of Slipboards phased out.
Opening of Empire Exhibition, Bellahouston Park.
Line Opened in Corkerhill Road from Mosspark Boulevard to Paisley Road West.
MOSSPARK terminus moved from Private Track west end to Corkerhill Road north end.
Curves Opened between Golspie Street to and from Govan Road westwards.
The following Temporary Service Alterations take place:
White Service 3 Weekdays and Saturdays: UNIVERSITY & DUMBRECK or MOSSPARK via POLLOKSHIELDS altered and extended to become
UNIVERSITY & DUMBRECK or MOSSPARK via POLLOKSHIELDS with through Circle Cars to and from Service 3A.
Sundays: UNIVERSITY & DUMBRECK or MOSSPARK Circle via POLLOKSHIELDS unaltered;
The following Service commences:

White Service 3A UNIVERSITY & MOSSPARK Circle via PAISLEY ROAD from University Avenue at Kelvin Way via University Avenue, Gibson Street, Eldon Street, Woodlands Road, St George's Road, Charing Cross, Sauchiehall Street, Renfield Street, Union Street, Jamaica Street, Glasgow Bridge, Nelson Street, Morrison Street, Paisley Road, Paisley Road West and Corkerhill Road with through Circle Cars to and from **Service 3**; No Sundays Service.

Yellow Service 12 Weekdays and Saturdays: MOUNT FLORIDA & PAISLEY ROAD TOLL via SHIELDS ROAD extended to become

MOUNT FLORIDA & PAISLEY ROAD TOLL or IBROX via SHIELDS ROAD via former route to Paisley Road Toll then via Paisley Road West, Broomloan Road to Broomloan Road south end;

Sundays: MOUNT FLORIDA & PAISLEY ROAD TOLL via SHIELDS ROAD unaltered.

The following Temporary Services commence:

Service 30/30A CIRCLE ST VINCENT STREET & EXHIBITION operates both ways from St Vincent Street between Hope Street and Renfield Street: (Part Day Only)

Service 30 Outer via St Vincent Street, Renfield Street, Union Street, Jamaica Street, Glasgow Bridge, Bridge Street, Eglinton Street, Eglinton Toll, Maxwell Road, Kenmure Street, Albert Drive, St Andrew's Drive, Nithsdale Road, Dumbreck Road, Private Track on north side of Mosspark Boulevard, Corkerhill Road returning via Corkerhill Road, Paisley Road West, Paisley Road, Morrison Street, Nelson Street, Commerce Street, George V Bridge, Oswald Street, Hope Street and St Vincent Street. No Sundays Service:

Service 30A Inner via St Vincent Street, Hope Street, Oswald Street George V Bridge, Commerce Street, Nelson Street, Morrison Street, Paisley Road, Paisley Road Toll, Paisley Road West, Corkerhill Road returning via Corkerhill Road, Private Track on north side of Mosspark Boulevard, Dumbreck Road, Nithsdale Road, St Andrew's Drive, Albert Drive, Kenmure Street, Maxwell Road, Eglinton Toll, Eglinton Street, Bridge Street, Glasgow Bridge, Jamaica Street, Union Street, Renfield Street and St Vincent Street. No Sundays Service.

Blue Service 31 LINTHOUSE & EXHIBITION from Holmfauld Road south end via Holmfauld Road, Govan Road, Golspie Street, Langlands Road, Elder Street, Crossloan Road, Craigton Road, Jura Street to Jura Street south end; (Part Day Only) No Sundays Service.

4th May 1938

The following Service Alterations take place:

White Service 3A Weekdays and Saturdays: UNIVERSITY & MOSSPARK Circle via PAISLEY ROAD altered to become KELVINGROVE or UNIVERSITY & MOSSPARK Circle via PAISLEY ROAD alternate cars from Radnor Street via Radnor Street via Sauchiehall Street, Charing Cross and former route; No Sundays Service.

Coronations were placed on Empire Exhibition Services as soon as they came off the production line. Here is one of the first, 1154, a Maryhill Depot car, on Mosspark Boulevard with the Exhibition buildings in the background.
(Courtesy, National Tramway Museum Archive)

Résumé
8th May 1938

The following Tram Services operating

1	Green	KNIGHTSWOOD or KELVINSIDE & DENNISTOUN, SHETTLESTON, BAILLIESTON, BARGEDDIE or AIRDRIE
1A	Green	DALMUIR WEST, SCOTSTOUN WEST or ANNIESLAND & PARKHEAD or SPRINGFIELD ROAD
2	White	PROVANMILL or GARNGAD & POLMADIE via GLASGOW CROSS
3	White	UNIVERSITY & DUMBRECK or MOSSPARK Circle via POLLOKSHIELDS
		Circle cars return as Service 3A (No Sundays Service)
		UNIVERSITY & MOSSPARK via POLLOKSHIELDS (Sundays only)
3A	White	KELVINGROVE or UNIVERSITY & MOSSPARK Circle via PAISLEY ROAD.
		Circle cars return as Service 3 (No Sundays Service)
4	Blue	KEPPOCHHILL ROAD & SHIELDHALL or RENFREW AERODROME
4A	Blue	SPRINGBURN & LINTHOUSE, SHIELDHALL or RENFREW CROSS via POSSILPARK, LORNE ST
		(Cars show "4" on journeys to LINTHOUSE, SHIELDHALL or RENFREW CROSS)
4B	Blue	LAMBHILL & LINTHOUSE, SHIELDHALL or RENFREW CROSS via POSSILPARK, LORNE ST
		(Cars show "4" on journeys to LINTHOUSE, SHIELDHALL or RENFREW CROSS)
5	Yellow	KIRKLEE Circle via BOTANIC GARDENS or Circle via HYNDLAND & CLARKSTON
		Circle Cars return via HYNDLAND or via BOTANIC GARDENS respectively.
5A	Yellow	JORDANHILL & LANGSIDE via HYNDLAND
6	Blue	DALMUIR WEST or SCOTSTOUN & ALEXANDRA PARK or RIDDRIE
7	Yellow	MILLERSTON or RIDDRIE & BELLAHOUSTON via BRIDGETON CROSS
8/8A/8B	Red	BISHOPBRIGGS (8) or SPRINGBURN (8) & POLLOKSHAWS WEST (8A) or ROUKEN GLEN Circle via THORNLIEBANK (8A)
		Circle Cars return to ALEXANDRA PARK (8A), RIDDRIE (8A) or MILLERSTON (8A).
		MILLERSTON (8A), RIDDRIE (8A) or ALEXANDRA PARK (8A), & MERRYLEE (8B), GIFFNOCK (8) or ROUKEN GLEN Circle via GIFFNOCK (8)
		Circle Cars return to SPRINGBURN (8) or BISHOPBRIGGS (8)
9	Red	DALMUIR WEST or SCOTSTOUN & LONDON ROAD or AUCHENSHUGGLE
9A	Red	DALMUIR WEST, CLYDEBANK or SCOTSTOUN & BURNSIDE via DALMARNOCK
		(Cars show "9" on journeys to SCOTSTOUN, CLYDEBANK or DALMUIR WEST)
9B	Red	DALMUIR WEST, CLYDEBANK or SCOTSTOUN & DALMARNOCK, RUTHERGLEN or CAMBUSLANG
		(Cars show "9" on journeys to SCOTSTOUN, CLYDEBANK or DALMUIR WEST)
10	Blue	KIRKLEE & OATLANDS or RUTHERGLEN via PARK ROAD, CROWN STREET
		PARTICK or ST VINCENT STREET & OATLANDS or RUTHERGLEN via CROWN STREET
11	Red	MARYHILL or GAIRBRAID AVENUE & SINCLAIR DRIVE via GARSCUBE ROAD
12	Yellow	MOUNT FLORIDA & PAISLEY ROAD TOLL or IBROX via SHIELDS ROAD
13	Red	MILNGAVIE, HILLFOOT or MARYHILL & MOUNT FLORIDA via NEW CITY ROAD
14	Blue	MILNGAVIE or MARYHILL & SHAWLANDS, PAISLEY CROSS or RENFREW FERRY via ST GEORGE'S CROSS, GORBALS, BARRHEAD
15	Green	FERGUSLIE MILLS or CROOKSTON & SHETTLESTON, BAILLIESTON or AIRDRIE
15A	Green	FERGUSLIE MILLS or CROOKSTON & TOLLCROSS, or UDDINGSTON
		(Cars show "15" on journeys to CROOKSTON or FERGUSLIE MILLS)
16	Green	KEPPOCHHILL ROAD & WHITEINCH or SCOTSTOUN via NORTH STREET
17	Red	ANNIESLAND & CAMBUSLANG via BOTHWELL STREET
18	White	SPRINGBURN, RUCHILL or KELVINSIDE AVENUE & RUTHERGLEN or BURNSIDE via BILSLAND DRIVE, RUTHERGLEN BRIDGE
19	White	SPRINGBURN & MOUNT FLORIDA or NETHERLEE via GLASGOW CROSS
20	Red	[Single Deck Cars] CLYDEBANK & RADNOR PARK or DUNTOCHER
-	Green	[Airdrie Local] LANGLOAN & AIRDRIE
-	Green	[Paisley Local] PAISLEY WEST or PAISLEY CROSS & HAWKHEAD ROAD (Part Day)
-	Blue	[Paisley Local] BRAIDS ROAD & PAISLEY CROSS (Part Day)
-	Blue	[Paisley Local] GLENFIELD or POTTERHILL & RENFREW FERRY
30	-	CIRCLE ST VINCENT STREET & EXHIBITION (OUTER) (No Sundays Service)
30A	-	CIRCLE ST VINCENT STREET & EXHIBITION (INNER) (No Sundays Service)
31	Blue	LINTHOUSE & EXHIBITION (No Sundays Service)

9th May 1938

Line Opened in Crookston Road north end.
CROOKSTON terminus moved from Paisley Road West at Crookston Road into Crookston Road north end.
Green Service 15 FERGUSLIE MILLS or CROOKSTON & SHETTLESTON, BAILLIESTON or AIRDRIE;
Green Service 15A FERGUSLIE MILLS or CROOKSTON & TOLLCROSS or UDDINGSTON
both adjusted accordingly.

8th August 1938

The following Service Alteration takes place:
White Service 3A Weekdays and Saturdays: KELVINGROVE or UNIVERSITY & MOSSPARK Circle via PAISLEY ROAD part-extended to become ANNIESLAND, KELVINGROVE or UNIVERSITY & MOSSPARK Circle via PAISLEY ROAD from Crow Road north end via Crow Road, Broomhill Cross, Clarence Drive, Hyndland Road, Highburgh Road, Byres Road, Church Street, Dumbarton Road, Argyle Street, Sauchiehall Street and former route;
No Sundays Service.

September 1938

GIFFNOCK terminus extended from Fenwick Road north of Eastwood Toll to Rouken Glen Road west of Eastwood Lodge.
Red Service 8/8A MILLERSTON, RIDDRIE or ALEXANDRA PARK & GIFFNOCK or ROUKEN GLEN Circle via GIFFNOCK section adjusted accordingly.

17th October 1938

Railway Bridge at Maryhill Station, Maryhill Road south of Caldercuilt Road closed for repairs.
All tram services from City curtailed at Celtic Street.
The following Temporary Service Alterations take place:
Red Service 11 Sundays: MARYHILL & SINCLAIR DRIVE via GARSCUBE ROAD;
Red Service 13 MILNGAVIE, HILLFOOT or MARYHILL & MOUNT FLORIDA via ST GEORGE'S CROSS;
Blue Service 14 MILNGAVIE or MARYHILL & SHAWLANDS, PAISLEY CROSS or RENFREW FERRY via ST GEORGE'S CROSS, GORBALS, BARRHEAD;
all curtailed to turn at MARYHILL using Celtic Street entrance to Maryhill Depot;
Motorbus Shuttle Service MILNGAVIE & MARYHILL introduced.

30th October 1938

Closure of Empire Exhibition, Bellahouston Park.
The following Service Alterations take place:
White Service 3 Weekdays and Saturdays: UNIVERSITY & DUMBRECK or MOSSPARK Circle via POLLOKSHIELDS
reverts to become
UNIVERSITY & DUMBRECK or MOSSPARK via POLLOKSHIELDS;
Sundays: UNIVERSITY & MOSSPARK via POLLOKSHIELDS unaltered;
White Service 3A ANNIESLAND, KELVINGROVE or UNIVERSITY & MOSSPARK Circle via PAISLEY ROAD withdrawn;
Yellow Service 5A JORDANHILL & LANGSIDE via HYNDLAND extended to become
ANNIESLAND & LANGSIDE via HYNDLAND from Crow Road north end via Crow Road and former route;
Service 30/30A CIRCLE ST VINCENT STREET & EXHIBITION withdrawn;
Blue Service 31 LINTHOUSE & EXHIBITION withdrawn.
The following Service commences:
Green Service 21 CROOKSTON & PROVANMILL via RENFIELD STREET from Crookston Road north end via Crookston Road, Paisley Road West, Paisley Road Toll, Paisley Road, Morrison Street, Nelson Street, Bridge Street, Glasgow Bridge, Jamaica Street, Union Street, Renfield Street, Sauchiehall Street, Parliamentary Road, Castle Street, Garngad Road to Garngad Road at Provanmill Road.
The following Operational Alteration takes place:

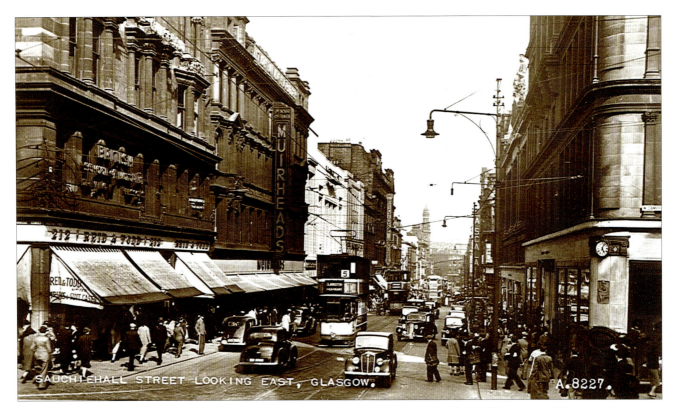

By the end of the Empire Exhibition, the new Service numbering scheme had settled down. This commercial postcard shows a Yellow Standard on Service 5. The fleet number is obliterated by reflected sun but the Green car in the distance is No.130. The Coronation is on Service 3A which was withdrawn on 30th October 1938.
(Commercial Postcard, BJ Cross Collection)

Yellow Service 12 MOUNT FLORIDA & PAISLEY ROAD TOLL or IBROX via SHIELDS ROAD operation of Service transferred from Govan Depot to Langside Depot.

21st November 1938

The following Service Alteration takes place:
Yellow Service 12 Weekdays and Saturdays: MOUNT FLORIDA & PAISLEY ROAD TOLL or IBROX via SHIELDS ROAD cut back to become
MOUNT FLORIDA & PAISLEY ROAD TOLL via SHIELDS ROAD;
Sundays: MOUNT FLORIDA & PAISLEY ROAD TOLL via SHIELDS ROAD unaltered.

25th December 1938

Repairs to Railway Bridge at Maryhill Station Maryhill Road south of Caldercuilt Road completed.
Red Service 11 Sundays: MARYHILL & SINCLAIR DRIVE via GARSCUBE ROAD
Red Service 13 MILNGAVIE, HILLFOOT or MARYHILL & MOUNT FLORIDA via ST GEORGE'S CROSS;
Blue Service 14 MILNGAVIE or MARYHILL & SHAWLANDS, PAISLEY CROSS or RENFREW FERRY via ST GEORGE'S CROSS, GORBALS, BARRHEAD all revert to normal routes;
Motorbus Shuttle Service MILNGAVIE & MARYHILL withdrawn.

4th February 1939

Tracks in Battlefield Road realigned between traffic islands to form paved reserved track. Layout at junction of Battlefield Road and Prospecthill Road redesigned to facilitate direct running from and to Langside Depot of cars on Depot Workings.

19th February 1939

The following Service Alteration takes place:
Red Service 11 MARYHILL or GAIRBRAID AVENUE & SINCLAIR DRIVE via GARSCUBE ROAD diverted to become RUCHILL & SINCLAIR DRIVE via GARSCUBE ROAD from Hawthorn Street west end at Lomond Street via Bilsland Drive, Maryhill Road and former route.

9th March 1939

Subsidence in Duke Street at Hunter Street.
The following Temporary Service Alterations take place:
Green Service 1 KNIGHTSWOOD or KELVINSIDE & DENNISTOUN, SHETTLESTON, BAILLIESTON, BARGEDDIE or AIRDRIE;

Green Service 1A DALMUIR WEST, SCOTSTOUN WEST or ANNIESLAND & PARKHEAD or SPRINGFIELD ROAD;
split to turn on either side at temporary crossovers in Duke Street, on the west at John Knox Street and on the east at Ladywell Street.

During 1939

Programme of repainting all Green and White Cars into Standard "bus" Green livery commences.

2nd April 1939

Sunday Repairs to Inchbelly railway overbridge in Springburn Road.
Tram Services turned on either side on temporary crossovers.
Red Service 8/8A Sundays: BISHOPBRIGGS & ROUKEN GLEN Circle via THORNLIEBANK section
White Service 19 Sundays: SPRINGBURN & NETHERLEE via GLASGOW CROSS
both altered accordingly.

4th April 1939

Duke Street reopened at Hunter Street.
Green Service 1 KNIGHTSWOOD or KELVINSIDE & DENNISTOUN, SHETTLESTON, BAILLIESTON, BARGEDDIE or AIRDRIE;
Green Service 1A DALMUIR WEST, SCOTSTOUN WEST or ANNIESLAND & PARKHEAD or SPRINGFIELD ROAD;
both revert to normal service.

7th May 1939

Repairs to Inchbelly railway overbridge in Springburn Road completed.
Red Service 8/8A Sundays: BISHOPBRIGGS & ROUKEN GLEN Circle via THORNLIEBANK section
White Service 19 Sundays: SPRINGBURN & NETHERLEE via GLASGOW CROSS
both revert to normal service.

3rd September 1939

Outbreak of Second World War.
Black-out conditions apply.

3rd September 1939

Lye Opened at Anderston Cross in Stobcross Street from Argyle Street as far as Stobcross Street at Warroch Street.
Loop in Argyle Street at Queen Street, still in use for City Centre cars from east, **closed** to trams.

By the summer of 1939, Coronation cars had appeared in Depots not previously associated with the Empire Exhibition. Seen at Dalmuir West is Partick's first, 1236, with Standard 235 on Service 1A. After Round Dash 292 was experimentally equipped the Hexagonal Dash Standards were the first to be fitted with roller blind Service Number indicators whereas the older Round Dash Standards, the ex-Paisley cars and Maximum Traction cars did not acquire them until after the war.
(Struan JT Robertson)

4th September 1939

ANDERSTON CROSS terminus opened.

City Centre shortworkings from east to Queen Street extended to run to Anderston Cross.

Peak-hour Cars and Specials on the following Services operate from Stobcross Street at Warroch Street via Stobcross Street, Argyle Street and former routes:

Red Service 9 QUEEN STREET & LONDON ROAD or AUCHENSHUGGLE extended to become ANDERSTON CROSS & LONDON ROAD or AUCHENSHUGGLE;

Red Service 9A QUEEN STREET & BURNSIDE via DALMARNOCK extended to become ANDERSTON CROSS & BURNSIDE via DALMARNOCK;

Red Service 9B QUEEN STREET & DALMARNOCK or RUTHERGLEN extended to become ANDERSTON CROSS & DALMARNOCK or RUTHERGLEN;

Green Service 15 QUEEN STREET & SHETTLESTON, BAILLIESTON or AIRDRIE extended to become ANDERSTON CROSS & SHETTLESTON, BAILLIESTON or AIRDRIE;

Green Service 15A QUEEN STREET & TOLLCROSS or UDDINGSTON extended to become ANDERSTON CROSS & TOLLCROSS or UDDINGSTON;

Red Service 17 QUEEN STREET & CAMBUSLANG extended to become ANDERSTON CROSS & CAMBUSLANG;

White Service 18 QUEEN STREET & RUTHERGLEN or BURNSIDE via RUTHERGLEN BRIDGE extended to become ANDERSTON CROSS & RUTHERGLEN or BURNSIDE via RUTHERGLEN BRIDGE.

18th September 1939

Second World War. War Emergency Service introduced.

Frequency reduced after 2230 hrs on Weekdays and Saturdays on all Services.

October 1939

Experimental Lightweight Cars start entering service, initially from Partick Depot on **Service 9**, and, subsequently, all from Newlands Depot on **Services 8 and 8A**.

15th October 1939

Due to Wartime Black-out Restrictions, daylight track renewal work carried out.

Sunday Relaying of junction at Sauchiehall Street/Renfield Street intersection.

The following Temporary Service Alterations take place during daylight hours:

Green Service 1 Sundays: KNIGHTSWOOD & BARGEDDIE or AIRDRIE

Green Service 1A Sundays: DALMUIR WEST & SPRINGFIELD ROAD

White Service 3 Sundays: UNIVERSITY & MOSSPARK via POLLOKSHIELDS;

Yellow Service 5 Sundays: KIRKLEE Circle via BOTANIC GARDENS or Circle via HYNDLAND & CLARKSTON;

Yellow Service 5A Sundays: ANNIESLAND & LANGSIDE via HYNDLAND

all diverted between Sauchiehall Street west of Hope Street and Renfield Street south of St Vincent Street via Hope Street, St Vincent Street and Renfield Street;

Blue Service 6 Sundays: DALMUIR WEST & ALEXANDRA PARK split to become

DALMUIR WEST & CHARING CROSS and

HANOVER STREET & ALEXANDRA PARK;

The Experimental "Lightweight" cars were constructed concurrently with the last of the Coronations and ran out of Newlands Depot for most of the first 10 years in service. Here is No.1003 at Elmvale Street, Springburn, on Service 8A, complete with wartime embellishments.
(W Fisher, Courtesy, DW Fisher)

Red Service 8/8A/8B Sundays: BISHOPBRIGGS & ROUKEN GLEN Circle via THORNLIEBANK split to become BISHOPBRIGGS & HANOVER STREET and ST VINCENT STREET & ROUKEN GLEN Circle via THORNLIEBANK;

Sundays: MILLERSTON & ROUKEN GLEN Circle via GIFFNOCK split to become
MILLERSTON & HANOVER STREET and ST VINCENT STREET & ROUKEN GLEN Circle via GIFFNOCK;

Green Service 21 Sundays: CROOKSTON & PROVANMILL via RENFIELD STREET split to become
CROOKSTON & ST VINCENT STREET and HANOVER STREET & PROVANMILL.

Kirkintilloch Road closed to trams north of Colston Road for track realignment work.

Red Service 8/8A BISHOPBRIGGS or SPRINGBURN & POLLOKSHAWS WEST or ROUKEN GLEN Circle via THORNLIEBANK temporarily cut back to become
SPRINGBURN & POLLOKSHAWS WEST or ROUKEN GLEN Circle via THORNLIEBANK;

Motorbus Shuttle Service: BISHOPBRIGGS & SPRINGBURN.

29th October 1939

Due to Wartime Black-out Restrictions, daylight track renewal work carried out.
Sunday relaying of junction at Alexandra Park.
The following Temporary Service Alterations take place between 0700 and 1800:

Blue Service 6 Sundays: DALMUIR WEST & ALEXANDRA PARK curtailed to DALMUIR WEST & MONKLAND STREET;

Yellow Service 7 Sundays: MILLERSTON, RIDDRIE or ALEXANDRA PARK & BELLAHOUSTON via BRIDGETON CROSS curtailed to
DENNISTOUN & BELLAHOUSTON via BRIDGETON CROSS from Carntyne Road west end via Carntyne Road, Duke Street and normal route;

Red Service 8/8A/8B Sundays: MILLERSTON & ROUKEN GLEN Circle via GIFFNOCK curtailed to
MONKLAND STREET & ROUKEN GLEN Circle via GIFFNOCK;

Motorbus Shuttle Services: MILLERSTON & DUKE STREET; MILLERSTON & MONKLAND STREET.

5th November 1939

Sunday Repairs to LNER Railway Bridge over Clarence Drive.

Yellow Service 5A Sundays: ANNIESLAND & LANGSIDE curtailed to become
HYNDLAND & LANGSIDE.

12th November 1939

Sunday Repairs to LNER Railway Bridge over Clarence Drive.

Yellow Service 5A Sundays: ANNIESLAND & LANGSIDE diverted between Broomhill Cross and Dumbarton Road at Church Street via Crow Road, Partick, Dumbarton Road;

Motorbus Shuttle Service: DUDLEY DRIVE & UNIVERSITY AVENUE connecting with
Yellow Service 5 KIRKLEE Circle & CLARKSTON in Byres Road at University Avenue.

16th November 1939

Burst Water Main in Great Western Road at Bank Street.
The following Temporary Service Alterations take place:

Green Service 1 KNIGHTSWOOD or KELVINSIDE & DENNISTOUN, SHETTLESTON, BAILLIESTON or AIRDRIE;
Green Service 1A DALMUIR WEST, SCOTSTOUN WEST or ANNIESLAND & PARKHEAD or SPRINGFIELD ROAD;
both diverted between Botanic Gardens and Sauchiehall Street at Cambridge Street via Byres Road, Church Street, Dumbarton Road, Sauchiehall Street, Charing Cross and Sauchiehall Street;

Blue Service 10 KIRKLEE & OATLANDS or RUTHERGLEN via PARK ROAD, CROWN STREET section curtailed to become
PARK ROAD & OATLANDS or RUTHERGLEN via CROWN STREET;

Motorbus Shuttle Service: BOTANIC GARDENS & RENFREW STREET.

18th November 1939

Burst Water Main in Great Western Road at Bank Street repairs near completion.

Green Service 1 KNIGHTSWOOD or KELVINSIDE & DENNISTOUN, SHETTLESTON, BAILLIESTON or AIRDRIE;
Green Service 1A DALMUIR WEST, SCOTSTOUN WEST or ANNIESLAND & PARKHEAD or SPRINGFIELD ROAD;
both revert to normal service.

20th November 1939

Burst Water Main in Great Western Road at Bank Street repairs completed.

Blue Service 10 KIRKLEE & OATLANDS or RUTHERGLEN via PARK ROAD, CROWN STREET section reverts to normal service.

7th January 1940

Sunday Repairs to LNER Railway Bridge over Clarence Drive.
Arrangements for 12th November 1939 repeated.

14th January 1940

Sunday Repairs to LNER Railway Bridge over Clarence Drive.
Arrangements for 12th November 1939 repeated.

21st January 1940

Sunday Repairs to LNER Railway Bridge over Clarence Drive.
Arrangements for 12th November 1939 repeated.

3rd February 1940

Due to staff shortages, Saturdays Timetables cancelled on all services and Weekdays Timetables operate on Saturdays until further notice.

11th February 1940

Service re-extended from Ferguslie Mills to Elderslie.
Line between Ferguslie Mills and Elderslie Depot reopened to Passenger Traffic.
The following Service Alterations take place:

Green Service 15 Weekdays: FERGUSLIE MILLS or CROOKSTON & SHETTLESTON or AIRDRIE extended to become
ELDERSLIE or CROOKSTON & SHETTLESTON or AIRDRIE from Ferguslie east of Fulbar Road via Ferguslie and former route;

Saturdays: FERGUSLIE MILLS or CROOKSTON & BAILLIESTON or AIRDRIE extended to become
ELDERSLIE or CROOKSTON & BAILLIESTON or AIRDRIE;

Sundays: FERGUSLIE MILLS & AIRDRIE extended to become
ELDERSLIE & AIRDRIE;

Green Service 15A Weekdays and Saturdays: FERGUSLIE MILLS or CROOKSTON & TOLLCROSS or UDDINGSTON extended to become
ELDERSLIE or CROOKSTON & TOLLCROSS or UDDINGSTON from Ferguslie east of Fulbar Road via Ferguslie and former route;

Sundays: FERGUSLIE MILLS & UDDINGSTON extended to become
ELDERSLIE & UDDINGSTON;

Cars show "15" on journeys to Crookston or Elderslie;
Cars proceeding from and to ELDERSLIE DEPOT again convey passengers between Elderslie Depot and Elderslie.
Regular cars resume operation on Main Road Elderslie and Ferguslie west of Thomas Street.

Line Opened at Carnwadric in Boydstone Road between Thornliebank Road and Boydstone Road at Cruachan Street.
CARNWADRIC terminus opened for shortworking cars.
The following Service Alteration takes place:

Red Service 8/8A SPRINGBURN & POLLOKSHAWS WEST or ROUKEN GLEN Circle via THORNLIEBANK shortworkings diverted to new Carnwadric terminus to become
SPRINGBURN & CARNWADRIC or ROUKEN GLEN Circle via THORNLIEBANK.

Extension of Green Car Service from Whiteinch to Scotstoun.
The following Service Alteration takes place:

Green Service 16 Weekdays: KEPPOCHHILL ROAD & WHITEINCH or SCOTSTOUN via NORTH STREET altered to become
KEPPOCHHILL ROAD & SCOTSTOUN via NORTH STREET;

Saturdays and Sundays: KEPPOCHHILL ROAD & WHITEINCH via NORTH STREET extended to become
KEPPOCHHILL ROAD & SCOTSTOUN via NORTH STREET via former route to Dumbarton Road then via Dumbarton Road, Balmoral Street to Balmoral Street north end.

12th February 1940

Second World War. Black-out Timetables introduced on all Services.
Extended Running Times allowed after 1830 hrs.
The following Service Alterations take place:

Blue Service [Paisley Local] BRAIDS ROAD & PAISLEY CROSS and
Blue Service [Paisley Local] GLENFIELD or POTTERHILL & RENFREW FERRY
combined to become
Blue Service [Paisley Local] POTTERHILL & RENFREW FERRY via former route.

1st March 1940

Kirkintilloch Road north of Colston Road reopened to trams.
Line Opened in Kenmure Avenue from Kirkintilloch Road to Kenmure Drive.
BISHOPBRIGGS terminus moved from Kirkintilloch Road north of Springfield Road to Kenmure Avenue east end.

Red Service 8/8A SPRINGBURN & CARNWADRIC or ROUKEN GLEN Circle via THORNLIEBANK
re-extended to become BISHOPBRIGGS or SPRINGBURN & CARNWADRIC or ROUKEN GLEN Circle via THORNLIEBANK from Kenmure Avenue east end via Kenmure Avenue, Kirkintilloch Road and former route;

Motorbus Shuttle Service: BISHOPBRIGGS & SPRINGBURN withdrawn.
Kirkintilloch Road north of Kenmure Avenue **closed** to trams.

3rd March 1940
Sunday Repairs to LNER Railway Bridge over Clarence Drive.
Arrangements for 12th November 1939 repeated.

31st March 1940
Sunday Repairs to LNER Railway Bridge over Clarence Drive.
Arrangements for 12th November 1939 repeated.

7th April 1940
Sunday Repairs to LNER Railway Bridge over Clarence Drive.
Arrangements for 12th November 1939 repeated.

4th May 1940
Staffing problems eased. Normal Saturdays Timetables restored on all services.

5th May 1940
Sunday Repairs to LNER Railway Bridge over Clarence Drive.
Arrangements for 12th November 1939 repeated.

23rd June 1940
The following Service Alterations take place:
Blue Service 4A SPRINGBURN & LINTHOUSE, SHIELDHALL or RENFREW CROSS via POSSILPARK, LORNE STREET; and
Blue Service 4B LAMBHILL & LINTHOUSE, SHIELDHALL or RENFREW CROSS via LORNE STREET both diverted between Paisley Road Toll and Lorne School to operate via Govan Road (Old Govan Road) instead of via Paisley Road West and Lorne Street;
Green Service 21 CROOKSTON & PROVANMILL via RENFIELD STREET diverted to become
HILLINGTON ROAD & PROVANMILL via LORNE STREET, RENFIELD STREET from Renfrew Road at Hillington Road via Renfrew Road, Govan Road, Lorne Street, Paisley Road West, Paisley Road Toll and former route.

A programme of replacing the ex-Paisley Single-Deckers on Service 20 with cut-down Semi-High Speed Standards was thwarted by the Second World War when only five had been completed. 975 is at Duntocher terminus early in the War. Note the absence of any Service number and the use of a destination slipboard.
(Struan JT Robertson)

14th July 1940

The following Service Alteration takes place:

Red Service 11 RUCHILL & SINCLAIR DRIVE via GARSCUBE ROAD diverted to become GAIRBRAID AVENUE & SINCLAIR DRIVE via GARSCUBE ROAD from Gairbraid Avenue east end via Gairbraid Avenue, Maryhill Road and former route.

19th January 1941

RADNOR PARK crossover replaced by PARKHALL crossover

The following Service Alteration takes place:

Red Service 20 Weekdays and Saturdays: CLYDEBANK & RADNOR PARK or DUNTOCHER altered to become CLYDEBANK & PARKHALL or DUNTOCHER;

PARKHALL terminus on Kilbowie Road just south of Great Western Road;

Sundays: CLYDEBANK & DUNTOCHER unaltered.

During 1941

The following Service Alteration takes place:

Blue Service 4 KEPPOCHHILL ROAD & SHIELDHALL or RENFREW AERODROME cut back to become KEPPOCHHILL ROAD & SHIELDHALL or RENFREW SOUTH via former route to Paisley Rd Renfrew at Porterfield Rd.

14th March 1941

Clydeside Blitz.

Two nights, Thursday 13/Friday 14 March and Friday 14/Saturday 15 March, of sustained bombing wrought considerable damage upon the Burgh of Clydebank and on parts of the City of Glasgow, particularly the Tradeston area as well as Partick, Maryhill, Townhead, Parkhead. 59 trams were damaged to varying degrees by blast or debris but only one car was totally destroyed.

The following interruptions to Services occurred:

Green Service 1 KNIGHTSWOOD or KELVINSIDE & DENNISTOUN, SHETTLESTON, BAILLIESTON or AIRDRIE service suspended;

Green Service 1A DALMUIR WEST, SCOTSTOUN WEST or ANNIESLAND & PARKHEAD or SPRINGFIELD ROAD service suspended, later operating SCOTSTOUN WEST & PARKHEAD;

Blue Service 4 KEPPOCHHILL ROAD & SHIELDHALL or RENFREW SOUTH service restricted to KEPPOCHHILL ROAD & ST VINCENT STREET;

Blue Service 4A SPRINGBURN & LINTHOUSE or RENFREW CROSS via POSSILPARK service restricted to SPRINGBURN & ST VINCENT STREET via POSSILPARK;

Blue Service 4B LAMBHILL & LINTHOUSE or RENFREW CROSS service restricted to LAMBHILL & ST VINCENT STREET;

Blue Service 6 SCOTSTOUN & ALEXANDRA PARK or RIDDRIE diverted from Sauchiehall Street via Renfield Street, St Vincent Street, St Vincent Place, George Square west and north, George Street, Duke Street, Cumbernauld Road and normal route;

Yellow Service 7 MILLERSTON or RIDDRIE & BELLAHOUSTON via BRIDGETON CROSS service restricted to MILLERSTON & BRIDGE STREET via BRIDGETON CROSS;

Red Services 8/8A BISHOPBRIGGS or SPRINGBURN & CARNWADRIC or ROUKEN GLEN Circle via THORNLIEBANK and MILLERSTON or RIDDRIE & GIFFNOCK or ROUKEN GLEN Circle via GIFFNOCK restricted as follows: BISHOPBRIGGS & MILLERSTON; MILLERSTON or RIDDRIE & GIFFNOCK or ROUKEN GLEN Circle via GIFFNOCK diverted from Alexandra Park via Cumbernauld Road, Duke Street, George Street, George Square north and west, St Vincent Place, St Vincent Street, Hope Street, Oswald Street, George V. Bridge, Commerce Street, Kingston Street, Bridge Street and normal route; and ST VINCENT STREET & POLLOKSHAWS WEST or ROUKEN GLEN Circle via THORNLIEBANK;

Red Service 9 DALMUIR WEST or SCOTSTOUN & LONDON ROAD or AUCHENSHUGGLE service restricted to SCOTSTOUN WEST & LONDON ROAD or AUCHENSHUGGLE;

Red Service 9A DALMUIR WEST, CLYDEBANK or SCOTSTOUN & BURNSIDE via DALMARNOCK restricted to SCOTSTOUN WEST or SCOTSTOUN & BURNSIDE via DALMARNOCK;

Red Service 9B DALMUIR WEST, CLYDEBANK or SCOTSTOUN & DALMARNOCK, RUTHERGLEN or CAMBUSLANG restricted to SCOTSTOUN WEST or SCOTSTOUN & DALMARNOCK, RUTHERGLEN or CAMBUSLANG;

Blue Service 14 MILNGAVIE or MARYHILL & SHAWLANDS, PAISLEY CROSS or RENFREW FERRY via ST GEORGE'S CROSS, GORBALS, BARRHEAD service restricted to MILNGAVIE or MARYHILL & SHAWLANDS or BARRHEAD via ST GEORGE'S CROSS, GORBALS (due to power failure in Paisley);

Green Service 15 ELDERSLIE or CROOKSTON & SHETTLESTON, BAILLIESTON or AIRDRIE service suspended;

Green Service 15A ELDERSLIE or PAISLEY CROSS & TOLLCROSS or UDDINGSTON service suspended;

Red Service 17 ANNIESLAND & CAMBUSLANG via BOTHWELL STREET service restricted to PARTICK & CAMBUSLANG via BOTHWELL STREET;

Red Service 20 CLYDEBANK & PARKHALL or DUNTOCHER service suspended;

Green Service 21 HILLINGTON ROAD & PROVANMILL via LORNE STREET, RENFIELD STREET service restricted to CASTLE STREET & PROVANMILL;
Blue Service [Paisley Local] POTTERHILL & RENFREW FERRY service suspended;
Green Service [Paisley Local] PAISLEY WEST or PAISLEY CROSS & HAWKHEAD ROAD service suspended.

15th March 1941

Clydeside Blitz.

The following interruptions to Services occurred:
Green Service 1 KNIGHTSWOOD or KELVINSIDE & DENNISTOUN, SHETTLESTON, BAILLIESTON or AIRDRIE normal service resumes;
Green Service 1A SCOTSTOUN WEST & PARKHEAD (and later SPRINGFIELD ROAD) only;
Blue Service 4 KEPPOCHHILL ROAD & ST VINCENT STREET only;
Blue Service 4A SPRINGBURN & ST VINCENT STREET via POSSILPARK only;
Blue Service 4B LAMBHILL & ST VINCENT STREET only;
Blue Service 6 SCOTSTOUN WEST or SCOTSTOUN & ALEXANDRA PARK or RIDDRIE only;
Yellow Service 7 MILLERSTON or RIDDRIE & BRIDGE STREET via BRIDGETON CROSS only;
Red Service 9 SCOTSTOUN WEST & LONDON ROAD or AUCHENSHUGGLE only;
Red Service 9A SCOTSTOUN WEST or SCOTSTOUN & BURNSIDE via DALMARNOCK only;
Red Service 9B SCOTSTOUN WEST or SCOTSTOUN & DALMARNOCK, RUTHERGLEN or CAMBUSLANG only;
Blue Service 14 MILNGAVIE or MARYHILL & SHAWLANDS or BARRHEAD via GORBALS only;
Green Service 15 CROOKSTON & CORKERHILL ROAD and ANDERSTON CROSS & AIRDRIE
Green Service 15A ANDERSTON CROSS & UDDINGSTON only;
Red Service 20 CLYDEBANK & PARKHALL or DUNTOCHER service suspended:
Green Service 21 BRIDGE STREET & PROVANMILL via RENFIELD STREET only;
Blue Service [Paisley Local] POTTERHILL & RENFREW FERRY service suspended;
Green Service [Paisley Local] PAISLEY WEST or PAISLEY CROSS & HAWKHEAD ROAD service suspended.

17th March 1941

Clydeside Blitz.

Power Restored in Paisley but street blockages still in Burgh of Clydebank, in Tradeston and in south Paisley.
The following interruptions to Services occurred:
Green Service 1A SCOTSTOUN WEST & PARKHEAD or SPRINGFIELD ROAD only;
Services 4, 4A, 4B, 6, 7, 9, 9A, 9B, 14, 20 and 21 restricted as before;
Green Service 15 CROOKSTON & SHETTLESTON or AIRDRIE via POLLOKSHIELDS and
Green Service 15A CROOKSTON & TOLLCROSS or UDDINGSTON via POLLOKSHIELDS both diverted between Paisley Road West at Corkerhill Road and Bridge Street via Corkerhill Road, Private Track on north side of Mosspark Boulevard, Dumbreck Road, Nithsdale Road, St Andrew's Drive, Albert Drive, Kenmure Street, Maxwell Road, Eglinton Toll, Eglinton Street, Bridge Street;
Blue Service [Paisley Local] POTTERHILL & RENFREW FERRY restricted to PAISLEY CROSS & RENFREW FERRY only;
Green Service [Paisley Local] operating ELDERSLIE & HAWKHEAD ROAD.

Some idea of the devastation, including tram tracks twisted skywards, that caused the prolonged suspension of Service 20 can be seen in this view of Kilbowie Road – completely unrecognisable today as all the property was razed to the ground.
(Strathclyde Regional Archives)

23rd March 1941
Clydeside Blitz.
Portion of Paisley Road West between Corkerhill Road and Paisley Road Toll reopened to traffic.
The following interruptions to Services occurred:
Services 4, 4A, 4B, 6, 7, 9, 9A, 9B, 14, 20, 21 and Blue Paisley Locals restricted as before;
Services 15 and 15A extended to ELDERSLIE and portions diverted at Corkerhill Road to run to and from PAISLEY ROAD TOLL via IBROX;
Green Service [Paisley Local] PAISLEY WEST or PAISLEY CROSS & HAWKHEAD ROAD resumes normal service.

28th March 1941
Clydeside Blitz.
Nelson Street, Morrison Street and Paisley Road reopened to traffic.
Blue Service 4 KEPPOCHHILL ROAD & SHIELDHALL or RENFREW SOUTH
Blue Service 4A SPRINGBURN & LINTHOUSE, SHIELDHALL or RENFREW CROSS via POSSILPARK
Blue Service 4B LAMBHILL & LINTHOUSE, SHIELDHALL or RENFREW CROSS
Yellow Service 7 MILLERSTON or RIDDRIE & BELLAHOUSTON via BRIDGETON CROSS
Green Service 15 ELDERSLIE or CROOKSTON & SHETTLESTON, BAILLIESTON or AIRDRIE
Green Service 15A ELDERSLIE or CROOKSTON & TOLLCROSS or UDDINGSTON
Green Service 21 HILLINGTON ROAD & PROVANMILL via LORNE STREET, RENFIELD STREET
all revert to normal service;
Services 1A, 6, 9A, 9B, 14, 20 and Blue Paisley Locals restricted as before.

April 1941
Clydeside Blitz.
Glasgow Road and Dumbarton Road Clydebank cleared for traffic.
Green Service 1A DALMUIR WEST, SCOTSTOUN WEST or ANNIESLAND & PARKHEAD or SPRINGFIELD ROAD
Blue Service 6 DALMUIR WEST or SCOTSTOUN & ALEXANDRA PARK or RIDDRIE
Red Service 9 DALMUIR WEST or SCOTSTOUN & LONDON ROAD or AUCHENSHUGGLE
Red Service 9A DALMUIR WEST, CLYDEBANK or SCOTSTOUN & BURNSIDE via DALMARNOCK
Red Service 9B DALMUIR WEST, CLYDEBANK or SCOTSTOUN & DALMARNOCK, RUTHERGLEN or CAMBUSLANG
all revert to normal service;
Neilston Road, Causeyside Street etc. Paisley cleared for traffic.
Blue Service 14 MILNGAVIE or MARYHILL & SHAWLANDS, PAISLEY CROSS or RENFREW FERRY via ST GEORGE'S CROSS, GORBALS, BARRHEAD
Blue Service [Paisley Local] POTTERHILL & RENFREW FERRY all revert to normal service;
Red Service 20 CLYDEBANK & PARKHALL or DUNTOCHER remains suspended.

4th May 1941
The following Service Alteration takes place:
Red Service 11 Summer Sundays: GAIRBRAID AVENUE & SINCLAIR DRIVE via GARSCUBE ROAD extended to become MARYHILL & SINCLAIR DRIVE via GARSCUBE ROAD;
Weekdays and Saturdays: GAIRBRAID AVENUE & SINCLAIR DRIVE via GARSCUBE ROAD unaltered.

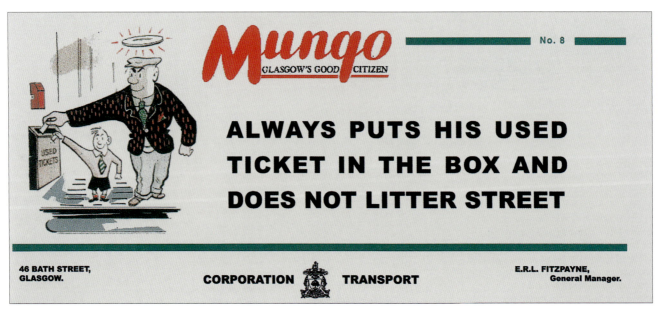

5th May 1941
Clydeside Blitz.
Kilbowie Road Clydebank cleared for traffic.
Red Service 20 CLYDEBANK & DUNTOCHER reintroduced on a restricted 15-minute frequency.

During 1941
Following Clydeside Blitz, allocation of Coronation Cars moved away from Govan Depot and from Partick Depot. (Depot buildings nearest to shipyards and dockland targets).

2nd June 1941
Clydeside Blitz.
Red Service 20 CLYDEBANK & PARKHALL or DUNTOCHER reverts to normal service.

June 1941
South Portland Street and Norfolk Street right-angled crossing lifted and replaced with plain rail for Norfolk Street cars.

24th August 1941
The following Service Alterations take place:
Red Service 13 Weekdays: MILNGAVIE, HILLFOOT or MARYHILL & MOUNT FLORIDA via ST GEORGE'S CROSS altered to become MILNGAVIE or MARYHILL & MOUNT FLORIDA via ST GEORGE'S CROSS;
Saturdays: MILNGAVIE, HILLFOOT or MARYHILL & MOUNT FLORIDA via ST GEORGE'S CROSS unaltered:
Sundays: MILNGAVIE & MOUNT FLORIDA via ST GEORGE'S CROSS unaltered;
Blue Service [Paisley Local] POTTERHILL & RENFREW FERRY extended to become
[Paisley Local] SPIERSBRIDGE & RENFREW FERRY from Spiersbridge Road north of Nitshill Road via Spiersbridge Road, Private Track on north side of Nitshill Road, Darnley, Private Track on north side of Parkhouse Road, Parkhouse, Darnley Road, Main Street Barrhead, Allan's Corner, Cross Arthurlie Street, Paisley Road Barrhead, Capelthill Road, Neilston Road and former route.

During the War, the Semi-High Speed Standard cars were not listed for repainting as they were not destined for long-term use. Most were Blue Cars and this view of 904 confirms that official policy was not always followed. This Car has been given the full paintshop treatment, rather than the "touch-up-and-varnish" that many got which, incidentally, prolonged the retention of earlier livery styles. It is seen here at Hillfoot.
(DLG Hunter, Courtesy AW Brotchie)

Like all good Citizens the Mungos have joined the Volunteer Air Force

APPLY:-
602 FIGHTER SQUADRON, 49 COPLAW STREET, S2
2602 L.A.A. SQUADRON
3602 FIGHTER CONTROL UNIT } R.A.F. STATION, BISHOPBRIGGS
101 RESERVE CENTRE

or

R.A.F. RECRUITING OFFICE, 38 SAUCHIEHALL STREET

2nd November 1941
Wartime Restrictions.
Last Cars on all Services from the City Centre timed for 2300 hrs instead of 2345.

During 1942
Programme of repainting all Green and White Cars into Standard Green livery completed. Remaining Yellow, Blue and Red Cars, where possible, operated on correct routes but increasing dependence on Service Numbers heralds eventual end of Route Colour system.

3rd May 1942
The following Service Alterations take place:
Blue Service 10 Sundays: ST VINCENT STREET & OATLANDS via CROWN STREET (Part Day) section altered to become
ANDERSTON CROSS & OATLANDS via CROWN STREET (Part Day) from Stobcross Street at Warroch Street via Stobcross Street, Argyle Street and former route,
KIRKLEE & RUTHERGLEN via PARK ROAD, CROWN STREET section unaltered;
Weekdays: KIRKLEE & OATLANDS or RUTHERGLEN via PARK ROAD, CROWN STREET split to become
KIRKLEE & RUTHERGLEN via PARK ROAD, CROWN STREET and
ANDERSTON CROSS & OATLANDS via CROWN STREET;
Saturdays: KIRKLEE & OATLANDS or RUTHERGLEN via PARK ROAD, CROWN STREET and
PARTICK & OATLANDS or RUTHERGLEN via CROWN STREET sections unaltered.
Closure of Kelvinside Avenue.
White Service 18 Weekdays and Saturdays: SPRINGBURN, RUCHILL or KELVINSIDE AVENUE & RUTHERGLEN or BURNSIDE via BILSLAND DRIVE, RUTHERGLEN BRIDGE altered to become
SPRINGBURN & BURNSIDE via BILSLAND DRIVE, RUTHERGLEN BRIDGE;
Sundays: SPRINGBURN & BURNSIDE via BILSLAND DRIVE, RUTHERGLEN BRIDGE unaltered.
Kelvinside Avenue **closed** to trams.
Blue Service [Paisley Local] SPIERSBRIDGE & RENFREW FERRY altered to become
[Paisley Local] SPIERSBRIDGE, GLENFIELD or POTTERHILL & RENFREW FERRY via former route.

4th May 1942
Wartime Restrictions.
Last Cars on all Services from City Centre restored to 2345, but at half normal service frequency after 2300.
Adjustments to services to Airdrie.
The following Service Alterations take place:

The ex-Paisley "Standard" cars were scattered around several Depots. Maryhill had two and here is their 1059 on Service 18 passing Central Station in 1942. By then the car had been repainted Standard "Bus" Green, having formerly been a White car. It was common for cars no longer carrying route colours to continue on their original Services.
(Courtesy, National Tramway Museum Archive)

Green Service 1 KNIGHTSWOOD or KELVINSIDE & DENNISTOUN, SHETTLESTON, BAILLIESTON, BARGEDDIE or AIRDRIE part extended to become
KNIGHTSWOOD or KELVINSIDE & DENNISTOUN or AIRDRIE;
Green Service 15 ELDERSLIE or CROOKSTON & SHETTLESTON, BAILLIESTON or AIRDRIE cut back to become
ELDERSLIE or CROOKSTON & SHETTLESTON via former route to Shettleston Road at Gartocher Road.

16th September 1942

Siding in Kessington Road to Bearsden Substation **closed** to trams.

1st November 1942

Wartime Restrictions. Last Cars on all Services from the City Centre again timed for 2300hrs. All Sunday Corporation Motorbus Services withdrawn and replaced by temporary Shuttle Services between key outlying areas and the nearest tram routes.

14th March 1943

Siding from Main Street Baillieston to Baillieston Substation **closed** to trams.
Junction to disused Aurs Road Depot access, Barrhead removed.

2nd May 1943

Various adjustments to Maryhill, Clarkston and Govan Services.
The following Service Alterations take place:
Red Service 11 MARYHILL or GAIRBRAID AVENUE & SINCLAIR DRIVE via GARSCUBE ROAD extended and rerouted to become
MILNGAVIE & SINCLAIR DRIVE via ST GEORGE'S CROSS from Main Street Milngavie at Park Road via Main Street Milngavie, Milngavie Road, Maryhill Road, Queen's Cross, Maryhill Road, St George's Cross, New City Road, Cowcaddens and former route;
Red Service 13 MILNGAVIE, HILLFOOT or MARYHILL & MOUNT FLORIDA via ST GEORGE'S CROSS altered to become
GAIRBRAID AVENUE & MOUNT FLORIDA or CLARKSTON via ST GEORGE'S CROSS from Gairbraid Avenue east end via Gairbraid Avenue, Maryhill Road and former route to Cathcart Road then via Cathcart Road, Holmlea Road, Clarkston Road, Busby Road, Mearns Road to Mearns Road west end;
Blue Service 14 MILNGAVIE or MARYHILL & SHAWLANDS, PAISLEY CROSS or RENFREW FERRY via ST GEORGE'S CROSS, GORBALS, BARRHEAD rerouted to become
MILNGAVIE or MARYHILL & SHAWLANDS, PAISLEY CROSS or RENFREW FERRY via GARSCUBE ROAD, GORBALS, BARRHEAD via former route to Queen's Cross then via Garscube Road, Cowcaddens and then former route;
White Service 19 SPRINGBURN & MOUNT FLORIDA or NETHERLEE via GLASGOW CROSS cut back to become SPRINGBURN & MOUNT FLORIDA via GLASGOW CROSS;
Yellow Service 12 MOUNT FLORIDA & PAISLEY ROAD TOLL via SHIELDS ROAD extended to become
MOUNT FLORIDA & LINTHOUSE via SHIELDS ROAD via former route to Paisley Road Toll then via Paisley Road West, Lorne Street, Govan Road, Holmfauld Road to Holmfauld Road south end;
Green Service 15 ELDERSLIE or CROOKSTON & SHETTLESTON extended to become
ELDERSLIE or CROOKSTON & GARROWHILL via former route to Shettleston Road at Gartocher Road then via Glasgow Road to Glasgow Road at Maxwell Avenue.
The following Operational Alteration takes place:
Operation of **Yellow Service 12** part transferred from Langside Depot to Govan Depot.
Yellow Service 12 MOUNT FLORIDA & LINTHOUSE via SHIELDS ROAD adjusted accordingly.

30th May 1943

Reintroduction of Mosspark circular service.

The southern termini of Service 19 were altered from time to time but Springburn always remained the northern terminus. Viewed from Balgray Hill, Springburn, when Service 19 was still operated with White cars, Car 833 is seen about to turn into Elmvale Street..
(Commercial Postcard, BJ Cross Collection)

The following Service Alteration takes place:
Service 3 UNIVERSITY & DUMBRECK or MOSSPARK altered to become
UNIVERSITY or ST VINCENT STREET & MOSSPARK Circle via POLLOKSHIELDS with through Circle Cars to and from **Service 3A**;

The following Service commences:
Service 3A UNIVERSITY or ST VINCENT STREET & MOSSPARK Circle via PAISLEY ROAD from University Avenue at Kelvin Way via University Avenue, Gibson Street, Eldon Street, Woodlands Road, St George's Road, Charing Cross, Sauchiehall Street, Renfield Street, Union Street, Jamaica Street, Glasgow Bridge, Bridge Street, Nelson Street, Morrison Street, Paisley Road, Paisley Road Toll, Paisley Road West, Corkerhill Road, with through Circle Cars to and from **Service 3**.

6th June 1943

The following Service Alteration takes place:
Service 21 HILLINGTON ROAD & PROVANMILL via LORNE STREET, RENFIELD STREET extended to become
RENFREW CROSS & PROVANMILL via LORNE STREET, RENFIELD STREET from Renfrew Cross via High Street Renfrew, Glasgow Road Renfrew, Renfrew Road and former route.

19th July 1943

The following Service Alteration takes place:
Service 19 Weekdays and Saturdays: SPRINGBURN & MOUNT FLORIDA via GLASGOW CROSS extended to become SPRINGBURN & NETHERLEE via GLASGOW CROSS via former route to Mount Florida then via Cathcart Road, Holmlea Road, Clarkston Road to Clarkston Road at Ormonde Drive;
Sundays: SPRINGBURN & MOUNT FLORIDA via GLASGOW CROSS unaltered.

Facing Page: Service 29 introduced in August 1943 as a replacement for the former Green Service 15A. Car 389 is loading at the Uddingston terminus. It was common for the "via" screens to be left blank around this time.
(David L Thomson Collection)

15th August 1943

Major alterations to services to cut the longer routes into more operationally manageable units particularly in view of Wartime conditions.

To make clearer use of Service Numbers and to depart from dependence on Route Colours, principal Services carrying suffix letters renumbered.

The following Service Alterations take place:

Service 1 KNIGHTSWOOD or KELVINSIDE & DENNISTOUN or AIRDRIE withdrawn

Service 1A DALMUIR WEST, SCOTSTOUN WEST or ANNIESLAND & PARKHEAD or SPRINGFIELD ROAD withdrawn

and replaced by the following three new **Services 1, 23 and 30** to become

Service 1 DALMUIR WEST or ANNIESLAND & DENNISTOUN via route of former **Service 1A** to Duke Street then Carntyne Road to Carntyne Road west end;

Service 23 KELVINGROVE & GARROWHILL or AIRDRIE from Radnor Street via Radnor Street, Sauchiehall Street, Charing Cross, Sauchiehall Street, Renfield Street, St Vincent Street, St Vincent Place, George Square west and north, George Street, Duke Street, Shettleston Road, Shettleston Sheddings, Shettleston Road, Glasgow Road, Main Street Baillieston, Private Track on south side of Coatbridge Road, Private Track on south side of Glasgow Road Coatbridge, Langloan, Bank Street Coatbridge, Main Street Coatbridge, Deedes Street, Alexander Street Airdrie, Stirling Street, Airdrie New Cross, Graham Street, Clark Street, Forrest Street to Forrest Street west end beyond Carlisle Road;

Service 30 KNIGHTSWOOD or KELVINSIDE & SPRINGFIELD ROAD from Great Western Road west of Knightswood Cross via Great Western Road and route of former **Service 1A**.

Service 4 KEPPOCHHILL ROAD & SHIELDHALL or RENFREW SOUTH altered to become
KEPPOCHHILL ROAD & RENFREW SOUTH.

Service 4A SPRINGBURN & LINTHOUSE, SHIELDHALL or RENFREW CROSS via POSSILPARK altered and renumbered to become

Service 27 SPRINGBURN & SHIELDHALL or RENFREW CROSS via POSSILPARK.

Service 4B LAMBHILL & LINTHOUSE, SHIELDHALL or RENFREW CROSS altered and renumbered to become

Service 31 LAMBHILL & HILLINGTON ROAD or RENFREW CROSS.

Service 5A ANNIESLAND & LANGSIDE via HYNDLAND renumbered to become

Service 24 ANNIESLAND & LANGSIDE via HYNDLAND via route of former **Service 5A**.

Service 5 KIRKLEE Circle via BOTANIC GARDENS or Circle via HYNDLAND & CLARKSTON.
Journeys to Kirklee via Hyndland renumbered 5A. All Cars show "5" on journeys to Clarkston

Service 8/8A/8B renumbered as **Services 8** and **25** to become

Service 8 MILLERSTON or RIDDRIE & MERRYLEE, GIFFNOCK or ROUKEN GLEN Circle via GIFFNOCK;
Circle Cars return as **Service 25** to SPRINGBURN or BISHOPBRIGGS.

117

Service 25 BISHOPBRIGGS or SPRINGBURN & CARNWADRIC or ROUKEN GLEN Circle via THORNLIEBANK; Circle Cars return as **Service 8** to RIDDRIE or MILLERSTON.

Service 9A DALMUIR WEST, CLYDEBANK or SCOTSTOUN & BURNSIDE via DALMARNOCK and

Service 9B DALMUIR WEST, CLYDEBANK or SCOTSTOUN & DALMARNOCK, RUTHERGLEN or CAMBUSLANG integrated and renumbered to become

Service 26 DALMUIR WEST, CLYDEBANK or SCOTSTOUN & RUTHERGLEN or BURNSIDE via DALMARNOCK;

Service 14 MILNGAVIE or MARYHILL & SHAWLANDS, PAISLEY CROSS or RENFREW FERRY via GARSCUBE ROAD, GORBALS, BARRHEAD split at Spiersbridge and part replaced by new **Service 28**, to become

Service 14 MILNGAVIE or MARYHILL & SHAWLANDS or SPIERSBRIDGE via GARSCUBE ROAD, GORBALS via former route to Spiersbridge Road north of Nitshill Road; and

Service 28 SPIERSBRIDGE & RENFREW FERRY from Spiersbridge Road north of Nitshill Road via Private Track on north side of Nitshill Road, Darnley, Private Track on north side of Parkhouse Road, Parkhouse, Darnley Road, Main Street Barrhead, Allan's Corner, Cross Arthurlie Street, Paisley Road Barrhead, Caplethill Road, Neilston Road, Causeyside Street, St Mirren Street, Paisley Cross, Gilmour Street, County Square, Gilmour Street, Old Sneddon Street, Renfrew Road Paisley, Paisley Road Renfrew, Hairst Street, Canal Street, Ferry Road to Ferry Road at London Street

Service [Paisley Local] SPIERSBRIDGE, GLENFIELD or POTTERHILL & RENFREW FERRY cut back, altered and split to become two services

Service [Paisley Local] GLENFIELD & RENFREW FERRY from Caplethill Road east of Glenfield Road via Caplethill Road, Neilston Road, Causeyside, St Mirren Street, Paisley Cross, Gilmour Street, County Square, Gilmour Street, Old Sneddon Street, Weir Street, Renfrew Road Paisley, Paisley Road Renfrew, Hairst Street Renfrew, Renfrew Cross, Canal Street, Ferry Road to Ferry Road south of London Street; and

Service [Paisley Local] BRAIDS ROAD & PAISLEY CROSS from Neilston Road at Braids Road via Neilston Road, Causeyside, St Mirren Street, Paisley Cross, Gilmour Street to County Square.

ELDERSLIE crossover relocated on Ferguslie from east of Fulbar Road to west of Fulbar Road.

Service 15 ELDERSLIE or CROOKSTON & GARROWHILL split in City Centre and part replaced by new **Services 21, 22** and **32** to become

Service 15 ANDERSTON CROSS & BAILLIESTON or AIRDRIE from Stobcross Street at Warroch Street via Stobcross Street, Argyle Street, Trongate, Glasgow Cross, Gallowgate, Parkhead Cross, Westmuir Street, Shettleston Sheddings, Shettleston Road, Glasgow Road Baillieston, Main Street Baillieston, Private Track on south side of Coatbridge Road, Private Track on south side of Glasgow Road Coatbridge, Langloan, Bank Street Coatbridge, Main Street Coatbridge, Deedes Street, Alexander Street Airdrie, Stirling Street, Airdrie Cross, Graham Street, Clark Street, Forrest Street to Forrest Street west end beyond Carlisle Road.

Service 15A ELDERSLIE or CROOKSTON & TOLLCROSS or UDDINGSTON split in City Centre and replaced by new **Services 21, 22, 29** and **32**.

Service 21 RENFREW CROSS & PROVANMILL via LORNE STREET, RENFIELD STREET diverted and renumbered to become

Service 32 ELDERSLIE & PROVANMILL via RENFIELD STREET from Ferguslie west of Fulbar Road via Ferguslie, Broomlands Street, West End Cross, Wellmeadow Street, High Street Paisley, Paisley Cross, St James Bridge, Smithhills, Gauze Street, Glasgow Road Paisley, Paisley Road West, Paisley Road Toll, Paisley Road, Morrison Street, Nelson Street, Bridge Street, Glasgow Bridge, Jamaica Street, Union Street, Renfield Street, Sauchiehall Street, Parliamentary Road, Castle Street, Garngad Road to Garngad Road east of Provanmill Road.

The following new Services commence:

Service 21 ELDERSLIE & ANNIESLAND via BOTHWELL STREET from Ferguslie west of Fulbar Road via Ferguslie, Broomlands Street, West End Cross, Wellmeadow Street, High Street Paisley, Paisley Cross, St James Bridge, Smithhills, Gauze Street, Glasgow Road Paisley, Paisley Road West, Paisley Road Toll, Paisley Road, Morrison Street, Nelson Street, Commerce Street, George V. Bridge, Oswald Street, Hope Street, Bothwell Street, St Vincent Street, Argyle Street, Dumbarton Road, Crow Road, Broomhill Cross, Crow Road to Crow Road at Anniesland Cross;

Service 22 CROOKSTON & ST VINCENT STREET from Crookston Road north end via Crookston Road, Paisley Road West, Paisley Road Toll, Paisley Road, Morrison Street, Nelson Street, Commerce Street, George V. Bridge, Oswald Street, Hope Street, St Vincent Street to St Vincent Street at Wellington Street;

Service 29 ANDERSTON CROSS & TOLLCROSS or UDDINGSTON from Stobcross Street at Warroch Street via Stobcross Street, Argyle Street, Trongate, Glasgow Cross Gallowgate, Parkhead Cross, Tollcross Road, Hamilton Road, Glasgow Road Uddingston, Main Street Uddingston to Main Street Uddingston north of Bellshill Road.

The following Service Alteration takes place:

Service 17 ANNIESLAND & CAMBUSLANG via BOTHWELL STREET altered to become ANDERSTON CROSS & CAMBUSLANG from Stobcross Street at Warroch Street via Stobcross Street, Argyle Street and former route.

Résumé

15th August 1943

The following Tram Services operating:

1	DALMUIR WEST or ANNIESLAND & DENNISTOUN
2	PROVANMILL or GARNGAD & POLMADIE via GLASGOW CROSS
3	UNIVERSITY or ST VINCENT STREET & MOSSPARK Circle via POLLOKSHIELDS
	Circle Cars return as Service 3A
3A	UNIVERSITY or ST VINCENT STREET & MOSSPARK Circle via PAISLEY ROAD
	Circle Cars return as Service 3
4	KEPPOCHHILL ROAD & RENFREW SOUTH
5	KIRKLEE Circle via BOTANIC GARDENS & CLARKSTON
	Circle Cars return as Service 5A route (All Cars show "5" on journeys to Clarkston.)
5A	KIRKLEE Circle via HYNDLAND & CLARKSTON
	Circle Cars return as Service 5 route (All Cars show "5" on journeys to Clarkston).
6	DALMUIR WEST or SCOTSTOUN & ALEXANDRA PARK or RIDDRIE
7	MILLERSTON or RIDDRIE & BELLAHOUSTON via BRIDGETON CROSS
8	MILLERSTON or RIDDRIE & GIFFNOCK or ROUKEN GLEN Circle via GIFFNOCK
	Circle Cars return as Service 25 to SPRINGBURN or BISHOPBRIGGS
9	DALMUIR WEST or SCOTSTOUN & LONDON ROAD or AUCHENSHUGGLE
10	KIRKLEE & OATLANDS or RUTHERGLEN via PARK ROAD, CROWN STREET
	PARTICK or ANDERSTON CROSS & OATLANDS or RUTHERGLEN via CROWN STREET
11	MILNGAVIE & SINCLAIR DRIVE via ST GEORGE'S CROSS
12	MOUNT FLORIDA & LINTHOUSE via SHIELDS ROAD
13	GAIRBRAID AVENUE & MOUNT FLORIDA or CLARKSTON via ST GEORGE'S CROSS
14	MILNGAVIE or MARYHILL & SHAWLANDS or SPIERSBRIDGE via GARSCUBE ROAD, GORBALS
15	ANDERSTON CROSS & BAILLIESTON or AIRDRIE
16	KEPPOCHHILL ROAD & SCOTSTOUN via NORTH STREET
17	ANDERSTON CROSS & CAMBUSLANG
18	SPRINGBURN & BURNSIDE via BILSLAND DRIVE, RUTHERGLEN BRIDGE
19	SPRINGBURN & MOUNT FLORIDA or NETHERLEE via GLASGOW CROSS
20	[Single Deck Cars] CLYDEBANK & PARKHALL or DUNTOCHER
21	ELDERSLIE & ANNIESLAND via BOTHWELL STREET
22	CROOKSTON & ST VINCENT STREET
23	KELVINGROVE & GARROWHILL or AIRDRIE
24	ANNIESLAND & LANGSIDE via HYNDLAND
25	BISHOPBRIGGS or SPRINGBURN & CARNWADRIC or ROUKEN GLEN Circle via THORNLIEBANK.
	Circle Cars return as Service 8 to RIDDRIE or MILLERSTON
26	DALMUIR WEST, CLYDEBANK or SCOTSTOUN & RUTHERGLEN or BURNSIDE via DALMARNOCK
27	SPRINGBURN & SHIELDHALL or RENFREW CROSS via POSSILPARK
28	SPIERSBRIDGE & RENFREW FERRY via PAISLEY CROSS
29	ANDERSTON CROSS & TOLLCROSS or UDDINGSTON
30	KNIGHTSWOOD or KELVINSIDE & SPRINGFIELD ROAD
31	LAMBHILL & HILLINGTON ROAD or RENFREW CROSS
32	ELDERSLIE & PROVANMILL via RENFIELD STREET
-	[Airdrie Local] LANGLOAN & AIRDRIE
-	[Paisley Local] PAISLEY WEST or PAISLEY CROSS & HAWKHEAD ROAD (Part Day)
-	[Paisley Local] BRAIDS ROAD & PAISLEY CROSS (Part Day)
-	[Paisley Local] GLENFIELD & RENFREW FERRY (Part Day)

7th November 1943

The following alterations take place:

Service 13 GAIRBRAID AVENUE & MOUNT FLORIDA or CLARKSTON via ST GEORGE'S CROSS part extended to become
MARYHILL or GAIRBRAID AVENUE & MOUNT FLORIDA or CLARKSTON via ST GEORGE'S CROSS from Caldercuilt Road west end via Caldercuilt Road, Maryhill Road and former route.

Service 14 MILNGAVIE or MARYHILL & SHAWLANDS or SPIERSBRIDGE via GARSCUBE ROAD, GORBALS altered to become
MILNGAVIE, MARYHILL or GAIRBRAID AVENUE & SHAWLANDS or SPIERSBRIDGE via GARSCUBE ROAD, GORBALS;

Service 18 SPRINGBURN & BURNSIDE via BILSLAND DRIVE, RUTHERGLEN BRIDGE cut back to become
SPRINGBURN & RUTHERGLEN via BILSLAND DRIVE, RUTHERGLEN BRIDGE;

Service 3 Weekdays: UNIVERSITY or ST VINCENT STREET & MOSSPARK Circle via POLLOKSHIELDS altered to become UNIVERSITY & MOSSPARK Circle via POLLOKSHIELDS;

Saturdays and Sundays: UNIVERSITY & MOSSPARK Circle via POLLOKSHIELDS unaltered;

Service 3A Weekdays: UNIVERSITY or ST VINCENT STREET & MOSSPARK Circle via PAISLEY ROAD altered to become UNIVERSITY & MOSSPARK Circle via PAISLEY ROAD;

Saturdays and Sundays: UNIVERSITY & MOSSPARK Circle via PAISLEY ROAD unaltered.

5th December 1943

Circular Services via Mosspark withdrawn.
The following Service Alterations take place:

Service 3 UNIVERSITY or ST VINCENT STREET & MOSSPARK Circle via POLLOKSHIELDS altered to become UNIVERSITY & MOSSPARK via POLLOKSHIELDS;

Service 3A UNIVERSITY or ST VINCENT STREET & MOSSPARK Circle via PAISLEY ROAD withdrawn.

The following Service commences:

Service 40 DUMBRECK & ST VINCENT STREET from Private Track east end via Private Track on north side of Mosspark Boulevard, Corkerhill Road, Paisley Road West, Paisley Road Toll, Paisley Road, Morrison Street, Nelson Street, Commerce Street, George V Bridge, Oswald Street, Hope Street, St Vincent Street.

2nd January 1944

Closure of Kirklee Road terminus.
KIRKLEE discontinued as terminal name.
The following Service Alterations take place:

Service 5 KIRKLEE Circle via BOTANIC GARDENS & CLARKSTON becomes
KELVINSIDE Circle via BOTANIC GARDENS & CLARKSTON (change in terminal name only).

Service 5A KIRKLEE Circle via HYNDLAND & CLARKSTON becomes
KELVINSIDE Circle via HYNDLAND & CLARKSTON (change in terminal name only)

Service 10 KIRKLEE & OATLANDS or RUTHERGLEN via PARK ROAD, CROWN STREET and
PARTICK or ANDERSTON CROSS & OATLANDS or RUTHERGLEN via CROWN STREET sections both extended to become KELVINSIDE Circle via PARK ROAD & OATLANDS or RUTHERGLEN via CROWN STREET from
Hyndland Road north end via Hyndland Road, Great Western Road and former route, with
through Circle Cars to and from new **Service 10A** at Kelvinside;

The following Service commences:

Service 10A KELVINSIDE Circle via CHURCH STREET & OATLANDS or RUTHERGLEN via CROWN STREET from Hyndland Road north end via Hyndland Road, Highburgh Road, Byres Road, Church Street, Dumbarton Road, Argyle Street, Sauchiehall Street, Charing Cross, Sauchiehall Street, Elmbank Street, Bothwell Street, Hope Street, Argyle Street, Trongate, Glasgow Cross, Saltmarket, Albert Bridge, Crown Street, Rutherglen Road, Glasgow Road Rutherglen, Main Street Rutherglen to Main Street Rutherglen west of Castle Street, with through circle cars to and from **Service 10** at Kelvinside.

Kirklee Road **closed** to trams.

During 1944

SPIERSBRIDGE crossover moved from Spiersbridge Road north of Nitshill Road to east end of
Private Track on north side of Nitshill Road.

Service 14 MILNGAVIE, MARYHILL or GAIRBRAID AVENUE & SHAWLANDS or SPIERSBRIDGE via GARSCUBE ROAD, GORBALS extended to east end of Private Track on north side of Nitshill Road;

Service 28 SPIERSBRIDGE & RENFREW FERRY via PAISLEY CROSS cut back to run from east end of
Private Track on north side of Nitshill Road and then former route.

During 1944

Loop in Cathcart Road at GOVANHILL turning point also called DIXON AVENUE removed.

5th March 1944

The following Service Alteration takes place:
Service 23 KELVINGROVE & GARROWHILL or AIRDRIE part extended to become
KELVINGROVE & BAILLIESTON or AIRDRIE.

30th April 1944

Further increase in frequency between Gairbraid Avenue and Maryhill.
Service 13 Weekdays and Saturdays: MARYHILL or GAIRBRAID AVENUE & MOUNT FLORIDA or CLARKSTON via ST GEORGE'S CROSS adjusted accordingly;
Sundays: MARYHILL or GAIRBRAID AVENUE & CLARKSTON via ST GEORGE'S CROSS unaltered.

1st May 1944

The following Service Alteration takes place:
Service 18 SPRINGBURN & RUTHERGLEN via BILSLAND DRIVE, RUTHERGLEN BRIDGE part extended to become SPRINGBURN & RUTHERGLEN or BURNSIDE via BILSLAND DRIVE, RUTHERGLEN BRIDGE via former route to Main Street Rutherglen then via Main Street Rutherglen, Stonelaw Road, Duke's Road to Duke's Road west end.

14th May 1944

Line opened in Maitland Street from Cowcaddens to Milton Street.
MAITLAND STREET available for cars turning short from the west and north.
Service trams extended over existing but unused section of London Road to Carmyle.
The following Service Alteration takes place:
Service 9 DALMUIR WEST or SCOTSTOUN & LONDON ROAD or AUCHENSHUGGLE extended to become
DALMUIR WEST or SCOTSTOUN & LONDON ROAD, AUCHENSHUGGLE or CARMYLE via existing route to Auchenshuggle then via London Road to London Road at Carmyle Avenue.

3rd September 1944

Further increase in frequency between Gairbraid Avenue and Maryhill.
Service 14 Weekdays and Saturdays: MILNGAVIE, MARYHILL or GAIRBRAID AVENUE & SHAWLANDS or SPIERSBRIDGE via GARSCUBE ROAD, GORBALS adjusted accordingly.

26th November 1944

The following Service commences:
Service 33 CIRCLE SPRINGBURN & CHARING CROSS operates both ways from Hawthorn Street east end:
Outer via Hawthorn Street, Springburn Road, Castle Street, Parliamentary Road, Sauchiehall Street, Charing Cross, St George's Road, St George's Cross, Maryhill Road, Queen's Cross, Maryhill Road, Bilsland Drive, Hawthorn Street;
Inner via Hawthorn Street, Bilsland Drive, Maryhill Road, Queen's Cross, Maryhill Road, St George's Cross, St George's Road, Charing Cross, Sauchiehall Street, Parliamentary Road, Castle Street, Springburn Road, Hawthorn Street.
The following Service Alteration takes place:
Service 12 MOUNT FLORIDA & LINTHOUSE via SHIELDS ROAD part cut back to become
MOUNT FLORIDA & PAISLEY ROAD TOLL or LINTHOUSE via SHIELDS ROAD.

Encapsulating the somewhat dreich days of immediate post-Second World War years but with a hopeful ray of sunshine striking through the buildings opposite, perhaps a harbinger of better times, the trams and the citizens intermingle in this city centre view of Renfield Street at the corner of Sauchiehall Street.
(David L Thomson Collection)

9th January 1945

Crossover in Shettleston Road at Gartocher Road closed.
SHETTLESTON terminus moved westwards to Shettleston Road at Muiryfauld Drive.
Service 15 ANDERSTON CROSS & AIRDRIE and
Service 23 KELVINGROVE & BAILLIESTON or AIRDRIE both adjusted accordingly.

12th February 1945

Single-line working on Duke Street east of Beardmore's Level Crossing and to Parkhead Cross.
Service 30 KNIGHTSWOOD or KELVINSIDE & SPRINGFIELD ROAD adjusted accordingly.

8th April 1945

The following Service Alterations take place:
Service 13 MARYHILL or GAIRBRAID AVENUE & CLARKSTON via ST GEORGE'S CROSS part cut back to become MARYHILL or GAIRBRAID AVENUE & MOUNT FLORIDA, NETHERLEE or CLARKSTON via ST GEORGE'S CROSS;
Service 17 Weekdays and Saturdays: ANDERSTON CROSS & CAMBUSLANG part cut back to become ANDERSTON CROSS & DALMARNOCK or CAMBUSLANG;
Sundays: ANDERSTON CROSS & CAMBUSLANG unaltered.
Service 30 KNIGHTSWOOD or KELVINSIDE & SPRINGFIELD ROAD part extended to become KNIGHTSWOOD or KELVINSIDE & SPRINGFIELD ROAD or CAMBUSLANG via former route to Springfield Road south end then via Springfield Road, Dalmarnock Road, Farme Cross, Cambuslang Road, Glasgow Road, Main Street Cambuslang to Main Street Cambuslang east end.

23rd April 1945

Second World War: Black-out restrictions lifted.

6th May 1945

The following Service Alteration takes place:
Service 40 DUMBRECK & ST VINCENT STREET via PAISLEY ROAD cut back to become MOSSPARK & ST VINCENT STREET via PAISLEY ROAD from Corkerhill Road via Corkerhill Road, Paisley Road West and former route.

8th May 1945

Second World War: cessation of hostilities in Europe. VE Day Celebrations.

4th and 5th June 1945

Major Engineering Works affecting water mains and Finnieston railway tunnel.
Track from city in Argyle Street at Kent Road temporarily closed.

When the black-out restrictions were lifted on 23rd April 1945 the white collision fenders and steps quickly returned to the former maroon. Anti-blast netting had gradually disappeared previous to this. Red Standard 336 is at Balmoral Street in August of the previous year. The white paint was difficult to keep clean as can be seen. *(Struan JT Robertson)*

The following diversions take place:

Service 9 DALMUIR WEST or SCOTSTOUN & LONDON ROAD, AUCHENSHUGGLE or CARMYLE

Service 26 DALMUIR WEST, CLYDEBANK or SCOTSTOUN & RUTHERGLEN or BURNSIDE via DALMARNOCK

westbound cars diverted from Argyle Street at Hope Street to Argyle Street at Sauchiehall Street via Hope Street, Bothwell Street, Elmbank Street, Sauchiehall Street, Charing Cross, Sauchiehall Street to Argyle Street.

Service 16 KEPPOCHHILL ROAD & SCOTSTOUN via NORTH STREET

westbound cars diverted from Sauchiehall Street at North Street to Argyle Street at Sauchiehall Street via Sauchiehall Street;

Service 21 ELDERSLIE & ANNIESLAND via BOTHWELL STREET

westbound cars diverted from Bothwell Street at Elmbank Street to Argyle Street at Sauchiehall Street via Elmbank Street, Sauchiehall Street, Charing Cross, Sauchiehall Street to Argyle Street.

9th and 10th June 1945

Major Engineering Works affecting water mains and Finnieston railway tunnel.
Tracks from City in Argyle Street at Kent Road temporarily closed
Arrangements for 4th and 5th June1945 repeated.

10th June 1945

Circular services at Hyndland withdrawn.
Services withdrawn from Hyndland Road between north end and Hyndland Station.

Service 5 KELVINSIDE Circle via BOTANIC GARDENS & CLARKSTON circular cars cease and altered to become
KELVINSIDE & CLARKSTON via BOTANIC GARDENS from Hyndland Road north end via Hyndland Road, Great Western Road, Byres Road and former route;

Service 5A KELVINSIDE Circle via HYNDLAND & CLARKSTON circular cars cease and altered to become
HYNDLAND & CLARKSTON via HIGHBURGH ROAD from Hyndland Road at Hyndland Station via Hyndland Road, Highburgh Road, Byres Road and former route;

Service 10 KELVINSIDE Circle via PARK ROAD & OATLANDS or RUTHERGLEN via CROWN STREET circular cars cease and altered to become
KELVINSIDE & OATLANDS or RUTHERGLEN via PARK ROAD, CROWN STREET from Hyndland Road north end via Hyndland Road via Great Western Road and former route;

Service 10A KELVINSIDE Circle via CHURCH STREET & OATLANDS or RUTHERGLEN via CROWN STREET circular cars cease and cut back to become
ANDERSTON CROSS & OATLANDS or RUTHERGLEN via CROWN STREET from Stobcross Street at Warroch Street via Stobcross Street, Argyle Street and former route;
(All cars show "10" on journeys to OATLANDS and RUTHERGLEN).
Regular cars cease to operate on Hyndland Road between Hyndland Station and Great Western Road.

15th and 16th June 1945

Major Engineering Works affecting water mains and Finnieston railway tunnel.
Both tracks in Argyle Street at Kent Road temporarily closed.
The following diversions take place:

Service 9 DALMUIR WEST or SCOTSTOUN & LONDON ROAD, AUCHENSHUGGLE or CARMYLE;

Service 26 DALMUIR WEST, CLYDEBANK or SCOTSTOUN & RUTHERGLEN or BURNSIDE via DALMARNOCK, diverted both ways between Argyle Street at Hope Street and Argyle Street at Sauchiehall Street via Hope Street, Bothwell Street, Elmbank Street, Sauchiehall Street, Charing Cross, Sauchiehall Street to Argyle Street;

Service 16 KEPPOCHHILL ROAD & SCOTSTOUN via NORTH STREET diverted both ways between Sauchiehall Street at North Street and Argyle Street at Sauchiehall Street via Sauchiehall Street to Argyle Street;

Service 21 ELDERSLIE & ANNIESLAND via BOTHWELL STREET diverted both ways between Bothwell Street at Elmbank Street and Argyle Street at Sauchiehall Street via Elmbank Street, Sauchiehall Street, Charing Cross, Sauchiehall Street to Argyle Street.

29th July 1945

Closure of North Street.
New curves Opened at St Vincent Cross linking Elmbank Street with St Vincent Street westwards.
The following Service Alteration takes place:

Service 16 KEPPOCHHILL ROAD & SCOTSTOUN via NORTH STREET diverted to become
KEPPOCHHILL ROAD & SCOTSTOUN via ELMBANK STREET via former route to Charing Cross, then via Sauchiehall Street, Elmbank Street, St Vincent Street and former route.
North Street and Kent Road siding **closed** to trams.

15th August 1945

Second World War. Surrender of Japan. VJ celebrations.

Time Frame 1945 – 1956: Recovery

World War II leaves Glasgow Corporation's tramways bloodied but unbowed. They have survived, albeit the poorer for reduced maintenance and general shortages. The next ten years are of recovery although some abandonments do take place. Scrapping of Standard trams in poor condition resumes but their place is largely filled by new trams – not rebuilds – and by a hesitant flirtation with trolleybuses, not forgetting what can now be seen as an unfortunate purchase of ex-Liverpool trams. During this period the tramcar fleet grows to its all-time maximum of 1208 cars in 1947. Remaining services continue to be developed and refined but 1956 has been selected as the date when the decisions that lead to inevitable decline become manifest. Tramway employees had seen it coming for some time.

26th August 1945
The following Operational Alterations take place:
Newlands Depot duties of **Service 40** transferred to Govan Depot.
Maryhill Depot duties of **Service 3** transferred to Newlands.
Service 3 UNIVERSITY & MOSSPARK via POLLOKSHIELDS and
Service 40 MOSSPARK & ST VINCENT STREET via PAISLEY ROAD
Depot workings adjusted accordingly.

8th September 1945
Major Engineering Works affecting water mains and Finnieston railway tunnel.
Track from city in Argyle Street at Kent Road temporarily closed.
Arrangements for 4th June 1945 for **Services 9, 21** and **26** repeated.
Service 16 KEPPOCHHILL ROAD & SCOTSTOUN via ELMBANK STREET diverted between St George's Road at Charing Cross and Argyle Street at Sauchiehall Street via Sauchiehall Street to Argyle Street.

9th September 1945
Further adjustments to the Hyndland Services.
Regular cars resume operation on Hyndland Road between Hyndland Station and Great Western Road.
The following Service Alterations take place:
Service 5 KELVINSIDE & CLARKSTON via BOTANIC GARDENS turning point (for Service 5 only) at
KELVINSIDE extended from Hyndland Road north end to Hyndland Station.

Clarkston was the most southerly point reached by Glasgow trams and was the terminus for Services 5 and 13, as seen here, with its facing crossover in Mearns Road. *(BJ Cross Collection)*

28th October 1945

Restoration of circular services at Hyndland.

KELVINSIDE terminus for **Services 10** and **30** moved from Hyndland Road north end to Hyndland Road at Hyndland Station.

The following Service Alterations take place:

Service 5 KELVINSIDE & CLARKSTON via BOTANIC GARDENS reverts to circular working to become

KELVINSIDE Circle via BOTANIC GARDENS & CLARKSTON from Hyndland Road at Hyndland Station via Hyndland Road, Great Western Road and former route;

Circle Cars return as **Service 5A** route; All Cars show "5" on journeys to Clarkston;

Service 5A HYNDLAND & CLARKSTON via HIGHBURGH ROAD reverts to circular working to become

KELVINSIDE Circle via HYNDLAND & CLARKSTON from Hyndland Road at Hyndland Station via Hyndland Road, Highburgh Road, Byres Road and former route;

Circle Cars return as **Service 5** route; All Cars show "5" on journeys to Clarkston;

Service 10 KELVINSIDE & OATLANDS or RUTHERGLEN via PARK ROAD, CROWN STREET extended to run from Hyndland Road at Hyndland Station via Hyndland Road and former route;

Service 30 KNIGHTSWOOD or KELVINSIDE & SPRINGFIELD ROAD or CAMBUSLANG

KELVINSIDE terminus extended on Hyndland Road to Hyndland Station.

Reduction in Milngavie Service and changes to Maryhill Road frequencies.

Service 14 Weekdays and Saturdays: MILNGAVIE, MARYHILL or GAIRBRAID AVENUE & SHAWLANDS or SPIERSBRIDGE via GARSCUBE ROAD, GORBALS cut back to become

MARYHILL or GAIRBRAID AVENUE & SHAWLANDS or SPIERSBRIDGE via GARSCUBE ROAD, GORBALS;

Sundays: MILNGAVIE or MARYHILL & SHAWLANDS or SPIERSBRIDGE via GARSCUBE ROAD, GORBALS cut back to become

HILLFOOT or MARYHILL & SHAWLANDS or SPIERSBRIDGE via GARSCUBE ROAD, GORBALS;

Service 40 MOSSPARK & ST VINCENT STREET via PAISLEY ROAD extended to become

DUMBRECK & GAIRBRAID AVENUE via CHARING CROSS from Private Track east end via Private Track on north side of Mosspark Boulevard, Corkerhill Road and former route to Hope Street, then via Hope Street, Bothwell Street, Elmbank Street, Sauchiehall Street, Charing Cross, St George's Road, St George's Cross, Maryhill Road, Queen's Cross, Maryhill Road, Gairbraid Avenue to Gairbraid Avenue east end.

7th November 1945

Completion of Major Engineering Works affecting water mains and Finnieston railway tunnel.

Argyle Street at Kent Road now fully re-opened.

Service 9 DALMUIR WEST or SCOTSTOUN & LONDON ROAD, AUCHENSHUGGLE or CARMYLE.

Service 16 KEPPOCHHILL ROAD & SCOTSTOUN via ELMBANK STREET

Service 21 ELDERSLIE & ANNIESLAND via BOTHWELL STREET

Service 26 DALMUIR WEST, CLYDEBANK or SCOTSTOUN & RUTHERGLEN or BURNSIDE via DALMARNOCK

all revert to normal service.

11th November 1945

Crossover at north end of Hyndland Road, formerly KELVINSIDE CROSS and former KELVINSIDE terminus, disconnected.

19th November 1945

POLLOKSHAWS WEST crossover disconnected.

29th November 1945

GREENVIEW STREET crossover disconnected.

9th December 1945

Temporary Shuttle Sunday Motorbus Services to and from tram routes withdrawn. Through Sunday Motorbus Services resume.

6th January 1946

POLLOKSHAWS WEST renamed POLLOKSHAWS and terminus sited at Greenview Street west end, cars using triangle to turn.

Service 14 Weekdays and Saturdays: MARYHILL or GAIRBRAID AVENUE & SHAWLANDS or SPIERSBRIDGE via GARSCUBE ROAD, GORBALS part extended to become

MARYHILL or GAIRBRAID AVENUE & POLLOKSHAWS or SPIERSBRIDGE via GARSCUBE ROAD, GORBALS;

Sundays: HILLFOOT or MARYHILL & SHAWLANDS or SPIERSBRIDGE via GARSCUBE ROAD, GORBALS part extended to become

HILLFOOT or MARYHILL & POLLOKSHAWS or SPIERSBRIDGE via GARSCUBE ROAD, GORBALS;

Service 25 BISHOPBRIGGS or SPRINGBURN & CARNWADRIC or ROUKEN GLEN Circle via THORNLIEBANK shortworkings adjusted accordingly.

Re-siting of ANNIESLAND terminus for **Service 1** westwards from Anniesland Cross to Anniesland Road at Chamberlain Road.
Service 1 DALMUIR WEST or ANNIESLAND & DENNISTOUN altered accordingly.

3rd March 1946

All Govan Depot journeys to city of Old Govan Road services rerouted to use Lorne Street, Paisley Road West.
Service 4 KEPPOCHHILL ROAD & RENFREW SOUTH
Service 7 MILLERSTON or RIDDRIE & BELLAHOUSTON via BRIDGETON CROSS
Service 27 SPRINGBURN & SHIELDHALL or RENFREW CROSS via POSSILPARK
Service 31 LAMBHILL & HILLINGTON ROAD or RENFREW CROSS all adjusted accordingly.

17th March 1946

Adjustments to Lambhill Service and increase in services in East End.
The following Service Alterations take place:
Service 22 CROOKSTON & ST VINCENT STREET extended to become
CROOKSTON & LAMBHILL via former route to Hope Street then via Hope Street, Cowcaddens, Garscube Road, Round Toll, Possil Road, Saracen Street, Saracen Cross, Balmore Road, Strachur Street to Strachur Street east end;
Service 31 LAMBHILL & HILLINGTON ROAD or RENFREW CROSS withdrawn and replaced by **Services 22** and **27**;
The following Service commences:
Service 34 CIRCLE PARKHEAD & BRIDGETON CROSS operates both ways from Springfield Road north end:
Outer via Springfield Road, Dalmarnock Road, Bridgeton Cross, London Road, Abercromby Street, Bellgrove Street, Duke Street, Parkhead Cross and Springfield Road;
Inner via Springfield Road, Parkhead Cross, Duke Street, Bellgrove Street, Abercromby Street, London Road, Bridgeton Cross, Dalmarnock Road and Springfield Road.

19th March 1946

LANGLOAN crossover moved from Bank Street Coatbridge at Woodside Street to Private Track on south side of Glasgow Road east end.
Service [Airdrie local] LANGLOAN & AIRDRIE extended to operate from Private Track east end and via former route.

1st April 1946

Special Service provided over further section of existing Line in London Road, lying unused, from Carmyle terminus at Carmyle Avenue to single track section at Kenmuirhill Road.
SCHOOLS SPECIALS commence to run to and from London Road at Kenmuirhill Road.

20th April 1946

The following Service Alteration takes place:
Service 27 Saturdays: SPRINGBURN & SHIELDHALL or RENFREW CROSS via POSSILPARK altered to become SPRINGBURN or POSSILPARK & SHIELDHALL or RENFREW CROSS;
Weekdays and Sundays: SPRINGBURN & SHIELDHALL or RENFREW CROSS via POSSILPARK unaltered.

28th April 1946

Sunday Engineering work on Dalmuir Canal Swing Bridge.
All services cut back to terminate at DALMUIR.
Service 1 Sundays: DALMUIR WEST & DENNISTOUN
Service 6 Sundays: DALMUIR WEST & ALEXANDRA PARK
Service 9 Sundays: DALMUIR WEST & CARMYLE all adjusted accordingly.

1st May 1946

Line Opened in Bogmoor Road.
SHIELDHALL terminus moved from Renfrew Road to Bogmoor Road north end
Service 4 KEPPOCHHILL ROAD & RENFREW SOUTH
Service 27 SPRINGBURN or POSSILPARK & SHIELDHALL or RENFREW CROSS both adjusted accordingly.

3rd June 1946

Resiting of crossover from Shettleston Road at Muiryfauld Drive to Shettleston Road between Chester Street and Amulree Street.
SHETTLESTON terminus moved to Shettleston Road between Chester Street and Amulree Street.
CARNTYNE and MUIRYFAULD DRIVE terminus withdrawn.
Service 15 ANDERSTON CROSS & BAILLIESTON or AIRDRIE and
Service 23 KELVINGROVE & BAILLIESTON or AIRDRIE adjusted accordingly.

18th August 1946

New Traffic Management scheme at Eglinton Toll. Barrier erected to segregate Pollokshaws Road<>Eglinton Street traffic from Victoria Road<>Pollokshaws Road traffic. Tram track layout altered.

The following Service Alterations take place:

Service 5 KELVINSIDE Circle via BOTANIC GARDENS & CLARKSTON
Service 5A KELVINSIDE Circle via HYNDLAND & CLARKSTON
Service 24 ANNIESLAND & LANGSIDE via HYNDLAND

all rerouted between Renfield Street at St Vincent Street and Victoria Road to run via St Vincent Street, St Vincent Place, George Square south, South Frederick Street, Ingram Street, Glassford Street, Stockwell Street, Victoria Bridge, Gorbals Street, Pollokshaws Road and Victoria Road to become

Service 5 KELVINSIDE Circle via BOTANIC GARDENS & CLARKSTON via GORBALS
Service 5A KELVINSIDE Circle via HYNDLAND & CLARKSTON via GORBALS
Service 24 ANNIESLAND & LANGSIDE via HYNDLAND, GORBALS;
Service 11 MILNGAVIE & SINCLAIR DRIVE via ST GEORGE'S CROSS

Northbound cars which proceed from Victoria Road via Eglinton Street and Turriff Street rerouted to follow original route directly from Victoria Road into Pollokshaws Road; Southbound Cars unaltered;

Service 14 HILLFOOT, MARYHILL or GAIRBRAID AVENUE & POLLOKSHAWS or SPIERSBRIDGE via GARSCUBE ROAD, GORBALS rerouted to become

HILLFOOT, MARYHILL or GAIRBRAID AVENUE & POLLOKSHAWS or SPIERSBRIDGE via GARSCUBE ROAD, RENFIELD STREET via former route to Cowcaddens then via Renfield Street, Union Street, Jamaica Street, Glasgow Bridge, Bridge Street, Eglinton Street, Eglinton Toll, Pollokshaws Road and former route.

Regular cars resume operation on Renfield Street between Sauchiehall Street and Cowcaddens.
Regular cars cease to operate on Turriff Street.

21st August 1946

TOLLCROSS crossover eastwards from Tollcross Road at Carmyle Avenue to Hamilton Road east of Carmyle Avenue.

Service 29 ANDERSTON CROSS & TOLLCROSS or UDDINGSTON adjusted accordingly.

25th August 1946

Tram Traffic Management scheme for city centre. One-way system introduced using existing track layout for Cars turning at the City Centre.

ST VINCENT STREET used by cars from the south and south-west now operates:
From Eglinton Street via Bridge Street, Glasgow Bridge, Jamaica Street, Union Street, Renfield Street, St Vincent Street, returning via St Vincent Street, Hope Street, Oswald Street, George V. Bridge, Commerce Street, Kingston Street, Bridge Street and Eglinton Street;
From Nelson Street via Nelson Street, Bridge Street, Glasgow Bridge, Jamaica Street, Union Street, Renfield Street, St Vincent Street returning via St Vincent Street, Hope Street, Oswald Street, George V. Bridge, Commerce Street and Nelson Street.

COMMERCE STREET used by Cars from the north now operates:
From Hope Street via Hope Street, Oswald Street, George V. Bridge, Commerce Street, Kingston Street, Bridge Street, Nelson Street, Commerce Street, George V. Bridge, Oswald Street and Hope Street.

Regular cars commence operation on Kingston Street.

28th August 1946

EGLINTON TOLL crossover in Eglinton Street south end removed

20th October 1946

Sunday repairs at Airdrie.
All Services temporarily curtailed at AIRDRIE CROSS.
Service 15 Sundays: ANDERSTON CROSS & BAILLIESTON or AIRDRIE
Service 23 Sundays: KELVINGROVE & BAILLIESTON or AIRDRIE
adjusted accordingly.

27th October 1946

Restoration of full service from city centre post 2300 until 2345 hrs.
All Night Tram Services from city centre replaced by Motorbuses. See separate list.

19th November 1946

New traffic management scheme at Castle Street.
Monkland Street made one-way westwards only, but tram-turning facilities retained allowing terminating eastbound trams from west to enter Monkland Street to use crossover.
Single Line Curve **Opened** eastbound from Parliamentary Road southwards into Castle Street.
All eastbound through trams proceeding from Monkland Street southwards into Castle Street diverted to continue via Parliamentary Road then turn right into Castle Street and via former route;
Cars travelling north in Castle Street on westbound services proceed directly into Monkland Street unaltered;

Service 6 DALMUIR WEST or SCOTSTOUN & ALEXANDRA PARK or RIDDRIE
Service 8 MILLERSTON or RIDDRIE & GIFFNOCK or ROUKEN GLEN Circle via GIFFNOCK
adjusted accordingly.

Cars from the city in Parliamentary Road shortworking to MONKLAND STREET or CASTLE STREET proceed, as before, turning right into Monkland Street to reverse at crossover.

Eastbound Curve from Monkland Street southwards into Castle Street **closed** to trams.

8th December 1946

The following Service Alteration takes place:

Service 17 ANDERSTON CROSS & DALMARNOCK or CAMBUSLANG extended to become
WHITEINCH & CAMBUSLANG via ANDERSTON CROSS from Primrose Street north end via Primrose Street, Dumbarton Road, Argyle Street, Trongate and former route.

Partick Depot recommences part-operation of Service.

12th January 1947

Rearrangement of Garscube Road and Maryhill Services.

GOVANHILL terminus moved from Cathcart Road at Dixon Avenue to Coplaw Street east end, Cars using triangle to turn.

Crossover remains in use as DIXON AVENUE for shortworkings.

The following Service Alterations take place:

Service 13 Weekdays and Saturdays: MARYHILL or GAIRBRAID AVENUE & MOUNT FLORIDA, NETHERLEE or CLARKSTON via ST GEORGE'S CROSS; altered to become
MARYHILL & MOUNT FLORIDA or CLARKSTON via ST GEORGE'S CROSS from Caldercuilt Road west end via Caldercuilt Road, Maryhill Road and former route;

Sundays: MARYHILL or GAIRBRAID AVENUE & CLARKSTON via ST GEORGE'S CROSS unaltered;

Service 14 HILLFOOT, MARYHILL or GAIRBRAID AVENUE & POLLOKSHAWS or SPIERSBRIDGE via GARSCUBE ROAD, RENFIELD STREET diverted to become
UNIVERSITY & POLLOKSHAWS or SPIERSBRIDGE from University Avenue at Kelvin Way via University Avenue, Gibson Street, Eldon Street, Woodlands Road, St George's Road, Charing Cross, Sauchiehall Street, Renfield Street and former route;

Service 23 KELVINGROVE & BAILLIESTON or AIRDRIE diverted to become
GAIRBRAID AVENUE & BAILLIESTON or AIRDRIE via GARSCUBE ROAD from Gairbraid Avenue east end via Gairbraid Avenue, Maryhill Road, Queen's Cross, Garscube Road, Round Toll, Garscube Road, Cowcaddens, West Nile Street, St Vincent Street and former route;

The following Services commence:

Service 13 Weekdays and Saturdays Auxiliary: GAIRBRAID AVENUE & GOVANHILL via ST GEORGE'S CROSS from Gairbraid Avenue east end via Gairbraid Avenue, Maryhill Road, Queen's Cross, Maryhill Road, St George's Cross, New City Road, Cowcaddens, West Nile Street, St Vincent Street, St Vincent Place, George Square south, South Frederick Street, Ingram Street, Glassford Street, Stockwell Street, Victoria Bridge, Gorbals Street, Cathcart Road to Cathcart Road at Coplaw Street;

Service 14A KELVINGROVE & POLLOKSHAWS or SPIERSBRIDGE from Radnor Street via Radnor Street, Sauchiehall Street, Charing Cross, Sauchiehall Street, Renfield Street, Union Street, Jamaica Street, Glasgow Bridge, Bridge Street, Eglinton Street, Eglinton Toll, Pollokshaws Road, Shawlands Cross, Pollokshaws Road to Pollokshaws at Greenview Street west end or via Pollokshaws Road, Cross Street, Harriet Street, Thornliebank Road, Main Street Thornliebank, Spiersbridge Road, Private Track on north side of Nitshill Road to east end of Private Track.

Regular cars cease to operate on Renfield Street between Sauchiehall Street and Cowcaddens.

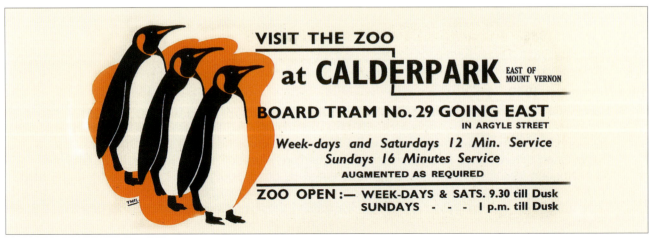

14th January 1947

Collapse of sewer at south end of Springfield Road. Single Line working instituted in Springfield Road at Baltic Street with temporary crossover.

Service 30 KNIGHTSWOOD or KELVINSIDE & SPRINGFIELD ROAD or CAMBUSLANG

Service 34 CIRCLE PARKHEAD & BRIDGETON CROSS adjusted accordingly.

15th February 1947

Road works at Eglinton Toll.
The following Temporary Service Alterations take place:

Service 5 KELVINSIDE Circle via BOTANIC GARDENS & CLARKSTON via GORBALS;

Service 5A KELVINSIDE Circle via HYNDLAND & CLARKSTON via GORBALS

Service 11 MILNGAVIE & SINCLAIR DRIVE via ST GEORGE'S CROSS

Service 24 ANNIESLAND & LANGSIDE via HYNDLAND, GORBALS

all diverted both ways between Pollokshaws Road at Turriff Street and Victoria Road at Coplaw Street via Turriff Street, Eglinton Street, Eglinton Toll, Pollokshaws Road, Coplaw Street and Victoria Road. (Northbound Cars reverse in Victoria Road and work single line under caution order via Coplaw Street).

19th February 1947

Road Works at Eglinton Toll completed.

Service 5 KELVINSIDE Circle via BOTANIC GARDENS & CLARKSTON via GORBALS;

Service 5A KELVINSIDE Circle via HYNDLAND & CLARKSTON via GORBALS

Service 11 MILNGAVIE & SINCLAIR DRIVE via ST GEORGE'S CROSS

Service 24 ANNIESLAND & LANGSIDE via HYNDLAND, GORBALS

all revert to normal route.

16th March 1947

Repairs to collapsed sewer at south end of Springfield Road commence.
Springfield Road closed to all traffic south of Baltic Street.
The following Temporary Service Alterations take place:

Service 30 KNIGHTSWOOD or KELVINSIDE & SPRINGFIELD ROAD or CAMBUSLANG cut back to become KNIGHTSWOOD or KELVINSIDE & SPRINGFIELD ROAD via former route to Springfield Road at Baltic Street;

Service 34 CIRCLE PARKHEAD & BRIDGETON CROSS altered to become

Weekdays and Saturdays: SPRINGFIELD ROAD & DALMARNOCK or CAMBUSLANG from Springfield Road at Baltic Street via Springfield Road, Parkhead Cross, Duke Street, Bellgrove Street, Abercromby Street, London Road, Bridgeton Cross, Dalmarnock Road, Farme Cross, Cambuslang Road, Glasgow Road Cambuslang, Main Street Cambuslang to Main Street Cambuslang east end;

Sundays: SPRINGFIELD ROAD & DALMARNOCK.

20th April 1947

Timetables for All Services recast with Special Workmen Cars now incorporated in Regular Timetables. Specials continue to operate independently of Regular Service Cars.
The following Service commences:

Service 11 Summer Sundays Auxiliary: MILNGAVIE & MAITLAND STREET from Main Street Milngavie at Park Road via Main Street Milngavie, Milngavie Road, Maryhill Road, Queen's Cross, Maryhill Road, St George's Cross, New City Road, Cowcaddens, Maitland Street to Maitland Street at Milton Street.

19th May 1947

The following Service Alteration takes place:

Part of the rearrangement of services to Maryhill involved the creation of new Service 14A on which Coronation 1281 is seen at the Spiersbridge terminus with Rouken Glen Park in the background.
(BJ Cross Collection)

Service 1 Weekdays and Saturdays: DALMUIR WEST or ANNIESLAND & DENNISTOUN altered to become DALMUIR WEST or SCOTSTOUN WEST & DENNISTOUN;
Sundays: DALMUIR WEST & DENNISTOUN unaltered.
ANNIESLAND terminus in Anniesland Road at Chamberlain Road disused.
Services 1 and 30 Cars shortworking to ANNIESLAND turn in Great Western Road east of Anniesland Cross.

15th July 1947

Resiting of GOVAN CROSS crossover in Govan Road 100 yards eastwards.

24th August 1947

BROOMHOUSE crossover resited eastwards from Hamilton Road at Broomhouse Post Office to Glasgow Road 300 yards east of Calderpark Zoo Gates at River Calder Bridge.

26th August 1947

Repairs to sewer at south end of Springfield Road near completion.
Temporary crossover in Springfield Road at Baltic Street removed and use of crossover at south end of Springfield Road resumes.
Temporary **Service 30** KNIGHTSWOOD or KELVINSIDE & SPRINGFIELD ROAD
Temporary **Service 34** SPRINGFIELD ROAD & DALMARNOCK or CAMBUSLANG
both extended to use normal Springfield Road crossover.

31st August 1947

Following completion of repairs to sewer in Springfield Road, street reopened.
Service 30 KNIGHTSWOOD or KELVINSIDE & SPRINGFIELD ROAD or CAMBUSLANG
Service 34 CIRCLE PARKHEAD & BRIDGETON CROSS both resume normal services.

9th October 1947

ARDOCH GROVE crossover in Main Street Cambuslang disconnected.

29th October 1947

Repairs to railway overbridge in Clarence Drive.
Single Line section provided through bridge.
Service 24 ANNIESLAND & LANGSIDE via HYNDLAND, GORBALS adjusted accordingly.

23rd November 1947

General Reduction in certain Sunday Service frequencies.
Service 2 Sundays: PROVANMILL & POLMADIE via GLASGOW CROSS
Service 13 Sundays: MARYHILL & NETHERLEE or CLARKSTON via ST GEORGE'S CROSS
both adjusted accordingly;
The following Service Alteration takes place:
Service 34 Sundays: CIRCLE PARKHEAD & BRIDGETON CROSS withdrawn;
Weekdays and Saturdays: CIRCLE PARKHEAD & BRIDGETON CROSS unaltered.

24th November 1947

The following Service Alterations take place:
Service 13 Weekdays Auxiliary: GAIRBRAID AVENUE & GOVANHILL via ST GEORGE'S CROSS extended to become MARYHILL & GOVANHILL via ST GEORGE'S CROSS from Caldercuilt Road west end via Caldercuilt Road, Maryhill Road and former route;
Saturdays Auxiliary: GAIRBRAID AVENUE & GOVANHILL via ST GEORGE'S CROSS unaltered;
Service 14 UNIVERSITY & POLLOKSHAWS or SPIERSBRIDGE altered to become Part Day only
Evening Service withdrawn and replaced by **Service 14A**;
Service 14A KELVINGROVE & POLLOKSHAWS or SPIERSBRIDGE adjusted accordingly.

22nd December 1947

Experimental Single-ended Car enters service from Possilpark Depot on **Service 33**.

Car 1005 entered service during the dark days of winter 1947-48 but Bob Clark managed to capture this scene opposite at Springburn when the car was brand new and going through its many teething problems. Its operation from Possilpark Depot was comparatively short-lived. It was transferred to Maryhill initially for operation on a hybrid circular service from St Vincent Street to Mosspark via Paisley Road West outbound and Pollokshields inbound, replicating the 1938 Empire Exhibition service. It is seen above at Dumbreck on a return journey to town. *(Opposite: RR Clark / STTS Collection; Above: R Morant collection)*

February 1948

The following Operational Alteration takes place:
Cars from All Services show "8" on journeys to NEWLANDS DEPOT.

11th February 1948

Repairs to railway overbridge in Clarence Drive completed.
Single Line working removed.
Service 24 ANNIESLAND & LANGSIDE via HYNDLAND, GORBALS reverts to normal service.

4th April 1948

The following Service Alteration takes place:
Service 40 DUMBRECK & GAIRBRAID AVENUE via CHARING CROSS extended to become DUMBRECK & MARYHILL via CHARING CROSS via former route then via Maryhill Road, Caldercuilt Road to Caldercuilt Road west end.

11th April 1948

Lyes 1 to 5 of Newlands Depot damaged by fire, along with 16 trams.

It took some time to repair or replace the Newlands Depot fire victims. In this view, taken two years afterwards, the preserved horse tram 543 can be seen with scorched paintwork. On the left is Lightweight car 6 with blackened panels and peeling paint. On the right are stored Daimler trolleybuses mothballed as a result of over-ordering, while behind 543 is Coronation 1239, by then repaired and showing its short-lived livery with the green panels carried straight round the front of the car, eliminating the streamlined effect. *(Photo: AP Tatt / Online Transport Archive)*

31st May 1948
Bogmoor Road temporarily closed for pipe-laying works.
Temporary crossover provided in Renfrew Road and SHIELDHALL terminus moved.
Service 27 SPRINGBURN or POSSILPARK & SHIELDHALL or RENFREW CROSS adjusted accordingly.

11th July 1948
PARKHEAD crossover at north end of Springfield Road moved southwards to opposite Newlands School.
The following Operational Alterations take place:
Service 15 ANDERSTON CROSS & BAILLIESTON or AIRDRIE
Service 29 ANDERSTON CROSS & TOLLCROSS or UDDINGSTON
Service 30 KNIGHTSWOOD or KELVINSIDE & SPRINGFIELD ROAD or CAMBUSLANG
Depot Workings to and from Parkhead Depot adjusted accordingly;
Service 34 CIRCLE PARKHEAD & BRIDGETON CROSS terminal lye-over point moved accordingly.

29th August 1948
Withdrawal of Uddingston trams.
The following Service Alterations take place:
Service 29 ANDERSTON CROSS & TOLLCROSS or UDDINGSTON cut back to become
ANDERSTON CROSS & TOLLCROSS or BROOMHOUSE via former route to Glasgow Road 330 yards east of Calderpark Zoo Gates at Calder Bridge;
Service 15 ANDERSTON CROSS & BAILLIESTON or AIRDRIE timetables adjusted accordingly.
Glasgow Road Uddingston and Main Street Uddingston **closed** to trams.

3rd October 1948
Line Opened in Porterfield Road Renfrew from Paisley Road Renfrew to Brown Street.
RENFREW SOUTH and PORTERFIELD ROAD terminus moved from Paisley Road Renfrew at Broadloan into Porterfield Road east end.
Service 4 KEPPOCHHILL ROAD & RENFREW SOUTH
Service 28 SPIERSBRIDGE & RENFREW FERRY via PAISLEY CROSS
Service [Paisley Local] GLENFIELD & RENFREW FERRY all adjusted accordingly.

17th October 1948
Crossover in Paisley Road Renfrew at Porterfield Road removed.
Crossover in Paisley Road West, west of Paisley Road Toll removed.

4th November 1948
CANNIESBURN crossover in Milngavie Road disconnected.

7th November 1948
Line Opened in Boydstone Road from Cruachan Street to short of Crebar Street.
Additional CARNWADRIC terminus in Boydstone Road at Crebar Street opened.
The following Service commences:
Service 14B CASTLE STREET & CARNWADRIC from Monkland Street via Monkland Street, Parliamentary Road, Sauchiehall Street, Renfield Street, Union Street, Jamaica Street, Glasgow Bridge, Bridge Street, Eglinton Street, Eglinton Toll, Pollokshaws Road, Shawlands Cross, Pollokshaws Road, Cross Street, Harriet Street, Thornliebank Road, Boydstone Road to Boydstone Road at shops near Crebar Street.
First CARNWADRIC terminus in Boydstone Road at Cruachan Street remains in use.
Service 25 BISHOPBRIGGS or SPRINGBURN & CARNWADRIC or ROUKEN GLEN Circle via THORNLIEBANK Shortworkings unaltered.

December 1948
Production models of Coronation Mark II Cars enter service from Newlands Depot.

26th December 1948
Provision of Sunday Afternoon Specials to and from Glasgow Zoo at Calderpark.
The following Service commences:
Service 29 Sunday Afternoon Specials: ANDERSTON CROSS & BROOMHOUSE introduced.

17th January 1949
Bogmoor Road reopened to traffic.
SHIELDHALL terminus reverts to normal position.
Service 27 SPRINGBURN or POSSILPARK & SHIELDHALL or RENFREW CROSS reverts to normal.

23rd January 1949
Preparations for introduction of Trolleybuses on High Street route.
Curves Opened linking Springfield Road westwards into Gallowgate.

The following Service Alterations take place:
Service 10 KELVINSIDE & OATLANDS or RUTHERGLEN via PARK ROAD, CROWN STREET altered to become
KELVINSIDE & PARKHEAD via PARK ROAD, Circle via GALLOWGATE returning via DALMARNOCK ROAD via former route to Trongate then via Glasgow Cross, Gallowgate, Springfield Road to Springfield Road at Newlands School returning via Springfield Road, Dalmarnock Road, Bridgeton Cross, London Road, Glasgow Cross, Trongate and former route;
Partick Depot recommences part-operation of **Service 10**;
Circle Cars in opposite direction provided by **Service 36**;
Service 10A ANDERSTON CROSS & OATLANDS or RUTHERGLEN via CROWN STREET withdrawn;
Part replaced by Temporary Motorbus Service 101.
Service 26 DALMUIR WEST, CLYDEBANK or SCOTSTOUN & RUTHERGLEN or BURNSIDE via DALMARNOCK altered to become
CLYDEBANK or SCOTSTOUN & OATLANDS or BURNSIDE via DALMARNOCK Oatlands cars via former route to Main Street Rutherglen then via Main Street Rutherglen, Glasgow Road Rutherglen, Rutherglen Road to Rutherglen Road east of Shawfield Drive;
Service 30 KNIGHTSWOOD or KELVINSIDE & SPRINGFIELD ROAD or CAMBUSLANG cut back to become
KNIGHTSWOOD or KELVINSIDE & DALMARNOCK via former route to Dalmarnock Road at Birkwood Street;
Service 34 CIRCLE PARKHEAD & BRIDGETON CROSS altered to become all week
DENNISTOUN & RUTHERGLEN Circle via DALMARNOCK ROAD returning via RUTHERGLEN BRIDGE from Carntyne Road west end via Carntyne Road, Duke Street, Bellgrove Street, Abercromby Street, London Road, Bridgeton Cross, Dalmarnock Road, Farme Cross, Farmeloan Road, Main Street Rutherglen to Main Street Rutherglen west of Castle Street returning via Main Street Rutherglen, Glasgow Road, Rutherglen Bridge, Main Street Bridgeton, Bridgeton Cross, London Road, Abercromby Street, Bellgrove Street, Duke Street and Carntyne Road to Carntyne Road west end;
Circle Cars in opposite direction provided by **Service 35**.
The following Services commence:
Service 35 DENNISTOUN & RUTHERGLEN Circle via RUTHERGLEN BRIDGE returning via DALMARNOCK ROAD from Carntyne Road west end via Carntyne Road, Duke Street, Bellgrove Street, Abercromby Street, London Road, Bridgeton Cross, Main Street Bridgeton, Rutherglen Bridge, Glasgow Road, Main Street Rutherglen to Main Street Rutherglen west of Castle Street returning via Main Street Rutherglen, Farmeloan Road, Farme Cross, Dalmarnock Road, Bridgeton Cross, London Road, Abercromby Street, Bellgrove Street, Duke Street and Carntyne Road to Carntyne Road west end;
Circle Cars in opposite direction provided by **Service 34**;
Service 36 KELVINSIDE & PARKHEAD via PARK ROAD, Circle via DALMARNOCK ROAD returning via GALLOWGATE from Hyndland Road at Hyndland Station via Hyndland Road, Great Western Road, Park Road, Woodlands Road, St George's Road, Charing Cross, Sauchiehall Street, Elmbank Street, Bothwell Street, Hope Street, Argyle Street, Trongate, Glasgow Cross, London Road, Bridgeton Cross, Dalmarnock Road, Springfield Road to Springfield Road at Newlands School returning via Springfield Road, Gallowgate, Glasgow Cross, Trongate, Argyle Street, Hope Street, Bothwell Street, Elmbank Street, Sauchiehall Street, Charing Cross, St George's Road, Woodlands Road, Park Road, Great Western Road, Hyndland Road to Hyndland Road at Hyndland Station;
Circle Cars in opposite direction provided by **Service 10**.
Rutherglen Road from Crown Street to east of Shawfield Drive **closed** to trams.

This view of Provanmill terminus was taken six months before Service 2 was withdrawn and replaced by temporary Motorbus Service 102 pending introduction of the trolleybus Service of the same number. Car 727 is seen here with 167 on Service 32, both cars carrying Standard or "Bus Green" route colours. The trolleybus poles were already in place.
(EC Haywood. Courtesy BJ Cross)

At the junction of Cathcart Road and Aikenhead Road, two cars on Services 19 and 13 are heading south while a Car on Service 2 waits to make a right turn into town. Poles for replacing trolleybuses have been planted but the overhead wiring remains to be strung. *(Dr Hugh Nicol, Courtesy BJ Cross)*

February 1949

Junction at St Vincent Street and North Street with former North Street route removed.

20th February 1949

Preparation for introduction of Trolleybuses on High Street route.
The following Service Alterations take place:
Service 2 PROVANMILL or GARNGAD & POLMADIE via GLASGOW CROSS withdrawn and replaced by Temporary Motorbus Service 102;
Service 19 SPRINGBURN & MOUNT FLORIDA or NETHERLEE via GLASGOW CROSS withdrawn and replaced by Motorbus Service 37;
Service 32 ELDERSLIE & PROVANMILL via RENFIELD STREET diverted to become
ELDERSLIE & BISHOPBRIGGS via RENFIELD STREET via former route to Castle Street then via Springburn Road, Kirkintilloch Road, Kenmure Avenue to Kenmure Avenue east end.
Service "Hampden Wheel" TRONGATE & FOOTBALL SPECIALS [Mount Florida] (one-way outwards via Gorbals and Victoria Road returning via Cathcart Road, Crown Street and Saltmarket) altered to become
ST VINCENT STREET & FOOTBALL SPECIALS [Mount Florida] from St Vincent Street at Wellington Street via St Vincent Street, St Vincent Place, George Square south, South Frederick Street, Ingram Street, Glassford Street, Stockwell Street, Victoria Bridge, Gorbals Street, Pollokshaws Road, Eglinton Toll, Victoria Road, Langside Road, Grange Road, Annan Street, Prospecthill Road, (Cars line up in Prospecthill Road during the Match), returning via Prospecthill Road, Cathcart Road, Gorbals Street, Victoria Bridge, Stockwell Street, Glassford Street, Ingram Street, South Frederick Street, George Square south, St Vincent Place and St Vincent Street to St Vincent Street at Wellington Street; [Operated for Football Internationals and Cup Finals at Hampden Park]
Garngad Road, Castle Street south of Alexandra Parade, High Street, Saltmarket, Albert Bridge, Crown Street and Aikenhead Road **closed** to trams.
Changes to CARNWADRIC services.
The following Service Alterations take place:
Service 14B CASTLE STREET & CARNWADRIC withdrawn and replaced by new **Service 31**.
The following Service commences:
Service 31 LAMBHILL & CARNWADRIC via CHARING CROSS from Strachur Street east end via Strachur Street, Balmore Road, Saracen Cross, Saracen Street, Mosshouse, Possil Road, Round Toll, St George's Road, St George's Cross, St George's Road, Charing Cross, Sauchiehall Street, Renfield Street, Union Street, Jamaica Street, Glasgow Bridge, Bridge Street, Eglinton Street, Eglinton Toll, Pollokshaws Road, Shawlands Cross, Pollokshaws Road, Cross Street, Harriet Street, Thornliebank Road, Boydstone Road to Boydstone Road at shops near Crebar Street.
Note: The first CARNWADRIC terminus in Boydstone Road at Cruachan Street remains in use for **Service 25**:
Service 25 BISHOPBRIGGS or SPRINGBURN & CARNWADRIC or ROUKEN GLEN Circle via THORNLIEBANK Shortworkings unaltered.

During 1949

To relieve congestion at Coplawhill Car Works, a considerable volume of maintenance transferred to Elderslie Workshops. Provision made for scrapping of redundant tramcars at Elderslie with the salvage of re-useable components. Elderslie Workshops re-equipped and modernised.

Résumé

1st March 1949

The following Tram Services operating:

1	DALMUIR WEST or SCOTSTOUN WEST & DENNISTOUN
3	UNIVERSITY & MOSSPARK via POLLOKSHIELDS
4	KEPPOCHHILL ROAD & RENFREW SOUTH
5	KELVINSIDE Circle via BOTANIC GARDENS & CLARKSTON via GORBALS
	Circle Cars return as Service 5A route (All Cars show "5" on journeys to CLARKSTON)
5A	KELVINSIDE Circle via HYNDLAND & CLARKSTON via GORBALS
	Circle Cars return as Service 5 route (All Cars show "5" on journeys to CLARKSTON)
6	DALMUIR WEST or SCOTSTOUN & ALEXANDRA PARK or RIDDRIE
7	MILLERSTON or RIDDRIE & BELLAHOUSTON via BRIDGETON CROSS
8	MILLERSTON or RIDDRIE & GIFFNOCK or ROUKEN GLEN Circle via GIFFNOCK
	Circle Cars return as Service 25 to SPRINGBURN or BISHOPBRIGGS
9	DALMUIR WEST or SCOTSTOUN & LONDON ROAD, AUCHENSHUGGLE or CARMYLE
10	KELVINSIDE & PARKHEAD via PARK ROAD, Circle via GALLOWGATE
	returning via DALMARNOCK ROAD
11	MILNGAVIE & SINCLAIR DRIVE via ST GEORGE'S CROSS
	MILNGAVIE & MAITLAND STREET via ST GEORGE'S CROSS (Sundays only)
12	MOUNT FLORIDA & PAISLEY ROAD TOLL or LINTHOUSE via SHIELDS ROAD
13	MARYHILL or GAIRBRAID AVENUE & MOUNT FLORIDA or CLARKSTON
	via ST GEORGE'S CROSS
	MARYHILL or GAIRBRAID AVENUE & GOVANHILL via ST GEORGE'S CROSS (No Sundays Service)
14	UNIVERSITY & POLLOKSHAWS or SPIERSBRIDGE (Part Day – No Evening Service)
14A	KELVINGROVE & POLLOKSHAWS or SPIERSBRIDGE
15	ANDERSTON CROSS & BAILLIESTON or AIRDRIE
16	KEPPOCHHILL ROAD & SCOTSTOUN via ELMBANK STREET
17	WHITEINCH & CAMBUSLANG via ANDERSTON CROSS
18	SPRINGBURN & RUTHERGLEN or BURNSIDE via BILSLAND DRIVE, RUTHERGLEN BRIDGE
20	[Single Deck Cars] CLYDEBANK & PARKHALL or DUNTOCHER
21	ELDERSLIE & ANNIESLAND via BOTHWELL STREET
22	CROOKSTON & LAMBHILL
23	GAIRBRAID AVENUE & BAILLIESTON or AIRDRIE via GARSCUBE ROAD
24	ANNIESLAND & LANGSIDE via HYNDLAND, GORBALS
25	BISHOPBRIGGS or SPRINGBURN & CARNWADRIC or ROUKEN GLEN Circle via THORNLIEBANK
	Circle Cars return as Service 8 to RIDDRIE or MILLERSTON
26	CLYDEBANK or SCOTSTOUN & OATLANDS or BURNSIDE via DALMARNOCK
27	SPRINGBURN or POSSILPARK & SHIELDHALL or RENFREW CROSS
28	SPIERSBRIDGE & RENFREW FERRY via PAISLEY CROSS
29	ANDERSTON CROSS & TOLLCROSS or BROOMHOUSE
30	KNIGHTSWOOD or KELVINSIDE & DALMARNOCK
31	LAMBHILL & CARNWADRIC via CHARING CROSS
32	ELDERSLIE & BISHOPBRIGGS via RENFIELD STREET
33	CIRCLE SPRINGBURN & CHARING CROSS
34	DENNISTOUN & RUTHERGLEN Circle via DALMARNOCK ROAD
	returning via RUTHERGLEN BRIDGE
35	DENNISTOUN & RUTHERGLEN Circle via RUTHERGLEN BRIDGE
	returning via DALMARNOCK ROAD
36	KELVINSIDE & PARKHEAD via PARK ROAD, Circle via DALMARNOCK ROAD
	returning via GALLOWGATE
40	DUMBRECK & MARYHILL via CHARING CROSS
-	[Airdrie Local] LANGLOAN & AIRDRIE
-	[Paisley Local] PAISLEY WEST or PAISLEY CROSS & HAWKHEAD ROAD (Part Day)
-	[Paisley Local] BRAIDS ROAD & PAISLEY CROSS (Part Day)
-	[Paisley Local] GLENFIELD & RENFREW FERRY (Part Day)

When Elderslie Depot's workshops were re-equipped and modernised this allowed cars overhauled there to display a certain amount of individuality and the Depot became the home of the last Semi-High Speed Standard cars and, as seen here, ex-Paisley cars like 1067. Behind the photographer is the railway overbridge which formed a barrier to Standard height top-covered cars trying to reach Johnstone and Kilbarchan. *(FNT Lloyd-Jones / Online Transport Archive)*

There was a stillborn scheme to resurrect the route colour system in 1949 that came to nothing although a handful of Coronation Mark I cars and one Cunarder were painted with red route colour panels. Here is the Cunarder, 1303, in Eglinton Street, shortly after entering service. *(AP Tatt / Online Transport Archive)*

25th March 1949
Crossover in Castle Street north of Parliamentary Road disconnected.

28th March 1949
Crossover in Castle Street north of Parliamentary Road unwired.

3rd April 1949
Withdrawal of trams from single track section between Cross Stobs and Glenfield.
The following Service Alterations take place:
Service 14 UNIVERSITY & POLLOKSHAWS or SPIERSBRIDGE (Part Day - No Evening Service) extended to become All Day
UNIVERSITY & POLLOKSHAWS or CROSSSTOBS via former route to Spiersbridge then via Private Track on north side of Nitshill Road, Darnley, Private Track on north side of Parkhouse Road, Parkhouse, Darnley Road, Main Street Barrhead, Allan's Corner, Cross Arthurlie Street, Paisley Road Barrhead, Caplethill Road to Caplethill Road south end just beyond Cross Stobs Inn;
Service 28 SPIERSBRIDGE & RENFREW FERRY via PAISLEY CROSS cut back to become
GLENFIELD & RENFREW FERRY from Caplethill Road east of Glenfield Road via Caplethill Road and former route.

136

Semi-High Speed Car 965 is on Brownside Loop about to enter the single track. After the Renfrewshire Council's insisting on the widening of this road, this section of Service 28 to Cross Stobs was withdrawn. Over sixty years later, the road has still to be widened. (Photo: Struan JT Robertson)

Service [Paisley Local] GLENFIELD & RENFREW FERRY cut back to become POTTERHILL & RENFREW FERRY from Neilston Road at Potterhill Station via Neilston Road and former route. Capplehill Road between Cross Stobs Inn and Glenfield **closed** to trams.

Frequency of service beyond Shieldhall reduced; Running Times to Rouken Glen reduced.

The following Operational Alterations take place:

Service 4 KEPPOCHHILL ROAD & RENFREW SOUTH

Service 27 SPRINGBURN or POSSILPARK & SHIELDHALL or RENFREW CROSS both adjusted accordingly;

Service 8 MILLERSTON or RIDDRIE & GIFFNOCK or ROUKEN GLEN Circle via GIFFNOCK

Service 25 BISHOPBRIGGS or SPRINGBURN & CARNWADRIC or ROUKEN GLEN Circle via THORNLIEBANK

both adjusted accordingly.

1st May 1949

Repairs commence to Strathbungo railway bridge Nithsdale Road.

Road closed, trams turned on special crossovers on either side of bridge.

Service 12 MOUNT FLORIDA & PAISLEY ROAD TOLL or LINTHOUSE via SHIELDS ROAD split accordingly.

The following Operational Alteration takes place:

Adjustment to Langside Depot Journeys.

Service 12 MOUNT FLORIDA & PAISLEY ROAD TOLL or LINTHOUSE via SHIELDS ROAD

Langside Depot Journeys via Prospecthill Road diverted to run via Holmlea Road and Garry Street crossover then via Cathcart Road.

15th May 1949

The following Service commences:

Service 7 Sundays Afternoon Specials: MILLERSTON & BRIDGETON CROSS via normal route to James Street east end.

Although now part of folklore, neither Auchenshuggle terminus is exactly full of character but this view of the earlier terminus is included because it features a Standard car on Service 34, not commonly captured on film. (Photo: AP Tatt / Online Transport Archive)

The single-decker cars on Service 20 only had over six months to go before withdrawal when this photograph was taken in the Coplawhill Car Works yet these trams were still receiving routine attention and overhaul.
(AP Tatt / Online Transport Archive)

29th May 1949

Further revision of Services in the East End.
The following Service Alterations take place:
Service 34 DENNISTOUN & RUTHERGLEN Circle via DALMARNOCK ROAD altered to become
ALEXANDRA PARK & AUCHENSHUGGLE from Aitken Street north end via Aitken Street, Cumbernauld Road, Duke Street, Bellgrove Street, Abercromby Street, London Road, Bridgeton Cross, London Road to London Road at Tollcross Station Road;
Service 35 DENNISTOUN & RUTHERGLEN Circle via RUTHERGLEN BRIDGE withdrawn.
Repairs to Strathbungo railway bridge Nithsdale Road.
Service 12 MOUNT FLORIDA & PAISLEY ROAD TOLL or LINTHOUSE via SHIELDS ROAD during closure of Strathbungo Bridge, split service extended to become
MOUNT FLORIDA & LINTHOUSE via SHIELDS ROAD.

19th June 1949

The following Operational Alteration takes place:
Adjustment to Langside Depot journeys.
Service 13 MARYHILL or GAIRBRAID AVENUE & GOVANHILL, MOUNT FLORIDA or CLARKSTON
Langside Depot Journeys via Prospecthill Road diverted to run via Holmlea Road and Garry Street crossover.

31st July 1949

Line Opened on Great Western Road from Knightswood to Blairdardie.
The following Service Alteration takes place:
Service 30 KNIGHTSWOOD or KELVINSIDE & DALMARNOCK extended to become
BLAIRDARDIE or KELVINSIDE & DALMARNOCK from Great Western Road east of Blairdardie Canal Bridge via Great Western Road Private Track, Knightswood Cross, Great Western Road Private Track and former route.

21st August 1949

Rearrangement of Pollokshaws and Carnwadric Services.
CARNWADRIC turning point consolidated at new terminus at Crebar Street.

Service 14 UNIVERSITY & POLLOKSHAWS or CROSSSTOBS altered to become
UNIVERSITY & SPIERSBRIDGE or CROSSSTOBS;

Service 14A KELVINGROVE & POLLOKSHAWS or SPIERSBRIDGE withdrawn;

Service 25 BISHOPBRIGGS or SPRINGBURN & CARNWADRIC or ROUKEN GLEN Circle via THORNLIEBANK cars turning at CARNWADRIC extended from first terminus in Boydstone Road at Cruachan Street via Boydstone Road to Boydstone Road at the shops just short of Crebar Street;

Service 31 LAMBHILL & CARNWADRIC [New terminus] via CHARING CROSS diverted to become
LAMBHILL & POLLOKSHAWS via CHARING CROSS via former route to Pollokshaws Road to Greenview Street west end.

1st September 1949

Crossover in St George's Road south of St George's Cross removed.

2nd September 1949

To ease congestion and remove traffic hazard, Line in Forrest Street Airdrie closed.
AIRDRIE terminus moved from Forrest Street west end to Clark Street east end (ie from further side to nearer side of Carlisle Road intersection).

To avoid trams crossing over the increasingly busy A73 road, the Airdrie terminus was cut back to the west side of the junction. Car 245 is at the old terminus unusually displaying a card service number – a practice more associated with Elderslie Depot.
(GS Hearse)

Service 20 to Duntocher must have been quite uneconomical with two-man crews and small capacity trams. The inevitable happened on 4th December 1949 when it was withdrawn and replaced by a Motorbus Service of the same number. Cut-down Standard car 923 is seen at Kilbowie Road terminus. Dumbarton Road is in the background.
(AP Tatt / Online Transport Archive)

Service 15 ANDERSTON CROSS & BAILLIESTON or AIRDRIE
Service 23 GAIRBRAID AVENUE & BAILLIESTON or AIRDRIE via GARSCUBE ROAD
Service [Airdrie Local] LANGLOAN & AIRDRIE all cut back accordingly.
Forrest Street Airdrie **closed** to trams.

23rd October 1949

In conjunction with widening and reconstruction of Paisley Road Renfrew, RENFREW DEPOT crossover in Paisley Road Renfrew at Newmains removed.

4th December 1949

Withdrawal of Duntocher trams.
Service 20 [Single Deck Cars] CLYDEBANK & PARKHALL or DUNTOCHER withdrawn and replaced by Motorbus Service 20.
Kilbowie Road, Glasgow Road Duntocher and Dumbarton Road Duntocher **closed** to trams.

5th March 1950

Frequency reduced to reflect drop in passenger traffic particularly between Spiersbridge and Barrhead.
Service 14 UNIVERSITY & SPIERSBRIDGE or CROSSSTOBS adjusted accordingly.

27th March 1950

Advertisements introduced on upper deck side panels.

15th April 1950

Repairs to Strathbungo railway bridge Nithsdale Road completed.
Road reopened and through tram traffic restored.
Service 12 MOUNT FLORIDA & LINTHOUSE via SHIELDS ROAD through running restored.

When advertisement panels first appeared there were still red, blue and yellow cars being turned out from the paint shop. Former Paisley car still has its red route colour band. Being a low-height car, it posed challenges for the sign-writer as the tenanted panels were much shallower than standard.
(AP Tatt / Online Transport Archive)

Service 40 was curtailed at Ibrox from 7th May 1950, sacrificing the run around three sides of Bellahouston Park to Dumbreck. At Paisley Road Toll, Car 528 leaves Paisley Road passing the policeman to head along Paisley Road West. *(RB Parr / STTS Collection)*

7th May 1950

The following Service Alteration takes place:

Service 40 DUMBRECK & MARYHILL via CHARING CROSS cut back to become
IBROX & MARYHILL via CHARING CROSS from Broomloan Road south end via Broomloan Road, Paisley Road West and former route.

12th May 1950

Burst Water Main at St Vincent Cross closing tracks linking Elmbank Street and Bothwell Street. Tracks between Elmbank Street and St Vincent Street and those between Bothwell Street and St Vincent Street unaffected.

Service 10 KELVINSIDE & PARKHEAD via PARK ROAD, Circle via GALLOWGATE
Service 18 SPRINGBURN & RUTHERGLEN or BURNSIDE via BILSLAND DRIVE, RUTHERGLEN BRIDGE
Service 36 KELVINSIDE & PARKHEAD via PARK ROAD, Circle via DALMARNOCK ROAD
Service 40 IBROX & MARYHILL via CHARING CROSS

all diverted between Sauchiehall Street at Elmbank Street and Hope Street at Bothwell Street to run via Sauchiehall Street and Hope Street.

Service 16 KEPPOCHHILL ROAD & SCOTSTOUN via ELMBANK STREET
Service 21 ELDERSLIE & ANNIESLAND via BOTHWELL STREET
both unaltered.

14th May 1950

Burst Water Main at St Vincent Cross repaired.

Service 10 KELVINSIDE & PARKHEAD via PARK ROAD, Circle via GALLOWGATE
Service 18 SPRINGBURN & RUTHERGLEN or BURNSIDE via BILSLAND DRIVE, RUTHERGLEN BRIDGE
Service 36 KELVINSIDE & PARKHEAD via PARK ROAD, Circle via DALMARNOCK ROAD
Service 40 IBROX & MARYHILL via CHARING CROSS all revert to normal routes.

21st May 1950

Crossovers at BRAIDS ROAD and at POTTERHILL removed and replaced by new crossover at LOCHFIELD ROAD.

Crossover in Renfrew Road Paisley at Arkleston Road removed and replaced by new crossover at Glencairn Road for use by Paisley Local cars shortworking to SANDYFORD.

Service [Paisley Local] BRAIDS ROAD & PAISLEY CROSS and
Service [Paisley Local] POTTERHILL & RENFREW FERRY combined to become
[Paisley Local] LOCHFIELD ROAD & PAISLEY CROSS or RENFREW FERRY from Neilston Road at Lochfield Road via Neilston Road and former route.

25th June 1950

Sunday Engineering Work at Dalmuir Canal Bridge.

Service 1 Sundays: DALMUIR WEST or SCOTSTOUN WEST & DENNISTOUN
Service 6 Sundays: DALMUIR WEST & ALEXANDRA PARK
Service 9 Sundays: DALMUIR WEST & AUCHENSHUGGLE or CARMYLE
all DALMUIR WEST Cars curtailed to turn at DALMUIR.

2nd July 1950

Sunday Engineering Work at Dalmuir Canal Bridge.
Arrangements for 25th June 1950 repeated.

Six months after the closure of the Duntocher route, the redundant single-deckers, including 1089, still languished in Partick Depot. Most of the small cars were sold off as garden sheds and the like but 1089 was transferred to Langside Depot for storage to re-emerge in 1952 as a crush-load car for shipyard specials.
(AP Tatt / Online Transport Archive)

This view should be compared with Dr Hugh Nicol's taken at the same location at the junction of Cathcart Road at Aikenhead Road in the previous year (page 134). By this time, trolleybuses had replaced Service 2 trams. TB3 is in trouble, trying to get back to Larkfield Garage. One boom has been taken down and it will proceed on battery power.
(Dewi Williams)

After the Cooperswell Street tracks were disused, they remained in situ for a while. This lower view looks north to Partick Cross.
(HB Priestley / NTM Archive)

During 1950

Siding in Cooperswell Street to Partick Substation **closed** to trams.
Sidings in Clyde Street and Customhouse Quay **closed** to trams.

17th December 1950

Running Times adjusted (mainly by reduction on Weekdays and Sundays and by increase on Saturdays) on All Services to meet changing traffic demands.
Adjustment in frequency on some services.
The following Operational Alterations take place:
Service 7 Weekdays: MILLERSTON or RIDDRIE & BELLAHOUSTON via BRIDGETON CROSS reduced in frequency;
Service 33 Weekdays and Saturdays: CIRCLE SPRINGBURN & CHARING CROSS reduced in frequency.
Reduction in certain Sunday Services.
The following Service Alteration takes place:
Service 17 Sundays: WHITEINCH & CAMBUSLANG via ANDERSTON CROSS cut back to become ANDERSTON CROSS & CAMBUSLANG from Stobcross Street at Warroch Street via Stobcross Street, Argyle Street and former route;
Weekdays and Saturdays: WHITEINCH & CAMBUSLANG via ANDERSTON CROSS unaltered;
Allocation of Sundays duties from Partick Depot transferred to Dalmarnock Depot.

3rd February 1951

Major Fire in premises on south side of Argyle Street between Jamaica Street and St Enoch Square breaks out in early hours of morning.
Argyle Street between Buchanan Street and Hope Street, Union Street and Jamaica Street closed to traffic all day.

Apart from the initial allocation of the experimental unidirectional tram 1005, until the last few months of operation, Service 33 was operated by Standard cars from Possilpark Depot. 467 was typical, seen turning right into Springburn Road on the clockwise circular service.
(RJS Wiseman)

The Service 17 terminal stub at Cambuslang was too short to accommodate two cars if one was a Coronation. Car 852 is featured.
(WD McMillan)

All tram services severely disrupted. Early attempts to divert east-west services via Sauchiehall Street, Renfield Street, St Vincent Street, St Vincent Place, George Square south, South Frederick Street, Ingram Street and Glassford Street abandoned in favour of turning services back at
ROBERTSON STREET and at DOUGLAS STREET on the west and at QUEEN STREET on the east;
North-south services between Charing Cross and Eglinton Street diverted via Hope Street, Oswald Street, George V. Bridge, Commerce Street and Kingston Street;
North-south services between Parliamentary Road and Eglinton Toll initially diverted from Renfield Street at St Vincent Street via St Vincent Street, St Vincent Place, George Square south, South Frederick Street, Ingram Street, Glassford Street, Stockwell Street, Victoria Bridge, Gorbals Street, Pollokshaws Road, Turriff Street to Eglinton Street at Turriff Street, but due to severe congestion cars turned back at
NORTH HANOVER STREET on the north and at BRIDGE STREET on the south.

4th February 1951

Argyle Street fire. Argyle Street between Buchanan Street and Hope Street, Union Street and Jamaica Street still closed to traffic all day.
Sunday Tram Services operate through workings following the diversions detailed above.

4th March 1951

The following Service Alteration takes place:

Service 34 ALEXANDRA PARK & AUCHENSHUGGLE diverted to become
ANDERSTON CROSS & AUCHENSHUGGLE from Stobcross Street at Warroch Street via Stobcross Street, Argyle Street, Trongate, Glasgow Cross, London Road and former route.

The following Operational Alterations take place:

Service 10 KELVINSIDE & PARKHEAD via PARK ROAD, Circle via GALLOWGATE
Service 36 KELVINSIDE & PARKHEAD via PARK ROAD, Circle via DALMARNOCK ROAD
both reduced in frequency.

Reduction in frequencies of Sundays Services:

Service 1 Sundays: DALMUIR WEST & DENNISTOUN
Service 3 Sundays: UNIVERSITY & MOSSPARK via POLLOKSHIELDS
Service 14 Sundays: UNIVERSITY & SPIERSBRIDGE or CROSSSTOBS
Service 16 Sundays: KEPPOCHHILL ROAD & SCOTSTOUN via ELMBANK STREET
Service 21 Sundays: ELDERSLIE & ANNIESLAND via BOTHWELL STREET
Service 22 Sundays: CROOKSTON & LAMBHILL
Service 30 Sundays: BLAIRDARDIE & DALMARNOCK
Service 31 Sundays: LAMBHILL & POLLOKSHAWS via CHARING CROSS
Service 32 Sundays: ELDERSLIE & BISHOPBRIGGS via RENFIELD STREET
Service 33 Sundays: CIRCLE SPRINGBURN & CHARING CROSS
Service 40 Sundays: IBROX & MARYHILL via CHARING CROSS
all reduced in frequency.

5th March 1951

The following Service Alteration takes place:

Service 40 Weekdays: IBROX & MARYHILL via CHARING CROSS part re-extended to become
DUMBRECK (1600-1800) or IBROX & MARYHILL via CHARING CROSS from Private Track east end via Mosspark Boulevard, Corkerhill Road, Paisley Road West and former route;
Saturdays and Sundays: IBROX & MARYHILL via CHARING CROSS unaltered.

10th March 1951

Frequency of Paisley town Services increased on Saturday forenoons.
The following Operational Alteration takes place:

Service 28 Saturdays: GLENFIELD & RENFREW FERRY
Service [Paisley Local] LOCHFIELD ROAD & PAISLEY CROSS or RENFREW FERRY
both adjusted accordingly.

12th March 1951

KEPPOCHHILL ROAD crossover in Springburn Road south of Keppochhill Road removed. Use to be made of Crossover in Keppochhill Road east end.
Citybound track provided from Springburn Road into Keppochhill Road.

1st April 1951

Extension of Keppochhill Road Services to Springburn.
Citybound track **Opened** from Springburn Road into Keppochhill Road.
The following Service Alterations take place:

Service 4 KEPPOCHHILL ROAD & RENFREW SOUTH extended to become
SPRINGBURN & RENFREW SOUTH via KEPPOCHHILL ROAD from Elmvale Street east end via Elmvale Street, Springburn Road, Keppochhill Road and former route;

Service 16 KEPPOCHHILL ROAD & SCOTSTOUN via ELMBANK STREET extended to become
SPRINGBURN & SCOTSTOUN via KEPPOCHHILL ROAD, ELMBANK STREET from Elmvale Street east end via Elmvale Street, Springburn Road, Keppochhill Road and former route.

1st July 1951

Preparations for introduction of Trolleybuses on Gorbals route.
Track layout access to and from Turriff Street reversed at each end and Line brought back into use for regular cars.
The following Service Alterations take place:

Service 5 KELVINSIDE Circle via BOTANIC GARDENS & CLARKSTON via GORBALS
Service 5A KELVINSIDE Circle via HYNDLAND & CLARKSTON via GORBALS
diverted between Renfield Street at St Vincent Street and Eglinton Toll to run via Renfield Street, Union Street, Jamaica Street, Glasgow Bridge, Bridge Street, Eglinton Street, Turriff Street, Pollokshaws Road, Eglinton Toll to become

Service 11 was withdrawn on 1st July 1951. Earlier that year Coronations were being operated as can be seen in this view of Maryhill Depot's 1286 coming off Stockwell Street. *(C Carter)*

Service 5 KELVINSIDE Circle via BOTANIC GARDENS & CLARKSTON
Service 5A KELVINSIDE Circle via HYNDLAND & CLARKSTON;
Service 11 MILNGAVIE & SINCLAIR DRIVE via ST GEORGE'S CROSS withdrawn and replaced by **Tram Services 13** and **24** and by **Motorbus Service 43**;
Service 11 Sundays Auxiliary: MILNGAVIE & MAITLAND STREET incorporated into **Service 13**;
Service 13 MARYHILL or GAIRBRAID AVENUE & MOUNT FLORIDA or CLARKSTON via ST GEORGE'S CROSS extended to become MILNGAVIE, MARYHILL or GAIRBRAID AVENUE & MOUNT FLORIDA or CLARKSTON via ST GEORGE'S CROSS from Main Street Milngavie at Park Road via Main Street Milngavie, Milngavie Road, Maryhill Road and former route;
Service 13 Saturdays Auxiliary: GAIRBRAID AVENUE & GOVANHILL via ST GEORGE'S CROSS extended to become MARYHILL & GOVANHILL via ST GEORGE'S CROSS;
Weekdays Auxiliary: MARYHILL & GOVANHILL via ST GEORGE'S CROSS unaltered;
Sundays Auxiliary: MILNGAVIE & MAITLAND STREET takes over from **Service 11**;
Service 24 ANNIESLAND & LANGSIDE via HYNDLAND, GORBALS diverted between Renfield Street at St Vincent Street and Eglinton Toll and half-diverted to become
ANNIESLAND & LANGSIDE or SINCLAIR DRIVE via HYNDLAND via former route to Renfield Street then via Renfield Street, Union Street, Jamaica Street, Glasgow Bridge, Bridge Street, Eglinton Street, Turriff Street, Pollokshaws Road, Eglinton Toll, Victoria Road, Langside Road to Battle Place; or via Langside Road, Grange Road, Sinclair Drive to Sinclair Drive at Cartside Street.
Service "Hampden Wheel" ST VINCENT STREET & FOOTBALL SPECIALS [Mount Florida] resumes full circular route operates one-way only from St Vincent Street westbound between Renfield Street and Hope Street via St Vincent Street, Hope Street, Oswald Street, George V. Bridge, Commerce Street, Kingston Street, Bridge Street, Eglinton Street, Turriff Street, Pollokshaws Road, Eglinton Toll, Victoria Road, Langside Road, Grange Road, Annan Street, Prospecthill Road, (Cars line up in Prospecthill Road during the Match),returning via Prospecthill Road, Cathcart Road, Gorbals Street, Victoria Bridge, Stockwell Street, Glassford Street, Ingram Street, South Frederick Street, George Square south, St Vincent Place, St Vincent Street to St Vincent Street between Renfield Street and Hope Street;
[Operated for Football Internationals and Cup Finals at Hampden Park].
Regular cars resume operation on Turriff Street.
Pollokshaws Road between Gorbals Street and Turriff Street **closed** to trams.

Service 28 has been described as "The Goldmine" as it enjoyed good loadings in both directions almost along the full length of the route. This is amply demonstrated in this view just to the south of Paisley's County Square. *(RJS Wiseman)*

5th August 1951

Rearrangement of Sinclair Drive Service.
The following Service Alteration takes place:
Service 24 ANNIESLAND & LANGSIDE or SINCLAIR DRIVE via HYNDLAND re-diverted reverting to become ANNIESLAND & LANGSIDE via HYNDLAND, part replaced by **Service 24A**.
The following Service commences:
Service 24A KELVINGROVE & SINCLAIR DRIVE from Radnor Street via Radnor Street, Sauchiehall Street, Charing Cross, Sauchiehall Street, Renfield Street, Union Street, Jamaica Street, Glasgow Bridge, Bridge Street, Eglinton Street, Turriff Street, Pollokshaws Road, Eglinton Toll, Victoria Road, Langside Road, Grange Road, Sinclair Drive to Sinclair Drive at Cartside Street.

30th August 1951

Lye at County Square Paisley taken out of use.

2nd September 1951

Reduction of tram service frequency to Sinclair Drive.
Service 24A KELVINGROVE & SINCLAIR DRIVE adjusted accordingly.

30th September 1951

NEWLANDS crossover moved southwards to Kilmarnock Road south of Corrour Road.

7th October 1951

The following Service Alteration takes place:
Service 6 Saturdays: DALMUIR WEST or SCOTSTOUN & ALEXANDRA PARK or RIDDRIE cut back to become SCOTSTOUN & ALEXANDRA PARK or RIDDRIE;
Sundays: DALMUIR WEST or SCOTSTOUN & ALEXANDRA PARK cut back to become SCOTSTOUN & ALEXANDRA PARK;
Weekdays: SCOTSTOUN & ALEXANDRA PARK or RIDDRIE unaltered.
The following Operational Alterations take place:
Following re-siting of NEWLANDS crossover, additional Running Time provided for cars proceeding to Newlands Depot;
Service 13 MILNGAVIE, MARYHILL or GAIRBRAID AVENUE & GOVANHILL, MOUNT FLORIDA or CLARKSTON frequency reduced;
Service 28 Sundays: GLENFIELD & RENFREW FERRY frequency reduced.

25th October 1951

Crossover in Paisley Road West at White City disconnected.

12th November 1951

The following Operational Alteration takes place:
Service 34 Weekdays: ANDERSTON CROSS & AUCHENSHUGGLE frequency reduced.

Standard car 64 was photographed on Service 36 negotiating the Charing Cross curves during their re-laying and realignment. The realigned single line curve for depot and special workings can be seen coming in on the left.
(WD McMillan)

2nd December 1951

Withdrawal of Sinclair Drive trams.

Service 24A KELVINGROVE & SINCLAIR DRIVE withdrawn and replaced by existing Motorbus Service 43.

Sinclair Drive **closed** to trams.

25th December 1951

Crossover at JORDANHILL removed.

April 1952

Junction at Charing Cross redesigned and re-laid with complete realignment of tracks at mouth of St George's Road and removal of track from St George's Road westbound into Sauchiehall Street (formerly used by Service 16 North Street cars).

Single line link from Sauchiehall Street eastbound into St George's Road northbound realigned and retained for Depot workings and Shipyard Specials.

4th May 1952

The following Service Alterations take place:

Service 15 Sundays: ANDERSTON CROSS & BAILLIESTON or AIRDRIE frequency increased;

Service 23 Weekdays and Saturdays: GAIRBRAID AVENUE & BAILLIESTON or AIRDRIE via GARSCUBE ROAD cut back to terminate at BAILLIESTON except at Peak-hours;

Sundays: GAIRBRAID AVENUE & BAILLIESTON or AIRDRIE via GARSCUBE ROAD cut back to become GAIRBRAID AVENUE & BAILLIESTON via GARSCUBE ROAD;

Service 34 ANDERSTON CROSS & AUCHENSHUGGLE withdrawn and replaced by Specials on Service 9.

The following Service commences:

Service 9 Specials: ANDERSTON CROSS & AUCHENSHUGGLE from Stobcross Street at Warroch Street via Stobcross Street, Argyle Street and normal route.

5th May 1952

Frequency reduced at off-peak times on Weekdays on most services.

The following Service Alteration takes place:

Service 3 Weekdays and Saturdays: UNIVERSITY & MOSSPARK via POLLOKSHIELDS part cut back to become UNIVERSITY or ST VINCENT STREET & MOSSPARK via POLLOKSHIELDS Cars from St Vincent Street proceeding via Hope Street, Oswald Street, George V. Bridge, Commerce Street, Kingston Street and Eglinton Street; Inwards Cars for ST VINCENT STREET run via Union Street, Renfield Street and St Vincent Street;

Sundays: UNIVERSITY & MOSSPARK via POLLOKSHIELDS unaltered;

Service 15 Weekdays: ANDERSTON CROSS & BAILLIESTON or AIRDRIE increased in frequency at peak times to replace **Service 23**;

The following Operational Alterations take place:

Service 1 DALMUIR WEST or SCOTSTOUN WEST & DENNISTOUN

Service 30 BLAIRDARDIE or KELVINSIDE & DALMARNOCK

both reduced in frequency and Running Times on Weekday off-peaks.

Coronation Mark I cars used on **Service 1** since no journeys now proceed east of Dennistoun.

10th May 1952

The following Operational Alterations take place:

Service 3 Saturdays: UNIVERSITY & MOSSPARK via POLLOKSHIELDS

Service 12 Saturdays: MOUNT FLORIDA & LINTHOUSE via SHIELDS ROAD reduced in frequency.

1st June 1952

Preparation for Trolleybuses on Cathcart Road.

DIXON AVENUE crossover unwired.

15th June 1952

Withdrawal of Carmyle trams.

AUCHENSHUGGLE terminus moved eastwards from London Road at Tollcross Station Road to London Road just west of Causewayside Street.

The following Service Alterations take place:

Service 9 DALMUIR WEST or SCOTSTOUN & LONDON ROAD, AUCHENSHUGGLE or CARMYLE cut back to become DALMUIR WEST & LONDON ROAD or AUCHENSHUGGLE via former route to London Road then via London Road to London Road just west of Causewayside Street;

Service 9 Specials: ANDERSTON CROSS & AUCHENSHUGGLE extended to London Road just west of Causewayside Street and frequency reduced.

Service SCHOOLS SPECIALS to London Road at Kenmuirhill Road withdrawn.

Regular cars cease to operate on London Road from Causewayside Street to Carmyle Avenue; Special cars cease to operate on London Road from Carmyle Avenue to Kenmuirhill Road;

The following Operational Alterations take place:

Service 17 Weekdays and Saturdays: WHITEINCH & CAMBUSLANG via ANDERSTON CROSS
Sundays: ANDERSTON CROSS & CAMBUSLANG

Service 26 CLYDEBANK or SCOTSTOUN & OATLANDS or BURNSIDE via DALMARNOCK
timetables altered to co-ordinate with revised **Service 9**.

London Road from Causewayside Street to Hamilton Road at Mount Vernon **closed** to trams.

20th July 1952

Turnouts at Gorbals Cross linking Crown Street northwards and Norfolk Street westwards removed in both directions.

September 1952

Junction at Battlefield linking Grange Road and the former route to Sinclair Drive removed.

2nd November 1952

Line Opened in Nether Auldhouse Road west end from Cross Street to Shawholm Street.

POLLOKSHAWS terminus moved from Greenview Street west end to Nether Auldhouse Road west end.

Greenview Street turning point named GREENVIEW STREET.

The following Service Alteration takes place:

Service 31 LAMBHILL & POLLOKSHAWS via CHARING CROSS extended to new terminus via former route to

The destination on this Service 31 car reads "Pollokshaws" but displays the frugality of the screen-painting department. It had formerly indicated "Pollokshaws West" but the blanking of the word "West" addressed the renaming of the terminal point and gave this evident lopsided appearance. Car 661 is at the Round Toll.
(WD McMillan)

Pollokshaws Road then via Pollokshaws Road, Cross Street, Nether Auldhouse Road to Nether Auldhouse Road west end.

Service 14 UNIVERSITY & SPIERSBRIDGE or CROSSSTOBS and
Service 25 BISHOPBRIGGS or SPRINGBURN & CARNWADRIC or ROUKEN GLEN Circle via THORNLIEBANK shortworkings adjusted accordingly to either GREENVIEW STREET or POLLOKSHAWS

17th November 1952

Points blocked and overhead removed from the following disused curves:
Junction of Hope Street and Cowcaddens both directions between Hope Street and Cowcaddens eastwards;
Junction of Trongate with Glassford Street and Stockwell Street:
both directions between Glassford Street and Trongate eastwards;
both directions between Stockwell Street and Trongate eastwards.

11th January 1953

Preparations for Trolleybuses in St Vincent Place.
To allow space for erection of Trolleybus overhead alongside trams,
ST VINCENT PLACE loop and crossover disconnected, terminal point for City Centre cars moved to
NORTH ALBION STREET for Cars from and to west and to ST VINCENT STREET (at Wellington Street) for cars from and to east.

Service 1 DALMUIR WEST or SCOTSTOUN WEST & DENNISTOUN
Service 5 KELVINSIDE Circle via BOTANIC GARDENS & CLARKSTON
Service 5A KELVINSIDE Circle via HYNDLAND & CLARKSTON
Service 13 MILNGAVIE, MARYHILL or GAIRBRAID AVENUE & MOUNT FLORIDA or CLARKSTON via ST GEORGE'S CROSS
Service 13 Auxiliary: MARYHILL & GOVANHILL via ST GEORGE'S CROSS
Service 23 GAIRBRAID AVENUE & BAILLIESTON or AIRDRIE via GARSCUBE ROAD
Service 24 ANNIESLAND & LANGSIDE via HYNDLAND
Service 30 BLAIRDARDIE or KELVINSIDE & DALMARNOCK.
Shortworkings all adjusted accordingly.

During 1953

Allocation of 56 newest Coronation Mark II Cars (1337-1392) transferred from Newlands Depot to Govan Depot.

**When the newest Cunarders started cascading from Newlands to Govan Depot in 1953 they became the first modern trams allocated there since the war. Note the reflection of the windscreen of the Wolseley car on the glossy side of 1384 on Service 21 at the junction of Bothwell Street and St Vincent Street – unrecognisable today.
(RJS Wiseman)**

1st March 1953

The following Service Alteration takes place:

Service 12 Weekdays: MOUNT FLORIDA & LINTHOUSE via SHIELDS ROAD part cut back to become
MOUNT FLORIDA & PAISLEY ROAD TOLL or LINTHOUSE via SHIELDS ROAD with service to LINTHOUSE at Morning and Evening Peak hours only;
Saturdays and Sundays: MOUNT FLORIDA & LINTHOUSE via SHIELDS ROAD cut back to become
MOUNT FLORIDA & PAISLEY ROAD TOLL via SHIELDS ROAD.

16th March 1953

Preparations for Trolleybuses in Glassford Street.
GLASSFORD STREET crossover removed.

19th April 1953

Further Adjustments to Services in the East End.
The following Service Alterations take place:

Service 1 DALMUIR WEST or SCOTSTOUN WEST & DENNISTOUN extended to become
Weekdays: DALMUIR WEST or SCOTSTOUN WEST & DENNISTOUN or DALMARNOCK via former route to Duke Street then at Peak Hours via Duke Street, Parkhead Cross, Springfield Road, Dalmarnock Road to Dalmarnock Road at Birkwood Street;
Saturdays: DALMUIR WEST or SCOTSTOUN WEST & DENNISTOUN, SPRINGFIELD ROAD or DALMARNOCK
(Dennistoun until 1130; Springfield Road 1130-1730; Dalmarnock from 1730 onwards) ;
Sundays: DALMUIR WEST or SCOTSTOUN WEST & DENNISTOUN or DALMARNOCK.
(Dennistoun until 1400; Dalmarnock from 1400 onwards);

Service 30 Weekdays and Saturdays: BLAIRDARDIE or KELVINSIDE & DALMARNOCK altered to become
BLAIRDARDIE or ANNIESLAND & DALMARNOCK Anniesland Cars from Great Western Road east of Anniesland Cross via Great Western Road;
Sundays: BLAIRDARDIE & DALMARNOCK unaltered;

Service 9 Specials: ANDERSTON CROSS & AUCHENSHUGGLE withdrawn, replaced by revised **Service 10**;

Service 10 KELVINSIDE & PARKHEAD via PARK ROAD, Circle via GALLOWGATE altered to become
Weekdays and Saturdays: KELVINSIDE & LONDON ROAD via PARK ROAD via former route to Trongate then via Glasgow Cross, London Road, Bridgeton Cross, London Road to London Road at Maukinfauld Road;
Sundays: KELVINSIDE & GLASGOW CROSS, LONDON ROAD or AUCHENSHUGGLE via PARK ROAD.
(Glasgow Cross until 1300; Auchenshuggle 1300-1900; London Road from 1900 onwards) for Glasgow Cross via London Road, Moir Street returning via same route;
for Auchenshuggle to London Road just west of Causewayside Street;

Service 36 KELVINSIDE & PARKHEAD via PARK ROAD, Circle via DALMARNOCK ROAD withdrawn.

The following Operational Alteration takes place:
Coronation Mark I cars withdrawn from working on **Service 1**.
Dalmarnock Depot commences part operation of **Service 1**.

2nd June 1953

Coronation of Queen Elizabeth. Special Timetables in operation on all Services.

The brief allocation of Coronation trams to Service 1 came to an end when Dennistoun ceased to be the normal terminus in the East End. Here is one passing Kelvin Court on Great Western Road. These luxury flats always looked as if they would have been more at home in West London rather than in Glasgow. Anniesland railway bridge can be seen in the distance.
(Dewi Williams)

25th June 1953

Official Visit of Queen Elizabeth to the city.
Various streets, including George Square, closed-off to traffic.
Various Services diverted and split accordingly, including:

Service 1 Weekdays: DALMUIR WEST or SCOTSTOUN WEST & DENNISTOUN or DALMARNOCK

Service 13 Weekdays: MILNGAVIE, MARYHILL or GAIRBRAID AVENUE & MOUNT FLORIDA or CLARKSTON via ST GEORGE'S CROSS.

Service 13 Auxiliary Weekdays: MARYHILL & GOVANHILL via ST GEORGE'S CROSS

Service 23 Weekdays: GAIRBRAID AVENUE & BAILLIESTON or AIRDRIE via GARSCUBE ROAD

Service 30 Weekdays: BLAIRDARDIE or ANNIESLAND & DALMARNOCK.

5th July 1953

Conversion of Clarkston route to Trolleybus operation.
The following Service Alterations take place:

Service 5 KELVINSIDE Circle via BOTANIC GARDENS & CLARKSTON cut back to become
KELVINSIDE Circle via BOTANIC GARDENS & HOLMLEA ROAD and

Service 5A KELVINSIDE Circle via HYNDLAND & CLARKSTON cut back to become
KELVINSIDE Circle via HYNDLAND & HOLMLEA ROAD (Cars show "5" on journeys to Holmlea Road)
both via former route to Holmlea Road then via Holmlea Road to Holmlea Road at new crossover at Morley Street;

Service 12 MOUNT FLORIDA & PAISLEY ROAD TOLL or LINTHOUSE Specials to NETHERLEE and to CLARKSTON withdrawn;

Service 13 MILNGAVIE, MARYHILL or GAIRBRAID AVENUE & MOUNT FLORIDA or CLARKSTON via ST GEORGE'S CROSS cut back and diverted to become
MILNGAVIE, MARYHILL or GAIRBRAID AVENUE & GLASGOW CROSS via ST GEORGE'S CROSS via former route to Cowcaddens then via Hope Street, Argyle Street, Trongate, Glasgow Cross, Gallowgate, Moir Street returning via same route;

Service 13 Weekdays and Saturdays Auxiliary: MARYHILL & GOVANHILL via ST GEORGE'S CROSS cut back to become MARYHILL & MAITLAND STREET;

Service 13 Sundays Auxiliary: MILNGAVIE & MAITLAND STREET unaltered;

Service 23 GAIRBRAID AVENUE & BAILLIESTON or AIRDRIE via GARSCUBE ROAD diverted to become
GAIRBRAID AVENUE & BAILLIESTON or AIRDRIE via ST GEORGE'S CROSS via former route to Queen's Cross then via Maryhill Road, St George's Cross, New City Road, Cambridge Street, Sauchiehall Street, Renfield Street, St Vincent Street, St Vincent Place and former route.
Garscube Road, West Nile Street, Gorbals, Cathcart Road, Clarkston trams replaced by **Trolleybus Service 105**.

To residents of Netherlee and Clarkston, the trolleybuses were no substitute for the trams. They bypassed the shops in Victoria Road as well as Central Station, Renfield and Sauchiehall Streets. They were also less reliable than the trams and it is little wonder that Western SMT buses benefited from increased custom. The trolleybuses tended to bunch as can be seen here at the Clincart Road junction where a Service 12 tram awaits its lonely journey along Cathcart Road. *(BJ Cross Collection)*

Service "Hampden Wheel" ST VINCENT STREET & FOOTBALL SPECIALS [Mount Florida] **withdrawn**.
The following Operational Alteration takes place:
Adjustment to Langside Depot Journeys.
Service 12 MOUNT FLORIDA & PAISLEY ROAD TOLL or LINTHOUSE via SHIELDS ROAD
Langside Depot Journeys via Holmlea Road, Garry Street crossover and Cathcart Road revert to former route via Prospecthill Road.
Garscube Road from Queen's Cross to Round Toll, Cowcaddens from Hope Street to West Nile Street, Renfield Street from Cowcaddens to Sauchiehall Street, West Nile Street, George Square south, South Frederick Street, Ingram Street, Glassford Street, Stockwell Street, Victoria Bridge, Gorbals Street, Cathcart Road from Gorbals Street to Allison Street, Cathcart Road from Clincart Road to Holmlea Road, Holmlea Road from Morley Street to Cathcart New Bridge, Clarkston Road, Busby Road and Mearns Road **closed** to trams.

2nd August 1953

The following Service Alteration takes place:
Service 32 ELDERSLIE & BISHOPBRIGGS via RENFIELD STREET cut back to become
ELDERSLIE & SPRINGBURN via RENFIELD STREET via former route to Springburn Road then Elmvale Street to Elmvale Street east end.

29th August 1953

Collapse of deeply-seated sewer in Park Road at Woodlands Road.
Intersection of Park Road and Woodlands Road closed to all traffic.
Service 10 KELVINSIDE & LONDON ROAD via PARK ROAD diverted between Botanic Gardens and Charing Cross via Byres Road, Church Street, Dumbarton Road, Argyle Street, Sauchiehall Street.

30th August 1953

Collapse of deeply-seated sewer in Park Road at Woodlands Road.
The following Temporary Service Alteration takes place:
Service 10 Weekdays and Saturdays: KELVINSIDE & LONDON ROAD via PARK ROAD split to become
KELVINSIDE & PARK ROAD via normal route to Park Road north end; and
UNIVERSITY & LONDON ROAD from University Avenue at Kelvin Way via University Avenue, Gibson Street, Eldon Street, Woodlands Road and normal route;
Sundays: KELVINSIDE via PARK ROAD & GLASGOW CROSS, LONDON ROAD or AUCHENSHUGGLE split to become
KELVINSIDE & PARK ROAD and UNIVERSITY & GLASGOW CROSS, LONDON ROAD or AUCHENSHUGGLE.

September 1953

Introduction of one-way operation for all trams turning at Glasgow Cross from the west.
All Cars now approach via Trongate, Glasgow Cross, London Road to Moir Street returning via Moir Street, Gallowgate, Glasgow Cross and Trongate.

Car 231 is heading east along Parliamentary Road to the short-lived Colston terminus in an area now totally razed and redeveloped.
(WD McMillan)

Service 10 Sundays: KELVINSIDE & GLASGOW CROSS via PARK ROAD
Service 13 MILNGAVIE, MARYHILL or GAIRBRAID AVENUE & GLASGOW CROSS via ST GEORGE'S CROSS
both altered accordingly.

4th October 1953

Rearrangement of Maryhill Road and Gallowgate services.
The following Service Alterations take place:
Service 13 MILNGAVIE, MARYHILL or GAIRBRAID AVENUE & GLASGOW CROSS via ST GEORGE'S CROSS withdrawn and replaced by revised **Service 29**;
Service 13 Weekdays and Saturdays Auxiliary: MARYHILL & MAITLAND STREET incorporated into **Service 29**;
Service 13 Sundays Auxiliary: MILNGAVIE & MAITLAND STREET incorporated into **Service 29**;
Service 29 ANDERSTON CROSS & TOLLCROSS or BROOMHOUSE diverted and extended to become
MILNGAVIE, MARYHILL or GAIRBRAID AVENUE & TOLLCROSS or BROOMHOUSE via NORMAL SCHOOL from Main Street Milngavie at Park Road via Main Street Milngavie, Milngavie Road, Maryhill Road, Queen's Cross, Maryhill Road, St George's Cross, New City Road, Cowcaddens, Hope Street, Argyle Street and former route;
Weekdays and Saturdays Auxiliary: MARYHILL & MAITLAND STREET per former **Service 13** route;
Sundays Auxiliary: MILNGAVIE & MAITLAND STREET per former **Service 13** route;
Sundays Afternoons only: ANDERSTON CROSS & BROOMHOUSE. (Cars show "15" on journeys to ANDERSTON CROSS).
Provision of Service to new housing area at Arden.
ARDEN crossover opened on Private Track on north side of Nitshill Road west of Kyleakin Road.
SPIERSBRIDGE crossover disused.
The following Service Alteration takes place:
Service 14 UNIVERSITY & SPIERSBRIDGE or CROSSSTOBS shortworkings extended to become
UNIVERSITY & ARDEN or CROSSSTOBS Arden cars proceed on Private Track on north side of Nitshill Road to Private Track west of Kyleakin Road.

October 1953

Ex-Liverpool Streamliner Cars start entering service from Maryhill Depot on **Service 29**.

Service 29 was initially the sole preserve of the ex-Liverpool "Streamliner" cars and they became a familiar sight in the city streets. The "destination" and "via" screens were soon transposed to make the ultimate destination easier to read when cars were running nose-to-tail in queues of rush-hour trams. Any enthusiast would have immediately known it was a 29 tram from its being a speck on the horizon!
(RR Clark / STTS Collection)

19th October 1953

Repairs to deeply-seated sewer in Park Road at Woodlands Road completed. Streets reopened to traffic.

Service 10 Weekdays and Saturdays: KELVINSIDE & LONDON ROAD via PARK ROAD

Sundays: KELVINSIDE & GLASGOW CROSS, LONDON ROAD or AUCHENSHUGGLE via PARK ROAD revert to normal service.

1st November 1953

SPIERSBRIDGE crossover disconnected.

2nd November 1953

The following Service Alteration takes place:

Service 29 Weekdays and Saturdays Auxiliary: MARYHILL & MAITLAND STREET extended to become MARYHILL & GLASGOW CROSS via NORMAL SCHOOL via former route to Cowcaddens then via Hope Street, Argyle Street, Trongate, Glasgow Cross, London Road, Moir Street returning via Moir Street, Gallowgate, Glasgow Cross, Trongate and outward route.

December 1953

Track lifted from MacKinlay Street, Abbotsford Place and South Portland Street on former Carlton Place route.

7th February 1954

SANDYFORD crossover also named PAISLEY NORTH for Cars turning from the City.

The following Service Alteration takes place:

Service 4 SPRINGBURN & RENFREW SOUTH via KEPPOCHHILL ROAD extended to become SPRINGBURN & PAISLEY NORTH via KEPPOCHHILL ROAD via former route to Paisley Road Renfrew then via Paisley Road Renfrew, Renfrew Road Paisley to Renfrew Road Paisley at Glencairn Road.

To accommodate ex-Liverpool trams, Caldercuilt Road closed.

MARYHILL terminus moved from Caldercuilt Road west end to Maryhill Road at Garscube Estate East Lodge Gate.

Service 29 MILNGAVIE, MARYHILL or GAIRBRAID AVENUE & TOLLCROSS or BROOMHOUSE via NORMAL SCHOOL

Service 29 Weekdays and Saturdays Auxiliary: MARYHILL & GLASGOW CROSS via NORMAL SCHOOL

Service 40 DUMBRECK or IBROX & MARYHILL via CHARING CROSS

all altered accordingly.

Caldercuilt Road **closed** to trams.

4th April 1954

The following Operational Alteration takes place:

Relief Point for crews from Partick Depot on **Services 5, 21** and **24** moved.

9th May 1954

The following Service Alteration takes place:

Service 40 Sundays: IBROX & MARYHILL via CHARING CROSS cut back to become DOUGLAS STREET & MARYHILL via CHARING CROSS from Bothwell Street at Douglas Street via Bothwell Street and former route;

Weekdays: DUMBRECK or IBROX & MARYHILL via CHARING CROSS unaltered;

Saturdays: IBROX & MARYHILL via CHARING CROSS unaltered.

28th June 1954

The following Operational Alterations take place:

Service 28 Weekdays and Saturdays: GLENFIELD & RENFREW FERRY

Service [Paisley Local] LOCHFIELD ROAD & PAISLEY CROSS or RENFREW FERRY

Running Times reduced.

15th August 1954

Sauchiehall Street/Renfield Street junction re-laid, severing disused tracks to top part of Renfield Street between Sauchiehall Street and Cowcaddens.

22nd August 1954

The following Service Alteration takes place:

Service 40 Sundays: DOUGLAS STREET & MARYHILL via CHARING CROSS withdrawn;

Weekdays: DUMBRECK or IBROX & MARYHILL via CHARING CROSS unaltered;

Saturdays: IBROX & MARYHILL via CHARING CROSS unaltered.

19th September 1954

Eastfield Permanent Way Coup **closed.**
Access Line from Springburn Road **closed.**
Line constructed in Hillcroft Terrace, Colston.
New Permanent Way Coup **opened** beyond Hillcroft Terrace, Colston.

As one coup closes, another one opens. When the Eastfield Permanent Way coup closed, just along the Springburn Road a new one was constructed at Hillcroft Terrace, Colston. This was over-looked by tenement property and one wonders what residents thought of night time activities such as these where PW Car No.51 has been unloading granite setts and rubble. (*AK Terry*)

29th September 1954

Further Alterations to Renfrew Ferry terminus to keep trams clear of waiting vehicular ferry traffic.

Service 28 GLENFIELD & RENFREW FERRY

Service [Paisley Local] LOCHFIELD ROAD & PAISLEY CROSS or RENFREW FERRY

both adjusted accordingly.

10th October 1954

COLSTON terminus **opened** in Hillcroft Terrace.

Rearrangement of Bishopbriggs and of Bothwell Street services.

The following Service Alterations take place:

Service 17 WHITEINCH or ANDERSTON CROSS & CAMBUSLANG altered reverting to become

ANNIESLAND & CAMBUSLANG via BOTHWELL STREET from Anniesland Cross via Crow Road, Dumbarton Road, Argyle Street, St Vincent Street, Bothwell Street, Hope Street, Argyle Street, Trongate and former route;

Service 21 ELDERSLIE & ANNIESLAND via BOTHWELL STREET cut back to become

ELDERSLIE & ST VINCENT STREET via former route to Nelson Street then via Nelson Street, Bridge Street, Glasgow Bridge, Jamaica Street, Union Street, Renfield Street, St Vincent Street returning via St Vincent Street, Hope Street, Oswald Street, George V. Bridge, Commerce Street and Nelson Street then inwards route;

Service 25 BISHOPBRIGGS or SPRINGBURN & CARNWADRIC or ROUKEN GLEN Circle via THORNLIEBANK cut back to become

COLSTON or SPRINGBURN & CARNWADRIC or ROUKEN GLEN Circle via THORNLIEBANK from Hillcroft Terrace west end via Hillcroft Terrace, Kirkintilloch Road and former route;

Service 32 ELDERSLIE & SPRINGBURN via RENFIELD STREET altered to become

CROOKSTON & BISHOPBRIGGS via RENFIELD STREET from Crookston Road north end via Crookston Road, Paisley Road West and former route to Springburn Road then via Springburn Road, Kirkintilloch Road, Kenmure Avenue to Kenmure Avenue east end.

The following Operational Alterations take place:

Service 16 Weekdays: SPRINGBURN & SCOTSTOUN via KEPPOCHHILL ROAD, ELMBANK STREET

Service 22 Saturdays: CROOKSTON & LAMBHILL

Service 28 Weekdays: GLENFIELD & RENFREW FERRY

Service 29 Saturdays: MILNGAVIE, MARYHILL or GAIRBRAID AVENUE & GLASGOW CROSS, TOLLCROSS or BROOMHOUSE via NORMAL SCHOOL

Service 31 Saturdays: LAMBHILL & POLLOKSHAWS via CHARING CROSS.

various adjustments to Running Times and/or frequencies at certain times.

11th October 1954

The following Service Alterations take place:

Service 15 Weekdays: ANDERSTON CROSS & BAILLIESTON or AIRDRIE frequency to AIRDRIE increased to replace Service 23;

Service 23 Weekdays: GAIRBRAID AVENUE & BAILLIESTON or AIRDRIE via ST GEORGE'S CROSS cut back to become

GAIRBRAID AVENUE & BAILLIESTON via ST GEORGE'S CROSS via former route to Private Track on south side of Coatbridge Road west end;

Saturdays and Sundays: GAIRBRAID AVENUE & BAILLIESTON via ST GEORGE'S CROSS unaltered.

155

Number 1243 was one of the Coronations that lasted until the very end. It is seen here on Service 15 at Bargeddie before reversing and returning to the city.
(RR Clark / STTS Collection)

8th November 1954

The following Operational Alteration takes place:

Service 29 Weekdays: MILNGAVIE, MARYHILL or GAIRBRAID AVENUE & GLASGOW CROSS, TOLLCROSS or BROOMHOUSE via NORMAL SCHOOL Running Times increased.

15th February 1955

Siding in East King Street, Rutherglen to Substation **closed** to trams.

28th February 1955

The following Operational Alteration takes place:

Service 17 Weekdays: ANNIESLAND & CAMBUSLANG via BOTHWELL STREET Running Times increased.

20th March 1955

Traffic management problems experienced at Hillcroft Terrace.

The following Service Alterations take place:

Service 25 COLSTON or SPRINGBURN & CARNWADRIC or ROUKEN GLEN Circle via THORNLIEBANK re-extended to become

BISHOPBRIGGS or SPRINGBURN & CARNWADRIC or ROUKEN GLEN Circle via THORNLIEBANK from Kenmure Avenue east end via Kenmure Avenue, Kirkintilloch Road and former route;

Service 32 CROOKSTON & BISHOPBRIGGS via RENFIELD STREET part cut back to become

CROOKSTON & SPRINGBURN or BISHOPBRIGGS via RENFIELD STREET Springburn Cars run to Elmvale Street east end. Hillcroft Terrace **closed** to service trams, retained for Permanent Way Department cars proceeding to and from Coup.

7th May 1955

The following Operational Alterations take place:

Service 8 Saturdays: MILLERSTON or RIDDRIE & GIFFNOCK or ROUKEN GLEN Circle via GIFFNOCK

Service 18A was created as part of the preparations for the introduction of trolleybuses to Rutherglen. Standard car 255 under the control of one of the Department's Motorwomen is about to turn east from Hope Street into Argyle Street. (RJS Wiseman)

Service 25 Saturdays: BISHOPBRIGGS or SPRINGBURN & CARNWADRIC or ROUKEN GLEN Circle via THORNLIEBANK frequency reduced.

7th August 1955

Preparations for introduction of Trolleybuses to Rutherglen.
The following Service Alterations take place:

Service 18 SPRINGBURN & RUTHERGLEN or BURNSIDE via BILSLAND DRIVE, RUTHERGLEN BRIDGE split, part-diverted and altered to become

Service 18 SPRINGBURN & BURNSIDE via BILSLAND DRIVE, DALMARNOCK via former route to Bridgeton Cross then via Dalmarnock Road, Farme Cross, Farmeloan Road, Stonelaw Road and former route;

Service 18A SPRINGBURN & SHAWFIELD via BILSLAND DRIVE, RUTHERGLEN BRIDGE via former route to Glasgow Road then via Glasgow Road to Glasgow Road north of Rutherglen Road;

Cars show "18" on journeys to Springburn;

Service 26 CLYDEBANK or SCOTSTOUN & OATLANDS or BURNSIDE via DALMARNOCK split, part-diverted and altered to become

Service 26 CLYDEBANK or SCOTSTOUN & BURNSIDE via DALMARNOCK via former route;

Service 26A CLYDEBANK or SCOTSTOUN & SHAWFIELD via RUTHERGLEN BRIDGE via former route to Bridgeton Cross then via Main Street Bridgeton, Rutherglen Bridge, Shawfield Road, Glasgow Road to Glasgow Road north of Rutherglen Road;

Cars show "26" on journeys to Scotstoun or Clydebank.

Main Street Rutherglen, Glasgow Road Rutherglen to north of Rutherglen Road, Rutherglen Road between Glasgow Road and east of Shawfield Drive **closed** to trams.

2nd November 1955

Line in Annan Street linking Grange Road and Prospecthill Road **closed** to trams and unwired.

Résumé

1st January 1956

The following Tram Services operating:

1	DALMUIR WEST or SCOTSTOUN WEST & DENNISTOUN, SPRINGFIELD ROAD or DALMARNOCK
3	UNIVERSITY or ST VINCENT STREET & MOSSPARK via POLLOKSHIELDS
4	SPRINGBURN & PAISLEY NORTH via KEPPOCHHILL ROAD
5	KELVINSIDE Circle via BOTANIC GARDENS & HOLMLEA ROAD
	Circle Cars return as Service 5A route (All Cars show "5" on journeys to HOLMLEA ROAD)
5A	KELVINSIDE Circle via HYNDLAND & HOLMLEA ROAD
	Circle Cars return as Service 5 route (All Cars show "5" on journeys to HOLMLEA ROAD)
6	SCOTSTOUN & ALEXANDRA PARK or RIDDRIE
7	MILLERSTON or RIDDRIE & BELLAHOUSTON via BRIDGETON CROSS
	MILLERSTON & BRIDGETON CROSS (Sundays Afternoons only)
8	MILLERSTON or RIDDRIE & GIFFNOCK or ROUKEN GLEN Circle via GIFFNOCK
	Circle Cars return as Service 25 to SPRINGBURN or BISHOPBRIGGS
9	DALMUIR WEST & LONDON ROAD or AUCHENSHUGGLE
10	KELVINSIDE & GLASGOW CROSS, LONDON ROAD or AUCHENSHUGGLE via PARK ROAD
12	MOUNT FLORIDA & PAISLEY ROAD TOLL or LINTHOUSE via SHIELDS ROAD
14	UNIVERSITY & ARDEN or CROSSSTOBS
15	ANDERSTON CROSS & BAILLIESTON or AIRDRIE
16	SPRINGBURN & SCOTSTOUN via KEPPOCHHILL ROAD, ELMBANK STREET
17	ANNIESLAND & CAMBUSLANG via BOTHWELL STREET
18	SPRINGBURN & BURNSIDE via BILSLAND DRIVE, DALMARNOCK
18A	SPRINGBURN & SHAWFIELD via BILSLAND DRIVE, RUTHERGLEN BRIDGE
	(Cars show "18" on journeys to SPRINGBURN)
21	ELDERSLIE & ST VINCENT STREET
22	CROOKSTON & LAMBHILL
23	GAIRBRAID AVENUE & BAILLIESTON via ST GEORGE'S CROSS
24	ANNIESLAND & LANGSIDE via HYNDLAND
25	BISHOPBRIGGS or SPRINGBURN & CARNWADRIC or ROUKEN GLEN Circle via THORNLIEBANK
	Circle Cars return as Service 8 to RIDDRIE or MILLERSTON
26	CLYDEBANK or SCOTSTOUN & BURNSIDE via DALMARNOCK
26A	CLYDEBANK or SCOTSTOUN & SHAWFIELD via RUTHERGLEN BRIDGE
	(Cars show "26" on journeys to SCOTSTOUN or CLYDEBANK)
27	SPRINGBURN or POSSILPARK & SHIELDHALL or RENFREW CROSS
28	GLENFIELD & RENFREW FERRY
29	MILNGAVIE, MARYHILL or GAIRBRAID AVENUE & TOLLCROSS or BROOMHOUSE via NORMAL SCHOOL
	MARYHILL & GLASGOW CROSS via NORMAL SCHOOL (No Sundays Service)
	MILNGAVIE & MAITLAND STREET via NORMAL SCHOOL (Sundays only)
	ANDERSTON CROSS & BROOMHOUSE (Sundays Afternoons only)
	(Cars show "15" on journeys to ANDERSTON CROSS)
30	BLAIRDARDIE or ANNIESLAND & DALMARNOCK
31	LAMBHILL & POLLOKSHAWS via CHARING CROSS
32	CROOKSTON & SPRINGBURN or BISHOPBRIGGS via RENFIELD STREET
33	CIRCLE SPRINGBURN & CHARING CROSS
40	DUMBRECK or IBROX & MARYHILL via CHARING CROSS (No Sundays Service)
-	[Airdrie Local] LANGLOAN & AIRDRIE
-	[Paisley Local] PAISLEY WEST or PAISLEY CROSS & HAWKHEAD ROAD (Part Day)
-	[Paisley Local] LOCHFIELD ROAD & PAISLEY CROSS or RENFREW FERRY (Part Day)

12th March 1956

The following Service Alteration takes place:
Service [Airdrie Local] LANGLOAN & AIRDRIE curtailed to Part Day only.

18th March 1956

YOKER crossover moved from Dumbarton Road west end at Yoker Burn eastwards to Dumbarton Road west of Yoker Ferry Road.
Service 1 DALMUIR WEST or SCOTSTOUN WEST & DENNISTOUN, SPRINGFIELD ROAD or DALMARNOCK.
Service 9 DALMUIR WEST & LONDON ROAD or AUCHENSHUGGLE
adjusted accordingly for shortworkings and late night cars.

8th April 1956

The following Service Alteration takes place:
Service 31 LAMBHILL & POLLOKSHAWS via CHARING CROSS diverted to become
LAMBHILL & MERRYLEE via CHARING CROSS via former route to Shawlands Cross then via Kilmarnock Road to Kilmarnock Road at Merrylee Road.

29th April 1956

The following Service Alteration takes place:
Service 1 Weekdays: DALMUIR WEST or SCOTSTOUN WEST & DENNISTOUN or DALMARNOCK cut back at off-peak times, proceeding to DALMUIR WEST (until 0830, 1600-1830) only east end unaltered, DALMARNOCK at Morning and Evening peaks only;
Saturdays: DALMUIR WEST or SCOTSTOUN WEST & DENNISTOUN, SPRINGFIELD ROAD or DALMARNOCK cut back to become
SCOTSTOUN WEST & DENNISTOUN, SPRINGFIELD ROAD or DALMARNOCK.
(Dennistoun until 1130; Springfield Road 1130-1730; Dalmarnock 1730 onwards);
Sundays: DALMUIR WEST or SCOTSTOUN WEST & DENNISTOUN or DALMARNOCK part cut back proceeding to
DALMUIR WEST (Until 0830; From 1500-1700) only, east end unaltered
(Dennistoun until 1400; Dalmarnock from 1400 onwards).

7th May 1956

The following Service Alteration takes place:
Service 1 Weekdays: DALMUIR WEST or SCOTSTOUN WEST & DENNISTOUN or DALMARNOCK part-re-extended to become
DALMUIR WEST, YOKER or SCOTSTOUN WEST & DENNISTOUN or DALMARNOCK
(Dalmuir West until 0830,1600-1830; Yoker 1200-1400) east end unaltered.

5th August 1956

BON ACCORD STREET crossover, Clydebank, removed.

The southern terminus of Service 31 was altered from Pollokshaws to Merrylee. Standard car 705 was heading for Merrylee when photographed on Balmore Road. This car was unusual in having silver Coronation-type numerals on the dash panel (at one end only!) instead of the normal green transfers.
(WD McMillan)

Time Frame 1956 – 1963: Decline and Demise

As long ago as November 1951 the Glasgow & District Transport Committee, under Sir Robert Inglis' chairmanship, had issued its Report on the future of Glasgow's Transport. Now known as "The Inglis Report" it recommended electrification of suburban railways and the quid pro quo was the curtailment of the tramways to within the City boundary – ultimately leading to their replacement. Whether or not this directly or indirectly led to the abandonment of the tram services is not completely clear but in this final Time Frame services beyond the boundary are indeed withdrawn, and in January 1957 it is announced that the system is to be completely eliminated, replaced mainly by motorbuses, but also by further trolleybus services. The latter would continue to use power generated by the recently modernised Pinkston Power Station but its sale to the South of Scotland Electricity Board in the following year suggests that the City's trolleybuses do not have a secure future either.

The closure of services beyond Arden eliminated the "white knuckle ride" to Barrhead and beyond via the undulating roadside reservation. Here is car 116 at the Board of Trade (compulsory) stop at the top of the hill beside Darnley Fire Station before descending the grade on which 976 came to grief in February 1941. (RJS Wiseman)

30th September 1956
Closure of Barrhead and Cross Stobs route.
The following Service Alteration takes place:
Service 14 UNIVERSITY & ARDEN or CROSSSTOBS cut back to become
UNIVERSITY & ARDEN.
Private Track on north side of Nitshill Road from west of Kyleakin Road westwards,
Private Track on north side of Parkhouse Road, Darnley Road, Main St Barrhead, Allan's Corner, Cross Arthurlie Street, Paisley Road Barrhead and south end of Capelthill Road **closed** to trams.
Langside Depot **closed** to trams; Cars to Newlands Depot.
Prospecthill Road retained out of use.
The following Operational Alterations take place:
Langside Depot Operation of
Service 5 KELVINSIDE Circle via BOTANIC GARDENS & HOLMLEA ROAD
Service 5 KELVINSIDE Circle via HYNDLAND & HOLMLEA ROAD
Service 24 ANNIESLAND & LANGSIDE via HYNDLAND
all transferred to Newlands Depot;
Langside Depot Operation of
Service 12 MOUNT FLORIDA & PAISLEY ROAD TOLL or LINTHOUSE via SHIELDS ROAD
transferred to Govan Depot.

4th November 1956
Withdrawal of tram services beyond the City Boundary to Milngavie, Cambuslang, Coatbridge and Airdrie.

Standard cars 609 and 124 pass on Milngavie Road when the Service was provided by the 13s. As was common practice the conductress is about to change the screens while 609 is still in motion.
(John H Meredith)

There is little visible in this view of Cambuslang Main Street that has survived the Millennium. About to pass Cambuslang Trinity Church of Scotland, Car 180 is heading for the terminus at the end of Main Street.
(RJS Wiseman)

The following Service Alterations take place:

Service 15 ANDERSTON CROSS & BAILLIESTON or AIRDRIE cut back to become
ANDERSTON CROSS & BAILLIESTON via former route to Private Track on south side of Coatbridge Road west end;

Service [Airdrie Local] LANGLOAN & AIRDRIE withdrawn without replacement;
Coatbridge Depot **closed** to trams; Cars to Dennistoun Depot and Parkhead Depot.

Service 17 ANNIESLAND & CAMBUSLANG via BOTHWELL STREET cut back to become
ANNIESLAND & FARME CROSS via BOTHWELL STREET via former route to Farme Cross then via Cambuslang Road to Cambuslang Road at Duchess Road;

Service 29 MILNGAVIE, MARYHILL or GAIRBRAID AVENUE & TOLLCROSS or BROOMHOUSE via NORMAL SCHOOL cut back to become
MARYHILL or GAIRBRAID AVENUE & TOLLCROSS or BROOMHOUSE via NORMAL SCHOOL from Maryhill Road at Garscube Estate East Lodge Gate via Maryhill Road and former route;

Weekdays and Saturdays Auxiliary: MARYHILL & GLASGOW CROSS via NORMAL SCHOOL unaltered;

Sundays Auxiliary: MILNGAVIE & MAITLAND STREET via NORMAL SCHOOL withdrawn without replacement;

Sundays Afternoons only: ANDERSTON CROSS & BROOMHOUSE unaltered;

Service 40 DUMBRECK or IBROX & MARYHILL via CHARING CROSS (No Sundays Service) withdrawn without replacement.

Private Track on south side of Coatbridge Road from east of Baillieston crossover, Private Track on south side of Glasgow Road, Bank Street Coatbridge, Main Street Coatbridge, Deedes Street, Alexander Street Airdrie, Stirling Street, Graham Street and Clark Street Airdrie, Cambuslang Road eastwards from Duchess Road, Glasgow Road Cambuslang, Main Street Cambuslang, Main Street Milngavie, Milngavie Road, Maryhill Road north of Garscube Estate East Lodge Gate **closed** to trams.

16th December 1956

Suez Crisis resulting in oil shortages.
Trams reintroduced on several Night Services. See separate list.
Planned withdrawal of Paisley and Renfrew tram services delayed.

10th February 1957

BAILLIESTON terminus moved westwards from Private Track on south side of Coatbridge Road to Main Street Baillieston just east of Martin Crescent
Service 15 ANDERSTON CROSS & BAILLIESTON
Service 23 GAIRBRAID AVENUE & BAILLIESTON via ST GEORGE'S CROSS
both adjusted accordingly.
Main Street Baillieston east of Martin Crescent and Private Track on south side of Coatbridge Road west end **closed** to trams.

9th March 1957

Mass X-Ray Campaign in city.
Illuminated Works Car tours system.

30th March 1957

Suez Crisis over, oil supplies restored.
Tram Night Services reconverted to Motorbus operation. See separate list.

13th April 1957

Mass X-Ray Campaign completed.

12th May 1957

Withdrawal of tram services beyond the City Boundary to Paisley and Renfrew.

The Suez Crisis gave the Paisley services a stay of execution. Service 21 had latterly run from St Vincent Street to Elderslie and Car 986 is seen here on Glasgow Road approaching the stop for the Kelbourne Cinema and the Paisley Ice Rink. This interurban service was handed over to Western SMT.
(WD McMillan, Courtesy Travel Lens Photographic)

162

About to take the plunge down St Mirren Brae at Paisley Cross is Coronation 1271 on Service 28. This car had, until then, never been allocated to any other depot than Elderslie and only had to visit the main Car Works for major work that Elderslie could not undertake in its own workshops.
(WD McMillan, Courtesy Travel Lens Photographic)

The abandonment of Paisley services also eliminated the last short stretch of single track used by regular service cars (as opposed to depot workings). This was in Weir Street and Standard car 104 is seen on the single line. Although displaying "28", it is out of service, probably on a test run.
(WD McMillan)

Service 21 ELDERSLIE & ST VINCENT STREET withdrawn without replacement;
Service 28 GLENFIELD & RENFREW FERRY withdrawn without replacement;
Service [Paisley Local] LOCHFIELD ROAD & PAISLEY CROSS or RENFREW FERRY (Part Day) withdrawn without replacement;
Service [Paisley Local] PAISLEY WEST or PAISLEY CROSS & HAWKHEAD ROAD (Part Day) withdrawn without replacement.
Elderslie Depot and Works **closed** to trams; Standard cars to Govan, Possilpark and Maryhill Depots, Coronation cars to Dalmarnock Depot, Lightweight cars to Govan Depot.
The following Service Alterations take place:
Service 4 SPRINGBURN & PAISLEY NORTH via KEPPOCHHILL ROAD cut back to become
SPRINGBURN & HILLINGTON ROAD via KEPPOCHHILL ROAD via former route to Renfrew Road at Hillington Road;
Service 22 CROOKSTON & LAMBHILL additional early morning journeys provided from Crookston to replace **Service 21**;

Service 27 SPRINGBURN or POSSILPARK & SHIELDHALL or RENFREW CROSS cut back to become
SPRINGBURN or POSSILPARK & SHIELDHALL via former route to Bogmoor Road north end.
Main Road Elderslie, Beith Road, Ferguslie, Broomlands Street, Wellmeadow Street, High Street Paisley, St James Bridge, Smithhills, Gauze Street, Glasgow Road, Paisley Road West west of Crookston Road, Caplethill Road from Glenfield Road, Nitshill Road, Causeyside Street, St Mirren Street, Gilmour Street, County Square, Old Sneddon Street, Abercorn Street, Weir Street, Renfrew Road Paisley, Paisley Road Renfrew, Hairst Street, Canal Street, Ferry Road, High Street Renfrew, Glasgow Road Renfrew **closed** to trams.

2nd August 1957

Line in Dalhousie Street to Substation **closed** to trams.

18th August 1957

MERRYLEE Crossover moved 180 yards south from Kilmarnock Road at Merrylee Road to Kilmarnock Road at Mulberry Road.
Service 31 LAMBHILL & MERRYLEE via CHARING CROSS extended accordingly.
The following Service Alteration takes place:
Service 23 GAIRBRAID AVENUE & BAILLIESTON via ST GEORGE'S CROSS extended to become
MARYHILL & BAILLIESTON via ST GEORGE'S CROSS from Maryhill Road at Garscube Estate East Lodge Gate via Maryhill Road and former route.

6th October 1957

Sunday Civil Engineering Works at Cambridge Street corner to raise the level of the roadway and citybound tram track with relaying of both tracks in asphalt.
Service 1 Sundays: DALMUIR WEST or SCOTSTOUN WEST & DENNISTOUN or DALMARNOCK
Service 23 Sundays: MARYHILL & BAILLIESTON via ST GEORGE'S CROSS
Service 30 Sundays: BLAIRDARDIE & DALMARNOCK
Eastbound cars diverted from New City Road at Cambridge Street to St Vincent Street at Renfield Street via New City Road, Cowcaddens, Hope Street, St Vincent Street and then normal route;
Westbound cars unaltered; Normal Service resumes 1900 hrs.

17th November 1957

Withdrawal of Victoria Road and Hyndland trams, first phase.
Service 5 KELVINSIDE Circle via BOTANIC GARDENS & HOLMLEA ROAD and
Service 5A KELVINSIDE Circle via HYNDLAND & HOLMLEA ROAD
withdrawn and replaced by Motorbus Service 43.
The following Service Alteration takes place:

In the West End, 1954-built Coronation 1397 turns from Highburgh Road into Byres Road. The tenements on the right have been partially razed to create a crossroad aligning with diverted University Avenue. Now controlled by traffic lights there are long tail-backs on all approaches to this very busy junction. *(RB Parr / STTS Collection)*

Service 5 from Holmlea Road to Kelvinside succumbed to bus operation on 17th November 1957. Car 472 has just left Holmlea Road terminus with Langside Depot in the background some two years earlier when it was still operational.
(RJS Wiseman)

The next withdrawal was Service 24. When Langside Depot gave up its operation of this Service to Newlands, Cunarders were introduced and 1299 is seen here on Highburgh Road. The large red sandstone tenements are still there but the "pre-fabs" have long gone.
(R Hamilton)

Service 24 ANNIESLAND & LANGSIDE via HYNDLAND increased in frequency at certain times to become ANNIESLAND or BROOMHILL CROSS & LANGSIDE via HYNDLAND.
Byres Road between Great Western Road and Highburgh Road, Grange Road, Prospecthill Road, Battlefield Road and Holmlea Road **closed** to trams.
Hyndland Road between Hyndland Station and Clarence Drive retained for Partick Depot workings of Service 10.

16th March 1958

Withdrawal of Victoria Road and Hyndland trams, second phase.
Service 24 ANNIESLAND or BROOMHILL CROSS & LANGSIDE via HYNDLAND withdrawn and replaced by **Motorbus Service 44.**
The following Operational Alterations take place:
Service 10 KELVINSIDE & GLASGOW CROSS, LONDON ROAD or AUCHENSHUGGLE via PARK ROAD
Partick Depot workings altered. See separate list.
Withdrawal of Possilpark and Govan trams, first phase.
Service 27 SPRINGBURN or POSSILPARK & SHIELDHALL withdrawn and replaced by **Motorbus Service 52.**
The following Operational Alteration takes place:
Service 16 SPRINGBURN & SCOTSTOUN via KEPPOCHHILL ROAD, ELMBANK STREET
Possilpark Depot duties transferred to Partick Depot.
Hyndland Road between Hyndland Station and Clarence Drive, Clarence Drive, Highburgh Road, Byres Road south of Highburgh Road, Church Street, Turriff Street, Pollokshaws Road between Turriff Street and

Eglinton Toll, Victoria Road, Langside Road **closed** to trams.
Saracen Street between Hawthorn Street and Saracen Cross retained for Possilpark Depot workings.

28th April 1958

Subsidence beneath citybound track in Possil Road at Canal Aqueduct.
The following Temporary Arrangements take place:
Service 4 SPRINGBURN & HILLINGTON ROAD southbound Cars diverted from Springburn Road at Keppochhill Road via Springburn Road, Parliamentary Road, Sauchiehall Street, Renfield Street, Union Street, Jamaica Street, Glasgow Bridge, Bridge Street, Nelson Street and normal route;
Service 16 SPRINGBURN & SCOTSTOUN via KEPPOCHHILL ROAD ELMBANK STREET Instead of turning in Elmvale Street northbound cars proceed via Springburn Road to Hawthorn Street east end; southbound cars leave from Hawthorn Street east end via Hawthorn Street, Bilsland Drive, Maryhill Road, Queen's Cross, Maryhill Road, St George's Cross, then via St George's Road and normal route;
Service 22 CROOKSTON & LAMBHILL and
Service 31 LAMBHILL & MERRYLEE via CHARING CROSS
southbound cars proceed via normal route to Saracen Cross, reverse and then via Saracen Street, Hawthorn Street to Possilpark Depot crossover, reverse and then via Hawthorn Street, Bilsland Drive, Maryhill Road, Queen's Cross, Maryhill Road, St George's Cross whence
Service 22 via New City Road, Cowcaddens and normal route;
Service 31 via St George's Road and normal route.
Special Service SPRINGBURN & MOSSHOUSE via KEPPOCHHILL ROAD from Elmvale Street east end via Elmvale Street, Springburn Road, Keppochhill Road, Possil Road to Possil Road north end.

29th April 1958

Subsidence in Possil Road at Canal Aqueduct repaired.
Service 4 SPRINGBURN & HILLINGTON ROAD via KEPPOCHHILL ROAD
Service 16 SPRINGBURN & SCOTSTOUN via KEPPOCHHILL ROAD, ELMBANK STREET
Service 22 CROOKSTON & LAMBHILL
Service 31 LAMBHILL & MERRYLEE via CHARING CROSS
revert to normal southbound routes.

15th June 1958

Conversion of Millerston-Bellahouston trams to trolleybus operation.
Service 7 MILLERSTON or RIDDRIE & BELLAHOUSTON via BRIDGETON CROSS withdrawn and replaced by
Trolleybus Service 106;
Service 7 Sundays Afternoon Specials: MILLERSTON & BRIDGETON CROSS withdrawn without replacement.
Cumbernauld Road between Alexandra Parade and Duke Street retained for Dennistoun Depot workings;
Abercromby Street south end retained for Dalmarnock Depot workings;
Points Control Tower at Bridgeton Cross closed.
Bellgrove Street, Abercromby Street, James Street, King's Drive, King's Bridge, Ballater Street, Norfolk Street, Golspie Street, Langlands Road, Elder Street, Crossloan Road, Craigton Road, Jura Street **closed** to trams.

18th July 1958

Subsidence in Cambridge Street south of Renfrew Street from 1900hrs.
The following Temporary Service Alterations take place:
Service 1 DALMUIR WEST, YOKER or SCOTSTOUN WEST & SPRINGFIELD ROAD or DALMARNOCK
Service 23 MARYHILL & BAILLIESTON via ST GEORGE'S CROSS
Service 30 BLAIRDARDIE or ANNIESLAND & DALMARNOCK
all diverted between New City Road at Cambridge Street and St Vincent Street at Renfield Street via New City Road, Cowcaddens, Hope Street and St Vincent Street.

21st July 1958

Subsidence in Cambridge Street south of Renfrew Street repaired, roadway reopened.
Service 1 DALMUIR WEST, YOKER or SCOTSTOUN WEST & SPRINGFIELD ROAD or DALMARNOCK
Service 23 MARYHILL & BAILLIESTON via ST GEORGE'S CROSS
Service 30 BLAIRDARDIE or ANNIESLAND & DALMARNOCK all revert to normal routes.

29th July 1958

Water Pipe Works in Corkerhill Road. Tram tracks closed.
MOSSPARK terminus temporarily moved from Corkerhill Road to former terminus at west end of Private Track in Mosspark Boulevard.
Service 3 UNIVERSITY or ST VINCENT STREET & MOSSPARK via POLLOKSHIELDS cut back accordingly.

Service 22 only appears infrequently in the chronology because it remained stable and virtually unaltered for much of its life. Here is the Lambhill terminus it shared with Service 31 cars. Note the use of an adjacent Standard car as a platform to aid adjustment of the rear view mirror on No. 45.
(BJ Cross Collection)

The terrain north of the Bellahouston terminus of Service 7 was hardly scenic as shown in this view of Cunarder 1366 crossing over the main railway line to Paisley and passing the City Cleansing Department's Destructor.
(RJS Wiseman)

Motorbus Service 53 took over operation of the Service 4 trams on 7th September 1958. Only four years earlier, major track repairs and reconstruction to raise the road level were taking place on the exposed Renfrew Road. Car 523 negotiates its way over the new rails yet to be surfaced.
(RJS Wiseman)

8th August 1958

Water Pipe Works in Corkerhill Road completed.

Service 3 UNIVERSITY or ST VINCENT STREET & MOSSPARK via POLLOKSHIELDS reverts to normal route.

7th September 1958

Withdrawal of trams from Possilpark and Govan, second phase.

Service 4 SPRINGBURN & HILLINGTON ROAD via KEPPOCHHILL ROAD withdrawn and replaced by Motorbus Service 53.

Govan Road between Paisley Road Toll and Lorne Street, Renfrew Road between Bogmoor Road and Hillington Road **closed** to trams.

Govan Road from Lorne Street and Renfrew Road to Bogmoor Road, Holmfauld Road and Bogmoor Road retained for Peak-hour workings only.

Sunday Gas Board Works in Duke Street between Carntyne Road and Shettleston Road.

The following Temporary Service Alterations take place:

Service 1 Sundays: DALMUIR WEST or SCOTSTOUN WEST & DENNISTOUN or DALMARNOCK curtailed to become DALMUIR WEST or SCOTSTOUN WEST & DENNISTOUN;

Service 23 Sundays: MARYHILL & BAILLIESTON via ST GEORGE'S CROSS curtailed to become MARYHILL & DENNISTOUN via ST GEORGE'S CROSS;

Service 30 Sundays: BLAIRDARDIE & DALMARNOCK curtailed to BLAIRDARDIE & DENNISTOUN;

Motorbus Shuttle Service : DENNISTOUN & SPRINGFIELD ROAD.

8th September 1958

Reconstruction work on sewer at Millerston.

Section from Riddrie to Millerston closed to trams.

The following Temporary Service Alteration takes place:

Service 8 MILLERSTON or RIDDRIE & GIFFNOCK or ROUKEN GLEN Circle via GIFFNOCK cut back to become RIDDRIE & GIFFNOCK or ROUKEN GLEN Circle via GIFFNOCK;

Millerston-Riddrie section covered by Trolleybus Service 106 with through booking facilities available at Riddrie between **Service 8** and Trolleybus Service 106.

Also Peak-hour Motorbus Shuttle Service MILLERSTON & RIDDRIE.

15th September 1958

Reconstruction work on sewer at Millerston completed.

Service 8 MILLERSTON or RIDDRIE & GIFFNOCK or ROUKEN GLEN Circle via GIFFNOCK resumes normal service.

Shared tracks: In September 1958, the steam locomotive from Alexander Stephens & Co. passes Car 345 on Renfrew Road between the shipyard and Shieldhall Goods Yard. Further east, Fairfields operated its own electric locomotive deriving power from the tramway overhead to convey wagons from their own shipyard to the Govan Goods Yard. To permit operation of railway rolling stock, Glasgow's tram tracks were laid to the 4'-7¾" gauge which allowed the heavier profiled railway wheels to run on their flanges in the tram-track grooves.
(Photos, Steam loco, GB Claydon: Fairfield's loco, AP Tatt / OTA)

17th September 1958

Increase in early morning service from Lambhill
Service 22 Weekdays and Saturdays: CROOKSTON & LAMBHILL adjusted accordingly.

27th September 1958

Burst Water Main in Springfield Road from 1200 hrs.
Service 1 Saturdays: DALMUIR WEST or SCOTSTOUN WEST & DENNISTOUN, SPRINGFIELD ROAD or DALMARNOCK
Service 30 Saturdays: BLAIRDARDIE & DALMARNOCK
both diverted at Parkhead Cross to run via Gallowgate to WHITEVALE turning in Rowchester Street;
Motorbus Shuttle Service: PARKHEAD & SPRINGFIELD ROAD.

28th September 1958

Water Main Repairs in Springfield Road completed by late afternoon.
Service 1 Sundays: DALMUIR WEST or SCOTSTOUN WEST & DENNISTOUN or DALMARNOCK
Service 30 Sundays: BLAIRDARDIE & DALMARNOCK
both diverted to WHITEVALE and resume normal service from 1600 hrs.
Motorbus Shuttle Service: PARKHEAD & SPRINGFIELD ROAD until 1600 hrs.

31st October 1958

Ownership of Pinkston Power Station transferred from Corporation Transport Department to South of Scotland Electricity Board.

The final cull of tram services on Paisley Road West took place on 16th November 1958. In happier times, at Paisley Road Toll, are 1050 on the rush hour extension of Service 12 trailing 282 on Service 22, both following a Service 40. It was quite common for trams on each service on this arterial route to run, like this, in convoy. *(RJS Wiseman)*

When trams to the Shawfield terminus were diverted to Farme Cross, Service 26A disappeared, being absorbed into Service 26. Here is 1137 at Shawfield in 1956 looking, then, like an industrial wasteland. Service 18A continued to serve Shawfield until June 1961. *(RB Parr / STTS Collection)*

14th November 1958

Withdrawal of Govan and Paisley Road West trams, final phase (first part).
Service 12 Weekdays: MOUNT FLORIDA & PAISLEY ROAD TOLL, LINTHOUSE via SHIELDS ROAD
Peak-hour service to LINTHOUSE and Specials to SHIELDHALL withdrawn and replaced by Trolleybus Service 108.
Govan Road from Lorne Street westwards, Holmfauld Road, Renfrew Road to Bogmoor Road and Bogmoor Road **closed** to trams.

16th November 1958

Withdrawal of Govan and Paisley Road West trams, final phase (second part).
Service 12 MOUNT FLORIDA & PAISLEY ROAD TOLL or LINTHOUSE via SHIELDS ROAD withdrawn and replaced by Trolleybus Service 108;
Service 22 CROOKSTON & LAMBHILL withdrawn and replaced by Motorbus Service 54;
Service 32 CROOKSTON & SPRINGBURN or BISHOPBRIGGS via RENFIELD STREET withdrawn and replaced by Motorbus Service 55.
Govan Depot **closed** to service trams; retained as store for cars awaiting disposal.

Serviceable fleet: Standard and Coronation Mark II Cars to Dalmarnock Depot; also a few Standard cars to Partick Depot.

Withdrawal of Crow Road trams.

Service 17 ANNIESLAND & FARME CROSS via BOTHWELL STREET withdrawn and replaced, in part, by **Service 26**;

Service 26A CLYDEBANK or SCOTSTOUN & SHAWFIELD via RUTHERGLEN BRIDGE diverted to
FARME CROSS and becomes part of **Service 26**;

Service 26 CLYDEBANK or SCOTSTOUN & BURNSIDE via DALMARNOCK altered to become
CLYDEBANK or SCOTSTOUN & FARME CROSS or BURNSIDE via DALMARNOCK Cars for Farme Cross run via Cambuslang Road to Cambuslang Road at Duchess Road;

The following Operational Alteration takes place:

Service 30 BLAIRDARDIE or ANNIESLAND & DALMARNOCK Partick Depot Workings altered.

The following Service Alterations take place:

ST VINCENT STREET circular turning arrangements cease, cars turning at City Centre from the south altered to operate:

approach via Union Street, Renfield Street, St Vincent Street to St Vincent Street at Wellington Street, returning via same route

Service 3 UNIVERSITY or ST VINCENT STREET & MOSSPARK via POLLOKSHIELDS

Service 8 MILLERSTON or RIDDRIE & GIFFNOCK or ROUKEN GLEN Circle via GIFFNOCK

Service 14 UNIVERSITY & ARDEN

Service 25 BISHOPBRIGGS or SPRINGBURN & CARNWADRIC or ROUKEN GLEN Circle via THORNLIEBANK

Service 31 LAMBHILL & MERRYLEE via CHARING CROSS

all altered accordingly for City Centre shortworkings from the south.

Clincart Road, Cathcart Road from Clincart Road to Allison Street, Allison Street, Nithsdale Street, Nithsdale Road from Nithsdale Street to Shields Road, Shields Road, Scotland Street, Seaward Street, Milnpark Street, Admiral Street, Crow Road, Oswald Street, George V. Bridge, Commerce Street, Kingston Street, Paisley Road West from Lorne Street to Crookston Road, Broomloan Road, Corkerhill Road north end north of crossover, Crookston Road **closed** to trams;

Nelson Street, Morrison Street, Paisley Road, Paisley Road West from Paisley Road Toll to Lorne Street, Lorne Street retained for access to and from Govan Depot for storage of cars awaiting disposal.

23rd November 1958

Sunday Water Main Repairs on London Road near Craignestock Street.

London Road closed to trams between Moir Street and Abercomby Street until 1600.

Service 9 Sundays: DALMUIR WEST & AUCHENSHUGGLE

Service 10 Sunday Afternoon and Evening: KELVINSIDE & LONDON ROAD or AUCHENSHUGGLE via PARK ROAD.

Service 18 Sundays: SPRINGBURN & BURNSIDE via BILSLAND DRIVE, DALMARNOCK

Service 18A Sundays: SPRINGBURN & SHAWFIELD via BILSLAND DRIVE, RUTHERGLEN BRIDGE

Service 26 Sundays: CLYDEBANK or SCOTSTOUN & FARME CROSS or BURNSIDE via DALMARNOCK

all split to operate from west to and from GLASGOW CROSS running via London Road to Moir Street and returning via Moir Street, Gallowgate, Glasgow Cross, Trongate and
from east to and from BRIDGETON CROSS turning in Abercromby Street south end.

Motorbus Shuttle Service: GLASGOW CROSS & BRIDGETON CROSS

4th January 1959

Closure of Eldon Street bridge over River Kelvin for reconstruction.

Abandonment of University trams.

The following Service Alterations take place:

Service 3 UNIVERSITY or ST VINCENT STREET & MOSSPARK or POLLOKSHIELDS diverted to become
PARK ROAD or ST VINCENT STREET & MOSSPARK via POLLOKSHIELDS from Park Road north end via Park Road, Woodlands Road and former route;

Service 14 UNIVERSITY & ARDEN diverted to become
KELVINGROVE & ARDEN from Radnor Street via Radnor Street, Sauchiehall Street, Charing Cross and former route.

University Avenue, Gibson Street, Eldon Street **closed** to trams.

15th February 1959

Road works under citybound track in Pollokshaws Road south of Shawlands Cross. Northbound journeys diverted between Pollokshaws Road at Greenview Street and Shawlands Cross by reversing into Greenview Street and then via Greenview Street, Pleasance Street, Coustonholm Road, Kilmarnock Road, Shawlands Cross and normal route.

Service 14 Sundays: KELVINGROVE & ARDEN
Service 25 Sundays: BISHOPBRIGGS or SPRINGBURN & CARNWADRIC or ROUKEN GLEN Circle via THORNLIEBANK
altered accordingly.
Fractured Gas Main in Renfield Street south of Sauchiehall Street.
The following Temporary Service Alterations take place:
Service 1 Sundays: DALMUIR WEST or SCOTSTOUN WEST & DENNISTOUN or DALMARNOCK
Service 3 Sundays: PARK ROAD & MOSSPARK via POLLOKSHIELDS
Service 14 Sundays: KELVINGROVE & ARDEN
Service 23 Sundays: MARYHILL & BAILLIESTON via ST GEORGE'S CROSS
Service 30 Sundays: BLAIRDARDIE & DALMARNOCK
Service 31 Sundays: LAMBHILL & MERRYLEE via CHARING CROSS
all diverted between Sauchiehall Street at Hope Street and St Vincent Street at Renfield Street via Hope Street and St Vincent Street.
Service 8 Sundays: MILLERSTON or RIDDRIE & GIFFNOCK or ROUKEN GLEN Circle via GIFFNOCK
Service 25 Sundays: BISHOPBRIGGS or SPRINGBURN & CARNWADRIC or ROUKEN GLEN Circle via THORNLIEBANK
split from and to the north at NORTH HANOVER STREET and from and to the south at ST VINCENT STREET cars proceeding to St Vincent Street at Wellington Street.
==Motorbus Shuttle Service== NORTH HANOVER STREET & ST VINCENT STREET.
Service 6 Sundays: SCOTSTOUN & ALEXANDRA PARK and
Service 33 Sundays: CIRCLE SPRINGBURN & CHARING CROSS both unaltered.

16th February 1959

Road Works in Pollokshaws Road south of Shawlands Cross and Fractured Gas Main in Renfield Street south of Sauchiehall Street both repaired.
All Services 1, 3, 8, 14, 23, 25, 30 and **31** return to normal from Monday morning.

28th February 1959

Govan Depot **closed** as store for cars awaiting disposal.
Nelson Street, Morrison Street, Paisley Road, Paisley Road West between Paisley Road Toll and Lorne Street, and Lorne Street **closed** to trams.

15th March 1959

Withdrawal of Giffnock trams.
Service 8 MILLERSTON or RIDDRIE & GIFFNOCK or ROUKEN Circle via GIFFNOCK withdrawn and replaced by ==Motorbus Service 38==. Circular runs at Rouken Glen cease.
ROUKEN GLEN terminus moved eastwards from Rouken Glen Road at Rowallan Road to the former Giffnock terminus in Rouken Glen Road at Milverton Road.
The following Service Alteration takes place:
Service 25 BISHOPBRIGGS or SPRINGBURN & CARNWADRIC or ROUKEN GLEN Circle via THORNLIEBANK extended to become
BISHOPBRIGGS or SPRINGBURN & CARNWADRIC or ROUKEN GLEN via THORNLIEBANK via former route to Rouken Glen Road at Rowallan Road then via Rouken Glen Road to Rouken Glen Road at Milverton Road;
Cars reverse and return via same route.
The following Operational Alterations take place:
Service 30 BLAIRDARDIE or ANNIESLAND & DALMARNOCK portion of Service operated by Parkhead Depot transferred to Dennistoun Depot;
Cars from All Services show "31" on journeys to NEWLANDS DEPOT;
Service 31 LAMBHILL & MERRYLEE via CHARING CROSS portion of Service operated by Possilpark Depot transferred to Newlands Depot. Last Car from City Centre to Lambhill departs 2315 instead of 2345;
Service 33 CIRCLE SPRINGBURN & CHARING CROSS operation transferred from Possilpark Depot to Maryhill Depot.
Station Road, Cumbernauld Road between Millerston and Smithycroft Road north end, Smithycroft Road north of Naver Street, Kilmarnock Road south of Mulberry Road, Fenwick Road, Rouken Glen Road between Eastwood Toll and Milverton Road **closed** to trams.
Smithycroft Road south of Naver Street and Cumbernauld Road between Smithycroft Road south end and Aitken Street retained for peak-hour journeys only.

29th March 1959

Burst Water Main in Great Western Road west of Park Road.
The following Temporary Service Alterations take place:
Service 1 Sundays: DALMUIR WEST or SCOTSTOUN WEST & DENNISTOUN or DALMARNOCK diverted to become
DALMUIR WEST & DALMARNOCK via PARTICK, CHARING CROSS via normal route to Scotstoun West then via Dumbarton Road, Argyle Street, Sauchiehall Street, Charing Cross, Sauchiehall Street and normal route;

Inroads into the services along Pollokshaws Road began with the substitution of Service 8 trams by Motorbus Service 38. Smart-looking 414 is on Eglinton Street, followed by 1295 on service 14, passing the Alexander "Greek" Thomson tenements that were later demolished to general dismay.
(WD McMillan)

and also split to operate SCOTSTOUN WEST & ANNIESLAND and MARYHILL & DENNISTOUN or DALMARNOCK from Maryhill Road at Garscube Estate East Lodge Gate via Maryhill Road, St George's Cross and normal route;
Service 10 Sundays: KELVINSIDE & GLASGOW CROSS, LONDON ROAD or AUCHENSHUGGLE cut back to become PARK ROAD & GLASGOW CROSS, LONDON ROAD or AUCHENSHUGGLE;
Service 30 Sundays: BLAIRDARDIE & DALMARNOCK split to become BLAIRDARDIE & ANNIESLAND and MARYHILL & DALMARNOCK from Maryhill Road at Garscube Estate East Lodge Gate via Maryhill Road, St George's Cross and normal route;
Motorbus Shuttle Service 1 ANNIESLAND & ST GEORGE'S CROSS.

30th March 1959

Burst Water Main in Great Western Road west of Park Road repaired.
Service 1 DALMUIR WEST, YOKER or SCOTSTOUN WEST & DENNISTOUN, SPRINGFIELD ROAD or DALMARNOCK
Service 10 KELVINSIDE & GLASGOW CROSS, LONDON ROAD or AUCHENSHUGGLE via PARK ROAD
Service 30 BLAIRDARDIE or ANNIESLAND & DALMARNOCK resume normal services.

3rd May 1959

Service 33 CIRCLE SPRINGBURN & CHARING CROSS withdrawn without replacement.

12th May 1959

Royal Visit of HRH Princess Margaret to George Square.
George Square closed to trams 1400-1530 hrs.
Special Timetables all day:
Service 1 DALMUIR WEST, YOKER or SCOTSTOUN WEST & DENNISTOUN or DALMARNOCK
Service 23 MARYHILL & BAILLIESTON via ST GEORGE'S CROSS
Service 30 BLAIRDARDIE or ANNIESLAND & DALMARNOCK
split between 1400 and 1530, cars from west diverted to CASTLE STREET running via Parliamentary Road to Monkland Street; cars from east turning back at NORTH ALBION STREET.
Special Timetables incorporate some journeys on **Services 1** and **30** to and from FARME CROSS.

May 1959

Last Motor School for Training Tramway Motormen.
Coplaw Street **closed** to trams.

Here are the Inspectors who operated the last Tram Motor School: (Centre, rear) J Edgar, (Middle row) W Wilson, J Black, (Front) D McMillan, R Stewart, R Simpson, J Fraser. *(DL Thomson Collection)*

7th June 1959

Withdrawal of Bishopbriggs, Pollokshaws and Rouken Glen trams.

Service 25 BISHOPBRIGGS or SPRINGBURN & CARNWADRIC or ROUKEN GLEN via THORNLIEBANK withdrawn and replaced by Motorbus Service 45. Motorbuses resume circular runs through Rouken Glen.

Possilpark Depot **closed** to trams; Cars to Partick Depot and Maryhill Depot.

The following Operational Alteration takes place:

Service 29 MARYHILL or GAIRBRAID AVENUE & TOLLCROSS or BROOMHOUSE via NORMAL SCHOOL

Service 29 Sundays Afternoons only: ANDERSTON CROSS & BROOMHOUSE

portion of Service operated by Parkhead Depot transferred to Dalmarnock Depot.

Kenmure Avenue, Kirkintilloch Road, Springburn Road north of Hawthorn Street, Hillcroft Terrace, Springburn Road from Keppochhill Road to Castle Street, Castle Street north of Parliamentary Road, Saracen Street from Hawthorn Street to Saracen Cross, Boydstone Road, Rouken Glen Road from Spiersbridge Road to Milverton Road **closed** to trams.

Regular cars cease to operate on Springburn Road between Hawthorn Street and Elmvale Street.

Permanent Way Coup in Hillcroft Terrace, Colston **closed**.

2nd July 1959

Repair works to sewer in Renfield Street at Drury Street.

The following Temporary Service Alterations take place:

Service 3 PARK ROAD or ST VINCENT STREET & MOSSPARK via POLLOKSHIELDS curtailed to become JAMAICA STREET & MOSSPARK via POLLOKSHIELDS;

Service 14 KELVINGROVE & ARDEN curtailed to become JAMAICA STREET & ARDEN;

Service 31 LAMBHILL & MERRYLEE via CHARING CROSS curtailed and diverted to become LAMBHILL & NORTH ALBION STREET via CHARING CROSS (operated by Partick Depot) via normal route to Renfield Street then via St Vincent Street, St Vincent Place, George Square west and north, George Street to George Street at North Albion Street.

No tram services provided to University, Kelvingrove nor Merrylee.

3rd July 1959

Renfield Street reopened to traffic.

Service 3 PARK ROAD or ST VINCENT STREET & MOSSPARK via POLLOKSHIELDS

Service 14 KELVINGROVE & ARDEN

Service 31 LAMBHILL & MERRYLEE via CHARING CROSS resume normal services.

Possilpark Depot was closed to trams on 7th June 1959 for conversion to a Motorbus Garage. Given that Coronation cars were only operated there between 1939 and 1941, No.1269's presence on the depot approach track suggests that it is defective and being run in off Service 16 for attention.
(BJ Cross Collection)

6th September 1959

Withdrawal of Springburn Road trams.
Service 16 SPRINGBURN & SCOTSTOUN via KEPPOCHHILL ROAD, ELMBANK STREET cut back to become KEPPOCHHILL ROAD & SCOTSTOUN via ELMBANK STREET from Keppochhill Road west end via Keppochhill Road and former route.
Elmvale Street and Springburn Road from Hawthorn Street to Keppochhill Road **closed** to trams.

7th September 1959

Dalmuir Canal Swing Bridge closed for repairs.
All cars curtailed at DALMUIR in Dumbarton Road Clydebank at Beardmore Street.
Service 1 DALMUIR WEST, YOKER or SCOTSTOUN WEST & DENNISTOUN, SPRINGFIELD ROAD or DALMARNOCK cut back to become
DALMUIR, YOKER or SCOTSTOUN WEST & DENNISTOUN, SPRINGFIELD ROAD or DALMARNOCK;
Service 9 DALMUIR WEST & LONDON ROAD or AUCHENSHUGGLE cut back to become
DALMUIR & LONDON ROAD or AUCHENSHUGGLE.

1st November 1959

Withdrawal of Alexandra Parade, Sauchiehall Street west and Pollokshaws trams.
Service 6 SCOTSTOUN & ALEXANDRA PARK or RIDDRIE withdrawn and replaced by Motorbus Service 56;
Service 14 KELVINGROVE & ARDEN withdrawn and replaced by Motorbus Service 57.
The following Operational Alterations take place:
Service 1 DALMUIR, YOKER or SCOTSTOUN WEST & DENNISTOUN, SPRINGFIELD ROAD or DALMARNOCK
Service 10 KELVINSIDE & GLASGOW CROSS, LONDON ROAD or AUCHENSHUGGLE via PARK ROAD
Service 30 BLAIRDARDIE or ANNIESLAND & DALMARNOCK Partick Depot workings altered.
Radnor Street, Sauchiehall Street from Argyle Street to Charing Cross, Sauchiehall Street from Renfield Street to Parliamentary Road, Parliamentary Road, Monkland Street, Castle Street from Parliamentary Road to Alexandra Parade, Alexandra Parade, Cumbernauld Road from Duke Street to Smithycroft Road south end, Aitken Street, Smithycroft Road south of Naver Street, Pollokshaws Road from Shawlands Cross to Cross Street, Greenview Street, Pleasance Street, Coustonholm Road, Cross Street, Nether Auldhouse Road, Thornliebank Road, Main Street Thornliebank, Spiersbridge Road, Private Track on north side of Nitshill Road to Arden **closed** to trams.

Service 6 was withdrawn on 1st November 1959 ending the tram service in Riddrie. 230 is joining Cumbernauld Road from Smithycroft Road, Riddrie with a Service 106 trolleybus in the distance, right.
(Iain M Hill / STS Collection)

6th December 1959

Withdrawal of Possilpark, Shawlands and Newlands trams.

Service 31 LAMBHILL & MERRYLEE via CHARING CROSS withdrawn without replacement.

The following Operational Alteration takes place:

Cars show "3" on journeys to NEWLANDS DEPOT.

Strachur Street, Balmore Road, Saracen Street south of Saracen Cross,

Kilmarnock Road from Corrour Road to Mulberry Road **closed** to trams.

Pollokshaws Road from Eglinton Toll to Shawlands Cross, Kilmarnock Road from Shawlands Cross to Corrour Road and Newlandsfield Road retained for Newlands Depot workings. Newlands Depot allocation of Standard Cars moved to Dennistoun Depot.

11th December 1959

Gas Main fracture at corner of St Vincent Place and George Square.

The following Temporary Service Alterations take place:

Service 1 Weekdays: DALMUIR, YOKER or SCOTSTOUN WEST & DENNISTOUN or DALMARNOCK

Service 23 Weekdays: MARYHILL & BAILLIESTON via ST GEORGE'S CROSS

Service 30 Weekdays: BLAIRDARDIE or ANNIESLAND & DALMARNOCK all split to operate from west to ST VINCENT STREET via normal routes to New City Road then via New City Road, Cowcaddens, Hope Street, St Vincent Street to St Vincent Street between Hope Street and Renfield Street;

and from east to NORTH ALBION STREET to George Street at North Albion Street;

Motorbus Shuttle Service ST VINCENT STREET & NORTH ALBION STREET.

12th December 1959

Gas Main fracture at corner of St Vincent Place and George Square repaired.

Service 1 DALMUIR, YOKER or SCOTSTOUN WEST & DENNISTOUN, SPRINGFIELD ROAD or DALMARNOCK

Service 23 MARYHILL & BAILLIESTON via ST GEORGE'S CROSS

Service 30 BLAIRDARDIE or ANNIESLAND & DALMARNOCK resume normal services.

Résumé

1st January 1960

The following Tram Services operating:

1		DALMUIR, YOKER or SCOTSTOUN WEST & DENNISTOUN, SPRINGFIELD ROAD or DALMARNOCK
3		PARK ROAD or ST VINCENT STREET & MOSSPARK via POLLOKSHIELDS
9		DALMUIR & LONDON ROAD or AUCHENSHUGGLE
10		KELVINSIDE & GLASGOW CROSS, LONDON ROAD or AUCHENSHUGGLE via PARK ROAD
15		ANDERSTON CROSS & BAILLIESTON
16		KEPPOCHHILL ROAD & SCOTSTOUN via ELMBANK STREET
18		SPRINGBURN & BURNSIDE via BILSLAND DRIVE, DALMARNOCK
18A		SPRINGBURN & SHAWFIELD via BILSLAND DRIVE, RUTHERGLEN BRIDGE
		(Cars show "18" on journeys to SPRINGBURN)
23		MARYHILL & BAILLIESTON via ST GEORGE'S CROSS
26		CLYDEBANK or SCOTSTOUN & FARME CROSS or BURNSIDE via DALMARNOCK
29		MARYHILL or GAIRBRAID AVENUE & TOLLCROSS or BROOMHOUSE via NORMAL SCHOOL
		MARYHILL & GLASGOW CROSS via NORMAL SCHOOL (No Sundays Services)
		ANDERSTON CROSS & BROOMHOUSE (Sundays Afternoons only)
		(Cars show "15" on journeys to ANDERSTON CROSS)
30		BLAIRDARDIE or ANNIESLAND & DALMARNOCK

A Service 1 tram on the paved reserved track on Great Western Road has run below the Anniesland Station girder bridge on its way to the City. Note the absence of road traffic. *(R Benton / NTM Archive)*

13th March 1960

Withdrawal of principal Great Western Road and Duke Street trams.
Service 1 DALMUIR, YOKER or SCOTSTOUN WEST & DENNISTOUN, SPRINGFIELD ROAD or DALMARNOCK and
Service 30 BLAIRDARDIE or ANNIESLAND & DALMARNOCK
both withdrawn and replaced by Motorbus Service 58.
Parkhead Depot **closed** to trams; Standard cars to Dalmarnock Depot, Coronation Mark I cars to Dennistoun Depot.

As was often the case, extremities of cross-city routes were in complete contrast to each other. The Great Western Road Services 1 and 30 were no exception. This view from the Points Control Tower at Parkhead Cross shows a Car on Service 30 turning into Springfield Road having just negiotiated the sharp curve to the right from Duke Street which was restricted to Standard cars only. (HB Priestley / NTM Archive)

The following Operational Alteration takes place:
Parkhead Depot operation of
Service 15 ANDERSTON CROSS & BALLIESTON transferred to Dennistoun Depot.
Kingsway, Anniesland Road, Great Western Road from Blairdardie to Hyndland Road, Great Western Road from Park Road to St George's Cross, Duke Street from Shettleston Road to Parkhead Cross **closed** to trams.
Springfield Road retained for Dalmarnock Depot workings.

15th March 1960

Points Control Tower at Parkhead Cross closed.

28th March 1960

Serious whisky bond warehouse fire in Cheapside Street Anderston from 2000 hrs.
The following Emergency Service Alterations take place:
Service 15 ANDERSTON CROSS & BAILLIESTON diverted to become
ST VINCENT STREET & BAILLIESTON from St Vincent Street between Renfield Street and Hope Street via St Vincent Street, Hope Street, Argyle Street and normal route;
Service 9 DALMUIR & LONDON ROAD or AUCHENSHUGGLE
Service 26 CLYDEBANK or SCOTSTOUN & FARME CROSS or BURNSIDE via DALMARNOCK
both diverted between Argyle Street at St Vincent Street and Argyle Street at Hope Street via St Vincent Street, Bothwell Street and Hope Street.

29th March 1960

Serious whisky bond warehouse fire in Cheapside Street Anderston.
Argyle Street reopened but Stobcross Street remains closed to traffic.
Service 9 DALMUIR & LONDON ROAD or AUCHENSHUGGLE
Service 26 CLYDEBANK or SCOTSTOUN & FARME CROSS or BURNSIDE via DALMARNOCK return to normal service.
Service 15 continues to operate as ST VINCENT STREET & BAILLIESTON;
All cars scheduled to turn at ANDERSTON CROSS from east diverted either to
ST VINCENT STREET or to DOUGLAS STREET.

1st April 1960

Serious whisky bond warehouse fire in Cheapside Street Anderston.
Stobcross Street reopened to tram traffic at 1600 hrs.
Service 15 ANDERSTON CROSS & BAILLIESTON and all
ANDERSTON CROSS short-workings revert to normal service.

5th June 1960

Withdrawal of Kelvinside, Sauchiehall Street, Renfield Street and Pollokshields trams
Service 3 PARK ROAD or ST VINCENT STREET & MOSSPARK via POLLOKSHIELDS withdrawn and replaced by
Motorbus Service 59;

The track east of Park Road used by Services 1 and 30 has been lifted but Service 10 trams continued along Great Western Road for twelve weeks. The tram is approaching Kelvinbridge, passing Lansdowne Parish Church. *(BJ Cross Collection)*

The last trams in south west Glasgow ran on Service 3. Here is Coronation 1220 passing the then Lord Provost's Pollokshields residence distinguished by its ornate lamp posts. *(BJ Cross Collection)*

Service 10 KELVINSIDE & GLASGOW CROSS, LONDON ROAD or AUCHENSHUGGLE via PARK ROAD. withdrawn and replaced, in part, by **Tram Service 9** and **Motorbus Service 59**;

Service 23 MARYHILL & BAILLIESTON via ST GEORGE'S CROSS diverted to become MARYHILL & BAILLIESTON via NORMAL SCHOOL via former route to New City Road then via New City Road, Cowcaddens, Hope Street, St Vincent Street, St Vincent Place and former route.

Newlands Depot **closed** to trams; Coronation Mark I cars to Dennistoun Depot, Coronation Mark II cars to Partick Depot.

Hyndland Road from Hyndland Station to Great Western Road, Great Western Road from Hyndland Road to Park Road, Park Road, Woodlands Road, Sauchiehall Street from Elmbank Street to Renfield Street, Cambridge Street, Renfield Street from Sauchiehall Street to St Vincent Street, Maxwell Road, Kenmure Street, Albert Drive from Kenmure Street to Nithsdale Road, Nithsdale Road, Dumbreck Road, Private Track on north side of Mosspark Boulevard, Corkerhill Road, Pollokshaws Road from Albert Drive to Shawlands Cross, Kilmarnock Road from Shawlands Cross to Corrour Road and Newlandsfield Road **closed** to trams.

Renfield Street south of St Vincent Street, Union Street, Jamaica Street, Glasgow Bridge, Bridge Street, Eglinton Street and Pollokshaws Road from Eglinton Toll to Albert Drive and Albert Drive retained for access to and from Coplawhill Works.

The Dalmuir Canal Bridge was unexpectedly re-opened to trams on 1st August 1960. A westbound Cunarder casts a reflection on the water of the Forth & Clyde Canal. *(David Hume / STTS Collection)*

Service 29 was cut back from Broomhouse to Tollcross on 6th November 1960. Here is Broomhouse a year or so earlier when ex-Liverpool trams were still allocated to this Service. Car 33 is reversing in the middle of the A74 trunk road. Note the speed de-restriction sign. *(BJ Cross Collection)*

1st August 1960

On completion of repairs, Dalmuir Canal Swing Bridge **reopened** to traffic.
All trams re-extended to DALMUIR WEST.
Service 9 DALMUIR & LONDON ROAD or AUCHENSHUGGLE re-extended to become
DALMUIR WEST & LONDON ROAD or AUCHENSHUGGLE via former route from Dalmuir West.

6th November 1960

Withdrawal of Duke Street and Broomhouse trams.
Service 23 MARYHILL & BAILLIESTON via NORMAL SCHOOL withdrawn and replaced by Motorbus Service 60;
Service 29 MARYHILL or GAIRBRAID AVENUE & TOLLCROSS or BROOMHOUSE via NORMAL SCHOOL cut back to become
MARYHILL or GAIRBRAID AVENUE & TOLLCROSS via NORMAL SCHOOL via former route to Hamilton Road east of Carmyle Avenue;
Sundays Afternoon Specials: ANDERSTON CROSS & BROOMHOUSE withdrawn without replacement;
Weekdays and Saturdays Auxiliary: MARYHILL & GLASGOW CROSS via NORMAL SCHOOL unaltered
Dennistoun Depot **closed** to trams; Cars to Dalmarnock Depot and Maryhill Depot.
The following Operational Alteration takes place:
Dennistoun Depot operation of

4th June 1961 at last saw the last of the Standard cars in use. Here is Car No.1088 coming out of the fire-ravaged section of Dalmarnock Depot, by then brought back into use but minus its roof. (BJ Cross Collection)

Service 15 ANDERSTON CROSS & BAILLIESTON transferred to Dalmarnock Depot.
St Vincent Street from Wellington Street to Hope Street and from Renfield Street to Buchanan Street, St Vincent Place, George Square west and north, George Street, Duke Street to Shettleston Road, Paton Street, Carntyne Road, Shettleston Road from Duke Street to Shettleston Sheddings, Hamilton Road from east of Carmyle Avenue, Glasgow Road to Calder Bridge **closed** to trams.
St Vincent Street from Hope Street to Renfield Street retained for access to and from Coplawhill Works.

12th March 1961

Withdrawal of Keppochhill Road trams.
Service 16 KEPPOCHHILL ROAD & SCOTSTOUN via ELMBANK STREET withdrawn and replaced by **Motorbus Service 32.** Keppochhill Road, Possil Road, St George's Road from Round Toll to St George's Cross, St Vincent Street from Elmbank Street to Argyle Street **closed** to trams.

22nd March 1961

Lyes 1 to 9 of Dalmarnock Depot destroyed, along with 50 trams, by fire breaking out at 0200 hrs.
The following Operational Alterations take place:
Cars withdrawn following **Service 16** abandonment made ready for return to service along with some cars set aside for preservation.
Special duties operated by Dalmarnock Depot transferred to Maryhill Depot and to Partick Depot.

Standard Car 127 is on a short-working to Vernon Street and is viewed from the Forth & Clyde Canal aqueduct at Bilsland Drive. *(WD McMillan)*

Coronation 1281 is crossing Sauchiehall Street, heading north up Hope Street. The curves in the foreground had not been used by normal service trams but were retained for diversions in emergency situations. *(BJ Cross Collection)*

16th April 1961

The following Operational Alterations take place:
Special duties previously transferred to Maryhill Depot and Partick Depot restored to Dalmarnock Depot.

4th June 1961

Withdrawal of Bilsland Drive, Bothwell Street, Rutherglen and Burnside trams.
Service 18 SPRINGBURN & BURNSIDE via BILSLAND DRIVE, DALMARNOCK and
Service 18A SPRINGBURN & SHAWFIELD via BILSLAND DRIVE, RUTHERGLEN BRIDGE withdrawn and replaced by
Motorbus Service 18.
The following Service Alteration takes place:
Service 26 CLYDEBANK or SCOTSTOUN & FARME CROSS or BURNSIDE via DALMARNOCK cut back to become CLYDEBANK or SCOTSTOUN & DALMARNOCK or FARME CROSS.
Hawthorn Street, Bilsland Drive, St George's Road from St George's Cross to Charing Cross, Sauchiehall Street from Charing Cross to Elmbank Street, Elmbank Street, Bothwell Street, Main Street Bridgeton, Rutherglen Bridge, Shawfield Road, Glasgow Road west of Rutherglen Road, Farmeloan Road, Stonelaw Road and Duke's Road **closed** to trams.
Operation of Standard trams in service ceases.

22nd October 1961

Withdrawal of Maryhill, Tollcross and Farme Cross trams.
Service 26 CLYDEBANK or SCOTSTOUN & DALMARNOCK or FARME CROSS cut back to become CLYDEBANK or SCOTSTOUN & DALMARNOCK via former route to Dalmarnock Road at Birkwood Street;
Service 29 MARYHILL or GAIRBRAID AVENUE & GLASGOW CROSS or TOLLCROSS via NORMAL SCHOOL withdrawn and replaced by **Motorbus Service 61**.
Maryhill Depot **closed** to trams; Cars to Dalmarnock Depot and to Partick Depot.
Maryhill Road from Garscube Estate East Lodge Gate southwards, Celtic Street, Gairbraid Avenue, New City Road, Cowcaddens, Hope Street from Cowcaddens to St Vincent Street, Tollcross Road, Hamilton Road, Dalmarnock Road from Birkwood Street to Farme Cross, Cambuslang Road from Farme Cross to Duchess Road **closed** to trams.
Hope Street from St Vincent Street to Argyle Street retained for access to and from Coplawhill Works.
Repairs to Water Main in Argyle Street at Bunhouse Road until 1230 hrs.
Service 9 Sundays: DALMUIR WEST & AUCHENSHUGGLE and
Service 26 Sundays: CLYDEBANK or SCOTSTOUN & DALMARNOCK both split to operate from and to the west at CHURCH STREET; and from and to the east at FINNIESTON;
Motorbus Shuttle Service PARTICK CROSS & FINNIESTON.

11th March 1962

Withdrawal of Parkhead, Shettleston and Baillieston trams.
Service 15 ANDERSTON CROSS & BAILLIESTON withdrawn and replaced by **Motorbus Service 62**.
Gallowgate from Moir Street to Parkhead Cross, Rowchester Street, Springfield Road, Westmuir Street, Shettleston Road from Shettleston Sheddings eastwards, Glasgow Road, Main Street Baillieston to Martin Crescent **closed** to trams.

GLASGOW'S LAST TRAM

The Last Tram route will be converted to motorbus operation on 1st September, 1962. There will be a procession of historical tramcars on the evening of 4th September, 1962. Limited accommodation will be available to the public.

On the 2nd, 3rd and 4th September, 1962, Special Trams will run for those interested in making a 'Last Tram' run.

Handbill available at
    Transport Offices, 46 Bath Street or at Information Bureau, George Square.

E. R. L. FITZPAYNE
General Manager

18th March 1962

Cessation of one-way operation for trams turning at Glasgow Cross from the west.

Cars turning at GLASGOW CROSS from the west previously proceeding via London Road to Moir Street and returning via Gallowgate run via London Road and Moir Street but altered to reverse in Moir Street and return via the same route.

Moir Street north of crossover, Gallowgate between Moir Street and Glasgow Cross and Trongate (north) between High Street and Albion Street **closed** to trams.

3rd June 1962

Withdrawal of Dalmarnock trams.

Service 26 CLYDEBANK or SCOTSTOUN & DALMARNOCK withdrawn and replaced by Motorbus Service 63.

A last day of full operation on Service 9 at Dalmuir West with the substation in the background, left. The photographer's car is in the foreground and would be a collector's item today.
(BJ Cross)

GLASGOW CORPORATION TRANSPORT

GLASGOW'S LAST TRAM

Vehicles taking part in the last tram procession will include the following:—

1	HORSE DRAWN TRAM	1896	5	RECONDITIONED STANDARD TRAM	1927
2	ROOM AND KITCHEN TRAM	1898	6	MARK I CORONATION TRAM	1937
3	DOUBLE-DECK OPEN VESTIBULE	1914	7	MARK II CUNARDER TYPE	1948
4	SINGLE-DECK TRAMCAR 1089	1926	8	MARK II	1948

Partick Depot **closed** to trams; Cars to Dalmarnock Depot.
The following Operational Alteration takes place:
Partick Depot operation of
Service 9 DALMUIR WEST & LONDON ROAD or AUCHENSHUGGLE
transferred to Dalmarnock Depot.
Dalmarnock Road from Ruby Street to Birkwood Street **closed** to trams.
Dalmarnock Road from Bridgeton Cross to Ruby Street retained for Dalmarnock Depot access.

2nd September 1962
Completion of Tramway Abandonment Programme.
Final Closure of Service Tramway System.

Clydebank was given the opportunity for its own last tram celebrations two days after the last trams ran in Glasgow. Number 1282 was selected for this event and is seen heading west from the Town Hall with its official party. The tram now resides at the National Tramway Museum. *(David Hume / STTS Collection)*

GLASGOW CORPORATION TRANSPORT

"The LAST TRAM"
By C. A. Oakley

124 PAGES OF AUTHORITATIVE AND ENTERTAINING HISTORY OF TRAMWAY SERVICES IN GLASGOW FROM 1872 TO 1962.

93 Photographs, Cartoons, Reproductions, etc. – Price 10/6

Available at all Booksellers

E. R. L. FITZPAYNE, *General Manager*

Service 9 DALMUIR WEST & LONDON ROAD or AUCHENSHUGGLE withdrawn and replaced by **Motorbus Service 64.**
The following Special Service commences:
Special Service 9 ANDERSTON CROSS & AUCHENSHUGGLE (Part Day) from Stobcross Street at Warroch Street via Stobcross Street, Argyle Street, Trongate, Glasgow Cross, London Road to London Road west of Causewayside Street, operating from 1200 until 1900 only, and at special flat-rate fare of 6d.
Dumbarton Road Clydebank, Glasgow Road Clydebank, Dumbarton Road, Balmoral Street, Primrose Street, Hayburn Street, Argyle Street between Partick Bridge and Stobcross Street **closed** to service trams.

4th September 1962

Final Closure of Tramway System.
Special Service 9 ANDERSTON CROSS & AUCHENSHUGGLE (Part Day) withdrawn.
Closing Procession from Dalmarnock Depot to Coplawhill Works.
Stobcross Street, Argyle Street from Stobcross Street to Glassford Street, Trongate, Moir Street, London Road, Abercromby Street, Bridgeton Cross, Dalmarnock Road from Bridgeton Cross to Ruby Street, Ruby Street **closed** to service trams. London Road from Bridgeton Cross to Causewayside Street **closed** to trams.

6th September 1962

Ceremony for Closure of Clydebank Tram System.
Special Car from Clydebank Town Hall to Dalmuir West and Yoker.
Dalmarnock Depot **closed** to trams.
Dumbarton Road Clydebank, Glasgow Road Clydebank, Dumbarton Road, Argyle Street, Trongate, London Road between Glasgow Cross and Bridgeton Cross, Bridgeton Cross, Dalmarnock Road between Bridgeton Cross and Ruby Street, Ruby Street, Hope Street between St Vincent Street and Argyle Street, St Vincent Street between Hope Street and Renfield Street, Renfield Street between St Vincent Street and Gordon Street, Union Street, Jamaica Street, Glasgow Bridge, Bridge Street, Eglinton Street, Pollokshaws Road between Eglinton Toll and Albert Drive **closed** to trams. Movement of remainder of the fleet from Dalmarnock Depot to Coplawhill took place over the few days following this date.

CLANG! CLANG! – B.B.C. OFF RAILS ON A GLASGOW TRAM

THE B.B.C. went right off the rails this morning — the Glasgow tram rails!

The 7 a.m. news bulletin referring to weather conditions intimated calmly—

"The only things running in Glasgow this morning are the trams."

Glasgow's reaction was delighted laughter and a few "more-in-sorrow-than-in-anger" complaints to the B.B.C. switchboard in Glasgow.

How did the mistake happen?

The B.B.C. got the "news" from the London office of the Automobile Association after some wag in the London office had phoned Glasgow and asked if the trams were still running!

The light-hearted reaction at the Glasgow end was "That will be right."

And that's how an early morning joke on a cold and wintry morning mis-fired!

E.T

5th/6th February 1963

Scotland experiences snow fall from 4.30pm on Tuesday 5th February that did not affect the Glasgow area much at all. However, in their 7am national news the following morning, the BBC Home Service from London reports that "only the trams are running". Local newspapers were quick to highlight the resultant embarrassment!

February 1963

Albert Drive between Pollokshaws Road and Kenmure Street used for movement of cars finally **closed** to trams and **traction power switched off**.

The last tramcar movements occurred on Albert Drive when Cunarder 1297 performed shunting duties to propel preserved cars into their final positions, either for display in what was to become the first Museum of Transport or ready for despatch. Here, 1297, later to return to Glasgow in 1988, is shunting Coronation 1274 on 4th January 1963 to be prepared for its long journey to the USA.
(J Stewart Jnr /STTS Collection)

APPENDIX 'A'
GLASGOW CORPORATION TRAMWAYS DEPOTS

This section which lists all Depots providing electric trams on the system, with the Services worked, should be read in conjunction with the accompanying Lists of Services. Very few tram services actually passed by the Depot Doors resulting in specific routes being followed by cars going into or coming off service. With the exception of Elderslie Depot between July 1932 and February 1940 such cars were always deemed to be in service and carry any passengers offering. The "Sorry, I'm not in service" indicator display is a contemporary phenomenon. These routes are described outwards from the Depots. Inwards journeys follow the same routes except where otherwise indicated.

BARRHEAD

Destination Displays: BARRHEAD (PRINCES SQUARE)

Services worked:
As from
01-08-1923 Blue P, Blue Paisley Local
04-10-1936 Depot closed
Blue P and Blue Paisley Local transferred to Elderslie Depot.
Cars transferred to Elderslie Depot.

Depot Workings:

All Services via Aurs Road to Main Street Barrhead.

COATBRIDGE

Destination Displays: JACKSON ST   COATBRIDGE DEPOT

Services worked:
As from
01-01-1922 Green Airdrie Local
03-06-1924 Depot closed temporarily during reconstruction of Airdrie & Coatbridge System.
Cars transferred to Elderslie Depot.
28-02-1926 Depot Reopened
Green B, Green D, Green Airdrie Local
03-05-1938 Green 1, Green 15, Green Airdrie Local
04-05-1942 Green 1, Green Airdrie Local
15-08-1943 **15, 23, Airdrie Local**
11-10-1954 **15, Airdrie Local**
04-11-1956 Depot closed.
Cars transferred to Dennistoun Depot and Parkhead Depot.

Depot Workings:

All Services pass Depot entrance

Car No. 808 is passing the Coatbridge Depot at Jackson Street on a through service from Glasgow to Airdrie.
(RB Parr / STTS Collection)

188

COPLAWHILL WORKS

Destination Displays: DEPOT ONLY   CAR SHED ONLY

Services worked:
As from
08-11-1899   White S
01-05-1901   Yellow C, White S
11-05-1901   Yellow C, Yellow H, White S
30-06-1901   Yellow C, Yellow H
06-01-1902   Yellow C
08-09-1902   Building ceases to serve as Depot
              Yellow C and Cars transferred to Langside Depot.

Depot workings:

All Services via Coplaw Street to Victoria Road or to Cathcart Road.

DALMARNOCK

Destination Displays: DALMARNOCK DEPOT

Services worked:
As from
08-04-1901   White Y
28-04-1901   Red F, Red L, White Y
06-08-1902   Red F, Red L, Blue O, White Y
02-12-1903   Red F, Red L, Blue O, Red X, White Y
03-05-1938   Red 9, Red 9A, Red 9B, Blue 10, Red 17, White 18,
15-08-1943   9, 10, 17, 18, 26
02-01-1944   9, 10, 10A, 17, 18, 26
17-03-1946   9, 10, 10A, 17, 18, 26, 34
23-01-1949   9, 10, 17, 18, 26, 34, 35, 36
29-05-1949   9, 10, 17, 18, 26, 34, 36
04-05-1952   9, 10, 17, 18, 26, 36
19-04-1953   1, 9, 10, 17, 18, 26
07-08-1955   1, 9, 10, 17, 18, 18A, 26, 26A
16-11-1958   1, 9, 10, 18, 18A, 26
07-06-1959   1, 9, 10, 18, 18A, 26, 29
13-03-1960   9, 10, 18, 18A, 26, 29
05-06-1960   9, 18, 18A, 26, 29
06-11-1960   9, 15, 18, 18A, 26, 29
22-03-1961   Half Depot (Lyes 1-9) destroyed by fire. Specials to Partick and Maryhill
16-04-1961   Specials restored
04-06-1961   9, 15, 26, 29
22-10-1961   9, 15, 26
11-03-1962   9, 26
02-06-1962   9
02-09-1962   **Special 9**
04-09-1962   Depot closed, System closed

Ruby Street would be a little known side street in Glasgow's East End were it not for its being home to Dalmarnock Depot. The last car in before the final procession on 4th September 1962 is seen here turning from Dalmarnock Road into Ruby Street amid the expectant crowds.
(David Hume / STTS Collection)

Depot Workings

All Services via Ruby Street to Dalmarnock Road.
The following Services pass along Dalmarnock Road:
Red F, Red X,
Red 9A, Red 9B, Red 17,
10 [from 23-01-1949 until 19-04-1953], **17, 18** [from 07-08-1955 until 04-06-1961], **26,**
34 [from 17-03-1946 until 29-05-1949], **35, 36.**
The following Services proceed:
Red L, Red 9, **9, 10** [from 19-04-1953 until 05-06-1960], **34** [from 04-03-1951 until 04-05-1952]:
via Dalmarnock Road, Bridgeton Cross, London Road then either continue to
ANDERSTON CROSS, WHITEINCH, SCOTSTOUN, CLYDEBANK, DALMUIR, DALMUIR WEST; or
via London Road, Abercromby Street to Abercromby Street south end (reverse) and return via London Road to LONDON ROAD, AUCHENSHUGGLE, CARMYLE.
1 [from 19-04-1953 until 13-03-1960]:
via Dalmarnock Road, Springfield Road south end and continue to SCOTSTOUN WEST, DALMUIR, DALMUIR WEST.
Blue O, Blue 10, **10** [until 23-01-1949], **10A**:
either via Dalmarnock Road, Farmeloan Road, Main Street Rutherglen and continue; or
via Dalmarnock Road, Bridgeton Cross, London Road, Glasgow Cross, Trongate and continue to
KIRKLEE, KELVINSIDE.
White Y, White 18, **18** [until 07-08-1955], **18A, 26A**:
via Dalmarnock Road, Bridgeton Cross, London Road then either continue to
KELVINSIDE AVENUE, RUCHILL, SPRINGBURN; or
via London Road, Abercromby Street to Abercromby Street south end (reverse) and return via London Road to
RUTHERGLEN, BURNSIDE, SHAWFIELD.
The following Service proceeds:
34 [from 29-05-1949 until 04-03-1951]:
via Dalmarnock Road, Bridgeton Cross, London Road then either continue to ALEXANDRA PARK; or
to Abercromby Street south end (reverse) and return via London Road to AUCHENSHUGGLE.

DENNISTOUN

Destination Displays: DENNISTOUN DEPOT

Services worked:
As from
13-06-1901	Green A
09-09-1901	Green A, Yellow J
02-10-1901	Green A, Yellow J, Red R
25-08-1902	Green A, Green D, Yellow J, Red R
12-09-1910	Green A, Green D, Yellow J, Red R, Blue Z
03-05-1938	Green 1, Green 1A, Blue 6, Yellow 7, Red 8/8A
15-08-1943	1, 6, 7, 8, 23, 25, 30
15-06-1958	1, 6, 8, 23, 25, 30
15-03-1959	1, 6, 23, 30
01-11-1959	1, 23, 30
13-03-1960	15, 23
06-11-1960	Depot closed. **15** transferred to Dalmarnock Depot. Cars transferred to Dalmarnock Depot and Maryhill Depot.

Depot Workings:

All Services via Paton Street to Duke Street.
The following Services pass along Duke Street:
Green A, Green D,
Green 1, Green 1A,
1, 23, 30.

The following Services proceed:
Red R, Blue Z
Blue 6, Red 8/8A,
6, 8:

190

via Duke Street to Duke Street at Bluevale Street (reverse) and return via Duke Street, Cumbernauld Road then either continue to ALEXANDRA PARK, RIDDRIE, MILLERSTON; or
to Aitken Street (reverse) and via Cumbernauld Road, Alexandra Parade to city and HYNDLAND, KELVINSIDE CROSS, SCOTSTOUN, DALMUIR WEST, POLLOKSHAWS EAST, NEWLANDS, GIFFNOCK,
ROUKEN GLEN Circle via GIFFNOCK, SPRINGBURN, BISHOPBRIGGS.

Yellow J,
Yellow 7,
7:
via Duke Street then either continue to PAISLEY ROAD TOLL, CRAIGTON ROAD, BELLAHOUSTON; or
to Duke Street at Bluevale Street (reverse) and return via Duke Street, Cumbernauld Road to ALEXANDRA PARK, RIDDRIE, MILLERSTON.

15:
either via Duke Street, Shettleston Road, Shettleston Sheddings and continue to SHETTLESTON, BAILLIESTON, or
via Duke Street, George Street, George Square north and west, St Vincent Place, St Vincent Street, Hope Street, Argyle Street and continue (show CITY CENTRE then SHETTLESTON, BAILLIESTON).

Temporary Alteration to Depot Workings:

Repairs to Railway Bridge at Duke Street Station, Duke Street closed.
From 30-11-1936 the following re-routings take place:

Yellow J:
via Duke Street, Parkhead Cross, Gallowgate, Glasgow Cross, Trongate, then either
via Glassford Street, Ingram Street, South Frederick Street, George Square south, St Vincent Place (reverse) then via St Vincent Place, George Square west and north, George Street, Duke Street and continue to ALEXANDRA PARK, RIDDRIE, MILLERSTON; or
via Argyle Street to Queen Street (reverse) return via Argyle Street, Trongate, Glasgow Cross, London Road, Bridgeton Cross and continue to BELLAHOUSTON.

Red R:
via Duke Street, Parkhead Cross, Gallowgate, Glasgow Cross, Trongate, Glassford Street, Ingram Street, South Frederick Street, George Square south, St Vincent Place, then either
(reverse) return via St Vincent Place, George Square west and north, George Street, Duke Street, Cumbernauld Road and continue to ALEXANDRA PARK, RIDDRIE, MILLERSTON; or
via St Vincent Street, Renfield Street and continue to SPRINGBURN, BISHOPBRIGGS; or
via St Vincent Street, (reverse) return via St Vincent Street, Renfield Street, Union Street and continue to SHAWLANDS, NEWLANDS, POLLOKSHAWS WEST, ROUKEN GLEN etc.

Blue Z:
via Duke Street, Parkhead Cross, Gallowgate, Glasgow Cross, Trongate, Glassford Street, Ingram Street, South Frederick Street, George Square south, St Vincent Place, then either
(reverse) return via St Vincent Place, George Square west and north, George Street, Duke Street, Cumbernauld Road and continue to ALEXANDRA PARK, RIDDRIE; or via St Vincent Street, Renfield Street, Sauchiehall Street
and continue to SCOTSTOUN, DALMUIR WEST.
25-12-1936   Duke Street Bridge reopened, normal Depot Workings resume.

CLOSING OF DENNISTOUN DEPOT

Following the closing of Dennistoun Depot on Sunday, 6th November, 1960, a number of early morning and late evening tram and trolleybus journeys will be withdrawn or altered.

Full information may be obtained from 46 BATH STREET during office hours.

46 Bath Street   GLASGOW CORPORATION TRANSPORT   E. R. L. FITZPAYNE,
General Manager

ELDERSLIE

Destination Displays: ELDERSLIE DEPOT

Services worked:

As from
01-08-1923	Green B, Green KIL, Green U, Green Paisley Local
21-02-1926	Green B, Green KIL, Green U
xx-XX-1928	Green B, Green KIL, Green U, Green Paisley Local
01-05-1932	Green B, Green U, Blue Paisley Local, Green Paisley Local
04 10-1936	Green B, Green U, Blue P, Blue Paisley Local, Green Paisley Local
03-05-1938	Blue 14, Green 15, Green 15A, Blue Paisley Local, Green Paisley Local,
15-08-1943	21, 28, 32, Blue Paisley Local, Green Paisley Local
10-10-1954	21, 28, (Blue) Paisley Local, (Green) Paisley Local
12-05-1957	Depot closed.

Cars transferred Standards to Govan Depot, Possilpark Depot and Maryhill Depot; Coronations to Dalmarnock Depot; Lightweights to Govan Depot.

Depot Workings:

The following Service passes Depot entrance:
Green KIL.

The following Services proceed:
Green B, Green U, Green Paisley Local
Green 15, Green 15A,
21, 32:
via Main Road Elderslie, Ferguslie and continue.
Blue P, Blue Paisley Local,
Blue 14, Blue Paisley Local,
28, Paisley Local:
via Main Road Elderslie, Ferguslie, Broomlands Street, Wellmeadow Street, High Street Paisley, Paisley Cross, Gilmour Street then either continue to RENFRW FERRY; or
to County Square (reverse) and return via Gilmour Street, Paisley Cross to POTTERHILL, GLENFIELD, BARRHEAD, SPIERSBRIDGE, GAIRBRAID AVENUE, MARYHILL, HILLFOOT, MILNGAVIE.

Special Instructions:

As from
17-07-1932	Cars operate Empty both ways between Elderslie Depot and Paisley West.
11-02-1940	Cars resume carriage of passengers on journeys from and to Elderslie Depot.

The former Paisley District Tramways main depot was at Elderslie. In the 1940s it was home to the declining numbers of Semi-High Speed Standard cars, like Blue 934, centre, and ex-Paisley low-height Standards such as Red 1067, six Coronations and a small fleet of buses for Motorbus Services 12 and 17. (RWA Jones / Online Transport Archive)

GOVAN

Destination Displays: LORNE SCHOOL   GOVAN DEPOT

Services worked:
As from
10-08-1915	Green B, Blue G, Yellow J, Blue K, Green U
29-01-1922	Green B, Blue G, Yellow J, Blue K, Yellow Q, Green U
03-05-1938	White 3, White 3A, Blue 4, Blue 4A, Blue 4B, Yellow 7, Yellow 12, Green 15, Green 15A, 30/30A, 31
30-10-1938	Blue 4, Blue 4A, Blue 4B, Yellow 7, Green 15, Green 15A, Green 21
02-05-1943	Blue 4, Blue 4A, Blue 4B, Yellow 7, Yellow 12, Green 15, Green 15A, Green 21
15-08-1943	4, 7, 12, 21, 22, 27, 31, 32
26-08-1945	4, 7, 12, 21, 22, 27, 31, 32, 40
17-03-1946	4, 7, 12, 21, 22, 27, 32, 40
01-03-1953	4, 7, 21, 22, 27, 32, 40
30-09-1956	4, 7, 12, 21, 22, 27, 32, 40
04-11-1956	4, 7, 12, 21, 22, 27, 32
12-05-1957	4, 7, 12, 22, 27, 32
16-03-1958	4, 7, 12, 22, 32
15-06-1958	4, 12, 22, 32
07-09-1958	12, 22, 32
16-11-1958	Depot closed to service trams. Standards, Mark II Coronation cars to Dalmarnock Depot, some Standard cars to Partick Depot. Building retained as storage for cars withdrawn for scrap.
28-02-1959	Depot closed.

Depot Workings:

All Services via Brand Street, Harvie Street to Lorne Street/Govan Road.
The following Services pass along Govan Road, Govan Road [Old Govan Road]:

Yellow J, Blue K,
Blue 4,
Blue 4A [from 23-06-1940 until 15-08-1943], Blue 4B [from 23-06-1940 until 15-08-1943],
Yellow 7,
4 [from 15-08-1943 until 03-03-1946], 7 [from 15-08-1943 until 03-03-1946], 27 [from 15-08-1943 until 03-03-1946],
31 [from 15-08-1943 until 03-03-1946]:
via Govan Road either to CRAIGTON ROAD, BELLAHOUSTON, LINTHOUSE, SHIELDHALL, HILLINGTON ROAD, RENFREW CROSS, RENFREW SOUTH, RENFREW AERODROME; or
via Govan Road (reverse) and return via Govan Road, Govan Road [Old Govan Road], Paisley Road Toll to RIDDRIE, MILLERSTON, KEPPOCHHILL ROAD, SPRINGBURN, LAMBHILL.

From June 1958 Govan Depot also accommodated its share of the trolleybuses operating Service 106 that had replaced Service 7 trams.
(IG Stewart Collection)

The following Services pass along Govan Road, Lorne Street:
Blue G,
Blue 4A [03-05-1938 until 23-06-1940], **Blue 4B** [03-05-1938 until 23-06-1940],
Green 21 [23-06-1940 until 15-08-1943],
4 [from 03-03-1946 until 07-09-1958], **7** [from 03-03-1946 until 15-06-1958], **27** [from 03-03-1946 until 16-03-1958],
31 [from 03-03-1946 until 17-03-1946]:
via Govan Road to BELLAHOUSTON, LINTHOUSE, SHIELDHALL, HILLINGTON ROAD, RENFREW CROSS, RENFREW SOUTH, PAISLEY NORTH; or
via Lorne Street, Paisley Road West, Paisley Road Toll and continue to RIDDRIE, MILLERSTON, PROVANMILL, KEPPOCHHILL ROAD, SPRINGBURN, LAMBHILL.

The following Services proceed:
Yellow Q [from 29-01-1922 until 24-11-1930 and from 09-01-1931 until 03-05-1938],
12 [from 01-05-1949 until 01-03-1953]:
either via Lorne Street, Paisley Road West to IBROX; or
via Govan Road to LINTHOUSE; or
via Lorne Street, Paisley Road West, Paisley Road Toll, Admiral Street and continue to MOUNT FLORIDA.
Yellow Q [from 24-11-1930 until 09-01-1931 and from 03-05-1938 until 30-10-1938]:
12 [from 30-09-1956 until 16-11-1958]:
via Govan Road to LINTHOUSE; or
via Lorne Street, Paisley Road West, Paisley Road Toll, Admiral Street and continue to MOUNT FLORIDA.
White 3 [from 03-05-1938 until 30-10-1938], **White 3A** [from 03-05-1938 until 30-10-1938],
Green 15, **Green 15A**, **Green 21** [from 30-10-1938 until 23-06-1940], **30/30A** [from 03-05-1938 until 30-10-1938],
21 [from 15-08-1943 until 12-05-1957], **22, 32, 40** [from 26-08-1945 until 04-11-1956]:
via Lorne Street either via Paisley Road West to IBROX, EXHIBITION, MOSSPARK, DUMBRECK, HALFWAY, CROOKSTON, PAISLEY CROSS, PAISLEY WEST, FERGUSLIE MILLS, ELDERSLIE; or
via Paisley Road West, Paisley Road Toll to ST VINCENT STREET, LAMBHILL, PROVANMILL, SPRINGBURN, BISHOPBRIGGS, PARKHEAD, TOLLCROSS, UDDINGSTON, SHETTLESTON, BAILLIESTON, AIRDRIE, GAIRBRAID AVENUE, MARYHILL.
31 [from 03-05-1938 until 30-10-1938]:
via Govan Road, Govan Cross, Govan Road and continue to LINTHOUSE; or
via Govan Road, Govan Cross, Govan Road, Golspie Street and continue to EXHIBITION.

KINNING PARK

Destination Displays: DEPOT ONLY   PAISLEY ROAD TOLL

Services worked:

As from
Date	Services
28-07-1901	Green B
10-08-1901	Green B, Blue G
24-03-1902	Green B, Blue G, Blue K
14-04-1902	Green B, Blue G, Blue K, Green U
20-08-1903	Green B, Blue G, Yellow J, Blue K, Green U
10-08-1915	Depot closed to service trams. Services and cars transferred to Govan Depot.

Depot Workings:

All Services via Admiral Street to Paisley Road Toll.
The following Services pass Paisley Road Toll:
Green B, Blue G, Yellow J, Blue K, Green U.

LANGSIDE

Destination Displays: BATTLEFIELD   LANGSIDE DEPOT

Services worked:

As from
Date	Services
05-05-1901	Yellow C, Yellow H
30-06-1901	Yellow C, Yellow H,, Red M
26-02-1902	Yellow C, Yellow H, Red M, White S
24-11-1902	Yellow C, Yellow H, Red M, Red N, White S
13-10-1906	Yellow C, Yellow H, Red M, Red N, Yellow Q, White S
12-11-1906	Yellow C, Yellow H, Red M, Red N, Yellow Q, White S, White V
10-09-1923	Yellow C, Yellow H, Red M, Red N, Yellow Q, White S, White V, Red CP
05-07-1926	Yellow C, Yellow H, Red M, Red N, Yellow Q, White S, White V
14-06-1930	Yellow C, Yellow H, Red M, Red N, Yellow Q, White S, White V, Red CP
06-09-1930	Yellow C, Yellow H, Red M, Red N, Yellow Q, White S, White V
20-11-1932	Yellow C, Yellow H, Red M, Yellow Q, White S, White V
11-12-1932	Yellow C, Yellow H, Red M, Red N, Yellow Q, White S, White V
03-05-1938	White 2, Yellow 5, Yellow 5A, Red 11, Yellow 12, Red 13, White 19

Facing Page: The curves in the foreground into Lorne Street from Paisley Road West provided access to Govan Depot. Standard car 45 is on Service 32 to Crookston. Stinsons specialised in naval uniforms – but would find little call for this today.
(BJ Cross Collection)

Right: Langside Depot was latterly the home of the Standard cars fitted with EMB Hornless trucks. Former White car 751 was typical, photographed at Provanmill terminus in August 1944.
(SJT Robertson)

195

15-08-1943	**2, 5, 5A, 11, 12, 13, 19, 24**
20-02-1949	**5, 5A, 11, 12, 13, 24**
01-07-1951	**5, 5A, 12, 13, 24**
05-08-1951	**5, 5A, 12, 13, 24, 24A**
02-12-1951	**5, 5A, 12, 13, 24**
05-07-1953	**5, 5A, 12, 24**
30-09-1956	Depot closed.

5, 5A, 24 transferred to Newlands Depot
12 transferred to Govan Depot
Cars transferred to Newlands Depot and Govan Depot.

Depot Workings:

The following Services pass Depot entrance:
Yellow C,
Yellow 5,
5, 5A

The following Services proceed:
White V
White 2,
2:
via Battlefield Road, Prospecthill Road, Cathcart Road, Crown Street then either continue to
GARNGAD, PROVANMILL; or
Crown Street (reverse) and return via Crown Street, Cathcart Road, Aikenhead Road to POLMADIE
Inwards cars run via Cathcart Road, Holmlea Road at Garry Street (reverse) and return via Holmlea Road to Battlefield Road.
Red M, White S,
Red 13, White 19,
13, 19:
via Battlefield Road, Prospecthill Road, Cathcart Road and continue to SPRINGBURN,
GAIRBRAID AVENUE, MARYHILL, MILNGAVIE; or
via Holmlea Road and continue to NETHERLEE, CLARKSTON.
Inwards cars from north run via Cathcart Road, Holmlea Road at Garry Street (reverse) and return via Holmlea Road to Battlefield Road.
13 [from 19-06-1949 until 05-07-1953]:
Northbound *Outwards* cars run via Holmlea Road to Garry Street (reverse) and return via Holmlea Road, Cathcart Road and continue to GAIRBRAID AVENUE, MARYHILL, MILNGAVIE.
Yellow H, Red N,
Yellow 5A, Red 11,
11, 24, 24A:
via Battlefield Road, Grange Road, Langside Road, Victoria Road then either continue to
KELVINGROVE, JORDANHILL, ANNIESLAND, RUCHILL, GAIRBRAID AVENUE, MARYHILL, MILNGAVIE; or
to Victoria Road at Queen's Park Gates (reverse) and return via Victoria Road, Langside Road to LANGSIDE
or via Grange Road, Sinclair Drive to SINCLAIR DRIVE.
Yellow Q,
Yellow 12,
12:
[until 01-05-1949 and from 05-07-1953] via Battlefield Road, Prospecthill Road, Cathcart Road and continue to
PAISLEY ROAD TOLL, LINTHOUSE, IBROX.
[from 01-05-1949 until 05-07-1953] via Holmlea Road to Holmlea Road at Garry Street (reverse) and return
via Holmlea Road, Cathcart Road and continue to PAISLEY ROAD TOLL, LINTHOUSE.

196

MARYHILL

Destination Displays: MARYHILL   MARYHILL DEPOT [From 07-02-1954]

Services worked:
As from
30-06-1901   White E, Red M, Red N, Red T
02-12-1903   White E, Red M, Red N, Red T, White Y
11-01-1914   White E, Red M, Red N, Blue P, Red T, White Y
27-03-1933   White E, Red M, Red N, Blue P, White Y
03-05-1938   White 3, White 3A, Red 11, Red 13, Blue 14, White 18,
30-10-1938   White 3, Red 11, Red 13, Blue 14, White 18,
30-05-1943   White 3, White 3A, Red 11, Red 13, Blue 14, White 18,
15-08-1943   3, 3A, 11, 13, 14, 18
05-12-1943   3, 11, 13, 14, 18
26-08-1945   11, 13, 14, 18, 40
12-01-1947   11, 13, 18, 23, 40
01-07-1951   13, 18, 23, 40
04-10-1953   18, 23, 29, 40
07-08-1955   18, 18A, 23, 29, 40
04-11-1956   18, 18A, 23, 29
15-03-1959   18, 18A, 23, 29, 33
03-05-1959   18, 18A, 23, 29
06-11-1960   18, 18A, 29
22-03-1961   18, 18A, 29, Dalmarnock Depot Specials
16-04-1961   18, 18A, 29
04-06-1961   29
22-10-1961   Depot closed.
             Cars to Dalmarnock Depot and Partick Depot.

Depot Workings:

All Services via Celtic Street to Maryhill Road.
The following Services pass along Maryhill Road:
Red M, Red N, Blue P, Red T,
Red 11, Red 13, Blue 14,
11, 13, 14, 23, 29, 40

Coronation 1148 in Maitland Street prepares to struggle through the congestion in Cowcaddens on its way back to Maryhill Depot. This car was rebodied after extensive damage in the Newlands Depot fire in 1948.
(RB Parr / STTS Collection)

The following Services proceed:
White E,
White 3, White 3A,
3, 3A:
via Maryhill Road, St George's Cross, St George's Road, Charing Cross, Sauchiehall Street then either continue to DUMBRECK, MOSSPARK; or
Sauchiehall Street (reverse) and return via Sauchiehall Street, Charing Cross either via Sauchiehall Street to KELVINGROVE, ANNIESLAND; or via St George's Road, Woodlands Road and to UNIVERSITY.
White Y,
White 18,
18, 18A, 33
via Maryhill Road, and continue to RUTHERGLEN, BURNSIDE, SHAWFIELD, CIRCLE SPRINGBURN; or
via Maryhill Road to Vernon Street (reverse) return via Maryhill Road, Bilsland Drive to SPRINGBURN, CIRCLE SPRINGBURN.

NEWLANDS

Destination Displays: NEWLANDS   NEWLANDS DEPOT

Services worked:
As from
xx-05-1910	White E, Red R
11-01-1914	White E, Blue P, Red R
20-11-1932	White E, Red N, Blue P, Red R
11-12-1932	White E, Blue P, Red R
03-05-1938	White 3, White 3A, Red 8, Red 8A, Blue 14, 30/30A
30-10-1938	White 3, Red 8, Red 8A, Blue 14
30-05-1943	White 3, White 3A, Red 8, Red 8A, Blue 14
15-08-1943	3, 3A, 8, 14, 25
05-12-1943	3, 8, 14, 25, 40
28-10-1945	3, 8, 14, 25
12-01-1947	3, 8, 14, 14A, 25
11-04-1948	Lyes 1-5 damaged by fire
07-11-1948	3, 8, 14, 14A, 14B, 25
20-02-1949	3, 8, 14, 14A, 25, 31
21-08-1949	3, 8, 14, 25, 31
30-09-1956	3, 5, 5A, 8, 14, 24, 25, 31
17-11-1957	3, 8, 14, 24, 25, 31
16-03-1958	3, 8, 14, 25, 31
15-03-1959	3, 14, 25, 31
07-06-1959	3, 14, 31
01-11-1959	3, 31
06-12-1959	**3** Remaining Standard Cars to Dennistoun Depot.
05-06-1960	Depot closed
	Coronation cars to Dennistoun Depot, Mark II Coronation and Replacement Mark I Coronation cars to Partick Depot.

Depot Workings:

All Services via Newlandsfield Road to Kilmarnock Road.
The following Services pass along Kilmarnock Road:
Red R,
Red 8/8A/8B,
8, 31 [from 08-04-1956 until 06-12-1959].
The following Services proceed:
White E,
White 3, White 3A, **30/30A**
3, 3A:
via Kilmarnock Road, Shawlands Cross, Pollokshaws Road, Eglinton Toll, Eglinton Street; either continue via Eglinton Street to ST VINCENT STREET, UNIVERSITY; or
via Pollokshaws Road to Pollokshaws Road at Albert Drive (reverse) and return via Albert Drive to POLLOKSHIELDS, DUMBRECK, MOSSPARK. *Inwards* cars run via Albert Drive, Kenmure Street,

Maxwell Road, Eglinton Toll, Eglinton Street, (reverse) and return via Eglinton Toll, Pollokshaws Road and outwards route.

40 [from 05-12-1943 until 26-08-1945]:
via Kilmarnock Road, Shawlands Cross, Pollokshaws Road, Eglinton Toll, Eglinton Street; either
via Eglinton Street, Bridge Street, Kingston Street, Commerce Street and continue to ST VINCENT STREET; or
via Pollokshaws Road to Pollokshaws Road at Albert Drive (reverse) and return via Albert Drive, St Andrew's Drive, Nithsdale Road, Dumbreck Road to DUMBRECK. *Inwards* cars run via Albert Drive, Kenmure Street, Maxwell Road, Eglinton Toll, Eglinton Street (reverse) and return via Eglinton Toll, Pollokshaws Road and outwards route.

Blue P, **Red R**,
Red 8A, **Blue 14**,
8A, 14, 14A, 14B, 25, 31 [from 20-02-1949 until 08-04-1956]:
either via Kilmarnock Road, Shawlands Cross, Pollokshaws Road and continue to MARYHILL, HILLFOOT, MILNGAVIE, CASTLE STREET, SPRINGBURN, COLSTON, BISHOPBRIGGS, KELVINGROVE, UNIVERSITY, LAMBHILL; or
via Kilmarnock Road (reverse at Coustonholm Road) and return via Coustonholm Road, Pleasance Street, Greenview Street, Pollokshaws Road to POLLOKSHAWS, CARNWADRIC, THORNLIEBANK, ROUKEN GLEN Circle via THORNLIEBANK, SPIERSBRIDGE, ARDEN, CROSSSTOBS, PAISLEY CROSS, RENFREW FERRY via BARRHEAD.

Red N [from 20-11-1932 until 11-12-1932 only]:
via Kilmarnock Road, Shawlands Cross, Pollokshaws Road, Eglinton Toll, Eglinton Street;
either via Turriff Street and continue to GAIRBRAID AVENUE, MARYHILL; or
to Eglinton Street (reverse at south end) and return via Eglinton Street, Eglinton Toll to SINCLAIR DRIVE.

5, 5A, 24:
via Kilmarnock Road, Shawlands Cross, Pollokshaws Road, Eglinton Toll, Eglinton Street;
either continue to KELVINSIDE, ANNIESLAND; or
via Eglinton Street, Bridge Street (reverse) and return via Bridge Street, Eglinton Street to HOLMLEA ROAD, LANGSIDE.

Special Instructions:

As from
xx-02-1948   All Services show "8" on *Inwards* journeys to NEWLANDS DEPOT.
15-03-1959   All Services show "31" on *Inwards* journeys to NEWLANDS DEPOT.
06-12-1959   All Services show "3" on *Inwards* journeys to NEWLANDS DEPOT.

In July 1954, Car 226 returns to Newlands Depot from duty on Service 14. Having reversed in Pollokshaws Road to gain Greenview Street, what had been the rear of the car now leads which will explain the display, at this end, of '14' rather than the mandatory '8' for the Depot Working. Passing Shawbridge Street and the final site of the former Pollokshaws East terminus, the car is entering Pleasance Street. It will reverse again on reaching Kilmarnock Road in order to head for Newlands Depot. *(RJS Wiseman)*

PARKHEAD

Destination Displays: PARKHEAD DEPOT

Services worked:
As from
15-10-1922 Green A, Green B, Green U
23-05-1925 Green A, Green Airdrie Local, Green B, Green U
21-06-1925 Green A, Green Airdrie Local, Green B, Green D, Green U
28-02-1926 Green A, Green B, Green D, Green U
28-10-1928 Green A, Green B, Green D, Green U, Green UM
01-11-1931 Green A, Green B, Green D, Green U
03-05-1938 Green 1, Green 1A, Green 15, Green 15A
15-08-1943 **15, 23, 29, 30**
12-01-1947 **15, 29, 30**
15-03-1959 **15, 29**
07-06-1959 **15**
13-03-1960 Depot closed.
transferred to Dennistoun Depot.
Standard cars to Dalmarnock Depot, Coronation cars to Dennistoun Depot.

Depot Workings:

The following Services pass the Depot entrance:
Green U, Green UM,
Green 15A
29.
The following Services proceed via Tollcross Road, Parkhead Cross:
Green B,
Green 15,
15:
either via Gallowgate and continue to IBROX, HALFWAY, CROOKSTON, PAISLEY CROSS, PAISLEY WEST, FERGUSLIE MILLS, ELDERSLIE, ANDERSTON CROSS; or
via Springfield Road to north end (reverse) and return via Springfield Road, Parkhead Cross, Westmuir Street to SHETTLESTON, BAILLIESTON, AIRDRIE.
Green 1
23 [from 15-08-1943 until 12-01-1947]:
via Springfield Road to north end (reverse) and return via Springfield Road, Parkhead Cross then either via Westmuir Street, Shettleston Sheddings to SHETTLESTON, BAILLIESTON, AIRDRIE; or
via Duke Street and continue to KELVINGROVE.
Green 1A,
30:
via Springfield Road and continue to SPRINGFIELD ROAD, DALMARNOCK, CAMBUSLANG; or
via Springfield Road to north end (reverse) and return via Springfield Road, Parkhead Cross, Duke Street and continue to KELVINSIDE, ANNIESLAND, KNIGHTSWOOD, BLAIRDARDIE.

PARTICK

Destination Displays: PARTICK

Services worked:
As from
28-04-1901 Red F, Red L
01-05-1901 Yellow C, Red F, White HS, Red L
05-06-1901 Yellow C, Red F, White HS, Red L, Blue O
xx-10-1901 Yellow C, Red F, Red L, Blue O
12-12-1901 Yellow C, Red F, Red L, Blue O, White Y
25-08-1902 Green A, Yellow C, Green D, Red F, Red L, Blue O, White Y
23-02-1903 Green A, Yellow C, Green D, Red F, Yellow H, Red L, Blue O, White Y
02-12-1903 Green A, Yellow C, Green D, Red F, Yellow H, Red L, Blue O, Red X
30-04-1905 Green A, Yellow C, Green D, Red F, Yellow H, Red L, Blue O, Green W, Red X
21-06-1909 Green A, Yellow C, Green D, Red F, Yellow H, Red L, Blue O, Green SF, Green W, Red X
12-09-1910 Green A, Yellow C, Green D, Red F, Yellow H, Red L, Blue O, Green SF,

200

	Green W, Red X, Blue Z
03-05-1911	Green A, Yellow C, Green D, Red F, Yellow H, White HS, Red L, Blue O, Green SF, Green W, Red X, Blue Z
06-11-1911	Green A, Yellow C, Green D, Red F, Yellow H, Red L, Blue O, Green SF, Green W, Red X, Blue Z
13-07-1924	Green A, Yellow C, Green D, Red F, Yellow H, Red L, Blue O, Red RP, Green SF, Green W, Red X, Blue Z
19-07-1924	Green A, Yellow C, Green D, Red F, Yellow H, Red L, Red RP, Green SF, Green W, Red X, Blue Z
04-05-1925	Green A, Yellow C, Green D, Red F, Yellow H, Red L, Red RP, Green W, Red X, Blue Z
03-05-1938	Green 1, Green 1A, Yellow 5, Yellow 5A, Blue 6, Red 9, Red 9A, Red 9B, Green 16, Red 17, Red 20
15-08-1943	1, 5, 5A, 6, 9, 16, 20, 21, 24, 26, 30
05-12-1943	1, 5, 5A, 6, 9, 16, 20, 21, 24, 26, 30, 40
28-10-1945	1, 5, 5A, 6, 9, 16, 20, 21, 24, 26, 30
08-12-1946	1, 5, 5A, 6, 9, 16, 17, 20, 21, 24, 26, 30
23-01-1949	1, 5, 5A, 6, 9, 10, 16, 17, 20, 21, 24, 26, 30, 36
04-12-1949	1, 5, 5A, 6, 9, 10, 16, 17, 21, 24, 26, 30, 36
19-04-1953	1, 5, 5A, 6, 9, 10, 16, 17, 21, 24, 26, 30
10-10-1954	1, 5, 5A, 6, 9, 10, 16, 17, 24, 26, 30
07-08-1955	1, 5, 5A, 6, 9, 10, 16, 17, 24, 26, 26A, 30
17-11-1957	1, 6, 9, 10, 16, 17, 24, 26, 26A, 30
16-03-1958	1, 6, 9, 10, 16, 17, 26, 26A, 30
16-11-1958	1, 6, 9, 10, 16, 26, 30
01-11-1959	1, 9, 10, 16, 26, 30
13-03-1960	9, 10, 16, 26
05-06-1960	9, 16, 26
12-03-1961	9, 26
03-06-1962	Depot closed 9 transferred to Dalmarnock Depot. Cars transferred to Dalmarnock Depot.

Partick Depot was in Hayburn Street and shared the Maximum Traction cars with Dalmarnock. It was also the home of 1089, the sole surviving Single-Decker after the Duntocher service was abandoned. It had re-entered service in 1952 adapted for use on shipyard specials as a standee car. *(RF Mack, Courtesy AD Packer)*

Depot Workings:

All Services via Hayburn Street to Dumbarton Road.
The following Services pass along Dumbarton Road:
Red F, Red L, Green W, Red X, Blue Z [from 08-08-1926],
Blue 6, Red 9, Red 9A, Red 9B, Green 16, Red 17,
6, 9, 16, 17, 21, 26, 26A.
The following Services proceed:
Green A, Green D:
via Dumbarton Road, Argyle Street, Sauchiehall Street, Charing Cross, Sauchiehall Street and continue to ST VINCENT PLACE, DENNISTOUN, PARKHEAD, SPRINGFIELD ROAD, SHETTLESTON, BAILLIESTON, AIRDRIE; or
via Dumbarton Road to Dumbarton Road at Church Street (reverse) and return via Church Street, Byres Road, Botanic Gardens, Great Western Road to KELVINSIDE, ANNIESLAND.
[from 10-07-1910] additionally via Dumbarton Road, Crow Road, Broomhill Cross, Crow Road to Anniesland Cross and continue
[from 15-09-1929] via Dumbarton Road to Scotstoun West either continue to DALMUIR WEST; or
to Dumbarton Road at Scotstoun West (reverse) and return via Kingsway to PARKHEAD, SPRINGFIELD ROAD.

The following Services proceed:
Green 1, Green 1A,
1, 30:
[until 01-11-1959] via Dumbarton Road, Argyle Street, Sauchiehall Street, Charing Cross, Sauchiehall Street and continue to ST VINCENT PLACE, NORTH ALBION STREET, DENNISTOUN etc; altered to become
[from 01-11-1959 until 13-03-1960] [show 9 MOIR STREET] via Dumbarton Road, Argyle Street, Anderston Cross, Argyle Street, Trongate, Glasgow Cross, London Road, Moir Street [show – ST VINCENT STREET]
then via Moir Street, Gallowgate, Glasgow Cross, Trongate, Argyle Street, Hope Street, St Vincent Street then continue to NORTH ALBION STREET, DENNISTOUN, SPRINGFIELD ROAD, DALMARNOCK; or
[until 15-11-1958] via Dumbarton Road, Crow Road, Broomhill Cross, Crow Road, Anniesland Cross, Great Western Road (reverse) and return via Anniesland Cross, Great Western Road to KNIGHTSWOOD, BLAIRDARDIE; altered to become
[from 15-11-1958 until 13-03-1960] via Dumbarton Road to Dumbarton Road at Scotstoun West (reverse) and return via Kingsway, Anniesland Road, Anniesland Cross, Great Western Road (reverse) and return via Anniesland Cross, Great Western Road to KNIGHTSWOOD, BLAIRDARDIE; or via Dumbarton Road to Scotstoun West either continue to DALMUIR WEST; or
to Dumbarton Road at Scotstoun West (reverse) and return via Kingsway to DENNISTOUN, PARKHEAD, SPRINGFIELD ROAD, DALMARNOCK.
Yellow C,
Yellow 5,
5, 5A:
via Dumbarton Road, Argyle Street and continue to city and to HOLMLEA ROAD, CLARKSTON; or
via Dumbarton Road to Dumbarton Road at Church Street (reverse) and return via Church Street to KIRKLEE, KELVINSIDE.
Yellow H
Yellow 5A [from 03-05-1938 until 15-08-1943],
24:
via Dumbarton Road, Argyle Street and continue to city and to LANGSIDE; or
via Dumbarton Road, Crow Road, Broomhill Cross, Crow Road and continue to JORDANHILL, ANNIESLAND.
Blue Z [from 12-09-1910 until 08-08-1926]:
via Dumbarton Road, Argyle Street and continue to ALEXANDRA PARK;
via Dumbarton Road to Dumbarton Road at Church Street (reverse) and return via Church Street to HYNDLAND, JORDANHILL, KELVINSIDE CROSS.
The following Services proceed:
Blue O [from 25-08-1902 until 19-07-1924]:
via Dumbarton Road, Argyle Street, Sauchiehall Street, Charing Cross, Sauchiehall Street and continue to OATLANDS, RUTHERGLEN; or
via Dumbarton Road to Dumbarton Road at Church Street (reverse) and return via Church Street, Byres Road, Botanic Gardens and to KIRKLEE.

10 [from 23-01-1949 until 19-04-1953], **36:**
via Dumbarton Road, Argyle Street, Sauchiehall Street, Charing Cross, Sauchiehall Street and continue to PARKHEAD; or
via Dumbarton Road to Dumbarton Road at Church St (reverse) and return via Church St, Byres Road, Highburgh Road, Hyndland Road to Hyndland Station and continue.
The following Services proceed:
10 [from 19-04-1953 until 16-03-1958]:
via Dumbarton Road, Argyle Street, Sauchiehall Street, Charing Cross, Sauchiehall Street and continue to LONDON ROAD; or
via Dumbarton Road to Dumbarton Road at Church Street (reverse) and return via Church Street, Byres Road, Highburgh Road, Hyndland Road to Hyndland Station and continue.
10 [from 16-03-1958 until 01-11-1959]:
via Dumbarton Road, Argyle Street, Sauchiehall Street, Charing Cross, Sauchiehall Street and continue to LONDON ROAD; or
via Dumbarton Road, Argyle Street, *outwards* via Sauchiehall Street, Charing Cross spur, St George's Road, Woodlands Road and continue to KELVINSIDE. *Inwards* cars run via same route to Charing Cross then via Sauchiehall Street, Elmbank Street, St Vincent Street, Finnieston, Argyle Street and Dumbarton Road.
10 [from 01-11-1959 until 05-06-1960]:
via Dumbarton Road, Argyle Street, Finnieston, St Vincent Street, Bothwell Street and continue to LONDON ROAD; or
via Dumbarton Road, Argyle Street, Finnieston, St Vincent Street, Elmbank Street, Sauchiehall Street and continue to KELVINSIDE.
Red RP,
Red 20,
20:
via Dumbarton Road, Glasgow Road Clydebank and continue to RADNOR PARK, PARKHALL, DUNTOCHER.
Green SF:
via Dumbarton Road, Argyle Street to Argyle Street at Finnieston (reverse) and return via Finnieston Street and continue to STOBCROSS FERRY.
40 [from 05-12-1943 until 26-08-1945]:
via Dumbarton Road, Argyle Street, Finnieston, St Vincent Street, Bothwell Street, Hope Street and continue to DUMBRECK.

POLLOKSHAWS

Destination Displays: DEPOT ONLY   POLLOKSHAWS EAST   POLLOKSHAWS WEST

Services worked:
As from
05-06-1901   **Red R**
09-05-1902   **White E**, **Red R**
xx-05-1910   Depot closed
              Services and Cars transferred to Newlands Depot.

Depot Workings:

All Services either via Coustonholm Road to Kilmarnock Road;
or via Pleasance Street, Greenview Street to Pollokshaws Road.
The following Services pass along Kilmarnock Road:
Red R (Pollokshaws East-Newlands-Giffnock section).
The following Services pass along Pollokshaws Road:
Red R (Pollokshaws West-Thornliebank section).
The following Service proceeds:
White E:
via Coustonholm Road, Kilmarnock Road, Shawlands Cross, Pollokshaws Road, Eglinton Toll, and either continue to UNIVERSITY; or
via Pollokshaws Road to Pollokshaws Road at Albert Drive (reverse) and return via Albert Drive, to POLLOKSHIELDS, DUMBRECK, MOSSPARK. *Inwards* cars run via Albert Drive, Kenmure Street, Maxwell Road, Eglinton Toll, Eglinton Street (reverse) and return via Eglinton Toll, Pollokshaws Road and outwards route.

Standard Car 31 is entering Possilpark Depot, as normal procedure, with the bow collector facing. Car 275 on Service 18 is waiting on Hawthorn Street for it to clear. *(BJ Cross Collection)*

POSSILPARK

Destination Displays: POSSILPARK DEPOT   SPRINGBURN   POSSILPARK
                                               POSSILPARK DEPOT   POSSILPARK DEPOT

Services worked:
As from
10-08-1901   Blue G
06-01-1902   Blue G, Red R, White S
24-03-1902   Blue G, Blue K, Red R, White S
04-06-1904   Blue G, Blue K, Red R, White S, Green W
12-11-1906   Blue G, Blue K, Red R, White S, White V, Green W
03-05-1938   White 2, Blue 4, Blue 4A, Blue 4B, Red 8, Red 8A, Green 16, White 19
30-10-1938   White 2, Blue 4, Blue 4A, Blue 4B, Red 8, Red 8A, Green 16, White 19, Green 21
15-08-1943   2, 4, 8, 16, 19, 25, 27, 31, 32
26-11-1944   2, 4, 8, 16, 19, 25, 27, 31, 32, 33
17-03-1946   2, 4, 8, 16, 19, 22, 25, 27, 32, 33
20-02-1949   4, 8, 16, 22, 25, 27, 31, 32, 33
16-03-1958   4, 8, 22, 25, 31, 32, 33
07-09-1958   8, 22, 25, 31, 32, 33
16-11-1958   8, 25, 31, 33
15-03-1959   25
07-06-1959   Depot closed
             Cars transferred to Maryhill Depot and Partick Depot.

Depot Workings:

The following Services pass Depot entrance:
Blue G [from 09-08-1925],
Blue 4A
27, 33
The following Services proceed:
Blue K, Green W,
Blue 4, Green 16,
4 [until 01-04-1951], **16** [until 01-04-1951]:

204

via Hawthorn Street, Saracen Street, Saracen Cross, Saracen Street, Mosshouse;
either via Possil Road and continue to SCOTSTOUN, LINTHOUSE, SHIELDHALL, RENFREW SOUTH; or
Mosshouse (reverse) and return via Keppochhill Road to KEPPOCHHILL ROAD.
Inwards cars run via Keppochhill Road, Springburn Road, Hawthorn Street

4 [from 01-04-1951 until 07-09-1958], **16** [from 01-04-1951 until 16-03-1958]:
via Hawthorn Street, Springburn Road and continue to SCOTSTOUN, SHIELDHALL, HILLINGTON ROAD, PAISLEY NORTH.

The following Services proceed:
Blue G [until 09-08-1925]
Blue 4B

22 [from 17-03-1946 until 16-11-1958], **31** [from 15-08-1943 until 17-03-1946 and from 20-02-1949 until 15-03-1959]:
via Hawthorn Street, Saracen Street, Saracen Cross then either continue to city and to CROOKSTON, LINTHOUSE, SHIELDHALL, HILLINGTON ROAD, RENFREW CROSS, POLLOKSHAWS, MERRYLEE; or
via Saracen Street, Mosshouse (reverse) and return via Saracen Street to LAMBHILL.

Red R, **White S**
Red 8, **Red 8A**, **White 19**,

8, 19, 25, 32 [from 20-02-1949 until 16-11-1958]:
via Hawthorn Street, Springburn Road and continue to city and to MOUNT FLORIDA, NETHERLEE, POLLOKSHAWS, CARNWADRIC, ROUKEN GLEN Circle via THORNLIEBANK, CROOKSTON, ELDERSLIE; or
to Springburn Road (reverse) and return via Springburn Road to COLSTON, BISHOPBRIGGS.

25 additional journeys [until 16-11-1958]:
certain CITY CENTRE journeys from north terminate at BRIDGE STREET and return *Inwards* to Depot as Service "27" via Nelson Street, Commerce Street, George V. Bridge, Oswald Street, Hope Street, Cowcaddens, Garscube Road, Round Toll, Possil Road, Mosshouse, Saracen Street, Saracen Cross, Saracen Street and Hawthorn Street.
Note: [from 16-03-1958] these journeys display "22".

White V,
White 2, **Green 21**,

2, 32 [from 15-08-1943 until 20-02-1949]:
via Hawthorn Street, Springburn Road, Castle Street;
then either continue to POLMADIE, CROOKSTON, ELDERSLIE, HILLINGTON ROAD, RENFREW CROSS; or
via Castle Street (reverse) and return via Castle Street, Garngad Road to GARNGAD, PROVANMILL.

Coronation 1269 is seen approaching Charing Cross on a Service 10 Depot Working back to Partick past Elder's "contemporary" furniture shop, long-since demolished to accommodate the M8 motorway cutting. *(R Hamilton)*

205

RENFREW

Destination Displays: RENFREW DEPOT

Services worked:
As from
- 01-08-1923   Green ABB, Green KIL, Blue Paisley Local
- 17-08-1924   Green ABB, Green KIL, Blue P, Blue Paisley Local
- 01-05-1932   Green ABB, Blue P, Blue Paisley Local
- 26-03-1933   Blue P, Blue Paisley Local
- 04-10-1936   Depot closed.
  Blue P and Blue Paisley Local transferred to Elderslie Depot.
  Cars transferred to Elderslie Depot, Govan Depot and Newlands Depot.

Depot Workings:

The following Services pass Depot entrance:
Green KIL, Blue P, Blue Paisley Local.
The following Service proceeds:
Green ABB:
via Paisley Road Renfrew, Renfrew Road Paisley, Weir Street, Old Sneddon Street, Gilmour Street to County Square.

SPRINGBURN

Destination Displays:

Services worked: DEPOT ONLY   CAR SHED ONLY
As from
- 13-10-1898   White S
- 05-06-1901   Red R, White S
- 06-01-1902   Depot closed.
  Services and Cars transferred to Possilpark Depot.

The original small Springburn Depot for the first electric cars was located at the east end of Keppochhill Road. It also housed the Power Plant for the first experimental electrified route. The Depot was closed in January 1902 when Possilpark Depot took over operation of its services. *(STTS Collection)*

Depot Workings:

All Services proceed via Keppochhill Road to Springburn Road:
then either northwards via Springburn Road to SPRINGBURN; or
Springburn Road (reverse) and return southwards via Springburn Road to MITCHELL STREET, GLASGOW CROSS, GOVANHILL, SHAWLANDS, POLLOKSHAWS.

WHITEVALE

Destination Displays: DEPOT ONLY   WHITEVALE

Services worked:
As from
28-07-1901   Green B
14-04-1902   Green B, Green U
17-04-1904   Green A, Green B, Green U
15-10-1922   Depot closed.
             Services and Cars transferred to Parkhead Depot.

Depot Workings:

All Services proceed via Rowchester Street to Gallowgate.
The following Services pass via Gallowgate:
Green B, Green U.
The following Service proceeds:
Green A:
via Gallowgate, Parkhead Cross, Duke Street and to ANNIESLAND;
or via Gallowgate, Glasgow Cross, Trongate, Glassford Street, Ingram Street, South Frederick Street, George Square south, St Vincent Place [ST VINCENT PL] then continue to ANNIESLAND;
or (reverse) and return via St Vincent Place, George Square west and north to DENNISTOUN, PARKHEAD or SPRINGFIELD ROAD.

On 8th May 1960, Car 83 pays a brief visit to Rowchester Street (Whitevale siding) during a special trip organised by the Light Railway Transport League. While a Glasgow urchin expresses his disdain for the photographer, in the background can be seen the façade of the former Whitevale Depot, still remaining at that time some 38 years after housing its last service cars.
(WDL Kerr – DL Thomson Collection)

TIM ticket machines were first experimented with in Glasgow in 1932. In advance of the general adoption of these machines, the Tram Fare Stages were numbered in March 1935 as shown on the accompanying map. The basis of the scheme of numbering, which resulted in the ubiquitous city centre stage-number of 29, will be apparent from a study of this.

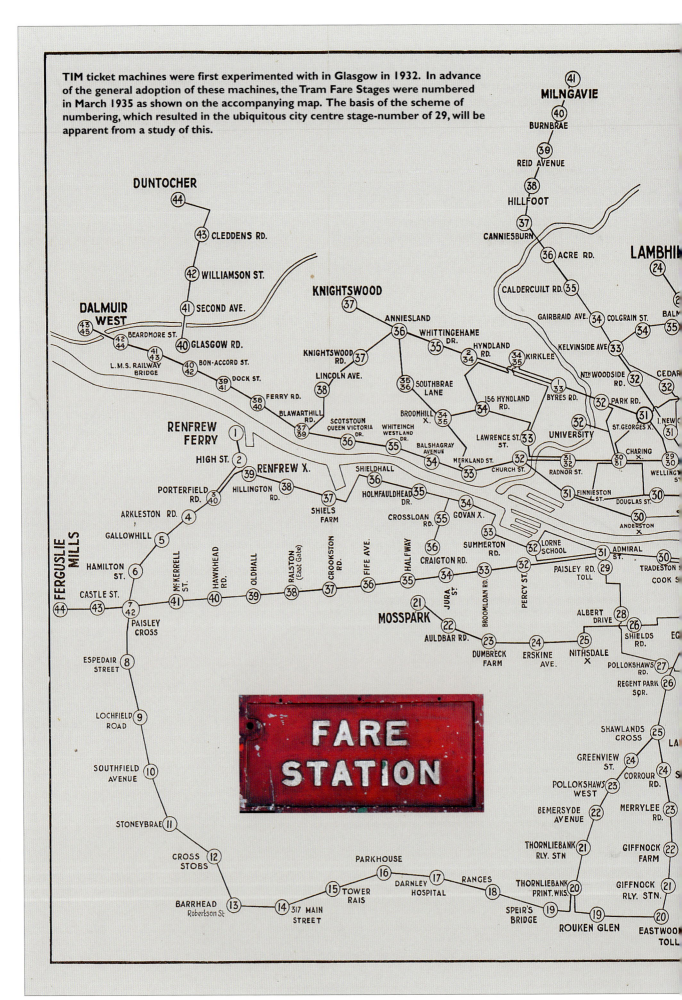

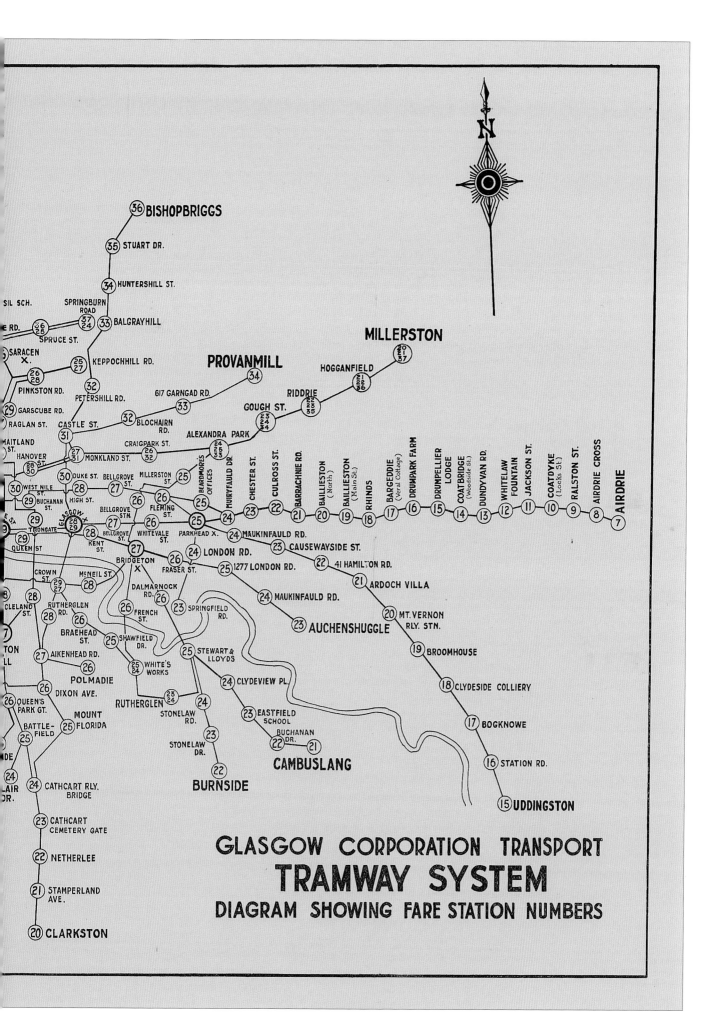

APPENDIX 'B'
GLASGOW CORPORATION TRAMWAYS SERVICES

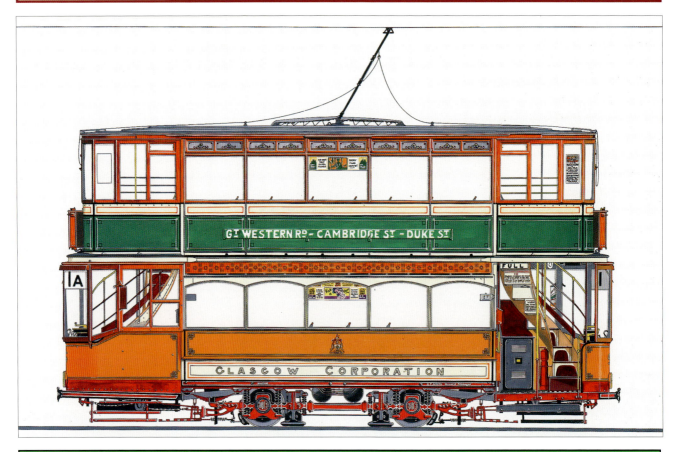

SERVICE A

COLOUR BAND Green   **Headcode** 19/20

Commencing

13-06-1901	Introduced KELVINSIDE & DENNISTOUN.
25-11-1901	Part-extended to become ANNIESLAND or KELVINSIDE & DENNISTOUN
25-08-1902	Altered to become Weekdays and Saturdays: ANNIESLAND & DENNISTOUN; Sundays: ANNIESLAND or BOTANIC GARDENS & CARNTYNE.
25-09-1902	Extended to become Weekdays and Saturdays: ANNIESLAND & CARNTYNE; Sundays: ANNIESLAND or BOTANIC GARDENS & CARNTYNE unaltered.
12-10-1902	Altered to become Sundays: ANNIESLAND & CARNTYNE; Weekdays and Saturdays: ANNIESLAND & CARNTYNE unaltered.
17-04-1904	Extended to become ANNIESLAND & PARKHEAD.
08-04-1906	Extended to become Weekdays and Saturdays: ANNIESLAND & SPRINGFIELD ROAD; Sundays: ANNIESLAND & DENNISTOUN or SPRINGFIELD ROAD.
16-01-1907	Altered to become Weekdays and Saturdays: ANNIESLAND & PARKHEAD or SPRINGFIELD ROAD; Sundays: ANNIESLAND & DENNISTOUN or SPRINGFIELD ROAD unaltered.
06-03-1910	Part-diverted to become ANNIESLAND & SPRINGFIELD ROAD or SHETTLESTON.
27-06-1910	Diverted to become Weekdays and Saturdays: ANNIESLAND & PARKHEAD or SPRINGFIELD RD; Sundays: ANNIESLAND & SPRINGFIELD ROAD or SHETTLESTON unaltered.
12-10-1924	Extended to become Weekdays and Saturdays: SCOTSTOUNHILL & PARKHEAD or SPRINGFIELD RD; Sundays: SCOTSTOUNHILL & SPRINGFIELD ROAD.
02-12-1928	Altered to become Weekdays and Saturdays: SCOTSTOUNHILL or ANNIESLAND & PARKHEAD or SPRINGFIELD ROAD; Sundays: SCOTSTOUNHILL & SPRINGFIELD ROAD unaltered.
15-09-1929	Extended to become Weekdays and Saturdays: DALMUIR WEST, SCOTSTOUNHILL or ANNIESLAND & PARKHEAD or SPRINGFIELD ROAD; Sundays: DALMUIR WEST & SPRINGFIELD ROAD.
25-08-1935	SCOTSTOUN WEST terminus introduced in Dumbarton Road west of Burnham Road.

	Altered to become Weekdays and Saturdays: DALMUIR WEST, SCOTSTOUN WEST or ANNIESLAND & PARKHEAD or SPRINGFIELD ROAD; Sundays: DALMUIR WEST & SPRINGFIELD ROAD unaltered.
29-09-1935	SCOTSTOUNHILL turning point withdrawn and crossover removed. SCOTSTOUN WEST terminus for Green Cars moved to Kingsway west end.
03-05-1938	Becomes **Green Service 1A**.
DEPOT	*Until August 1902:* **Dennistoun** *August 1902 until April 1904:* **Partick and Dennistoun** *April 1904 until October 1922:* **Partick, Dennistoun and Whitevale** *From October 1922:* **Partick, Dennistoun and Parkhead**

TYPES OF CAR	*Until 1903:* **Standard**
	1903 until November 1913: **Standard, Electrified Horse Car only**
	   (Clearance restricted at Parkhead Cross)
	November 1913 until 1931: **Standard only**
	   (Clearance restricted at Parkhead Cross)
	From 1931: **Standard, ex-Paisley District only**
	   (Clearance restricted at Parkhead Cross)

SERVICE ABB

COLOUR BAND	Green	**Headcode**	--

Commencing	
01-08-1923	Acquired from Paisley District Tramways Company PAISLEY CROSS & SPRINGBANK ROAD or ABBOTSINCH.
14-04-1928	Converted to Pay-As-You-Enter fare collection and altered to become PAISLEY CROSS & ABBOTSINCH; (No Sundays Service).
19-09-1929	PAISLEY CROSS terminus extended (to facilitate reversal of bow collector) at Gilmour Street from under railway bridge to County Square.
26-03-1933	Withdrawn and replaced by **Motorbus Service 17**.
DEPOT	**Renfrew**
TYPES OF CAR	*Until May 1925:* **Ex-Paisley District** *From May 1925:* **Single-Decker [Cut-down Electrified Horse Car],** **Ex-Paisley District**

SERVICE AL

COLOUR BAND	Green	**Headcode**	--

Commencing	
01-01-1922	Acquired from Airdrie & Coatbridge Tramways Company: LANGLOAN & AIRDRIE.
03-06-1924	**Temporarily operated by Motorbuses** during reconstruction of tracks.
23-05-1925	Recommences LANGLOAN & AIRDRIE.

Former Horse Car No. 92 was transferred to operate the quiet Abbotsinch service for which one-man operation was more economical. Here is the car at County Square, Paisley.
(BJ Cross Collection)

The Airdrie Local Services were operated by both Standard and Coronation cars. Here Car 872 heads through Coatbridge on a hot summer's day with the young passenger on the top deck enjoying the breeze through the open drop-light.
(RJS Wiseman)

19-03-1946	LANGLOAN terminus moved from Bank Street Coatbridge at Woodside Street to Private Track on south side of Glasgow Road east end.
02-09-1949	AIRDRIE terminus moved west from Forrest Street west end to Clark Street east end.
12-03-1956	Curtailed to become Weekdays and Saturdays: LANGLOAN & AIRDRIE (Part Day only). (No Sundays Service).
04-11-1956	Withdrawn without replacement.
DEPOT	*Until June 1924:* **Coatbridge**
	May 1925 until February 1926: **Parkhead**
	From February 1926: **Coatbridge**
TYPES OF CAR	*Until June 1924:* **Ex-Airdrie & Coatbridge**
	From May 1925 until Summer 1941: **Standard**
	From Summer 1941: **Standard, Coronation**

SERVICE B

COLOUR BAND Green   **Headcode** 21/22

Commencing

28-07-1901	Introduced PAISLEY ROAD & PARKHEAD.
17-08-1901	Extended to become Weekdays and Saturdays: HALFWAY, IBROX or PAISLEY ROAD TOLL & PARKHEAD;
	Sundays: HALFWAY or PAISLEY ROAD TOLL & PARKHEAD.
26-02-1902	Extended to become Weekdays and Saturdays: HALFWAY or IBROX & PARKHEAD or SHETTLESTON;
	Split to become Sundays: HALFWAY & SHETTLESTON; and
	IBROX & PARKHEAD.
14-04-1902	Extended, split and **Green Service U** introduced.
	Altered to become Weekdays: IBROX & SHETTLESTON or BARRACHNIE;
	Saturdays and Sundays: IBROX & BARRACHNIE.
17-04-1904	Introduced Saturdays Specials: QUEEN STREET & BARRACHNIE.
13-08-1904	Extended to become Saturdays: PAISLEY & SHETTLESTON or BARRACHNIE;
	Weekdays: IBROX & SHETTLESTON or BARRACHNIE and Sundays: IBROX & BARRACHNIE unaltered.

212

26-11-1904	Saturdays Specials: QUEEN STREET & BARRACHNIE withdrawn.
20-03-1905	PAISLEY terminus moved westwards from Glasgow Road at Hawkhead Road to PAISLEY CROSS.
03-03-1906	Extended to become Weekdays: IBROX & SHETTLESTON or BAILLIESTON; Saturdays: PAISLEY CROSS or IBROX & SHETTLESTON or BAILLIESTON; Sundays: IBROX & BAILLIESTON.
08-04-1906	Extended to become Sundays: PAISLEY CROSS & BAILLIESTON
11-09-1911	Extended to become Weekdays: CROOKSTON & SHETTLESTON or BAILLIESTON; Saturdays: PAISLEY CROSS or CROOKSTON & SHETTLESTON or BAILLIESTON; Sundays: PAISLEY CROSS & BAILLIESTON unaltered.
12-11-1911	Cut back to become Weekdays: IBROX & SHETTLESTON or BAILLIESTON; Saturdays: PAISLEY CROSS or IBROX & SHETTLESTON or BAILLIESTON; Sundays: PAISLEY CROSS & BAILLIESTON unaltered.
15-10-1922	Altered to become Weekdays: HALFWAY or IBROX & SHETTLESTON or BAILLIESTON; Saturdays: PAISLEY CROSS or IBROX & SHETTLESTON or BAILLIESTON unaltered; Sundays: PAISLEY CROSS & BAILLIESTON unaltered.
03-06-1923	IBROX terminus moved from Paisley Road West at Copland Road to existing siding in Broomloan Road south end.
18-11-1923	Extended to become PAISLEY CROSS, HALFWAY or IBROX & SHETTLESTON, BAILLIESTON or BARGEDDIE.
30-12-1923	Extended to become PAISLEY CROSS, HALFWAY or IBROX & SHETTLESTON, BAILLIESTON or COATBRIDGE [Langloan].
17-01-1925	Extended to become FERGUSLIE MILLS, CROOKSTON, HALFWAY or IBROX & SHETTLESTON, BAILLIESTON or COATBRIDGE [Langloan]
23-05-1925	Extended to become FERGUSLIE MILLS, CROOKSTON, HALFWAY or IBROX & SHETTLESTON, BAILLIESTON or AIRDRIE.
05-07-1926	Cut back to become Weekdays and Saturdays: PAISLEY WEST, PAISLEY CROSS, CROOKSTON, or IBROX & SHETTLESTON or AIRDRIE; Sundays: IBROX & SHETTLESTON or AIRDRIE.
05-06-1927	Altered to become Weekdays: PAISLEY WEST, PAISLEY CROSS, CROOKSTON, HALFWAY or IBROX & SHETTLESTON or AIRDRIE and Saturdays: PAISLEY WEST, CROOKSTON, HALFWAY or IBROX & BAILLIESTON or AIRDRIE; Sundays: PAISLEY WEST & AIRDRIE unaltered.
28-10-1928	Altered to become Weekdays: PAISLEY WEST, CROOKSTON, HALFWAY or IBROX & SHETTLESTON or AIRDRIE. Saturdays: PAISLEY WEST, CROOKSTON, HALFWAY or IBROX & BAILLIESTON or AIRDRIE and Sundays: PAISLEY WEST & AIRDRIE unaltered.
16-09-1934	Extended to become FERGUSLIE MILLS, CROOKSTON, HALFWAY or IBROX & SHETTLESTON, BAILLIESTON or AIRDRIE.
06-09-1936	BAILLIESTON terminus moved eastwards from Main Street Baillieston east of Dyke Street to west end of Private Track on south side of Coatbridge Road.
29-08-1937	Cars shortworking to IBROX extended to CROOKSTON.
03-05-1938	Becomes Green Service 15.
DEPOT	*Until August 1915:* **Kinning Park and Whitevale** *August 1915 until October 1922:* **Govan and Whitevale** *October 1922 until January 1925:* **Govan and Parkhead** *January 1925 until February 1926:* **Elderslie, Govan and Parkhead** *From February 1926:* **Elderslie, Govan, Parkhead and Coatbridge**
TYPES OF CAR	*Until February 1902:* **Standard** *February 1902 until January 1914:* **Standard, Electrified Horse Car**

January 1914 until October 1928: **Standard**
October 1928 until 1932: **Standard, Standard Double-Bogie**
1932 until February 1938: **Standard, Experimental Bogie Car**
From February 1938: **Standard, Experimental Bogie Car, Coronation**

SERVICE C

| COLOUR BAND | Yellow | Headcode | 3/4 |

Commencing

01-05-1901	Introduced KELVINGROVE & QUEEN'S PARK.
05-05-1901	Extended to become KELVINGROVE & LANGSIDE [Battlefield].
08-06-1901	Extended to become BOTANIC GARDENS or KELVINGROVE & LANGSIDE [Battlefield].
08-09-1902	Altered and extended to become BOTANIC GARDENS & CATHCART and KELVINGROVE & LANGSIDE [Battlefield].
01-12-1902	Alteration to terminal names in Langside and Battlefield area. LANGSIDE terminus renamed BATTLEFIELD. BATTLE PLACE terminus renamed LANGSIDE. Becomes KELVINGROVE & BATTLEFIELD; BOTANIC GARDENS & CATHCART unaltered
23-02-1903	Section KELVINGROVE & BATTLEFIELD replaced by Yellow Service H. BOTANIC GARDENS & CATHCART section unaltered.
26-01-1908	Altered to become Weekdays: BOTANIC GARDENS or HYNDLAND & CATHCART; Saturdays and Sundays: BOTANIC GARDENS & CATHCART unaltered.
10-04-1910	Extended to become Weekdays: BOTANIC GARDENS or BROOMHILL CROSS & CATHCART; Saturdays and Sundays: BOTANIC GARDENS & CATHCART unaltered.
15-05-1910	Part-extended to become Weekdays: BOTANIC GARDENS or JORDANHILL & CATHCART; Saturdays and Sundays: BOTANIC GARDENS & CATHCART unaltered.
27-06-1910	Part cut back to become Weekdays: BOTANIC GARDENS or HYNDLAND & CATHCART; Saturdays and Sundays: BOTANIC GARDENS & CATHCART unaltered.
25-06-1911	Altered and extended to become KIRKLEE & CATHCART via BOTANIC GARDENS.
06-11-1911	Part diverted to become Weekdays: KIRKLEE or HYNDLAND & CATHCART; Saturdays and Sundays: KIRKLEE & CATHCART via BOTANIC GARDENS unaltered.
18-04-1915	Extended to become Weekdays: KIRKLEE or HYNDLAND & NETHERLEE; Saturdays and Sundays: KIRKLEE & NETHERLEE via BOTANIC GARDENS.
16-08-1921	Extended to become Weekdays: KIRKLEE or HYNDLAND & CLARKSTON; Saturdays and Sundays: KIRKLEE & CLARKSTON via BOTANIC GARDENS.
01-10-1921	CLARKSTON terminus extended from temporary Stamperland site to Mearns Road.
08-08-1926	Introduction of Circle Services for Hyndland. KIRKLEE terminus for Yellow Cars moved from Kirklee Road to Hyndland Road north end. Extended to become KIRKLEE Circle via BOTANIC GARDENS or Circle via HYNDLAND & NETHERLEE or CLARKSTON.
19-11-1934	Altered to become KIRKLEE Circle via BOTANIC GARDENS or Circle via HYNDLAND & CLARKSTON.
03-05-1938	Becomes Yellow Service 5.

DEPOT
Until May 1901: **Partick and Coplawhill**
May 1901 until January 1902: **Partick, Coplawhill and Langside**
From January 1902: **Partick and Langside**

TYPES OF CAR
Until January 1914: **Standard, Electrified Horse Car**
From January 1914: **Standard**

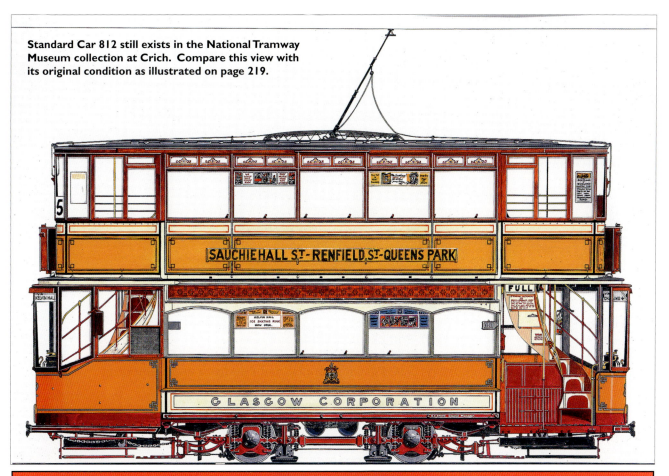

Standard Car 812 still exists in the National Tramway Museum collection at Crich. Compare this view with its original condition as illustrated on page 219.

SERVICE CP

| COLOUR BAND | Red | Headcode | -- |

Commencing

10-09-1923	Introduced CARLTON PLACE & BATTLEFIELD (Part Day).
05-07-1926	Withdrawn without replacement.
14-06-1930	Reintroduced Saturdays and Sundays: CARLTON PLACE & ROUKEN GLEN Circle via GIFFNOCK or Circle via THORNLIEBANK. (No Weekdays service)
06-09-1930	Withdrawn without replacement.
DEPOT	**Langside**
TYPES OF CAR	**Standard**

SERVICE D

| COLOUR BAND | Green | Headcode | 19/20 |

Commencing

25-08-1902	Introduced BOTANIC GARDENS & CARNTYNE (No Sundays Service)
25-09-1902	Extended and altered to become KELVINSIDE & DENNISTOUN (No Sundays Service).
17-04-1904	DENNISTOUN terminus moved eastwards to Duke Street at Fleming Street.
06-03-1910	Introduced Sundays: ANNIESLAND & DENNISTOUN; Weekdays and Saturdays: KELVINSIDE & DENNISTOUN unaltered.
30-05-1910	Part-extended to become Weekdays and Saturdays: KELVINSIDE & DENNISTOUN or PARKHEAD; Sundays: ANNIESLAND & DENNISTOUN unaltered.
27-06-1910	Diverted to become Weekdays and Saturdays: KELVINSIDE & DENNISTOUN or SHETTLESTON; Sundays: ANNIESLAND & DENNISTOUN unaltered.
10-08-1924	KELVINSIDE terminus moved from Great Western Road into Hyndland Road north end.
12-10-1924	Extended to become Sundays: ANNIESLAND & SHETTLESTON; Weekdays and Saturdays: KELVINSIDE & DENNISTOUN or SHETTLESTON unaltered.
21-06-1925	Extended to become Weekdays and Saturdays: KELVINSIDE & DENNISTOUN, SHETTLESTON or AIRDRIE; Sundays: ANNIESLAND & AIRDRIE.
14-11-1926	Altered to become Sundays: ANNIESLAND & DENNISTOUN or AIRDRIE; Weekdays and Saturdays: KELVINSIDE & DENNISTOUN, SHETTLESTON or AIRDRIE unaltered.

30-11-1926	Extended to become Weekdays and Saturdays: KNIGHTSWOOD or KELVINSIDE & DENNISTOUN, SHETTLESTON or AIRDRIE; Sundays: KNIGHTSWOOD & DENNISTOUN or AIRDRIE.
02-12-1926	New KNIGHTSWOOD extension closed upon instruction of Master of Works.
03-12-1926	New KNIGHTSWOOD extension reopened.
05-03-1928	KNIGHTSWOOD terminus extended from Munro Place to Knightswood Cross.
13-03-1929	DENNISTOUN terminus moved eastwards to Carntyne Road west end.
24-06-1929	Altered to become Sundays: KNIGHTSWOOD & SHETTLESTON or AIRDRIE. Weekdays and Saturdays: KNIGHTSWOOD or KELVINSIDE & DENNISTOUN, SHETTLESTON or AIRDRIE unaltered.
13-11-1933	Altered to become Weekdays and Saturdays: KNIGHTSWOOD or KELVINSIDE & DENNISTOUN, SHETTLESTON, BARRACHNIE or AIRDRIE; Sundays: KNIGHTSWOOD & SHETTLESTON or AIRDRIE unaltered.
06-09-1936	BAILLIESTON terminus moved eastwards to Private Track Coatbridge Road west end. Altered to become Weekdays and Saturdays: KNIGHTSWOOD or KELVINSIDE & DENNISTOUN, SHETTLESTON, BAILLIESTON or AIRDRIE; Sundays: KNIGHTSWOOD & SHETTLESTON or AIRDRIE unaltered.
14-11-1937	Altered to become Sundays: KNIGHTSWOOD & BARGEDDIE or AIRDRIE; Weekdays and Saturdays: KNIGHTSWOOD or KELVINSIDE & DENNISTOUN, SHETTLESTON, BAILLIESTON or AIRDRIE unaltered.
03-05-1938	Becomes Green Service 1
DEPOT	*Until June 1925*: **Partick and Dennistoun** *June 1925 until February 1926*: **Partick, Dennistoun and Parkhead** *From February 1926*: **Partick, Dennistoun, Parkhead and Coatbridge**
TYPES OF CAR	*Until November 1913*: **Standard, Electrified Horse Car** *November 1913 until January 1929*: **Standard** *January 1929 until 1932*: **Standard, Standard Double-Bogie** *From 1932*: **Standard, Experimental Bogie Car**

SERVICE E

COLOUR BAND	White	Headcode	7/8

Commencing

09-05-1901	Introduced UNIVERSITY & POLLOKSHIELDS (No Sundays Service).
14-07-1901	Introduced Sundays: UNIVERSITY & POLLOKSHIELDS.
23-02-1903	Altered to become UNIVERSITY or NEW CITY ROAD [Seamore Street] & POLLOKSHIELDS.
02-12-1903	Altered to become UNIVERSITY & POLLOKSHIELDS; Specials introduced:

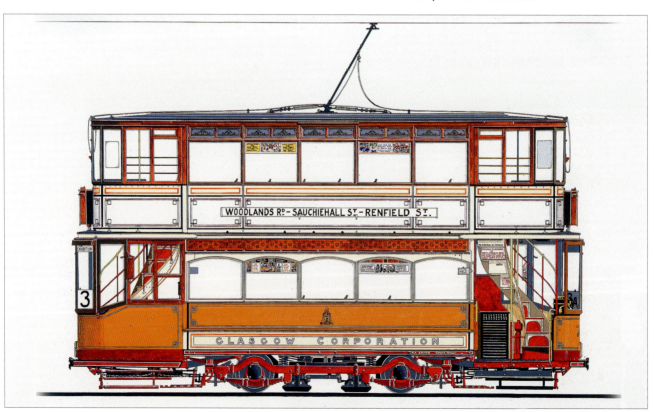

	Weekdays and Saturdays: GORDON STREET & POLLOKSHIELDS (0830-0930 and 1300-1815).
xx-XX-1904	Specials extended to become ST VINCENT STREET & POLLOKSHIELDS.
16-02-1906	POLLOKSHIELDS terminus extended to Nithsdale Road at Sherbrooke Avenue.
13-08-1906	Extended to become UNIVERSITY & DUMBRECK via POLLOKSHIELDS; POLLOKSHIELDS terminus reverts to St Andrew's Drive north of Nithsdale Road.
13-12-1909	Altered to become Weekdays and Saturdays: UNIVERSITY & POLLOKSHIELDS or DUMBRECK; Sundays: UNIVERSITY & DUMBRECK via POLLOKSHIELDS unaltered.
03-05-1911	Temporary Specials introduced UNIVERSITY & ST VINCENT STREET.
06-11-1911	Temporary Specials UNIVERSITY & ST VINCENT STREET withdrawn.
12-08-1923	Extended to become UNIVERSITY & MOSSPARK via POLLOKSHIELDS.
15-02-1926	Altered to become Weekdays and Saturdays: UNIVERSITY & DUMBRECK or MOSSPARK via POLLOKSHIELDS; Sundays: UNIVERSITY & MOSSPARK via POLLOKSHIELDS unaltered.
22-03-1926	Restored to become Weekdays and Saturdays: UNIVERSITY & MOSSPARK via POLLOKSHIELDS; Sundays: UNIVERSITY & MOSSPARK via POLLOKSHIELDS unaltered.
23-11-1930	Altered to become UNIVERSITY & POLLOKSHIELDS or MOSSPARK.
15-12-1930	Altered to become Weekdays and Saturdays: UNIVERSITY & DUMBRECK or MOSSPARK via POLLOKSHIELDS; Sundays: UNIVERSITY & POLLOKSHIELDS or MOSSPARK unaltered.
03-05-1938	Becomes *White Service 3*.
DEPOT	*Until May 1910*: **Maryhill and Pollokshaws**
	From May 1910: **Maryhill and Newlands**
TYPES OF CAR	*Until 1902:* **Standard**
	1902 until May 1913: **Standard, Electrified Horse Car**
	May 1913 until October 1937: **Standard**
	From October 1937: **Standard, Coronation**

SERVICE F

COLOUR BAND	Red	Headcode	23/24

Commencing

28-04-1901	Introduced PARTICK & DALMARNOCK.
12-05-1901	Extended to become Sundays: WHITEINCH & DALMARNOCK. Weekdays and Saturdays: PARTICK & DALMARNOCK unaltered.
02-04-1902	Extended to become Weekdays and Saturdays: PARTICK & DALMARNOCK or RUTHERGLEN. Sundays: WHITEINCH & RUTHERGLEN via DALMARNOCK.

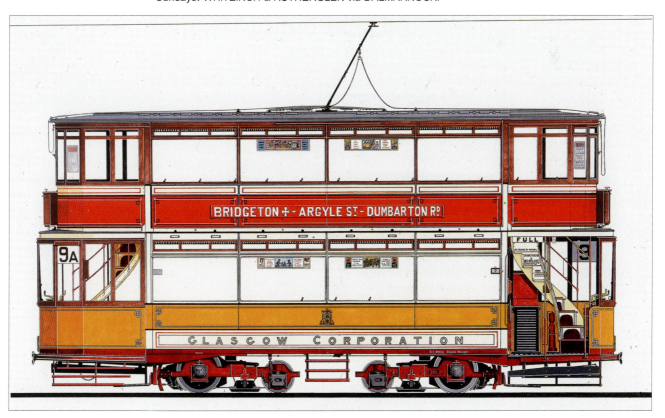

05-07-1902	Extended to become Saturdays: WHITEINCH or PARTICK & DALMARNOCK or RUTHERGLEN; Weekdays: PARTICK & DALMARNOCK or RUTHERGLEN unaltered; Sundays: WHITEINCH & RUTHERGLEN via DALMARNOCK unaltered.
30-05-1903	Extended to become Weekdays and Saturdays: WHITEINCH & DALMARNOCK or RUTHERGLEN; Sundays: WHITEINCH & RUTHERGLEN via DALMARNOCK unaltered.
23-01-1904	Extended to become Saturdays: WHITEINCH & DALMARNOCK, RUTHERGLEN or CAMBUSLANG with *alternate* cars after 1300 proceeding to Cambuslang; Weekdays: WHITEINCH & DALMARNOCK or RUTHERGLEN unaltered; Sundays: WHITEINCH & RUTHERGLEN via DALMARNOCK unaltered.
30-04-1905	Extended to become Weekdays: SCOTSTOUN & DALMARNOCK or RUTHERGLEN; Saturdays: SCOTSTOUN & DALMARNOCK, RUTHERGLEN or CAMBUSLANG; Sundays: DALMUIR (Summer only), SCOTSTOUN & RUTHERGLEN via DALMARNOCK.
19-11-1905	Cut back to become Sundays: WHITEINCH & RUTHERGLEN via DALMARNOCK.
27-11-1905	Altered to become Weekdays: WHITEINCH & DALMARNOCK or RUTHERGLEN; Saturdays: WHITEINCH & DALMARNOCK, RUTHERGLEN or CAMBUSLANG; Sundays: WHITEINCH & RUTHERGLEN via DALMARNOCK unaltered.
19-12-1909	Extended to become Weekdays: WHITEINCH & DALMARNOCK, RUTHERGLEN or BURNSIDE; Saturdays: DALMUIR or WHITEINCH & DALMARNOCK, RUTHERGLEN, BURNSIDE or CAMBUSLANG; Sundays: WHITEINCH & RUTHERGLEN or BURNSIDE via DALMARNOCK.
08-05-1910	Extended to become Summer Sundays: DALMUIR or WHITEINCH & RUTHERGLEN or BURNSIDE via DALMARNOCK.
24-02-1913	Altered to become Weekdays: SCOTSTOUN & DALMARNOCK, RUTHERGLEN or BURNSIDE; Saturdays: DALMUIR or SCOTSTOUN & DALMARNOCK, RUTHERGLEN, BURNSIDE or CAMBUSLANG; Sundays: DALMUIR (Summer only) or WHITEINCH & RUTHERGLEN or BURNSIDE via DALMARNOCK unaltered.
11-02-1915	Extended to become Weekdays: DALMUIR WEST & DALMARNOCK, RUTHERGLEN or BURNSIDE; Saturdays: DALMUIR WEST or SCOTSTOUN & DALMARNOCK, RUTHERGLEN, BURNSIDE or CAMBUSLANG; Sundays: DALMUIR WEST (Summer only) or WHITEINCH & RUTHERGLEN or BURNSIDE via DALMARNOCK.
08-03-1915	Altered to become Weekdays: DALMUIR & DALMARNOCK, RUTHERGLEN or BURNSIDE; Saturdays: DALMUIR or SCOTSTOUN & DALMARNOCK, RUTHERGLEN, BURNSIDE or CAMBUSLANG; Sundays: DALMUIR WEST (Summer only) or WHITEINCH & RUTHERGLEN or BURNSIDE via DALMARNOCK unaltered.
06-03-1922	Altered to become Saturdays: CLYDEBANK or SCOTSTOUN & DALMARNOCK, RUTHERGLEN, BURNSIDE or CAMBUSLANG; Weekdays: DALMUIR & DALMARNOCK, RUTHERGLEN or BURNSIDE unaltered; Sundays: DALMUIR WEST (Summer only) or WHITEINCH & RUTHERGLEN or BURNSIDE via DALMARNOCK unaltered
18-09-1922	WHITEINCH terminus moved into Primrose Street north end
05-11-1922	Altered to become Weekdays: SCOTSTOUN & DALMARNOCK, RUTHERGLEN or BURNSIDE; Saturdays: CLYDEBANK or SCOTSTOUN & DAMARNOCK, RUTHERGLEN, BURNSIDE or CAMBUSLANG; and Sundays: DALMUIR WEST (Summer only), or WHITEINCH & RUTHERGLEN or BURNSIDE via DALMARNOCK unaltered.
06-10-1923	SCOTSTOUN terminus moved into Balmoral Street north end.
07-06-1925	BURNSIDE terminus moved into Duke's Road west end.
01-05-1926	CLYDEBANK terminus moved from Glasgow Road at Bon-Accord Street to Kilbowie Road south end.
13-12-1935	Lying time position at CAMBUSLANG terminus moved to ease traffic congestion.
25-12-1935	CLYDEBANK terminus moved to Dumbarton Road just east of LMS railway overbridge.
03-05-1938	Becomes **Red Services 9A and 9B**
DEPOT	**Partick and Dalmarnock**
TYPES OF CAR	*Until 1930:* **Standard**
	From 1930: **Standard, Standard Double-Bogie**
	Note: Standard only on Cambuslang section (Length restricted at Cambuslang lye)

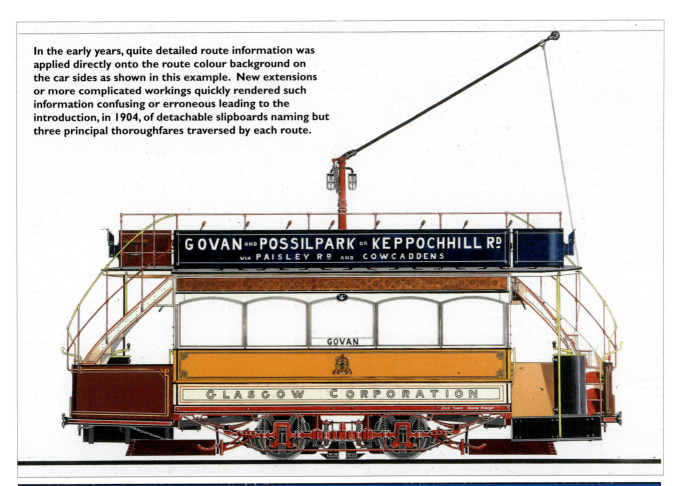

In the early years, quite detailed route information was applied directly onto the route colour background on the car sides as shown in this example. New extensions or more complicated workings quickly rendered such information confusing or erroneous leading to the introduction, in 1904, of detachable slipboards naming but three principal thoroughfares traversed by each route.

SERVICE G

COLOUR BAND	Blue	**Headcode**	5/6

Commencing

10-08-1901 — Introduced POSSILPARK & GOVAN [Linthouse] via LORNE STREET

02-12-1901 — Part-divided and extended to become KEPPOCHHILL ROAD or POSSILPARK & GOVAN [Linthouse] via LORNE STREET;

24-03-1902 — GOVAN terminus renamed LINTHOUSE becomes POSSILPARK & LINTHOUSE via LORNE STREET. Keppochhill Road section replaced by new Blue Service K.

27-04-1903 — Part-extended to become Sundays: POSSILPARK & LINTHOUSE or RENFREW via LORNE STREET; Weekdays and Saturdays: POSSILPARK & LINTHOUSE via LORNE STREET unaltered.

13-07-1906 — Extended to become Weekdays and Saturdays: LAMBHILL or POSSILPARK & LINTHOUSE via LORNE STREET; Sundays: LAMBHILL or POSSILPARK & LINTHOUSE or RENFREW via LORNE STREET.

10-08-1913 — Altered to become Sundays: LAMBHILL & LINTHOUSE via LORNE STREET; Weekdays and Saturdays: LAMBHILL or POSSILPARK & LINTHOUSE via LORNE STREET unaltered.

xx-05-1922 — LINTHOUSE terminus moved into Holmfauld Road south end.

09-08-1925 — Extended to become Weekdays and Saturdays: LAMBHILL or SPRINGBURN & LINTHOUSE, SHIELDHALL or RENFREW via POSSILPARK, LORNE STREET; and Sundays: LAMBHILL or SPRINGBURN & LINTHOUSE via POSSILPARK, LORNE STREET.

26-03-1926 — Construction of new deep-water King George V Dock at Shieldhall. Renfrew Road realigned from Shieldhall crossover to High Street Renfrew near intersection of Glebe Street.

28-10-1926 — Rerouted between Cowcaddens and Nelson Street to run via Hope Street, Oswald Street, George V. Bridge, Commerce Street.

01-05-1932 — RENFREW terminus renamed RENFREW CROSS.

03-05-1938 — Becomes Blue Services 4A and 4B.

DEPOT — *Until August 1915:* **Possilpark and Kinning Park**
From August 1915: **Possilpark and Govan**

TYPES OF CAR — *Until May 1913:* **Standard, Electrified Horse Car**
From May 1913: **Standard**

219

SERVICE H

COLOUR BAND	Yellow	**Headcode**	3/4

Commencing

11-05-1901	Introduced NEW CITY ROAD [Seamore Street] & LANGSIDE [Battlefield]
10-10-1902	Diverted to become NEW CITY ROAD [Seamore Street] & BATTLE PLACE.
01-12-1902	Alteration to terminal names in Langside and Battlefield area, LANGSIDE terminus renamed BATTLEFIELD. BATTLE PLACE terminus renamed LANGSIDE. Becomes NEW CITY ROAD [Seamore Street] & LANGSIDE.
23-02-1903	Diverted to become KELVINGROVE & LANGSIDE.
04-12-1907	Extended to become HYNDLAND & LANGSIDE.
10-04-1910	Extended to become BROOMHILL CROSS & LANGSIDE via HYNDLAND.
15-05-1910	Extended to become JORDANHILL & LANGSIDE via HYNDLAND.
27-06-1910	Altered to become Weekdays: JORDANHILL or HYNDLAND & LANGSIDE; Saturdays and Sundays: JORDANHILL & LANGSIDE via HYNDLAND unaltered
25-06-1911	Altered to become Weekdays: JORDANHILL & LANGSIDE via HYNDLAND; Saturdays and Sundays: JORDANHILL & LANGSIDE via HYNDLAND unaltered.
16-11-1911	Altered to become Weekdays: JORDANHILL or HYNDLAND & LANGSIDE; Saturdays and Sundays: JORDANHILL & LANGSIDE via HYNDLAND unaltered.
10-02-1913	Altered to become Weekdays: JORDANHILL & LANGSIDE via HYNDLAND; Saturdays and Sundays: JORDANHILL & LANGSIDE via HYNDLAND unaltered.
23-04-1934	JORDANHILL terminus moved from Jordanhill Station to Crow Road north of Southbrae Drive.
03-05-1938	Becomes Yellow Service 5A.
DEPOT	*Until January 1902*: **Coplawhill** *January 1902 until February 1903*: **Langside** *From February 1903*: **Partick and Langside**
TYPES OF CAR	*Until January 1914*: **Standard, Electrified Horse Car** *From January 1914*: **Standard**

SERVICE HS

COLOUR BAND	White	**Headcode**	---

Commencing

03-05-1901	Opening of International Exhibition in Kelvingrove Park. Special Service introduced QUEEN STREET & ST VINCENT PLACE via RADNOR STREET. *(Cars show* EXHIBITION *on leaving Queen Street or St Vincent Place).*
xx-10-1901	Closure of International Exhibition in Kelvingrove Park. Withdrawn.
03-05-1911	Opening of Scottish National Exhibition in Kelvingrove Park. Special Services introduced QUEEN STREET & ST VINCENT PLACE via RADNOR STREET and QUEEN STREET & ST VINCENT PLACE via KELVINGROVE; STREET (both Part Day only). *(Cars show* EXHIBITION *on leaving Queen Street and St Vincent Place).*
13-05-1911	Special Service; QUEEN STREET & ST VINCENT PLACE via KELVINGROVE STREET withdrawn; all cars operate as QUEEN STREET & ST VINCENT PLACE via RADNOR STREET (Part Day only).
05-07-1911	Cut back to become RADNOR STREET [EXHIBITION] & ST VINCENT PLACE (Part Day only).
06-11-1911	Closure of Scottish National Exhibition in Kelvingrove Park. Withdrawn.
DEPOT	**Partick**
TYPES OF CAR	*1901*: **Standard** *1911*: **Standard, Electrified Horse Car**

SERVICE HW

COLOUR BAND	Various	**Headcode**	---

Commencing

xx-XX-1906	Special Service established "Hampden Wheel" TRONGATE & FOOTBALL SPECIALS [Mount Florida]; [Operated for Football Internationals and Cup Finals at Hampden Park] operates one-way (anticlockwise) only.
08-02-1935	Rerouted between Grange Road and Prospecthill Road to run via Annan Street.

20-02-1949	Rerouted to become ST VINCENT STREET & FOOTBALL SPECIALS [Mount Florida].
01-07-1951	Rerouted to resume full one-way circular service.
05-07-1953	Withdrawn without replacement.
DEPOT	*Until May 1910:* **Dalmarnock, Dennistoun, Kinning Park, Langside, Maryhill, Partick, Pollokshaws, Possilpark and Whitevale.**
	May 1910 until August 1915: **Dalmarnock, Dennistoun, Kinning Park, Langside, Maryhill, Newlands, Partick, Possilpark and Whitevale.**
	August 1915 until October 1922: **Dalmarnock, Dennistoun, Govan, Langside, Maryhill, Newlands, Partick, Possilpark and Whitevale.**
	From October 1922: **Dalmarnock, Dennistoun, Govan, Langside, Maryhill, Newlands, Parkhead, Partick and Possilpark.**
TYPES OF CAR	**Standard**

SERVICE J

COLOUR BAND	Yellow	**Headcode** 31/32

Commencing

09-09-1901	Introduced ALEXANDRA PARK & BRIDGETON CROSS (No Sundays Service).
29-03-1903	Introduced Sundays: ALEXANDRA PARK & BRIDGETON CROSS.
20-08-1903	Extended to become ALEXANDRA PARK & PAISLEY ROAD TOLL via BRIDGETON CROSS.
07-09-1903	Extended to become Saturdays: ALEXANDRA PARK & PAISLEY ROAD TOLL or LINTHOUSE via BRIDGETON CROSS; Weekdays and Sundays: ALEXANDRA PARK & PAISLEY ROAD TOLL via BRIDGETON CROSS unaltered.
23-12-1905	Altered to become Saturdays: ALEXANDRA PARK & PAISLEY ROAD TOLL via BRIDGETON CROSS; Weekdays and Sundays: ALEXANDRA PARK & PAISLEY ROAD TOLL via BRIDGETON CROSS unaltered
04-08-1907	Extended to become RIDDRIE or ALEXANDRA PARK & PAISLEY ROAD TOLL via BRIDGETON CROSS.
xx-05-1912	ALEXANDRA PARK terminus moved from Cumbernauld Road at Kennyhill Square into Aitken Street north end.
16-09-1923	Extended to become RIDDRIE or ALEXANDRA PARK & CRAIGTON ROAD via BRIDGETON CROSS.
05-07-1925	Extended to become MILLERSTON, RIDDRIE or ALEXANDRA PARK & CRAIGTON ROAD via BRIDGETON CROSS.

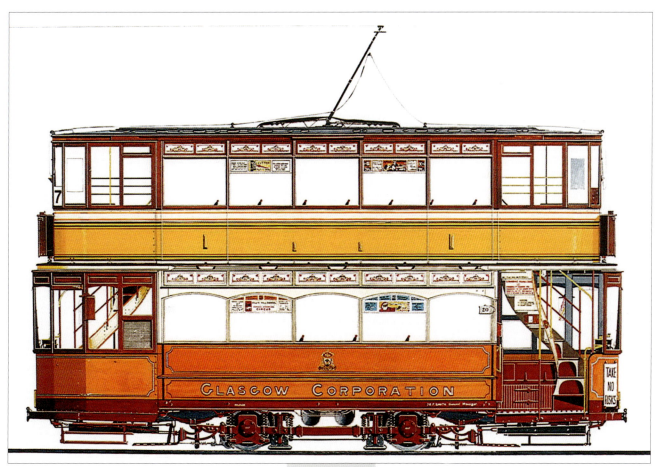

04-11-1929	Altered to become Weekdays and Saturdays: MILLERSTON or RIDDRIE & CRAIGTON ROAD via BRIDGETON CROSS; Sundays: MILLERSTON, RIDDRIE or ALEXANDRA PARK & CRAIGTON ROAD via BRIDGETON CROSS unaltered.
22-09-1930	King's Bridge (James Street Bridge) closed for major reconstruction.
21-10-1933	Completion of reconstruction of King's Bridge - normal services resume.
06-02-1938	Extended to become Weekdays and Saturdays: MILLERSTON or RIDDRIE & BELLAHOUSTON via BRIDGETON CROSS; Sundays: MILLERSTON, RIDDRIE or ALEXANDRA PARK & BELLAHOUSTON via BRIDGETON CROSS.
03-05-1938	Becomes Yellow Service 7.
DEPOT	*Until August 1903:* **Dennistoun**
	August 1903 until August 1915: **Dennistoun and Kinning Park**
	From August 1915: **Dennistoun and Govan**
TYPES OF CAR	*Until January 1914:* **Standard, Electrified Horse Car**
	January 1914 until February 1938: **Standard**
	From February 1938: **Standard, Coronation**

SERVICE K

COLOUR BAND	Blue	Headcode	5/6

Commencing	
24-03-1902	Introduced KEPPOCHHILL ROAD & SHIELDHALL.
22-11-1902	Extended to become Weekdays and Saturdays: KEPPOCHHILL ROAD & SHIELDHALL or RENFREW; Sundays: KEPPOCHHILL ROAD & RENFREW.
27-12-1903	Altered to become Sundays: KEPPOCHHILL ROAD & LINTHOUSE or RENFREW; Weekdays and Saturdays: KEPPOCHHILL ROAD & SHIELDHALL or RENFREW unaltered.
10-08-1913	Altered to become Sundays: KEPPOCHHILL ROAD & RENFREW; Weekdays and Saturdays: KEPPOCHHILL ROAD & SHIELDHALL or RENFREW unaltered.
26-03-1926	Construction of new deep-water King George V Dock at Shieldhall. Renfrew Road realigned from Shieldhall crossover to High Street Renfrew near intersection of Glebe Street.
28-10-1928	Rerouted between Cowcaddens and Nelson Street to run via Hope Street, Oswald Street, George V. Bridge and Commerce Street.
01-05-1932	Extended to become Weekdays and Saturdays: KEPPOCHHILL ROAD & SHIELDHALL or PORTERFIELD ROAD; Sundays: KEPPOCHHILL ROAD & PORTERFIELD ROAD.
06-12-1936	Extended to become KEPPOCHHILL ROAD & SHIELDHALL or RENFREW AERODROME (RENFREW DEPOT).
03-05-1938	Becomes Blue Service 4
DEPOT	*Until August 1915:* **Possilpark and Kinning Park**
	From August 1915: **Possilpark and Govan**
TYPES OF CAR	*Until November 1913:* **Standard, Electrified Horse Car**
	From November 1913: **Standard**

SERVICE KIL

COLOUR BAND	Green/Red *	Headcode	---

Commencing	
01-08-1923	Acquired from Paisley District Tramways Company. KILBARCHAN or JOHNSTONE CENTRE & RENFREW FERRY.
21-02-1926	Split to become KILBARCHAN & RENFREW FERRY and JOHNSTONE CENTRE & HAWKHEAD ROAD or RENFREW FERRY.
20-03-1927	Altered to become Sundays: JOHNSTONE CENTRE & PAISLEY CROSS or RENFREW FERRY; Sundays: KILBARCHAN & RENFREW FERRY section unaltered; Weekdays and Saturdays: JOHNSTONE CENTRE & HAWKHEAD ROAD or RENFREW FERRY section and KILBARCHAN & RENFREW FERRY section both unaltered.
10-04-1927	Altered at off-peak to become Weekdays and Saturdays: JOHNSTONE CENTRE & PAISLEY CROSS, HAWKHEAD ROAD or RENFREW FERRY; Sundays: KILBARCHAN or JOHNSTONE CENTRE & PAISLEY CROSS or RENFREW FERRY unaltered; KILBARCHAN & RENFREW FERRY section unaltered.
xx-XX-1928	All HAWKHEAD ROAD journeys withdrawn, replaced by Green Paisley Local Service.
01-05-1932	Withdrawn and replaced by Motorbus Service 12 and revised Paisley Local Service.
DEPOT	**Elderslie and Renfrew**

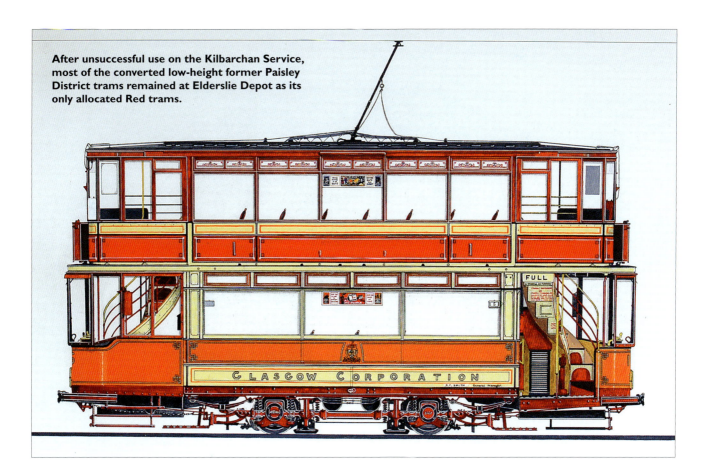

After unsuccessful use on the Kilbarchan Service, most of the converted low-height former Paisley District trams remained at Elderslie Depot as its only allocated Red trams.

TYPES OF CAR   *Until April 1930:* **Ex-Paisley District [Open Top], Ex-Airdrie & Coatbridge [Open Top] only (Low Bridge at Elderslie)**
From April 1930: **Ex-Paisley District [Open Top], Ex-Airdrie & Coatbridge [Open Top], Ex-Paisley District [low-height covered tops.]***
Experimental Single-Decker, only (Low Bridge at Elderslie)#
Notes: * Distinguished by a red route colour band, Ex-Paisley District [low-height cars] operated limited period only (longer w/b incompatible with passing loops). # Experimental Single-Decker on Johnstone-Paisley Cross service only.

SERVICE L

COLOUR BAND	Red	Headcode	23/24

Commencing	
28-04-1901	Introduced WHITEINCH & LONDON ROAD.
05-06-1902	Extended to become Weekdays and Saturdays: SCOTSTOUN or WHITEINCH & LONDON ROAD; Sundays: SCOTSTOUN & LONDON ROAD
29-10-1902	Extended to become Weekdays and Saturdays: YOKER or WHITEINCH & LONDON ROAD; Sundays: YOKER & LONDON ROAD.
30-05-1903	Extended to become Weekdays and Saturdays: CLYDEBANK or WHITEINCH & LONDON ROAD; Sundays: CLYDEBANK & LONDON ROAD.
20-06-1903	Extended to become Saturdays: CLYDEBANK & LONDON ROAD; Weekdays: CLYDEBANK or WHITEINCH & LONDON ROAD unaltered; Sundays: CLYDEBANK & LONDON ROAD unaltered.
10-10-1904	Extended to become Weekdays: DALMUIR or WHITEINCH & LONDON ROAD; Saturdays and Sundays: DALMUIR & LONDON ROAD.
30-04-1905	Altered to become Weekdays: DALMUIR or SCOTSTOUN & LONDON ROAD; Saturdays and Sundays: DALMUIR & LONDON ROAD unaltered.
27-11-1905	Altered to become Weekdays: DALMUIR or WHITEINCH & LONDON ROAD; Saturdays and Sundays: DALMUIR & LONDON ROAD unaltered.
08-04-1911	LONDON ROAD terminus moved east from London Road at Kinnear Road to London Road at Williamson Street.
24-02-1913	Altered to become Weekdays and Saturdays: DALMUIR or SCOTSTOUN & LONDON ROAD; Sundays: DALMUIR & LONDON ROAD unaltered.

11-02-1915	Extended to become Weekdays and Saturdays: DALMUIR WEST or SCOTSTOUN & LONDON ROAD; Sundays: DALMUIR WEST & LONDON ROAD.	
05-11-1922	Extended to become Weekdays and Saturdays: DALMUIR WEST & LONDON ROAD or AUCHENSHUGGLE; Sundays: DALMUIR WEST & AUCHENSHUGGLE.	
08-08-1926	Altered to become Saturdays: DALMUIR WEST, CLYDEBANK or SCOTSTOUN & LONDON ROAD or AUCHENSHUGGLE; Sundays: WHITEINCH & LONDON ROAD or AUCHENSHUGGLE and Weekdays: DALMUIR WEST or SCOTSTOUN & LONDON ROAD or AUCHENSHUGGLE both unaltered.	
31-10-1926	Altered to become Saturdays: DALMUIR WEST & LONDON ROAD or AUCHENSHUGGLE; Sundays: DALMUIR WEST & AUCHENSHUGGLE; Weekdays: DALMUIR WEST or SCOTSTOUN & LONDON ROAD or AUCHENSHUGGLE unaltered.	
01-11-1936	LONDON ROAD terminus moved eastwards from crossover at Williamson Street to London Road at Maukinfauld Road.	
22-01-1938	Altered to become Saturdays: DALMUIR WEST & AUCHENSHUGGLE; Weekdays: DALMUIR WEST or SCOTSTOUN & LONDON ROAD or AUCHENSHUGGLE and Sundays: DALMUIR WEST & AUCHENSHUGGLE both unaltered.	
03-05-1938	Becomes Red Service 9.	
DEPOT	**Partick and Dalmarnock**	
TYPES OF CAR	*Until July 1902:* **Standard** *July 1902 until November 1905:* **Standard, Single-Decker ['Room and Kitchen']** *November 1905 until 1930:* **Standard** *From 1930:* **Standard, Standard Double-Bogie**	

SERVICE M

COLOUR BAND	Red	Headcode	9/10

Commencing	
30-06-1901	Introduced MARYHILL & MOUNT FLORIDA via NEW CITY ROAD
14-05-1903	MOUNT FLORIDA terminus extended southwards from Cathcart Road at McLennan Street to Clincart Road at Florida Street.
13-04-1906	Extended to become KILLERMONT & MOUNT FLORIDA via NEW CITY ROAD.
19-11-1906	Altered to become Weekdays and Saturdays: KILLERMONT or MARYHILL & MOUNT FLORIDA via NEW CITY ROAD; Sundays: KILLERMONT & MOUNT FLORIDA via NEW CITY ROAD unaltered.
06-03-1911	MOUNT FLORIDA terminus extended to Clincart Road at Bolton Drive.
03-04-1915	MARYHILL terminus moved from Maryhill Station to Caldercuilt Road west end
01-10-1922	Extended to become Weekdays and Saturdays: CANNIESBURN or MARYHILL & MOUNT FLORIDA via NEW CITY ROAD; Sundays: CANNIESBURN & MOUNT FLORIDA via NEW CITY ROAD.
21-04-1923	Altered to become Saturdays: CANNIESBURN & MOUNT FLORIDA via NEW CITY ROAD; Weekdays: CANNIESBURN or MARYHILL & MOUNT FLORIDA via NEW CITY ROAD and Sundays: CANNIESBURN & MOUNT FLORIDA via NEW CITY ROAD both unaltered.
25-11-1923	Extended to become Weekdays: HILLFOOT or MARYHILL & MOUNT FLORIDA via NEW CITY ROAD; Saturdays and Sundays: HILLFOOT & MOUNT FLORIDA via NEW CITY ROAD.

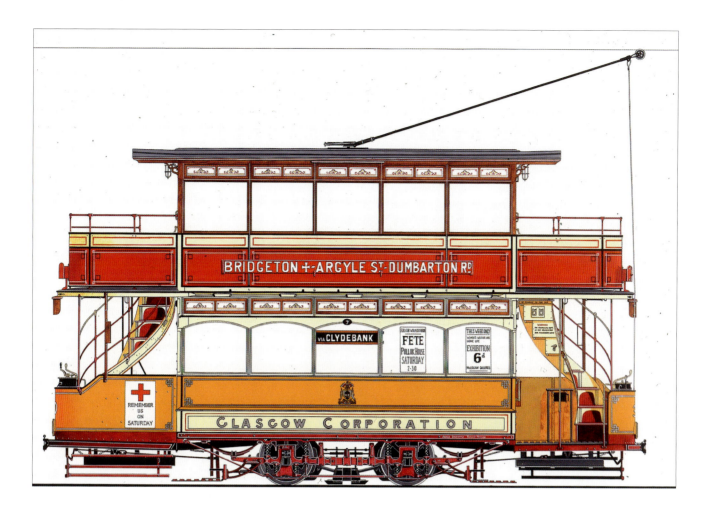

26-03-1933	Red Service T integrated into Red Service M.
07-10-1934	Extended to become Weekdays: MILNGAVIE, HILLFOOT or MARYHILL & MOUNT FLORIDA via NEW CITY ROAD;
	Saturdays and Sundays: MILNGAVIE & MOUNT FLORIDA via NEW CITY ROAD.
03-05-1938	Becomes Red Service 13.
DEPOT	**Maryhill and Langside**
TYPES OF CAR	Until January 1914: **Standard, Electrified Horse Car**
	From January 1914: **Standard**

SERVICE N

COLOUR BAND Red   Headcode   11/12

Commencing

30-06-1901	Introduced GAIRBRAID STREET & QUEEN'S PARK via NEW CITY ROAD.
05-07-1901	Rerouted between Queen's Cross and Cowcaddens to become GAIRBRAID STREET & QUEEN'S PARK via GARSCUBE ROAD.
24-11-1902	Extended to become Weekdays and Saturdays: BARRACKS GATE & LANGSIDE [Battlefield] via GARSCUBE ROAD; Sundays: MARYHILL & LANGSIDE [Battlefield] via GARSCUBE ROAD.
01-12-1902	Alteration to terminal names in Langside and Battlefield area.
	LANGSIDE terminus renamed BATTLEFIELD.
	BATTLE PLACE terminus renamed LANGSIDE.
	Extended to become Weekdays and Saturdays: BARRACKS GATE & BATTLEFIELD via GARSCUBE ROAD; Sundays: MARYHILL & BATTLEFIELD via GARSCUBE ROAD.
28-05-1905	Altered to become Summer Sundays: MARYHILL & CATHCART via GARSCUBE ROAD;
	Weekdays and Saturdays: BARRACKS GATE & BATTLEFIELD via GARSCUBE ROAD unaltered.
20-12-1909	GAIRBRAID STREET terminus renamed QUEEN'S CROSS.
	Altered to become Weekdays and Saturdays: QUEEN'S CROSS & BATTLEFIELD via GARSCUBE ROAD; Sundays: MARYHILL & BATTLEFIELD or CATHCART via GARSCUBE ROAD unaltered.
01-05-1910	Altered to become Summer Sundays: MARYHILL & BATTLEFIELD via GARSCUBE ROAD;
	Weekdays and Saturdays: QUEEN'S CROSS & BATTLEFIELD via GARSCUBE ROAD unaltered.

21-11-1910	New terminus KELVINSIDE AVENUE provided in Kelvinside Avenue north end. Extended to become Weekdays and Saturdays: KELVINSIDE AVENUE & BATTLEFIELD via GARSCUBE ROAD; Sundays: MARYHILL & BATTLEFIELD via GARSCUBE ROAD unaltered.
06-09-1914	Extended to become Weekdays and Saturdays: KELVINSIDE AVENUE & SINCLAIR DRIVE via GARSCUBE ROAD; Sundays: MARYHILL & SINCLAIR DRIVE via GARSCUBE ROAD.
03-04-1915	MARYHILL terminus moved from Maryhill Station to Caldercuilt Road west end.
25-04-1927	Extended to become Weekdays and Saturdays: GAIRBRAID AVENUE & SINCLAIR DRIVE via GARSCUBE ROAD; Sundays: MARYHILL & SINCLAIR DRIVE via GARSCUBE ROAD unaltered.
27-05-1928	Altered to become Sundays: HILLFOOT or MARYHILL & SINCLAIR DRIVE via GARSCUBE ROAD; Weekdays and Saturdays: GAIRBRAID AVENUE & SINCLAIR DRIVE via GARSCUBE ROAD unaltered.
21-10-1929	Altered to become Weekdays and Saturdays: KELVINSIDE AVENUE & SINCLAIR DRIVE via GARSCUBE ROAD; Sundays: GAIRBRAID AVENUE & SINCLAIR DRIVE via GARSCUBE ROAD.
16-03-1930	Re-extended to become Sundays: MARYHILL & SINCLAIR DRIVE via GARSCUBE ROAD; Weekdays and Saturdays: KELVINSIDE AVENUE & SINCLAIR DRIVE via GARSCUBE ROAD unaltered.
23-06-1930	Re-extended to become Weekdays and Saturdays: GAIRBRAID AVENUE & SINCLAIR DRIVE via GARSCUBE ROAD; Sundays: MARYHILL & SINCLAIR DRIVE via GARSCUBE ROAD unaltered.
17-06-1936	Northbound cars rerouted at Eglinton Toll to proceed from Victoria Road via Eglinton Street, Turriff Street, Pollokshaws Road and former route. Southbound cars unaltered continue to run directly from Pollokshaws Road to Victoria Road.
03-05-1938	Becomes Red Service 11.
DEPOT	*Until November 1932:* **Maryhill and Langside** *November 1932 until December 1932:* **Maryhill and Newlands** *From December 1932:* **Maryhill and Langside**
TYPES OF CAR	*Until January 1914*: **Standard, Electrified Horse Car** *From January 1914:* **Standard**

SERVICE O

COLOUR BAND	Blue	**Headcode**	27/28

Commencing

15-06-1901	Introduced BOTANIC GARDENS & OATLANDS via PARK ROAD, CROWN STREET.
06-08-1902	Extended to become Weekdays and Saturdays: BOTANIC GARDENS & OATLANDS or RUTHERGLEN via PARK ROAD, CROWN STREET; Sundays: BOTANIC GARDENS & RUTHERGLEN via PARK ROAD, CROWN STREET.
28-03-1906	OATLANDS crossover moved from Rutherglen Road at Braehead Street eastwards to Rutherglen Road at Shawfield Drive.
24-12-1922	Extended to become Weekdays and Saturdays: KIRKLEE & OATLANDS or RUTHERGLEN via PARK ROAD, CROWN STREET; Sundays: KIRKLEE & RUTHERGLEN via PARK ROAD, CROWN STREET.
21-07-1929	Part-extended to become Weekdays and Saturdays: KIRKLEE & OATLANDS, RUTHERGLEN or BURNSIDE via PARK ROAD, CROWN STREET; Sundays: RUTHERGLEN or BURNSIDE via PARK ROAD, CROWN STREET.
16-11-1930	Altered to become Weekdays and Saturdays: KIRKLEE & OATLANDS or RUTHERGLEN via PARK ROAD, CROWN STREET; Altered and split to become Sundays: KIRKLEE & RUTHERGLEN via PARK ROAD, CROWN STREET and QUEEN STREET & OATLANDS via CROWN STREET (Part Day only).
10-12-1933	Extended to become Sundays: ST VINCENT STREET & OATLANDS via CROWN STREET (Part Day); Sundays: KIRKLEE & RUTHERGLEN via PARK ROAD, CROWN STREET main section unaltered; Weekdays and Saturdays: KIRKLEE & OATLANDS or RUTHERGLEN via PARK ROAD, CROWN STREET unaltered.
14-04-1934	Altered to become Saturdays: KIRKLEE or ST VINCENT STREET & OATLANDS or RUTHERGLEN via PARK ROAD, CROWN STREET; Weekdays: KIRKLEE & OATLANDS or RUTHERGLEN via PARK ROAD, CROWN STREET unaltered; Sundays: KIRKLEE & RUTHERGLEN via PARK ROAD, CROWN STREET and ST VINCENT STREET & OATLANDS via CROWN STREET (Part Day) both unaltered.
10-11-1934	Part diverted and extended to become Saturdays: KIRKLEE or PARTICK & OATLANDS or RUTHERGLEN via CROWN STREET.
03-05-1938	Becomes **Blue Service 10**.
DEPOT	*Until July 1924:* **Partick and Dalmarnock** *From July 1924:* **Dalmarnock**
TYPES OF CAR	**Standard**

SERVICE P

COLOUR BAND	Blue	**Headcode**	9/14

Commencing

05-02-1912	Introduced ST VINCENT PLACE & SHAWLANDS via GORBALS (No Sundays Service).
11-01-1914	Extended to become MARYHILL & SHAWLANDS via ST GEORGE'S CROSS GORBALS; Sundays Service introduced.
26-04-1914	Extended to become Sundays: KILLERMONT & SHAWLANDS via ST GEORGE'S CROSS, GORBALS Weekdays and Saturdays: MARYHILL & SHAWLANDS via ST GEORGE'S CROSS, GORBALS unaltered.
03-04-1915	MARYHILL terminus moved from Maryhill Station into Caldercuilt Road west end.
25-03-1923	Extended to become Sundays: CANNIESBURN & SHAWLANDS via ST GEORGE'S CROSS, GORBALS; Weekdays and Saturdays: MARYHILL & SHAWLANDS via ST GEORGE'S CROSS, GORBALS unaltered.
08-12-1923	Extended to become Weekdays and Saturdays: MARYHILL & SHAWLANDS or BARRHEAD CENTRE via ST GEORGE'S CROSS, GORBALS; Sundays: CANNIESBURN & SHAWLANDS or BARRHEAD CENTRE via ST GEORGE'S CROSS, GORBALS.
20-04-1924	Extended to become Sundays: HILLFOOT & SHAWLANDS or BARRHEAD CENTRE via ST GEORGE'S CROSS, GORBALS; Weekdays and Saturdays: MARYHILL & SHAWLANDS or BARRHEAD CENTRE via ST GEORGE'S CROSS, GORBALS unaltered.
10-05-1924	Altered Saturdays: All SHAWLANDS cars extended to BARRHEAD CENTRE.

Botanic Gardens in 1932 shows two Kirklee cars. On the left an outbound Blue Car passes an inbound Yellow Car about to turn right into Byres Road. The twin turrets of Botanic Gardens railway station are prominent in this view as is the diminutive Alexanders single-decker bus.
(T&R Annan)

The Blue Renfrew Ferry–Milngavie Service was the last routed through the city to rely on Semi-High Speed Standard cars such as No. 963 seen here in 1940 taking layover time at Caldercuilt Road by then numbered Service 14.
(SJT Robertson)

17-08-1924	Extended to become Weekdays: MARYHILL & SHAWLANDS, PAISLEY CROSS or RENFREW FERRY via ST GEORGE'S CROSS, GORBALS, BARRHEAD; Saturdays: HILLFOOT & PAISLEY CROSS or RENFREW FERRY via ST GEORGE'S CROSS, GORBALS, BARRHEAD; Sundays: HILLFOOT & SHAWLANDS, PAISLEY CROSS or RENFREW FERRY via ST GEORGE'S CROSS, GORBALS, BARRHEAD.
07-10-1934	Extended to become Saturdays: MILNGAVIE & PAISLEY CROSS or RENFREW FERRY via ST GEORGE'S CROSS, GORBALS, BARRHEAD; Sundays: MILNGAVIE & SHAWLANDS, PAISLEY CROSS or RENFREW FERRY via ST GEORGE'S CROSS, GORBALS, BARRHEAD; Weekdays: MARYHILL & SHAWLANDS, PAISLEY CROSS or RENFREW FERRY via ST GEORGE'S CROSS, BARRHEAD unaltered.
15-01-1936	SHAWLANDS terminus moved from Pollokshaws Road north of Shawlands Cross to Pollokshaws Road south of Shawlands Cross at Shawlands Academy.
xx-05-1936	RENFREW FERRY terminus moved back from Ferry Road south of Clyde Street to Ferry Road south of London Street.
03-05-1938	Becomes **Blue Service 14**.
DEPOT	*Until January 1914:* **Maryhill**
	January 1914 until December 1923: **Maryhill and Newlands**
	December 1923 until August 1924: **Maryhill, Newlands and Barrhead**
	August 1924 until October 1936: **Maryhill, Newlands, Barrhead, Elderslie and Renfrew**
	From October 1936: **Maryhill, Newlands and Elderslie**
TYPES OF CAR	**Standard**
	Note: Standard only (Clearance restricted on loops CrossStobs-Glenfield)

SERVICE PL

COLOUR BAND	Blue / Standard Green Headcode --
Commencing	
01-08-1923	Acquired from Paisley District Tramways Company:
	ROUKEN GLEN [Spiersbridge], BARRHEAD (PRINCES SQUARE), BARRHEAD CENTRE or POTTERHILL & RENFREW FERRY and
	POTTERHILL & PAISLEY CROSS or SPRINGBANK ROAD.
08-12-1923	Cut back and split to become
	BARRHEAD (PRINCES SQUARE), BARRHEAD CENTRE or POTTERHILL & RENFREW FERRY and
	PAISLEY CROSS & RENFREW FERRY;
	POTTERHILL & PAISLEY CROSS or SPRINGBANK ROAD section unaltered.
17-08-1924	Altered and combined to become
	BARRHEAD (PRINCES SQUARE), BARRHEAD CENTRE or POTTERHILL & PAISLEY CROSS;
	PAISLEY CROSS & RENFREW FERRY section unaltered.
25-01-1931	Altered to become GLENFIELD & PAISLEY CROSS and POTTERHILL & RENFREW FERRY;
	PAISLEY CROSS & RENFREW FERRY section Withdrawn.
11-10-1931	Cut back to become POTTERHILL & PAISLEY CROSS;
	POTTERHILL & RENFREW FERRY unaltered.
01-05-1932	Revised to become
	POTTERHILL & PAISLEY CROSS;
	BRAIDS ROAD & RENFREW FERRY;
	PAISLEY CROSS & RENFREW FERRY to replace Green Service KIL cars.
01-10-1932	Altered to become
	BRAIDS ROAD & PAISLEY CROSS;
	GLENFIELD or POTTERHILL & RENFREW FERRY.
xx-05-1936	RENFREW FERRY terminus moved back from Ferry Road south of Clyde Street to Ferry Road south of London Street.
03-05-1938	Services carry Blank Service Numbers under new system of numbering.
12-02-1940	Combined to become POTTERHILL & RENFREW FERRY.
24-08-1941	Extended to become SPIERSBRIDGE & RENFREW FERRY via BARRHEAD.
03-05-1942	Altered to become GLENFIELD or POTTERHILL & RENFREW FERRY.
15-08-1943	Split to become GLENFIELD & RENFREW FERRY and
	BRAIDS ROAD & PAISLEY CROSS.
03-04-1949	Cut back to become POTTERHILL & RENFREW FERRY;
	BRAIDS ROAD & PAISLEY CROSS section unaltered.

While illustrating the far-flung nature of the "Specials" worked on the Glasgow system, Govan Depot-based Car 101 turns at Lochfield Road, Paisley, to return to Renfrew South to collect workers from the Babcocks & Wilcox works, then to bring them back through the Burgh, effectively an integral part of the Paisley Local Service. *(RB Parr / STTS Collection)*

21-05-1950	Crossovers at BRAIDS ROAD and at POTTERHILL removed and replaced by new crossover at LOCHFIELD ROAD.
	Crossover in Renfrew Road Paisley at Arkleston Road removed and replaced by one at Glencairn Road for use by Paisley Local cars shortworking to SANDYFORD.
	Combined to become LOCHFIELD ROAD & PAISLEY CROSS or RENFREW FERRY.
12-05-1957	Withdrawn without replacement.
DEPOT	*Until May 1932:* **Barrhead and Renfrew**
	May 1932 until October 1936: **Barrhead, Elderslie and Renfrew**
	From October 1936: **Elderslie**
TYPES OF CAR	*Until August 1924:* **Ex-Paisley District only (Low bridges in Barrhead and at Brownside Loop; Clearance restricted on loops Cross Stobs - Glenfield)**
	August 1924 until May 1932: **Ex-Paisley District, Standard**
	May 1932 until August 1934: **Ex-Paisley District, Ex-Airdrie & Coatbridge, Standard**
	August 1934 until May 1950: **Ex-Paisley District, Standard**
	May 1950 until May 1951: **Ex-Paisley District, Standard, Coronation**
	May 1951 until August 1953: **Ex-Paisley District, Standard, Coronation, Experimental Lightweight**
	From August 1953: **Standard, Coronation, Experimental Lightweight**

SERVICE PLG

COLOUR BAND	Green / Standard Green	Headcode	---
Commencing			
01-08-1923	Acquired from Paisley District Tramways Company: PAISLEY CROSS & HAWKHEAD ROAD.		
21-02-1926	Withdrawn and replaced by section of **Green Service KIL**.		
xx-XX-1928	Reintroduced PAISLEY WEST or PAISLEY CROSS & HAWKHEAD ROAD (Part Day).		
03-05-1938	Service carries Blank Service Number under new system of numbering.		
12-05-1957	Withdrawn without replacement.		
DEPOT	**Elderslie**		

TYPES OF CAR	*Until February 1926:* **Ex-Paisley District, Ex-Airdrie & Coatbridge**
From 1928 until August 1934: **Ex-Paisley District, Ex-Airdrie & Coatbridge, Standard**
August 1934 until May 1951: **Standard, Ex-Paisley District**
May 1951 until August 1953: **Standard, Ex-Paisley District, Coronation, Experimental Lightweight**
From August 1953: **Standard, Coronation, Experimental Lightweight**

SERVICE Q

COLOUR BAND	Yellow	**Headcode**	33/34

Commencing	
13-10-1906	Introduced MOUNT FLORIDA & PAISLEY ROAD TOLL via SHIELDS ROAD.
06-03-1911	MOUNT FLORIDA terminus extended from Clincart Road at Florida Street to Clincart Road at Bolton Drive.
24-11-1930	Extended to become Weekdays and Saturdays: MOUNT FLORIDA & PAISLEY ROAD TOLL or IBROX via SHIELDS ROAD; Sundays: MOUNT FLORIDA & PAISLEY ROAD TOLL via SHIELDS ROAD unaltered.
09-11-1931	Cut back to become MOUNT FLORIDA & PAISLEY ROAD TOLL via SHIELDS ROAD.
03-05-1938	Becomes Yellow Service 12 and extended to become
Weekdays and Saturdays: MOUNT FLORIDA & PAISLEY ROAD TOLL or IBROX via SHIELDS ROAD; Sundays: MOUNT FLORIDA & PAISLEY ROAD TOLL via SHIELDS ROAD unaltered.
DEPOT	*Until January 1922:* **Langside**
From January 1922: **Langside and Govan**
TYPES OF CAR	*Until January 1914:* **Standard, Electrified Horse Car only**
From January 1914: **Standard only (Clearances restricted in Kinning Park at Seaward Street, Milnpark Street, Admiral Street)**

SERVICE R

COLOUR BAND	Red	**Headcode**	1/2

Commencing	
05-06-1901	Introduced SPRINGBURN & SHAWLANDS or POLLOKSHAWS.
02-10-1901	Split and extended to become SPRINGBURN or ALEXANDRA PARK & POLLOKSHAWS; and SPRINGBURN & SHAWLANDS.
14-06-1902	POLLOKSHAWS terminus renamed POLLOKSHAWS EAST.
Section altered to become ALEXANDRA PARK & POLLOKSHAWS EAST;
Section extended to become SPRINGBURN & SHAWLANDS or POLLOKSHAWS WEST.
17-07-1902	POLLOKSHAWS WEST terminus extended from Pollokshaws Road at Greenview Street to Pollokshaws Road at Barrhead Road.
02-02-1903	Section extended to become BISHOPBRIGGS or SPRINGBURN & SHAWLANDS or POLLOKSHAWS WEST;
ALEXANDRA PARK & POLLOKSHAWS EAST section unaltered.
23-03-1903	Section extended to become RIDDRIE or ALEXANDRA PARK & POLLOKSHAWS EAST;
BISHOPBRIGGS or SPRINGBURN & SHAWLANDS or POLLOKSHAWS WEST section unaltered.
21-02-1904	POLLOKSHAWS EAST terminus extended from Coustonholm Road east end to Coustonholm Road at Coustonhill Street.
17-06-1905	Section extended to become Weekdays and Saturdays: RIDDRIE or ALEXANDRA PARK & POLLOKSHAWS EAST or GIFFNOCK; Sundays: RIDDRIE or ALEXANDRA PARK & GIFFNOCK.
BISHOPBRIGGS or SPRINGBURN & SHAWLANDS or POLLOKSHAWS WEST section unaltered.
10-12-1905	Section altered to become Sundays: RIDDRIE or ALEXANDRA PARK & POLLOKSHAWS EAST or GIFFNOCK.
13-04-1906	Extended to become Weekdays and Saturdays: RIDDRIE or ALEXANDRA PARK & POLLOKSHAWS EAST or ROUKEN GLEN via GIFFNOCK;
Sundays: RIDDRIE or ALEXANDRA PARK & ROUKEN GLEN via GIFFNOCK.
20-05-1906	RIDDRIE terminus extended from Cumbernauld Road at Lomax Street to Smithycroft Street at Naver Street.
30-04-1909	Section extended and altered to become Weekdays and Saturdays: BISHOPBRIGGS or SPRINGBURN & POLLOKSHAWS WEST or ROUKEN GLEN Circle via THORNLIEBANK;
Sundays: BISHOPBRIGGS & ROUKEN GLEN Circle via THORNLIEBANK;
Through running instituted at Rouken Glen with Circle Cars returning via Giffnock to ALEXANDRA PARK or RIDDRIE.

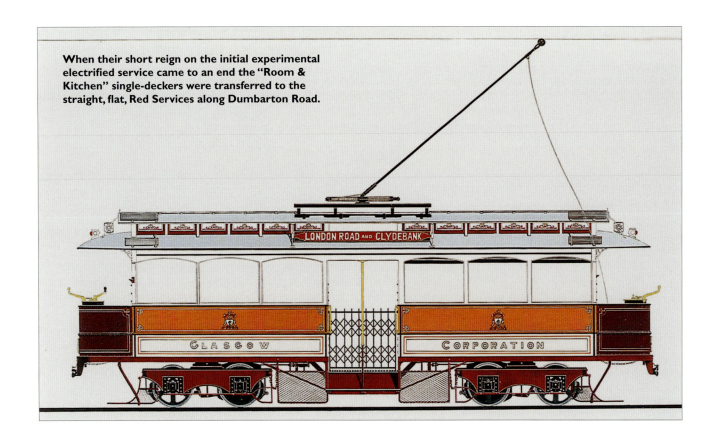

When their short reign on the initial experimental electrified service came to an end the "Room & Kitchen" single-deckers were transferred to the straight, flat, Red Services along Dumbarton Road.

	Section altered to become RIDDRIE or ALEXANDRA PARK & POLLOKSHAWS EAST or ROUKEN GLEN Circle via GIFFNOCK;
	Through running instituted at Rouken Glen with Circle Cars returning via Thornliebank to SPRINGBURN or BISHOPBRIGGS.
15-08-1910	POLLOKSHAWS EAST terminus moved from Coustonholm Road at Coustonhill Street to Pollokshaws Town House at corner of Pleasance Street and Shawbridge Street.
08-04-1911	POLLOKSHAWS EAST section withdrawn.
	Section altered to become RIDDRIE or ALEXANDRA PARK & NEWLANDS or ROUKEN GLEN Circle via GIFFNOCK.
03-07-1911	MERRYLEE terminus provided on Kilmarnock Road at Merrylee Road.
	Section altered to become RIDDRIE or ALEXANDRA PARK & MERRYLEE or ROUKEN GLEN Circle via GIFFNOCK.
xx-05-1912	ALEXANDRA PARK terminus moved from Cumbernauld Road at Kennyhill Square into Aitken Street north end.
05-10-1912	SPRINGBURN terminus for cars from the south moved from Springburn Road at Balgrayhill into Elmvale Street east end.
04-07-1924	Section extended to become Weekdays and Saturdays: MILLERSTON, RIDDRIE or ALEXANDRA PARK & MERRYLEE or ROUKEN GLEN Circle via GIFFNOCK;
	Sundays: MILLERSTON, RIDDRIE or ALEXANDRA PARK & ROUKEN GLEN Circle via GIFFNOCK.
30-11-1931	Some POLLOKSHAWS WEST shortworking cars extended to SPIERSBRIDGE.
27-09-1932	SPIERSBRIDGE shortworkings cut back to POLLOKSHAWS WEST.
15-01-1936	SHAWLANDS terminus moved from Pollokshaws Road north of Shawlands Cross to Pollokshaws Road south of Shawlands Cross at Shawlands Academy.
24-02-1936	Section altered to become Weekdays and Saturdays: MILLERSTON, RIDDRIE or ALEXANDRA PARK & GIFFNOCK or ROUKEN GLEN Circle via GIFFNOCK; Sundays: MILLERSTON, RIDDRIE or ALEXANDRA PARK & ROUKEN GLEN Circle via GIFFNOCK unaltered.
03-05-1938	Becomes **Red Service 8/8A**
DEPOT	*Until June 1901*: **Springburn and Pollokshaws**
	June 1901 until January 1902: **Springburn, Dennistoun and Pollokshaws**
	January 1902 until May 1910: **Possilpark, Dennistoun and Pollokshaws**
	From May 1910: **Possilpark, Dennistoun and Newlands**
TYPES OF CAR	*Until July 1902*: **Standard, Single-Decker ['Room and Kitchen']**
	From July 1902: **Standard**

SERVICE RP

| COLOUR BAND | Red* | Headcode | 39/40 |

Commencing
- 13-07-1924 Introduced YOKER & RADNOR PARK.
- 01-02-1925 Extended to become YOKER & DUNTOCHER.
- 01-02-1926 Cut back to become Weekdays and Saturdays: CLYDEBANK & RADNOR PARK or DUNTOCHER; Sundays: CLYDEBANK & DUNTOCHER.
- 03-05-1938 Becomes Red Service 20.

DEPOT Partick

TYPES OF CAR *Until August 1932:* **Single-Decker [Cut-down Ex-Paisley District] only (Low Bridge Kilbowie Road)**
From August 1932: **Single-Decker [Cut-down Ex-Paisley District], Experimental Single-Decker only (Low Bridge Kilbowie Road)**
* not displayed

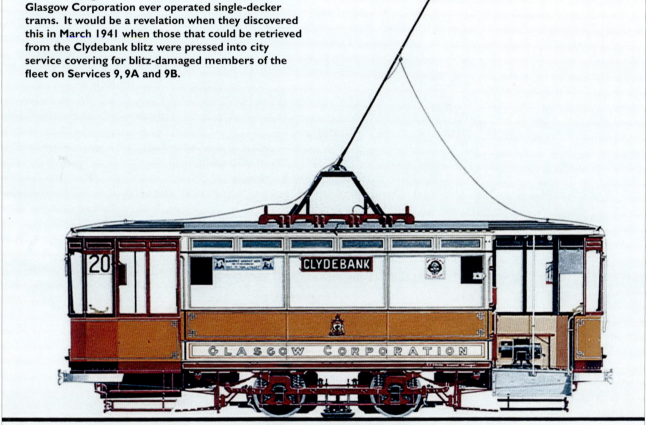

Most Glaswegians were oblivious to the fact that Glasgow Corporation ever operated single-decker trams. It would be a revelation when they discovered this in March 1941 when those that could be retrieved from the Clydebank blitz were pressed into city service covering for blitz-damaged members of the fleet on Services 9, 9A and 9B.

SERVICE S

| COLOUR BAND | White | Headcode | 15/16 |

Commencing
- 13-10-1898 Introduced SPRINGBURN & MITCHELL STREET.
- 23-01-1899 Split and extended to become SPRINGBURN & GLASGOW CROSS and SPRINGBURN & MITCHELL STREET.
- 08-11-1899 Extended to become SPRINGBURN & GOVANHILL via GLASGOW CROSS; SPRINGBURN & MITCHELL STREET section unaltered.
- 30-06-1901 SPRINGBURN & MITCHELL STREET section Withdrawn replaced by Red Service R; SPRINGBURN & GOVANHILL via GLASGOW CROSS section unaltered.
- 26-02-1902 Extended to become SPRINGBURN & GOVANHILL or MOUNT FLORIDA via GLASGOW CROSS.
- 25-08-1902 Diverted, altered, split and part-extended to become SPRINGBURN & MOUNT FLORIDA via GLASGOW CROSS and SPRINGBURN & POLMADIE via GLASGOW CROSS.

14-05-1903	MOUNT FLORIDA terminus moved southwards from Cathcart Road at McLennan Street to Clincart Road at Florida Street.	
12-11-1906	Section SPRINGBURN & POLMADIE via GLASGOW CROSS withdrawn and replaced by new White Service V. SPRINGBURN & MOUNT FLORIDA via GLASGOW CROSS section unaltered.	
01-05-1910	Extended to become SPRINGBURN & MOUNT FLORIDA or CATHCART via GLASGOW CROSS.	
06-03-1911	MOUNT FLORIDA terminus extended southwards to Clincart Road at Bolton Drive.	
05-10-1912	SPRINGBURN terminus for cars from the south moved from Springburn Road at Balgrayhill Road to Elmvale Street east end.	
10-06-1922	Extended to become Saturdays: SPRINGBURN & MOUNT FLORIDA, CATHCART or NETHERLEE via GLASGOW CROSS; Sundays: SPRINGBURN & NETHERLEE via GLASGOW CROSS; Weekdays: SPRINGBURN & MOUNT FLORIDA or CATHCART via GLASGOW CROSS unaltered.	
11-03-1923	Demolition of Tolbooth Buildings (apart from Tolbooth Steeple) on north side of Trongate at corner of High Street, Glasgow Cross. High Street closed to all traffic.	
31-03-1924	High Street reopened to traffic-normal service resumes.	
10-10-1927	Extended to become Weekdays: SPRINGBURN & MOUNT FLORIDA, CATHCART or NETHERLEE via GLASGOW CROSS; Saturdays: SPRINGBURN & MOUNT FLORIDA, CATHCART or NETHERLEE via GLASGOW CROSS; Sundays: SPRINGBURN & NETHERLEE via GLASGOW CROSS both unaltered.	
14-11-1927	Cut back to become Weekdays: SPRINGBURN & MOUNT FLORIDA or CATHCART via GLASGOW CROSS.	
19-11-1934	Altered to become Weekdays and Saturdays: SPRINGBURN & MOUNT FLORIDA or NETHERLEE via GLASGOW CROSS; Sundays: SPRINGBURN & NETHERLEE via GLASGOW CROSS unaltered.	
03-05-1938	Becomes White Service 19.	
DEPOT	*Until November 1899:* **Springburn** *November 1899 until June 1901:* **Springburn and Coplawhill** *June 1901 until January 1902:* **Springburn and Langside** *From January 1902:* **Possilpark and Langside**	
TYPES OF CAR	*Until June 1901:* **Standard, Single-Decker ['Room and Kitchen']** *From June 1901 until 1931:* **Standard** *From 1931:* **Standard, Ex-Paisley District**	

SERVICE SF

COLOUR BAND	Green	Headcode	--
Commencing			
21-06-1909	Introduced STOBCROSS FERRY & FINNIESTON.		
01-08-1910	Converted to one-man operation, with Pay-As-You-Enter fare collection.		
04-05-1925	Withdrawn and replaced by Motorbus Service.		
DEPOT	**Partick**		
TYPES OF CAR	*Until May 1910:* **Standard** *From May 1910:* **Single-Decker [Cut-down Electrified Horse Car]**		

Actually caught on the last day of Service S, by then 19, Car 617 is seen on Cathcart Road at the juntion with Allison Street.
(RR Clark / STTS Collection)

234

SERVICE T

COLOUR BAND Red	**Headcode** 9/10

Commencing

30-06-1901 — Introduced Weekdays and Saturdays: GAIRBRAID STREET & TRONGATE via NEW CITY ROAD; Sundays: MARYHILL & TRONGATE via NEW CITY ROAD.

24-11-1902 — Extended to become Weekdays and Saturdays: BARRACKS GATE & TRONGATE via NEW CITY ROAD; Sundays: MARYHILL & TRONGATE via NEW CITY ROAD unaltered.

03-04-1905 — Extended to become MARYHILL & TRONGATE via NEW CITY ROAD.

13-04-1906 — Extended to become Weekdays and Saturdays: MARYHILL & TRONGATE or GORBALS via NEW CITY ROAD; Sundays: MARYHILL & TRONGATE via NEW CITY ROAD unaltered.

27-05-1906 — Extended to become Summer Sundays: KILLERMONT or MARYHILL & TRONGATE via NEW CITY ROAD; Weekdays and Saturdays: MARYHILL & TRONGATE or GORBALS via NEW CITY ROAD unaltered.

19-11-1906 — Some peak journeys to GORBALS cut back to TRONGATE.

01-04-1909 — Extended to become Weekdays and Saturdays: MARYHILL & TRONGATE or JAMIESON STREET via NEW CITY ROAD; Sundays: KILLERMONT or MARYHILL & TRONGATE via NEW CITY ROAD unaltered.

28-09-1909 — Altered to become Weekdays: BARRACKS GATE & TRONGATE or GOVANHILL via NEW CITY ROAD; Saturdays: MARYHILL or BARRACKS GATE & TRONGATE or GOVANHILL via NEW CITY ROAD; Sundays: KILLERMONT or MARYHILL & TRONGATE via NEW CITY ROAD unaltered.

05-06-1910 — Split to become
Weekdays and Saturdays: MARYHILL or BARRACKS GATE & GOVANHILL via NEW CITY ROAD and KILLERMONT & TRONGATE via NEW CITY ROAD;
Sundays: KILLERMONT MARYHILL & TRONGATE via NEW CITY ROAD unaltered.

11-01-1914 — Cut back to become
Weekdays and Saturdays: MARYHILL or BARRACKS GATE & GOVANHILL via NEW CITY ROAD; No Sundays Service.

03-04-1915 — MARYHILL terminus moved from Maryhill Station to Caldercuilt Road west end.

01-03-1925 — Extended to become HILLFOOT or MARYHILL & MOUNT FLORIDA via NEW CITY ROAD.

26-03-1933 — Integrated into **Red Service M**.

DEPOT Maryhill

TYPES OF CAR *Until 1903:* **Standard**
1903 until November 1913: **Standard, Electrified Horse Car**
From November 1913: **Standard**

SERVICE U

COLOUR BAND Green	**Headcode** 21/22

Commencing

14-04-1902 — Introduced Weekdays and Saturdays: HALFWAY or IBROX & PARKHEAD; IBROX & TOLLCROSS; Sundays: HALFWAY & TOLLCROSS.

03-11-1902 — Extended to become Weekdays and Saturdays: CROOKSTON or IBROX & PARKHEAD; IBROX & TOLLCROSS section unaltered; Sundays: CROOKSTON & TOLLCROSS.

26-11-1903 — Extended to become Weekdays and Saturdays: PAISLEY & PARKHEAD; IBROX & TOLLCROSS section unaltered; Sundays: PAISLEY & TOLLCROSS.

29-02-1904 — Altered to become Weekdays: PAISLEY or IBROX & PARKHEAD; IBROX & TOLLCROSS unaltered. Saturdays and Sundays unaltered.

17-04-1904 — Introduced Saturdays and Sundays Specials: PAISLEY & QUEEN STREET.

13-08-1904 — Altered Saturdays: PAISLEY & TOLLCROSS replacing PAISLEY & QUEEN STREET Specials.

20-03-1905 — PAISLEY terminus moved westwards to PAISLEY CROSS. Altered to become PAISLEY CROSS & TOLLCROSS.

26-08-1905 — Altered to become Saturdays: PAISLEY CROSS or IBROX & TOLLCROSS; Weekdays and Sundays: PAISLEY CROSS & TOLLCROSS unaltered.

15-10-1905 — Altered to become Weekdays: PAISLEY CROSS or IBROX & TOLLCROSS.

15-12-1906 — Extended to become PAISLEY CROSS or IBROX & TOLLCROSS or BROOMHOUSE.

21-04-1907 — Altered on Saturdays: All cars extended to BROOMHOUSE after 1200.

04-05-1907 — Extended to become Weekdays and Saturdays: PAISLEY CROSS or IBROX & TOLLCROSS or UDDINGSTON; Sundays: PAISLEY CROSS & TOLLCROSS or UDDINGSTON.

235

Two views of car 975: above, as an open-topper turning into Jamaica Street from Argyle Srteet in 1902 and, below, at Powburn Toll in Uddingston around ten years later, by which time it had acquired a top cover. In both cases, 975 is on Green Service U. A view of this same car as a single-decker is on page 109. *(above: NTM Archive; below: STTS Collection)*

08-06-1907	UDDINGSTON terminus extended south from Caledonian Railway Station to Main Street Uddingston north of Bellshill Road.
10-11-1907	Altered on Sundays: Frequency beyond TOLLCROSS reduced.
11-09-1911	Altered to become Weekdays and Saturdays: PAISLEY CROSS, CROOKSTON or IBROX & TOLLCROSS or UDDINGSTON;
	Sundays: PAISLEY CROSS & TOLLCROSS or UDDINGSTON unaltered.
12-11-1911	Altered to become Weekdays and Saturdays: PAISLEY CROSS & TOLLCROSS or UDDINGSTON;
	Sundays: PAISLEY CROSS & TOLLCROSS or UDDINGSTON unaltered.
17-01-1925	Extended to become Weekdays and Saturdays: FERGUSLIE MILLS CROOKSTON or IBROX & TOLLCROSS or UDDINGSTON;
	Sundays: FERGUSLIE MILLS & TOLLCROSS or UDDINGSTON.
05-07-1926	Altered to become Weekdays: PAISLEY CROSS, CROOKSTON or IBROX & TOLLCROSS or UDDINGSTON;
	Saturdays: PAISLEY WEST or IBROX & TOLLCROSS or UDDINGSTON;
	Sundays: PAISLEY CROSS & TOLLCROSS or UDDINGSTON.
18-07-1926	Altered to become Sundays: PAISLEY WEST & UDDINGSTON;
	Weekdays: PAISLEY CROSS, CROOKSTON or IBROX & TOLLCROSS or UDDINGSTON unaltered;
	Saturdays: PAISLEY WEST or IBROX & TOLLCROSS or UDDINGSTON unaltered.
11-10-1926	Altered to become Weekdays and Saturdays: PAISLEY WEST & TOLLCROSS or UDDINGSTON;
	Sundays: PAISLEY WEST & UDDINGSTON unaltered.
05-06-1927	Altered to become Weekdays and Saturdays: PAISLEY WEST, CROOKSTON, HALFWAY or IBROX & TOLLCROSS or UDDINGSTON;
	Sundays: PAISLEY WEST & UDDINGSTON unaltered.
18-03-1928	TOLLCROSS terminus moved from Tollcross Road at Causewayside Street to Tollcross Road at Carmyle Avenue.
28-10-1928	Cut back to become Weekdays: PAISLEY WEST or IBROX & TOLLCROSS;
	Uddingston service replaced by new Green Service UM;
	Saturdays: PAISLEY WEST, CROOKSTON, HALFWAY or IBROX & TOLLCROSS or UDDINGSTON and Sundays: PAISLEY WEST & UDDINGSTON both unaltered.
01-11-1931	Re-extended to become Weekdays: PAISLEY WEST or IBROX & TOLLCROSS or UDDINGSTON following withdrawal of Green Service UM;
	Saturdays: PAISLEY WEST, CROOKSTON, HALFWAY or IBROX & TOLLCROSS or UDDINGSTON and Sundays: PAISLEY WEST & UDDINGSTON both increased in frequency to UDDINGSTON to replace Green Service UM.
16-09-1934	Extended to become Weekdays: FERGUSLIE MILLS or IBROX & TOLLCROSS or UDDINGSTON;

	Saturdays: FERGUSLIE MILLS, CROOKSTON, HALFWAY or IBROX & TOLLCROSS or UDDINGSTON; Sundays: FERGUSLIE MILLS & UDDINGSTON.
29-08-1937	Altered to become Weekdays and Saturdays: FERGUSLIE MILLS or CROOKSTON & TOLLCROSS or UDDINGSTON; Sundays: FERGUSLIE MILLS & UDDINGSTON unaltered.
03-05-1938	Becomes Green Service 15A.
DEPOT	*Until August 1915:* **Kinning Park and Whitevale**
	August 1915 until October 1922: **Govan and Whitevale**
	October 1922 until January 1925: **Govan and Parkhead**
	From January 1925: **Elderslie, Govan and Parkhead**
TYPES OF CAR	*Until January 1914:* **Standard, Electrified Horse Car**
	January 1914 until October 1928: **Standard**
	October 1928 until 1932: **Standard, Standard Double-Bogie**
	1932 until February 1938: **Standard, Experimental Bogie Car**
	From February 1938: **Standard, Experimental Bogie Car, Coronation**

SERVICE UM

COLOUR BAND	Green	**Headcode**	---
Commencing			
28-10-1928	Introduced UDDINGSTON & HOPE STREET via GLASSFORD STREET		
06-04-1930	Extended to become UDDINGSTON & GAIRBRAID AVENUE via GLASSFORD STREET.		
01-11-1931	Withdrawn.		
DEPOT	**Parkhead**		
TYPES OF CAR	**Standard, Standard Double-Bogie**		

Service UM lasted just over three years and the new Standard Double-Bogie cars were employed on it. Car 1101 was still a Green Car when this photograph was taken in St. Vincent Street at West Nile Street, probably early in 1929. These cars had been re-allocated to Red Services before Service UM was withdrawn. *(Whitcombe/Science & Society Picture Library)*

It was not uncommon for ex-Paisley Standard trams to be rostered to the White Service 2. This is 1064 in August 1944, clearly showing its wartime headlamp mask and white fender, at Provanmill terminus.
(SJT Robertson)

	SERVICE V		
COLOUR BAND	White	**Headcode**	17/18

Commencing	
12-11-1906	Introduced GARNGAD & POLMADIE via GLASGOW CROSS to replace, in part, White Service S.
30-01-1908	POLMADIE terminus extended southwards from Aikenhead Road at Govanhill Street to Aikenhead Road at Polmadie Street.
16-07-1922	Extended to become PROVANMILL & POLMADIE via GLASGOW CROSS.
11-03-1923	Demolition of Tolbooth Buildings (apart from Tolbooth Steeple) on north side of Trongate at corner of High Street, Glasgow Cross. High Street closed to all traffic.
31-03-1924	High Street reopened to traffic-normal service resumes.
24-05-1930	Altered to become Saturdays: PROVANMILL or GARNGAD & POLMADIE via GLASGOW CROSS; Weekdays and Sundays: PROVANMILL & POLMADIE via GLASGOW CROSS unaltered.
02-11-1930	POLMADIE terminus extended southwards from Aikenhead Road at Polmadie Street to Aikenhead Road north of Calder Street.
16-01-1933	GARNGAD terminus moved eastwards from Garngad Road at Blochairn Road to Garngad Road at LNER railway tunnel.
30-03-1937	Altered to become Weekdays: PROVANMILL or GARNGAD & POLMADIE via GLASGOW CROSS Saturdays: PROVANMILL & POLMADIE via GLASGOW CROSS; Sundays: PROVANMILL & POLMADIE via GLASGOW CROSS unaltered.
03-05-1938	Becomes White Service 2.
DEPOT	**Possilpark and Langside**
TYPES OF CAR	*Until 1931:* **Standard**
	From 1931: **Standard, Ex-Paisley District**

SERVICE W

COLOUR BAND	Green	Headcode	35/36

Commencing

04-06-1904	Introduced ST GEORGE'S CROSS & STOBCROSS FERRY via NORTH STREET.
14-09-1904	Extended to become KEPPOCHHILL ROAD & STOBCROSS FERRY via NORTH STREET
30-04-1905	Diverted to become KEPPOCHHILL ROAD & WHITEINCH via NORTH STREET.
24-01-1916	Extended to become Weekdays: KEPPOCHHILL ROAD & WHITEINCH or SCOTSTOUN via NORTH STREET; Saturdays and Sundays: KEPPOCHHILL ROAD & WHITEINCH via NORTH STREET unaltered.
03-09-1917	Extended to become Weekdays and Saturdays: KEPPOCHHILL ROAD & WHITEINCH or CLYDEBANK via NORTH STREET; Sundays: KEPPOCHHILL ROAD & WHITEINCH via NORTH STREET unaltered.
23-11-1918	Altered to become Saturdays: KEPPOCHHILL ROAD & WHITEINCH via NORTH STREET; Weekdays: KEPPOCHHILL ROAD & WHITEINCH or CLYDEBANK via NORTH STREET unaltered; Sundays: KEPPOCHHILL ROAD & WHITEINCH via NORTH STREET unaltered.
19-12-1921	Altered to become Weekdays: KEPPOCHHILL ROAD & WHITEINCH, SCOTSTOUN or CLYDEBANK via NORTH STREET; Saturdays and Sundays: KEPPOCHHILL ROAD & WHITEINCH via NORTH STREET unaltered.
18-09-1922	WHITEINCH terminus moved from Dumbarton Road at Westland Drive into Primrose Street north end.
16-10-1923	SCOTSTOUN terminus moved from Dumbarton Road west of Queen Victoria Drive into Balmoral Street north end.
17-08-1925	Altered to become Weekdays: KEPPOCHHILL ROAD & WHITEINCH or SCOTSTOUN via NORTH STREET; Saturdays and Sundays: KEPPOCHHILL ROAD & WHITEINCH via NORTH STREET unaltered.
03-05-1938	Becomes Green Service 16.
DEPOT	*Until April 1905:* **Possilpark** *From April 1905:* **Possilpark and Partick**
TYPES OF CAR	*Until November 1913:* **Standard, Electrified Horse Car** *From November 1913:* **Standard**

SERVICE X

COLOUR BAND	Red	Headcode	25/26

Commencing

02-12-1903	Introduced PARTICK & CAMBUSLANG via BOTHWELL STREET.
30-04-1905	Rerouted between Finnieston and Argyle Street at Hope Street and diverted to replace, in part, Green Service W to become STOBCROSS FERRY & CAMBUSLANG via ANDERSTON CROSS.

A Red Standard car waits to depart from the Anniesland terminus at the top of Crow Road with Green cars on Great Western Road in the background, left. *(C Carter)*

03-09-1905	Rerouted between Finnieston and Argyle Street at Hope Street to become STOBCROSS FERRY & CAMBUSLANG via BOTHWELL STREET.
30-05-1909	Diverted to become PARTICK & CAMBUSLANG via BOTHWELL STREET.
06-03-1910	Extended to become BROOMHILL CROSS & CAMBUSLANG via BOTHWELL STREET
15-05-1910	Extended to become JORDANHILL & CAMBUSLANG via BOTHWELL STREET.
10-07-1910	Extended to become ANNIESLAND & CAMBUSLANG via BOTHWELL STREET.
13-12-1935	Lying time position at CAMBUSLANG terminus moved to ease traffic congestion.
03-05-1938	Becomes **Red Service 17**.
DEPOT	*Until April 1905:* **Partick and Dalmarnock**
	April 1905 until May 1909: **Dalmarnock**
	From May 1909: **Partick and Dalmarnock**
TYPES OF CAR	**Standard only (Length restricted at Cambuslang lye)**

SERVICE Y

COLOUR BAND	White	**Headcode**	29/30

Commencing

28-04-1901	Introduced FINNIESTON & RUTHERGLEN BRIDGE.
09-05-1901	Extended to become EXHIBITION & RUTHERGLEN BRIDGE
xx-10-1901	EXHIBITION terminus in Radnor Street renamed KELVINGROVE. Becomes KELVINGROVE & RUTHERGLEN BRIDGE.
12-12-1901	Extended to become WHITEINCH & RUTHERGLEN BRIDGE
05-06-1902	Altered to become Weekdays and Saturdays: PARTICK & RUTHERGLEN BRIDGE; Sundays: WHITEINCH & RUTHERGLEN BRIDGE unaltered.
19-06-1902	Altered to become Weekdays and Saturdays: WHITEINCH or PARTICK & RUTHERGLEN BRIDGE; Sundays: WHITEINCH & RUTHERGLEN BRIDGE unaltered.
16-02-1903	Extended to become Weekdays and Saturdays: WHITEINCH or PARTICK & RUTHERGLEN BRIDGE or RUTHERGLEN; Sundays: WHITEINCH & RUTHERGLEN via RUTHERGLEN BRIDGE unaltered.
27-04-1903	Altered to become Weekdays and Saturdays: WHITEINCH or PARTICK & RUTHERGLEN via RUTHERGLEN BRIDGE; Sundays: WHITEINCH & RUTHERGLEN via RUTHERGLEN BRIDGE unaltered.

Green Standard car 318 on Service A enters the north side of George Square in 1938 shortly before the introduction of the new Service Numbering scheme. The headcode displays have already been removed. *(STTS Collection)*

30-05-1903	Cut back to become PARTICK & RUTHERGLEN via RUTHERGLEN BRIDGE all week.
02-12-1903	Diverted to become SEAMORE STREET & RUTHERGLEN via RUTHERGLEN BRIDGE.
09-06-1907	Extended to become BARRACKS GATE & RUTHERGLEN via RUTHERGLEN BRIDGE.
15-10-1908	Extended to become BARRACKS GATE & BURNSIDE via RUTHERGLEN BRIDGE.
09-01-1909	Diverted and extended to become SPRINGBURN & BURNSIDE via BILSLAND DRIVE, RUTHERGLEN BRIDGE.
19-12-1909	Altered to become Weekdays and Saturdays: SPRINGBURN or VERNON STREET & RUTHERGLEN or BURNSIDE via BILSLAND DRIVE, RUTHERGLEN BRIDGE; Sundays: SPRINGBURN & RUTHERGLEN or BURNSIDE via BILSLAND DRIVE, RUTHERGLEN BRIDGE.
21-11-1910	Altered to become Weekdays and Saturdays: SPRINGBURN or KELVINSIDE AVENUE & RUTHERGLEN or BURNSIDE via BILSLAND DRIVE, RUTHERGLEN BRIDGE; Sundays: SPRINGBURN & RUTHERGLEN or BURNSIDE via BILSLAND DRIVE, RUTHERGLEN BRIDGE unaltered.
11-06-1911	Altered to become Sundays: SPRINGBURN & BURNSIDE via BILSLAND DRIVE, RUTHERGLEN BRIDGE; Weekdays and Saturdays: SPRINGBURN or KELVINSIDE AVENUE & RUTHERGLEN or BURNSIDE via BILSLAND DRIVE, RUTHERGLEN BRIDGE unaltered.
05-10-1912	SPRINGBURN (Balgrayhill) terminus moved northwards in Springburn Road to a position between Elmvale Street and Hawthorn Street.
07-06-1925	BURNSIDE terminus extended from Stonelaw Road at Duke's Road into Duke's Road west end. SPRINGBURN terminus cut back from Springburn Road between Hawthorn Street and Elmvale Street to Hawthorn Street east end.
27-04-1931	Altered to become Weekdays and Saturdays: SPRINGBURN or BALMORE ROAD & RUTHERGLEN or BURNSIDE via BILSLAND DRIVE, RUTHERGLEN BRIDGE; Sundays: SPRINGBURN & BURNSIDE via BILSLAND DRIVE, RUTHERGLEN BRIDGE unaltered.
29-01-1934	Altered to become Weekdays and Saturdays: SPRINGBURN, RUCHILL (BALMORE ROAD) or KELVINSIDE AVENUE & RUTHERGLEN or BURNSIDE via BILSLAND DRIVE, RUTHERGLEN BRIDGE; Sundays: SPRINGBURN & BURNSIDE via BILSLAND DRIVE, RUTHERGLEN BRIDGE unaltered.
03-05-1938	Becomes White Service 18.
DEPOT	*Until December 1901:* **Dalmarnock** *December 1901 until December 1903:* **Partick and Dalmarnock** *From December 1903:* **Maryhill and Dalmarnock**
TYPES OF CAR	*Until November 1913:* **Standard, Electrified Horse Car** *November 1913 until 1931:* **Standard** *From 1931:* **Standard, Ex-Paisley District**

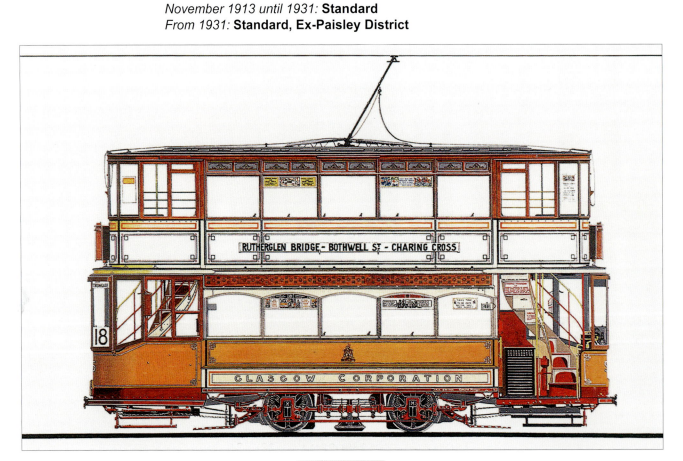

SERVICE Z

COLOUR BAND Blue	**Headcode** 37/38

Commencing

12-09-1910 — Introduced HYNDLAND & ALEXANDRA PARK for an experimental period of three months.

12-12-1910 — Confirmed HYNDLAND & ALEXANDRA PARK.

11-03-1912 — Extended to become Weekdays: JORDANHILL or HYNDLAND & ALEXANDRA PARK;
Saturdays and Sundays: HYNDLAND & ALEXANDRA PARK unaltered.

xx-05-1912 — ALEXANDRA PARK terminus moved from Cumbernauld Road at Kennyhill Square to Aitken Street north end.

10-02-1913 — Cut back to become Weekdays: HYNDLAND & ALEXANDRA PARK;
Saturdays and Sundays: HYNDLAND & ALEXANDRA PARK unaltered.

10-08-1924 — Extended to become Weekdays: KELVINSIDE CROSS & ALEXANDRA PARK.
Saturdays and Sundays: HYNDLAND & ALEXANDRA PARK unaltered.

17-08-1925 — Part-extended and part-diverted to become
Weekdays: JORDANHILL or KELVINSIDE CROSS & ALEXANDRA PARK or RIDDRIE;
Saturdays and Sundays: HYNDLAND & ALEXANDRA PARK unaltered

08-08-1926 — Diverted and extended to become Weekdays: DALMUIR WEST & ALEXANDRA PARK or RIDDRIE;
Saturdays and Sundays: DALMUIR WEST & ALEXANDRA PARK.

08-11-1926 — Altered to become Weekdays: DALMUIR WEST or SCOTSTOUN & ALEXANDRA PARK or RIDDRIE;
Saturdays: DALMUIR WEST or SCOTSTOUN & ALEXANDRA PARK;
Sundays: DALMUIR WEST & ALEXANDRA PARK unaltered.

03-05-1938 — Becomes **Blue Service 6**.

DEPOT **Partick and Dennistoun**

TYPES OF CAR *Until November 1913:* **Standard, Electrified Horse Car**
From November 1913: **Standard**

Eastbound Car 658 on Service 1 approaches the curve in Cambridge Street where the track had been re-set in tarmac in October 1957.
(WDL Kerr / STTS Collection)

SERVICE 1

COLOUR BAND   Green / Standard Green

Commencing

03-05-1938	Former **Green Service D** KNIGHTSWOOD or KELVINSIDE & DENNISTOUN, SHETTLESTON, BARGEDDIE or AIRDRIE.
04-05-1942	Altered to become KNIGHTSWOOD or KELVINSIDE & DENNISTOUN or AIRDRIE.
15-08-1943	Withdrawn along with Service 1A and replaced by new **Services 1, 23 and 30**. Becomes DALMUIR WEST or ANNIESLAND & DENNISTOUN.
06-01-1946	ANNIESLAND terminus moved westwards from Anniesland Cross to Anniesland Road at Chamberlain Road.
19-05-1947	Altered to become Weekdays and Saturdays: DALMUIR WEST or SCOTSTOUN WEST & DENNISTOUN; Sundays: DALMUIR WEST & DENNISTOUN unaltered.
19-04-1953	Extended to become Weekdays: DALMUIR WEST or SCOTSTOUN WEST & DENNISTOUN or DALMARNOCK; Saturdays: DALMUIR WEST or SCOTSTOUN WEST & DENNISTOUN, SPRINGFIELD ROAD or DALMARNOCK (Dennistoun until 1130; Springfield Road 1130-1730; Dalmarnock from 1730); Sundays: DALMUIR WEST or SCOTSTOUN WEST & DENNISTOUN or DALMARNOCK (Dennistoun until 1400; Dalmarnock from 1400 onwards).
29-04-1956	Altered to become Weekdays: DALMUIR WEST or SCOTSTOUN WEST & DENNISTOUN or DALMARNOCK, proceeding to DALMUIR WEST (until 0830, 1630-1830) only, east end unaltered; Saturdays: SCOTSTOUN WEST & DENNISTOUN, SPRINGFIELD ROAD or DALMARNOCK (Dennistoun until 1130; Springfield Road 1130-1730; Dalmarnock from 1730 onwards); Sundays: DALMUIR WEST or SCOTSTOUN WEST & DENNISTOUN or DALMARNOCK (Dalmuir West until 0830; 1500-1700) only, east end unaltered (Dennistoun until 1400; Dalmarnock from 1400 onwards).
07-05-1956	Altered to become Weekdays: DALMUIR WEST, YOKER or SCOTSTOUN WEST & DENNISTOUN or DALMARNOCK (Dalmuir West until 0830; 1600-1830; Yoker 1200-1400), east end unaltered.
07-09-1959	Dalmuir Canal Swing Bridge closed for repairs. All DALMUIR WEST Cars curtailed at DALMUIR.
13-03-1960	Withdrawn and replaced by **Motorbus Service 58**.
DEPOT	*Until August 1943:* **Partick, Dennistoun, Parkhead and Coatbridge**
	August 1943 until April 1953: **Partick and Dennistoun**
	From April 1953: **Partick, Dennistoun and Dalmarnock**
TYPES OF CAR	*Until July 1939:* **Standard, Experimental Bogie Car**
	July 1939 until 1940: **Standard, Experimental Bogie Car, Coronation**
	1940 until September 1941: **Standard, Coronation**
	September 1941 until May 1952: **Standard**
	May 1952 until April 1953: **Standard, Coronation**
	From April 1953: **Standard only**
	(Clearance restricted at Parkhead Cross)

SERVICE 1A

COLOUR BAND   Green / Standard Green

Commencing

03-05-1938	Former **Green Service A** DALMUIR WEST, SCOTSTOUN WEST or ANNIESLAND & PARKHEAD or SPRINGFIELD ROAD.
15-08-1943	Withdrawn along with Service 1 and replaced by new **Services 1, 23** and **30**.
DEPOT	**Partick, Dennistoun and Parkhead**
TYPES OF CAR	**Standard, Ex-Paisley District only (Clearance restricted at Parkhead Cross)**

SERVICE 2

COLOUR BAND   White / Standard Green

Commencing

03-05-1938	Former **White Service V** PROVANMILL or GARNGAD & POLMADIE via GLASGOW CROSS.
20-02-1949	Withdrawn and replaced by **Temporary Motorbus Service 102**.
DEPOT	**Possilpark and Langside**
TYPES OF CAR	**Standard, Ex-Paisley District**

SERVICE 3

COLOUR BAND White / Red / Standard Green

Commencing

03-05-1938 — Former White Service E becomes Weekdays and Saturdays: UNIVERSITY & DUMBRECK or MOSSPARK Circle via POLLOKSHIELDS (Circle Cars return as Service 3A);
Sundays: UNIVERSITY & MOSSPARK via POLLOKSHIELDS.

30-10-1938 — Altered to become Weekdays and Saturdays: UNIVERSITY & DUMBRECK or MOSSPARK via POLLOKSHIELDS;
Sundays: UNIVERSITY & MOSSPARK via POLLOKSHIELDS unaltered.

30-05-1943 — Altered to become UNIVERSITY or ST VINCENT STREET & MOSSPARK Circle via POLLOKSHIELDS with through Circle Cars to and from Service 3A.

07-11-1943 — Altered to become Weekdays: UNIVERSITY & MOSSPARK Circle via POLLOKSHIELDS;
Saturdays and Sundays: UNIVERSITY & MOSSPARK Circle via POLLOKSHIELDS unaltered.

05-12-1943 — Altered to become UNIVERSITY & MOSSPARK via POLLOKSHIELDS.

05-05-1952 — Altered to become Weekdays and Saturdays: UNIVERSITY or ST VINCENT STREET & MOSSPARK via POLLOKSHIELDS;
Sundays: UNIVERSITY & MOSSPARK via POLLOKSHIELDS unaltered.

04-01-1959 — Closure of Eldon Street bridge over River Kelvin for reconstruction.
Diverted to become PARK ROAD or ST VINCENT STREET & MOSSPARK via POLLOKSHIELDS.

05-06-1960 — Withdrawn and replaced by Motorbus Service 59.

DEPOT *Until August 1945:* **Maryhill and Newlands**
From August 1945: **Newlands**

TYPES OF CAR *Until December 1948:* **Standard, Coronation**
December 1948 until July 1954: **Standard, Coronation, Mark II Coronation ['Cunarder']**
July 1954 until December 1959: **Standard, Coronation, Mark II Coronation ['Cunarder'], Replacement Mark I Coronation**
From December 1959: **Coronation, Mark II Coronation ['Cunarder'], Replacement Mark I Coronation**
Also During 1948: **Experimental One-Way on Special Service 40>3 St Vincent Street-Mosspark-St Vincent Street only**

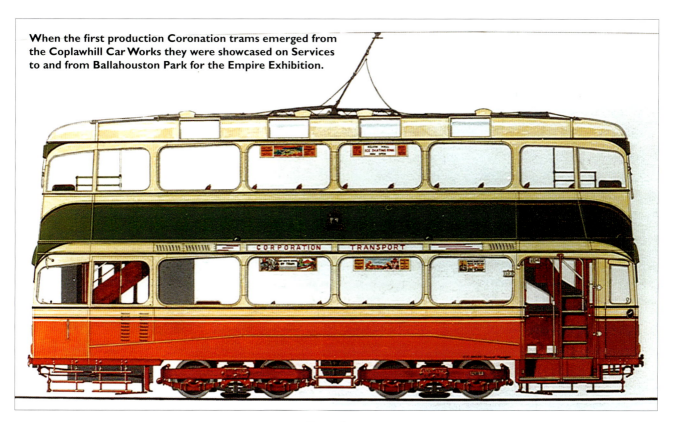

When the first production Coronation trams emerged from the Coplawhill Car Works they were showcased on Services to and from Ballahouston Park for the Empire Exhibition.

SERVICE 3A

COLOUR BAND White / Standard Green
Commencing
03-05-1938 Introduced UNIVERSITY & MOSSPARK Circle via PAISLEY ROAD (Circle Cars return as Service 3) No Sundays Service.
04-05-1938 Extended to become KELVINGROVE or UNIVERSITY & MOSSPARK Circle via PAISLEY ROAD (Circle Cars return as Service 3) No Sundays Service.
08-08-1938 Part-extended to become ANNIESLAND, KELVINGROVE or UNIVERSITY & MOSSPARK Circle via PAISLEY ROAD (Circle Cars return as Service 3) No Sundays Service.
30-10-1938 Withdrawn.
30-05-1943 Reintroduced UNIVERSITY or ST VINCENT STREET & MOSSPARK Circle via PAISLEY ROAD with through Circle Cars to and from Service 3.
07-11-1943 Altered to become Weekdays: UNIVERSITY & MOSSPARK Circle via PAISLEY ROAD; Saturdays and Sundays: UNIVERSITY & MOSSPARK Circle via PAISLEY ROAD unaltered.
05-12-1943 Withdrawn replaced by new **Service 40**.
DEPOT *1938:* **Maryhill, Newlands and Govan**
1943: **Maryhill and Newlands**
TYPES OF CAR **Standard, Coronation**

SERVICE 4

COLOUR BAND Blue / Standard Green
Commencing
03-05-1938 Former **Blue Service K** KEPPOCHHILL ROAD & SHIELDHALL or RENFREW AERODROME.
xx-XX-1941 Cut back to become KEPPOCHHILL ROAD & SHIELDHALL or RENFREW SOUTH.
15-08-1943 Altered to become KEPPOCHHILL ROAD & RENFREW SOUTH.
03-10-1948 RENFREW SOUTH and PORTERFIELD ROAD terminus moved from Paisley Road Renfrew at Broadloan into Porterfield Road east end.
01-04-1951 Extended to become SPRINGBURN & RENFREW SOUTH via KEPPOCHHILL ROAD.
07-02-1954 SANDYFORD terminus also named PAISLEY NORTH for Cars turning from the City.
Extended to become
SPRINGBURN & PAISLEY NORTH via KEPPOCHHILL ROAD.
12-05-1957 Cut back to become SPRINGBURN & HILLINGTON ROAD via KEPPOCHHILL ROAD.
07-09-1958 Withdrawn and replaced by **Motorbus Service 53**.
DEPOT **Possilpark and Govan**
TYPES OF CAR *Until October 1938:* **Standard**
October 1938 until October 1941: **Standard, Coronation**
October 1941 until March 1953: **Standard**
From March 1953: **Standard, Mark II Coronation ['Cunarder']**

SERVICE 4A

COLOUR BAND	**Blue**
Commencing	
03-05-1938	Part of former **Blue Service G** SPRINGBURN & LINTHOUSE, SHIELDHALL or RENFREW CROSS via POSSILPARK, LORNE STREET.
23-06-1940	Rerouted between Paisley Road Toll and Lorne School to operate via Govan Road (Old Govan Road) to become
	SPRINGBURN & LINTHOUSE, SHIELDHALL or RENFREW CROSS via POSSILPARK.
15-08-1943	Renumbered **Service 27**.
DEPOT	**Possilpark and Govan**
TYPES OF CAR	*Until October 1938:* **Standard**
	October 1938 until October 1941: **Standard, Coronation**
	From October 1941: **Standard**

SERVICE 4B

COLOUR BAND	**Blue**
Commencing	
03-05-1938	Part of former **Blue Service G** LAMBHILL & LINTHOUSE, SHIELDHALL or RENFREW CROSS via POSSILPARK, LORNE STREET.
23-06-1940	Rerouted between Paisley Road Toll and Lorne School to operate via Govan Road (Old Govan Road) to become
	LAMBHILL & LINTHOUSE, SHIELDHALL or RENFREW CROSS via POSSILPARK.
15-08-1943	Renumbered **Service 31**.
DEPOT	**Possilpark and Govan**
TYPES OF CAR	*Until October 1938:* **Standard**
	October 1938 until October 1941: **Standard, Coronation**
	From October 1941: **Standard**

Car 842 has around ½ mile to go before reaching its Clarkston terminus and is seen in 1952 at Stamperland. Note the number indicator has been set by a lazy conductor who has simply turned the "A" from "5A" out of vision (almost).
(John H Meredith)

SERVICE 5

COLOUR BAND Yellow / Standard Green

Commencing

03-05-1938	Former Yellow Service C KIRKLEE Circle via BOTANIC GARDENS or Circle via HYNDLAND & CLARKSTON.
15-08-1943	Altered to become KIRKLEE Circle via BOTANIC GARDENS & CLARKSTON; Cars return as Service 5A route; journeys to Kirklee via Hyndland renumbered 5A; All Cars show "5" on journeys to Clarkston.
02-01-1944	KIRKLEE discontinued as terminal name. Becomes KELVINSIDE Circle via BOTANIC GARDENS & CLARKSTON.
10-06-1945	Circular runs cease, becomes KELVINSIDE & CLARKSTON via BOTANIC GARDENS.
09-09-1945	KELVINSIDE terminus moved from Hyndland Road north end to Hyndland Station.
28-10-1945	Circular runs resume, reverts to KELVINSIDE Circle via BOTANIC GARDENS & CLARKSTON; Cars return as Service 5A route; journeys to Kelvinside via Hyndland numbered 5A; All Cars show "5" on journeys to Clarkston.
18-08-1946	Rerouted between Renfield Street at St Vincent Street and Victoria Road to become KELVINSIDE Circle via BOTANIC GARDENS & CLARKSTON via GORBALS.
01-07-1951	Rerouted between Renfield Street at St Vincent Street and Eglinton Toll to run via Bridge Street and Turriff Street to become KELVINSIDE Circle via BOTANIC GARDENS & CLARKSTON.
05-07-1953	Cut back to become KELVINSIDE Circle via BOTANIC GARDENS & HOLMLEA ROAD.
17-11-1957	Withdrawn and replaced by Motorbus Service 43.
DEPOT	*Until September 1956:* **Partick and Langside** *From September 1956:* **Partick and Newlands**
TYPES OF CAR	*Until September 1938:* **Standard** *September 1938 until September 1956:* **Standard, Coronation** *From September 1956:* **Standard, Coronation, Mark II Coronation ['Cunarder'], Replacement Mark I Coronation**

SERVICE 5A

COLOUR BAND Yellow / Standard Green

Commencing

03-05-1938	Former Yellow Service H JORDANHILL & LANGSIDE via HYNDLAND.
30-10-1938	Extended to become ANNIESLAND & LANGSIDE via HYNDLAND.
15-08-1943	Renumbered **Service 24**. Portion of Service 5 renumbered to become KIRKLEE Circle via HYNDLAND & CLARKSTON; Circle Cars return as Service 5. All Cars show "5" on journeys to Clarkston.
02-01-1944	KIRKLEE discontinued as terminal name. Becomes KELVINSIDE Circle via HYNDLAND & CLARKSTON.
10-06-1945	Circular runs cease, becomes HYNDLAND & CLARKSTON via HIGHBURGH ROAD.
28-10-1945	Circular runs resume, reverts to KELVINSIDE Circle via HYNDLAND & CLARKSTON; Circle Cars return as Service 5. All Cars show "5" on journeys to Clarkston.
18-08-1946	Rerouted between Renfield Street at St Vincent Street and Victoria Road to run via Gorbals to become KELVINSIDE Circle via HYNDLAND & CLARKSTON via GORBALS.
01-07-1951	Rerouted between Renfield Street at St Vincent Street and Eglinton Toll to become KELVINSIDE Circle via HYNDLAND & CLARKSTON.
05-07-1953	Cut back to become KELVINSIDE Circle via HYNDLAND & HOLMLEA ROAD.
17-11-1957	Withdrawn and replaced by Motorbus Service 43.
DEPOT	*Until September 1956:* **Partick and Langside** *From September 1956:* **Partick and Newlands**
TYPES OF CAR	*Until September 1938:* **Standard** *September 1938 until September 1956:* **Standard, Coronation** *From September 1956:* **Standard, Coronation, Mark II Coronation ['Cunarder'], Replacement Mark I Coronation**

SERVICE 6

COLOUR BAND	**Blue / Standard Green**
Commencing	
03-05-1938	Former **Blue Service Z** DALMUIR WEST or SCOTSTOUN & ALEXANDRA PARK or RIDDRIE.
19-11-1946	All eastbound trams proceeding from Monkland Street southwards into Castle Street rerouted to continue via Parliamentary Road then turn right into Castle Street. Westbound Cars unaltered.
07-10-1951	Cut back to become Weekdays and Saturdays: SCOTSTOUN & ALEXANDRA PARK or RIDDRIE; Sundays: SCOTSTOUN & ALEXANDRA PARK.
01-11-1959	Withdrawn and replaced by **Motorbus Service 56**.
DEPOT	**Partick and Dennistoun**
TYPES OF CAR	*Until May 1950:* **Standard**
	May 1950 until January 1959: **Standard, Coronation**
	From January 1959: **Standard, Coronation, Mark II Coronation ['Cunarder']**

SERVICE 7

COLOUR BAND	**Yellow / Standard Green**
Commencing	
03-05-1938	Former **Yellow Service J** MILLERSTON. RIDDRIE or ALEXANDRA PARK & BELLAHOUSTON.
15-05-1949	Introduced Sundays Afternoon Specials: MILLERSTON & BRIDGETON CROSS.
15-06-1958	Withdrawn and replaced by **Trolleybus Service 106**.
	Sundays Afternoon Specials: MILLERSTON & BRIDGETON CROSS withdrawn without replacement.
DEPOT	**Dennistoun and Govan**
TYPES OF CAR	*Until September 1939:* **Standard**
	September 1939 until August 1943: **Standard, Coronation**
	August 1943 until March 1953: **Standard**
	From March 1953: **Standard, Mark II Coronation ['Cunarder']**

In 1943 Govan Depot lost all its modern trams. Presumably the proximity to the docks was seen to render the premises vulnerable to air bombardment. A case of shutting the stable door after the horse had bolted perhaps? Small consolation came in the allocation of rebuilt Standard cars such as 679 below. *(DLG Hunter, courtesy AW Brotchie)*

SERVICE 8

COLOUR BAND	**Red / Standard Green**
Commencing	
03-05-1938	Former Red Service R becomes Red Service 8/8A: BISHOPBRIGGS (8) or SPRINGBURN (8) & POLLOKSHAWS WEST (8A) or ROUKEN GLEN Circle via THORNLIEBANK (8A). Circle Cars return to ALEXANDRA PARK (8A), RIDDRIE (8A) or MILLERSTON (8A); MILLERSTON (8A), RIDDRIE (8A) or ALEXANDRA PARK (8A) & MERRYLEE (8B), GIFFNOCK (8) or ROUKEN GLEN Circle via GIFFNOCK (8). Circle Cars return to SPRINGBURN (8) or BISHOPBRIGGS (8).
xx-09-1938	GIFFNOCK terminus extended from Fenwick Road north of Eastwood Toll to Rouken Glen Road west of Eastwood Lodge.
01-03-1940	BISHOPBRIGGS terminus moved from Kirkintilloch Road north of Springfield Road to Kenmure Avenue east end.
15-08-1943	Renumbered as **Services 8** and **25**. Service 8 becomes MILLERSTON, RIDDRIE or ALEXANDRA PARK & GIFFNOCK or ROUKEN GLEN Circle via GIFFNOCK. Circle Cars return as Service 25 to Springburn or Bishopbriggs.
19-11-1946	All eastbound through trams proceeding from Monkland Street southwards into Castle Street rerouted to continue via Parliamentary Road then turn right into Castle Street and via former route. Westbound Cars unaltered.
15-03-1959	Withdrawn and replaced by Motorbus Service 38.
DEPOT	**Possilpark, Dennistoun and Newlands**
TYPES OF CAR	*Until September 1938:* **Standard**
	September 1938 until January 1940: **Standard, Coronation**
	January 1940 until December 1948: **Standard, Coronation, Experimental Lightweight**
	December 1948 until May 1951: **Standard, Coronation, Experimental Lightweight, Mark II Coronation ['Cunarder']**
	May 1951 until July 1954: **Standard, Coronation, Mark II Coronation ['Cunarder']**
	From July 1954: **Standard, Coronation, Mark II Coronation ['Cunarder'], Replacement Mark I Coronation**

When first placed in service the Coronation Mark II or 'Cunarder' trams were all allocated to Newlands Depot. Until problems with stability were overcome they were kept off Services 3 and 14 with sleeper track, and figured prominently on Services 8 and 25.

SERVICE 8A

COLOUR BAND	**Red**
Commencing	
03-05-1938	Former Red Service R becomes Red Service 8/8A:
	BISHOPBRIGGS (8) or SPRINGBURN (8) & POLLOKSHAWS WEST (8A) or ROUKEN GLEN Circle via THORNLIEBANK (8A). Circle Cars return to ALEXANDRA PARK (8A), RIDDRIE (8A) or MILLERSTON (8A). MILLERSTON (8A), RIDDRIE (8A) or ALEXANDRA PARK (8A) & MERRYLEE (8B) GIFFNOCK (8) or ROUKEN GLEN Circle via GIFFNOCK (8).
	Circle Cars return to SPRINGBURN (8) or BISHOPBRIGGS (8).
xx-09-1938	GIFFNOCK terminus extended from Fenwick Road north of Eastwood Toll to Rouken Glen Road west of Eastwood Lodge.
11-02-1940	CARNWADRIC terminus opened in Boydstone Road at Cruachan Street.
	Becomes BISHOPBRIGGS (8) or SPRINGBURN (8) & CARNWADRIC (8A) or ROUKEN GLEN Circle via THORNLIEBANK (8A).
01-03-1940	BISHOPBRIGGS terminus moved from Kirkintilloch Road north of Springfield Road to Kenmure Avenue east end.
15-08-1943	Renumbered as **Services 8** and **25**.
DEPOT	**Possilpark, Dennistoun and Newlands**
TYPES OF CAR	*Until October 1938:* **Standard**
	October 1938 until January 1940: **Standard, Coronation**
	From January 1940: **Standard, Coronation, Experimental Lightweight**

SERVICE 8B

COLOUR BAND	**Red**
Commencing	
03-05-1938	*[See entries under Services 8 and 8A]*
15-08-1943	*[See entries under Services 8 and 8A]*
DEPOT	**Possilpark, Dennistoun and Newlands**
TYPES OF CAR	*Until October 1938:* **Standard**
	October 1938 until January 1940: **Standard, Coronation**
	From January 1940: **Standard, Coronation, Experimental Lightweight**

This 'red over green' livery style, seen right, was the first manifestation of the abandonment of the route colour system. This had mixed success and only around forty trams were treated in this way.

The quintet of 'Lightweight' experimental trams, as seen below, spent the first ten years of service at Newlands Depot.

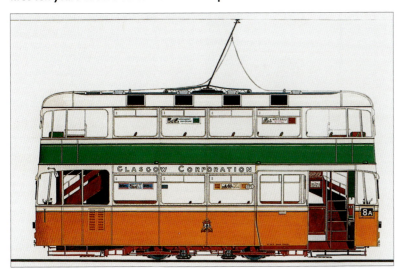

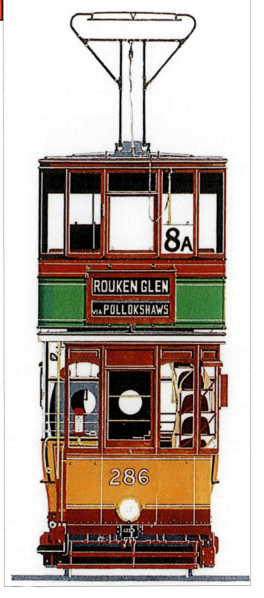

SERVICE 9

COLOUR BAND Red / Standard Green

Commencing

03-05-1938	Former **Red Service L** DALMUIR WEST or SCOTSTOUN & LONDON ROAD or AUCHENSHUGGLE.
14-05-1944	Extended to become DALMUIR WEST or SCOTSTOUN & LONDON ROAD, AUCHENSHUGGLE or CARMYLE.
04-05-1952	Introduced Specials: ANDERSTON CROSS & AUCHENSHUGGLE to replace **Service 34**.
15-06-1952	AUCHENSHUGGLE terminus moved eastwards from London Road at Tollcross Station Road to London Road just west of Causewayside Street. Cut back to become DALMUIR WEST or SCOTSTOUN & LONDON ROAD or AUCHENSHUGGLE.
19-04-1953	Specials: ANDERSTON CROSS & AUCHENSHUGGLE withdrawn replaced by **Service 10**
07-09-1959	Dalmuir Canal Swing Bridge closed for repairs. All cars curtailed at DALMUIR.
01-08-1960	Dalmuir Canal Swing Bridge reopened to traffic. Re-extended to DALMUIR WEST.
02-09-1962	Withdrawn replaced by **Motorbus Service 64**. Introduced Special Service ANDERSTON CROSS & AUCHENSHUGGLE (Part Day).
04-09-1962	Withdrawn.

DEPOT *Until June 1962:* **Partick and Dalmarnock**
From June 1962: **Dalmarnock**

TYPES OF CAR *Until December 1938:* **Standard, Standard Double-Bogie**
December 1938 until October 1939: **Standard, Standard Double-Bogie, Coronation**
October 1939 until January 1940: **Standard, Standard Double-Bogie, Coronation, Experimental Lightweight**
January 1940 until Spring 1942: **Standard, Standard Double-Bogie, Coronation**
Note: During late March, April and part of May 1941 **Single-Decker [Cut-down Ex-Paisley District], Single-Decker [Cut-down Standard]** *available due to temporary suspension of Service 20, operated substituting for blitz-damaged members of the fleet being repaired.*
Spring 1942 until May 1950: **Standard, Standard Double-Bogie**
May 1950 until June 1958: **Standard, Standard Double-Bogie, Coronation**
June 1958 until June 1960: **Standard, Standard Double-Bogie, Coronation, Mark II Coronation ['Cunarder']**
June 1960 until June 1961: **Standard, Standard Double-Bogie, Coronation, Mark II Coronation ['Cunarder'], Replacement Mark I Coronation**
June 1961 until August 1961: **Standard Double-Bogie, Coronation, Mark II Coronation ['Cunarder'], Replacement Mark I Coronation**
August 1961 until 2 September 1962: **Coronation, Mark II Coronation, ['Cunarder'], Replacement Mark I Coronation**
2 until 4 September 1962: **Coronation, Mark II Coronation [Cunarder']**
Also from May 1941 until November 1961: **Experimental Bogie Car***

The embarrassment and disruption caused by the frequent derailments of Standard Double-Bogie cars, particularly at the Jamaica Street/Argyle Street junction had to be speedily addressed and, as early as the summer of 1929, some of the cars were being tried out on alternative services. Repainted with a Red route band and based at Newlands Depot, 1119 makes its way citywards in Main Street Thornliebank bound for Bishopbriggs on Service R. Trials are also known to have taken place on Red Service N. By the early 1930s all of the class with the exception of Car 1100 which remained at Parkhead, had gravitated to Partick and Dalmarnock Depots.
(Courtesy East Renfrewshire Council Libraries)

and from 1952 until August 1960: **Experimental Single-Decker***
and from March 1961 until June 1961: **Experimental Single-Decker***
Notes: * principally running only between Partick and Dalmuir West.

SERVICE 9A

COLOUR BAND	**Red**
Commencing	
03-05-1938	Part of former **Red Service F** DALMUIR WEST, CLYDEBANK or SCOTSTOUN & BURNSIDE via DALMARNOCK. (Cars show "9" on journeys to SCOTSTOUN, CLYDEBANK or DALMUIR WEST).
15-08-1943	Integrated with **Red Service 9B** and renumbered **Service 26**.
DEPOT	**Partick and Dalmarnock**
TYPES OF CAR	**Standard, Standard Double-Bogie**
	Note: During late March, April and part of May 1941 **[Cut-down Ex-Paisley District] Single-Decker [Cut-down Standard]** *available due to temporary suspension of Service 20, operated substituting for blitz-damaged members of the fleet being repaired.*

SERVICE 9B

COLOUR BAND	**Red**
Commencing	
03-05-1938	Part of former **Red Service F** DALMUIR WEST, CLYDEBANK or SCOTSTOUN & RUTHERGLEN or CAMBUSLANG via DALMARNOCK. (Cambuslang Saturdays after 1300 only) (Cars show "9" on journeys to SCOTSTOUN, CLYDEBANK or DALMUIR WEST)
15-08-1943	Integrated with **Red Service 9A** and renumbered **Service 26**.
DEPOT	**Partick and Dalmarnock**
TYPES OF CAR	**Standard, Standard Double-Bogie**
	Standard only on Cambuslang section (Length restricted at Cambuslang Iye)
	Note: During late March, April and part of May 1941 **[Cut-down Ex-Paisley District] Single-Decker [Cut-down Standard]** *available due to temporary suspension of Service 20, operated substituting for blitz-damaged members of the fleet being repaired.*

Although newer and more robust, the Maximum Traction "Kilmarnock Bogie" cars were not listed to receive full repaints as continued to be specified until 1958 for the ubiquitous Standard cars. Policy was not always followed, however, as can be seen with this very smart No.1118 on Service 9, Dumbarton Road. *(John H Meredith)*

253

Service 10 was another East End-West End service and is represented here by Car 733 at the junction of Eldon Street and Woodlands Road in the West End.
(RJS Wiseman)

SERVICE 10

COLOUR BAND Blue / Standard Green

Commencing

03-05-1938 — Former **Blue Service O** KIRKLEE & OATLANDS or RUTHERGLEN via PARK ROAD, CROWN STREET and
PARTICK or ST VINCENT STREET & OATLANDS or RUTHERGLEN via CROWN STREET.

03-05-1942 — Altered Sundays: ST VINCENT STREET & OATLANDS via CROWN STREET (Part Day) section to become ANDERSTON CROSS & OATLANDS via CROWN STREET (Part Day);
Sundays: KIRKLEE & RUTHERGLEN via PARK ROAD, CROWN STREET section unaltered;
Split to become
Weekdays: KIRKLEE & RUTHERGLEN via PARK ROAD, CROWN STREET and
ANDERSTON CROSS & OATLANDS via CROWN STREET;
Saturdays: KIRKLEE & OATLANDS or RUTHERGLEN via PARK ROAD, CROWN STREET and
PARTICK & OATLANDS or RUTHERGLEN via CROWN STREET sections unaltered.

02-01-1944 — Altered to become KELVINSIDE Circle via PARK ROAD & OATLANDS or RUTHERGLEN via CROWN STREET with through Circle Cars at Kelvinside returning as **Service 10A** route.

10-06-1945 — Altered to become KELVINSIDE & OATLANDS or RUTHERGLEN via PARK ROAD, CROWN STREET.

28-10-1945 — KELVINSIDE terminus moved from Hyndland Road north end to Hyndland Road at Hyndland Station.

23-01-1949 — Altered to become KELVINSIDE & PARKHEAD via PARK ROAD, Circle via GALLOWGATE returning via DALMARNOCK ROAD. Circle Cars in opposite direction by **Service 36**.

19-04-1953 — Altered to become Weekdays and Saturdays: KELVINSIDE & LONDON ROAD via PARK ROAD;
Sundays: KELVINSIDE & GLASGOW CROSS, LONDON ROAD or AUCHENSHUGGLE via PARK ROAD.
(Glasgow Cross until 1300; Auchenshuggle 1300-1900; London Road from 1900 onwards).

29-08-1953 — Park Road closed by collapse of deeply-seated sewer.

xx-09-1953 — Introduced one-way operation for cars turning at GLASGOW CROSS.

19-10-1953 — Park Road reopened - normal service resumes.

05-06-1960 — Withdrawn replaced in part by **Service 9** and by **Motorbus Service 59**.

DEPOT — *Until January 1949:* **Dalmarnock**
From January 1949: **Partick and Dalmarnock**

TYPES OF CAR	*Until 1955:* **Standard**
	1955 until January 1959: **Standard, Coronation**
	From January 1959: **Standard, Coronation, Mark II Coronation ['Cunarder']**

SERVICE 10A

COLOUR BAND	**Blue / Standard Green**
Commencing	
02-01-1944	Introduced KELVINSIDE Circle via CHURCH STREET & OATLANDS or RUTHERGLEN via CROWN STREET with through Circle Cars at Kelvinside returning as **Service 10**.
10-06-1945	Cut back to become ANDERSTON CROSS & OATLANDS or RUTHERGLEN via CROWN STREET; (All Cars show "10" on journeys to OATLANDS and RUTHERGLEN).
23-01-1949	Withdrawn without replacement.
DEPOT	**Dalmarnock**
TYPES OF CAR	**Standard**

SERVICE 11

COLOUR BAND	**Red / Standard Green**
Commencing	
03-05-1938	Former **Red Service N** MARYHILL or GAIRBRAID AVENUE & SINCLAIR DRIVE via GARSCUBE ROAD.
19-02-1939	Diverted to become RUCHILL & SINCLAIR DRIVE via GARSCUBE ROAD.
14-07-1940	Diverted to become GAIRBRAID AVENUE & SINCLAIR DRIVE via GARSCUBE ROAD.
04-05-1941	Extended to become Summer Sundays: MARYHILL & SINCLAIR DRIVE via GARSCUBE ROAD; Weekdays and Saturdays: GAIRBRAID AVENUE & SINCLAIR DRIVE via GARSCUBE ROAD unaltered.
02-05-1943	Rerouted between Queen's Cross and Cowcaddens and extended to become MILNGAVIE & SINCLAIR DRIVE via ST GEORGE'S CROSS.
18-08-1946	Northbound cars rerouted to run directly from Victoria Road into Pollokshaws Road; Southbound cars unaltered.
20-04-1947	Introduced Summer Sundays Auxiliary: MILNGAVIE & MAITLAND STREET.
01-07-1951	Withdrawn replaced by **Services 13** and **24** and by **Motorbus Service 43**. Sundays Auxiliary: MILNGAVIE & MAITLAND STREET incorporated into **Service 13**.
DEPOT	**Maryhill and Langside**
TYPES OF CAR	*Until October 1941:* **Standard**
	From October 1941: **Standard, Coronation**

Milngavie terminus in 1947 with cars on Service 11. The terminus was just short of the town centre.
(BJ Cross Collection)

Service 12 never entered the city centre, hiding itself away between Paisley Road Toll and Mount Florida, scurrying across Pollokshaws Road and Victoria Road before heading for Crosshill. Car 29 is seen here passing Strathbungo Station, heading into Pollokshields.
(RJS Wiseman)

SERVICE 12

COLOUR BAND	Yellow / Standard Green
Commencing	
03-05-1938	Former Yellow Service Q Weekdays and Saturdays: MOUNT FLORIDA & PAISLEY ROAD TOLL or IBROX via SHIELDS ROAD; Sundays: MOUNT FLORIDA & PAISLEY ROAD TOLL via SHIELDS ROAD.
21-11-1938	Cut back to become Weekdays and Saturdays: MOUNT FLORIDA & PAISLEY ROAD TOLL via SHIELDS ROAD; Sundays: MOUNT FLORIDA & PAISLEY ROAD TOLL via SHIELDS ROAD unaltered.
02-05-1943	Extended to become MOUNT FLORIDA & LINTHOUSE via SHIELDS ROAD.
26-11-1944	Part Cut Back to become MOUNT FLORIDA & PAISLEY ROAD TOLL or LINTHOUSE via SHIELDS ROAD.
01-05-1949	Strathbungo railway bridge repairs - service split.
29-05-1949	During closure of Strathbungo bridge, all cars extended to LINTHOUSE.
15-04-1950	Strathbungo railway bridge repairs completed-through service resumes.
01-03-1953	Altered to become Weekdays: MOUNT FLORIDA & PAISLEY ROAD TOLL or LINTHOUSE via SHIELDS ROAD (Linthouse Morning and Evening Peak-hours only); Saturdays and Sundays: MOUNT FLORIDA & PAISLEY ROAD TOLL via SHIELDS ROAD.
14-11-1958	Peak-hour workings to LINTHOUSE and Specials to SHIELDHALL withdrawn.
16-11-1958	Withdrawn replaced by Trolleybus Service 108.
DEPOT	*Until October 1938:* **Langside and Govan**
	October 1938 until May 1943: **Langside**
	May 1943 until March 1953: **Langside and Govan**
	March 1953 until September 1956: **Langside**
	From September 1956: **Govan**
TYPES OF CAR	Standard only (Clearances restricted in Kinning Park at Seaward Street, Milnpark Street, Admiral Street)

SERVICE 13

COLOUR BAND   Red / Standard Green

Commencing

03-05-1938	Former **Red Service M** MILNGAVIE, HILLFOOT or MARYHILL & MOUNT FLORIDA via NEW CITY ROAD.
17-10-1938	Railway Bridge at Maryhill Station closed for repairs.
25-12-1938	Railway Bridge at Maryhill Station repairs completed - normal service resumes.
24-08-1941	Altered to become Weekdays: MILNGAVIE or MARYHILL & MOUNT FLORIDA via ST GEORGE'S CROSS; Saturdays: MILNGAVIE, HILLFOOT or MARYHILL & MOUNT FLORIDA via ST GEORGE'S CROSS and Sundays: MILNGAVIE & MOUNT FLORIDA via ST; GEORGE'S CROSS unaltered.
02-05-1943	Altered to become GAIRBRAID AVENUE & MOUNT FLORIDA or CLARKSTON via ST GEORGE'S CROSS; Milngavie section replaced by **Service 11**.
07-11-1943	Part extended to become MARYHILL or GAIRBRAID AVENUE & MOUNT FLORIDA or CLARKSTON via ST GEORGE'S CROSS.
08-04-1945	Altered to become MARYHILL or GAIRBRAID AVENUE & MOUNT FLORIDA, NETHERLEE or CLARKSTON via ST GEORGE'S CROSS.
12-01-1947	GOVANHILL terminus moved from Cathcart Road at Dixon Avenue to Coplaw Street east end using triangle to turn. Altered to become Weekdays and Saturdays: MARYHILL or GAIRBRAID AVENUE & MOUNT FLORIDA or CLARKSTON via ST GEORGE'S CROSS; Sundays: MARYHILL or GAIRBRAID AVENUE & CLARKSTON via ST GEORGE'S CROSS unaltered; Introduced Weekdays and Saturdays Auxiliary Service: GAIRBRAID AVENUE & GOVANHILL via ST GEORGE'S CROSS.
24-11-1947	Altered to become Weekdays Auxiliary: MARYHILL & GOVANHILL via ST GEORGE'S CROSS; Saturdays Auxiliary: GAIRBRAID AVENUE & GOVANHILL via ST GEORGE'S CROSS unaltered.
01-07-1951	Extended to become MILNGAVIE, MARYHILL or GAIRBRAID AVENUE & MOUNT FLORIDA or CLARKSTON via ST GEORGE'S CROSS to replace **Service 11** to Milngavie; Saturdays Auxiliary: GAIRBRAID AVENUE & GOVANHILL via ST GEORGE'S CROSS; and Weekdays Auxiliary: MARYHILL & GOVANHILL via ST GEORGE'S CROSS both unaltered.

05-07-1953	Introduced Sundays Auxiliary: MILNGAVIE & MAITLAND STREET to replace **Service 11** Auxiliary. Rerouted between Cowcaddens and Glassford Street/Trongate and diverted to become MILNGAVIE, MARYHILL or GAIRBRAID AVENUE & GLASGOW CROSS via ST GEORGE'S CROSS; Cut back to become Weekdays and Saturdays Auxiliary: MARYHILL & MAITLAND STREET; Sundays Auxiliary: MILNGAVIE & MAITLAND STREET unaltered.
xx-09-1953	Introduced one-way operation for cars turning at GLASGOW CROSS.
04-10-1953	Withdrawn replaced by revised **Service 29**. Auxiliary Services incorporated into revised **Service 29**.
DEPOT	*Until July 1953:* **Maryhill and Langside** *From July 1953:* **Maryhill**
TYPES OF CAR	**Standard, Coronation**

SERVICE 14

COLOUR BAND	**Blue / Standard Green**
Commencing	
03-05-1938	Former **Blue Service P** MILNGAVIE or MARYHILL & SHAWLANDS, PAISLEY CROSS or RENFREW FERRY via ST GEORGE'S CROSS, GORBALS, BARRHEAD.
17-10-1938	Railway Bridge at Maryhill Station closed for repairs.
25-12-1938	Railway Bridge at Maryhill Station repairs completed-normal service resumes.
02-05-1943	Rerouted between Queen's Cross and Cowcaddens to become MILNGAVIE or MARYHILL & SHAWLANDS, PAISLEY CROSS or RENFREW FERRY via GARSCUBE ROAD, GORBALS, BARRHEAD.
15-08-1943	Split at Spiersbridge to become MILNGAVIE or MARYHILL & SHAWLANDS or SPIERSBRIDGE via GARSCUBE ROAD, GORBALS; Section beyond Spiersbridge replaced by new **Service 28**.
07-11-1943	Altered to become MILNGAVIE, MARYHILL or GAIRBRAID AVENUE & SHAWLANDS or SPIERSBRIDGE via GARSCUBE ROAD, GORBALS.
xx-XX-1944	SPIERSBRIDGE terminus moved from Spiersbridge Road north of Nitshill Road to east end of Private Track on north side of Nitshill Road.
28-10-1945	Cut back to become Weekdays and Saturdays: MARYHILL or GAIRBRAID AVENUE & SHAWLANDS or SPIERSBRIDGE via GARSCUBE ROAD, GORBALS; Sundays: HILLFOOT or MARYHILL & SHAWLANDS or SPIERSBRIDGE via GARSCUBE ROAD, GORBALS.
06-01-1946	POLLOKSHAWS WEST renamed POLLOKSHAWS and terminus resited at Greenview Street west end, cars using triangle to turn. Altered to become Weekdays and Saturdays: MARYHILL or GAIRBRAID AVENUE & POLLOKSHAWS or SPIERSBRIDGE via GARSCUBE ROAD, GORBALS; Sundays: HILLFOOT or MARYHILL & POLLOKSHAWS or SPIERSBRIDGE via GARSCUBE ROAD, GORBALS.
18-08-1946	Rerouted between Cowcaddens at Renfield Street and Eglinton Street at Turriff Street to become HILLFOOT, MARYHILL or GAIRBRAID AVENUE & POLLOKSHAWS or SPIERSBRIDGE via GARSCUBE ROAD, RENFIELD STREET.
12-01-1947	Diverted to become UNIVERSITY & POLLOKSHAWS or SPIERSBRIDGE.
24-11-1947	Altered to become Part-Day. Evening Service replaced by new **Service 14A**.
03-04-1949	Extended to become All Day UNIVERSITY & POLLOKSHAWS or CROSSSTOBS to replace, in part, **Service 28**.
21-08-1949	Altered to become UNIVERSITY & SPIERSBRIDGE or CROSSSTOBS.

04-10-1953	ARDEN terminus opened on Private Track on north side of Nitshill Road west of Kyleakin Road. SPIERSBRIDGE terminus disused. Altered to become UNIVERSITY & ARDEN or CROSSSTOBS.
30-09-1956	Cut back to become UNIVERSITY & ARDEN.
04-01-1959	Closure of Eldon Street bridge over River Kelvin for reconstruction. Diverted to become KELVINGROVE & ARDEN.
01-11-1959	Withdrawn replaced by Motorbus Service 57.
DEPOT	*Until August 1943:* **Maryhill, Newlands and Elderslie** *August 1943 until January 1947:* **Maryhill and Newlands** *From January 1947:* **Newlands**
TYPES OF CAR	*Until August 1943:* **Standard only (Clearance restricted on loops Cross Stobs-Glenfield)** *August 1943 until January 1947:* **Standard** *January.1947 until December 1948:* **Standard, Coronation** *December 1948 until July 1954:* **Standard, Coronation, Mark II Coronation ['Cunarder']** *From July 1954:* **Standard, Coronation, Mark II Coronation ['Cunarder'], Replacement Mark I Coronation**

SERVICE 14A

COLOUR BAND	**Standard Green**
Commencing	
12-01-1947	Introduced KELVINGROVE & POLLOKSHAWS or SPIERSBRIDGE.
21-08-1949	Withdrawn.
DEPOT	**Newlands**
TYPES OF CAR	**Standard, Coronation**

SERVICE 14B

COLOUR BAND	**Standard Green**
Commencing	
07-11-1948	Introduced CASTLE STREET & CARNWADRIC.
20-02-1949	Withdrawn replaced by new Service 31
DEPOT	**Newlands**
TYPES OF CAR	**Standard, Coronation**

SERVICE 15

COLOUR BAND	**Green / Standard Green**
Commencing	
03-05-1938	Former Green Service B FERGUSLIE MILLS or CROOKSTON & SHETTLESTON, BAILLIESTON or AIRDRIE.
09-05-1938	CROOKSTON terminus moved from Paisley Road West at Crookston Road into Crookston Road north end.
11-02-1940	Extended to become Weekdays: ELDERSLIE or CROOKSTON & SHETTLESTON or AIRDRIE; Saturdays: ELDERSLIE or CROOKSTON & BAILLIESTON or AIRDRIE; Sundays: ELDERSLIE & AIRDRIE.
04-05-1942	Cut back to become ELDERSLIE or CROOKSTON & SHETTLESTON.
02-05-1943	Extended to become ELDERSLIE or CROOKSTON & GARROWHILL.
15-08-1943	Split in City Centre to become ANDERSTON CROSS & BAILLIESTON or AIRDRIE; Part replaced by new Services 21, 22 and 32.
02-09-1949	AIRDRIE terminus moved from Forrest Street west end to Clark Street east end.
04-11-1956	Cut back to become ANDERSTON CROSS & BAILLIESTON.
10-02-1957	BAILLIESTON terminus moved westwards from Private Track on south side of Coatbridge Road to Main Street Baillieston just east of Martin Crescent.
11-03-1962	Withdrawn replaced by Motorbus Service 62.
DEPOT	*Until May 1942:* **Elderslie, Govan, Parkhead and Coatbridge** *May 1942 until August 1943:* **Elderslie, Govan and Parkhead** *August 1943 until November 1956:* **Parkhead and Coatbridge** *November 1956 until March 1960:* **Parkhead** *March 1960 until November 1960:* **Dennistoun**

Standard Car No.1 is seen at Parkhead Cross on a short-working to Shettleston. Note the pointsman's two-storey "hut" in the distance. Judging by the crowds, Celtic have been playing at home.
(RJS Wiseman)

TYPES OF CAR	*From November 1960:* **Dalmarnock** *Until 1940:* **Standard, Experimental Bogie-Car, Coronation** *1940 until March 1957:* **Standard, Coronation** *March 1957 until June 1960:* **Standard, Coronation, Ex-Liverpool Streamliner** *June 1960 until November 1960:* **Standard, Coronation** *November 1960 until June 1961:* **Standard, Coronation, Mark II Coronation ['Cunarder'], Replacement Mark I Coronation** *From June 1961:* **Coronation, Mark II Coronation ['Cunarder'], Replacement Mark I Coronation**

SERVICE 15A

COLOUR BAND	Green / Standard Green
Commencing	
03-05-1938	Former Green Service U FERGUSLIE MILLS or CROOKSTON & TOLLCROSS or UDDINGSTON.
09-05-1938	CROOKSTON terminus moved from Paisley Road West at Crookston Road into Crookston Road north end.
11-02-1940	Extended to become Weekdays and Saturdays: ELDERSLIE or CROOKSTON & TOLLCROSS or UDDINGSTON; Sundays: ELDERSLIE & UDDINGSTON.
15-08-1943	Split in City Centre and replaced by new **Services 21, 22, 29** and **32**.
DEPOT	**Elderslie, Govan and Parkhead**
TYPES OF CAR	*Until 1940:* **Standard, Experimental Bogie-Car, Coronation** *From 1940:* **Standard, Coronation**

Car 434 on Service 16 in typical Springburn tenement territory turning from Springburn Road into Keppochhill Road, followed by Car 101 on Service 4 in May 1957. *(WD McMillan, Courtesy Travel Lens)*

SERVICE 16

COLOUR BAND	Green / Standard Green
Commencing	
03-05-1938	Former **Green Service W** Weekdays: KEPPOCHHILL ROAD & WHITEINCH or SCOTSTOUN via NORTH STREET;
	Saturdays and Sundays: KEPPOCHHILL ROAD & WHITEINCH via NORTH STREET.
11-02-1940	Extended to become KEPPOCHHILL ROAD & SCOTSTOUN via NORTH STREET.
29-07-1945	Rerouted between Charing Cross and St Vincent Street at North Street to become KEPPOCHHILL ROAD & SCOTSTOUN via ELMBANK STREET.
01-04-1951	Extended to become SPRINGBURN & SCOTSTOUN via KEPPOCHHILL ROAD, ELMBANK STREET.
06-09-1959	Cut back to become KEPPOCHHILL ROAD & SCOTSTOUN via ELMBANK STREET.
12-03-1961	Withdrawn replaced by **Motorbus Service 32**.
DEPOT	*Until March 1958:* **Possilpark and Partick**
	From March 1958: **Partick**
TYPES OF CAR	*Until March 1958:* **Standard**
	March 1958 until January 1959: **Standard, Coronation**
	From January 1959: **Standard, Coronation, Mark II Coronation ['Cunarder']**

SERVICE 17

COLOUR BAND Red / Standard Green

Commencing

03-05-1938 — Former **Red Service X** ANNIESLAND & CAMBUSLANG via BOTHWELL STREET.

15-08-1943 — Cut back to become ANDERSTON CROSS & CAMBUSLANG. Part replaced by new **Service 21**.

08-04-1945 — Altered to become Weekdays and Saturdays: ANDERSTON CROSS & DALMARNOCK or CAMBUSLANG;
Sundays: ANDERSTON CROSS & CAMBUSLANG unaltered.

08-12-1946 — Extended to become WHITEINCH & CAMBUSLANG via ANDERSTON CROSS.

17-12-1950 — Altered to become Sundays: ANDERSTON CROSS & CAMBUSLANG;
Weekdays and Saturdays: WHITEINCH & CAMBUSLANG via ANDERSTON CROSS unaltered.

10-10-1954 — Rerouted between Finnieston and Argyle Street at Hope Street and diverted to become ANNIESLAND & CAMBUSLANG via BOTHWELL STREET in part to replace **Service 21**.

04-11-1956 — Cut back to become ANNIESLAND & FARME CROSS via BOTHWELL STREET.

16-11-1958 — Withdrawn replaced, in part, by **Service 26**.

DEPOT *Until August 1943:* **Partick and Dalmarnock**
August 1943 until December 1946: **Dalmarnock**
From December 1946: **Partick and Dalmarnock**

TYPES OF CAR *Until November 1956:* **Standard only (Length restricted at Cambuslang lye)**
From November 1956 until June 1958: **Standard, Coronation**
From June 1958: **Standard, Coronation, Mark II Coronation ['Cunarder']**

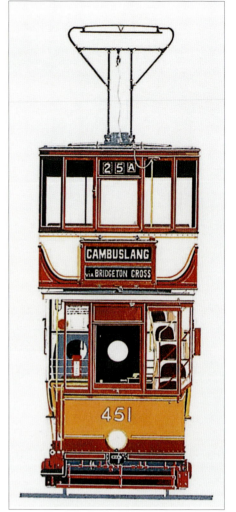

SERVICE 18

COLOUR BAND White / Red / Standard Green

Commencing

03-05-1938 — Former **White Service Y** SPRINGBURN, RUCHILL or KELVINSIDE AVENUE & RUTHERGLEN or BURNSIDE via BILSLAND DRIVE, RUTHERGLEN BRIDGE.

03-05-1942 — Altered to become SPRINGBURN & BURNSIDE via BILSLAND DRIVE, RUTHERGLEN BRIDGE.

07-11-1943 — Cut back to become SPRINGBURN & RUTHERGLEN via BILSLAND DRIVE, RUTHERGLEN BRIDGE.

01-05-1944 — Re-extended to become SPRINGBURN & RUTHERGLEN or BURNSIDE via BILSLAND DRIVE, RUTHERGLEN BRIDGE.

07-08-1955 — Rerouted between Bridgeton Cross and Rutherglen Cross and split to become
SPRINGBURN & BURNSIDE via BILSLAND DRIVE, DALMARNOCK; and
18A SPRINGBURN & SHAWFIELD via BILSLAND DRIVE, RUTHERGLEN BRIDGE; (Cars show "18" on journeys to SPRINGBURN).

04-06-1961 — Withdrawn replaced by **Motorbus Service 18**.

DEPOT **Maryhill and Dalmarnock**

TYPES OF CAR *Until October 1941:* **Standard, Ex-Paisley District**
October 1941 until May 1952: **Standard, Ex-Paisley District, Coronation**
May 1952 until June 1958: **Standard, Coronation**
June 1958 until June 1960: **Standard, Coronation, Mark II Coronation ['Cunarder']**
From June 1960: **Standard, Coronation, Mark II Coronation ['Cunarder'], Replacement Mark I Coronation**
Also from 1948 until October 1953: **Experimental One-Way on Special Service between Maryhill Depot and Glasgow Cross**

Car 517 picks up a load of passengers in Bilsland Drive. The terminus "Shawfield" has been added to the existing screens and employed a template of letters suitable for both Standard Car screens and the narrower Coronation blinds, resulting in this compressed effect. (RJS Wiseman)

SERVICE 18A

COLOUR BAND	Standard Green
Commencing	
07-08-1955	Introduced SPRINGBURN & SHAWFIELD via BILSLAND DRIVE. RUTHERGLEN BRIDGE (Cars show "18" on journeys to SPRINGBURN).
04-06-1961	Withdrawn replaced by Motorbus Service 18.
DEPOT	**Maryhill and Dalmarnock**
TYPES OF CAR	*Until June 1958:* **Standard, Coronation**
	June 1958 until June 1960: **Standard, Coronation, Mark II Coronation ['Cunarder']**
	From June 1960: **Standard, Coronation, Mark II Coronation 'Cunarder'], Replacement Mark I Coronation**

SERVICE 19

COLOUR BAND	White / Standard Green
Commencing	
03-05-1938	Former White Service S SPRINGBURN & MOUNT FLORIDA or NETHERLEE via GLASGOW CROSS.
02-05-1943	Cut back to become SPRINGBURN & MOUNT FLORIDA via GLASGOW CROSS.
19-07-1943	Extended to become Weekdays and Saturdays: SPRINGBURN & NETHERLEE via GLASGOW CROSS;
	Sundays: SPRINGBURN & MOUNT FLORIDA via GLASGOW CROSS unaltered.
20-02-1949	Withdrawn replaced by Motorbus Service 37
DEPOT	**Possilpark and Langside**
TYPES OF CAR	*Until November 1938:* **Standard, Ex-Paisley District**
	November 1938 until October 1941: **Standard, Ex-Paisley District, Coronation**
	From October 1941: **Standard, Ex-Paisley District**

Southbound single-decker 1024 comes off the Forth & Clyde Canal bridge in Kilbowie Road. It was the proximity of this to an adjacent low railway bridge that prevented the roadway from being lowered any further and therefore restricted operation to single-deckers. *(BJ Cross Collection)*

SERVICE 20

COLOUR BAND Red* / Standard Green#

Commencing
- 03-05-1938 Former **Red Service RP** CLYDEBANK & RADNOR PARK or DUNTOCHER.
- 19-01-1941 RADNOR PARK crossover replaced by PARKHALL crossover.
  Altered to become Weekdays and Saturdays: CLYDEBANK & PARKHALL or DUNTOCHER; Sundays: CLYDEBANK & DUNTOCHER unaltered.
- 04-12-1949 Withdrawn replaced by **Motorbus Service 20**.

DEPOT Partick

TYPES OF CAR *Until May 1939:* **Single-Decker [Cut-down Ex-Paisley District], Experimental Single-Decker** only (Low Bridge Kilbowie Road)
From May 1939: **Single-Decker [Cut-down Ex-Paisley District], Experimental Single-Decker, Single-Decker [Cut-down Standard]** only (Low Bridge Kilbowie Road)

* not displayed

\# displayed only on Cut-down Standard cars.

SERVICE 21

COLOUR BAND Green / Standard Green

Commencing
- 30-10-1938 Introduced CROOKSTON & PROVANMILL via RENFIELD STREET.
- 23-06-1940 Diverted to become HILLINGTON ROAD & PROVANMILL via LORNE STREET, RENFIELD STREET.
- 06-06-1943 Extended to become RENFREW CROSS & PROVANMILL via LORNE STREET, RENFIELD STREET.
- 15-08-1943 Diverted and renumbered to become **Service 32**.
  New Service introduced ELDERSLIE & ANNIESLAND via BOTHWELL STREET to replace, in part, Services **15, 15A** and **17**.
- 10-10-1954 Cut back to become ELDERSLIE & ST VINCENT STREET. Anniesland section replaced by revised **Service 17**.
- 12-05-1957 Withdrawn without replacement.

DEPOT *Until August 1943:* **Govan and Possilpark**
August 1943 until October 1954: **Elderslie, Govan and Partick**
From October 1954: **Elderslie and Govan**

TYPES OF CAR *Until October 1941:* **Standard, Coronation**
October 1941 until August 1943: **Standard**
August 1943 until March 1953: **Standard, Coronation**
From March 1953: **Standard, Coronation, Mark II Coronation ['Cunarder']**

SUBSIDENCE IN MARYHILL ROAD

DIVERSION OF TRAM SERVICES

HILLFOOT and MOUNT FLORIDA, GAIRBRAID AVENUE and SINCLAIR DRIVE, MARYHILL and RENFREW FERRY, SPRINGBURN and BURNSIDE.

Passengers might please note that, while repairs are being carried out, an

EMERGENCY BUS SERVICE

will be operated between Queen's Cross and Hope Street, via Maryhill Road, St. George's Road, Sauchiehall Street, Elmbank Street, and Bothwell Street, returning via Hope Street, St Vincent Street, Elmbank Street and as on outward journey, at the undernoted times:

7.0 a.m. till 9.30 a.m.   12 noon till 2.30 p.m.   4.30 p.m. till 7.30 p.m.

The Service will be at 4-minute intervals.   Fare, Queen's Cross to Hope Street, 1½d.

46 Bath Street, May, 1934.   **GLASGOW CORPORATION TRANSPORT.**   L. MACKINNON, General Manager.

On some sets of screens, certain Destination points appeared only on the lower screen. This resulted in varying layouts of displays even on the same service as illustrated here by two Service 22 cars passing on Paisley Road West at the foot of Cokerhill Road. *(John H Meredith)*

SERVICE 22

COLOUR BAND Blue / Standard Green

Commencing

15-08-1943	Introduced CROOKSTON & ST VINCENT STREET to replace, in part, **Services 15** and **15A**.
17-03-1946	Extended to become CROOKSTON & LAMBHILL to replace, in part, **Service 31**.
16-11-1958	Withdrawn replaced by Motorbus Service 54.

DEPOT *Until March 1946:* **Govan**
From March 1946: **Govan and Possilpark**

TYPES OF CAR *Until March 1953:* **Standard**
From March 1953: **Standard, Mark II Coronation ['Cunarder']**

SERVICE 23

COLOUR BAND Standard Green

Commencing

15-08-1943	Introduced KELVINGROVE & GARROWHILL or AIRDRIE to replace, in part, **Service 1**.
05-03-1944	Altered to become KELVINGROVE & BAILLIESTON or AIRDRIE.
12-01-1947	Diverted to become GAIRBRAID AVENUE & BAILLIESTON or AIRDRIE via GARSCUBE ROAD to replace part of **Service 14**.
02-09-1949	AIRDRIE terminus moved from Forrest Street west end to Clark Street east end.
04-05-1952	Altered to become Weekdays: GAIRBRAID AVENUE & BAILLIESTON or AIRDRIE via GARSCUBE ROAD (Airdrie cars at Peak-hours only); Saturdays and Sundays: GAIRBRAID AVENUE & BAILLIESTON via GARSCUBE ROAD.
05-07-1953	Rerouted between Queen's Cross and St Vincent Street to become GAIRBRAID AVENUE & BAILLIESTON or AIRDRIE via ST GEORGE'S CROSS.
11-10-1954	Altered to become Weekdays: GAIRBRAID AVENUE & BAILLIESTON via ST GEORGE'S CROSS; Saturdays and Sundays: GAIRBRAID AVENUE & BAILLIESTON via ST GEORGE'S CROSS unaltered.
10-02-1957	BAILLIESTON terminus moved westwards from Private Track on south side of Coatbridge Road to Main Street Baillieston just east of Martin Crescent.
18-08-1957	Extended to become MARYHILL & BAILLIESTON via ST GEORGE'S CROSS.
05-06-1960	Rerouted between St George's Road and St Vincent Street to become MARYHILL & BAILLIESTON via NORMAL SCHOOL.

06-11-1960	Withdrawn replaced by Motorbus Service 60.
DEPOT	*Until January 1947:* **Dennistoun, Parkhead and Coatbridge** *January 1947 until October 1954:* **Maryhill, Dennistoun and Coatbridge** *From October 1954:* **Maryhill and Dennistoun**
TYPES OF CAR	**Standard, Coronation**

SERVICE 24

COLOUR BAND	Yellow / Standard Green
Commencing	
15-08-1943	Former Yellow Service 5A ANNIESLAND & LANGSIDE via HYNDLAND.
18-08-1946	Rerouted between Renfield Street at St Vincent Street and Eglinton Toll to become ANNIESLAND & LANGSIDE via HYNDLAND, GORBALS.
01-07-1951	Rerouted between Renfield Street at St Vincent Street and Eglinton Toll to run via Bridge Street and Turriff Street and half-diverted to replace, in part, Service 11 to become ANNIESLAND & LANGSIDE or SINCLAIR DRIVE via HYNDLAND.
15-08-1951	Rediverted to become ANNIESLAND & LANGSIDE via HYNDLAND; Sinclair Drive section replaced by Service 24A.
17-11-1957	Altered to become ANNIESLAND or BROOMHILL CROSS & LANGSIDE via HYNDLAND.
16-03-1958	Withdrawn replaced by Motorbus Service 44.
DEPOT	*Until September 1956:* **Partick and Langside** *From September 1956:* **Partick and Newlands**
TYPES OF CAR	*Until September 1956:* **Standard, Coronation** *From September 1956:* **Standard, Coronation, Mark II Coronation ['Cunarder'], Replacement Mark I Coronation**

Former Red car 223 created a minor sensation in 1949 when it was repainted with cadmium upper panels. It operated on Service 24 from Langside Depot.

 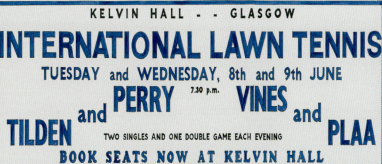 

SERVICE 24A

COLOUR BAND	Standard Green
Commencing	
05-08-1951	Introduced KELVINGROVE & SINCLAIR DRIVE to replace part of Service 24.
02-12-1951	Withdrawn replaced by existing Motorbus Service 43.
DEPOT	Langside
TYPES OF CAR	Standard, Coronation

Service 24A was very short lived and very few photographs exist of trams allocated to it. Car 28 is at its Sinclair Drive terminus with the Conductor in the process of setting the lower screen to KELVINGROVE for the return journey. *(Iain M Hill/STTS Collection)*

SERVICE 25

COLOUR BAND	Red / Standard Green
Commencing	
15-08-1943	Former Service 8/8A renumbered as Services 8 and 25. Service 25 becomes BISHOPBRIGGS or SPRINGBURN & CARNWADRIC or ROUKEN GLEN Circle via THORNLIEBANK; Circle Cars return as Service 8 to Riddrie or Millerston.
07-11-1948	Additional CARNWADRIC terminus in Boydstone Road at Crebar Street opened and served by new Service 14B. First CARNWADRIC terminus in Boydstone Road at Cruachan Street remains in use for Service 25.
21-08-1949	CARNWADRIC turning point consolidated at new terminus at Crebar Street. CARNWADRIC terminus extended to Boydstone Road at Crebar Street.

Car 231 heads citywards down Springburn Road on Service 25 with two Corporation buses in pursuit. Judging by the encroaching yellow paint on the tram stop, this is likely to be a last-day photograph.
(WD McMillan, Courtesy Travel Lens)

10-10-1954	New COLSTON terminus opened in Hillcroft Terrace. Cut back to become COLSTON or SPRINGBURN & CARNWADRIC or ROUKEN GLEN Circle via THORNLIEBANK; Bishopbriggs section replaced by revised **Service 32**.
20-03-1955	Re-extended to become BISHOPBRIGGS or SPRINGBURN & CARNWADRIC or ROUKEN GLEN Circle via THORNLIEBANK.
15-03-1959	Withdrawal of Giffnock trams. Circular runs at Rouken Glen cease. ROUKEN GLEN terminus moved eastwards from Rouken Glen Road at Rowallan Road to the former Giffnock terminus in Rouken Glen Road at Milverton Road becomes BISHOPBRIGGS or SPRINGBURN & CARNWADRIC or ROUKEN GLEN via THORNLIEBANK.
07-06-1959	Withdrawn replaced by Motorbus Service 45
DEPOT	*Until March 1959:* **Possilpark, Dennistoun and Newlands** *From March 1959:* **Possilpark and Newlands**
TYPES OF CAR	*Until December 1948:* **Standard, Coronation, Experimental Lightweight** *December 1948 until May 1951:* **Standard, Coronation, Experimental Lightweight, Mark II Coronation ['Cunarder']** *May 1951 until July 1954:* **Standard, Coronation, Mark II Coronation ['Cunarder']** *From July 1954:* **Standard, Coronation, Mark II Coronation ['Cunarder'], Replacement Mark I Coronation**

SERVICE 26

COLOUR BAND	**Red/ Standard Green**
Commencing	
15-08-1943	Former Red Services 9A and 9B become DALMUIR WEST, CLYDEBANK or SCOTSTOUN & RUTHERGLEN or BURNSIDE via DALMARNOCK.
23-01-1949	Altered to become CLYDEBANK or SCOTSTOUN & OATLANDS or BURNSIDE via DALMARNOCK.
07-08-1955	Part-diverted and altered to become CLYDEBANK or SCOTSTOUN & BURNSIDE via DALMARNOCK and **26A**;CLYDEBANK or SCOTSTOUN & SHAWFIELD via RUTHERGLEN BRIDGE; (Cars show "26" on journeys to SCOTSTOUN or CLYDEBANK).
16-11-1958	**Service 26A** diverted to FARME CROSS and integrated with **Service 26** to replace part of **Service 17**.

This Maximum Traction car at Oatlands terminus is still carrying red route colour panels. The conductor is more concerned about holding on to his hat as he changes the indicator display.
(DL Thomson Collection)

269

	Altered to become CLYDEBANK or SCOTSTOUN & FARME CROSS or BURNSIDE via DALMARNOCK.
04-06-1961	Cut back to become CLYDEBANK or SCOTSTOUN & DALMARNOCK or FARME CROSS.
22-10-1961	Cut back to become CLYDEBANK or SCOTSTOUN & DALMARNOCK.
03-06-1962	Withdrawn replaced by Motorbus Service 63.
DEPOT	**Partick and Dalmarnock**
TYPES OF CAR	*Until May 1950:* **Standard, Standard Double-Bogie**
	May 1950 until June 1958: **Standard, Standard Double-Bogie, Coronation**
	June 1958 until June 1960: **Standard, Standard Double-Bogie, Coronation, Mark II Coronation ['Cunarder']**
	June 1960 until June 1961: **Standard, Standard Double-Bogie, Coronation, Mark II Coronation ['Cunarder'], Replacement Mark I Coronation**
	June 1961 until August 1961: **Standard Double-Bogie, Coronation, Mark II Coronation ['Cunarder'], Replacement Mark I Coronation**
	From August 1961: **Coronation, Mark II Coronation ['Cunarder'], Replacement Mark I Coronation**

SERVICE 26A

COLOUR BAND	**Standard Green**
Commencing	
07-08-1955	Introduced CLYDEBANK or SCOTSTOUN & SHAWFIELD via RUTHERGLEN BRIDGE; (Cars show "26" on journeys to SCOTSTOUN or CLYDEBANK).
16-11-1958	Diverted to FARME CROSS and integrated with Service 26. Shawfield service covered by existing Service 18A.
DEPOT	**Partick and Dalmarnock**
TYPES OF CAR	*Until June 1958:* **Standard, Standard Double-Bogie, Coronation**
	From June 1958: **Standard, Standard Double-Bogie, Coronation, Mark II Coronation ['Cunarder']**

Car 111 on Service 26A, is followed by Car 91, passing the Tron Steeple, taking the right fork for London Road.
(RB Parr / STTS Collection)

Paisley Road Toll is the setting for Car 449 on Service 27 with the Angel Building in the background. The third track in the foreground provided access for the Departmental cars from the main line to the Sand Drier building in the former Kinning Park Depot in Admiral Street, to the left of this view. The tram is about to fork right into Govan Road, the section formerly known as Old Govan Road. *(RJS Wiseman)*

SERVICE 27

COLOUR BAND Blue / Standard Green
Commencing
15-08-1943 — Former Blue Service 4A SPRINGBURN & SHIELDHALL or RENFREW CROSS via POSSILPARK.
20-04-1946 — Altered to become Saturdays: SPRINGBURN or POSSILPARK & SHIELDHALL or RENFREW CROSS. Weekdays and Sundays: SPRINGBURN & SHIELDHALL or RENFREW CROSS via POSSILPARK unaltered.
01-05-1946 — SHIELDHALL terminus moved from Renfrew Road to Bogmoor Road north end.
12-05-1957 — Cut back to become SPRINGBURN or POSSILPARK & SHIELDHALL.
16-03-1958 — Withdrawn replaced by Motorbus Service 52.
DEPOT **Possilpark and Govan**
TYPES OF CAR *Until March 1953:* **Standard**
From March 1953: **Standard, Mark II Coronation ['Cunarder']**

SERVICE 28

COLOUR BAND Blue / Standard Green
Commencing
15-08-1943 — Introduced SPIERSBRIDGE & RENFREW FERRY via PAISLEY CROSS to replace, in part, Service 14.
xx-XX-1944 — SPIERSBRIDGE terminus moved from Spiersbridge Road north of Nitshill Road to east end of Private Track on north side of Nitshill Road.
03-04-1949 — Cut back to become GLENFIELD & RENFREW FERRY, replaced, in part, by Service 14 and by Motorbus Service 41.
12-05-1957 — Withdrawn without replacement.
DEPOT **Elderslie**
TYPES OF CAR *Until April 1949:* **Ex-Paisley District, Standard only (Clearance restricted on loops Cross Stobs-Glenfield)**
April 1949 until May 1950: **Ex-Paisley District, Standard**
May 1950 until May 1951: **Ex-Paisley District, Standard, Coronation**
May 1951 until August 1953: **Ex-Paisley District, Standard, Coronation, Experimental Lightweight**
From August 1953: **Standard, Coronation, Experimental Lightweight**

Once the long Service 14 was split, there was no longer any need to roster Semi-high speed Standards on regular city services. Many ended their days on Service 28 as here.

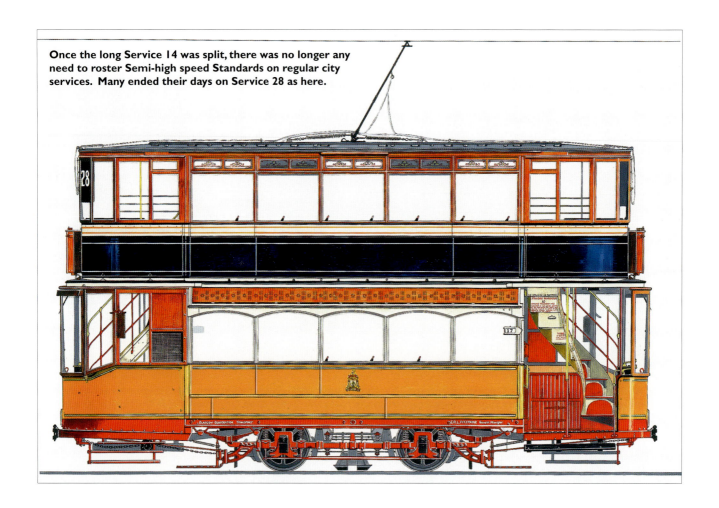

The cramped confines of Caldercuilt Road proved too tight for the Ex-Liverpool cars which had to use the Depot triangle in Celtic Street as their Maryhill turning point. The Maryhill terminus for Services 29 and 40 was soon moved to Garscube Estate East Lodge Gate. *(RB Parr / STTS Collection)*

SERVICE 29

COLOUR BAND	Standard Green

Commencing

15-08-1943	Introduced ANDERSTON CROSS & TOLLCROSS or UDDINGSTON to replace, in part, **Service 15A**
21-08-1946	TOLLCROSS terminus moved eastwards from Tollcross Road at Carmyle Avenue to Hamilton Road east of Carmyle Avenue.
24-08-1947	BROOMHOUSE crossover resited eastwards from Hamilton Road at Broomhouse Post Office to Hamilton Road 300 yards east of Calderpark Zoo Gates at River Calder Bridge.
29-08-1948	Cut back to become ANDERSTON CROSS & TOLLCROSS or BROOMHOUSE.
26-12-1948	Introduced Sundays Afternoon Specials: ANDERSTON CROSS & BROOMHOUSE.
04-10-1953	Diverted and extended to replace **Service 13** to become MILNGAVIE, MARYHILL or GAIRBRAID AVENUE & TOLLCROSS or BROOMHOUSE via NORMAL SCHOOL; Introduced: Weekdays and Saturdays Auxiliary: MARYHILL & MAITLAND STREET via NORMAL SCHOOL and Sundays Auxiliary: MILNGAVIE & MAITLAND STREET via NORMAL SCHOOL. Sundays Afternoons only: ANDERSTON CROSS & BROOMHOUSE (Cars show "15" on journeys to ANDERSTON CROSS) unaltered.
02-11-1953	Extended to become Weekdays and Saturdays Auxiliary: MARYHILL & GLASGOW CROSS via NORMAL SCHOOL.
07-02-1954	MARYHILL terminus moved from Caldercuilt Road west end to Maryhill Road at Garscube Estate East Lodge Gate.
04-11-1956	Cut back to become MARYHILL or GAIRBRAID AVENUE & TOLLCROSS or BROOMHOUSE via NORMAL SCHOOL; Weekdays and Saturdays Auxiliary: MARYHILL & GLASGOW CROSS via NORMAL SCHOOL unaltered; Sundays Auxiliary: MILNGAVIE & MAITLAND STREET withdrawn without replacement; Sundays Afternoons only: ANDERSTON CROSS & BROOMHOUSE unaltered.
06-11-1960	Cut back to become MARYHILL or GAIRBRAID AVENUE & TOLLCROSS via NORMAL SCHOOL; Sundays Afternoons: ANDERSTON CROSS & BROOMHOUSE withdrawn without replacement. Weekdays and Saturdays Auxiliary: MARYHILL & GLASGOW CROSS via NORMAL SCHOOL unaltered.

Hillfoot terminus sees two ex-Liverpool "Streamliners". With the closure of the section beyond Maryhill Park these cars were denied one of the few opportunities to show their turn of speed.
(HB Priestley / National Tramway Museum Archive)

22-10-1961	Withdrawn replaced by Motorbus Service 61.
DEPOT	*Until October 1953:* **Parkhead**
	October 1953 until June 1959: **Maryhill and Parkhead**
	From June 1959: **Maryhill and Dalmarnock**
TYPES OF CAR	*Until Autumn 1953:* **Standard, Coronation**
	Autumn 1953 until February 1954: **Standard, Coronation, Ex-Liverpool Streamliner (Ex-Liverpool Streamliner turning at Maryhill use Celtic Street)**
	February 1954 until June 1959: **Standard, Coronation, Ex-Liverpool Streamliner**
	June 1959 until June 1960: **Standard, Coronation, Mark II Coronation ['Cunarder'], Ex-Liverpool Streamliner**
	June 1960 until July 1960: **Standard, Coronation, Mark II Coronation ['Cunarder'], Replacement Mark I Coronation, Ex-Liverpool Streamliner**
	July 1960 until June 1961: **Standard, Coronation, Mark II Coronation ['Cunarder'], Replacement Mark I Coronation**
	From June 1961: **Coronation, Mark II Coronation ['Cunarder'], Replacement Mark I Coronation**
	Also from October 1953 until November 1955: **Experimental One-Way on Maryhill Depot-Glasgow Cross service only**

SERVICE 30

COLOUR BAND	Various / Standard Green	
Commencing		
03-05-1938	Introduced CIRCLE ST VINCENT STREET & EXHIBITION (OUTER) temporary service. Cars in opposite direction by **Service 30A**.	
30-10-1938	Withdrawn	

In Duke Street at the junction of Shettleston Road Standard Tramcar 190 passes through the industrial East End of the city with Parkhead Forge on the left, from which a connecting railway line crosses the tram track a right angles immediately in front of the tram. *(RB Parr / STTS Collection)*

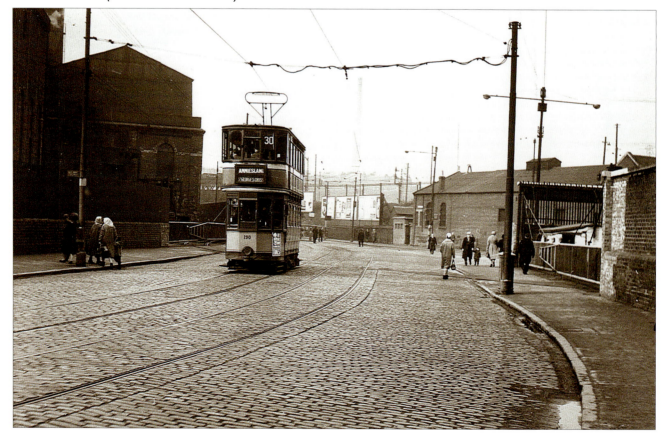

15-08-1943	Introduced KNIGHTSWOOD or KELVINSIDE & SPRINGFIELD ROAD to replace, in part, **Services 1, 1A**.
08-04-1945	Extended to become KNIGHTSWOOD or KELVINSIDE & SPRINGFIELD ROAD or CAMBUSLANG.
28-10-1945	KELVINSIDE terminus moved from Hyndland Road north end to Hyndland Road at Hyndland Station.
23-01-1949	Cut back to become KNIGHTSWOOD or KELVINSIDE & DALMARNOCK.
31-07-1949	Extended to become BLAIRDARDIE or KELVINSIDE & DALMARNOCK.
19-04-1953	Altered to become Weekdays and Saturdays: BLAIRDARDIE or ANNIESLAND & DALMARNOCK; Sundays: BLAIRDARDIE & DALMARNOCK unaltered.
13-03-1960	Withdrawn replaced, in part, by Motorbus Service 58.
DEPOT	*1938:* **Newlands and Govan**
	August 1943 until March 1959: **Partick, Dennistoun and Parkhead**
	From March 1959: **Partick and Dennistoun**
TYPES OF CAR	*1938:* **Standard, Coronation**
	From August 1943 until November 1952: **Standard, Ex-Paisley District only (Clearance restricted at Parkhead Cross and, also, length restricted at Cambuslang lye)**
	From November 1952: **Standard only (Clearance restricted at Parkhead Cross)**

SERVICE 30A

COLOUR BAND	Various
Commencing	
03-05-1938	Introduced CIRCLE ST VINCENT STREET & EXHIBITION (INNER) temporary service. Cars in opposite direction by **Service 30**.
30-10-1938	Withdrawn.
DEPOT	**Newlands and Govan**
TYPES OF CAR	**Standard, Coronation**

This panoramic view of Parkhead Cross from Tollcross Road illustrates the complicated tramway junction and the need for the Pointsman's Control Tower (foreground, centre). The two Standard trams are negotiating the sharp curve from Duke Street denied to Coronation trams. *(Commercial postcard / STTS Collection)*

SERVICE 31

COLOUR BAND Blue / Standard Green

Commencing

03-05-1938	Introduced LINTHOUSE & EXHIBITION temporary service.
30-10-1938	Withdrawn.
15-08-1943	Introduced former **Blue Service 4B** LAMBHILL & HILLINGTON ROAD or RENFREW CROSS.
17-03-1946	Withdrawn replaced by **Services 22** and **27**.
20-02-1949	Introduced LAMBHILL & CARNWADRIC via CHARING CROSS to replace **Service 14B**.
21-08-1949	Cut back to become LAMBHILL & POLLOKSHAWS via CHARING CROSS. Carnwadric service replaced by **Service 25**.
02-11-1952	POLLOKSHAWS terminus extended from Greenview Street west end to Nether Auldhouse Road west end.
08-04-1956	Diverted to become LAMBHILL & MERRYLEE via CHARING CROSS.
18-08-1957	MERRYLEE terminus moved 180 yards south from Kilmarnock Road at Merrylee Road to Kilmarnock Road at Mulberry Road.
06-12-1959	Withdrawn without replacement.
DEPOT	*1938:* **Govan**
	August 1943 until March 1946: **Possilpark and Govan**
	February 1949 until March 1959: **Possilpark and Newlands**
	From March 1959: **Newlands**
TYPES OF CAR	*1938:* **Standard, Coronation**
	August 1943 until March 1946: **Standard**
	February 1949 until July 1954: **Standard, Coronation, Mark II Coronation ['Cunarder']**
	From July 1954: **Standard, Coronation, Mark II Coronation ['Cunarder'], Replacement Mark I Coronation**

SERVICE 32

COLOUR BAND Standard Green

Commencing

15-08-1943	Former **Green Service 21** diverted to become ELDERSLIE & PROVANMILL via RENFIELD STREET to replace, in part, **Services 15** and **15A**
20-02-1949	Diverted to become ELDERSLIE & BISHOPBRIGGS via RENFIELD STREET.
02-08-1953	Cut back to become ELDERSLIE & SPRINGBURN via RENFIELD STREET.
10-10-1954	Altered to become CROOKSTON & BISHOPBRIGGS via RENFIELD STREET.
20-03-1955	Altered to become CROOKSTON & SPRINGBURN or BISHOPBRIGGS via RENFIELD STREET.
16-11-1958	Withdrawn replaced by **Motorbus Service 55**.
DEPOT	*Until October 1954:* **Elderslie, Govan and Possilpark**
	From October 1954: **Govan and Possilpark**
TYPES OF CAR	*Until March 1953:* **Standard, Coronation**
	March 1953 until October 1954: **Standard, Coronation, Mark II Coronation ['Cunarder']**
	From October 1954: **Standard, Mark II Coronation ['Cunarder']**

After October 1954 Service 32 trams ceased to run west of Crookston leaving the trunk service to Paisley and beyond to Service 21 cars. Car 562 is at Paisley Cross heading for Springburn, having been curtailed from Bishopbriggs in August of the previous year. *(RJS Wiseman)*

SERVICE 33

COLOUR BAND	**Standard Green**
Commencing	
26-11-1944	Introduced CIRCLE SPRINGBURN & CHARING CROSS.
03-05-1959	Withdrawn without replacement.
DEPOT	*Until March 1959:* **Possilpark**
	From March 1959: **Maryhill**
TYPES OF CAR	*Until December 1947:* **Standard**
	December 1947 until 1948: **Standard, Experimental One-Way**
	1948 until March 1959: **Standard**
	From March 1959: **Standard, Coronation**

SERVICE 34

COLOUR BAND	**Standard Green**
Commencing	
17-03-1946	Introduced CIRCLE PARKHEAD & BRIDGETON CROSS.
23-11-1947	Sundays Service withdrawn.
11-07-1948	PARKHEAD terminal point at north end of Springfield Road moved southwards to opposite Newlands School.
23-01-1949	Altered to become DENNISTOUN & RUTHERGLEN Circle via DALMARNOCK ROAD returning via RUTHERGLEN BRIDGE; Sundays service reintroduced. Cars in opposite direction by **Service 35**.
29-05-1949	Altered to become ALEXANDRA PARK & AUCHENSHUGGLE.
04-03-1951	Diverted to become ANDERSTON CROSS & AUCHENSHUGGLE.
04-05-1952	Withdrawn replaced by Specials on **Service 9**.
DEPOT	**Dalmarnock**
TYPES OF CAR	**Standard**

SERVICE 35

COLOUR BAND	**Standard Green**
Commencing	
23-01-1949	Introduced DENNISTOUN & RUTHERGLEN Circle via RUTHERGLEN BDGE returning via DALMARNOCK RD. Cars in opposite direction by **Service 34**.
29-05-1949	Withdrawn.
DEPOT	**Dalmarnock**
TYPES OF CAR	**Standard**

Car 333 is seen here on Service 36 in Hope Street passing the Central Hotel and Malmaison Restaurant when they were the place to be in 1952.
(AWV Mace / National Tramway Museum Archive)

SERVICE 36

COLOUR BAND	**Blue / Standard Green**
Commencing	
23-01-1949	Introduced KELVINSIDE & PARKHEAD via PARK ROAD, Circle via DALMARNOCK ROAD returning via GALLOWGATE.
	Cars in opposite direction by **Service 10**.
19-04-1953	Withdrawn.
DEPOT	**Partick and Dalmarnock**
TYPES OF CAR	**Standard**

SERVICE 40

COLOUR BAND	**Blue/Red/Standard Green**
Commencing	
05-12-1943	Introduced DUMBRECK & ST VINCENT STREET via PAISLEY ROAD to replace **Service 3A**.
06-05-1945	Cut back to become MOSSPARK & ST VINCENT STREET via PAISLEY ROAD.
28-10-1945	Extended to become DUMBRECK & GAIRBRAID AVENUE via CHARING CROSS.
04-04-1948	Extended to become DUMBRECK & MARYHILL via CHARING CROSS.
07-05-1950	Cut back to become IBROX & MARYHILL via CHARING CROSS.
05-03-1951	Re-extended to become Weekdays: DUMBRECK or IBROX & MARYHILL via CHARING CROSS; (Dumbreck 1600-1800 only);
	Saturdays and Sundays: IBROX & MARYHILL via CHARING CROSS unaltered.
07-02-1954	MARYHILL terminus moved from Caldercuilt Road west end to Garscube Estate East Lodge Gate.
09-05-1954	Cut back to become Sundays: DOUGLAS STREET & MARYHILL via CHARING CROSS;
	Weekdays: DUMBRECK or IBROX & MARYHILL via CHARING CROSS unaltered;
	Saturdays: IBROX & MARYHILL via CHARING CROSS unaltered.
22-08-1954	Sundays service withdrawn.
04-11-1956	Withdrawn without replacement.
DEPOT	*Until August 1945:* **Newlands and Partick**
	August 1945 until October 1945: **Govan and Partick**
	From October 1945: **Govan and Maryhill**

278

The Grand Hotel is the backdrop for this view of Standard Car 13 at Charing Cross heading for Maryhill on Service 40. *(RB Parr / STTS Collection)*

TYPES OF CAR *Until October 1945:* **Standard**
October 1945 until March 1953: **Standard, Coronation**
From March 1953: **Standard, Coronation, Mark II Coronation ['Cunarder']**
Also during 1948: **Experimental One-Way on Special Service 40>3 St Vincent Street-Mosspark-St Vincent Street only**

To explain a couple of mysteries

When Services 3 and 3A were altered in December 1943 the next available Service Number was 33 but, because the new Service DUMBRECK & ST VINCENT STREET being introduced would shadow Service 3 between Dumbreck and Mosspark, it was decided, to avoid a perceived confusion by the travelling public between similar numbers, to allocate it the number 40.

When the next new Service CIRCLE SPRINGBURN & CHARING CROSS was introduced in November 1944 it became 33.

In January 1949, it had been the plan to retain Service 10 KELVINSIDE & OATLANDS OR RUTHERGLEN by the expedient of diverting it between the south end of Hope Street and Rutherglen Road operating via Oswald Street, George V Bridge, Commerce Street, Nelson Street, Norfolk Street, Ballater Street and Crown Street using the curves from Ballater Street into Crown Street already in place for emergency use. The portion of the Service operating from Dalmarnock Depot would have been transferred to Govan Depot. To this end, indeed, the Govan Screens had '10' and the appropriate destinations added.

However, at the very last minute, the Ministry of Transport indicated it was not prepared to allow trams and trolleybuses to co-exist over the even relatively short stretch of Crown Street between Ballater Street and Rutherglen Road. This ruling came about because at that time the Ministry was nervous about allowing the operation of Bow Collectors alongside Trolley Poles. In later years a less stringent view was taken and indeed some sections where trams and trolleybuses were sanctioned to co-exist were considerably longer.

This directive resulted in a very hurried rearrangement of plans for the tram services in the east end of the city, bringing about changes to Service 34 and the introduction of Services 35 and 36. The new Services 34/35 so formed were soon found to be an over-provision only lasting some 18 weeks.

It is interesting to speculate the different form the tram system would have taken had Service 10 continued to run between Kelvinside and Oatlands/Rutherglen until the trolleybuses reached Rutherglen in the mid-fifties.

No new Services justifying a fresh number were introduced and, hence, 37, 38 and 39 remained unused.

Reference is made to the "Hampden Wheel" Service, but Football Specials were provided for all major fixtures at other senior football club grounds. In this view taken in March 1933, some thirty-odd Cars are lined up on both tracks in Broomloan Road, Ibrox, awaiting supporters from a *Rangers FC* home match. The eleventh car from the left still retains its open balcony. Most Cars will carry their passengers as far as Trongate, some running via Norfolk Street, Gorbals Cross, Victoria Bridge and Stockwell Street. Football Specials were also regularly operated to and from Celtic Park *(Celtic FC)*, Shawfield Park *(Clyde FC)*, Kelvinside Avenue *(Partick Thistle FC)*, Mount Florida, for Hampden Park *(Queen's Park FC)*, and, in earlier years, Cathkin Park *(Third Lanark FC)*. *(BJ Cross Collection)*

APPENDIX 'C'
GLASGOW CORPORATION TRAMWAY SLIPBOARDS

Slipboards were carried along the upper sides of trams from 1904 until the practice was discontinued during the Summer of 1938. So that the three places could appear in the correct geographical order on the appropriate side of the car, a reverse version was also provided. Note: Blue Service Z, unusually, originally carried deep boards listing nine points of interest.

Green A, D	GT WESTERN RD. - CAMBRIDGE ST. - DUKE ST.
	DUKE ST. - CAMBRIDGE ST. - GT WESTERN RD
Green ABB	No boards
Green B, U	PAISLEY RD. - JAMAICA ST. – GALLOWGATE
	GALLOWGATE - JAMAICA ST. - PAISLEY RD.
Yellow C, H	SAUCHIEHALL ST. - RENFIELD ST. - EGLINTON TOLL
	EGLINTON TOLL - RENFIELD ST. - SAUCHIEHALL ST.
	SAUCHIEHALL ST. - RENFIELD ST. - QUEEN'S PARK
	QUEEN'S PARK - RENFIELD ST. - SAUCHIEHALL ST.
Red CP	No Boards
White E	WOODLANDS RD. - SAUCHIEHALL ST. - RENFIELD ST.
	RENFIELD ST. - SAUCHIEHALL ST. - WOODLANDS RD.
Red F, L	DUMBARTON RD. - ARGYLE ST. - BRIDGETON +
	BRIDGETON + - ARGYLE ST. - DUMBARTON RD.
Blue G, K	COWCADDENS - PAISLEY RD. – GOVAN
	GOVAN - PAISLEY RD. - COWCADDENS
Green KIL	RENFREW FERRY AND KILBARCHAN] (mounted within saloon)
	RENFREW FERRY AND JOHNSTONE]
White HS	No boards
Yellow J	BELLGROVE - BRIDGETON - GLASGOW GREEN
	GLASGOW GREEN - BRIDGETON - BELLGROVE
Red M	NEW CITY RD. - STOCKWELL - CATHCART RD.
	CATHCART RD. - STOCKWELL - NEW CITY RD.
Red N	GARSCUBE RD. - STOCKWELL - POLLOKSHAWS RD.
	POLLOKSHAWS RD. - STOCKWELL - GARSCUBE RD.
Blue O	WOODLANDS ROAD - BOTHWELL ST. - SALTMARKET
	SALTMARKET - BOTHWELL ST. - WOODLANDS ROAD
Blue P	GORBALS - SHAWLANDS - BARRHEAD
	BARRHEAD - SHAWLANDS – GORBALS
	ST GEORGE'S + - GORBALS - SHAWLANDS
	SHAWLANDS - GORBALS - ST GEORGE'S +
Yellow Q	SHIELDS RD – NITHSDALE RD – ALLISON ST
	ALLISON ST – NITHSDALE RD – SHIELDS RD
Red R	Until April 1909 only:
	SPRINGBURN RD.- RENFIELD ST. - EGLINTON ST.
	EGLINTON ST. - RENFIELD ST. - SPRINGBURN RD.
	ALEXANDRA PARADE - RENFIELD ST. - EGLINTON ST.
	EGLINTON ST. - RENFIELD ST. -ALEXANDRA PARADE
	From April 1909: No Boards
Red RP	No Boards
White S, V	HIGH ST. - GLASGOW CROSS - CROWN ST.
	CROWN ST. - GLASGOW CROSS - HIGH ST.
Green SF	No boards
Red T	NEW CITY RD. - WEST NILE ST. - GLASSFORD ST.
	GLASSFORD ST. - WEST NILE ST. - NEW CITY RD.
Green UM	No boards
Green W	Until April 1905:
	ST GEORGE'S + - NORTH ST. - ST. VINCENT ST.
	ST VINCENT ST. - NORTH ST. - ST GEORGE'S +
	From April 1905:
	ST GEORGE'S + - NORTH ST. - DUMBARTON RD.
	DUMBARTON RD. - NORTH ST. - ST GEORGE'S +
Red X	ST. VINCENT ST. - BOTHWELL ST. - HOPE ST
	HOPE ST. - BOTHWELL ST. - ST. VINCENT ST
White Y	CHARING CROSS - BOTHWELL ST. - RUTHERGLEN BRIDGE
	RUTHERGLEN BRIDGE - BOTHWELL ST. - CHARING CROSS
Blue Z	Until August 1926:
	ROYAL INFIRMARY CHARING CROSS KELVINGROVE PARK
	CATHEDRAL THE MITCHELL LIBRARY ART GALLERIES
	FINE ART INSTITUTE ST ANDREW'S HALLS WESTERN INFIRMARY
	From August 1926:
	DUMBARTON RD. - CHARING CROSS - ALEXANDRA PARADE
	ALEXANDRA PARADE - CHARING CROSS - DUMBARTON RD.

APPENDIX 'D'
GLASGOW CORPORATION TRAMWAY HEADCODES

In parallel with the Route Colour System, prior to the introduction of Servcie Numbers in 1938, trams displayed, from the beginning of 1925, the following Headcodes. As can be seen, the system was over-complicated and invariably ignored by crews and the public alike.

Red R	*Northbound*		*Southbound*
1A	ALEXANDRA PARK	2	SHAWLANDS
1B	RIDDRIE	2A	NEWLANDS
1C	MILLERSTON	2B	MERRYLEE
1E	SPRINGBURN via CASTLE STREET	2C	GIFFNOCK via NEWLANDS
		2D	ROUKEN GLEN via GIFFNOCK
1J	BISHOPBRIGGS	2E	ROUKEN GLEN via POLLOKSHAWS
		2H	THORNLIEBANK via POLLOKSHAWS
		2J	POLLOKSHAWS WEST

Yellow C, H	*Northbound*		*Southbound*
3A	HYNDLAND	4A	BATTLEFIELD
3B	JORDANHILL	4B	CATHCART
3C	KIRKLEE	4C	NETHERLEE
		4D	CLARKSTON
		4E	LANGSIDE

Blue G, K	*Northbound*		*Southbound*
5A	POSSILPARK	6	LINTHOUSE
5B	LAMBHILL	6A	SHIELDHALL
5C	KEPPOCHHILL ROAD	6B	RENFREW
5D	SPRINGBURN via POSSILPARK	6C	PORTERFIELD ROAD
		6D	RENFREW DEPOT (later RENFREW SOUTH)

White E	*Northbound*		*Southbound*
7	UNIVERSITY	8	POLLOKSHIELDS
		8A	DUMBRECK
		8B	MOSSPARK

Red M, T	*Northbound*		*Southbound*
9	KELVINSIDE AVENUE via NEW CITY ROAD	10	MOUNT FLORIDA
9A	GAIRBRAID AVENUE		
9B	MARYHILL via NEW CITY ROAD		
9C	HILLFOOT via NEW CITY ROAD		
9D	MILNGAVIE via NEW CITY ROAD		

Red N	*Northbound*		*Southbound*
11	KELVINSIDE AVENUE via GARSCUBE ROAD	12	BATTLEFIELD
11A	GAIRBRAID AVENUE via GARSCUBE ROAD	12A	SINCLAIR DRIVE
11B	MARYHILL via GARSCUBE ROAD		
11C	HILLFOOT via GARSCUBE ROAD		

Blue P	Northbound		Southbound
9	KELVINSIDE AVENUE	14	SHAWLANDS
	via NEW CITY ROAD	14A	POLLOKSHAWS WEST
9A	GAIRBRAID AVENUE	14B	THORNLIEBANK
9B	MARYHILL via NEW CITY ROAD	14C	BARRHEAD
9C	HILLFOOT via NEW CITY ROAD	14D	PAISLEY CROSS via BARRHEAD
9D	MILNGAVIE via NEW CITY ROAD	14E	RENFREW FERRY via BARRHEAD

White S	Northbound		Southbound
15	SPRINGBURN	16	MOUNT FLORIDA
	via GLASGOW CROSS	16A	CATHCART
		16B	NETHERLEE

White V	Northbound		Southbound
17	GARNGAD	18	POLMADIE
17A	PROVANMILL		

Green A, D	Eastbound		Westbound
19	DENNISTOUN	20	BOTANIC GARDENS
19A	SHETTLESTON	20A	KELVINSIDE
19B	PARKHEAD	20B	ANNIESLAND
19C	SPRINGFIELD ROAD	20C	SCOTSTOUNHILL
			(later SCOTSTOUN WEST)
19E	BAILLIESTON		
19H	COATBRIDGE	20D	DALMUIR WEST
19J	AIRDRIE	20E	KNIGHTSWOOD

Green B, U, UM	Eastbound		Westbound
21	PARKHEAD	22	IBROX
21A	SHETTLESTON	22A	HALFWAY
21B	BAILLIESTON	22B	PAISLEY CROSS
21C	COATBRIDGE	22C	PAISLEY WEST
21D	AIRDRIE	22D	FERGUSLIE MILLS
21E	TOLLCROSS		
21H	BROOMHOUSE		
21J	UDDINGSTON		

Red F, L	Eastbound		Westbound
23A	DALMARNOCK	24	PARTICK
23B	RUTHERGLEN via DALMARNOCK	24A	SCOTSTOUN
23C	BURNSIDE via DALMARNOCK	24B	CLYDEBANK
23D	CAMBUSLANG	24C	DALMUIR
23E	LONDON ROAD	24D	DALMUIR WEST
23H	AUCHENSHUGGLE		

Red X	Eastbound		Westbound
25	DALMARNOCK	26	PARTICK via BOTHWELL STREET
25A	CAMBUSLANG	26A	ANNIESLAND

Blue O	Eastbound		Westbound
27	OATLANDS	28	KIRKLEE via PARK ROAD
27A	RUTHERGLEN via OATLANDS		
27B	BURNSIDE via OATLANDS		

White Y	Eastbound		Westbound
29	RUTHERGLEN	30	KELVINSIDE AVENUE
	via RUTHERGLEN BRIDGE		via CHARING CROSS
29A	BURNSIDE	30A	SPRINGBURN via BILSLAND DRIVE
	via RUTHERGLEN BRIDGE		

Yellow J	Eastbound		Westbound
31	ALEXANDRA PARK	32	PAISLEY ROAD TOLL
31A	RIDDRIE	32A	CRAIGTON ROAD
31B	MILLERSTON		(later BELLAHOUSTON)

Yellow Q		Westbound			Eastbound
33		PAISLEY ROAD TOLL	34		MOUNT FLORIDA
33A		IBROX			

Green W		Eastbound			Westbound
35		KEPPOCHHILL ROAD	36		WHITEINCH
			36A		SCOTSTOUN
			36B		CLYDEBANK

Blue Z		Eastbound			Westbound
37		ALEXANDRA PARK	38		KELVINSIDE CROSS
37A		RIDDRIE	38A		JORDANHILL

		Eastbound			Westbound
37		ALEXANDRA PARK	38		PARTICK
37A		RIDDRIE	38A		SCOTSTOUN
			38B		CLYDEBANK
			38C		DALMUIR
			38D		DALMUIR WEST

Red RP		Eastbound			Westbound
39		CLYDEBANK (KILBOWIE ROAD)	40		RADNOR PARK
39A		YOKER	40A		DUNTOCHER

Green ABB	No Code
Red CP	No Code
Green KIL	No Code
Green SF	No Code

LAST TRAM PROCESSION

We regret that no more applications for reserved seats on the vehicles in the LAST TRAM PROCESSION can be accepted.

APPENDIX 'E'
GLASGOW CORPORATION TRAMWAYS
NIGHT SERVICES

The very small number of trams required to operate the night services did not constitute the best use of Pinkston Power Station's massive potential. Motormen were pleased, however, to avail themselves of the higher Voltage that enabled high-speed running.

xx-09-1914	Proposals for Night Tram Services shelved due to outbreak of First World War
07-02-1921	Night Tram Services introduced. No Service on Sunday mornings.
	From City 0030, 0130, 0230, 0330. From outer termini 0100, 0200, 0300.
	Night Service ST VINCENT PLACE & POSSILPARK via Blue G route
	Night Service ST VINCENT PLACE & ANNIESLAND via Green D route
	Night Service ST VINCENT PLACE & ALEXANDRA PARK via DENNISTOUN via Green A Route then Yellow J route
	Night Service ST VINCENT PLACE & JORDANHILL via Yellow H route
	Night Service ST VINCENT PLACE & MOUNT FLORIDA via Red M route
	Night Service ST VINCENT PLACE & SPRINGBURN via Red R route
	Night Service TRONGATE & MARYHILL via Red T route
	Night Service ST VINCENT STREET & CATHCART via Yellow C route
	Night Service ST VINCENT STREET & LINTHOUSE via Blue K route
	Night Service ST VINCENT STREET & MERRYLEE via Red R route
	Night Service QUEEN STREET & SHETTLESTON via Green B route
	Night Service QUEEN STREET & CROOKSTON via Green U route
	Night Service QUEEN STREET & RUTHERGLEN via DALMARNOCK via Red F route.
	Night Service QUEEN STREET & SCOTSTOUN via Red L route
	Night Service QUEEN STREET & OATLANDS via Blue O route
21-02-1921	Night Service QUEEN STREET & OATLANDS via Blue O route withdrawn
	Night Service ST VINCENT PLACE & POSSILPARK via Blue G route withdrawn
01-11-1922	Night Service ST VINCENT PLACE & ALEXANDRA PARK via DENNISTOUN extended to become
	ST VINCENT PLACE & RIDDRIE via DENNISTOUN via Green A then Yellow J routes
28-02-1927	Night Service QUEEN STREET & RUTHERGLEN via DALMARNOCK extended to become
	QUEEN STREET & BURNSIDE via DALMARNOCK via Red F route
26-03-1928	Night Service ST VINCENT PLACE & ANNIESLAND extended to become
	ST VINCENT PLACE & KNIGHTSWOOD via Green D route
07-04-1930	Night Service QUEEN STREET & SCOTSTOUN extended to become
	QUEEN STREET & YOKER via Red L route
25-01-1932	The following Night Service commences:
	Night Service ST VINCENT PLACE & LAMBHILL via Blue G route.
01-04-1932	Night Service ST VINCENT PLACE & LAMBHILL via Blue G route withdrawn.
25-12-1932 only	Special Sunday Morning Service departs 0115 after Alhambra Theatre Charity Show to the usual Night Service Destinations with the following changes:
	Night Service QUEEN STREET & YOKER cut back to QUEEN STREET to SCOTSTOUN;
	Night Service ST VINCENT PLACE & RIDDRIE via DENNISTOUN diverted to become
	ST VINCENT PLACE to RIDDRIE via PARLIAMENTARY ROAD via Red R route;
	Night Service ST VINCENT STREET & MERRYLEE extended to become ST VINCENT STREET to GIFFNOCK via Red R route;
	The following Additional Services run:
	Night Service ST VINCENT STREET to MOSSPARK via POLLOKSHIELDS via White E route;
	Night Service ST VINCENT PLACE to POLLOKSHAWS WEST via GORBALS via Blue P route;
	Night Service ST VINCENT PLACE to POSSILPARK via Blue G route;
	Night Service QUEEN STREET to RUTHERGLEN via OATLANDS via Blue O route;
	Night Service QUEEN STREET to TOLLCROSS via Green U route;
	Night Service QUEEN STREET to KIRKLEE via PARK ROAD via Blue O route
27-12-1932 only	All Normal Night Services operate to a 30-minute frequency from City 0030-0330 and from outer termini 0100-0300.
01-01-1933 only	All Normal Night Services operate to a 10-minute frequency from City 0010-0400 and from outer termini 0010-0330.
	The following Additional Services run:
	Night Service GLASGOW CROSS & PROVANMILL via White V route;
	Night Service ST VINCENT PLACE & LAMBHILL via Blue G route.

285

03-01-1933 and 04-01-1933 only	All Normal Night Services operate to a 30-minute frequency from City 0030-0400 and from outer termini 0100-0330. The following Additional Service runs: Night Service ST VINCENT PLACE & LAMBHILL via **Blue G** route.
26-12-1933 only	All Normal Night Services operate to a 30-minute frequency from City 0030-0330 and from outer termini 0100-0300.
31-12-1933 only	Special Sunday Morning Service departs 0115 after Alhambra Theatre Charity Show to the usual Night Service Destinations with the following changes: Night Service ST VINCENT PLACE & RIDDRIE via DENNISTOUN diverted to become ST VINCENT PLACE to RIDDRIE via PARLIAMENTARY ROAD via **Red R** route; Night Service ST VINCENT STREET & MERRYLEE extended to become ST VINCENT STREET to GIFFNOCK via **Red R** route; The following Additional Services run: Night Service ST VINCENT STREET to MOSSPARK via POLLOKSHIELDS via **White E** route; Night Service ST VINCENT PLACE to POLLOKSHAWS WEST via GORBALS via **Blue P** route; Night Service ST VINCENT PLACE to POSSILPARK via **Blue G** route; Night Service QUEEN STREET to RUTHERGLEN via OATLANDS via **Blue O** route; Night Service QUEEN STREET to TOLLCROSS via **Green U** route; Night Service QUEEN STREET to KIRKLEE via PARK ROAD via **Blue O** route
01-01-1934 only	All Normal Night Services operate to a 10-minute frequency from City 2340-0400 and from outer termini 0010-0330. The following Additional Services run: Night Service GLASGOW CROSS & PROVANMILL via **White V** route; Night Service ST VINCENT PLACE & LAMBHILL via **Blue G** route.
02-01-1934 and 03-01-1934 only	All Normal Night Services operate to a 30-minute frequency from City 0030-0400 and from outer termini 0010-0330. The following Additional Service runs: Night Service ST VINCENT PLACE & LAMBHILL via **Blue G** route.
15-04-1934 only	Special Sunday Morning Service provided to cater for returning London Football traffic from England-v-Scotland International at Wembley: Night Service ST VINCENT PLACE to CLYDEBANK via **Green A** route; Night Service ST VINCENT PLACE to HILLFOOT via **Red M** route; Night Service ST VINCENT PLACE to SPRINGFIELD ROAD via **Green A** route; Night Service ST VINCENT PLACE to SHETTLESTON via **Green D** route; Night Service QUEEN STREET to CLYDEBANK via **Red L** route; Night Service QUEEN STREET to SHETTLESTON via **Green B** route; Night Service QUEEN STREET to OATLANDS via **Blue O** route; Night Service QUEEN STREET to CROOKSTON via **Green U** route; Night Service ST VINCENT STREET to SPRINGBURN via **Red R** route; Night Service ST VINCENT STREET to ALEXANDRA PARK via **Green A** route then **Yellow J** route; Night Service ST VINCENT STREET to LAMBHILL via **Blue G** route; Night Service ST VINCENT STREET to LINTHOUSE via **Blue K** route; Night Service ST VINCENT STREET to CATHCART via **Yellow C** route; Night Service ST VINCENT PLACE to POLLOKSHAWS WEST via **Blue P** route;
04-06-1934	Night Service ST VINCENT STREET & CATHCART extended to become ST VINCENT STREET & NETHERLEE via **Yellow C** route;
26-12-1934 only	All Normal Night Services operate to a 30-minute frequency from City 0030-0330 and from outer termini 0100-0300.
01-01-1935 only	All Normal Night Services operate to a 10-minute frequency from City 0010-0400 and from outer termini 0010-0330. The following Additional Services run: Night Service GLASGOW CROSS & PROVANMILL via **White V** route; Night Service ST VINCENT PLACE & LAMBHILL via **Blue G** route.
02-01-1935 only	All Normal Night Services operate to a 30-minute frequency from City 0030-0400 and from outer termini 0100-0300. The following Additional Service runs: Night Service ST VINCENT PLACE & LAMBHILL via **Blue G** route.
25-01-1935	Night Service ST VINCENT PLACE & MARYHILL extended experimentally to become ST VINCENT PLACE & HILLFOOT via **Red M** route.
04-02-1935	Night Service ST VINCENT PLACE & HILLFOOT via **Red M** route confirmed.
04-03-1935	Night Service ST VINCENT STREET & MERRYLEE extended to become ST VINCENT STREET & GIFFNOCK via **Red R** route;
07-10-1935	Night Service ST VINCENT STREET & NETHERLEE extended to become ST VINCENT STREET & CLARKSTON via **Yellow C** route; Night Service ST VINCENT STREET & SPRINGBURN extended to become ST VINCENT STREET & RUCHILL (BALMORE ROAD) via **Red R** route then **White Y** route
16-11-1935	Night Service QUEEN STREET & SHETTLESTON extended to become QUEEN STREET & BAILLIESTON via **Green B** route.
29-12-1935 only	Special Sunday Morning Service departs 0115 after Alhambra Theatre Charity Show to the usual Night Service Destinations with the following changes:

	Night Service ST VINCENT PLACE & RIDDRIE via DENNISTOUN diverted to become ST VINCENT PLACE to RIDDRIE via PARLIAMENTARY ROAD via **Red R** route
	Night Service ST VINCENT STREET & RUCHILL (BALMORE ROAD) cut back to become ST VINCENT STREET to SPRINGBURN via **Red R** route
	Night Service QUEEN STREET & BAILLIESTON cut back to become QUEEN STREET to SHETTLESTON via **Green B** route.
	The following Additional Services run:
	Night Service ST VINCENT STREET to MOSSPARK via POLLOKSHIELDS via **White E** route;
	Night Service ST VINCENT PLACE to POLLOKSHAWS WEST via GORBALS via **Blue P** route;
	Night Service ST VINCENT PLACE to POSSILPARK via **Blue G** route;
	Night Service QUEEN STREET to RUTHERGLEN via OATLANDS via **Blue O** route;
	Night Service QUEEN STREET to TOLLCROSS via **Green U** route;
	Night Service QUEEN STREET to KIRKLEE via PARK ROAD via **Blue O** route
14-12-1936	Night Service ST VINCENT PLACE & RIDDRIE via DENNISTOUN extended to become ST VINCENT PLACE & MILLERSTON via DENNISTOUN via **Green A** route then **Yellow J** route.
18-01-1937	Sandyhills Railway Bridge closed for repairs. Night Service QUEEN STREET & BAILLIESTON temporarily curtailed to become QUEEN STREET & SANDYHILLS BRIDGE via **Green B** route.
01-03-1937	Sandyhills Railway Bridge repairs completed. Night Service QUEEN STREET & BAILLIESTON via **Green B** route resumes normal route.
04-10-1937	Night Service ST VINCENT PLACE & MILLERSTON via DENNISTOUN diverted to become ST VINCENT PLACE & MILLERSTON via PARLIAMENTARY ROAD via **Red R** route. Night Service QUEEN STREET & BAILLIESTON diverted to become ST VINCENT PLACE & BAILLIESTON via **Green D** route The following Services introduced: Night Service QUEEN STREET & TOLLCROSS via **Green U** route; Night Service ST VINCENT STREET & THORNLIEBANK via **Red R** route.
20-12-1937	Night Service ST VINCENT PLACE & HILLFOOT extended to become ST VINCENT PLACE & MILNGAVIE via **Red M** route.
17-01-1938	Night Service ST VINCENT PLACE & MILNGAVIE cut back to become ST VINCENT PLACE & HILLFOOT via **Red M** route.
17-10-1938	Caldercuilt Railway Bridge at Maryhill Station closed for repairs. Night Service ST VINCENT PLACE & HILLFOOT temporarily curtailed to become ST VINCENT PLACE & MARYHILL via **Red 13** route. **Shuttle Motorbus Service** MARYHILL & HILLFOOT.
12-12-1938	The following Service commences: Night Service ST VINCENT STREET & RUCHILL (BALMORE ROAD) via CHARING CROSS via Renfield Street, Sauchiehall Street then **White 18** route.
26-12-1938	Caldercuilt Railway Bridge at Maryhill Station reopened. Night Service ST VINCENT PLACE & HILLFOOT via **Red 13** route reverts to normal route.
09-03-1939	Subsidence at Duke Street at Hunter Street. Cars turn on temporary crossovers on either side at John Street and at Ladywell Street. Night Service ST VINCENT PLACE & BAILLIESTON split accordingly.
04-04-1939	Duke Street reopened at Hunter Street Night Service ST VINCENT PLACE & BAILLIESTON via **Green 1** route reverts to normal route.
12-02-1940	Night Service ST VINCENT PLACE & MOUNT FLORIDA extended to become ST VINCENT PLACE & NETHERLEE via **Service 13** route. Black-out timetables commence on all services. Revised times for Night Services: From City 0030, 0200, 0330; From outer termini 0115, 0245.
08-04-1940	The following Service commences: Night Service QUEEN STREET & PAISLEY CROSS via **Service 15** route with times: From City 0145, 0245; From outer terminus to City 0150, to Lorne School 0332.
11-11-1940	Night Service ST VINCENT STREET & LINTHOUSE extended to become ST VINCENT STREET & SHIELDHALL via **Service 4** route.
14-03-1941 and 15-03-1941	Clydeside Blitz. Night Services seriously disrupted. The following Services suspended: Night Service ST VINCENT STREET & SHIELDHALL via **Service 4** route. Night Service QUEEN STREET & CROOKSTON via **Service 15** route. Night Service QUEEN STREET & PAISLEY CROSS via **Service 15** route Night Service QUEEN STREET & YOKER via **Service 9** route.

28-03-1941	Clydeside Blitz.
	The following Services resume:
	Night Service ST VINCENT STREET & SHIELDHALL via **Service 4** route.
	Night Service QUEEN STREET & CROOKSTON via **Service 15** route.
	Night Service QUEEN STREET & PAISLEY CROSS via **Service 15** route
xx-04-1941	Clydeside Blitz.
	The following Service resumes:
	Night Service QUEEN STREET & YOKER via **Service 9** route.
24-11-1941	Revisal of times for Night Services:
	All Night Services except Paisley: From City 0000, 0130, 0330:
	From outer termini: 0120
30-11-1941	Introduction of Sunday Services.
	All Night Services commence operation on Sunday mornings.
07-03-1943	Night Services numbered.
	Night Service ST VINCENT PLACE & JORDANHILL extended to become
	ST VINCENT PLACE & ANNIESLAND via HYNDLAND via **Service 5A** route.
	Night Service ST VINCENT STREET & THORNLIEBANK extended to become
	ST VINCENT STREET & ROUKEN GLEN via THORNLIEBANK via **Service 8A** route.
	Night Service QUEEN STREET & BURNSIDE via DALMARNOCK diverted to become
	QUEEN STREET & BURNSIDE via CROWN STREET, OATLANDS via **Service 10** route
	The following Service commences:
	Night Service QUEEN STREET & CAMBUSLANG via **Service 17** route.
	All Night Services except Paisley: From City 0030, 0200, 0330.
	From outer termini: 0115, 0245.
	PAISLEY CROSS Night Service: From City 0100, 0245;
	From outer terminus to City 0150; to Lorne School 0332.
15-08-1943	Night Service QUEEN STREET & CROOKSTON diverted to become ST VINCENT STREET & CROOKSTON via **Service 22** route.
	Night Service QUEEN STREET & PAISLEY CROSS diverted to become ST VINCENT STREET & PAISLEY CROSS via **Service 21** route.
04-03-1945	The following Service commences:
	Night Service ST VINCENT PLACE & PROVANMILL via RENFIELD STREET via **Service 32** route.
16-06-1945	Water Mains Pipe Works in Argyle Street at Kent Road.
	Night Service QUEEN STREET & YOKER diverted via Hope Street, Bothwell Street, Elmbank Street, Sauchiehall Street.
23-09-1945	Duplicate cars provided at 0400 hrs on the following services from City:
	Night Service ST VINCENT STREET & CROOKSTON;
	Night Service ST VINCENT STREET & SHIELDHALL;
	Night Service ST VINCENT PLACE & BAILLIESTON;
	Night Service QUEEN STREET & YOKER;
	Night Service ST VINCENT PLACE & SPRINGBURN via PARLIAMENTARY ROAD
05-11-1945	Night Service QUEEN STREET & BURNSIDE via CROWN STREET, OATLANDS rediverted to become
	QUEEN STREET & BURNSIDE via DALMARNOCK via **Service 26** route.
	Night Service ST VINCENT STREET & ROUKEN GLEN via THORNLIEBANK cut back to become
	ST VINCENT STREET & THORNLIEBANK via **Service 25** route.
07-11-1945	Water mains pipe works in Argyle Street at Kent Road completed.
	Night Service QUEEN STREET & YOKER via **Service 9** route resumes normal working.
26-11-1945	The following Service commences:
	Night Service BAILLIESTON & AIRDRIE connecting with ST VINCENT PLACE & BAILLIESTON service.
03-02-1946	Reduction in Night Tram Services with expansion of Night Motorbus Services.
	Revisal of times of Night Tram Services.
	All Night Services except Paisley. From City 0030 only.
	From outer termini withdrawn.
	Night Service ST VINCENT STREET & PAISLEY CROSS extended to become
	ST VINCENT STREET to ELDERSLIE via **Service 21** route. From City only 0030.
15-06-1946	Night Service ST VINCENT PLACE to BAILLIESTON duplicated on Saturday and Sunday mornings.
18-08-1946	Erection of Traffic Barrier at Eglinton Toll.
	Night Service ST VINCENT STREET to CLARKSTON diverted to become
	ST VINCENT PLACE to CLARKSTON via GORBALS, BATTLEFIELD via revised **Service 5** route.
27-10-1946	Last Cars on all daytime tram services revert to 2345. Night Tram Services (except Airdrie) withdrawn:
	Night Service ST VINCENT PLACE to KNIGHTSWOOD via **Service 30** route;
	Night Service ST VINCENT PLACE to MILLERSTON via PARLIAMENTARY ROAD via **Service 8** route;
	Night Service ST VINCENT PLACE to ANNIESLAND via HYNDLAND via **Service 24** route;
	Night Service ST VINCENT PLACE to NETHERLEE via **Service 13** route;

	Night Service ST VINCENT PLACE to SPRINGBURN via PARLIAMENTARY ROAD via **Service 25** route;
	Night Service ST VINCENT PLACE to BAILLIESTON via **Service 23** route;
	Night Service ST VINCENT PLACE to CLARKSTON via GORBALS, BATTLEFIELD via **Service 5** route;
	Night Service ST VINCENT PLACE to RUCHILL (BALMORE ROAD) via CHARING CROSS via Sauchiehall Street and **Service 18** route;
	Night Service ST VINCENT PLACE to PROVANMILL via **Service 32** route;
	Night Service TRONGATE to HILLFOOT via **Service 13** route;
	Night Service ST VINCENT STREET to SHIELDHALL via **Service 4** route;
	Night Service ST VINCENT STREET to THORNLIEBANK via **Service 25** route;
	Night Service ST VINCENT STREET to GIFFNOCK via **Service 8** route;
	Night Service ST VINCENT STREET to CROOKSTON via **Service 22** route;
	Night Service ST VINCENT STREET to ELDERSLIE via **Service 21** route;
	Night Service QUEEN STREET to YOKER via **Service 9** route;
	Night Service QUEEN STREET to TOLLCROSS via **Service 29** route;
	Night Service QUEEN STREET to CAMBUSLANG via **Service 17** route;
	Night Service QUEEN STREET to BURNSIDE via DALMARNOCK via **Service 26** route;
	All withdrawn.
	Night Service at BAILLIESTON & AIRDRIE continues to connect with Night Motorbus Service at BAILLIESTON; From Airdrie 0058; From Baillieston 0132.
26-11-1948	Coatbridge Depot Staff Car becomes Night Service: COATBRIDGE DEPOT & DENNISTOUN DEPOT. From Coatbridge Depot 0303; From Dennistoun Depot 0350 for Airdrie, then to Coatbridge Depot.
04-11-1956	Withdrawal of Airdrie and Coatbridge trams. Night Service BAILLIESTON & AIRDRIE withdrawn.
16-12-1956	Suez Crisis: rationing of Oil Supplies Certain Motorbus Night Services converted to tram operation. The following Services commence: **Night Service 1** QUEEN STREET & TOLLCROSS via **Service 29** route; **Night Service 9** QUEEN STREET & YOKER **Night Service 16** QUEEN STREET & BURNSIDE via DALMARNOCK via **Service 26** route; **Night Service 19** QUEEN STREET & MARYHILL via **Service 29** route; **Night Service 23** ST VINCENT STREET & BAILLIESTON from St Vincent St at Wellington St. From City 0100, 0215, 0330 and approx 0430 to Depot (except NS 16 and NS 19). From outer termini 0137, 0252 and approx 0400.
01-01-1957	Increased frequencies on all Services as follows: **Night Service 1** Every 10 minutes 0010-0210; every 12 minutes until 0346 then 0357, 0407 and 0430 to PARKHEAD DEPOT; **Night Service 9** Every 10 minutes 0010-0330; every 10 minutes to PARTICK until 0440 **Night Service 16** Every 15 minutes 0015-0100; every 12 minutes until 0324; every 15 minutes until 0409; **Night Service 19** Every 15 minutes 0045-0330; then to MARYHILL DEPOT until 0415 and 0426; **Night Service 23** at 0010, 0020, then every 20 minutes until 0340 then at 0400, 0412, 0432, 0444 to DENNISTOUN DEPOT.
02-01-1957	Increased frequencies on all Services as follows: **Night Service 1** Every 15 minutes 0015-0345; then to PARKHEAD DEPOT until 0430; **Night Service 9** Every 15 minutes 0015-0330; then to PARTICK every 15 minutes 0337-0437; **Night Service 16** As 01-01-1957 **Night Service 19** As 01-01-1957 **Night Service 23** at 0011, 0040, 0055, 0155 and every 15 minutes until 0345 then to DENNISTOUN DEPOT 0402, 0432.
24-02-1957	**Night Service 16** QUEEN STREET & BURNSIDE via DALMARNOCK withdrawn and replaced by Motorbus Night Service 16.
17-03-1957	**Night Service 23** ST VINCENT STREET & BAILLIESTON withdrawn and replaced by Motorbus Night Service 23.
31-03-1957	**Night Service 1** QUEEN STREET & TOLLCROSS withdrawn and replaced by Motorbus Night Service 1. **Night Service 9** QUEEN STREET & YOKER withdrawn and replaced by Motorbus Night Service 9. **Night Service 19** QUEEN STREET & MARYHILL withdrawn and replaced by Motorbus Night Service 19.
Note:	*Throughout the operation of Night Tram Services there were occasions when engineering operations on the track necessitated substitution of tramcars by motorbuses.*

APPENDIX 'F'
GLASGOW CORPORATION TRAMWAYS
DESTINATION DISPLAYS

Originally, Destinations were displayed on boards on the front and rear augmented by Route/Via boards mounted in the centre window of the lower saloon. These were soon replaced by roller blind screens in similar positions, supplemented for a while by additional boards hung at the end windows for which brackets survived on cars until the end. At the time of modernisation of Standard Cars, new Destination Boxes combining both screens were provided. At that time, the Side Route Screen boxes were removed, only being retained on Single-Deck cars for use of Destination Screens. Screen lists were compiled, per Depot, but according to the Colour of the Car carrying them. This restricted the Cars' route availability, hence individual cars became associated with particular routes. Each Depot had Screens for "Specials" and Cars allocated to these duties would have their screens switched over. Instructions detailing the Route or "Via" displays to be used were published to the Staff and those form the basis of the lists below.

SERVICE/ROUTE

Route	Colour	Headcode	Number	DESTINATION	VIA DISPLAY
ABB	Green		--	ABBOTSINCH	(None)
			--	SPRINGBANK ROAD	(None)
			--	PAISLEY CROSS	(None)
AD	Green	20D	1A	DALMUIR WEST	VIA ANNIESLAND
			1A	DALMUIR	VIA ANNIESLAND
			1A	CLYDEBANK	VIA ANNIESLAND
			1A	YOKER	VIA ANNIESLAND
		20C	1A	SCOTSTOUN WEST	VIA BOTANIC GARDENS
		20C	1A	SCOTSTOUNHILL	VIA BOTANIC GARDENS
		20E	1	KNIGHTSWOOD	VIA BOTANIC GARDENS
		20B	1/1A	ANNIESLAND	VIA KELVINSIDE
		20A	1/1A	KELVINSIDE	VIA ST GEORGE'S CROSS
		20	1/1A	BOTANIC GARDENS	VIA ST GEORGE'S CROSS
			1/1A	PARTICK	
			1/1A	ST VINCENT PL	VIA ST GEORGE'S CROSS
			1/1A	GEORGE SQUARE	VIA ST GEORGE'S CROSS
			1/1A	NORTH ALBION ST	VIA ST VINCENT PL
		19	1	DENNISTOUN	VIA ST VINCENT PL
			1	CARNTYNE	VIA DENNISTOUN
		19A	1	SHETTLESTON	VIA DENNISTOUN
			1	BARRACHNIE	VIA SHETTLESTON
			1	GARROWHILL	VIA SHETTLESTON
		19E	1	BAILLIESTON	VIA SHETTLESTON
			1	BARGEDDIE	VIA SHETTLESTON
		19H	1	COATBRIDGE	VIA SHETTLESTON
		19J	1	AIRDRIE	VIA SHETTLESTON
		19B	1A	PARKHEAD	VIA DENNISTOUN
		19C	1A	SPRINGFIELD RD	VIA DENNISTOUN
BU	Green	-	15/15A	ELDERSLIE	VIA PAISLEY
		22D	15/15A	FERGUSLIE MILLS	VIA PAISLEY
		22C	15/15A	PAISLEY WEST	VIA IBROX
		22B	15/15A	PAISLEY CROSS	VIA IBROX
			15/15A	CROOKSTON	VIA IBROX
		22A	15/15A	HALFWAY	VIA PAISLEY RD TOLL
		22	15/15A	IBROX	VIA PAISLEY RD TOLL
			15/15A	LORNE SCHOOL	VIA PAISLEY RD TOLL
			15/15A	LORNE SCHOOL	VIA IBROX
			15/15A	ANDERSTON CROSS	VIA PARKHEAD
			15/15A	QUEEN STREET	VIA PARKHEAD
			15/15A	GLASGOW CROSS	
			15/15A	WHITEVALE	
		21	15/15A	PARKHEAD	VIA GLASGOW BRIDGE
		21A	15	SHETTLESTON	VIA PARKHEAD

290

			15	BARRACHNIE	VIA SHETTLESTON
			15	GARROWHILL	VIA SHETTLESTON
		21B	15	BAILLIESTON	VIA SHETTLESTON
			15	BARGEDDIE	VIA SHETTLESTON
		21C	15	COATBRIDGE	VIA SHETTLESTON
		21D	15	AIRDRIE	VIA SHETTLESTON
		21E	15A	TOLLCROSS	VIA PARKHEAD
		21H	15A	BROOMHOUSE	VIA TOLLCROSS
		21J	15A	UDDINGSTON	VIA TOLLCROSS
CH	Yellow	3C	5	KIRKLEE	VIA BOTANIC GARDENS
		3C	5	KIRKLEE	VIA HYNDLAND
			5	BOTANIC GARDENS	VIA CHARING CROSS
			5A	ANNIESLAND	VIA HYNDLAND
		3B	5A	JORDANHILL	VIA HYNDLAND
			5A	BROOMHILL CROSS	VIA HYNDLAND
		3A	5A	HYNDLAND	VIA CHARING CROSS
			5A	PARTICK	(None)
			5/5A	PARTICK	VIA CHARING CROSS
			5/5A	ST VINCENT ST	VIA GLASGOW BRIDGE
		4E	5A	LANGSIDE	VIA QUEEN'S PARK
		4A	5	BATTLEFIELD	VIA QUEEN'S PARK
		4B	5	CATHCART	VIA BATTLEFIELD
		4C	5	NETHERLEE	VIA CATHCART
		4D	5	CLARKSTON	VIA CATHCART
E	White	7	3	UNIVERSITY	VIA CHARING CROSS
			3	CHARING CROSS	VIA GLASGOW BRIDGE
			3	MARYHILL	VIA CHARING CROSS
			3	ST VINCENT ST	VIA GLASGOW BRIDGE
			3	EGLINTON TOLL	VIA GLASGOW BRIDGE
			3	NEWLANDS	VIA GLASGOW BRIDGE
		8	3	POLLOKSHIELDS	VIA GLASGOW BRIDGE
		8A	3	DUMBRECK	VIA POLLOKSHIELDS
		8B	3	MOSSPARK	VIA POLLOKSHIELDS
			3	EXHIBITION	VIA POLLOKSHIELDS

Car 289, below, was photographed at Uddingston terminus in 1936 and illustrates very well why the Headcode system fell out of use. Quite apart from the hard work in changing the screens in non-geared indicator boxes the displays were not readily seen in an approaching tram.
(MJ O'Connor / National Tramway Museum Archive)

When the first Coronation trams were placed in service, the Headcodes became prominent for the first time and indeed the apertures within the indicator boxes were designed to accommodate them.

	White		3A	ANNIESLAND	VIA CHARING CROSS
			3A	JORDANHILL	VIA CHARING CROSS
			3A	HYNDLAND	VIA CHARING CROSS
			3A	KELVINGROVE	VIA CHARING CROSS
			3A	MOSSPARK	VIA PAISLEY RD
			3A	EXHIBITION	VIA PAISLEY RD
FL	Red	24D	9	DALMUIR WEST	VIA SCOTSTOUN
		24C	9	DALMUIR	VIA SCOTSTOUN
		24B	9	CLYDEBANK	VIA SCOTSTOUN
			9	YOKER	VIA SCOTSTOUN
			9	SCOTSTOUN WEST	VIA PARTICK
		24A	9	SCOTSTOUN	VIA PARTICK
			9	WHITEINCH	VIA PARTICK
		24	9	PARTICK	VIA SCOTSTOUN
		24	9	PARTICK	VIA ARGYLE ST
			9	FINNIESTON	VIA ANDERSTON CROSS
			9	ANDERSTON CROSS	VIA ARGYLE ST
			9	QUEEN STREET	VIA ANDERSTON CROSS
			9	GLASGOW CROSS	VIA ANDERSTON CROSS
		23E	9	LONDON ROAD	VIA BRIDGETON CROSS
		23H	9	AUCHENSHUGGLE	VIA BRIDGETON CROSS
		23A	9B	DALMARNOCK	VIA BRIDGETON CROSS
		23B	9B	RUTHERGLEN	VIA DALMARNOCK
		23C	9A	BURNSIDE	VIA DALMARNOCK
		23D	9B	CAMBUSLANG	VIA DALMARNOCK
GK	Blue	5B	4B	LAMBHILL	VIA POSSILPARK
		5D	4A	SPRINGBURN	VIA POSSILPARK
		5A	4A	POSSILPARK	VIA MOSSHOUSE
		5C	4	KEPPOCHHILL RD	VIA MOSSHOUSE
			4	MOSSHOUSE	VIA NORMAL SCHOOL
			4	NORMAL SCHOOL	VIA COWCADDENS
			4	ST VINCENT ST	VIA GLASGOW BRIDGE
			4	ST VINCENT ST	VIA GEORGE V. BRIDGE
			4	COMMERCE ST	VIA GEORGE V. BRIDGE
G			4A/4B	LORNE SCHOOL	VIA PAISLEY RD
K			4	LORNE SCHOOL	VIA OLD GOVAN ROAD
K		6	4	LINTHOUSE	VIA OLD GOVAN ROAD
G		6	4A/4B	LINTHOUSE	VIA PAISLEY RD
K		6A	4	SHIELDHALL	VIA OLD GOVAN ROAD
G		6A	4A/4B	SHIELDHALL	VIA PAISLEY RD
			4	HILLINGTON ROAD	VIA OLD GOVAN ROAD
		6B	4	RENFREW	VIA OLD GOVAN ROAD
		6C	4	PORTERFIELD ROAD	VIA RENFREW
			4	RENFREW SOUTH	VIA LINTHOUSE
		6D	4	RENFREW AERODROME	VIA RENFREW
		6D	4	RENFREW DEPOT	VIA LINTHOUSE
J	Yellow	31B	7	MILLERSTON	VIA BRIDGETON CROSS
		31A	7	RIDDRIE	VIA BRIDGETON CROSS
		31	7	ALEXANDRA PARK	VIA BRIDGETON CROSS
			7	DENNISTOUN	VIA BRIDGETON CROSS
			-	JAMES ST BRIDGE	VIA BRIDGETON CROSS
			-	JAMES ST BRIDGE	VIA PAISLEY RD TOLL
		32	7	PAISLEY RD TOLL	VIA BRIDGETON CROSS
		32A	-	CRAIGTON ROAD	VIA OLD GOVAN ROAD
		32A	7	BELLAHOUSTON	VIA OLD GOVAN ROAD
KIL	Green		-	RENFREW FERRY	VIA PAISLEY CROSS
			-	RENFREW DEPOT	VIA PAISLEY CROSS
			-	PAISLEY CROSS	(None)
			-	HAWKHEAD ROAD	VIA PAISLEY CROSS
			-	JOHNSTONE CENTRE	VIA PAISLEY CROSS
			-	KILBARCHAN	VIA PAISLEY CROSS
M	Red	9D	13	MILNGAVIE	VIA ST GEORGE'S CROSS
		9C	13	HILLFOOT	VIA ST GEORGE'S CROSS
			13	CANNIESBURN	VIA MARYHILL
			13	KILLERMONT	VIA MARYHILL
		9B	13	MARYHILL	VIA ST GEORGE'S CROSS
		9A	13	GAIRBRAID AVENUE	VIA NEW CITY RD
			-	BARRACKS GATE	VIA NEW CITY RD

			13	GLASSFORD ST	VIA NORMAL SCHOOL
			13	GORBALS	VIA STOCKWELL ST
			13	GOVANHILL	VIA STOCKWELL ST
		10	13	MOUNT FLORIDA	VIA GOVANHILL
			13	CATHCART	VIA MOUNT FLORIDA
			13	NETHERLEE	VIA MOUNT FLORIDA
			13	CLARKSTON	VIA MOUNT FLORIDA
N	Red	11C	-	HILLFOOT	VIA GARSCUBE RD
		11B	11	MARYHILL	VIA GARSCUBE RD
		11A	11	GAIRBRAID AVENUE	VIA GARSCUBE RD
			11	RUCHILL	VIA GARSCUBE RD
		11	11	KELVINSIDE AVENUE	VIA GARSCUBE RD
			-	QUEEN'S CROSS	VIA GARSCUBE RD
			-	GLASSFORD ST	VIA GARSCUBE RD
			11	GORBALS	VIA STOCKWELL ST
		12	11	BATTLEFIELD	VIA QUEEN'S PARK
		12A	11	SINCLAIR DRIVE	VIA QUEEN'S PARK
			11	MILNGAVIE	VIA ST GEORGE'S CROSS
			11	HILLFOOT	VIA ST GEORGE'S CROSS
			11	CANNIESBURN	VIA ST GEORGE'S CROSS
			11	MARYHILL	VIA ST GEORGE'S CROSS
			11	GAIRBRAID AVENUE	VIA ST GEORGE'S CROSS
			11	KELVINSIDE AVENUE	VIA ST GEORGE'S CROSS
O	Blue	28	10	KIRKLEE	VIA CHARING CROSS
					or VIA PARK ROAD
			10	BOTANIC GARDENS	VIA PARK ROAD
			10	PARK ROAD	VIA WOODLANDS RD
			10	ST VINCENT ST	VIA HOPE STREET
			10	PARTICK	VIA ANDERSTON CROSS
			10	ANDERSTON CROSS	VIA CROWN STREET
			10	QUEEN STREET	VIA CROWN STREET
			10	GLASGOW CROSS	VIA CHARING CROSS
		27	10	OATLANDS	VIA CROWN STREET
		27A	10	RUTHERGLEN	VIA OATLANDS
		27B	-	BURNSIDE	VIA RUTHERGLEN
P	Blue	9D	14	MILNGAVIE	VIA GORBALS ***
		9C	14	HILLFOOT	VIA GORBALS ***
			14	CANNIESBURN	VIA NEW CITY RD
			14	KILLERMONT	VIA NEW CITY RD
		9B	14	MARYHILL	VIA GORBALS ***
		9A	14	GAIRBRAID AVENUE	VIA NEW CITY RD
		9	14	KELVINSIDE AVENUE	VIA NEW CITY RD
			-	ST VINCENT PLACE	VIA GORBALS
			14	ST VINCENT PLACE	VIA NEW CITY RD
			14	GORBALS	VIA NEW CITY RD
		14	14	SHAWLANDS	VIA GORBALS
			14	NEWLANDS	VIA GORBALS
		14A	14	POLLOKSHAWS WEST	VIA GORBALS
		14B	14	THORNLIEBANK	VIA POLLOKSHAWS WEST
			14	SPIERSBRIDGE	VIA THORNLIEBANK
			14	SPIERSBRIDGE	VIA BARRHEAD
		14C	14	BARRHEAD	VIA POLLOKSHAWS WEST
			14	POTTERHILL	VIA PAISLEY CROSS
			14	ELDERSLIE	VIA PAISLEY CROSS
		14D	14	PAISLEY CROSS	VIA BARRHEAD
			14	RENFREW DEPOT	VIA BARRHEAD
			14	PORTERFIELD ROAD	VIA PAISLEY CROSS
			14	RENFREW	VIA BARRHEAD
		14E	14	RENFREW FERRY	VIA BARRHEAD
			14	MILNGAVIE	VIA GARSCUBE RD
			14	HILLFOOT	VIA GARSCUBE RD
			14	CANNIESBURN	VIA GARSCUBE RD
			14	MARYHILL	VIA GARSCUBE RD
			14	GAIRBRAID AVENUE	VIA GARSCUBE RD
			14	ST VINCENT PL	VIA GARSCUBE RD
			14	GORBALS	VIA GARSCUBE RD

***   On journeys from Renfrew Ferry and Paisley show VIA BARRHEAD until arrival there then VIA GORBALS.

Q	Yellow	34	12	MOUNT FLORIDA	VIA SHIELDS ROAD
		33	12	PAISLEY RD TOLL	VIA SHIELDS ROAD
		33A	12	IBROX	VIA PAISLEY RD TOLL
			12	LINTHOUSE	VIA PAISLEY RD TOLL
			12	SHIELDHALL	VIA PAISLEY RD TOLL
R	Red	1C	8A	MILLERSTON	VIA ALEXANDRA PARK
		1B	8A	RIDDRIE	VIA ALEXANDRA PARK
		1A	8A	ALEXANDRA PARK	VIA CASTLE STREET
		1J	8	BISHOPBRIGGS	VIA SPRINGBURN
		1E	8	SPRINGBURN	VIA CASTLE STREET
			8/8A	ST VINCENT ST	VIA GLASGOW BRIDGE
			8/8A	BRIDGE STREET	VIA GLASGOW BRIDGE
		2	8/8A	SHAWLANDS	VIA GLASGOW BRIDGE
		2A	8	NEWLANDS	VIA SHAWLANDS
		2B	8B	MERRYLEE	VIA SHAWLANDS
		2C	8	GIFFNOCK	VIA NEWLANDS
		2D	8	ROUKEN GLEN	VIA GIFFNOCK
		2J	8A	POLLOKSHAWS WEST	VIA SHAWLANDS
			8A	CARNWADRIC	VIA POLLOKSHAWS WEST
		2H	8A	THORNLIEBANK	VIA POLLOKSHAWS WEST
		2E	8A	ROUKEN GLEN	VIA THORNLIEBANK
RP	Red	40A	20	DUNTOCHER	(None)
			20	PARKHALL	(None)
		40	20	RADNOR PARK	(None)
		39	20	CLYDEBANK	(None)
		39A	20	YOKER	(None)
			20	PARTICK	(None)
S	White	15	19	SPRINGBURN	VIA GLASGOW CROSS
			19	GLASGOW CROSS	(None)
		16	19	MOUNT FLORIDA	VIA GLASGOW CROSS
		16A	19	CATHCART	VIA MOUNT FLORIDA
		16B	19	NETHERLEE	VIA MOUNT FLORIDA
T	Red	9C	-	HILLFOOT	VIA NEW CITY RD
			-	CANNIESBURN	VIA NEW CITY RD
			-	KILLERMONT	VIA NEW CITY RD
		9B	-	MARYHILL	VIA NEW CITY RD
		9A	-	GAIRBRAID AVENUE	VIA NEW CITY RD
			-	BARRACKS GATE	VIA NEW CITY RD
		9	-	KELVINSIDE AVENUE	VIA NEW CITY RD
			-	QUEEN'S CROSS	VIA NEW CITY RD
			-	SEAMORE ST	VIA ST GEORGE'S CROSS
			-	GLASSFORD ST	VIA NEW CITY RD
			-	TRONGATE	VIA NEW CITY RD
			-	GORBALS	VIA STOCKWELL ST
			-	JAMIESON STREET	VIA STOCKWELL ST
			-	GOVANHILL	VIA STOCKWELL ST
		10	-	MOUNT FLORIDA	VIA GOVANHILL
UM	Green	21J	-	UDDINGSTON	VIA TOLLCROSS
		21H	-	BROOMHOUSE	VIA TOLLCROSS
			-	HOPE STREET	VIA GLASSFORD ST
			-	GAIRBRAID AVENUE	VIA MARYHILL RD
V	White	17A	2	PROVANMILL	VIA GARNGAD
		17	2	GARNGAD	VIA GLASGOW CROSS
			-	MONKLAND ST	VIA GLASGOW CROSS
			2	GLASGOW CROSS	(None)
			2	AIKENHEAD RD	VIA GLASGOW CROSS
		18	2	POLMADIE	VIA GLASGOW CROSS
			2	HOLMLEA RD	(None)
W	Green	35	16	KEPPOCHHILL ROAD	VIA ST GEORGE'S CROSS
			16	POSSILPARK	VIA MOSSHOUSE
			16	MOSSHOUSE	VIA ST GEORGE'S CROSS
			16	FINNIESTON	VIA CHARING CROSS
			-	STOBCROSS FERRY	VIA FINNIESTON ST.
			16	PARTICK	VIA FINNIESTON
			16	PARTICK	
		36	16	WHITEINCH	VIA FINNIESTON

294

		36A	16	SCOTSTOUN	VIA FINNIESTON
		36B	16	CLYDEBANK	VIA YOKER
X	Red	26A	17	ANNIESLAND	VIA BOTHWELL ST
			17	JORDANHILL	VIA CROW ROAD
			17	BROOMHILL CROSS	VIA CROW ROAD
		26	17	PARTICK	VIA BOTHWELL ST
			17	FINNIESTON	VIA BOTHWELL ST
			-	STOBCROSS FERRY	VIA ANDERSTON CROSS
			-	STOBCROSS FERRY	VIA BOTHWELL ST
		25	17	DALMARNOCK	VIA BOTHWELL ST
		25A	17	CAMBUSLANG	VIA BOTHWELL ST
Y	White		-	PARTICK	VIA ANDERSTON CROSS
			-	WHITEINCH	VIA PARTICK
		30A	18	SPRINGBURN	VIA BILSLAND DRIVE
			-	BALMORE ROAD	VIA BILSLAND DRIVE
			18	RUCHILL	VIA ST GEORGE'S CROSS
			18	MARYHILL	VIA SEAMORE ST
			-	BARRACKS GATE	VIA SEAMORE ST
		30	18	KELVINSIDE AVENUE	VIA ST GEORGE'S CROSS
			-	SEAMORE ST	VIA ST GEORGE'S CROSS
			18	RUTHERGLEN BRIDGE	VIA ST GEORGE'S CROSS
		29	18	RUTHERGLEN	VIA RUTHERGLEN BRIDGE
		29A	18	BURNSIDE	VIA RUTHERGLEN BRIDGE
Z	Blue	37A	6	RIDDRIE	VIA ALEXANDRA PARK
		37	6	ALEXANDRA PARK	VIA CASTLE STREET
			6	MONKLAND ST	VIA CHARING CROSS
			6	KELVINGROVE	VIA CHARING CROSS
			-	HYNDLAND	VIA CHARING CROSS
		38	-	KELVINSIDE CROSS	VIA HYNDLAND
		38A	-	JORDANHILL	VIA HYNDLAND
		38	6	PARTICK	VIA CHARING CROSS
			6	WHITEINCH	VIA PARTICK
		38A	6	SCOTSTOUN	VIA PARTICK
		38B	6	CLYDEBANK	VIA PARTICK
		38C	6	DALMUIR	VIA PARTICK
		38D	6	DALMUIR WEST	VIA PARTICK
-	Blue		-	RENFREW FERRY	VIA PAISLEY CROSS
			-	RENFREW CROSS	VIA PAISLEY CROSS
			-	PORTERFIELD ROAD	VIA PAISLEY CROSS
			-	RENFREW DEPOT	VIA PAISLEY CROSS
			-	SPRINGBANK ROAD	VIA PAISLEY CROSS
			-	PAISLEY CROSS	VIA POTTERHILL
			-	BRAIDS ROAD	VIA PAISLEY CROSS
			-	FALSIDE	VIA PAISLEY CROSS
			-	POTTERHILL	VIA PAISLEY CROSS
			-	GLENFIELD	VIA POTTERHILL
			-	BARRHEAD	VIA POTTERHILL
			-	BARRHEAD (PRINCES SQUARE)	VIA POTTERHILL
			-	SPIERSBRIDGE	VIA BARRHEAD
			-	ROUKEN GLEN	VIA BARRHEAD
-	Green		-	HAWKHEAD ROAD	VIA PAISLEY CROSS
			-	PAISLEY CROSS	(None)
			-	PAISLEY WEST	VIA PAISLEY CROSS
-	Green	-	21	PROVANMILL	VIA RENFIELD ST or VIA GARNGAD
			21	GARNGAD	VIA RENFIELD ST
			21	SHIELDHALL	VIA PAISLEY RD
			21	HILLINGTON ROAD	VIA GOVAN CROSS
			21	RENFREW	VIA GOVAN CROSS
			21	CROOKSTON	VIA PAISLEY RD
	Various	-	30	EXHIBITION	VIA MOSSPARK
			30A	EXHIBITION	VIA PAISLEY RD
			30A	ST VINCENT ST	VIA GLASGOW BRIDGE
			30	ST VINCENT ST	VIA GEORGE V. BRIDGE

Car 243, left, was one of the earliest Standard cars to undergo modernisation (May 1928). Note that there are no grab-rails or step-irons to assist in accessing the roof. The bow-springs had yet to acquire canvass protection. Significantly, changing the screens in the indicator box had to be effected by use of the two handles on one side and the lower one was virtually out of reach!
(STTS Collection)

Car 89, right, illustrates the improvement made to the conductor's lot. The absence of the Headcode display suggests that the tram was photographed in 1938. The changing of displays is now achieved by handles mounted on top of the destination box. That on the right is contained within a cup to prevent the handle fouling the trailing bow-rope. The ultimate destination incorporated 5in characters while those for the "via" display were only 4½in. The cowl mounted on the corner vestibule frame housed illumination for a small slipboard (eg "via Kelvin Hall")
(W Fisher, Courtesy, DW Fisher)

The post-war Cunarders had the Service Number well placed to the nearside aiding recognition from the tram stop when a line of trams approached. The destination indicators, however, were not as clear. The appertures were inset in curved panels and as the glazing was flat, this created a dirt trap that impaired clarity as can be seen in the left hand view.
(RB Parr / STTS Collection)

To increase flexibility, "universal" screens were provided for each depot from 1943 and dedicated "via" displays abandoned. Henceforward the lettering was of equal size in the upper and lower apertures. A typical display is seen on car 257 as it prepares to turn at Yoker. GCT mainly printed its own screens in a loft above the paintshop but from 1943 they bought some in ready-made from Norco (Standard cars and some Coronation Mark I cars) and Eco (Coronation Mark I and II cars). Apart from the digital number displays of the latter (supplied by Eco) Service numbers were invariably made at Coplawhill apart from a few inserts for Services 1, 10, 31, 35 and 36 around 1949-50 that were spliced in to existing screens.
(DL Thomson Collection)

	Colour		Number	Destination	Via
-	Blue	-	31	EXHIBITION	(None)
			31	LINTHOUSE	(None)
-	Green	-	-	STOBCROSS FERRY	VIA FINNIESTON ST
			-	FINNIESTON	VIA FINNIESTON ST
			-	PARTICK	(None)
-	Red	-	-	BATTLEFIELD	VIA QUEEN'S PARK
			-	CARLTON PLACE	(None)
-	Red	-	-	ROUKEN GLEN	VIA GIFFNOCK
	-			ROUKEN GLEN	VIA THORNLIEBANK
			-	CARLTON PLACE	(None)
-	White	-	-	EXHIBITION	VIA CHARING CROSS
			-	EXHIBITION	VIA ANDERSTON CROSS
			-	QUEEN STREET	VIA ANDERSTON CROSS
			-	ST VINCENT PL	VIA CHARING CROSS

In August 1943, the major changes in the services and the increasing availability of Cars in Standard Green livery brought about the introduction of universal screens for each Depot superseding the Colour-orientated lists. The word "VIA" was dropped from the lower screen lists although that screen was, in the main, still used for a route description when appearing with the destination on the top screen. In 1947, instructions were issued listing the lower displays to be used. In quite a number of instances the required displays were not available on the lower screens of the Depots concerned resulting, for a number of years, in a reduction of displayed information. However, later screens were provided with more carefully compiled lists bringing about the return of Route information. The displays in the following section list the normal usage and the 1947 instructions are highlighted with an asterisk (*), along with those 1947 instructions (marked #) which it was never, or hardly ever, possible to show! At some Depots, certain Destinations appeared only on the lower screens. In these instances the top screen would be left blank. The only exception to this was for journeys to Possilpark Depot. Because "Possilpark Depot" appeared only on the lower screen, the route to be taken was distinguished by showing either "Springburn" or "Possilpark" on the top screen.

SERVICE/ROUTE

Colour
Standard

DESTINATION POST-1943 LOWER

Number		
1	DALMUIR WEST	ST VINCENT PLACE or ST GEORGE'S CROSS or BOTANIC GARDENS*
1	DALMUIR	(As Dalmuir West)
1	CLYDEBANK	(As Dalmuir West)
1	YOKER	(As Dalmuir West)
1	SCOTSTOUN WEST	(As Dalmuir West)
30	BLAIRDARDIE	(As Dalmuir West)
30	KNIGHTSWOOD	(As Dalmuir West)
1/30	ANNIESLAND	(As Dalmuir West)
1/30	KELVINSIDE	(As Dalmuir West)
1/30	PARTICK	CHARING CROSS
1/30	ST VINCENT PLACE	CHARING CROSS
1/30	PARTICK	
1/30	ST VINCENT PLACE	BOTANIC GARDENS or ST GEORGE'S CROSS
1/30	NORTH ALBION ST	(As St Vincent Place)
1/30	DENNISTOUN DEPOT	
1	DENNISTOUN	BOTANIC GARDENS or ST GEORGE'S CROSS or ST VINCENT PLACE*
30	PARKHEAD	ST GEORGE'S CROSS or ST VINCENT PLACE or DENNISTOUN
30	PARKHEAD DEPOT	(As Parkhead)
1/30	SPRINGFIELD ROAD	(As Parkhead) or PARKHEAD*
1/30	DALMARNOCK	ST GEORGE'S CROSS or ST VINCENT PLACE or DENNISTOUN or PARKHEAD or SPRINGFIELD ROAD*
1	DALMARNOCK DEPOT	(As Dalmarnock)
30	CAMBUSLANG	(As Dalmarnock)

Standard

2	PROVANMILL	GARNGAD or GLASGOW CROSS*
2	GARNGAD	GLASGOW CROSS
2	GLASGOW CROSS	
2	POLMADIE	GLASGOW CROSS*
2	SPRINGBURN	POSSILPARK DEPOT
2	LANGSIDE DEPOT	

Standard / Red

3	UNIVERSITY	CHARING CROSS*
3A	UNIVERSITY	PAISLEY ROAD TOLL
3	ST VINCENT STREET	POLLOKSHIELDS
3	MARYHILL	CHARING CROSS
3	DUMBRECK	POLLOKSHIELDS
3	MOSSPARK	POLLOKSHIELDS*
3A	MOSSPARK	PAISLEY ROAD TOLL
8	NEWLANDS	SHAWLANDS
31	NEWLANDS	SHAWLANDS
3	NEWLANDS	SHAWLANDS

Blue / Standard

KEPPOCHHILL ROAD / MOSSHOUSE — Service No. 4

HILLINGTON ROAD / PAISLEY ROAD TOLL — Service No. 27

RENFREW SOUTH / SHIELDHALL — Service No. 4

Yellow / Standard

KELVINSIDE / BOTANIC GARDENS — Service No. 5

ANNIESLAND / HYNDLAND — Service No. 24

LANGSIDE / QUEENS PARK — Service No. 24

HOLMLEA Rd / BATTLEFIELD — Service No. 5

CLARKSTON / CATHCART — Service No. 5

Blue / Standard

RIDDRIE / CASTLE STREET — Service No. 6

ALEXANDRA PARK / CHARING CROSS — Service No. 6

KELVINGROVE / CHARING CROSS — Service No. 6

Yellow / Standard

MILLERSTON / BRIDGETON CROSS — Service No. 7

BELLAHOUSTON / PAISLEY ROAD TOLL — Service No. 7

4	SPRINGBURN	KEPPOCHHILL ROAD
4	KEPPOCHHILL ROAD	MOSSHOUSE*
4	SPRINGBURN	POSSILPARK DEPOT
27	POSSILPARK	POSSILPARK DEPOT
27	SPRINGBURN	POSSILPARK or SARACEN CROSS
27	POSSILPARK	MOSSHOUSE
27	SARACEN CROSS	MOSSHOUSE
4/27	COMMERCE ST	
4/27	LORNE SCHOOL	
4/27	GOVAN DEPOT	
27	LINTHOUSE	PAISLEY ROAD TOLL or GOVAN CROSS
4/27	SHIELDHALL	(As Linthouse)
4/27	HILLINGTON ROAD	PAISLEY ROAD TOLL or SHIELDHALL
27	RENFREW CROSS	(As Hillington Road)
4	RENFREW SOUTH	SHIELDHALL* or RENFREW CROSS or RENFREW AIRPORT
4	PAISLEY NORTH	(As Renfrew South)
5	KIRKLEE	BOTANIC GARDENS
5A	KIRKLEE	HYNDLAND
5A	HYNDLAND	HIGHBURGH ROAD
5	KELVINSIDE	BOTANIC GARDENS*
5A	KELVINSIDE	HYNDLAND*
24	ANNIESLAND	HYNDLAND
24	JORDANHILL	HYNDLAND
5/24	PARTICK	
24A	KELVINGROVE	
5/24	ST VINCENT PLACE	
5/24	NORTH ALBION ST	
24	LANGSIDE	QUEEN'S PARK
24	SINCLAIR DRIVE	QUEEN'S PARK or EGLINTON TOLL
24A	SINCLAIR DRIVE	QUEEN'S PARK
5/24/24A	LANGSIDE DEPOT	BATTLEFIELD
5	HOLMLEA RD	BATTLEFIELD or EGLINTON TOLL
5	CATHCART	BATTLEFIELD
5	NETHERLEE	(As Clarkston)
5	CLARKSTON	BATTLEFIELD* or CATHCART
8	NEWLANDS	SHAWLANDS
24	ANNIESLAND	ST VINCENT PLACE #
24	LANGSIDE	ST VINCENT PLACE # or GORBALS
5	CLARKSTON	ST VINCENT PLACE or GORBALS
6	RIDDRIE	CASTLE STREET or CHARING CROSS* or WHITEINCH
6	ALEXANDRA PARK	(As Riddrie)
6	DENNISTOUN DEPOT	
6	CASTLE STREET	CHARING CROSS
6	KELVINGROVE	CHARING CROSS
6	PARTICK	
6	WHITEINCH	CHARING CROSS
6	SCOTSTOUN	CHARING CROSS* or PARTICK or WHITEINCH
6	SCOTSTOUN WEST	(As Scotstoun)
6	DALMUIR WEST	(As Scotstoun)
7	MILLERSTON	BRIDGETON CROSS*
7	RIDDRIE	BRIDGETON CROSS
7	ALEXANDRA PARK	BRIDGETON CROSS
7	DENNISTOUN DEPOT	
7	BRIDGETON CROSS	
7	LORNE STREET	PAISLEY ROAD TOLL
7	GOVAN DEPOT	
7	LORNE SCHOOL	
7	BELLAHOUSTON	PAISLEY ROAD TOLL or GOVAN ROAD #
7	LINTHOUSE	PAISLEY ROAD TOLL
7	SHIELDHALL	PAISLEY ROAD TOLL

Red / Standard

8	MILLERSTON	ALEXANDRA PARK*
		or CASTLE STREET
8	RIDDRIE	(As Millerston)
8	ALEXANDRA PARK	CASTLE STREET
8	DENNISTOUN DEPOT	(None)
25	BISHOPBRIGGS	SPRINGBURN*
		or CASTLE STREET
25	COLSTON	(As Bishopbriggs)
25	SPRINGBURN	CASTLE STREET*
8/25	CASTLE STREET	SHAWLANDS
8/25	MONKLAND STREET	SHAWLANDS
8/25	SHAWLANDS	EGLINTON TOLL
8	NEWLANDS	SHAWLANDS*
8	MERRYLEE	SHAWLANDS
8	GIFFNOCK	NEWLANDS*
		or SHAWLANDS
		or EGLINTON TOLL
8	ROUKEN GLEN	GIFFNOCK*
25	GREENVIEW STREET	SHAWLANDS
25	POLLOKSHAWS WEST	SHAWLANDS
25	POLLOKSHAWS	SHAWLANDS*
25	CARNWADRIC	POLLOKSHAWS*
		or SHAWLANDS
25	ROUKEN GLEN	POLLOKSHAWS*
		or CARNWADRIC
		or THORNLIEBANK
25	SPRINGBURN	POSSILPARK DEPOT

Red / Standard

9	DALMUIR WEST	PARTICK or SCOTSTOUN*
9	DALMUIR	(As Dalmuir West)
9/26	CLYDEBANK	PARTICK
		or SCOTSTOUN*
9/26	YOKER	(As Dalmuir West)
26	SCOTSTOUN	PARTICK*
		or FINNIESTON
9/26	PARTICK	FINNIESTON
9/26	ANDERSTON CROSS	BRIDGETON CROSS
		or GLASGOW CROSS
9/26	GLASGOW CROSS	PARTICK
9	LONDON ROAD	GLASGOW CROSS
		or BRIDGETON CROSS
9	AUCHENSHUGGLE	BRIDGETON CROSS*
		or GLASGOW CROSS
9	CARMYLE	BRIDGETON CROSS*
26A	SHAWFIELD	BRIDGETON CROSS
9/26	DALMARNOCK DEPOT	BRIDGETON CROSS
26	DALMARNOCK	BRIDGETON CROSS
26	FARME CROSS	BRIDGETON CROSS
		or DALMARNOCK
		or DALMARNOCK ROAD
26	RUTHERGLEN	(As Burnside)
26	OATLANDS	(As Burnside)
26	BURNSIDE	DALMARNOCK*
		or DALMARNOCK ROAD

Blue / Standard

10	KIRKLEE	PARK ROAD
10	KELVINSIDE	PARK ROAD*
10A	KELVINSIDE	CHURCH STREET
10/10A	ANDERSTON CROSS	CROWN STREET
10	OATLANDS	CROWN STREET*
10	RUTHERGLEN	CROWN STREET*
10A	RUTHERGLEN	CROWN STREET
10	DALMARNOCK DEPOT	
10	KELVINSIDE	DALMARNOCK ROAD
36	KELVINSIDE	GALLOWGATE
10	PARKHEAD	GALLOWGATE
36	PARKHEAD	DALMARNOCK ROAD
10/36	PARTICK	CHARING CROSS
10	KELVINSIDE	CHARING CROSS
		or PARK ROAD
		or BOTANIC GARDENS
10	PARTICK	CHARING CROSS
10	DOUGLAS ST	
10	MOIR STREET	CHARING CROSS
10	LONDON ROAD	GLASGOW CROSS
		or BRIDGETON CROSS
10	AUCHENSHUGGLE	(As London Road)

299

Red / Standard

Yellow / Standard

Blue / Standard

Standard

11/13	MILNGAVIE	ST GEORGE'S CROSS*
11/13	HILLFOOT	ST GEORGE'S CROSS
11/13	CANNIESBURN	ST GEORGE'S CROSS
11/13	MARYHILL	ST GEORGE'S CROSS*
11/13	GAIRBRAID AVENUE	ST GEORGE'S CROSS
11	KELVINSIDE AVENUE	ST GEORGE'S CROSS
11/13	MAITLAND ST.	ST GEORGE'S CROSS
11/13	GORBALS	ST GEORGE'S CROSS
11	BATTLEFIELD	QUEEN'S PARK
11	LANGSIDE DEPOT	QUEEN'S PARK
11	SINCLAIR DRIVE	ST GEORGE'S CROSS*
		or GORBALS
		or EGLINTON TOLL
		or QUEEN'S PARK
13	GOVANHILL	GORBALS
13	MOUNT FLORIDA	GORBALS*
		or GOVANHILL
13	LANGSIDE DEPOT	
13	CATHCART	GOVANHILL
13	NETHERLEE	GOVANHILL
13	CLARKSTON	MOUNT FLORIDA*
		or GOVANHILL
13	GLASGOW CROSS	NORMAL SCHOOL
12	MOUNT FLORIDA	SHIELDS ROAD*
12	PAISLEY ROAD TOLL	SHIELDS ROAD
12	GOVAN DEPOT	
12	LORNE SCHOOL	
12	IBROX	PAISLEY ROAD TOLL
12	LINTHOUSE	PAISLEY ROAD TOLL*
		or SHIELDS ROAD
12	SHIELDHALL	(As Linthouse)
12	CLARKSTON	SHIELDS ROAD
12	NETHERLEE	SHIELDS ROAD
12	LANGSIDE DEPOT	
14	MILNGAVIE	GARSCUBE ROAD
14	HILLFOOT	GARSCUBE ROAD
14	MARYHILL	GARSCUBE ROAD
14	GAIRBRAID AVENUE	GARSCUBE ROAD
14	SHAWLANDS	GORBALS
14	POLLOKSHAWS	GORBALS
14	SPIERSBRIDGE	GORBALS
14	SHAWLANDS	EGLINTON TOLL
14	POLLOKSHAWS	EGLINTON TOLL
14	SPIERSBRIDGE	EGLINTON TOLL
14	UNIVERSITY	CHARING CROSS*
14/14A	KELVINGROVE	CHARING CROSS*
14B	CASTLE STREET	SHAWLANDS
14	SHAWLANDS	
8	NEWLANDS	SHAWLANDS
14/14A	POLLOKSHAWS	SHAWLANDS*
14B	CARNWADRIC	SHAWLANDS
		or POLLOKSHAWS
14/14A	SPIERSBRIDGE	SHAWLANDS
		or POLLOKSHAWS*
14	ARDEN	(As Spiersbridge)
14	PRINCES SQUARE	(As Spiersbridge)
14	BARRHEAD CENTRE	(As Spiersbridge)
14	CROSSSTOBS	(As Spiersbridge)
31	NEWLANDS	SHAWLANDS
15	AIRDRIE	PARKHEAD
		or SHETTLESTON*
		or (None) [Airdrie Local]
15	COATBRIDGE	(As Airdrie)
15	JACKSON STREET	(As Airdrie)
15	COATBRIDGE DEPOT	(As Airdrie)
15	LANGLOAN	(As Airdrie)
15	BARGEDDIE	(As Airdrie)
15	BAILLIESTON	PARKHEAD
		or SHETTLESTON
15	GARROWHILL	(As Baillieston)
15	SHETTLESTON	PARKHEAD
15	PARKHEAD DEPOT	PARKHEAD
15	PARKHEAD	
15	GLASGOW CROSS	(As Baillieston)

Standard

Service No.	From	To
15	ROBERTSON ST	(As Baillieston)
15	ANDERSTON CROSS	(As Baillieston)
15	CITY CENTRE*	PARKHEAD*
15	DENNISTOUN DEPOT	
15	DALMARNOCK DEPOT	SPRINGFIELD ROAD
16	SPRINGBURN	KEPPOCHHILL ROAD
16	KEPPOCHHILL ROAD	MOSSHOUSE or CHARING CROSS*
16	FINNIESTON	CHARING CROSS
16	FINNIESTON	PARTICK
16	PARTICK	FINNIESTON
16	WHITEINCH	(As Scotstoun)
16	SCOTSTOUN	CHARING CROSS* or FINNIESTON or PARTICK
16	SPRINGBURN	POSSILPARK DEPOT
16	POSSILPARK	POSSILPARK DEPOT

Red / Standard

Service No.	From	To
17	WHITEINCH	PARTICK*
17	ANDERSTON CROSS	BRIDGETON CROSS
17	ANNIESLAND	BOTHWELL ST or PARTICK
17	JORDANHILL	(As Anniesland)
17	PARTICK	
17	DOUGLAS ST	BRIDGETON CROSS
17	DALMARNOCK DEPOT	
17	DALMARNOCK	BRIDGETON CROSS
17	FARME CROSS	(As Cambuslang)
17	ARDOCH GROVE	
17	CAMBUSLANG	BRIDGETON CROSS or DALMARNOCK ROAD or DALMARNOCK*

Red / Standard

Service No.	From	To
18	SPRINGBURN	CHARING CROSS or RUCHILL or BILSLAND DRIVE # ‡
18	RUCHILL	CHARING CROSS
18	MARYHILL	CHARING CROSS
18	DOUGLAS ST	CHARING CROSS
18	GLASGOW CROSS	CHARING CROSS
18	RUTHERGLEN	RUTHERGLEN BRIDGE
18	BURNSIDE	RUTHERGLEN BRIDGE*
18	DALMARNOCK DEPOT	BRIDGETON CROSS
18A	SHAWFIELD	BRIDGETON CROSS
18	BURNSIDE	DALMARNOCK ROAD or DALMARNOCK

Standard

Service No.	From	To
19	SPRINGBURN	GLASGOW CROSS*
19	GLASGOW CROSS	
19	MOUNT FLORIDA	GLASGOW CROSS*
19	NETHERLEE	GLASGOW CROSS*
19	SPRINGBURN	POSSILPARK DEPOT
19	LANGSIDE DEPOT	

Standard

Service No.	From	To
20	DUNTOCHER	(None)
20	PARKHALL	(None)
20	RADNOR PARK	(None)
20	CLYDEBANK	(None)
20	YOKER	(None)
20	PARTICK	(None)

Standard / Red / Blue

Service No.	From	To
21/32	ELDERSLIE	PAISLEY ROAD TOLL or CROOKSTON or PAISLEY CROSS #
21/32	FERGUSLIE MILLS	(As Elderslie)
21/32	PAISLEY WEST	(As Elderslie)
32	CROOKSTON	PAISLEY ROAD TOLL
21/32	GOVAN DEPOT	
21/32	LORNE SCHOOL	
21	DOUGLAS ST	PAISLEY ROAD TOLL
21	PARTICK	PAISLEY ROAD TOLL
21	ANNIESLAND	BOTHWELL ST # or PARTICK
32	CASTLE STREET	PAISLEY ROAD TOLL
32	PROVANMILL	CASTLE STREET*
32	SPRINGBURN	CASTLE STREET

Blue / Standard

CROOKSTON
PAISLEY ROAD WEST
Service No. 22

Standard

BAILLIESTON
SHETTLESTON
Service No. 23

MARYHILL
St GEORGE'S CROSS
Service No. 23

Blue / Red / Standard

Standard

32	BISHOPBRIGGS	CASTLE STREET
21	CITY CENTRE	(None)
21/32	ELDERSLIE DEPOT	(As Elderslie)
22	CROOKSTON	PAISLEY ROAD WEST#‡ or PAISLEY ROAD TOLL
22	GOVAN DEPOT	
22	LORNE SCHOOL	PAISLEY ROAD TOLL
22	CITY CENTRE	(None)
22	POSSILPARK	MOSSHOUSE
22	LAMBHILL	GEORGE V BRIDGE #‡ or MOSSHOUSE or POSSILPARK
22	POSSILPARK	POSSILPARK DEPOT
23	AIRDRIE	(None)
23	COATBRIDGE	(None)
23	JACKSON ST	(None)
23	COATBRIDGE DEPOT	(None)
23	LANGLOAN	(None)
23	BARGEDDIE	(None)
23	BAILLIESTON	(None)
23	GARROWHILL	(None)
23	SHETTLESTON	(None)
23	DENNISTOUN	(None)
23	DENNISTOUN DEPOT	(None)
23	ST VINCENT STREET	(None)
23	KELVINGROVE	(None)
23	AIRDRIE	GARSCUBE ROAD* or SHETTLESTON or (None)
23	JACKSON ST	(As Airdrie)
23	COATBRIDGE DEPOT	(As Airdrie)
23	LANGLOAN	(As Airdrie)
23	BARGEDDIE	(As Airdrie)
23	BAILLIESTON	(As Airdrie)
23	GARROWHILL	(As Airdrie)
23	SHETTLESTON	(As Airdrie)
23	DENNISTOUN	(As Airdrie)
23	DENNISTOUN DEPOT	(As Airdrie)
23	NORTH ALBION ST	GARSCUBE ROAD
23	ST VINCENT PLACE	GARSCUBE ROAD
23	ST VINCENT STREET	(None)
23	GAIRBRAID AVENUE	GARSCUBE ROAD*
23	MARYHILL	GARSCUBE ROAD
23	AIRDRIE	ST GEORGE'S CROSS or SHETTLESTON
23	BAILLIESTON	(As Airdrie)
23	DENNISTOUN DEPOT	(As Airdrie)
23	GAIRBRAID AVENUE	ST GEORGE'S CROSS
23	MARYHILL DEPOT	ST GEORGE'S CROSS
23	MARYHILL	ST GEORGE'S CROSS
23	BAILLIESTON	NORMAL SCHOOL or DENNISTOUN
23	DENNISTOUN DEPOT	NORMAL SCHOOL
23	MARYHILL	NORMAL SCHOOL
23	MARYHILL DEPOT	NORMAL SCHOOL
28	RENFREW FERRY	BARRHEAD #
28	RENFREW CROSS	(None)
28	RENFREW SOUTH	(None)
28	PORTERFIELD ROAD	(None)
28	SANDYFORD	(None)
28	PAISLEY CROSS	(None)
28	ELDERSLIE DEPOT	(None)
28	CAUSEYSIDE	(None)
28	BRAIDS ROAD	(None)
28	LOCHFIELD ROAD	(None)
28	FALSIDE	(None)
28	POTTERHILL	(None)
28	GLENFIELD	(None)
28	BARRHEAD	(None)
28	PRINCES SQUARE	(None)
28	SPIERSBRIDGE	BARRHEAD #
29	UDDINGSTON	PARKHEAD or TOLLCROSS* or ZOO

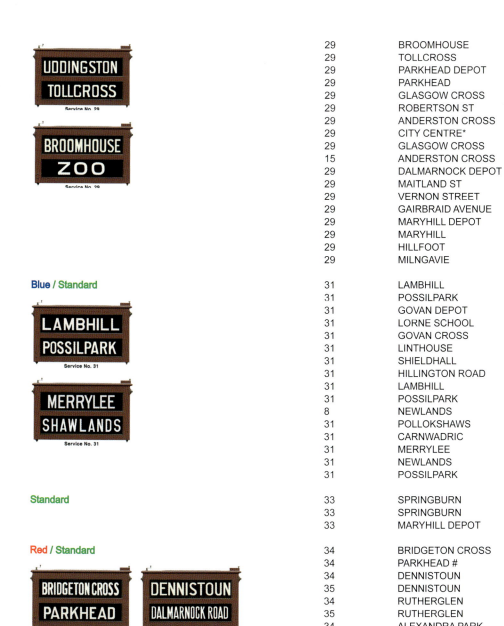

Service	From	To
29	BROOMHOUSE	(As Uddingston)
29	TOLLCROSS	PARKHEAD*
29	PARKHEAD DEPOT	PARKHEAD
29	PARKHEAD	
29	GLASGOW CROSS	PARKHEAD
29	ROBERTSON ST	PARKHEAD
29	ANDERSTON CROSS	PARKHEAD
29	CITY CENTRE*	PARKHEAD*
29	GLASGOW CROSS	NORMAL SCHOOL
15	ANDERSTON CROSS	PARKHEAD
29	DALMARNOCK DEPOT	SPRINGFIELD ROAD
29	MAITLAND ST	NORMAL SCHOOL
29	VERNON STREET	
29	GAIRBRAID AVENUE	NORMAL SCHOOL
29	MARYHILL DEPOT	NORMAL SCHOOL
29	MARYHILL	NORMAL SCHOOL
29	HILLFOOT	NORMAL SCHOOL
29	MILNGAVIE	NORMAL SCHOOL

Blue / Standard

Service	From	To
31	LAMBHILL	POSSILPARK
31	POSSILPARK	MOSSHOUSE
31	GOVAN DEPOT	
31	LORNE SCHOOL	
31	GOVAN CROSS	PAISLEY ROAD TOLL
31	LINTHOUSE	PAISLEY ROAD TOLL
31	SHIELDHALL	PAISLEY ROAD TOLL
31	HILLINGTON ROAD	PAISLEY ROAD TOLL
31	LAMBHILL	CHARING CROSS
31	POSSILPARK	CHARING CROSS
8	NEWLANDS	SHAWLANDS
31	POLLOKSHAWS	SHAWLANDS
31	CARNWADRIC	SHAWLANDS
31	MERRYLEE	SHAWLANDS
31	NEWLANDS	SHAWLANDS
31	POSSILPARK	POSSILPARK DEPOT

Standard

Service	From	To
33	SPRINGBURN	CHARING CROSS*
33	SPRINGBURN	POSSILPARK DEPOT
33	MARYHILL DEPOT	CHARING CROSS

Red / Standard

Service	From	To
34	BRIDGETON CROSS	PARKHEAD
34	PARKHEAD #	BRIDGETON CROSS #
34	DENNISTOUN	BRIDGETON CROSS
35	DENNISTOUN	DALMARNOCK ROAD
34	RUTHERGLEN	DALMARNOCK ROAD
35	RUTHERGLEN	RUTHERGLEN BRIDGE
34	ALEXANDRA PARK	BRIDGETON CROSS
34	AUCHENSHUGGLE	BRIDGETON CROSS
34	ANDERSTON CROSS	BRIDGETON CROSS
34	AUCHENSHUGGLE	BRIDGETON CROSS
34	DALMARNOCK DEPOT	BRIDGETON CROSS

Blue / Standard

Service	From	To
40	DUMBRECK	PAISLEY ROAD TOLL*
40	IBROX	PAISLEY ROAD TOLL
40	LORNE SCHOOL	PAISLEY ROAD TOLL
40	GOVAN DEPOT	
40	CITY CENTRE	(None)
40	PARTICK	
40	DOUGLAS ST	CHARING CROSS
40	GAIRBRAID AVENUE	CHARING CROSS*
40	MARYHILL	CHARING CROSS
40	MARYHILL DEPOT	CHARING CROSS
Various	CITY CENTRE **	

NOTES

* As per June 1947 Instructions
\# As per June 1947 Instructions but not available for display on most, or in some cases any, Screens.
‡ Subsequently appeared on new Screens printed in the mid- to late-fifties
** "City Centre" was introduced on all post-August 1943 Screens, usually, but not always, on the lower screen. This was, ostensibly, to assist visiting armed forces and others in the city during the war years. It continued in lessening use after hostilities ceased and could apply to Anderston Cross, Robertson Street, Douglas Street, St Vincent Street, St Vincent Place, North Albion Street, North Hanover Street, Monkland Street, Castle Street, Glassford Street, Glasgow Cross, Trongate, Jamaica Street, Commerce Street or Bridge Street, but not to Maitland Street or Charing Cross.

Route colour bands were gradually superseded from 1939 by Standard (Bus) Green. The last White Car ran in May 1942, the last Green in November 1942 while Red Cars finally disappeared in 1952, Yellow in 1953 and Blue in 1954. Thereafter all cars were Standard (Bus) Green. The references above to colours reflects the usage of Cars on particular Services, however, it should be noted that there was no pre-determined pattern for the colour allocation of Cars to duties. All Coronation Cars – except three Mark I and one Mark II painted Red in 1950 – carried the Standard (Bus) Green livery and after August 1943 there was more and more dependence for route recognition on the Service Number as, particularly at Peak Hours, there could be considerable inter-working of different colours.

Sometimes commercial photographers, as with this example from Leyland Motors, reproduced by Courtesy of The British Commercial Vehicle Museum Ltd, unwittingly record for posterity what in later years become gems for the enthusiasts. In this view taken in 1929 Leyland TD1 133 heads into New City Road at St George's Cross passing none other than Blue car 22 heading for Maryhill and displaying Headcode 9. The bus was new in 1928 and car 22, towering over its low height was built in 1922. It would called in the following year for modernisation. The bus service had been numbered 3 in 1928 and extended to Mosspark in January 1929. This number would also be allocated some nine years later to the White tram service to Mosspark when the numbering scheme for tram services shadowing the then exisiting bus service numbers was introduced preparatory to the Empire Exhibition. By good fortune, a bus of this type, No. 111, has survived in preservation, as has Car 22 which regularly operates at the National Tramway Museum, Crich in Derbyshire. Back home in Glasgow, sadly however, it is a case of ...

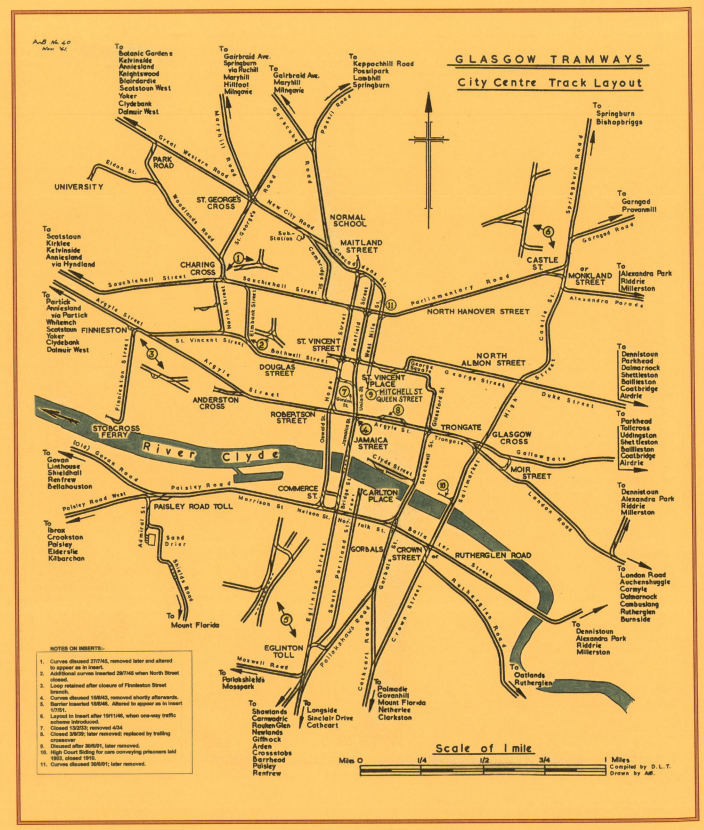

This map should be read in conjunction with that reproduced on the inside end papers which comprises the whole system.
(Drawn by Alan Brotchie and used with his courtesy)